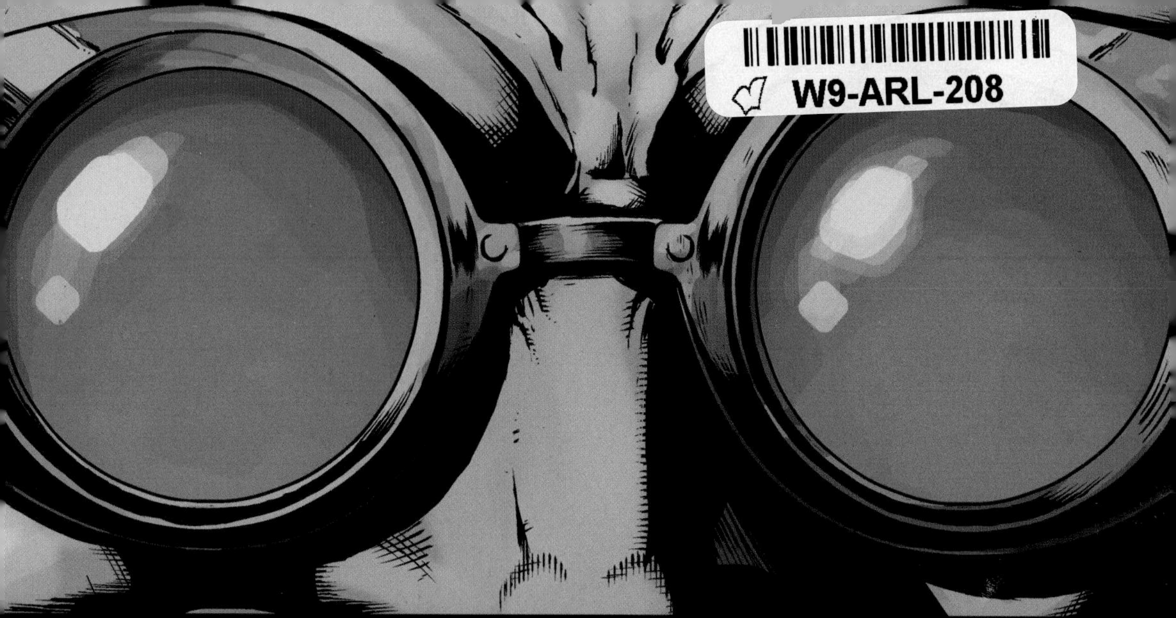

BATMAN ARKHAM

MISTER FREEZE

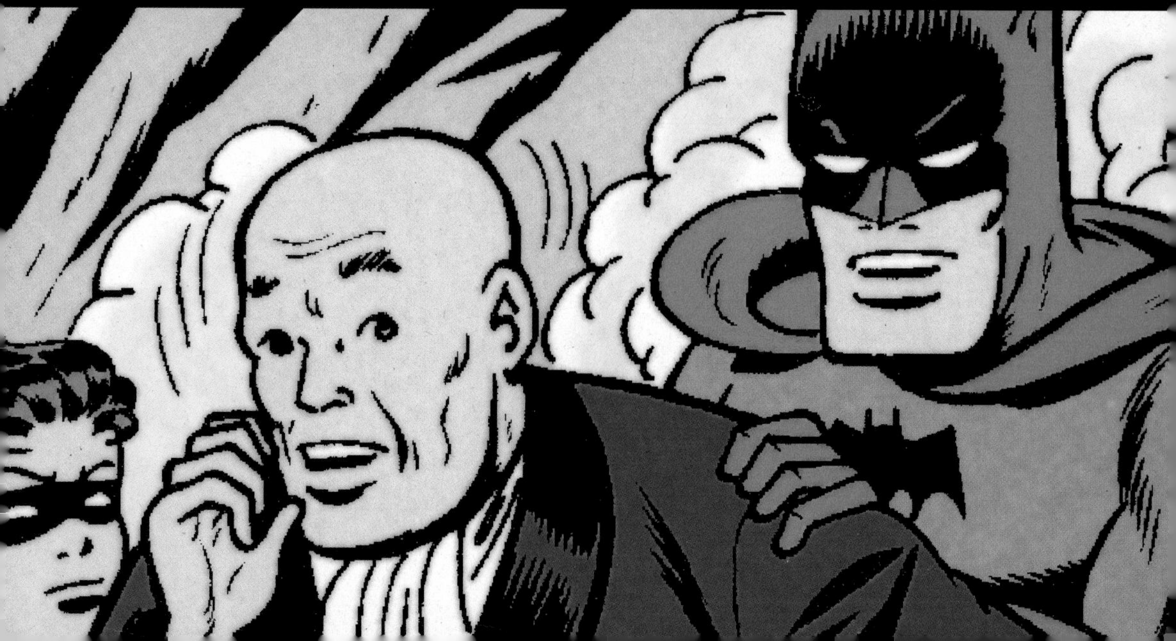

TABLE OF CONTENTS

Brian Stelfreeze
Collection Cover Artist

BATMAN created by BOB KANE with BILL FINGER

WHITNEY ELLSWORTH JULIUS SCHWARTZ LEN WEIN JOEY CAVALIERI
DENNY O'NEIL SCOTT PETERSON MATT IDELSON MIKE MARTS EDITORS – ORIGINAL SERIES
E. NELSON BIRDWELL JORDAN GORFINKEL DARREN VINCENZO ASSOCIATE EDITORS – ORIGINAL SERIES
NACHIE CASTRO KATIE KUBERT ASSISTANT EDITORS – ORIGINAL SERIES
JEB WOODARD GROUP EDITOR – COLLECTED EDITIONS
PAUL SANTOS EDITOR – COLLECTED EDITION
STEVE COOK DESIGN DIRECTOR – BOOKS
LOUIS PRANDI PUBLICATION DESIGN

BOB HARRAS SENIOR VP – EDITOR-IN-CHIEF, DC COMICS

DIANE NELSON PRESIDENT
DAN DiDIO PUBLISHER
JIM LEE PUBLISHER
GEOFF JOHNS PRESIDENT & CHIEF CREATIVE OFFICER
AMIT DESAI EXECUTIVE VP – BUSINESS & MARKETING STRATEGY, DIRECT TO CONSUMER & GLOBAL FRANCHISE MANAGEMENT
SAM ADES SENIOR VP – DIRECT TO CONSUMER
BOBBIE CHASE VP – TALENT DEVELOPMENT
MARK CHIARELLO SENIOR VP – ART, DESIGN & COLLECTED EDITIONS
JOHN CUNNINGHAM SENIOR VP – SALES & TRADE MARKETING
ANNE DePIES SENIOR VP – BUSINESS STRATEGY, FINANCE & ADMINISTRATION
DON FALLETTI VP – MANUFACTURING OPERATIONS
LAWRENCE GANEM VP – EDITORIAL ADMINISTRATION & TALENT RELATIONS
ALISON GILL SENIOR VP – MANUFACTURING & OPERATIONS
HANK KANALZ SENIOR VP – EDITORIAL STRATEGY & ADMINISTRATION
JAY KOGAN VP – LEGAL AFFAIRS
THOMAS LOFTUS VP – BUSINESS AFFAIRS
JACK MAHAN VP – BUSINESS AFFAIRS
NICK J. NAPOLITANO VP – MANUFACTURING ADMINISTRATION
EDDIE SCANNELL VP – CONSUMER MARKETING
COURTNEY SIMMONS SENIOR VP – PUBLICITY & COMMUNICATIONS
JIM (SKI) SOKOLOWSKI VP – COMIC BOOK SPECIALTY SALES & TRADE MARKETING
NANCY SPEARS VP – MASS, BOOK, DIGITAL SALES & TRADE MARKETING

BATMAN ARKHAM: MISTER FREEZE

DC COMICS, 2900 WEST ALAMEDA AVE., BURBANK, CA 91505
PRINTED BY SOLISCO PRINTERS, SCOTT, QC, CANADA. 4/7/17. FIRST PRINTING.
ISBN: 978-1-4012-6887-9

LIBRARY OF CONGRESS CATALOGING-IN-PUBLICATION DATA IS AVAILABLE.

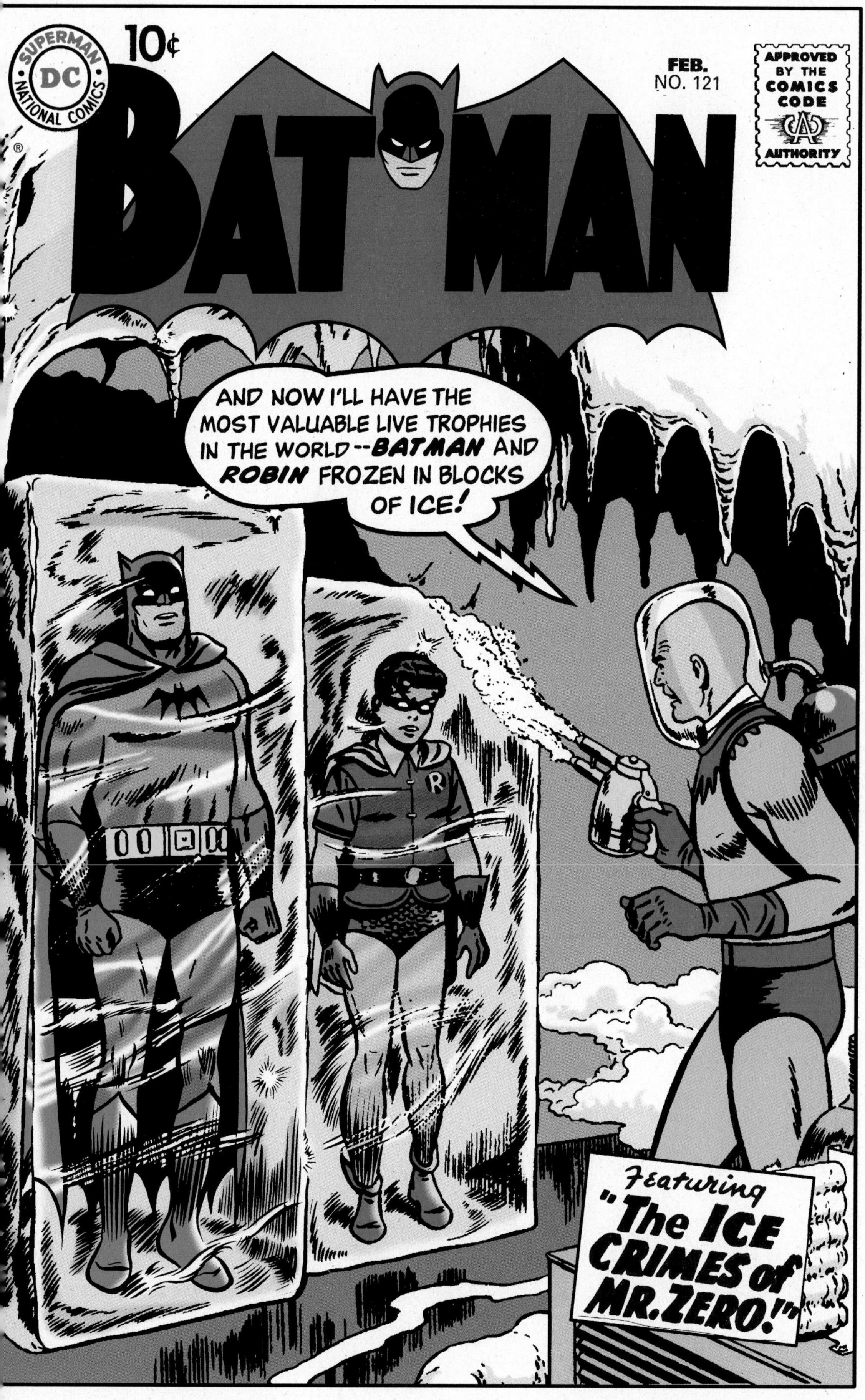
SUPERMAN DC NATIONAL COMICS
10¢
FEB.
NO. 121
APPROVED BY THE COMICS CODE AUTHORITY
BATMAN
AND NOW I'LL HAVE THE MOST VALUABLE LIVE TROPHIES IN THE WORLD--BATMAN AND ROBIN FROZEN IN BLOCKS OF ICE!
Featuring "The ICE CRIMES of MR. ZERO!"

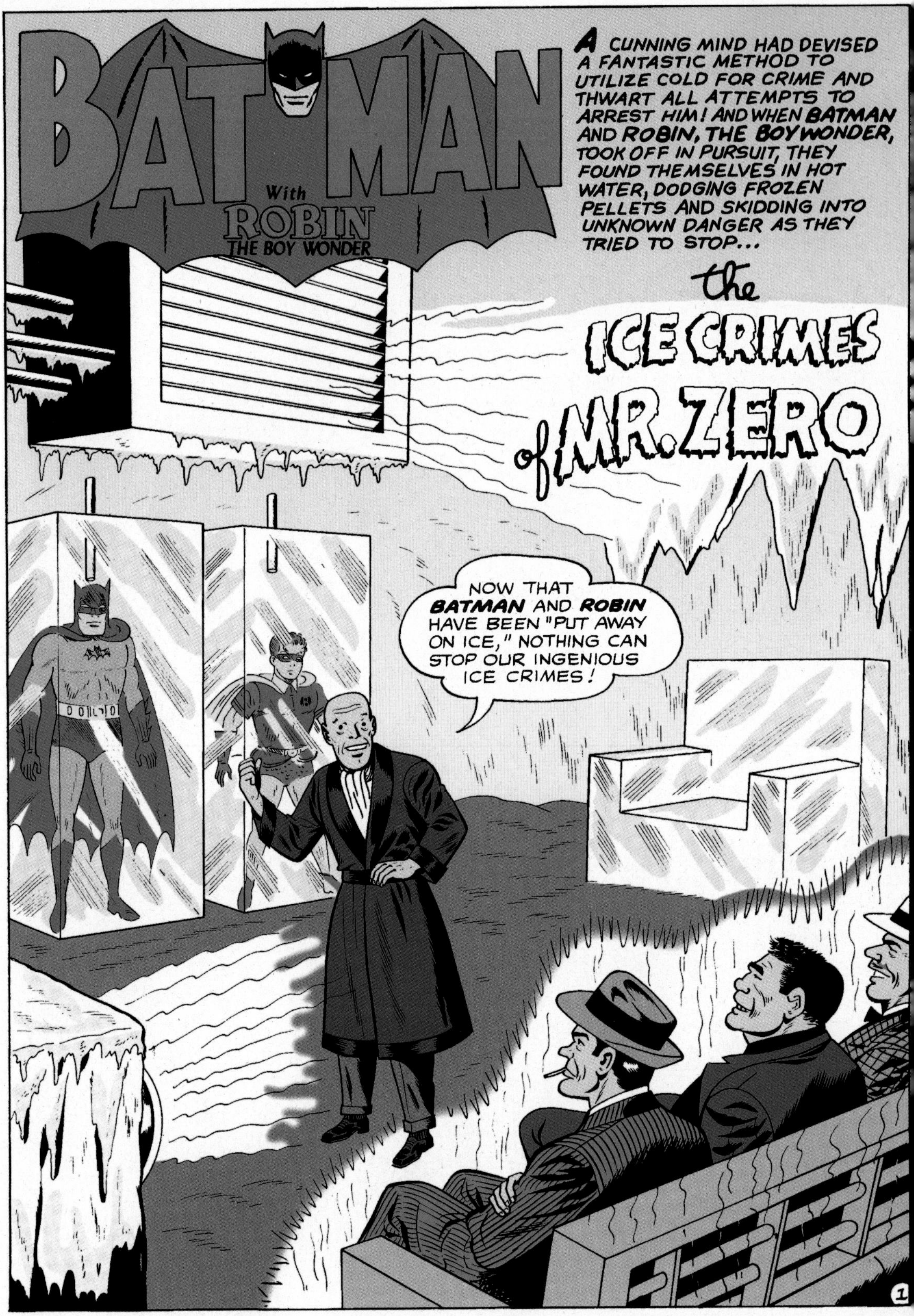
BATMAN
With ROBIN THE BOY WONDER
A CUNNING MIND HAD DEVISED A FANTASTIC METHOD TO UTILIZE COLD FOR CRIME AND THWART ALL ATTEMPTS TO ARREST HIM! AND WHEN BATMAN AND ROBIN, THE BOY WONDER, TOOK OFF IN PURSUIT, THEY FOUND THEMSELVES IN HOT WATER, DODGING FROZEN PELLETS AND SKIDDING INTO UNKNOWN DANGER AS THEY TRIED TO STOP...
the ICE CRIMES of MR. ZERO
NOW THAT BATMAN AND ROBIN HAVE BEEN "PUT AWAY ON ICE," NOTHING CAN STOP OUR INGENIOUS ICE CRIMES!
1

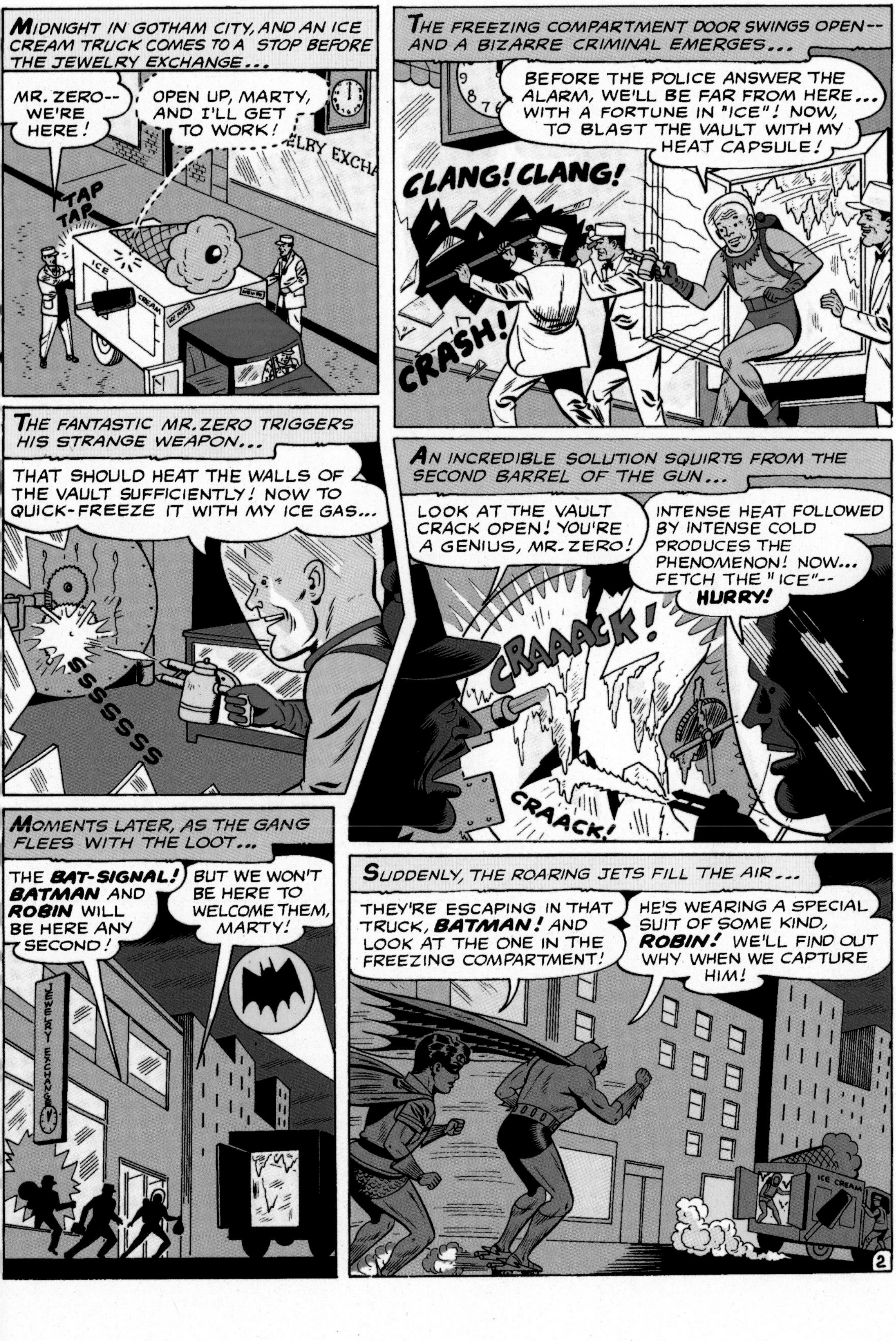
MIDNIGHT IN GOTHAM CITY, AND AN ICE CREAM TRUCK COMES TO A STOP BEFORE THE JEWELRY EXCHANGE...
MR. ZERO-- WE'RE HERE!
OPEN UP, MARTY, AND I'LL GET TO WORK!
TAP TAP
THE FREEZING COMPARTMENT DOOR SWINGS OPEN-- AND A BIZARRE CRIMINAL EMERGES...
BEFORE THE POLICE ANSWER THE ALARM, WE'LL BE FAR FROM HERE... WITH A FORTUNE IN "ICE"! NOW, TO BLAST THE VAULT WITH MY HEAT CAPSULE!
CLANG! CLANG!
CRASH!
CRASH
THE FANTASTIC MR. ZERO TRIGGERS HIS STRANGE WEAPON...
THAT SHOULD HEAT THE WALLS OF THE VAULT SUFFICIENTLY! NOW TO QUICK-FREEZE IT WITH MY ICE GAS...
SSSSSSSS
AN INCREDIBLE SOLUTION SQUIRTS FROM THE SECOND BARREL OF THE GUN...
LOOK AT THE VAULT CRACK OPEN! YOU'RE A GENIUS, MR. ZERO!
INTENSE HEAT FOLLOWED BY INTENSE COLD PRODUCES THE PHENOMENON! NOW... FETCH THE "ICE"-- HURRY!
CRAAACK!
CRAACK!
MOMENTS LATER, AS THE GANG FLEES WITH THE LOOT...
THE BAT-SIGNAL! BATMAN AND ROBIN WILL BE HERE ANY SECOND!
BUT WE WON'T BE HERE TO WELCOME THEM, MARTY!
JEWELRY EXCHANGE
SUDDENLY, THE ROARING JETS FILL THE AIR...
THEY'RE ESCAPING IN THAT TRUCK, BATMAN! AND LOOK AT THE ONE IN THE FREEZING COMPARTMENT!
HE'S WEARING A SPECIAL SUIT OF SOME KIND, ROBIN! WE'LL FIND OUT WHY WHEN WE CAPTURE HIM!
ICE CREAM
2

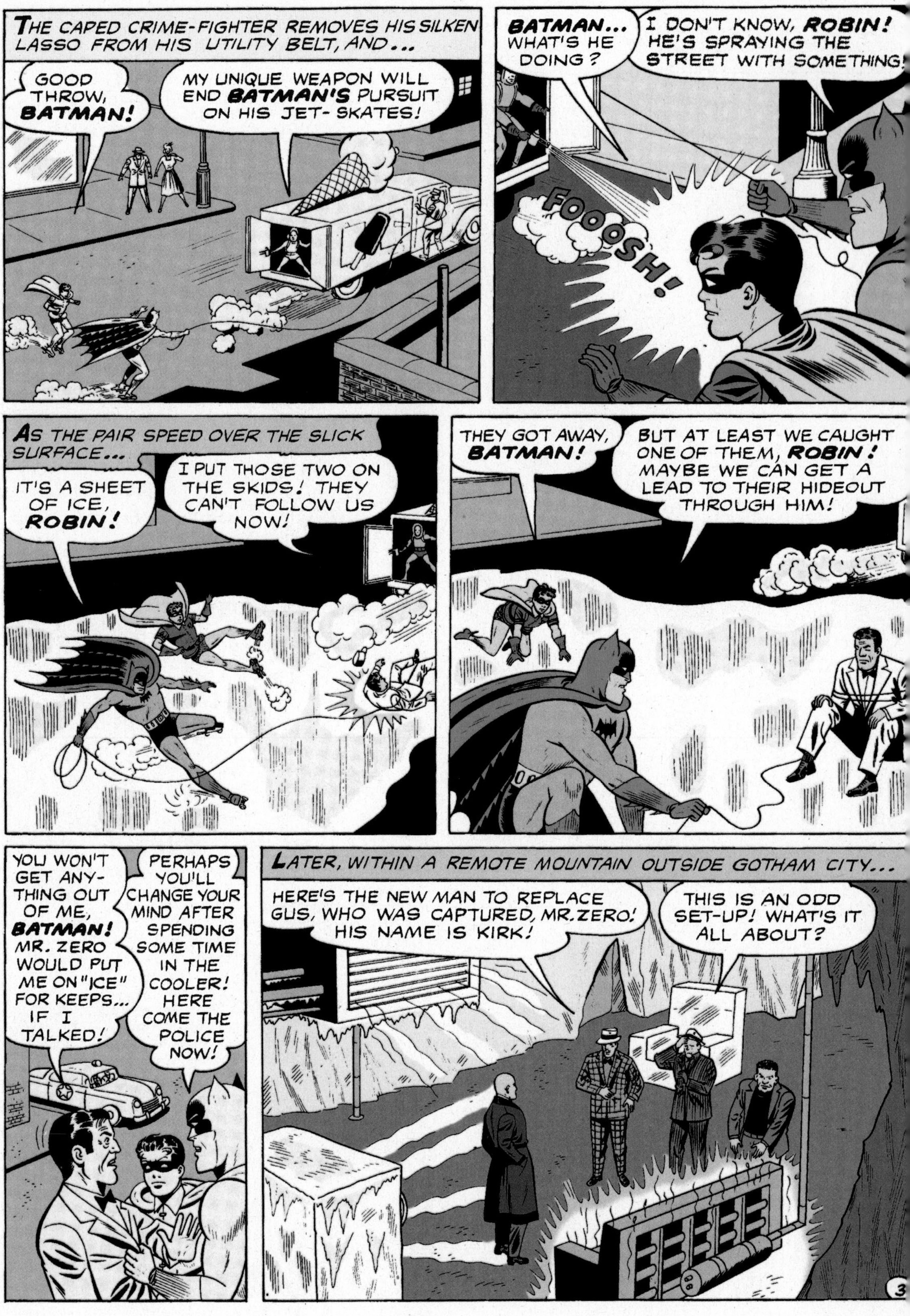
THE CAPED CRIME-FIGHTER REMOVES HIS SILKEN LASSO FROM HIS UTILITY BELT, AND...
GOOD THROW, BATMAN!
MY UNIQUE WEAPON WILL END BATMAN'S PURSUIT ON HIS JET-SKATES!
BATMAN... WHAT'S HE DOING?
I DON'T KNOW, ROBIN! HE'S SPRAYING THE STREET WITH SOMETHING!
FOOOSH!
AS THE PAIR SPEED OVER THE SLICK SURFACE...
IT'S A SHEET OF ICE, ROBIN!
I PUT THOSE TWO ON THE SKIDS! THEY CAN'T FOLLOW US NOW!
THEY GOT AWAY, BATMAN!
BUT AT LEAST WE CAUGHT ONE OF THEM, ROBIN! MAYBE WE CAN GET A LEAD TO THEIR HIDEOUT THROUGH HIM!
YOU WON'T GET ANY-THING OUT OF ME, BATMAN! MR. ZERO WOULD PUT ME ON "ICE" FOR KEEPS... IF I TALKED!
PERHAPS YOU'LL CHANGE YOUR MIND AFTER SPENDING SOME TIME IN THE COOLER! HERE COME THE POLICE NOW!
LATER, WITHIN A REMOTE MOUNTAIN OUTSIDE GOTHAM CITY...
HERE'S THE NEW MAN TO REPLACE GUS, WHO WAS CAPTURED, MR. ZERO! HIS NAME IS KIRK!
THIS IS AN ODD SET-UP! WHAT'S IT ALL ABOUT?
3

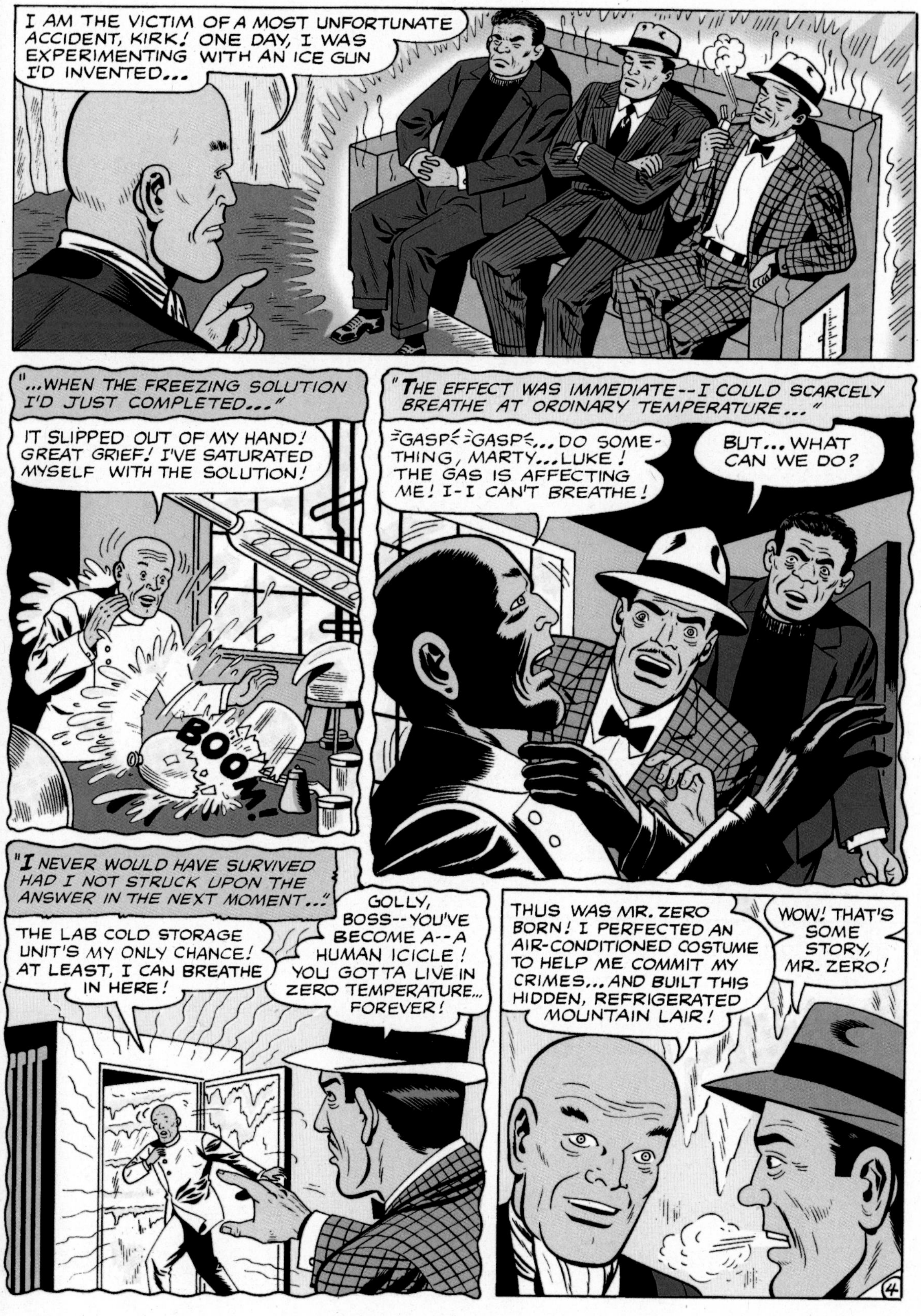
I AM THE VICTIM OF A MOST UNFORTUNATE ACCIDENT, KIRK! ONE DAY, I WAS EXPERIMENTING WITH AN ICE GUN I'D INVENTED...
"...WHEN THE FREEZING SOLUTION I'D JUST COMPLETED..."
IT SLIPPED OUT OF MY HAND! GREAT GRIEF! I'VE SATURATED MYSELF WITH THE SOLUTION!
BOOM!
"THE EFFECT WAS IMMEDIATE--I COULD SCARCELY BREATHE AT ORDINARY TEMPERATURE..."
GASP GASP... DO SOMETHING, MARTY...LUKE! THE GAS IS AFFECTING ME! I-I CAN'T BREATHE!
BUT... WHAT CAN WE DO?
"I NEVER WOULD HAVE SURVIVED HAD I NOT STRUCK UPON THE ANSWER IN THE NEXT MOMENT..."
THE LAB COLD STORAGE UNIT'S MY ONLY CHANCE! AT LEAST, I CAN BREATHE IN HERE!
GOLLY, BOSS--YOU'VE BECOME A--A HUMAN ICICLE! YOU GOTTA LIVE IN ZERO TEMPERATURE... FOREVER!
THUS WAS MR. ZERO BORN! I PERFECTED AN AIR-CONDITIONED COSTUME TO HELP ME COMMIT MY CRIMES... AND BUILT THIS HIDDEN, REFRIGERATED MOUNTAIN LAIR!
WOW! THAT'S SOME STORY, MR. ZERO!
4

NOW, GENTLEMEN, WE WILL CONTINUE WITH OUR PLANS TO "FREEZE" THE WEALTH OF GOTHAM CITY! HERE IS PLAN C!

NEXT DAY, OUTSIDE THE EXCLUSIVE GOTHAM CITY HOTEL...

SPECIAL FROZEN MEAT SHIPMENT FOR THE VISITING PRINCE AND PRINCESS!

OKAY--THE STORAGE LOCKERS ARE STRAIGHT AHEAD!

FROZEN FOOD STORAGE

RVICE ENTRAN

SHORTLY, A FANTASTIC CRIME PLAN TAKES FORM...

GUARDS ARE ALL OVER THE PLACE, PROTECTING THE VISITING ROYALTY, BUT THANKS TO MR. ZERO, WE'LL GET INSIDE JUST THE SAME!

QUIET! GET READY TO MOVE AS SOON AS HE'S FINISHED!

THEN, AS MR. ZERO FIRES THE FREEZING JET...

GRAB THE PRINCESS' TIARA AND HER DIAMOND PENDANT! HURRY!

OH-H-H!

NEARBY, AS BATMAN AND ROBIN HEAR A POLICE BULLETIN...

...AND THE THIEVES HAVE SMASHED INTO THE GRAND BALL ROOM...

THERE'S THE HOTEL--AND MR. ZERO ESCAPING ON THE TERRACE, ROBIN!

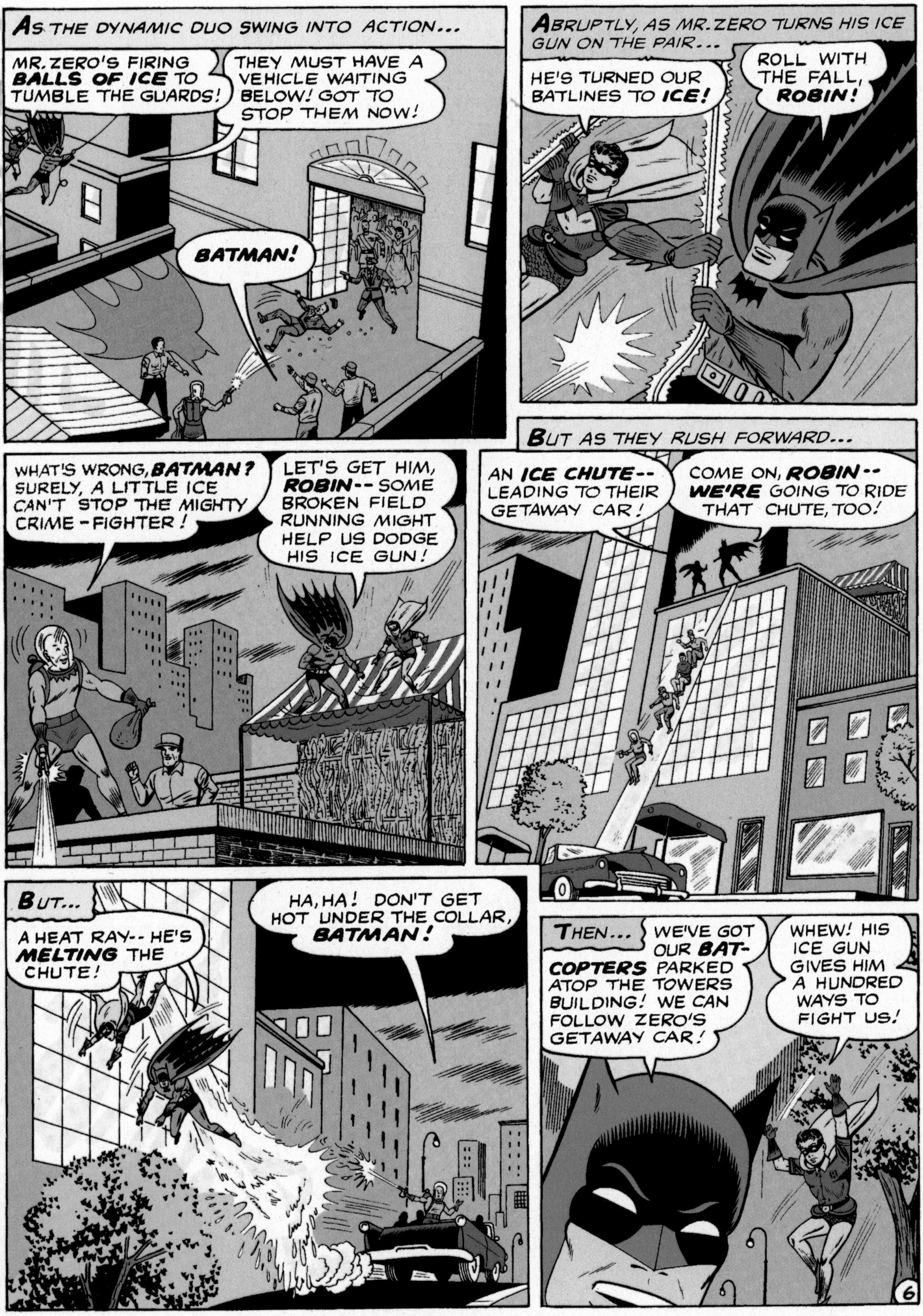
AS THE DYNAMIC DUO SWING INTO ACTION...
MR. ZERO'S FIRING BALLS OF ICE TO TUMBLE THE GUARDS!
THEY MUST HAVE A VEHICLE WAITING BELOW! GOT TO STOP THEM NOW!
BATMAN!
ABRUPTLY, AS MR. ZERO TURNS HIS ICE GUN ON THE PAIR...
HE'S TURNED OUR BATLINES TO ICE!
ROLL WITH THE FALL, ROBIN!
WHAT'S WRONG, BATMAN? SURELY, A LITTLE ICE CAN'T STOP THE MIGHTY CRIME-FIGHTER!
LET'S GET HIM, ROBIN-- SOME BROKEN FIELD RUNNING MIGHT HELP US DODGE HIS ICE GUN!
BUT AS THEY RUSH FORWARD...
AN ICE CHUTE-- LEADING TO THEIR GETAWAY CAR!
COME ON, ROBIN-- WE'RE GOING TO RIDE THAT CHUTE, TOO!
BUT...
A HEAT RAY-- HE'S MELTING THE CHUTE!
HA, HA! DON'T GET HOT UNDER THE COLLAR, BATMAN!
THEN...
WE'VE GOT OUR BAT-COPTERS PARKED ATOP THE TOWERS BUILDING! WE CAN FOLLOW ZERO'S GETAWAY CAR!
WHEW! HIS ICE GUN GIVES HIM A HUNDRED WAYS TO FIGHT US!
6

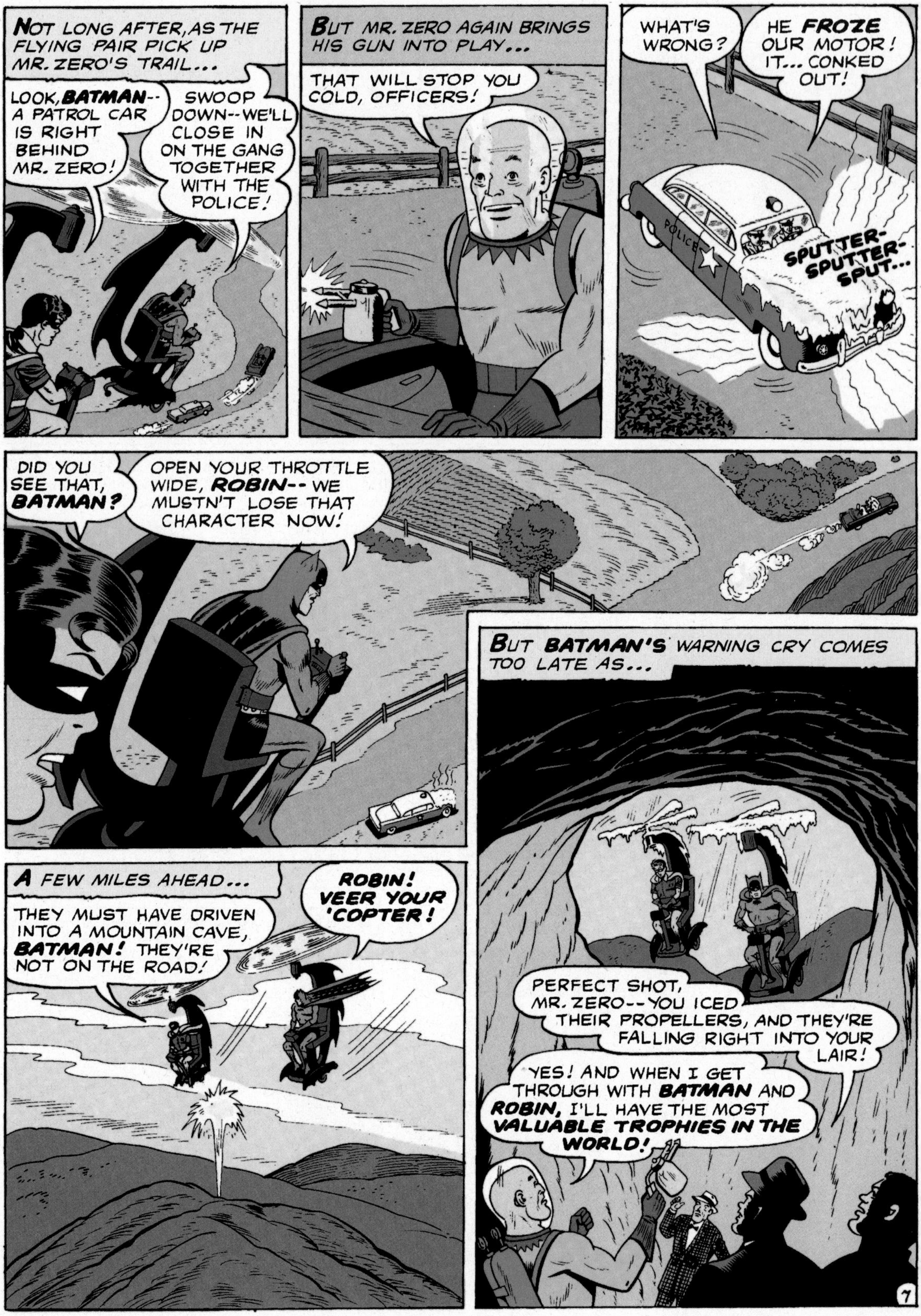
NOT LONG AFTER, AS THE FLYING PAIR PICK UP MR. ZERO'S TRAIL...
LOOK, BATMAN-- A PATROL CAR IS RIGHT BEHIND MR. ZERO!
SWOOP DOWN--WE'LL CLOSE IN ON THE GANG TOGETHER WITH THE POLICE!
BUT MR. ZERO AGAIN BRINGS HIS GUN INTO PLAY...
THAT WILL STOP YOU COLD, OFFICERS!
WHAT'S WRONG?
HE FROZE OUR MOTOR! IT... CONKED OUT!
POLICE
SPUTTER-SPUTTER-SPUT...
DID YOU SEE THAT, BATMAN?
OPEN YOUR THROTTLE WIDE, ROBIN-- WE MUSTN'T LOSE THAT CHARACTER NOW!
A FEW MILES AHEAD...
THEY MUST HAVE DRIVEN INTO A MOUNTAIN CAVE, BATMAN! THEY'RE NOT ON THE ROAD!
ROBIN! VEER YOUR 'COPTER!
BUT BATMAN'S WARNING CRY COMES TOO LATE AS...
PERFECT SHOT, MR. ZERO--YOU ICED THEIR PROPELLERS, AND THEY'RE FALLING RIGHT INTO YOUR LAIR!
YES! AND WHEN I GET THROUGH WITH BATMAN AND ROBIN, I'LL HAVE THE MOST VALUABLE TROPHIES IN THE WORLD!
7

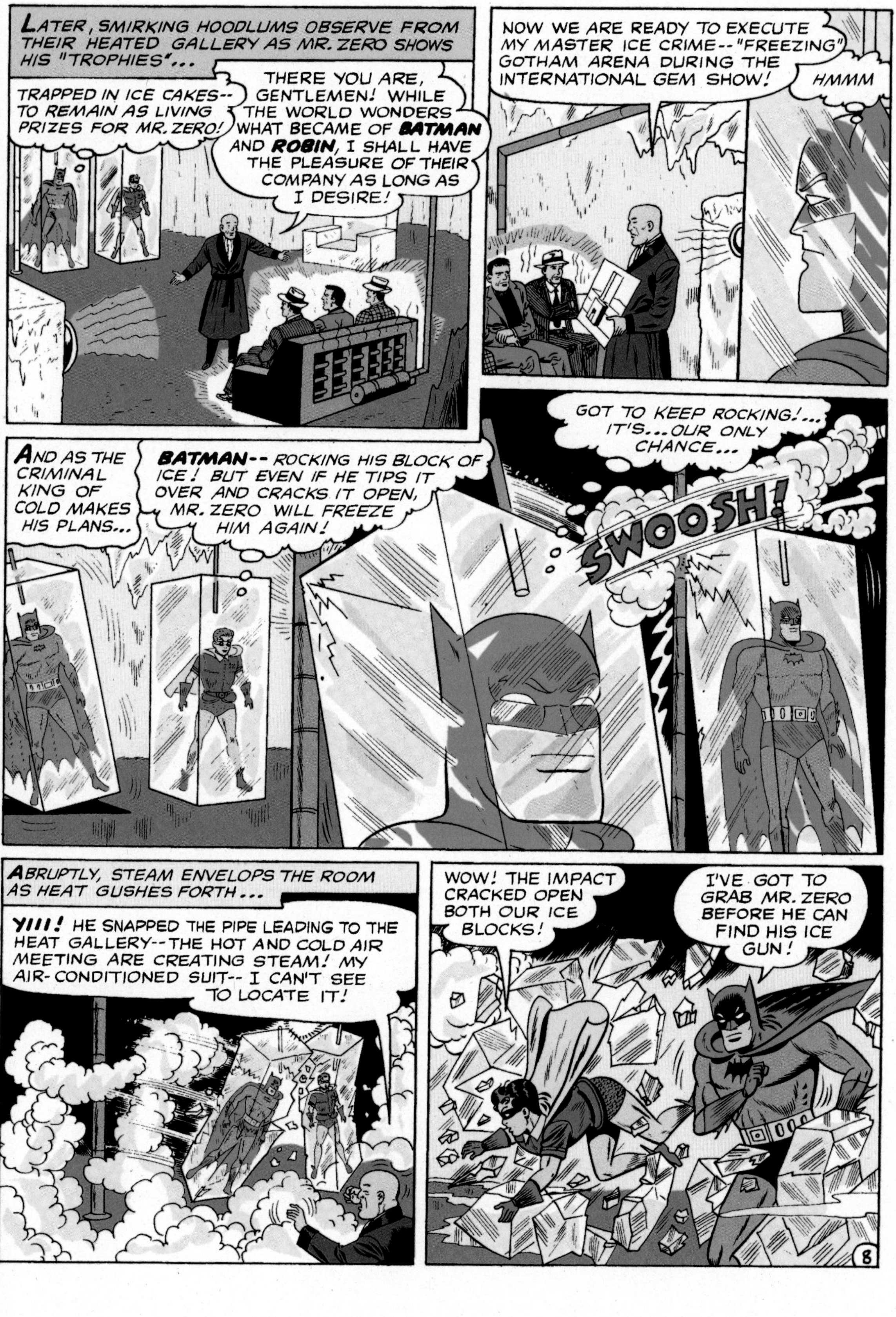

LATER, SMIRKING HOODLUMS OBSERVE FROM THEIR HEATED GALLERY AS MR. ZERO SHOWS HIS "TROPHIES"...
TRAPPED IN ICE CAKES-- TO REMAIN AS LIVING PRIZES FOR MR. ZERO!
THERE YOU ARE, GENTLEMEN! WHILE THE WORLD WONDERS WHAT BECAME OF BATMAN AND ROBIN, I SHALL HAVE THE PLEASURE OF THEIR COMPANY AS LONG AS I DESIRE!
NOW WE ARE READY TO EXECUTE MY MASTER ICE CRIME--"FREEZING" GOTHAM ARENA DURING THE INTERNATIONAL GEM SHOW!
HMMM
AND AS THE CRIMINAL KING OF COLD MAKES HIS PLANS...
BATMAN-- ROCKING HIS BLOCK OF ICE! BUT EVEN IF HE TIPS IT OVER AND CRACKS IT OPEN, MR. ZERO WILL FREEZE HIM AGAIN!
GOT TO KEEP ROCKING!... IT'S...OUR ONLY CHANCE...
SWOOSH!
ABRUPTLY, STEAM ENVELOPS THE ROOM AS HEAT GUSHES FORTH...
YIII! HE SNAPPED THE PIPE LEADING TO THE HEAT GALLERY--THE HOT AND COLD AIR MEETING ARE CREATING STEAM! MY AIR-CONDITIONED SUIT-- I CAN'T SEE TO LOCATE IT!
WOW! THE IMPACT CRACKED OPEN BOTH OUR ICE BLOCKS!
I'VE GOT TO GRAB MR. ZERO BEFORE HE CAN FIND HIS ICE GUN!
8

THE STEAM IS WEAKENING MR. ZERO-- BUT HE'S FOUND THAT ICE GUN!
I'VE... G-G-GOT... THE... ICE G-GUN...
COLD... M-M-MUST HAVE COLD!
THIS'LL MAKE YOU STIFF AS A BOARD!
THEN, AS THE PANICKY GANG IS LED OUT OF THE ICE CHAMBER...
YOU DON'T UNDERSTAND! I CAN'T SURVIVE IN NORMAL TEMPERATURES! GET ME MY AIR-CONDITIONED SUIT!
IF YOU NEED IT, YOU'LL HAVE IT! MOVE!
9
BUT ONCE OUTSIDE...
WHY...I--CAN BREATHE NORMALLY AGAIN!
YES, MR. ZERO, THAT STEAM TREATMENT MUST HAVE CHANGED YOU BACK TO NORMAL! NOW WE'LL SEE IF THE LAW CAN STRAIGHTEN OUT YOUR DISTORTED MIND!
THE END

BATMAN

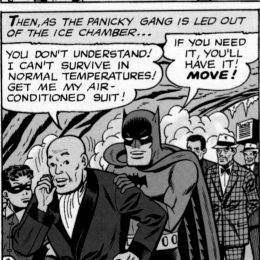

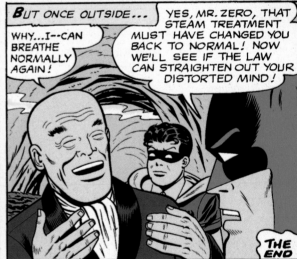

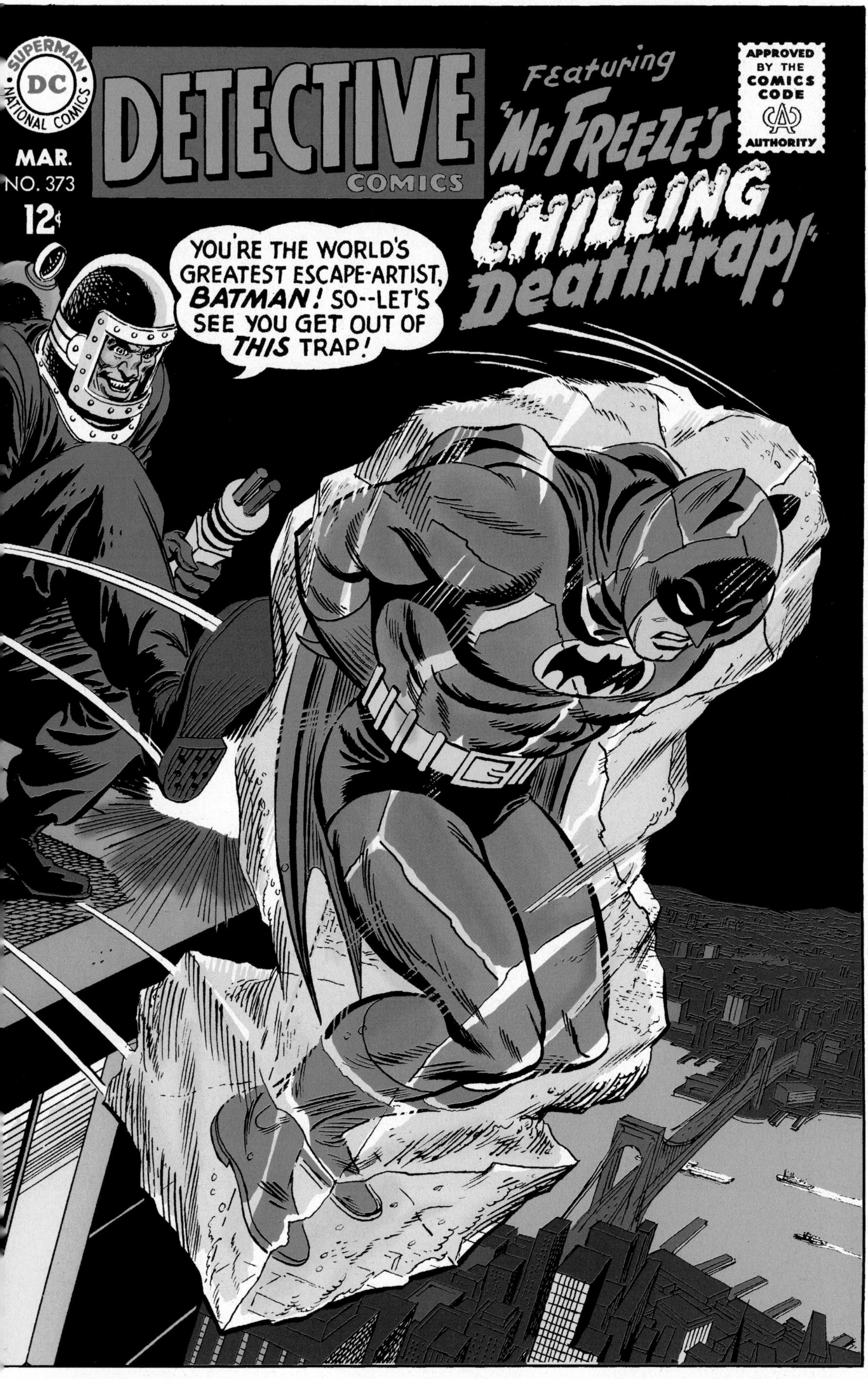
SUPERMAN DC NATIONAL COMICS
DETECTIVE COMICS
MAR.
NO. 373
12¢
APPROVED BY THE COMICS CODE AUTHORITY
Featuring "Mr. Freeze's Chilling Deathtrap!"
YOU'RE THE WORLD'S GREATEST ESCAPE-ARTIST, BATMAN! SO--LET'S SEE YOU GET OUT OF THIS TRAP!

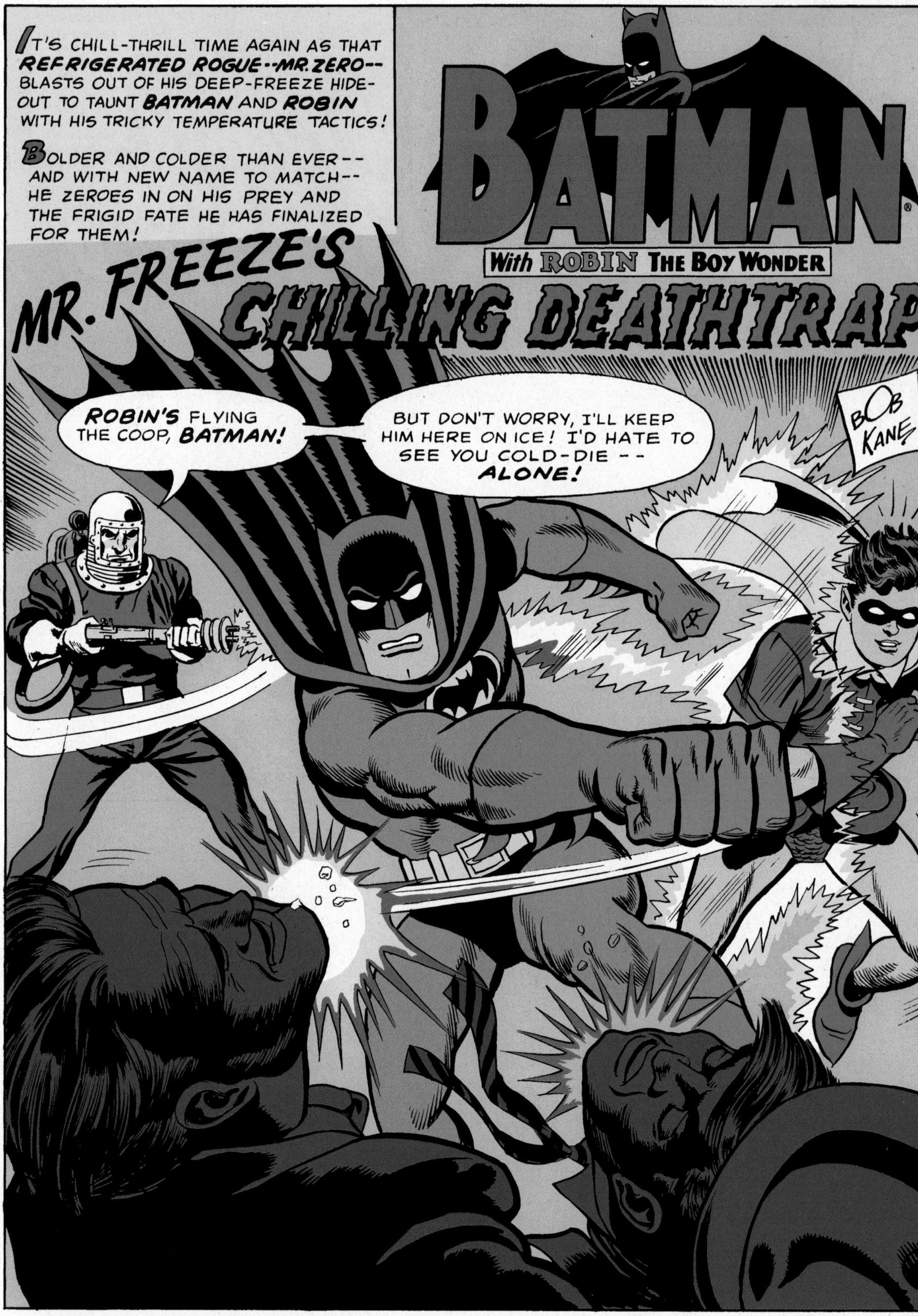
IT'S CHILL-THRILL TIME AGAIN AS THAT REFRIGERATED ROGUE--MR. ZERO--BLASTS OUT OF HIS DEEP-FREEZE HIDE-OUT TO TAUNT BATMAN AND ROBIN WITH HIS TRICKY TEMPERATURE TACTICS!
BOLDER AND COLDER THAN EVER--AND WITH NEW NAME TO MATCH--HE ZEROES IN ON HIS PREY AND THE FRIGID FATE HE HAS FINALIZED FOR THEM!
BATMAN®
With ROBIN THE BOY WONDER
MR. FREEZE'S CHILLING DEATHTRAP!
BOB KANE
ROBIN'S FLYING THE COOP, BATMAN!
BUT DON'T WORRY, I'LL KEEP HIM HERE ON ICE! I'D HATE TO SEE YOU COLD-DIE -- ALONE!

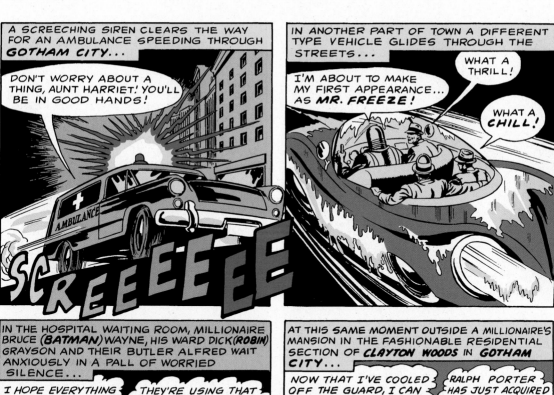

A SCREECHING SIREN CLEARS THE WAY FOR AN AMBULANCE SPEEDING THROUGH *GOTHAM CITY*...

DON'T WORRY ABOUT A THING, AUNT HARRIET! YOU'LL BE IN GOOD HANDS!

SCREEEEE

IN ANOTHER PART OF TOWN A DIFFERENT TYPE VEHICLE GLIDES THROUGH THE STREETS...

I'M ABOUT TO MAKE MY FIRST APPEARANCE... AS *MR. FREEZE!*

WHAT A THRILL!

WHAT A CHILL!

IN THE HOSPITAL WAITING ROOM, MILLIONAIRE BRUCE (*BATMAN*) WAYNE, HIS WARD DICK (*ROBIN*) GRAYSON AND THEIR BUTLER ALFRED WAIT ANXIOUSLY IN A PALL OF WORRIED SILENCE...

I HOPE EVERYTHING GOES WELL!

THEY'RE USING THAT NEW MEDICAL TECHNIQUE ON AUNT HARRIET-- *CRYOSURGERY**.

DR. NOSTRAND IS THE COUNTRY'S FINEST *CRYOSURGEON!*

*CRYOSURGERY IS OPERATING BY USE OF INTENSE COLD.

AT THIS SAME MOMENT OUTSIDE A MILLIONAIRE'S MANSION IN THE FASHIONABLE RESIDENTIAL SECTION OF *CLAYTON WOODS* IN *GOTHAM CITY*...

NOW THAT I'VE COOLED OFF THE GUARD, I CAN BLAST MY WAY IN HERE!

RALPH PORTER HAS JUST ACQUIRED THE VERY PAINTING I WANT--A WINTER SCENE THAT RANKS WITH THE BEST MASTERS!

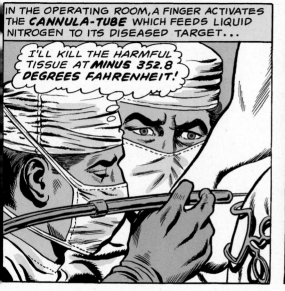

IN THE OPERATING ROOM, A FINGER ACTIVATES THE *CANNULA-TUBE* WHICH FEEDS LIQUID NITROGEN TO ITS DISEASED TARGET...

I'LL KILL THE HARMFUL TISSUE AT *MINUS 352.8 DEGREES FAHRENHEIT!*

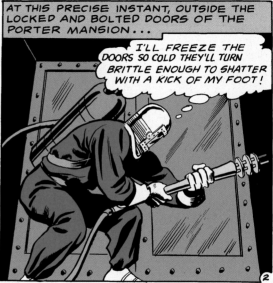

AT THIS PRECISE INSTANT, OUTSIDE THE LOCKED AND BOLTED DOORS OF THE PORTER MANSION...

I'LL FREEZE THE DOORS SO COLD THEY'LL TURN BRITTLE ENOUGH TO SHATTER WITH A KICK OF MY FOOT!

DR. NOSTRAND PAUSES--GASPS IN PUZZLED DISMAY! AGAIN HE PRESSES THE CANNULA ACTIVATION SWITCH--AND AGAIN...

IT--SUDDENLY STOPPED WORKING! AND THERE ISN'T ANOTHER MACHINE LIKE IT WITHIN A THOUSAND MILES!

IN SIMILAR SHOCK, *MR. FREEZE* STARES AT HIS OWN INVENTION, THE *CRYOTHERMAL* GUN WHICH CAN FOCUS INTENSE HEAT OR UTTER COLD FROM ITS TWIN BARRELS...

WHAT'S WRONG? THE COLD BARREL OF MY WEAPON NEVER CONKED OUT ON ME BEFORE!--IT'S AS IF ITS POWER CYLINDER HAS BEEN SHORT-CIRCUITED!

OH, WELL--I'LL SIMPLY SWITCH TO THE *HEAT* SECTION AND BURN MY WAY IN!

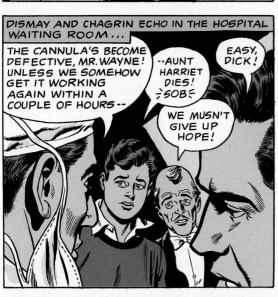

DISMAY AND CHAGRIN ECHO IN THE HOSPITAL WAITING ROOM...

THE CANNULA'S BECOME DEFECTIVE, MR. WAYNE! UNLESS WE SOMEHOW GET IT WORKING AGAIN WITHIN A COUPLE OF HOURS--

--AUNT HARRIET DIES! ≶SOB≶

EASY, DICK!

WE MUSN'T GIVE UP HOPE!

WHILE WARM DELIGHT AND COOL CHEERFULNESS RESOUND IN THE VOICE OF THE *FRIGID FELON*...

AT LAST! THIS PERFECT REPRESENTATION OF A WINTER WONDERLAND IS--*ALL MINE!*

BRRR! IT MAKES ME *SHIVER* JUST TO *LOOK* AT IT!

SCANT MOMENTS AFTER THEY HAVE RECEIVED THE BAD NEWS FROM THE SURGEON, BRUCE AND DICK ARE AGAIN SHAKEN BY...

THE *BAT-SIGNAL!* OHH--*NO!* NOT AT A TIME LIKE *THIS!*

HOW CAN WE GO INTO ACTION AS *BATMAN* AND *ROBIN* -- WHEN AUNT HARRIET'S LIFE IS HANGING IN THE BALANCE?

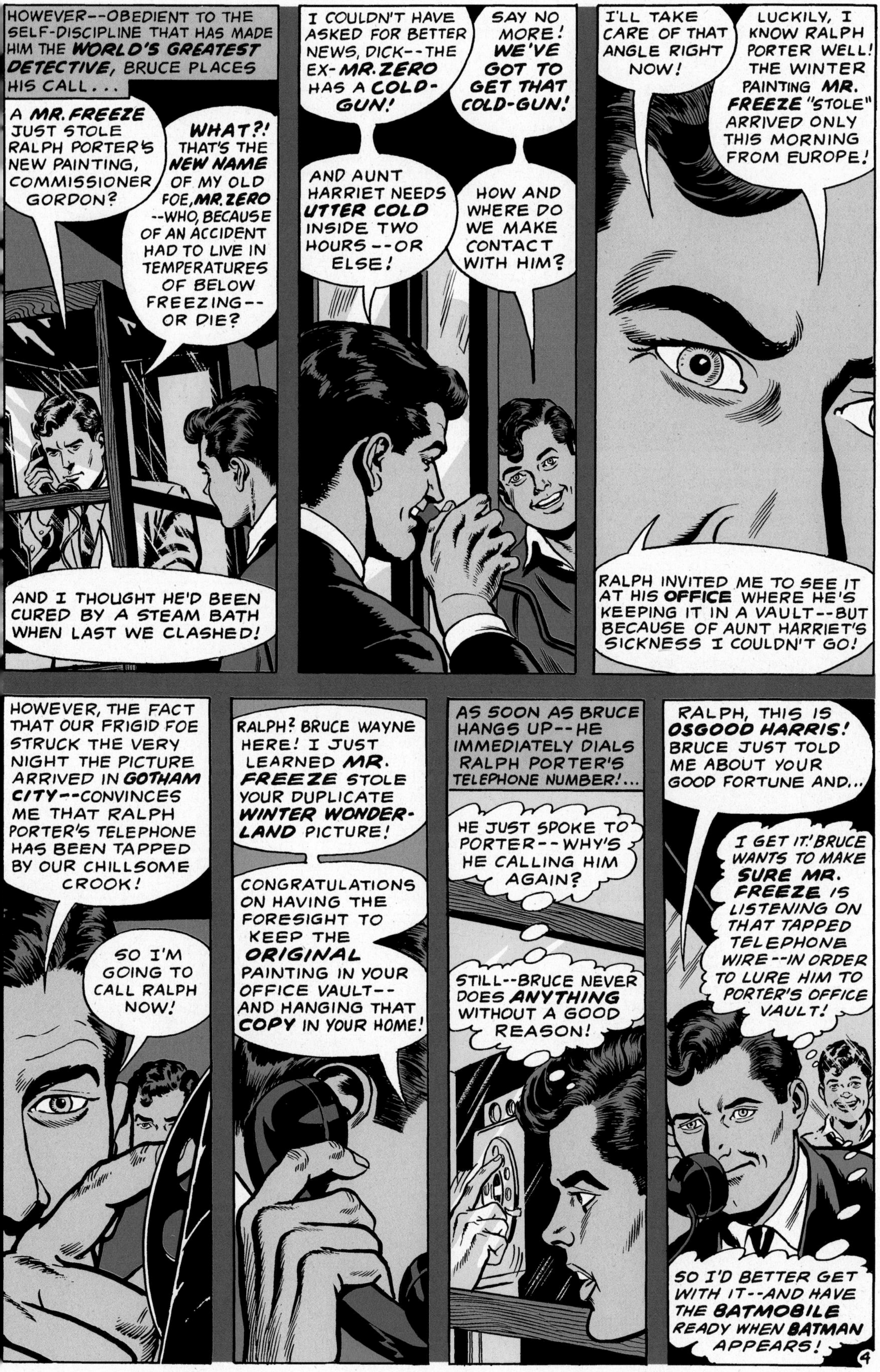

HOWEVER--OBEDIENT TO THE SELF-DISCIPLINE THAT HAS MADE HIM THE **WORLD'S GREATEST DETECTIVE,** BRUCE PLACES HIS CALL...
A **MR. FREEZE** JUST STOLE RALPH PORTER'S NEW PAINTING, COMMISSIONER GORDON?
WHAT?! THAT'S THE **NEW NAME** OF MY OLD FOE, **MR. ZERO** --WHO, BECAUSE OF AN ACCIDENT HAD TO LIVE IN TEMPERATURES OF BELOW FREEZING--OR DIE?
AND I THOUGHT HE'D BEEN CURED BY A STEAM BATH WHEN LAST WE CLASHED!
I COULDN'T HAVE ASKED FOR BETTER NEWS, DICK--THE EX-**MR. ZERO** HAS A **COLD-GUN!**
AND AUNT HARRIET NEEDS **UTTER COLD** INSIDE TWO HOURS--OR ELSE!
SAY NO MORE! **WE'VE GOT TO GET THAT COLD-GUN!**
HOW AND WHERE DO WE MAKE CONTACT WITH HIM?
I'LL TAKE CARE OF THAT ANGLE RIGHT NOW!
LUCKILY, I KNOW RALPH PORTER WELL! THE WINTER PAINTING **MR. FREEZE** "STOLE" ARRIVED ONLY THIS MORNING FROM EUROPE!
RALPH INVITED ME TO SEE IT AT HIS **OFFICE** WHERE HE'S KEEPING IT IN A VAULT--BUT BECAUSE OF AUNT HARRIET'S SICKNESS I COULDN'T GO!
HOWEVER, THE FACT THAT OUR FRIGID FOE STRUCK THE VERY NIGHT THE PICTURE ARRIVED IN **GOTHAM CITY**--CONVINCES ME THAT RALPH PORTER'S TELEPHONE HAS BEEN TAPPED BY OUR CHILLSOME CROOK!
SO I'M GOING TO CALL RALPH NOW!
RALPH? BRUCE WAYNE HERE! I JUST LEARNED **MR. FREEZE** STOLE YOUR DUPLICATE **WINTER WONDERLAND** PICTURE!
CONGRATULATIONS ON HAVING THE FORESIGHT TO KEEP THE **ORIGINAL** PAINTING IN YOUR OFFICE VAULT--AND HANGING THAT **COPY** IN YOUR HOME!
AS SOON AS BRUCE HANGS UP--HE IMMEDIATELY DIALS RALPH PORTER'S TELEPHONE NUMBER!...
HE JUST SPOKE TO PORTER--WHY'S HE CALLING HIM AGAIN?
STILL--BRUCE NEVER DOES **ANYTHING** WITHOUT A GOOD REASON!
RALPH, THIS IS **OSGOOD HARRIS!** BRUCE JUST TOLD ME ABOUT YOUR GOOD FORTUNE AND...
I GET IT! BRUCE WANTS TO MAKE **SURE MR. FREEZE** IS LISTENING ON THAT TAPPED TELEPHONE WIRE--IN ORDER TO LURE HIM TO PORTER'S OFFICE VAULT!
SO I'D BETTER GET WITH IT--AND HAVE THE **BATMOBILE** READY WHEN **BATMAN** APPEARS!
4

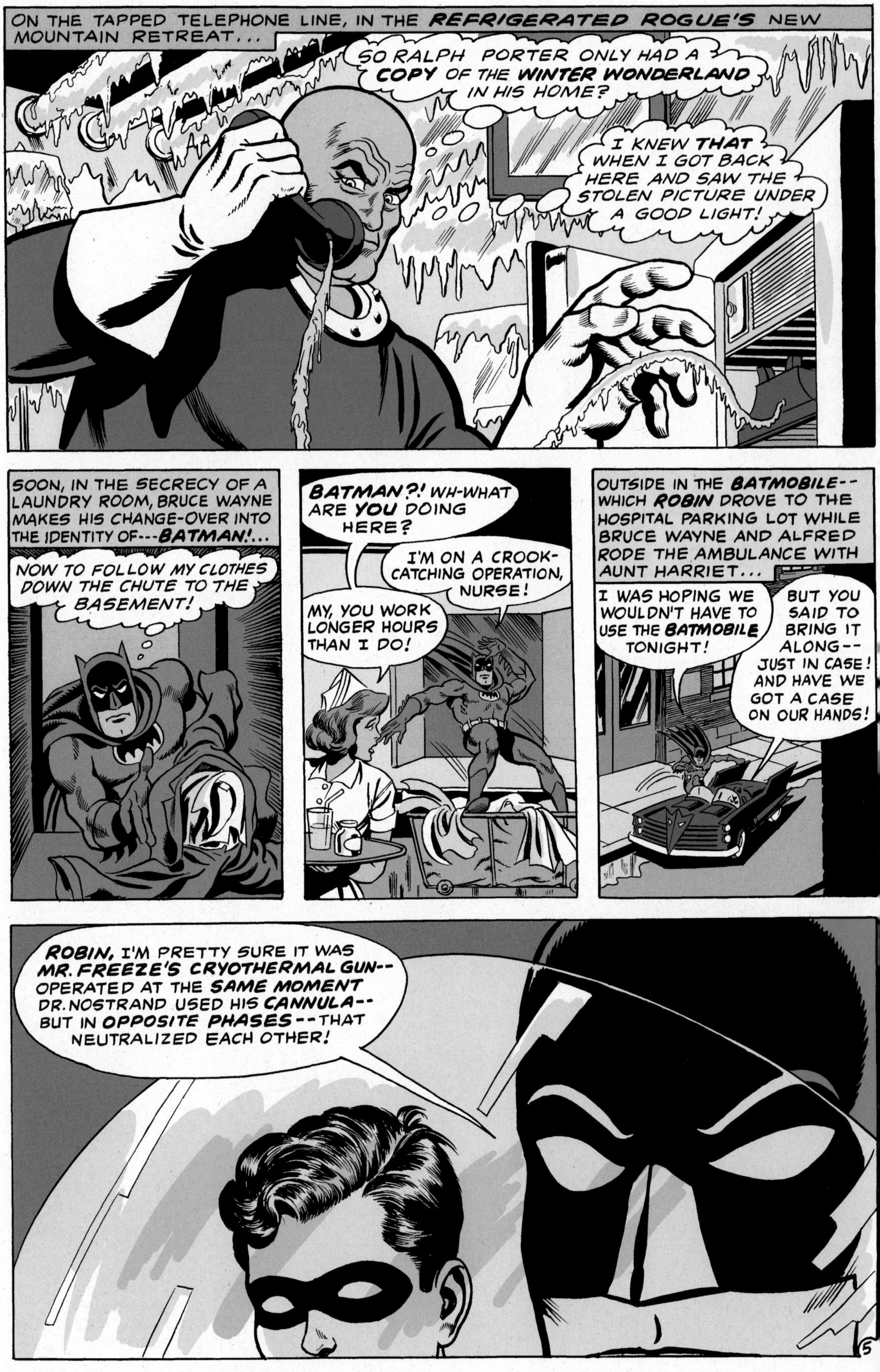
ON THE TAPPED TELEPHONE LINE, IN THE REFRIGERATED ROGUE'S NEW MOUNTAIN RETREAT...
SO RALPH PORTER ONLY HAD A COPY OF THE WINTER WONDERLAND IN HIS HOME?
I KNEW THAT WHEN I GOT BACK HERE AND SAW THE STOLEN PICTURE UNDER A GOOD LIGHT!
SOON, IN THE SECRECY OF A LAUNDRY ROOM, BRUCE WAYNE MAKES HIS CHANGE-OVER INTO THE IDENTITY OF---BATMAN!...
NOW TO FOLLOW MY CLOTHES DOWN THE CHUTE TO THE BASEMENT!
BATMAN?! WH-WHAT ARE YOU DOING HERE?
I'M ON A CROOK-CATCHING OPERATION, NURSE!
MY, YOU WORK LONGER HOURS THAN I DO!
OUTSIDE IN THE BATMOBILE--WHICH ROBIN DROVE TO THE HOSPITAL PARKING LOT WHILE BRUCE WAYNE AND ALFRED RODE THE AMBULANCE WITH AUNT HARRIET...
I WAS HOPING WE WOULDN'T HAVE TO USE THE BATMOBILE TONIGHT!
BUT YOU SAID TO BRING IT ALONG--JUST IN CASE! AND HAVE WE GOT A CASE ON OUR HANDS!
ROBIN, I'M PRETTY SURE IT WAS MR. FREEZE'S CRYOTHERMAL GUN--OPERATED AT THE SAME MOMENT DR. NOSTRAND USED HIS CANNULA--BUT IN OPPOSITE PHASES--THAT NEUTRALIZED EACH OTHER!
5

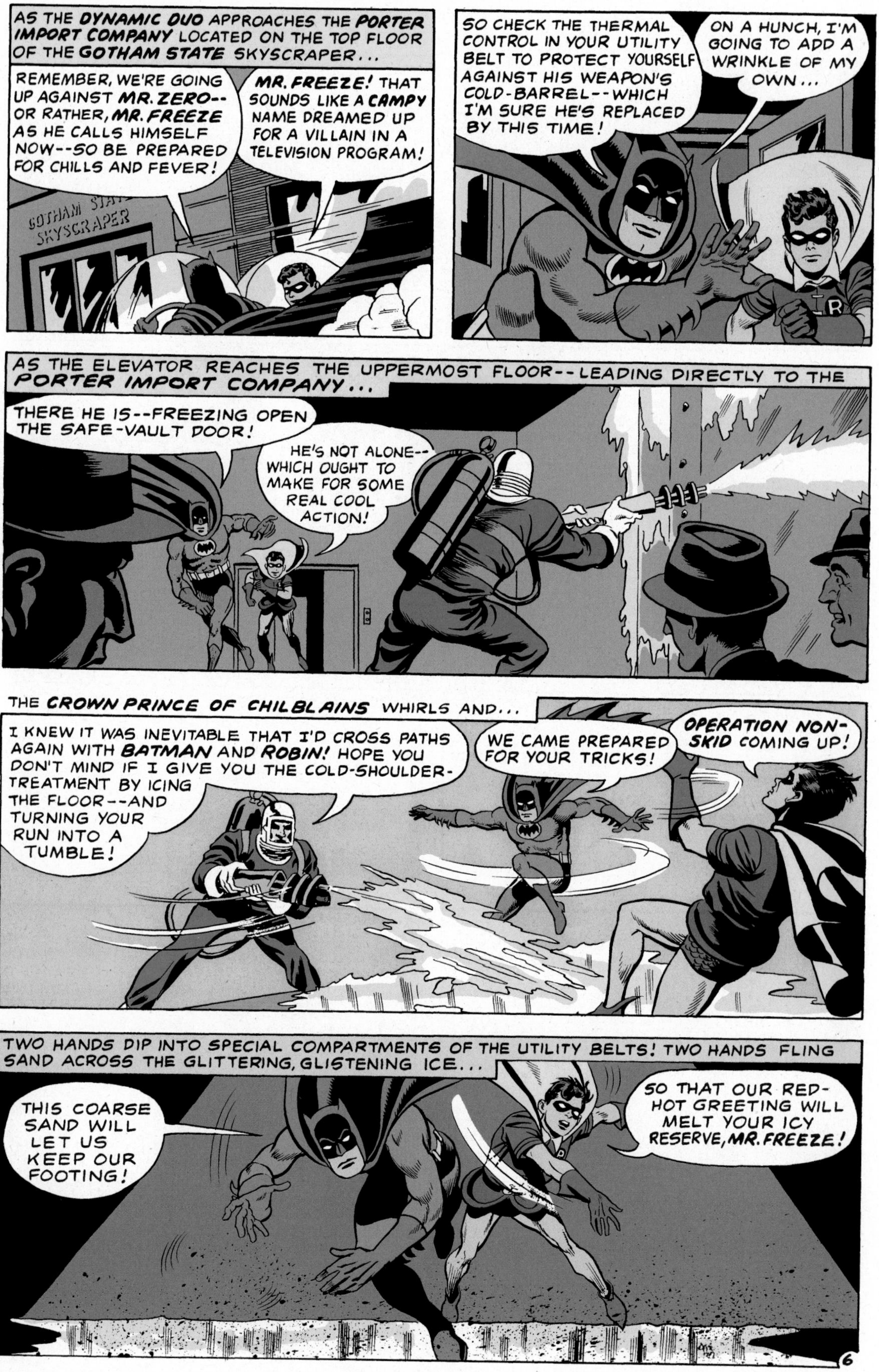
AS THE DYNAMIC DUO APPROACHES THE PORTER IMPORT COMPANY LOCATED ON THE TOP FLOOR OF THE GOTHAM STATE SKYSCRAPER...
REMEMBER, WE'RE GOING UP AGAINST MR. ZERO-- OR RATHER, MR. FREEZE AS HE CALLS HIMSELF NOW--SO BE PREPARED FOR CHILLS AND FEVER!
MR. FREEZE! THAT SOUNDS LIKE A CAMPY NAME DREAMED UP FOR A VILLAIN IN A TELEVISION PROGRAM!
GOTHAM STATE SKYSCRAPER
SO CHECK THE THERMAL CONTROL IN YOUR UTILITY BELT TO PROTECT YOURSELF AGAINST HIS WEAPON'S COLD-BARREL--WHICH I'M SURE HE'S REPLACED BY THIS TIME!
ON A HUNCH, I'M GOING TO ADD A WRINKLE OF MY OWN...
AS THE ELEVATOR REACHES THE UPPERMOST FLOOR--LEADING DIRECTLY TO THE PORTER IMPORT COMPANY...
THERE HE IS--FREEZING OPEN THE SAFE-VAULT DOOR!
HE'S NOT ALONE-- WHICH OUGHT TO MAKE FOR SOME REAL COOL ACTION!
THE CROWN PRINCE OF CHILBLAINS WHIRLS AND...
I KNEW IT WAS INEVITABLE THAT I'D CROSS PATHS AGAIN WITH BATMAN AND ROBIN! HOPE YOU DON'T MIND IF I GIVE YOU THE COLD-SHOULDER-TREATMENT BY ICING THE FLOOR--AND TURNING YOUR RUN INTO A TUMBLE!
WE CAME PREPARED FOR YOUR TRICKS!
OPERATION NON-SKID COMING UP!
TWO HANDS DIP INTO SPECIAL COMPARTMENTS OF THE UTILITY BELTS! TWO HANDS FLING SAND ACROSS THE GLITTERING, GLISTENING ICE...
THIS COARSE SAND WILL LET US KEEP OUR FOOTING!
SO THAT OUR RED-HOT GREETING WILL MELT YOUR ICY RESERVE, MR. FREEZE!
6

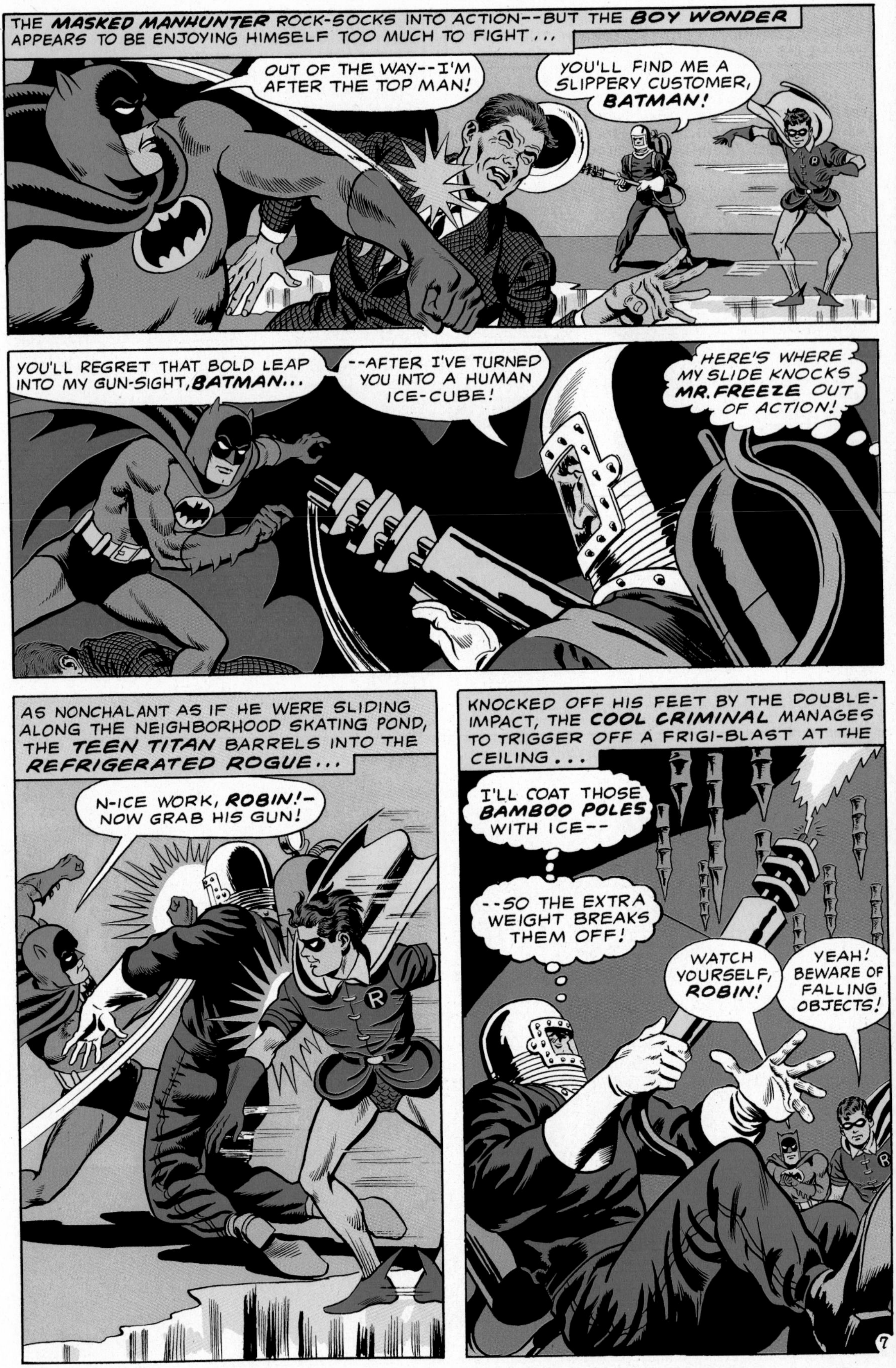
THE MASKED MANHUNTER ROCK-SOCKS INTO ACTION--BUT THE BOY WONDER APPEARS TO BE ENJOYING HIMSELF TOO MUCH TO FIGHT...
OUT OF THE WAY--I'M AFTER THE TOP MAN!
YOU'LL FIND ME A SLIPPERY CUSTOMER, BATMAN!
YOU'LL REGRET THAT BOLD LEAP INTO MY GUN-SIGHT, BATMAN...
--AFTER I'VE TURNED YOU INTO A HUMAN ICE-CUBE!
HERE'S WHERE MY SLIDE KNOCKS MR. FREEZE OUT OF ACTION!
AS NONCHALANT AS IF HE WERE SLIDING ALONG THE NEIGHBORHOOD SKATING POND, THE TEEN TITAN BARRELS INTO THE REFRIGERATED ROGUE...
N-ICE WORK, ROBIN!-NOW GRAB HIS GUN!
KNOCKED OFF HIS FEET BY THE DOUBLE-IMPACT, THE COOL CRIMINAL MANAGES TO TRIGGER OFF A FRIGI-BLAST AT THE CEILING...
I'LL COAT THOSE BAMBOO POLES WITH ICE--
--SO THE EXTRA WEIGHT BREAKS THEM OFF!
WATCH YOURSELF, ROBIN!
YEAH! BEWARE OF FALLING OBJECTS!
7

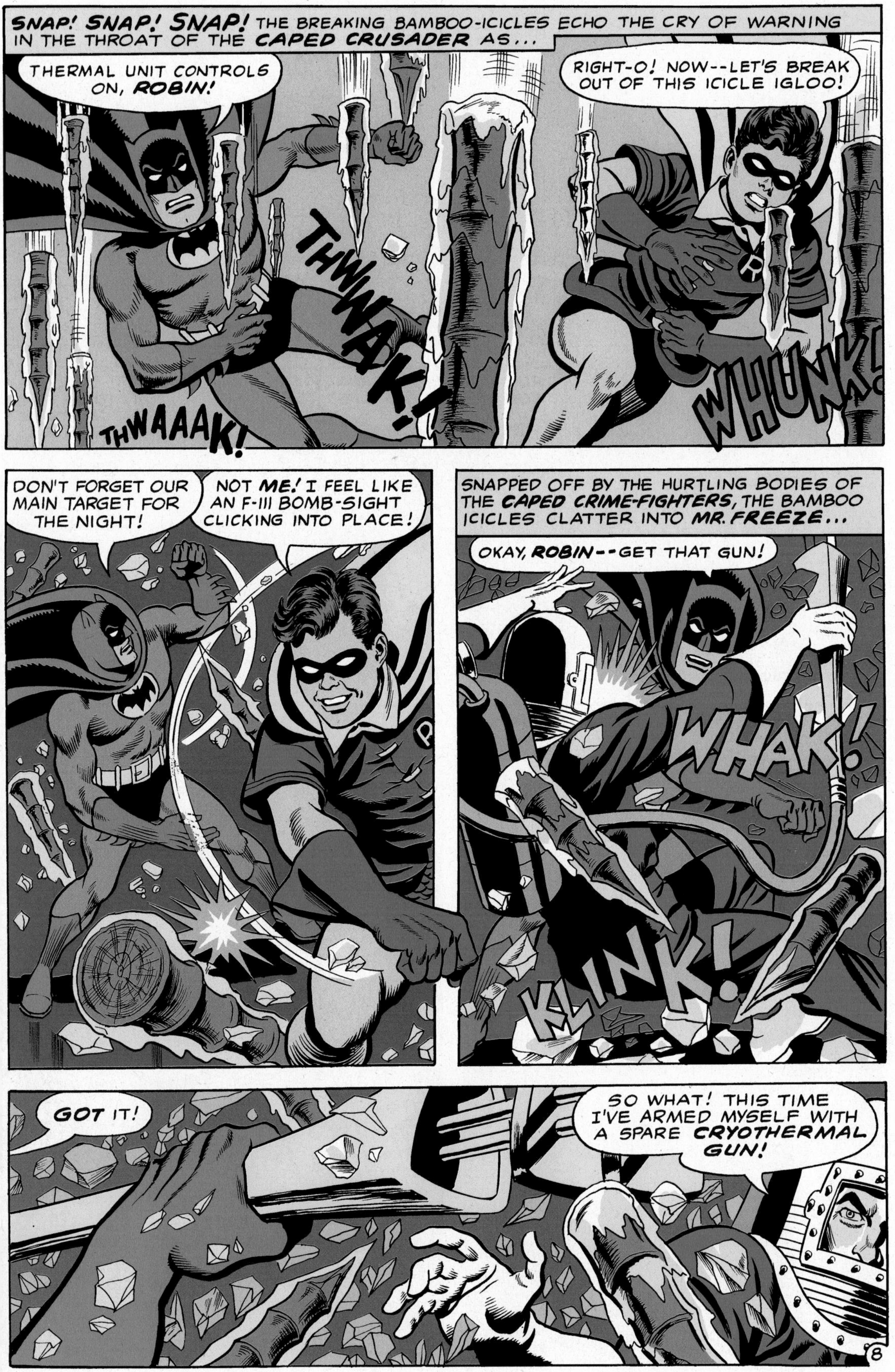
SNAP! SNAP! SNAP! THE BREAKING BAMBOO-ICICLES ECHO THE CRY OF WARNING IN THE THROAT OF THE CAPED CRUSADER AS...
THERMAL UNIT CONTROLS ON, ROBIN!
RIGHT-O! NOW--LET'S BREAK OUT OF THIS ICICLE IGLOO!
THWWAK!
THWAAAK!
WHUNK!
DON'T FORGET OUR MAIN TARGET FOR THE NIGHT!
NOT ME! I FEEL LIKE AN F-III BOMB-SIGHT CLICKING INTO PLACE!
SNAPPED OFF BY THE HURTLING BODIES OF THE CAPED CRIME-FIGHTERS, THE BAMBOO ICICLES CLATTER INTO MR. FREEZE...
OKAY, ROBIN--GET THAT GUN!
WHAK!
KLINK!
GOT IT!
SO WHAT! THIS TIME I'VE ARMED MYSELF WITH A SPARE CRYOTHERMAL GUN!
8

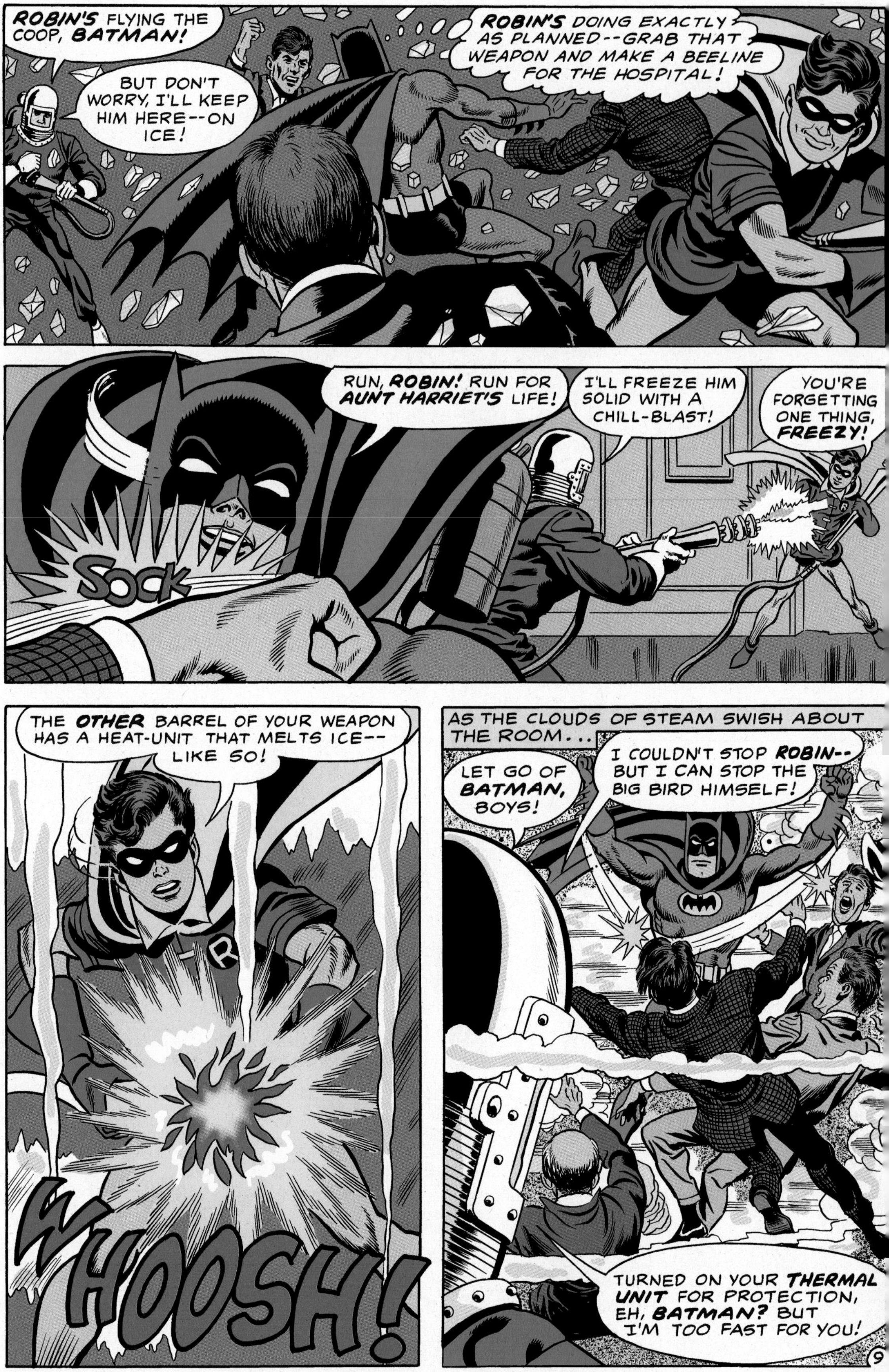
ROBIN'S FLYING THE COOP, BATMAN!
BUT DON'T WORRY, I'LL KEEP HIM HERE--ON ICE!
ROBIN'S DOING EXACTLY AS PLANNED--GRAB THAT WEAPON AND MAKE A BEELINE FOR THE HOSPITAL!
SOCK
RUN, ROBIN! RUN FOR AUNT HARRIET'S LIFE!
I'LL FREEZE HIM SOLID WITH A CHILL-BLAST!
YOU'RE FORGETTING ONE THING, FREEZY!
THE OTHER BARREL OF YOUR WEAPON HAS A HEAT-UNIT THAT MELTS ICE-- LIKE SO!
WHOOSH!
AS THE CLOUDS OF STEAM SWISH ABOUT THE ROOM...
LET GO OF BATMAN, BOYS!
I COULDN'T STOP ROBIN-- BUT I CAN STOP THE BIG BIRD HIMSELF!
TURNED ON YOUR THERMAL UNIT FOR PROTECTION, EH, BATMAN? BUT I'M TOO FAST FOR YOU!
9

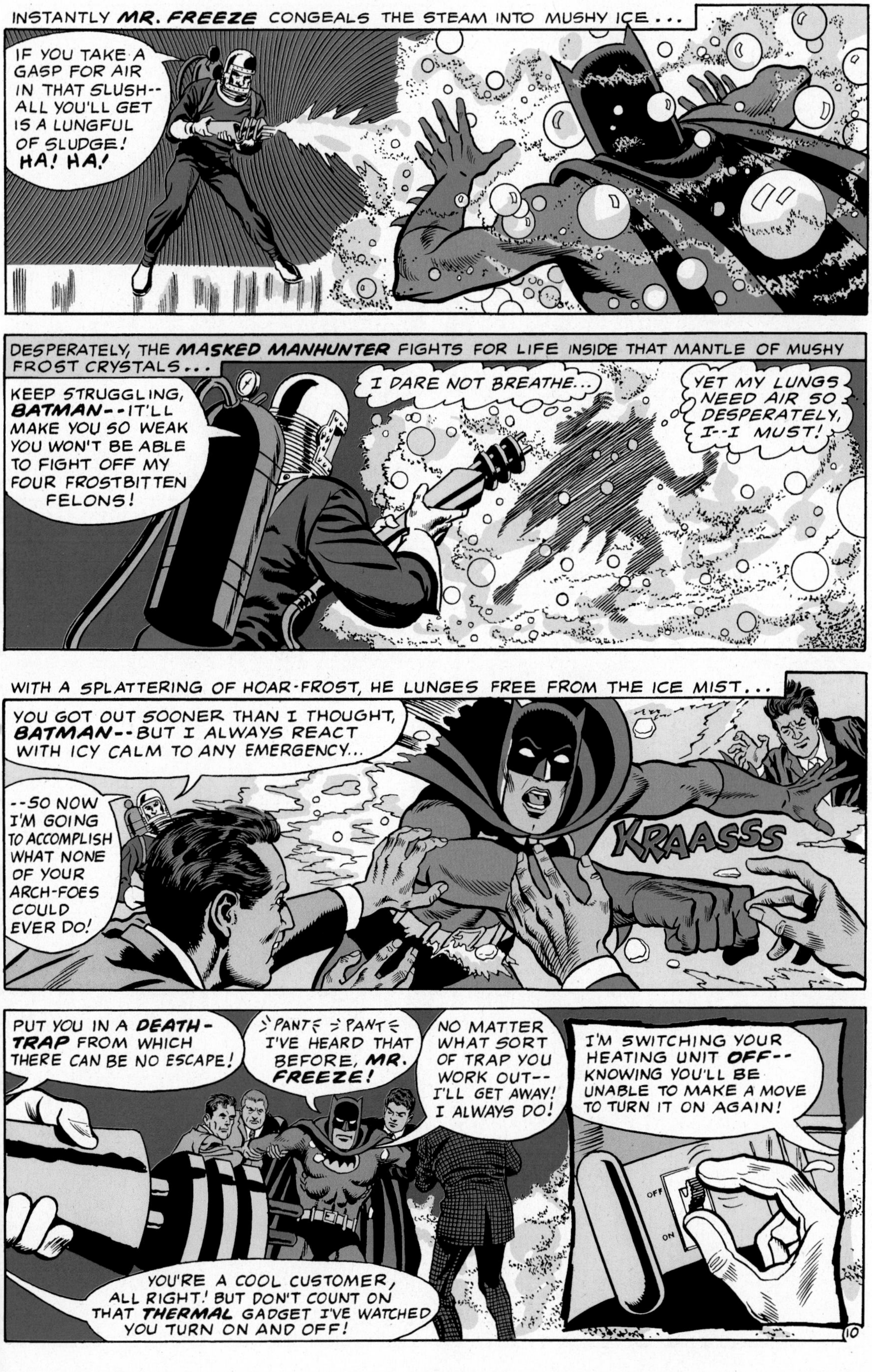
INSTANTLY MR. FREEZE CONGEALS THE STEAM INTO MUSHY ICE...
IF YOU TAKE A GASP FOR AIR IN THAT SLUSH-- ALL YOU'LL GET IS A LUNGFUL OF SLUDGE! HA! HA!
DESPERATELY, THE MASKED MANHUNTER FIGHTS FOR LIFE INSIDE THAT MANTLE OF MUSHY FROST CRYSTALS...
KEEP STRUGGLING, BATMAN--IT'LL MAKE YOU SO WEAK YOU WON'T BE ABLE TO FIGHT OFF MY FOUR FROSTBITTEN FELONS!
I DARE NOT BREATHE...
YET MY LUNGS NEED AIR SO DESPERATELY, I--I MUST!
WITH A SPLATTERING OF HOAR-FROST, HE LUNGES FREE FROM THE ICE MIST...
YOU GOT OUT SOONER THAN I THOUGHT, BATMAN--BUT I ALWAYS REACT WITH ICY CALM TO ANY EMERGENCY...
--SO NOW I'M GOING TO ACCOMPLISH WHAT NONE OF YOUR ARCH-FOES COULD EVER DO!
KRAASSS
PUT YOU IN A DEATH-TRAP FROM WHICH THERE CAN BE NO ESCAPE!
PANT PANT I'VE HEARD THAT BEFORE, MR. FREEZE!
NO MATTER WHAT SORT OF TRAP YOU WORK OUT-- I'LL GET AWAY! I ALWAYS DO!
YOU'RE A COOL CUSTOMER, ALL RIGHT! BUT DON'T COUNT ON THAT THERMAL GADGET I'VE WATCHED YOU TURN ON AND OFF!
I'M SWITCHING YOUR HEATING UNIT OFF-- KNOWING YOU'LL BE UNABLE TO MAKE A MOVE TO TURN IT ON AGAIN!
OFF
ON
10

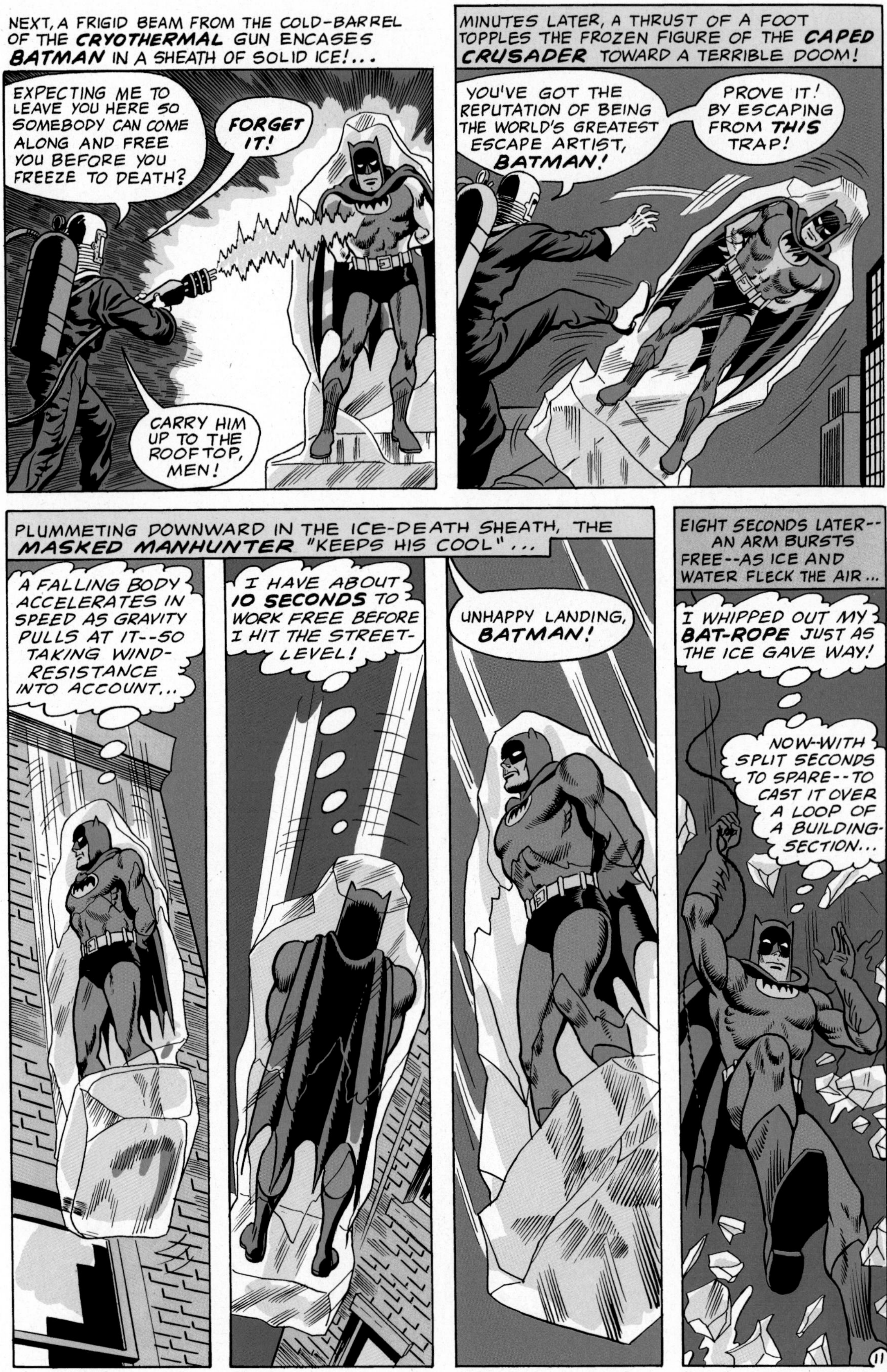
NEXT, A FRIGID BEAM FROM THE COLD-BARREL OF THE CRYOTHERMAL GUN ENCASES BATMAN IN A SHEATH OF SOLID ICE!...
EXPECTING ME TO LEAVE YOU HERE SO SOMEBODY CAN COME ALONG AND FREE YOU BEFORE YOU FREEZE TO DEATH?
FORGET IT!
CARRY HIM UP TO THE ROOFTOP, MEN!
MINUTES LATER, A THRUST OF A FOOT TOPPLES THE FROZEN FIGURE OF THE CAPED CRUSADER TOWARD A TERRIBLE DOOM!
YOU'VE GOT THE REPUTATION OF BEING THE WORLD'S GREATEST ESCAPE ARTIST, BATMAN!
PROVE IT! BY ESCAPING FROM THIS TRAP!
PLUMMETING DOWNWARD IN THE ICE-DEATH SHEATH, THE MASKED MANHUNTER "KEEPS HIS COOL"...
A FALLING BODY ACCELERATES IN SPEED AS GRAVITY PULLS AT IT--SO TAKING WIND-RESISTANCE INTO ACCOUNT...
I HAVE ABOUT 10 SECONDS TO WORK FREE BEFORE I HIT THE STREET-LEVEL!
UNHAPPY LANDING, BATMAN!
EIGHT SECONDS LATER-- AN ARM BURSTS FREE--AS ICE AND WATER FLECK THE AIR...
I WHIPPED OUT MY BAT-ROPE JUST AS THE ICE GAVE WAY!
NOW--WITH SPLIT SECONDS TO SPARE--TO CAST IT OVER A LOOP OF A BUILDING-SECTION...
11

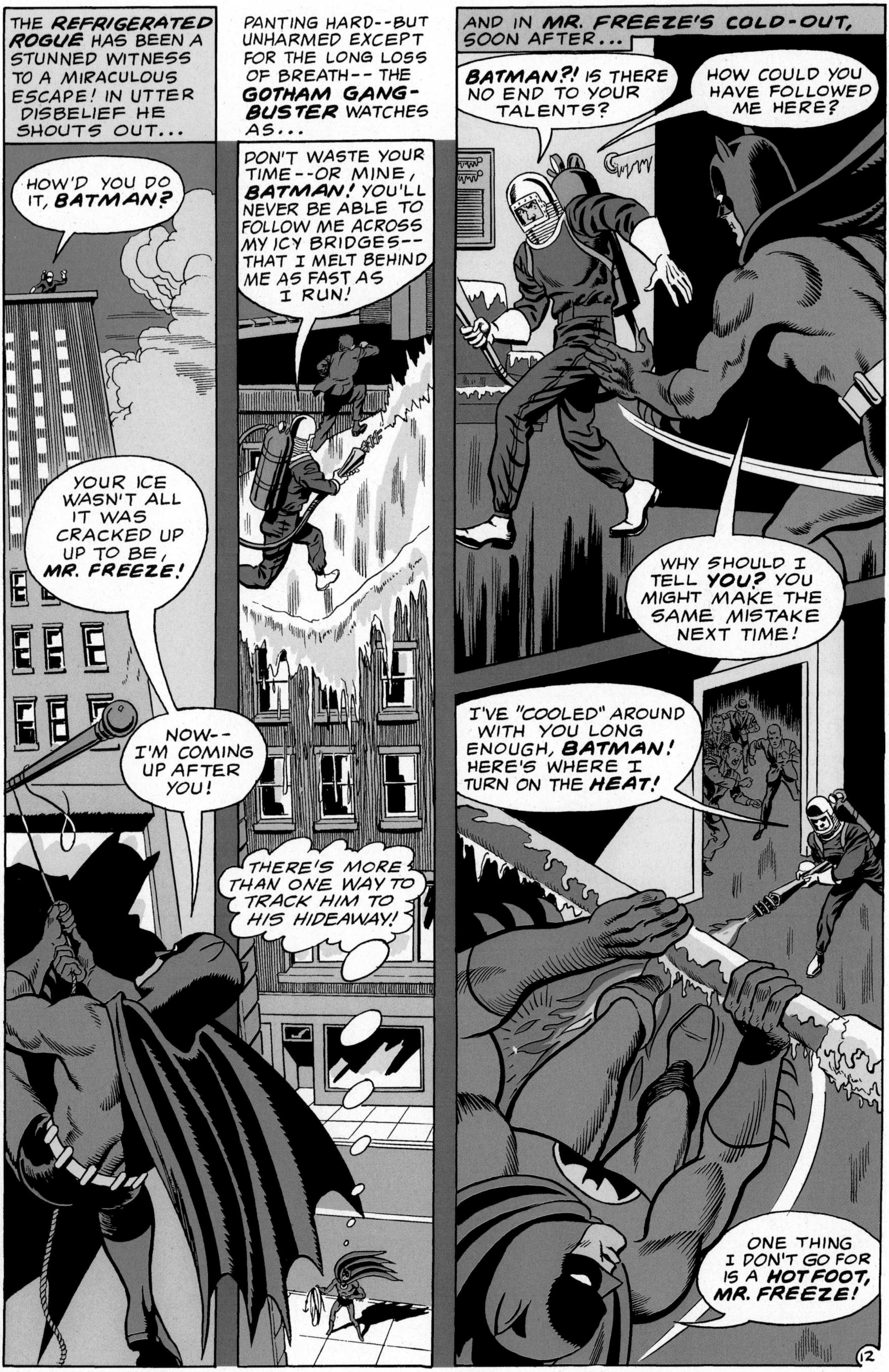

THE REFRIGERATED ROGUE HAS BEEN A STUNNED WITNESS TO A MIRACULOUS ESCAPE! IN UTTER DISBELIEF HE SHOUTS OUT...
HOW'D YOU DO IT, BATMAN?
YOUR ICE WASN'T ALL IT WAS CRACKED UP UP TO BE, MR. FREEZE!
NOW-- I'M COMING UP AFTER YOU!
PANTING HARD--BUT UNHARMED EXCEPT FOR THE LONG LOSS OF BREATH-- THE GOTHAM GANG-BUSTER WATCHES AS...
DON'T WASTE YOUR TIME--OR MINE, BATMAN! YOU'LL NEVER BE ABLE TO FOLLOW ME ACROSS MY ICY BRIDGES-- THAT I MELT BEHIND ME AS FAST AS I RUN!
THERE'S MORE THAN ONE WAY TO TRACK HIM TO HIS HIDEAWAY!
AND IN MR. FREEZE'S COLD-OUT, SOON AFTER...
BATMAN?! IS THERE NO END TO YOUR TALENTS?
HOW COULD YOU HAVE FOLLOWED ME HERE?
WHY SHOULD I TELL YOU? YOU MIGHT MAKE THE SAME MISTAKE NEXT TIME!
I'VE "COOLED" AROUND WITH YOU LONG ENOUGH, BATMAN! HERE'S WHERE I TURN ON THE HEAT!
ONE THING I DON'T GO FOR IS A HOTFOOT, MR. FREEZE!
12

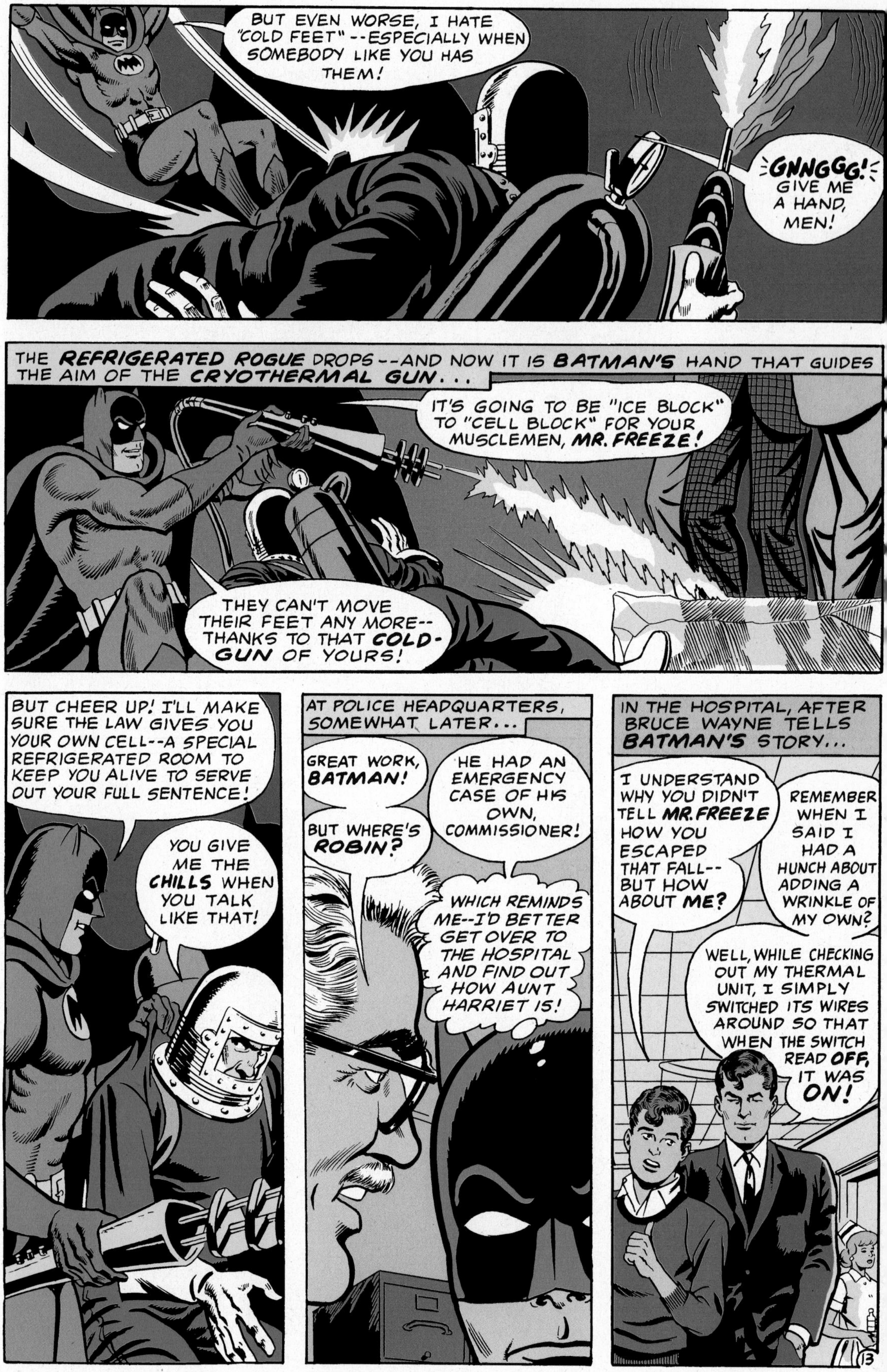

BUT EVEN WORSE, I HATE "COLD FEET"--ESPECIALLY WHEN SOMEBODY LIKE YOU HAS THEM!
GNNGGG! GIVE ME A HAND, MEN!
THE REFRIGERATED ROGUE DROPS--AND NOW IT IS BATMAN'S HAND THAT GUIDES THE AIM OF THE CRYOTHERMAL GUN...
IT'S GOING TO BE "ICE BLOCK" TO "CELL BLOCK" FOR YOUR MUSCLEMEN, MR. FREEZE!
THEY CAN'T MOVE THEIR FEET ANY MORE--THANKS TO THAT COLD-GUN OF YOURS!
BUT CHEER UP! I'LL MAKE SURE THE LAW GIVES YOU YOUR OWN CELL--A SPECIAL REFRIGERATED ROOM TO KEEP YOU ALIVE TO SERVE OUT YOUR FULL SENTENCE!
YOU GIVE ME THE CHILLS WHEN YOU TALK LIKE THAT!
AT POLICE HEADQUARTERS, SOMEWHAT LATER...
GREAT WORK, BATMAN!
BUT WHERE'S ROBIN?
HE HAD AN EMERGENCY CASE OF HIS OWN, COMMISSIONER!
WHICH REMINDS ME--I'D BETTER GET OVER TO THE HOSPITAL AND FIND OUT HOW AUNT HARRIET IS!
IN THE HOSPITAL, AFTER BRUCE WAYNE TELLS BATMAN'S STORY...
I UNDERSTAND WHY YOU DIDN'T TELL MR. FREEZE HOW YOU ESCAPED THAT FALL--BUT HOW ABOUT ME?
REMEMBER WHEN I SAID I HAD A HUNCH ABOUT ADDING A WRINKLE OF MY OWN?
WELL, WHILE CHECKING OUT MY THERMAL UNIT, I SIMPLY SWITCHED ITS WIRES AROUND SO THAT WHEN THE SWITCH READ OFF, IT WAS ON!
13

SO ACTUALLY--*MR. FREEZE* HELPED ME TO ESCAPE UNKNOWINGLY BY SWITCHING MY THERMAL UNIT *ON!* WHILE I WAS BEING CARRIED TO THE ROOF, THE HEATED UNIFORM BEGAN MELTING THE ICE--SO DURING THE 10-SECOND FALL I MANAGED TO GET AN ARM FREE AND HURL MY *BAT-ROPE!*

I ATTACHED A COUNTER-TRACER TO THE PHONE-LINE HE TAPPED AND USED ELECTRONIC SIGNALS TO LEAD ME BACK TO *MR. FREEZE'S* PHONE IN HIS RETREAT!

BUT AFTER THAT-- HOW'D YOU LOCATE *MR. FREEZE'S COLD-OUT?*

DOCTOR NOSTRAND EXPLAINED HOW *BATMAN* AND *ROBIN* SAVED MY LIFE, BRUCE! YOU MUST ARRANGE FOR ME TO THANK THEM *PERSONALLY!*

THEY'LL SEE TO THAT--I ASSURE YOU, MRS. COOPER!

THEY'LL BE YOUR FIRST VISITORS TOMORROW MORNING, AUNT HARRIET--

The End.

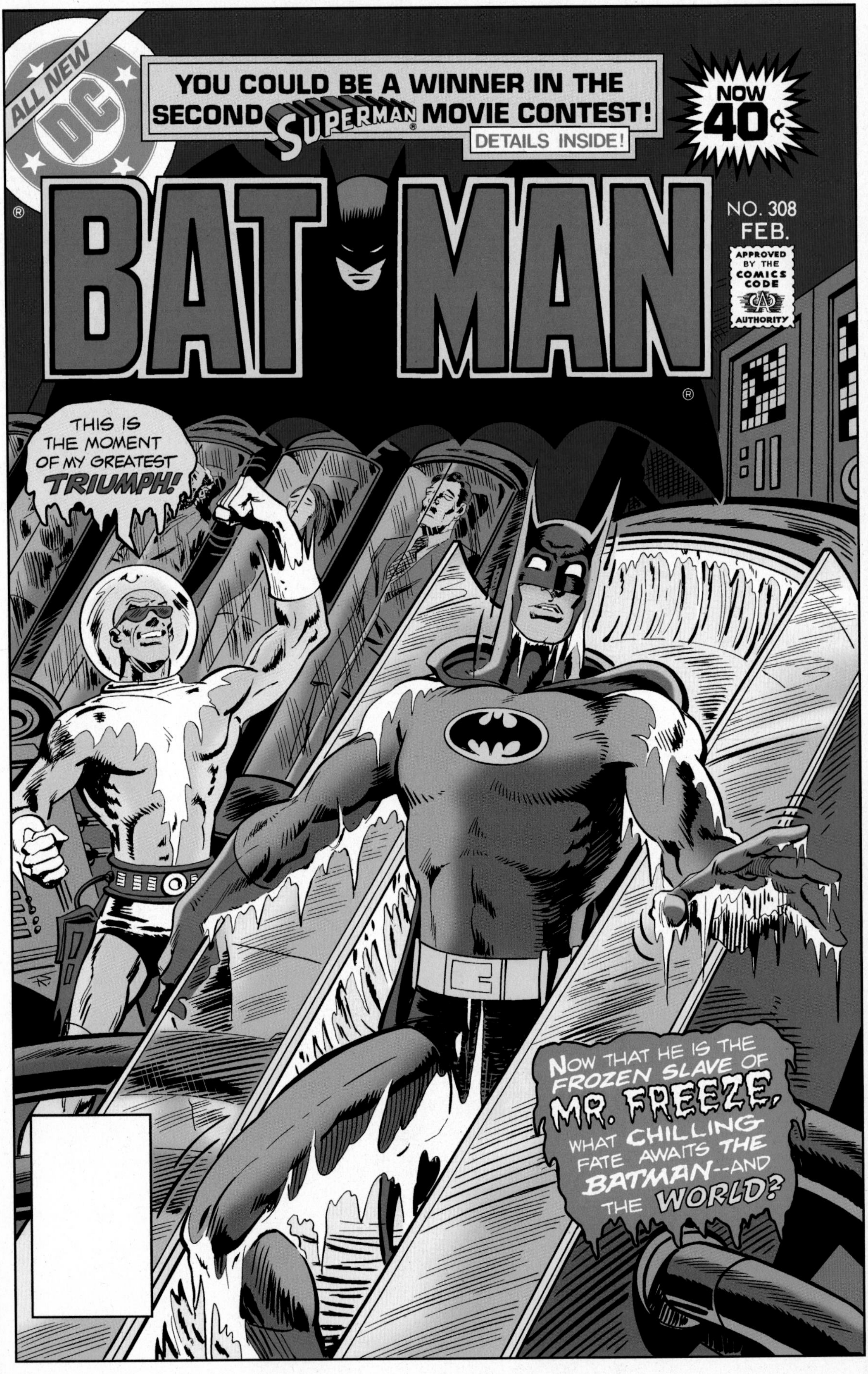
ALL NEW DC
YOU COULD BE A WINNER IN THE SECOND SUPERMAN MOVIE CONTEST!
DETAILS INSIDE!
NOW 40¢
BATMAN
NO. 308
FEB.
APPROVED BY THE COMICS CODE AUTHORITY
THIS IS THE MOMENT OF MY GREATEST TRIUMPH!
NOW THAT HE IS THE FROZEN SLAVE OF MR. FREEZE, WHAT CHILLING FATE AWAITS THE BATMAN--AND THE WORLD?

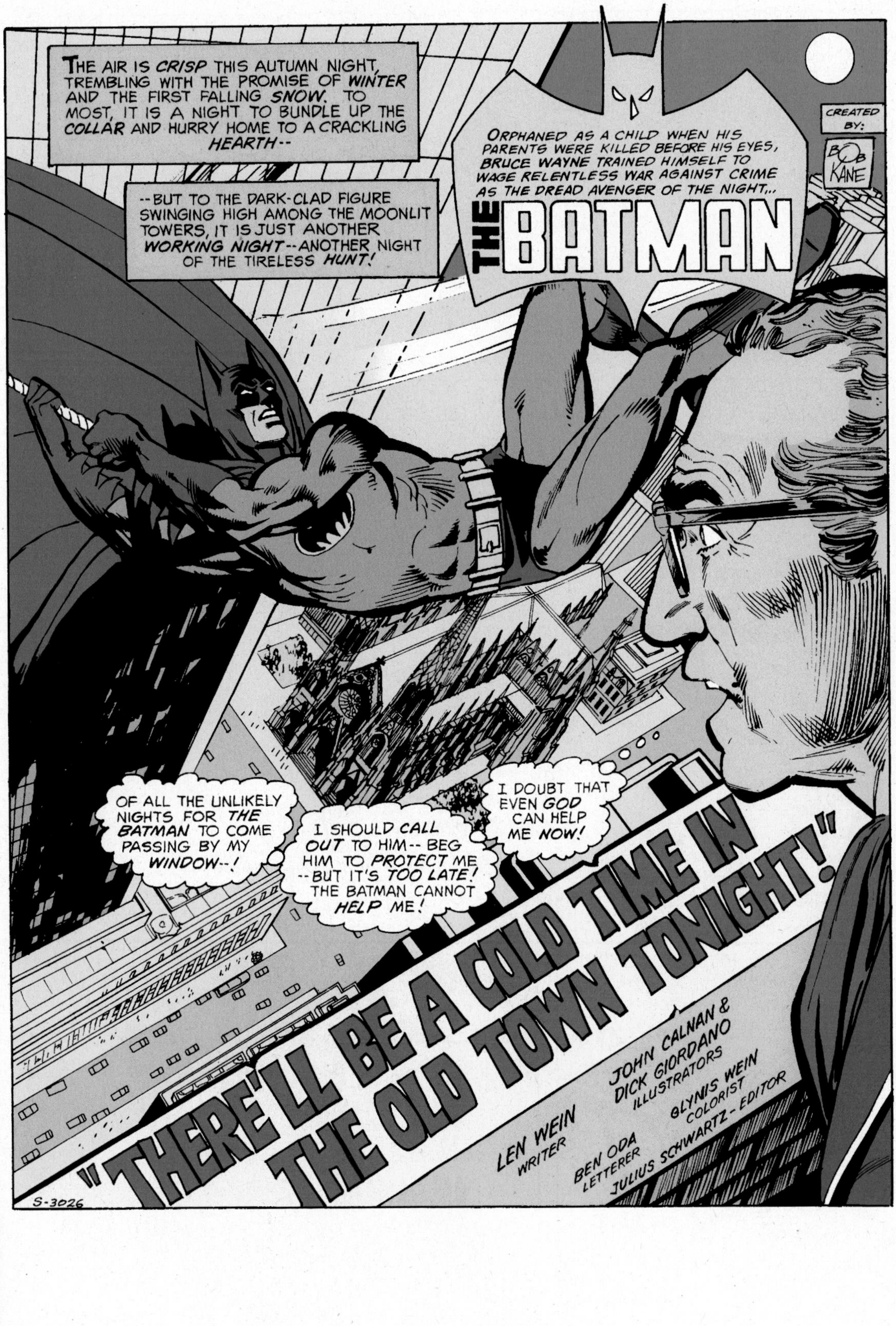

THE AIR IS CRISP THIS AUTUMN NIGHT, TREMBLING WITH THE PROMISE OF WINTER AND THE FIRST FALLING SNOW. TO MOST, IT IS A NIGHT TO BUNDLE UP THE COLLAR AND HURRY HOME TO A CRACKLING HEARTH--
--BUT TO THE DARK-CLAD FIGURE SWINGING HIGH AMONG THE MOONLIT TOWERS, IT IS JUST ANOTHER WORKING NIGHT--ANOTHER NIGHT OF THE TIRELESS HUNT!
ORPHANED AS A CHILD WHEN HIS PARENTS WERE KILLED BEFORE HIS EYES, BRUCE WAYNE TRAINED HIMSELF TO WAGE RELENTLESS WAR AGAINST CRIME AS THE DREAD AVENGER OF THE NIGHT...
THE BATMAN
CREATED BY: BOB KANE
OF ALL THE UNLIKELY NIGHTS FOR THE BATMAN TO COME PASSING BY MY WINDOW--!
I SHOULD CALL OUT TO HIM-- BEG HIM TO PROTECT ME --BUT IT'S TOO LATE! THE BATMAN CANNOT HELP ME!
I DOUBT THAT EVEN GOD CAN HELP ME NOW!
"THERE'LL BE A COLD TIME IN THE OLD TOWN TONIGHT!"
LEN WEIN WRITER
JOHN CALNAN & DICK GIORDANO ILLUSTRATORS
BEN ODA LETTERER
GLYNIS WEIN COLORIST
JULIUS SCHWARTZ - EDITOR
S-3026

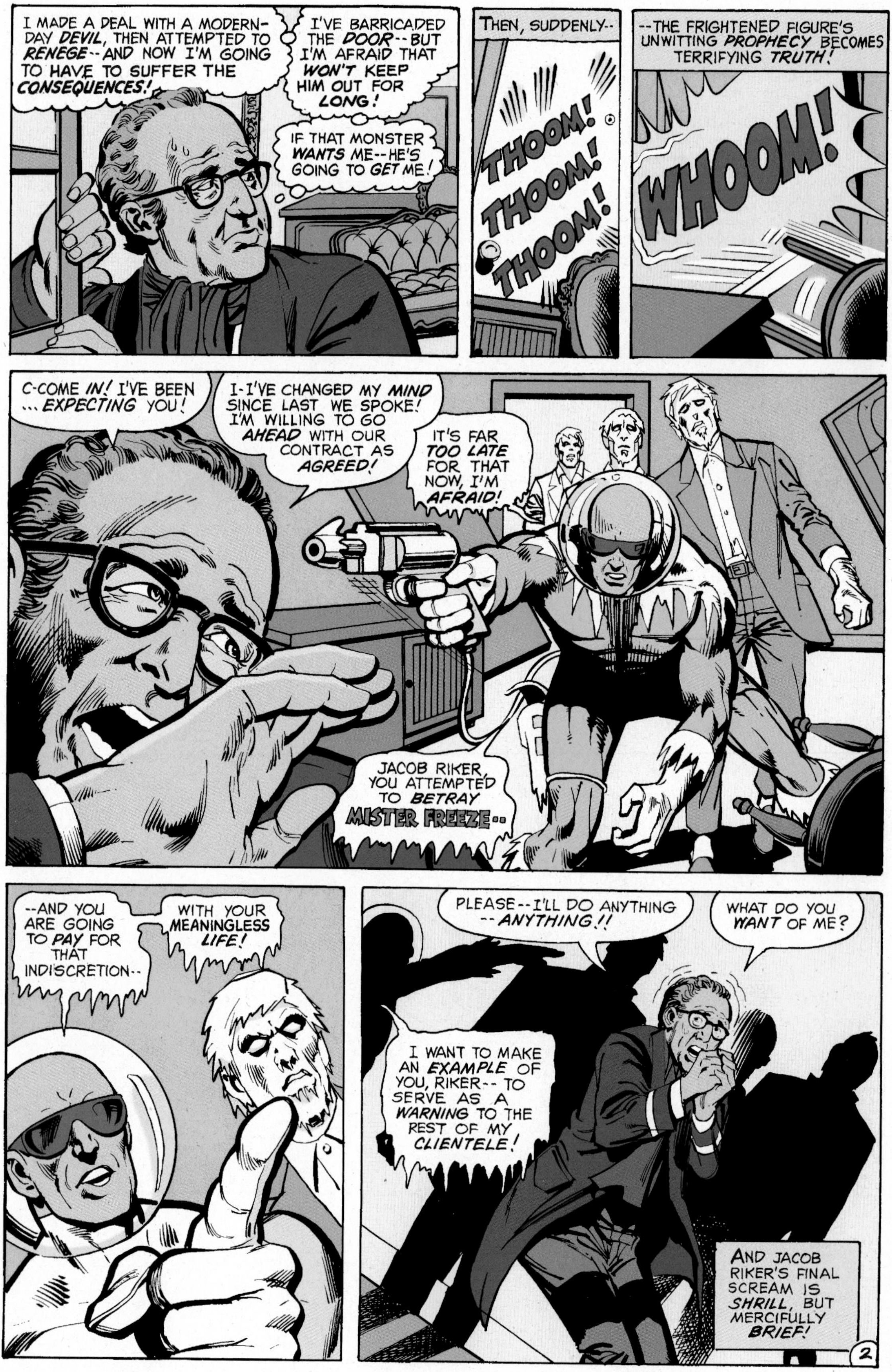
I MADE A DEAL WITH A MODERN-DAY DEVIL, THEN ATTEMPTED TO RENEGE--AND NOW I'M GOING TO HAVE TO SUFFER THE CONSEQUENCES!
I'VE BARRICADED THE DOOR--BUT I'M AFRAID THAT WON'T KEEP HIM OUT FOR LONG!
IF THAT MONSTER WANTS ME--HE'S GOING TO GET ME!
THEN, SUDDENLY--
THOOM! THOOM! THOOM!
--THE FRIGHTENED FIGURE'S UNWITTING PROPHECY BECOMES TERRIFYING TRUTH!
WHOOM!
C-COME IN! I'VE BEEN ...EXPECTING YOU!
I-I'VE CHANGED MY MIND SINCE LAST WE SPOKE! I'M WILLING TO GO AHEAD WITH OUR CONTRACT AS AGREED!
IT'S FAR TOO LATE FOR THAT NOW, I'M AFRAID!
JACOB RIKER, YOU ATTEMPTED TO BETRAY MISTER FREEZE--
--AND YOU ARE GOING TO PAY FOR THAT INDISCRETION--
WITH YOUR MEANINGLESS LIFE!
PLEASE--I'LL DO ANYTHING --ANYTHING!!
WHAT DO YOU WANT OF ME?
I WANT TO MAKE AN EXAMPLE OF YOU, RIKER-- TO SERVE AS A WARNING TO THE REST OF MY CLIENTELE!
AND JACOB RIKER'S FINAL SCREAM IS SHRILL, BUT MERCIFULLY BRIEF!
2

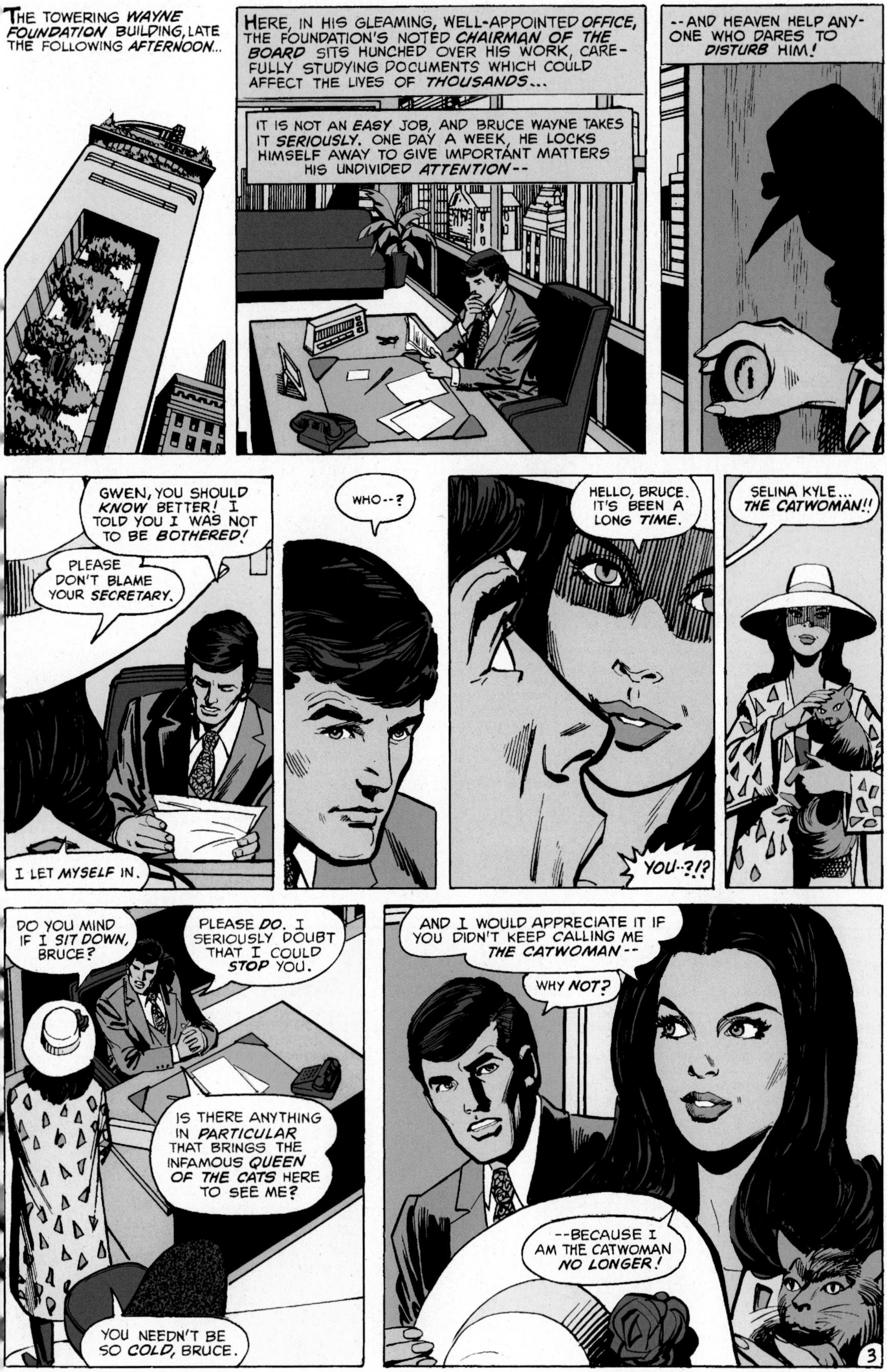
THE TOWERING WAYNE FOUNDATION BUILDING, LATE THE FOLLOWING AFTERNOON...
HERE, IN HIS GLEAMING, WELL-APPOINTED OFFICE, THE FOUNDATION'S NOTED CHAIRMAN OF THE BOARD SITS HUNCHED OVER HIS WORK, CAREFULLY STUDYING DOCUMENTS WHICH COULD AFFECT THE LIVES OF THOUSANDS...
IT IS NOT AN EASY JOB, AND BRUCE WAYNE TAKES IT SERIOUSLY. ONE DAY A WEEK, HE LOCKS HIMSELF AWAY TO GIVE IMPORTANT MATTERS HIS UNDIVIDED ATTENTION--
--AND HEAVEN HELP ANYONE WHO DARES TO DISTURB HIM!
GWEN, YOU SHOULD KNOW BETTER! I TOLD YOU I WAS NOT TO BE BOTHERED!
PLEASE DON'T BLAME YOUR SECRETARY.
I LET MYSELF IN.
WHO--?
HELLO, BRUCE. IT'S BEEN A LONG TIME.
YOU--?!?
SELINA KYLE... THE CATWOMAN!!
DO YOU MIND IF I SIT DOWN, BRUCE?
PLEASE DO. I SERIOUSLY DOUBT THAT I COULD STOP YOU.
IS THERE ANYTHING IN PARTICULAR THAT BRINGS THE INFAMOUS QUEEN OF THE CATS HERE TO SEE ME?
YOU NEEDN'T BE SO COLD, BRUCE.
AND I WOULD APPRECIATE IT IF YOU DIDN'T KEEP CALLING ME THE CATWOMAN--
WHY NOT?
--BECAUSE I AM THE CATWOMAN NO LONGER!
3

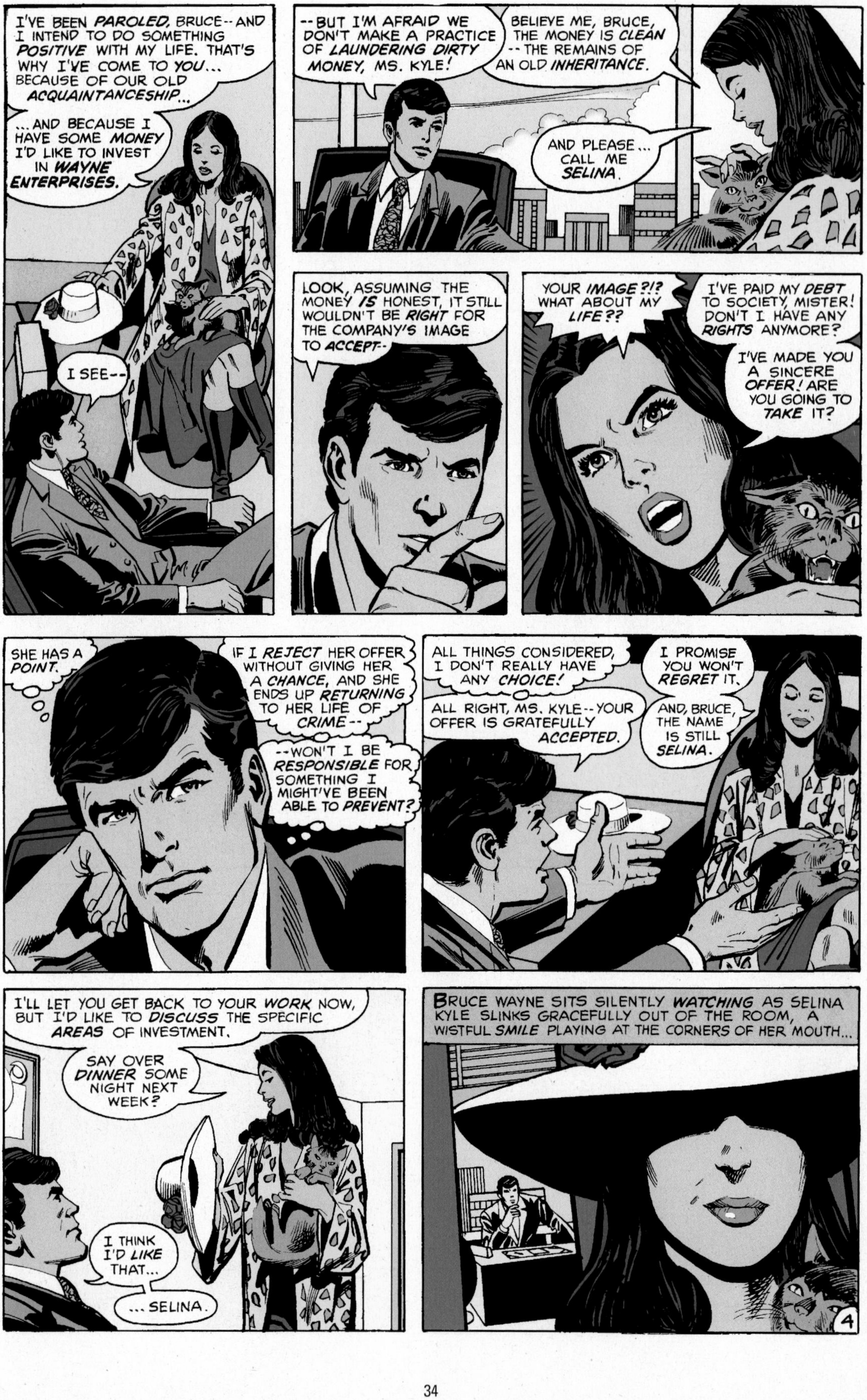
I'VE BEEN PAROLED, BRUCE--AND I INTEND TO DO SOMETHING POSITIVE WITH MY LIFE. THAT'S WHY I'VE COME TO YOU... BECAUSE OF OUR OLD ACQUAINTANCESHIP...
...AND BECAUSE I HAVE SOME MONEY I'D LIKE TO INVEST IN WAYNE ENTERPRISES.
I SEE--
--BUT I'M AFRAID WE DON'T MAKE A PRACTICE OF LAUNDERING DIRTY MONEY, MS. KYLE!
BELIEVE ME, BRUCE, THE MONEY IS CLEAN --THE REMAINS OF AN OLD INHERITANCE.
AND PLEASE... CALL ME SELINA.
LOOK, ASSUMING THE MONEY IS HONEST, IT STILL WOULDN'T BE RIGHT FOR THE COMPANY'S IMAGE TO ACCEPT--
YOUR IMAGE?!? WHAT ABOUT MY LIFE??
I'VE PAID MY DEBT TO SOCIETY, MISTER! DON'T I HAVE ANY RIGHTS ANYMORE?
I'VE MADE YOU A SINCERE OFFER! ARE YOU GOING TO TAKE IT?
SHE HAS A POINT.
IF I REJECT HER OFFER WITHOUT GIVING HER A CHANCE, AND SHE ENDS UP RETURNING TO HER LIFE OF CRIME--
--WON'T I BE RESPONSIBLE FOR SOMETHING I MIGHT'VE BEEN ABLE TO PREVENT?
ALL THINGS CONSIDERED, I DON'T REALLY HAVE ANY CHOICE!
ALL RIGHT, MS. KYLE--YOUR OFFER IS GRATEFULLY ACCEPTED.
I PROMISE YOU WON'T REGRET IT.
AND, BRUCE, THE NAME IS STILL SELINA.
I'LL LET YOU GET BACK TO YOUR WORK NOW, BUT I'D LIKE TO DISCUSS THE SPECIFIC AREAS OF INVESTMENT.
SAY OVER DINNER SOME NIGHT NEXT WEEK?
I THINK I'D LIKE THAT...
...SELINA.
BRUCE WAYNE SITS SILENTLY WATCHING AS SELINA KYLE SLINKS GRACEFULLY OUT OF THE ROOM, A WISTFUL SMILE PLAYING AT THE CORNERS OF HER MOUTH...
4

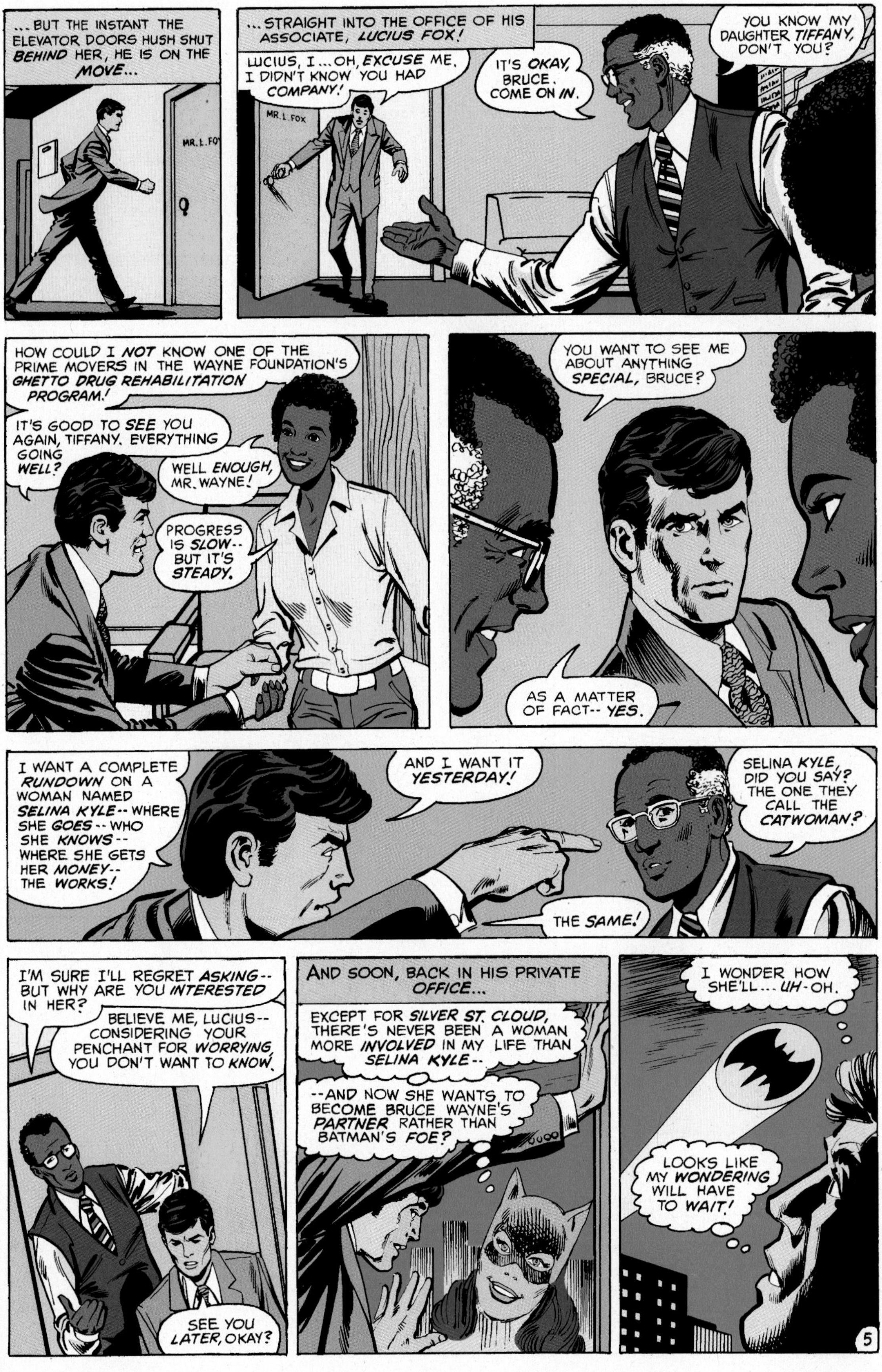

...BUT THE INSTANT THE ELEVATOR DOORS HUSH SHUT BEHIND HER, HE IS ON THE MOVE...
MR. L. FOX
...STRAIGHT INTO THE OFFICE OF HIS ASSOCIATE, LUCIUS FOX!
LUCIUS, I...OH, EXCUSE ME. I DIDN'T KNOW YOU HAD COMPANY!
IT'S OKAY, BRUCE. COME ON IN.
YOU KNOW MY DAUGHTER TIFFANY, DON'T YOU?
HOW COULD I NOT KNOW ONE OF THE PRIME MOVERS IN THE WAYNE FOUNDATION'S GHETTO DRUG REHABILITATION PROGRAM!
IT'S GOOD TO SEE YOU AGAIN, TIFFANY. EVERYTHING GOING WELL?
WELL ENOUGH, MR. WAYNE!
PROGRESS IS SLOW-- BUT IT'S STEADY.
YOU WANT TO SEE ME ABOUT ANYTHING SPECIAL, BRUCE?
AS A MATTER OF FACT-- YES.
I WANT A COMPLETE RUNDOWN ON A WOMAN NAMED SELINA KYLE-- WHERE SHE GOES-- WHO SHE KNOWS-- WHERE SHE GETS HER MONEY-- THE WORKS!
AND I WANT IT YESTERDAY!
SELINA KYLE, DID YOU SAY? THE ONE THEY CALL THE CATWOMAN?
THE SAME!
I'M SURE I'LL REGRET ASKING-- BUT WHY ARE YOU INTERESTED IN HER?
BELIEVE ME, LUCIUS-- CONSIDERING YOUR PENCHANT FOR WORRYING, YOU DON'T WANT TO KNOW.
SEE YOU LATER, OKAY?
AND SOON, BACK IN HIS PRIVATE OFFICE...
EXCEPT FOR SILVER ST. CLOUD, THERE'S NEVER BEEN A WOMAN MORE INVOLVED IN MY LIFE THAN SELINA KYLE--
--AND NOW SHE WANTS TO BECOME BRUCE WAYNE'S PARTNER RATHER THAN BATMAN'S FOE?
I WONDER HOW SHE'LL... UH-OH.
LOOKS LIKE MY WONDERING WILL HAVE TO WAIT!
5

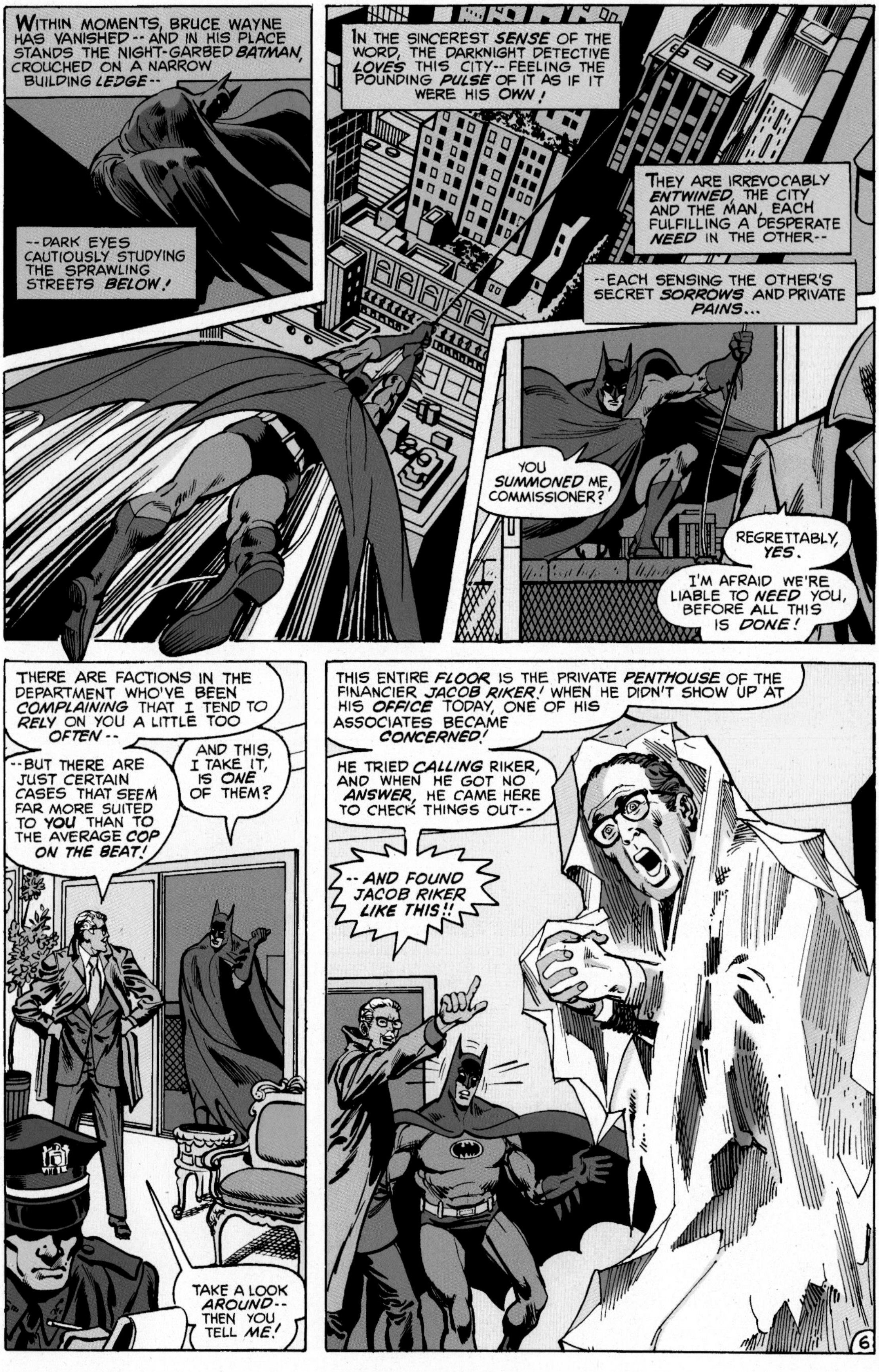
WITHIN MOMENTS, BRUCE WAYNE HAS VANISHED-- AND IN HIS PLACE STANDS THE NIGHT-GARBED BATMAN, CROUCHED ON A NARROW BUILDING LEDGE--
--DARK EYES CAUTIOUSLY STUDYING THE SPRAWLING STREETS BELOW!
IN THE SINCEREST SENSE OF THE WORD, THE DARKNIGHT DETECTIVE LOVES THIS CITY-- FEELING THE POUNDING PULSE OF IT AS IF IT WERE HIS OWN!
THEY ARE IRREVOCABLY ENTWINED, THE CITY AND THE MAN, EACH FULFILLING A DESPERATE NEED IN THE OTHER--
--EACH SENSING THE OTHER'S SECRET SORROWS AND PRIVATE PAINS...
YOU SUMMONED ME, COMMISSIONER?
REGRETTABLY, YES.
I'M AFRAID WE'RE LIABLE TO NEED YOU, BEFORE ALL THIS IS DONE!
THERE ARE FACTIONS IN THE DEPARTMENT WHO'VE BEEN COMPLAINING THAT I TEND TO RELY ON YOU A LITTLE TOO OFTEN--
--BUT THERE ARE JUST CERTAIN CASES THAT SEEM FAR MORE SUITED TO YOU THAN TO THE AVERAGE COP ON THE BEAT!
AND THIS, I TAKE IT, IS ONE OF THEM?
TAKE A LOOK AROUND-- THEN YOU TELL ME!
THIS ENTIRE FLOOR IS THE PRIVATE PENTHOUSE OF THE FINANCIER JACOB RIKER! WHEN HE DIDN'T SHOW UP AT HIS OFFICE TODAY, ONE OF HIS ASSOCIATES BECAME CONCERNED!
HE TRIED CALLING RIKER, AND WHEN HE GOT NO ANSWER, HE CAME HERE TO CHECK THINGS OUT--
--AND FOUND JACOB RIKER LIKE THIS!!
6

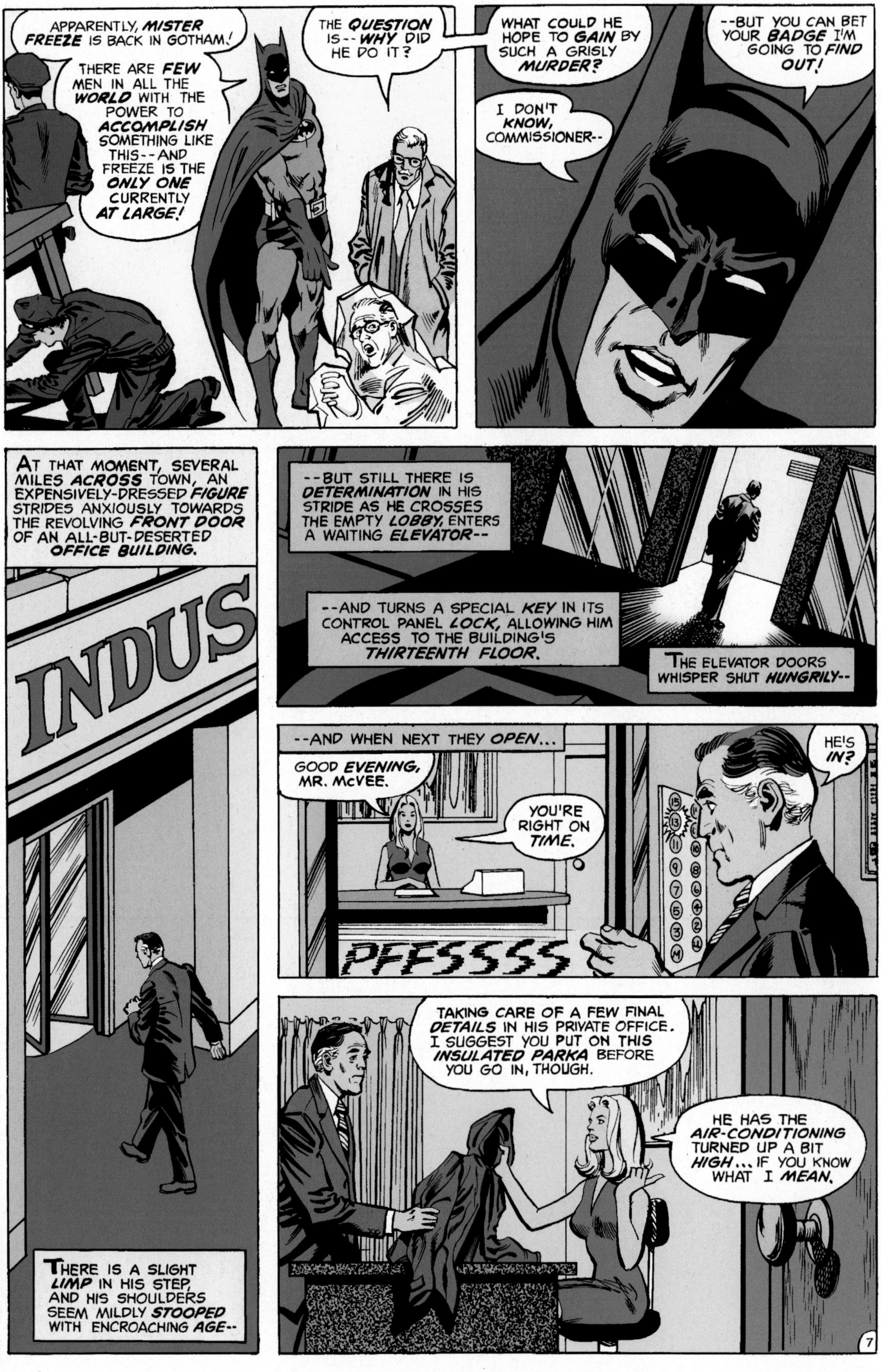
APPARENTLY, MISTER FREEZE IS BACK IN GOTHAM!
THERE ARE FEW MEN IN ALL THE WORLD WITH THE POWER TO ACCOMPLISH SOMETHING LIKE THIS--AND FREEZE IS THE ONLY ONE CURRENTLY AT LARGE!
THE QUESTION IS--WHY DID HE DO IT?
WHAT COULD HE HOPE TO GAIN BY SUCH A GRISLY MURDER?
I DON'T KNOW, COMMISSIONER--
--BUT YOU CAN BET YOUR BADGE I'M GOING TO FIND OUT!
AT THAT MOMENT, SEVERAL MILES ACROSS TOWN, AN EXPENSIVELY-DRESSED FIGURE STRIDES ANXIOUSLY TOWARDS THE REVOLVING FRONT DOOR OF AN ALL-BUT-DESERTED OFFICE BUILDING.
INDUS
THERE IS A SLIGHT LIMP IN HIS STEP, AND HIS SHOULDERS SEEM MILDLY STOOPED WITH ENCROACHING AGE--
--BUT STILL THERE IS DETERMINATION IN HIS STRIDE AS HE CROSSES THE EMPTY LOBBY, ENTERS A WAITING ELEVATOR--
--AND TURNS A SPECIAL KEY IN ITS CONTROL PANEL LOCK, ALLOWING HIM ACCESS TO THE BUILDING'S THIRTEENTH FLOOR.
THE ELEVATOR DOORS WHISPER SHUT HUNGRILY--
--AND WHEN NEXT THEY OPEN...
PFFSSSS
GOOD EVENING, MR. McVEE.
YOU'RE RIGHT ON TIME.
HE'S IN?
TAKING CARE OF A FEW FINAL DETAILS IN HIS PRIVATE OFFICE. I SUGGEST YOU PUT ON THIS INSULATED PARKA BEFORE YOU GO IN, THOUGH.
HE HAS THE AIR-CONDITIONING TURNED UP A BIT HIGH... IF YOU KNOW WHAT I MEAN.
7

DONNING THE PARKA AS INSTRUCTED, JOHN McVEE STEPS *INTO* THE INNER OFFICE--AND IS *STUNNED* BY A SUDDEN GUST OF AIR AS *COLD* AS AN *ARCTIC WIND!*

I CONVERTED SEVERAL MILLION DOLLARS WORTH OF *NEGOTIABLE BONDS* INTO CASH--DEPOSITED *FIVE HUNDRED THOUSAND* INTO YOUR NUMBERED *SWISS ACCOUNT*--

--AND INFORMED ALL MY FRIENDS AND ASSOCIATES THAT I AM TAKING AN EXTENDED *LEAVE OF ABSENCE!*

BUT FRANKLY, I'M STILL NOT CERTAIN WHY ALL THIS WAS *NECESSARY!*

HE *HESITATES*, AWED BY THE FROZEN *TABLEAU* HE SEES BEFORE HIM--THEN THE DOOR AUTOMATICALLY CLICKS SHUT *BEHIND* HIM--

--AND HE *KNOWS* THERE IS NO *TURNING BACK!*

WELCOME, MR. McVEE!

HAVE YOU *DONE* AS I *INSTRUCTED?*

I D-DIDN'T BUILD A MULTI-MILLION-DOLLAR *EMPIRE* BY BEING *INEFFICIENT*, SIR.

I ASSURE YOU, IT IS ALL FOR YOUR *BENEFIT*, MR. McVEE.

AFTER TONIGHT, THERE WILL BE NO WAY FOR YOU TO *RETURN* TO YOUR FORMER *LIFE!*

IT JUST S-SEEMS SO *EXTREME!*

GENIUS IS EXTREME BY ITS VERY *DEFINITION*, MY FRIEND.

BUT TO GIVE UP THE WORK OF A *LIFETIME!*

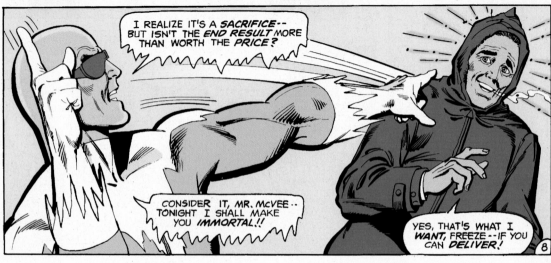

I REALIZE IT'S A *SACRIFICE*--BUT ISN'T THE *END RESULT* MORE THAN WORTH THE *PRICE?*

CONSIDER IT, MR. McVEE--TONIGHT I SHALL MAKE YOU *IMMORTAL!!*

YES, THAT'S WHAT I *WANT*, FREEZE--IF YOU CAN *DELIVER!*

8

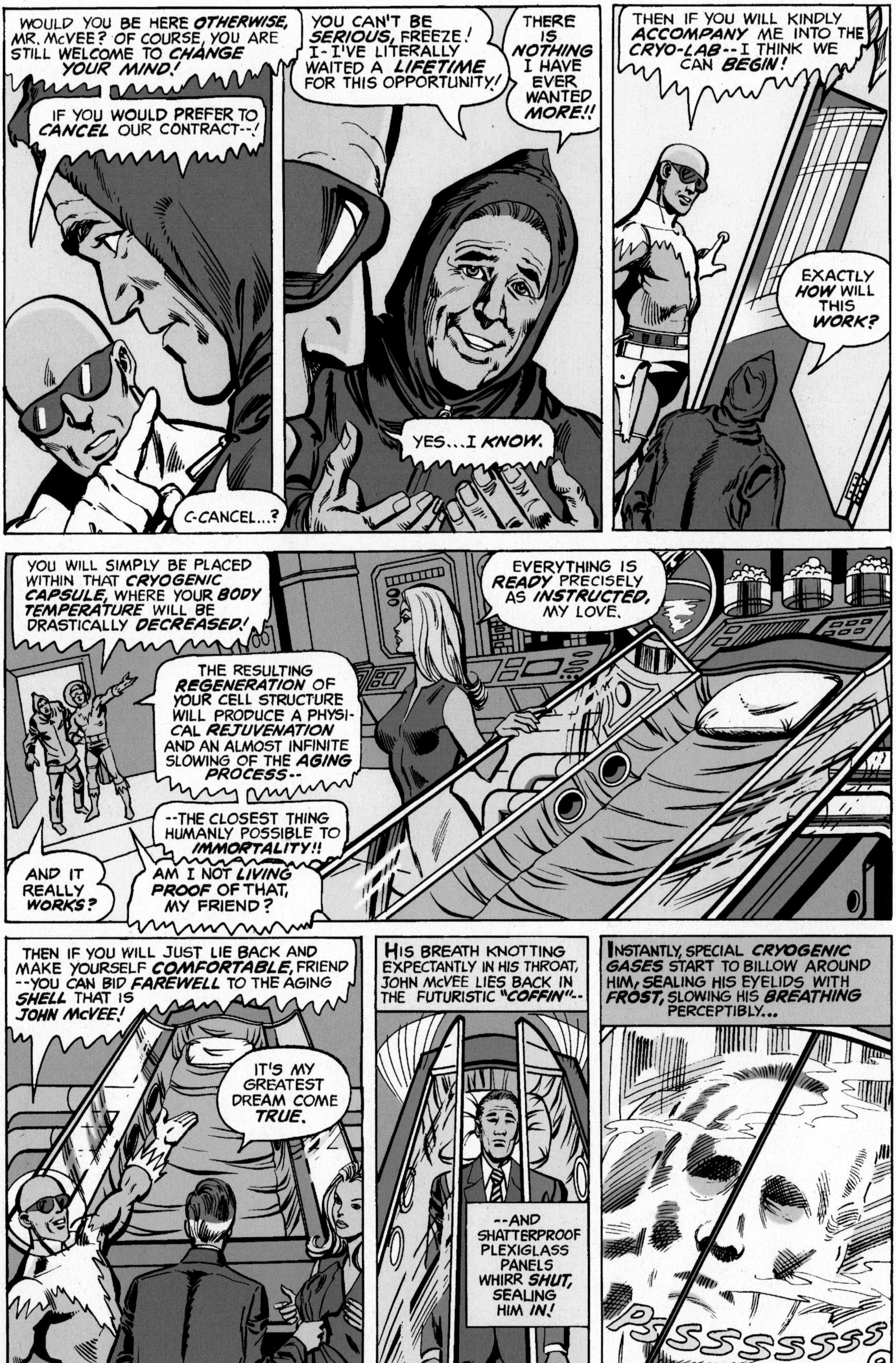
WOULD YOU BE HERE OTHERWISE, MR. McVEE? OF COURSE, YOU ARE STILL WELCOME TO CHANGE YOUR MIND!
IF YOU WOULD PREFER TO CANCEL OUR CONTRACT--!
C-CANCEL...?
YOU CAN'T BE SERIOUS, FREEZE! I-I'VE LITERALLY WAITED A LIFETIME FOR THIS OPPORTUNITY!
THERE IS NOTHING I HAVE EVER WANTED MORE!!
YES...I KNOW.
THEN IF YOU WILL KINDLY ACCOMPANY ME INTO THE CRYO-LAB--I THINK WE CAN BEGIN!
EXACTLY HOW WILL THIS WORK?
YOU WILL SIMPLY BE PLACED WITHIN THAT CRYOGENIC CAPSULE, WHERE YOUR BODY TEMPERATURE WILL BE DRASTICALLY DECREASED!
THE RESULTING REGENERATION OF YOUR CELL STRUCTURE WILL PRODUCE A PHYSICAL REJUVENATION AND AN ALMOST INFINITE SLOWING OF THE AGING PROCESS--
--THE CLOSEST THING HUMANLY POSSIBLE TO IMMORTALITY!!
EVERYTHING IS READY PRECISELY AS INSTRUCTED, MY LOVE.
AND IT REALLY WORKS?
AM I NOT LIVING PROOF OF THAT, MY FRIEND?
THEN IF YOU WILL JUST LIE BACK AND MAKE YOURSELF COMFORTABLE, FRIEND --YOU CAN BID FAREWELL TO THE AGING SHELL THAT IS JOHN McVEE!
IT'S MY GREATEST DREAM COME TRUE.
HIS BREATH KNOTTING EXPECTANTLY IN HIS THROAT, JOHN McVEE LIES BACK IN THE FUTURISTIC "COFFIN"--
--AND SHATTERPROOF PLEXIGLASS PANELS WHIRR SHUT, SEALING HIM IN!
INSTANTLY, SPECIAL CRYOGENIC GASES START TO BILLOW AROUND HIM, SEALING HIS EYELIDS WITH FROST, SLOWING HIS BREATHING PERCEPTIBLY...
PSSSSSSSSS
9

WITHIN SECONDS, THE FROST HAS *COATED* THE CAPSULE ENTIRELY, *OBSCURING* THE STATIONARY FORM WITHIN.

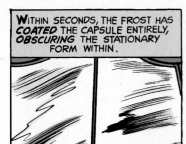

FOR SEVERAL MINUTES, THE ONLY *SOUNDS* WHICH CAN BE HEARD ARE THE *HISS* OF SWIRLING GASES, AND THE *HUM* OF ELECTRONIC CIRCUITRY--

--THEN, AT LAST, THE PLEXIGLASS PANELS WHIRR *OPEN* ONCE MORE TO REVEAL THE *NEW* JOHN McVEE--

TSSSSSSSS

--A MAN WHOSE ONCE-AGING BODY IS QUITE A BIT *YOUNGER* NOW, SEVERAL INCHES *TALLER*, AND INFINITELY MORE *POWERFUL* BY FAR--

--BUT, ALAS, NO LONGER *HUMAN*!!

NO! McVEE'S LIKE ALL THE *OTHERS!* HIS BODY HAS *SURVIVED* THE CRYOGENIC TREATMENT--BUT HIS *BRAIN CELLS* ARE IRREVOCABLY *FROZEN!*

HE'S BECOME LITTLE MORE THAN A LIVING *ZOMBIE!*

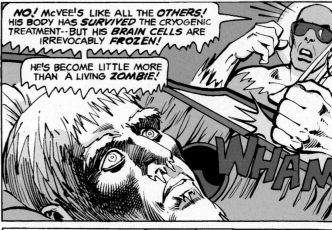

WHAM

I'VE FAILED *AGAIN*--BUT EACH ATTEMPT BRINGS ME CLOSER TO *PERFECTING* MY PROCESS!

SOON, HILDY MY LOVE, YOU WILL BE ABLE TO *JOIN* ME IN MY SUB-ZERO EXISTENCE--AND YOUR *BEAUTY* SHALL ENDURE *FOREVER!*

DON'T *WORRY*, DARLING--I HAVE *FAITH* IN YOU.

BUT ONCE I'VE *GAINED* THE IMMORTALITY YOU'VE PROMISED ME, I WILL GLADLY STEP ON YOU LIKE THE OBNOXIOUS *INSECT* THAT YOU ARE!

10

WHILE, HALF A CITY *AWAY*, AT THE GOTHAM CITY BRANCH OF *S.T.A.R.*LABS...

--AND IT TOOK *NINE* MEN TO HOLD OUR FRIEND HERE *STILL* LONG ENOUGH TO ADMINISTER THE *ANESTHESIA!*

NOT EXACTLY THE *LEAST VIOLENT* PATIENT WE'VE EVER HAD HERE, IS HE?

THE *WAYNE FOUNDATION* SEEMED ALMOST *GLAD* TO GET HIM OFF ITS *HANDS!*

*AS IN *SCIENTIFIC* AND *TECHNOLOGICAL* ADVANCED *RESEARCH.* --J.S.

WELL, THERE REALLY WASN'T ANYTHING THEY COULD *DO* FOR HIM THERE--EXCEPT KEEP HIM *CONTAINED.*

AT LEAST, *HERE*, WE HAVE A CHANCE OF RESTORING HIM TO *NORMAL.*

YEAH, THIS NEW *RADIATION TREATMENT* WILL EITHER *CURE* HIM-- OR *KILL* HIM!

BUTTONS ARE *PRESSED*--AND INSTANTLY, THE SHROUDED FIGURE IS ENVELOPED IN CORUSCATING *ENERGIES...*

FOR SEVERAL SECONDS, NOTHING *HAPPENS*--THEN THE MASSIVE BODY BENEATH THE STERILE SHEET BEGINS TO *WRITHE* IN TERRIBLE *AGONY*--

ARRGGH

--UNTIL IT *SUNDERS* ITS THICK METAL *BONDS* IN A FIT OF UNIMAGINABLE *FURY!*

SNAP

STAGGERING TO ITS FEET, THE TOWERING FIGURE GOES *BERSERK* --LASHING OUT BLINDLY AT THE SOURCE OF ITS MIND-SHATTERING *PAIN...*

KRAM

THEN, MOANING LIKE SOME LOST AND LONELY *CHILD*, THE FIGURE STUMBLES FORWARD--

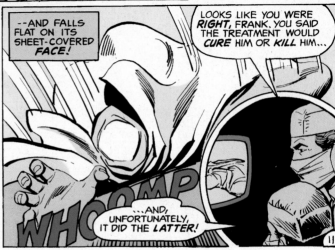

--AND FALLS FLAT ON ITS SHEET-COVERED *FACE!*

LOOKS LIKE YOU WERE *RIGHT*, FRANK. YOU SAID THE TREATMENT WOULD *CURE* HIM OR *KILL* HIM...

WHOOMP

...AND, UNFORTUNATELY, IT DID THE *LATTER!*

11

41

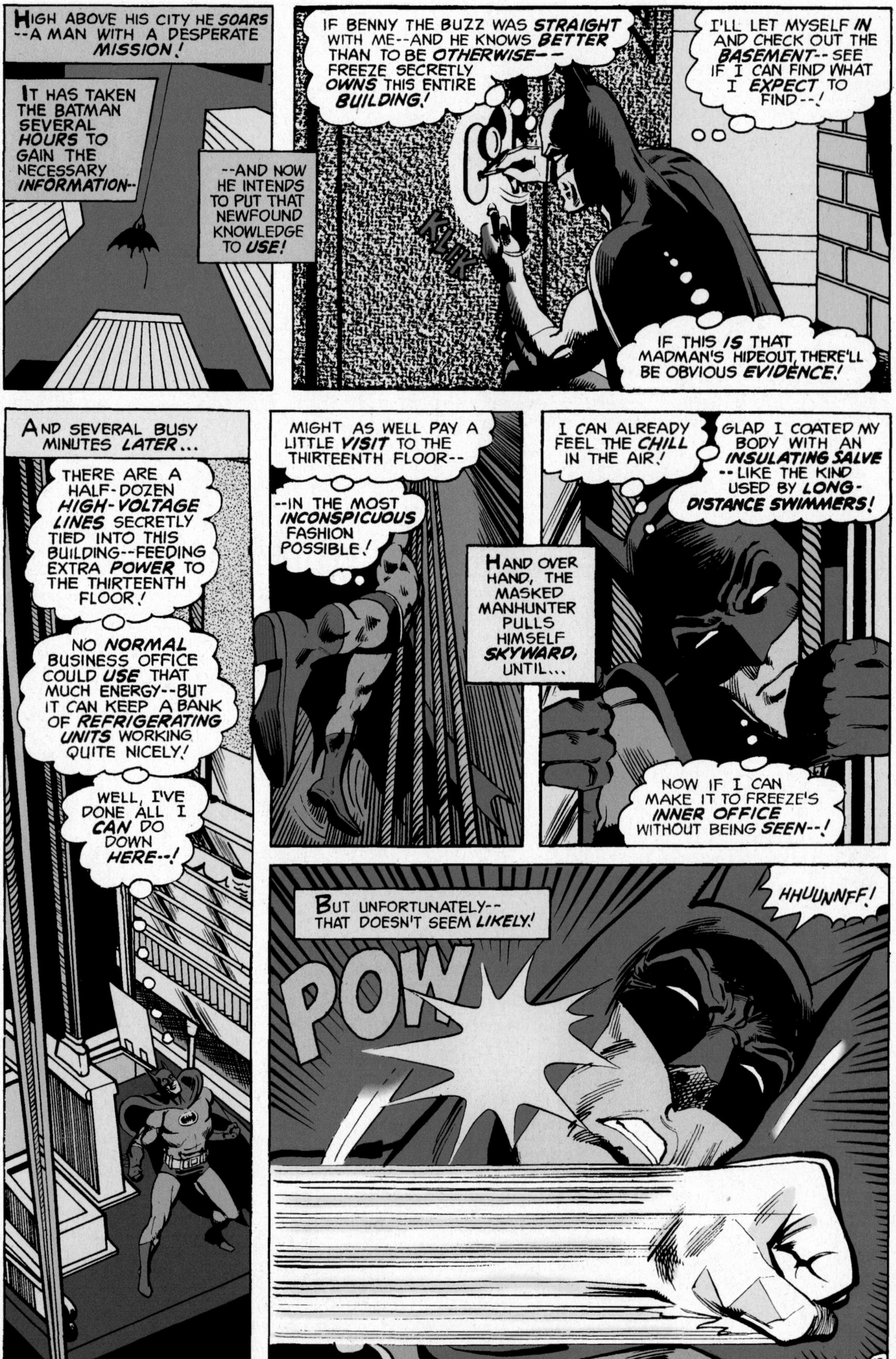
HIGH ABOVE HIS CITY HE SOARS --A MAN WITH A DESPERATE MISSION!
IT HAS TAKEN THE BATMAN SEVERAL HOURS TO GAIN THE NECESSARY INFORMATION--
--AND NOW HE INTENDS TO PUT THAT NEWFOUND KNOWLEDGE TO USE!
IF BENNY THE BUZZ WAS STRAIGHT WITH ME--AND HE KNOWS BETTER THAN TO BE OTHERWISE-- FREEZE SECRETLY OWNS THIS ENTIRE BUILDING!
I'LL LET MYSELF IN AND CHECK OUT THE BASEMENT--SEE IF I CAN FIND WHAT I EXPECT TO FIND--!
KLIK
IF THIS IS THAT MADMAN'S HIDEOUT, THERE'LL BE OBVIOUS EVIDENCE!
AND SEVERAL BUSY MINUTES LATER...
THERE ARE A HALF-DOZEN HIGH-VOLTAGE LINES SECRETLY TIED INTO THIS BUILDING--FEEDING EXTRA POWER TO THE THIRTEENTH FLOOR!
NO NORMAL BUSINESS OFFICE COULD USE THAT MUCH ENERGY--BUT IT CAN KEEP A BANK OF REFRIGERATING UNITS WORKING QUITE NICELY!
WELL, I'VE DONE ALL I CAN DO DOWN HERE--!
MIGHT AS WELL PAY A LITTLE VISIT TO THE THIRTEENTH FLOOR--
--IN THE MOST INCONSPICUOUS FASHION POSSIBLE!
HAND OVER HAND, THE MASKED MANHUNTER PULLS HIMSELF SKYWARD, UNTIL...
I CAN ALREADY FEEL THE CHILL IN THE AIR!
GLAD I COATED MY BODY WITH AN INSULATING SALVE --LIKE THE KIND USED BY LONG-DISTANCE SWIMMERS!
NOW IF I CAN MAKE IT TO FREEZE'S INNER OFFICE WITHOUT BEING SEEN--!
BUT UNFORTUNATELY-- THAT DOESN'T SEEM LIKELY!
HHUUNNFF!
POW
12

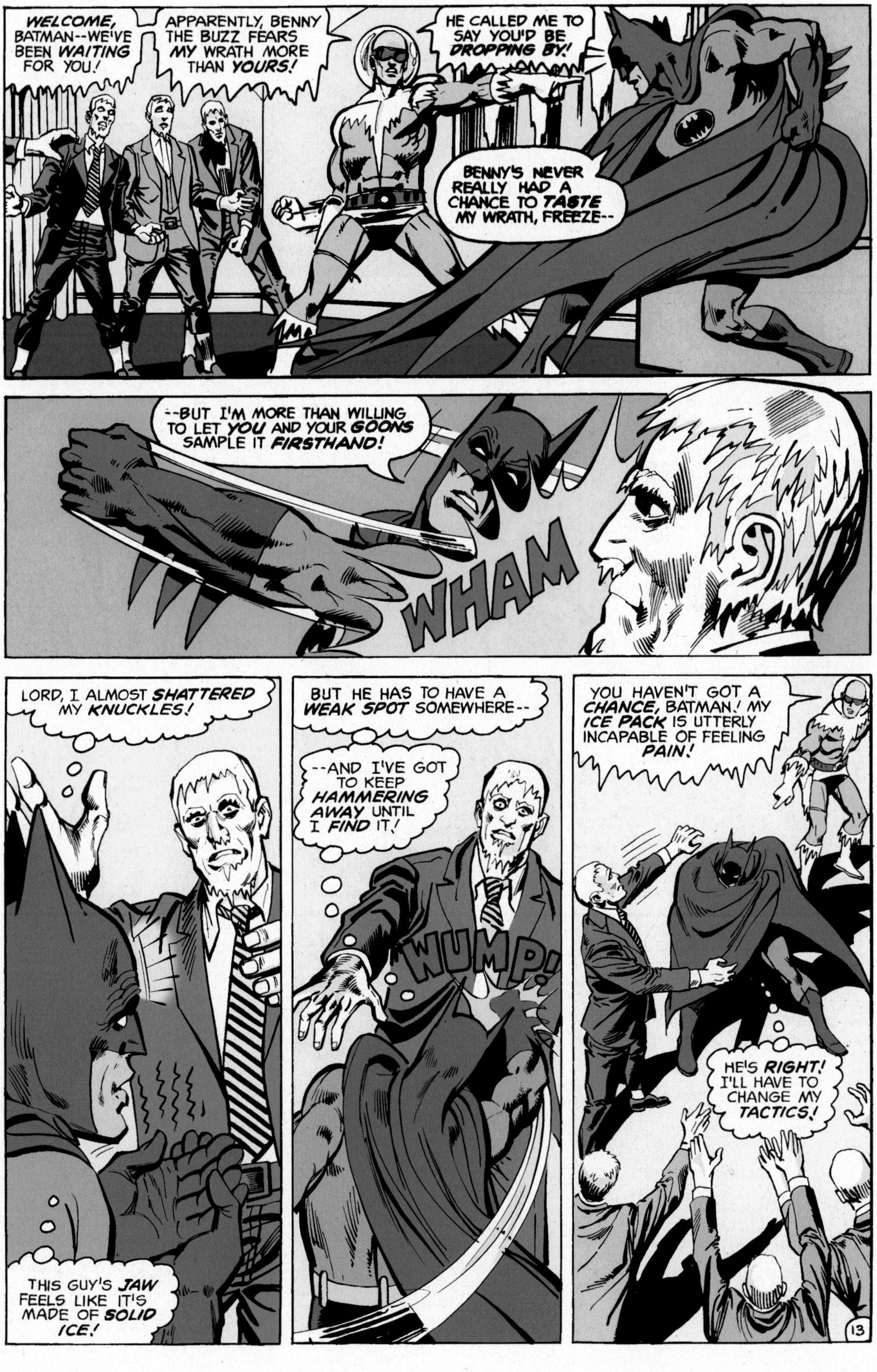
WELCOME, BATMAN--WE'VE BEEN WAITING FOR YOU!
APPARENTLY, BENNY THE BUZZ FEARS MY WRATH MORE THAN YOURS!
HE CALLED ME TO SAY YOU'D BE DROPPING BY!
BENNY'S NEVER REALLY HAD A CHANCE TO TASTE MY WRATH, FREEZE--
--BUT I'M MORE THAN WILLING TO LET YOU AND YOUR GOONS SAMPLE IT FIRSTHAND!
WHAM
LORD, I ALMOST SHATTERED MY KNUCKLES!
THIS GUY'S JAW FEELS LIKE IT'S MADE OF SOLID ICE!
BUT HE HAS TO HAVE A WEAK SPOT SOMEWHERE--
--AND I'VE GOT TO KEEP HAMMERING AWAY UNTIL I FIND IT!
WUMP!
YOU HAVEN'T GOT A CHANCE, BATMAN! MY ICE PACK IS UTTERLY INCAPABLE OF FEELING PAIN!
HE'S RIGHT! I'LL HAVE TO CHANGE MY TACTICS!
13

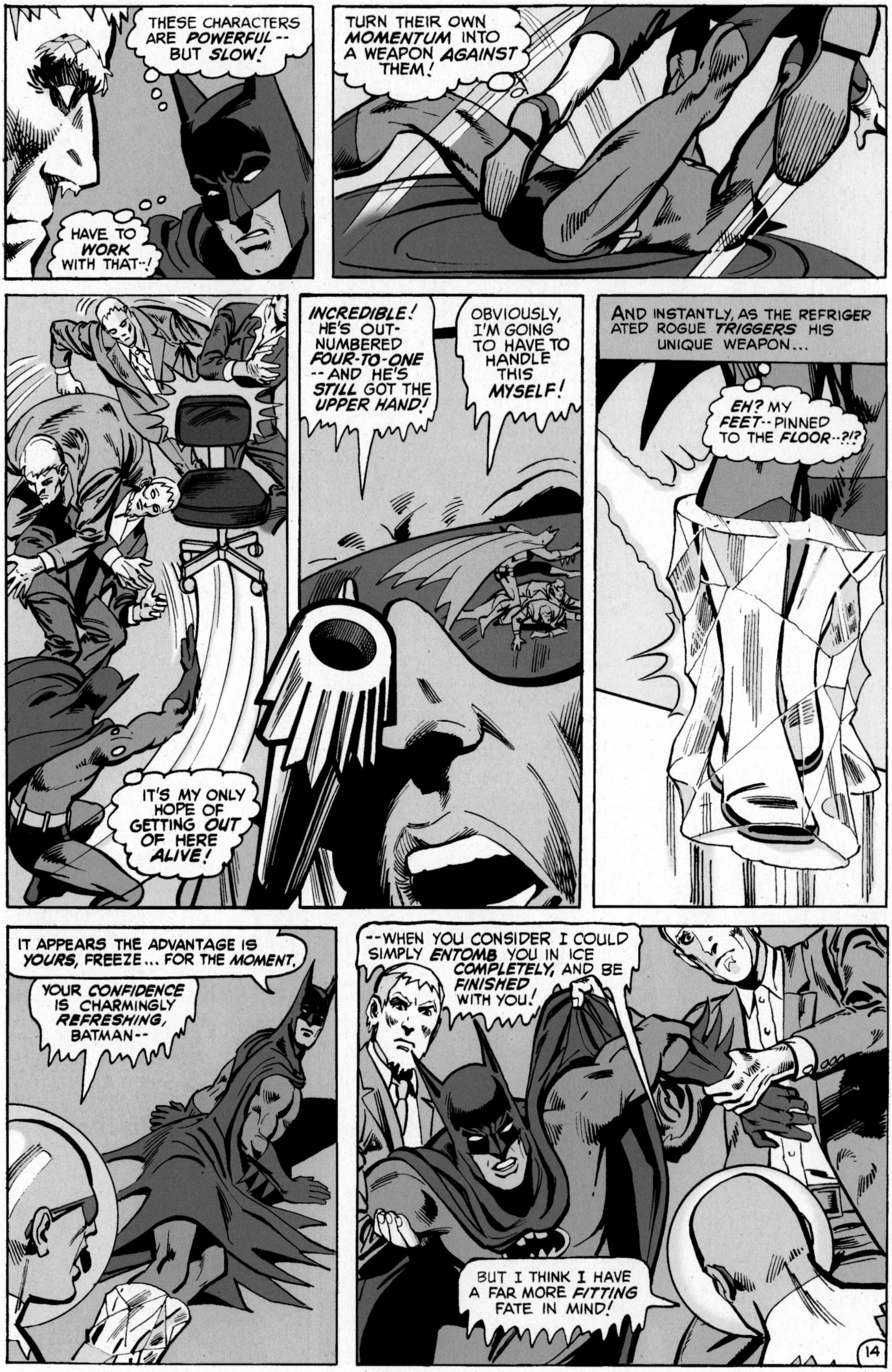
THESE CHARACTERS ARE POWERFUL -- BUT SLOW!
HAVE TO WORK WITH THAT--!
TURN THEIR OWN MOMENTUM INTO A WEAPON AGAINST THEM!
IT'S MY ONLY HOPE OF GETTING OUT OF HERE ALIVE!
INCREDIBLE! HE'S OUT-NUMBERED FOUR-TO-ONE -- AND HE'S STILL GOT THE UPPER HAND!
OBVIOUSLY, I'M GOING TO HAVE TO HANDLE THIS MYSELF!
AND INSTANTLY, AS THE REFRIGER ATED ROGUE TRIGGERS HIS UNIQUE WEAPON...
EH? MY FEET--PINNED TO THE FLOOR--?!?
IT APPEARS THE ADVANTAGE IS YOURS, FREEZE... FOR THE MOMENT.
YOUR CONFIDENCE IS CHARMINGLY REFRESHING, BATMAN--
--WHEN YOU CONSIDER I COULD SIMPLY ENTOMB YOU IN ICE COMPLETELY, AND BE FINISHED WITH YOU!
BUT I THINK I HAVE A FAR MORE FITTING FATE IN MIND!
14

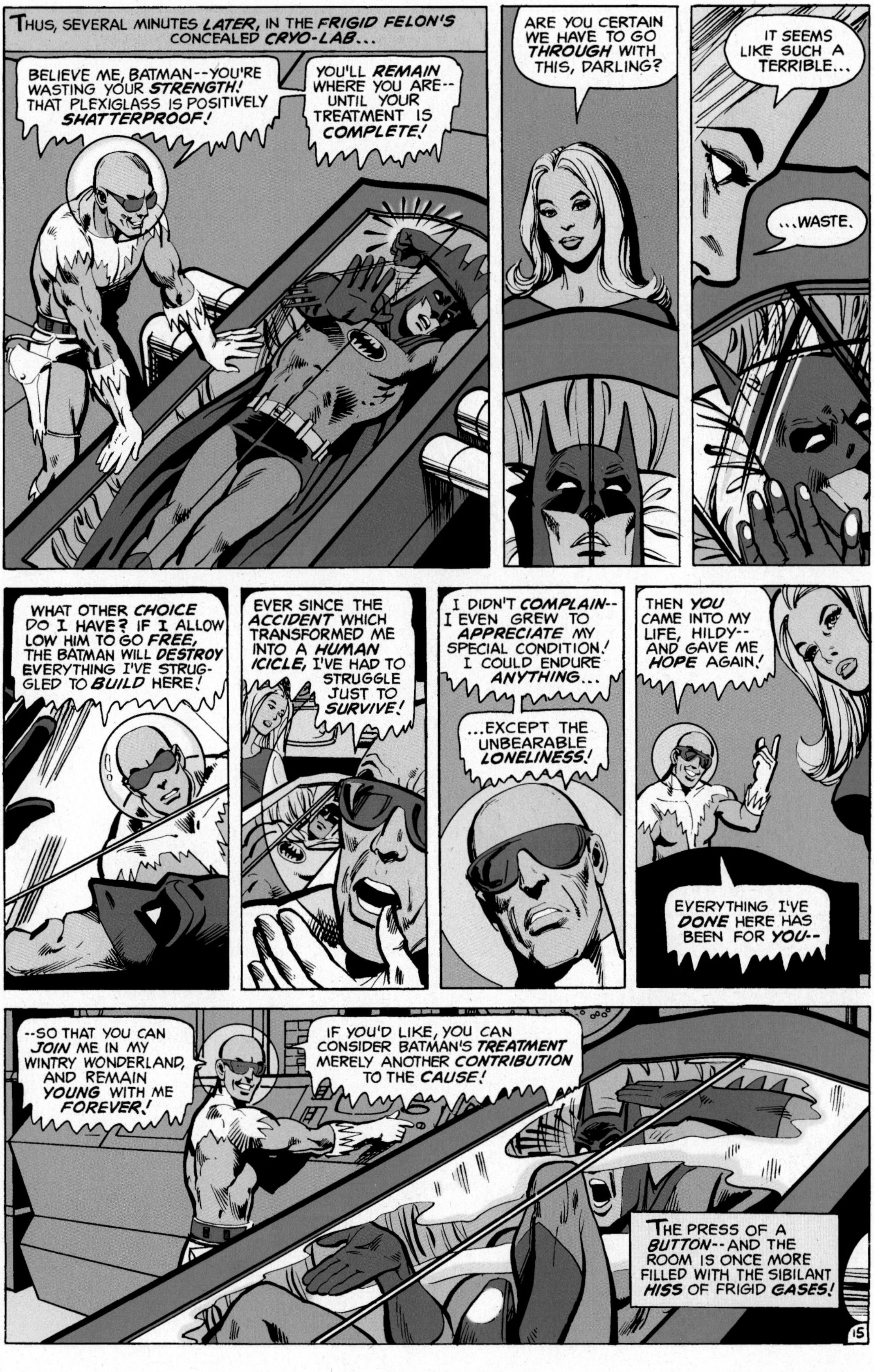
THUS, SEVERAL MINUTES LATER, IN THE FRIGID FELON'S CONCEALED CRYO-LAB...
BELIEVE ME, BATMAN--YOU'RE WASTING YOUR STRENGTH! THAT PLEXIGLASS IS POSITIVELY SHATTERPROOF!
YOU'LL REMAIN WHERE YOU ARE--UNTIL YOUR TREATMENT IS COMPLETE!
ARE YOU CERTAIN WE HAVE TO GO THROUGH WITH THIS, DARLING?
IT SEEMS LIKE SUCH A TERRIBLE...
...WASTE.
WHAT OTHER CHOICE DO I HAVE? IF I ALLOW LOW HIM TO GO FREE, THE BATMAN WILL DESTROY EVERYTHING I'VE STRUGGLED TO BUILD HERE!
EVER SINCE THE ACCIDENT WHICH TRANSFORMED ME INTO A HUMAN ICICLE, I'VE HAD TO STRUGGLE JUST TO SURVIVE!
I DIDN'T COMPLAIN--I EVEN GREW TO APPRECIATE MY SPECIAL CONDITION! I COULD ENDURE ANYTHING...
...EXCEPT THE UNBEARABLE LONELINESS!
THEN YOU CAME INTO MY LIFE, HILDY--AND GAVE ME HOPE AGAIN!
EVERYTHING I'VE DONE HERE HAS BEEN FOR YOU--
--SO THAT YOU CAN JOIN ME IN MY WINTRY WONDERLAND, AND REMAIN YOUNG WITH ME FOREVER!
IF YOU'D LIKE, YOU CAN CONSIDER BATMAN'S TREATMENT MERELY ANOTHER CONTRIBUTION TO THE CAUSE!
THE PRESS OF A BUTTON--AND THE ROOM IS ONCE MORE FILLED WITH THE SIBILANT HISS OF FRIGID GASES!
15

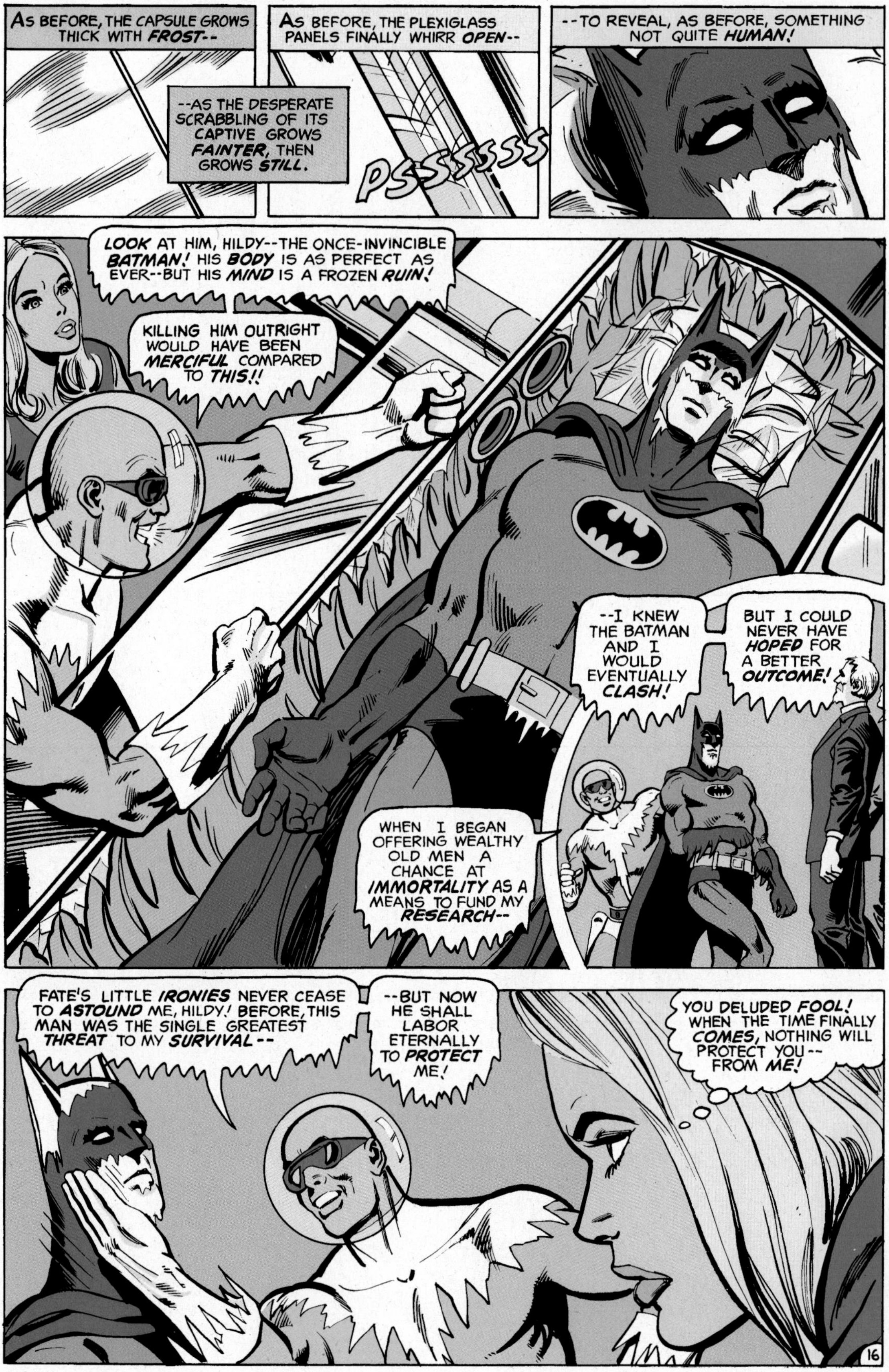

AS BEFORE, THE CAPSULE GROWS THICK WITH FROST--
--AS THE DESPERATE SCRABBLING OF ITS CAPTIVE GROWS FAINTER, THEN GROWS STILL.
AS BEFORE, THE PLEXIGLASS PANELS FINALLY WHIRR OPEN--
PSSSSSSS
--TO REVEAL, AS BEFORE, SOMETHING NOT QUITE HUMAN!
LOOK AT HIM, HILDY--THE ONCE-INVINCIBLE BATMAN! HIS BODY IS AS PERFECT AS EVER--BUT HIS MIND IS A FROZEN RUIN!
KILLING HIM OUTRIGHT WOULD HAVE BEEN MERCIFUL COMPARED TO THIS!!
WHEN I BEGAN OFFERING WEALTHY OLD MEN A CHANCE AT IMMORTALITY AS A MEANS TO FUND MY RESEARCH--
--I KNEW THE BATMAN AND I WOULD EVENTUALLY CLASH!
BUT I COULD NEVER HAVE HOPED FOR A BETTER OUTCOME!
FATE'S LITTLE IRONIES NEVER CEASE TO ASTOUND ME, HILDY! BEFORE, THIS MAN WAS THE SINGLE GREATEST THREAT TO MY SURVIVAL--
--BUT NOW HE SHALL LABOR ETERNALLY TO PROTECT ME!
YOU DELUDED FOOL! WHEN THE TIME FINALLY COMES, NOTHING WILL PROTECT YOU-- FROM ME!
16

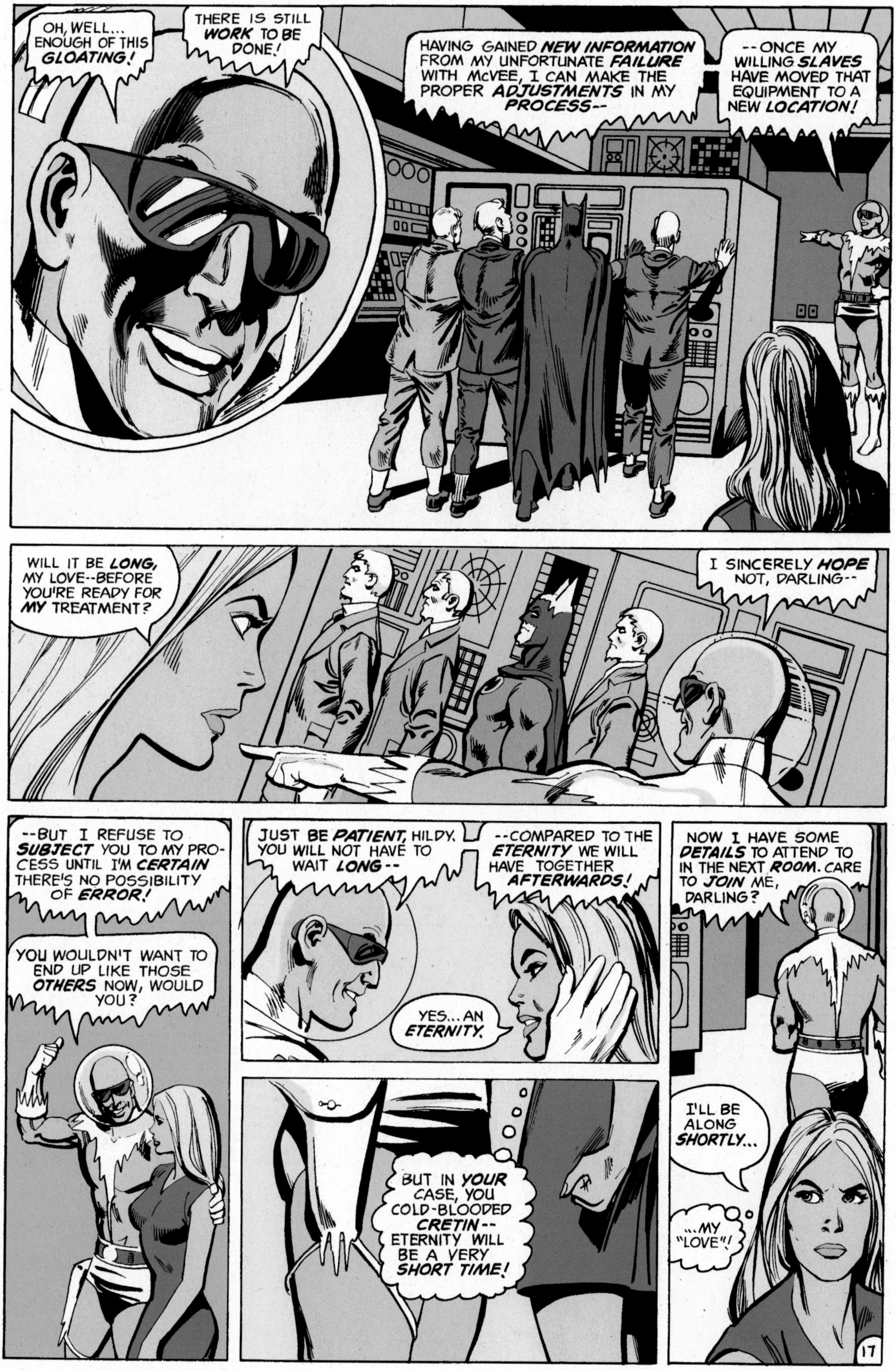
OH, WELL... ENOUGH OF THIS GLOATING!
THERE IS STILL WORK TO BE DONE!
HAVING GAINED NEW INFORMATION FROM MY UNFORTUNATE FAILURE WITH McVEE, I CAN MAKE THE PROPER ADJUSTMENTS IN MY PROCESS--
--ONCE MY WILLING SLAVES HAVE MOVED THAT EQUIPMENT TO A NEW LOCATION!
WILL IT BE LONG, MY LOVE--BEFORE YOU'RE READY FOR MY TREATMENT?
I SINCERELY HOPE NOT, DARLING--
--BUT I REFUSE TO SUBJECT YOU TO MY PROCESS UNTIL I'M CERTAIN THERE'S NO POSSIBILITY OF ERROR!
YOU WOULDN'T WANT TO END UP LIKE THOSE OTHERS NOW, WOULD YOU?
JUST BE PATIENT, HILDY. YOU WILL NOT HAVE TO WAIT LONG--
--COMPARED TO THE ETERNITY WE WILL HAVE TOGETHER AFTERWARDS!
YES...AN ETERNITY.
BUT IN YOUR CASE, YOU COLD-BLOODED CRETIN--ETERNITY WILL BE A VERY SHORT TIME!
NOW I HAVE SOME DETAILS TO ATTEND TO IN THE NEXT ROOM. CARE TO JOIN ME, DARLING?
I'LL BE ALONG SHORTLY...
...MY "LOVE"!
17

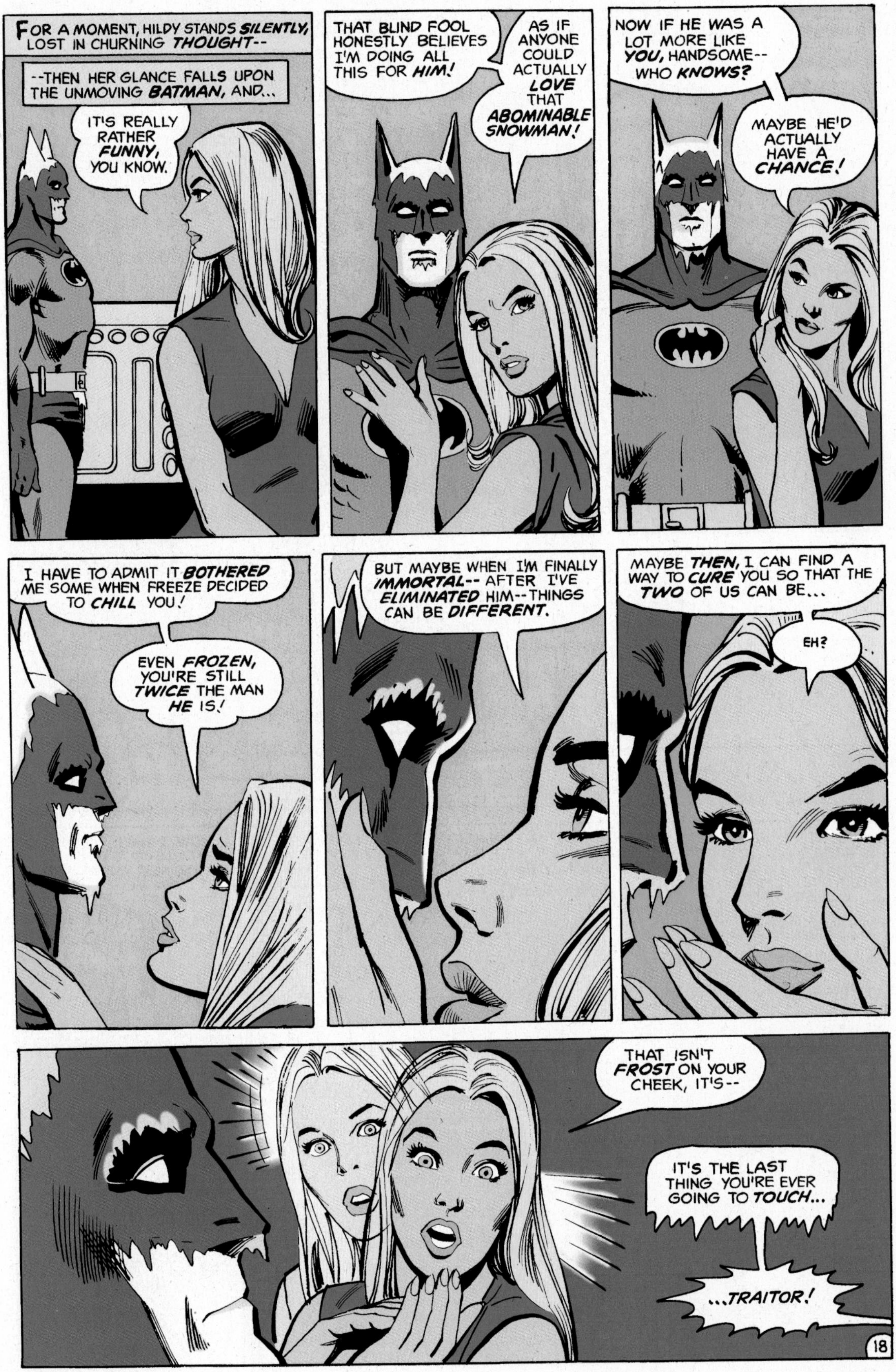

FOR A MOMENT, HILDY STANDS SILENTLY, LOST IN CHURNING THOUGHT--
--THEN HER GLANCE FALLS UPON THE UNMOVING BATMAN, AND...
IT'S REALLY RATHER FUNNY, YOU KNOW.
THAT BLIND FOOL HONESTLY BELIEVES I'M DOING ALL THIS FOR HIM!
AS IF ANYONE COULD ACTUALLY LOVE THAT ABOMINABLE SNOWMAN!
NOW IF HE WAS A LOT MORE LIKE YOU, HANDSOME-- WHO KNOWS?
MAYBE HE'D ACTUALLY HAVE A CHANCE!
I HAVE TO ADMIT IT BOTHERED ME SOME WHEN FREEZE DECIDED TO CHILL YOU!
EVEN FROZEN, YOU'RE STILL TWICE THE MAN HE IS!
BUT MAYBE WHEN I'M FINALLY IMMORTAL-- AFTER I'VE ELIMINATED HIM--THINGS CAN BE DIFFERENT.
MAYBE THEN, I CAN FIND A WAY TO CURE YOU SO THAT THE TWO OF US CAN BE...
EH?
THAT ISN'T FROST ON YOUR CHEEK, IT'S--
IT'S THE LAST THING YOU'RE EVER GOING TO TOUCH...
...TRAITOR!
18

YOU REALLY SHOULDN'T EXPRESS YOUR THOUGHTS SO *VOCALLY*, HILDY! EVEN IN THE NEXT ROOM, I COULDN'T HELP *OVERHEARING*!

YOU PLAYED ME FOR A *FOOL* -- AND NOW YOU'RE GOING TO *SUFFER* FOR IT!

DARLING -- *WAIT!* YOU DON'T *UNDERSTAND*--!

I DIDN'T *MEAN* WHAT I SAID! I WAS ONLY TRYING TO *TRICK* THE BATMAN!

HE ISN'T WHAT HE *APPEARS* TO BE! HE'S REALLY--

HILDY-- *PLEASE!*

DON'T INSULT ME BY *BEGGING!* I'D PREFER TO REMEMBER YOU JUST THE WAY YOU *WERE*--

--A CONNIVING, SCHEMING, UNFAITHFUL *WITCH!*

N-NO... PLEASE...

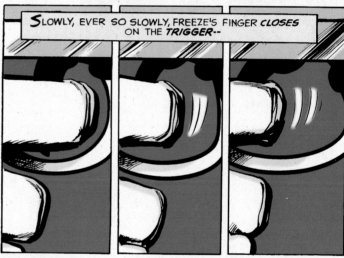

*S*LOWLY, EVER SO SLOWLY, FREEZE'S FINGER *CLOSES* ON THE *TRIGGER*--

--BUT BEFORE HE CAN SQUEEZE IT *TIGHT*...

ALL RIGHT, FREEZE-- THAT'S *ENOUGH!*

IF YOU'RE LOOKING FOR A *TARGET*-- TRY *ME!!*

I WAS *RIGHT!* THE BATMAN IS STILL *ALIVE!*

19

BUT HOW--?!?

BEFORE I CAME *UP* HERE, I *DISCONNECTED* SEVERAL OF YOUR EXTRA *POWER* LINES, FREEZE!

YOU HAD *VOLTAGE* ENOUGH TO MAINTAIN YOUR *REFRIGERATING* UNITS, BUT NOT *NEARLY* ENOUGH TO POWER YOUR *CRYOGENIC* CAPSULE!

I *FAKED* BECOMING ONE OF YOUR *VICTIMS* SO I COULD FIND OUT *WHAT* THIS WAS ALL ABOUT--

--AND IT WOULD'VE *WORKED* IF YOUR LADY FRIEND HADN'T DISCOVERED THE *MAKE-UP* ON MY CHEEK!

THAT'S *TWICE* I'VE BEEN FOOLED-- BUT *NO MORE!* ICE PACK-- KILL HIM!!

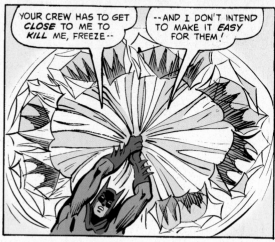

YOUR CREW HAS TO GET *CLOSE* TO ME TO *KILL* ME, FREEZE--

--AND I DON'T INTEND TO MAKE IT *EASY* FOR THEM!

INCREDIBLE! THAT BLOCK OF ICE WOULD'VE FLATTENED A *RHINO*--

--BUT IT BARELY EVEN *SLOWED* THESE *ZOMBIES!*

WHAM

KROOM

THUK-THUK THUK

HAVE TO KEEP *MOVING*-- CAN'T LET THEM GET THEIR *HANDS* ON ME--!

BUT EVEN USING THEIR *SLUGGISHNESS* AGAINST THEM--

--THE *BEST* I CAN HOPE FOR IS A *STAND-OFF!*

GOT TO FIND A WAY TO STOP THEM PERMANENTLY--

--BEFORE THEY DO THE SAME TO *ME!*

20

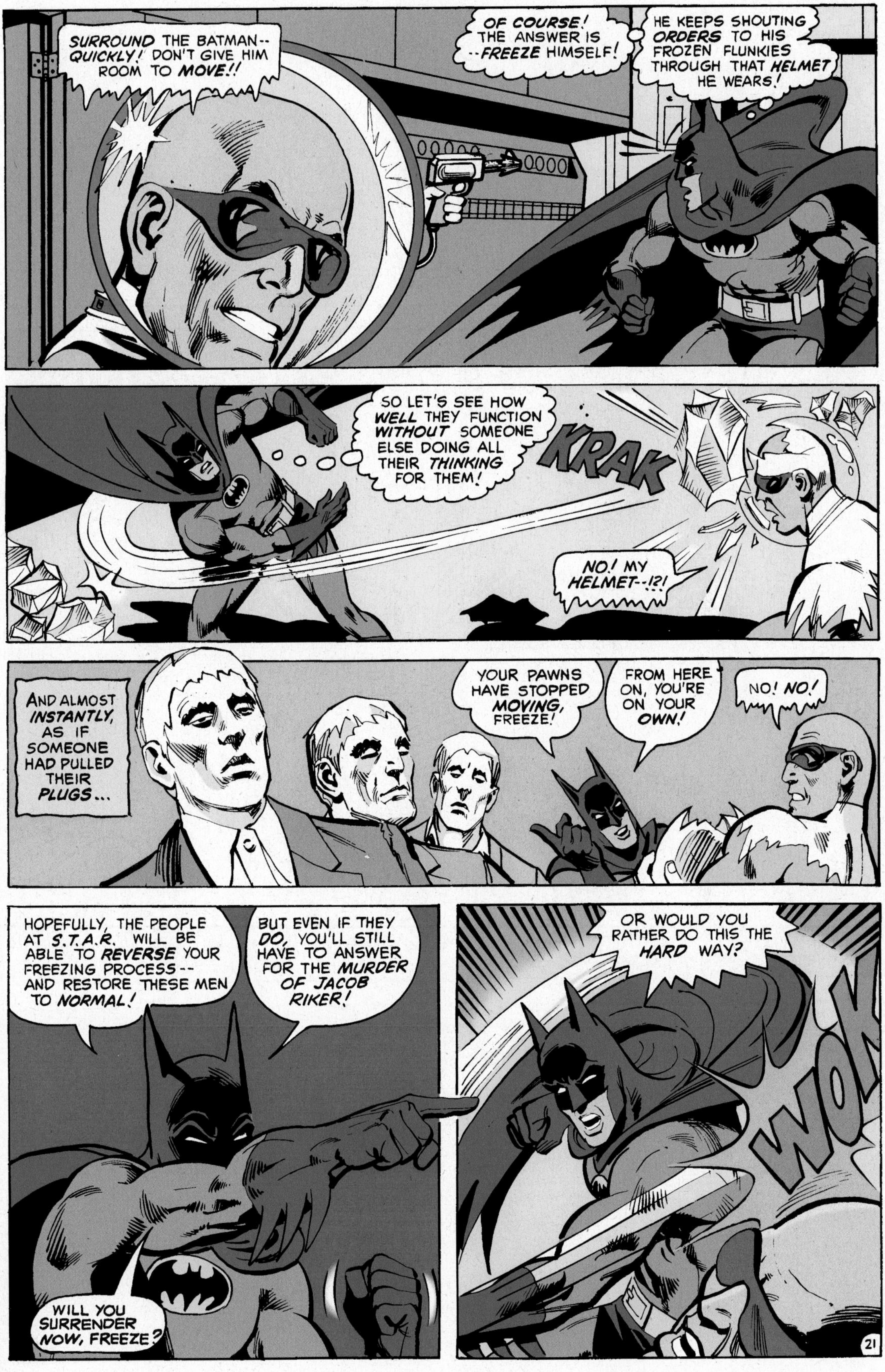

SURROUND THE BATMAN-- QUICKLY! DON'T GIVE HIM ROOM TO MOVE!!
OF COURSE! THE ANSWER IS --FREEZE HIMSELF!
HE KEEPS SHOUTING ORDERS TO HIS FROZEN FLUNKIES THROUGH THAT HELMET HE WEARS!
SO LET'S SEE HOW WELL THEY FUNCTION WITHOUT SOMEONE ELSE DOING ALL THEIR THINKING FOR THEM!
KRAK
NO! MY HELMET--!?!
AND ALMOST INSTANTLY, AS IF SOMEONE HAD PULLED THEIR PLUGS...
YOUR PAWNS HAVE STOPPED MOVING, FREEZE!
FROM HERE ON, YOU'RE ON YOUR OWN!
NO! NO!
HOPEFULLY, THE PEOPLE AT S.T.A.R. WILL BE ABLE TO REVERSE YOUR FREEZING PROCESS-- AND RESTORE THESE MEN TO NORMAL!
BUT EVEN IF THEY DO, YOU'LL STILL HAVE TO ANSWER FOR THE MURDER OF JACOB RIKER!
WILL YOU SURRENDER NOW, FREEZE?
OR WOULD YOU RATHER DO THIS THE HARD WAY?
WOK
21

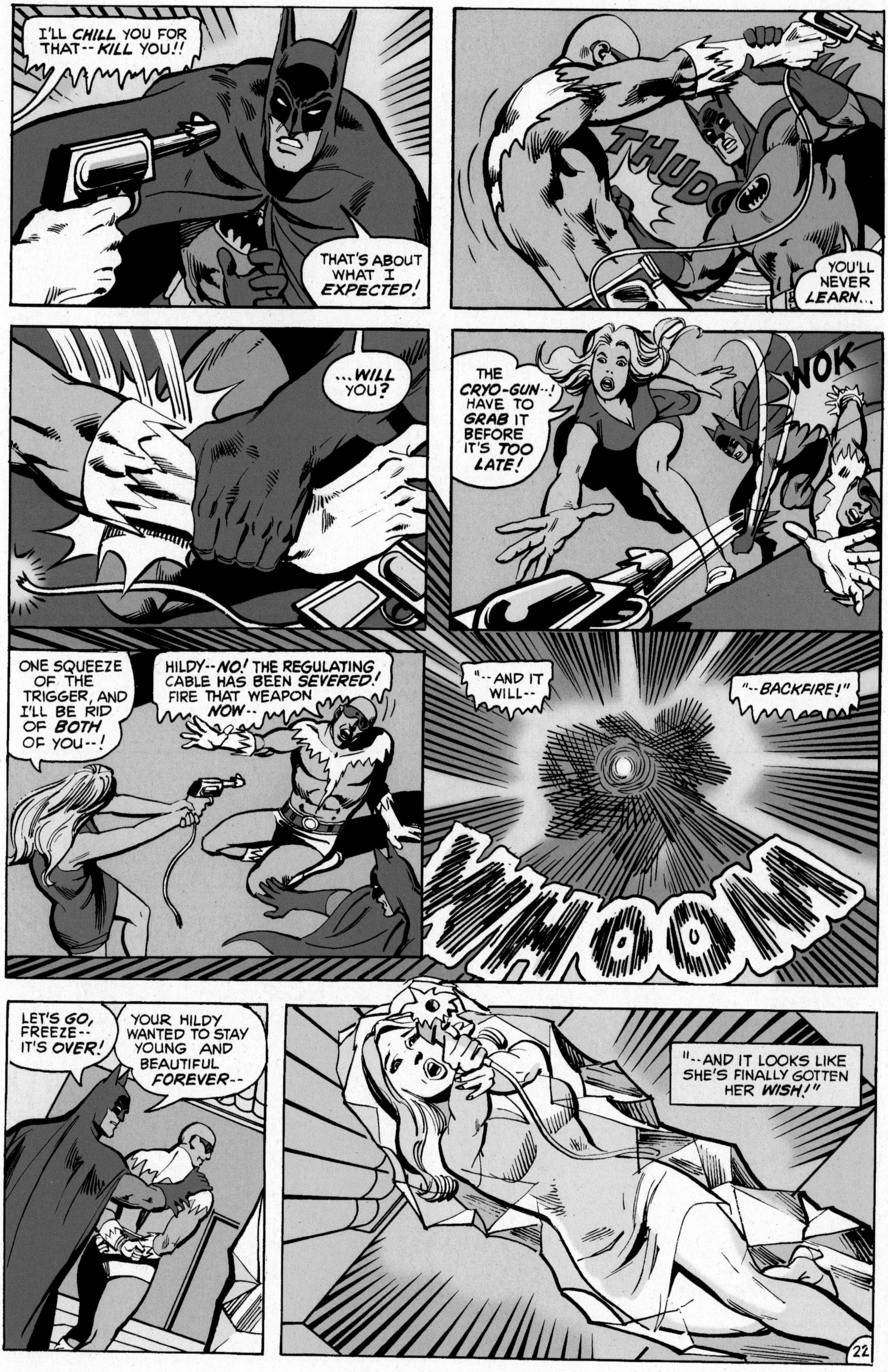
I'LL CHILL YOU FOR THAT--KILL YOU!!
THAT'S ABOUT WHAT I EXPECTED!
THUD
YOU'LL NEVER LEARN...
...WILL YOU?
THE CRYO-GUN--! HAVE TO GRAB IT BEFORE IT'S TOO LATE!
WOK
ONE SQUEEZE OF THE TRIGGER, AND I'LL BE RID OF BOTH OF YOU--!
HILDY--NO! THE REGULATING CABLE HAS BEEN SEVERED! FIRE THAT WEAPON NOW--
"--AND IT WILL--
"--BACKFIRE!"
WHOOM
LET'S GO, FREEZE-- IT'S OVER!
YOUR HILDY WANTED TO STAY YOUNG AND BEAUTIFUL FOREVER--
"--AND IT LOOKS LIKE SHE'S FINALLY GOTTEN HER WISH!"
22

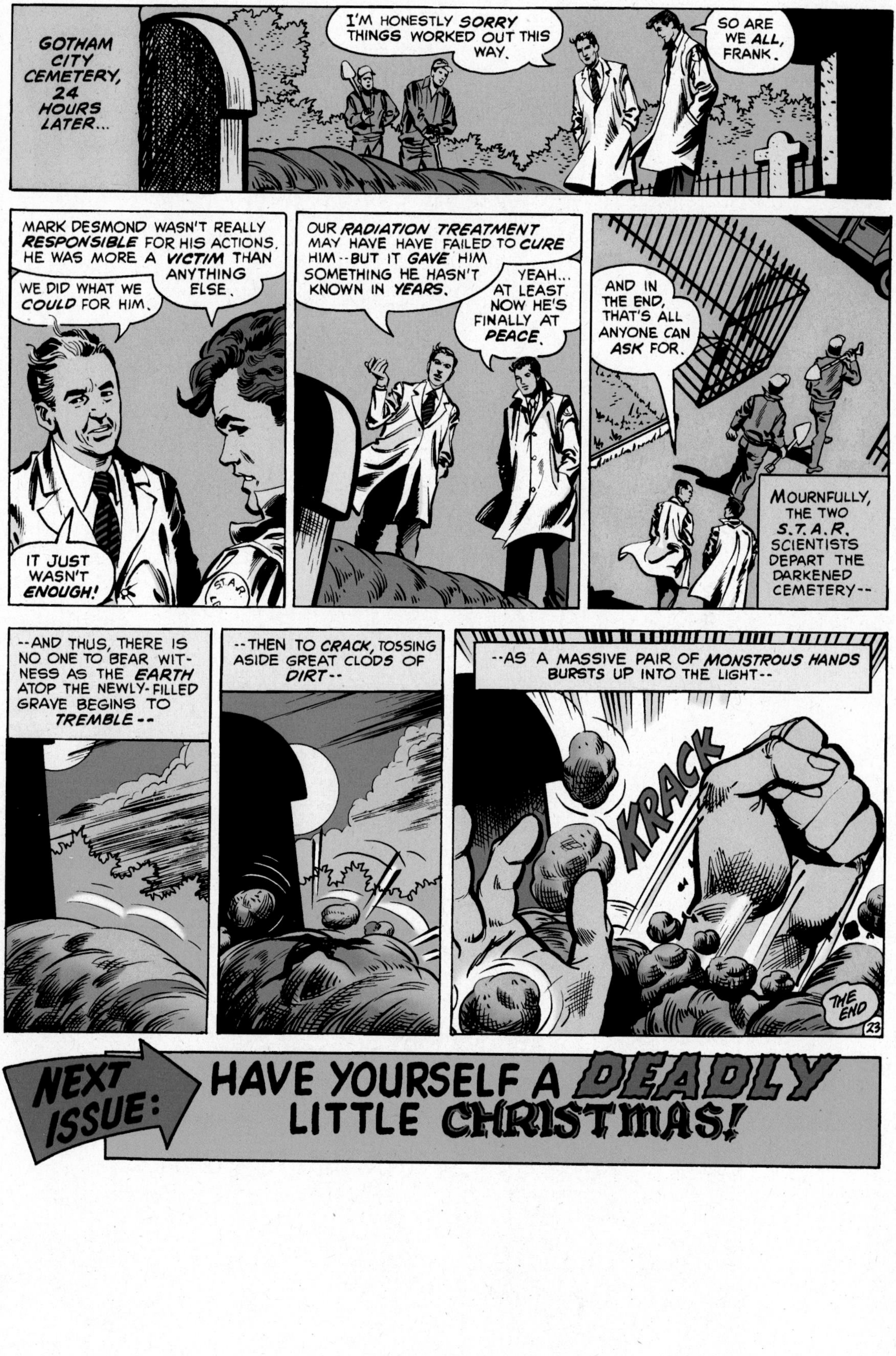
GOTHAM CITY CEMETERY, 24 HOURS LATER...
I'M HONESTLY SORRY THINGS WORKED OUT THIS WAY.
SO ARE WE ALL, FRANK.
MARK DESMOND WASN'T REALLY RESPONSIBLE FOR HIS ACTIONS. HE WAS MORE A VICTIM THAN ANYTHING ELSE.
WE DID WHAT WE COULD FOR HIM.
IT JUST WASN'T ENOUGH!
S.T.A.R.
OUR RADIATION TREATMENT MAY HAVE HAVE FAILED TO CURE HIM--BUT IT GAVE HIM SOMETHING HE HASN'T KNOWN IN YEARS.
YEAH... AT LEAST NOW HE'S FINALLY AT PEACE.
AND IN THE END, THAT'S ALL ANYONE CAN ASK FOR.
MOURNFULLY, THE TWO S.T.A.R. SCIENTISTS DEPART THE DARKENED CEMETERY--
--AND THUS, THERE IS NO ONE TO BEAR WITNESS AS THE EARTH ATOP THE NEWLY-FILLED GRAVE BEGINS TO TREMBLE--
--THEN TO CRACK, TOSSING ASIDE GREAT CLODS OF DIRT--
--AS A MASSIVE PAIR OF MONSTROUS HANDS BURSTS UP INTO THE LIGHT--
KRACK
THE END
23
NEXT ISSUE: HAVE YOURSELF A DEADLY LITTLE CHRISTMAS!

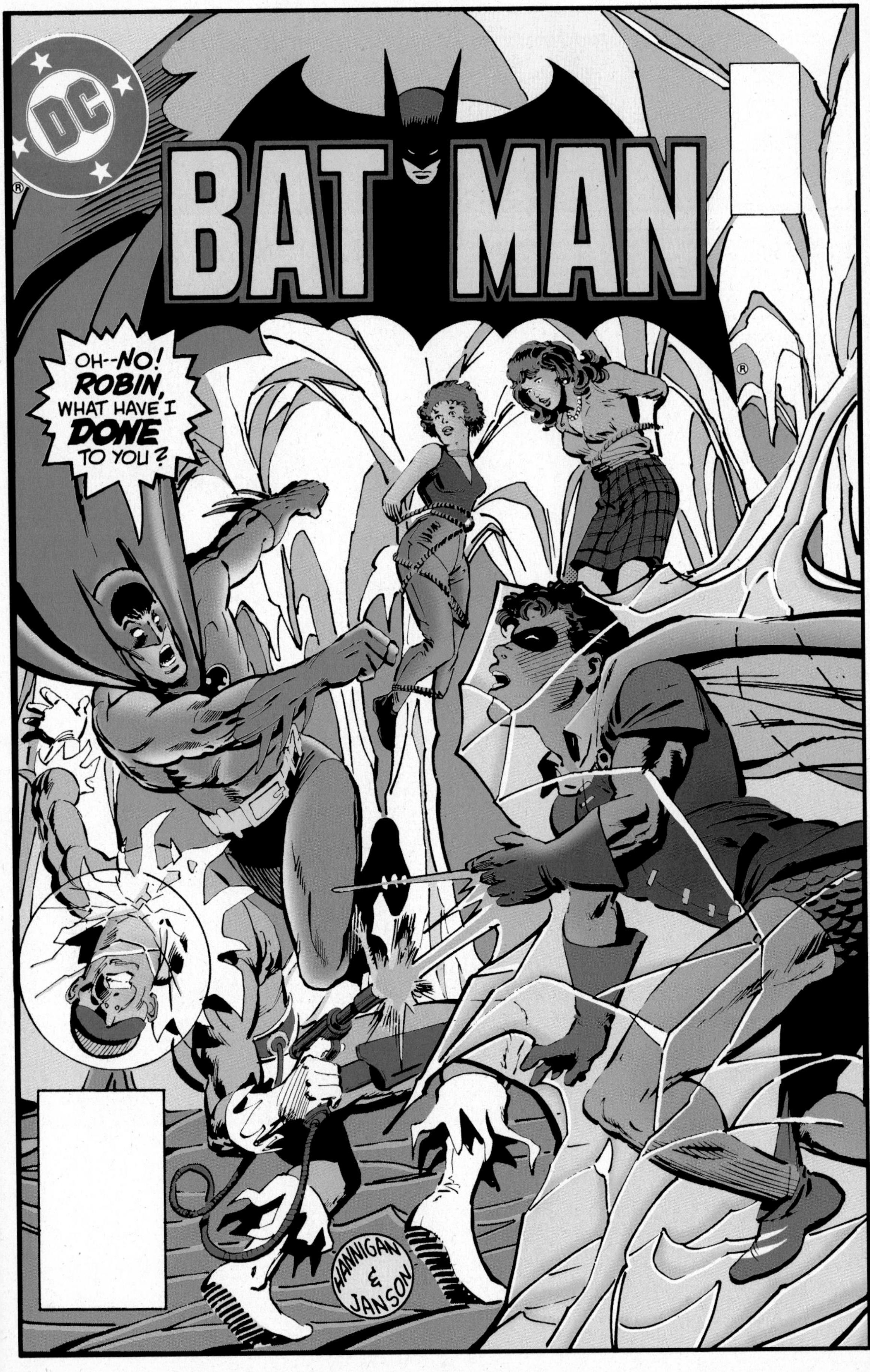
BATMAN
OH--NO! ROBIN, WHAT HAVE I DONE TO YOU?
HANNIGAN & JANSON

BAT MAN
CREATED BY BOB KANE ®

Let me tell you a tale of old Gotham-town
'Pon whose spires lies a cast of deep cold
So chill and rigid to eternally drown
All who dared the ice of its hold.
    So if still you must visit fair Gotham-town
    Hurry, before it cracks, and falls down
    Ending this, my tale, told with long frown...

The Glacier Under Gotham!

DOUG MOENCH	DON NEWTON	ALFREDO ALCALA	TODD KLEIN	ADRIENNE ROY	LEN WEIN
WRITER	ARTIST	INKER	LETTERER	COLORIST	EDITOR

1

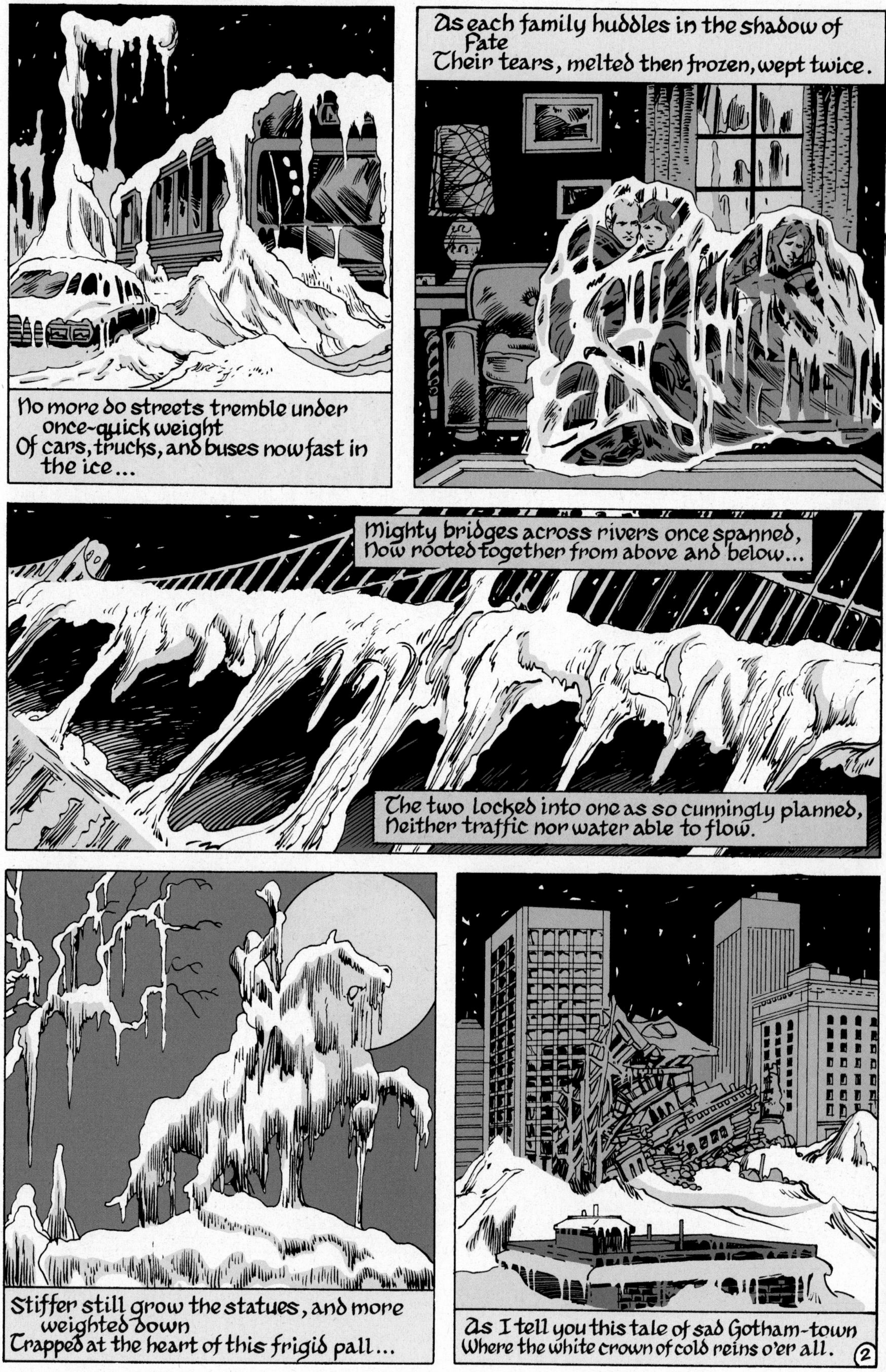
No more do streets tremble under once-quick weight
Of cars, trucks, and buses now fast in the ice...
As each family huddles in the shadow of Fate
Their tears, melted then frozen, wept twice.
Mighty bridges across rivers once spanned,
Now rooted together from above and below...
The two locked into one as so cunningly planned,
Neither traffic nor water able to flow.
Stiffer still grow the statues, and more weighted down
Trapped at the heart of this frigid pall...
As I tell you this tale of sad Gotham-town
Where the white crown of cold reins o'er all.
2

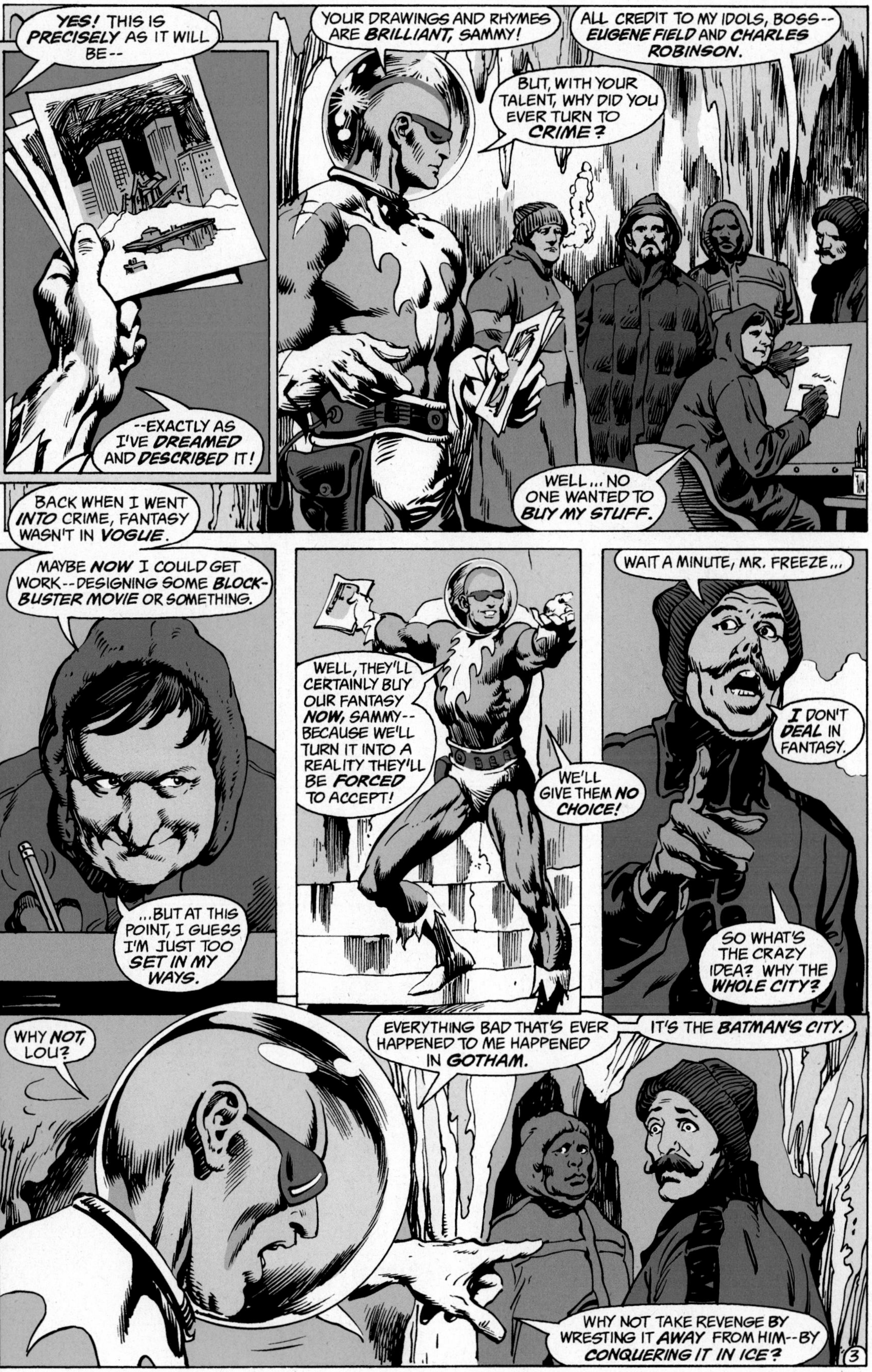

YES! THIS IS PRECISELY AS IT WILL BE--
--EXACTLY AS I'VE DREAMED AND DESCRIBED IT!
YOUR DRAWINGS AND RHYMES ARE BRILLIANT, SAMMY!
ALL CREDIT TO MY IDOLS, BOSS-- EUGENE FIELD AND CHARLES ROBINSON.
BUT, WITH YOUR TALENT, WHY DID YOU EVER TURN TO CRIME?
WELL... NO ONE WANTED TO BUY MY STUFF.
BACK WHEN I WENT INTO CRIME, FANTASY WASN'T IN VOGUE.
MAYBE NOW I COULD GET WORK--DESIGNING SOME BLOCK-BUSTER MOVIE OR SOMETHING.
...BUT AT THIS POINT, I GUESS I'M JUST TOO SET IN MY WAYS.
WELL, THEY'LL CERTAINLY BUY OUR FANTASY NOW, SAMMY-- BECAUSE WE'LL TURN IT INTO A REALITY THEY'LL BE FORCED TO ACCEPT!
WE'LL GIVE THEM NO CHOICE!
WAIT A MINUTE, MR. FREEZE...
I DON'T DEAL IN FANTASY.
SO WHAT'S THE CRAZY IDEA? WHY THE WHOLE CITY?
WHY NOT, LOU?
EVERYTHING BAD THAT'S EVER HAPPENED TO ME HAPPENED IN GOTHAM.
IT'S THE BATMAN'S CITY.
WHY NOT TAKE REVENGE BY WRESTING IT AWAY FROM HIM--BY CONQUERING IT IN ICE?
3

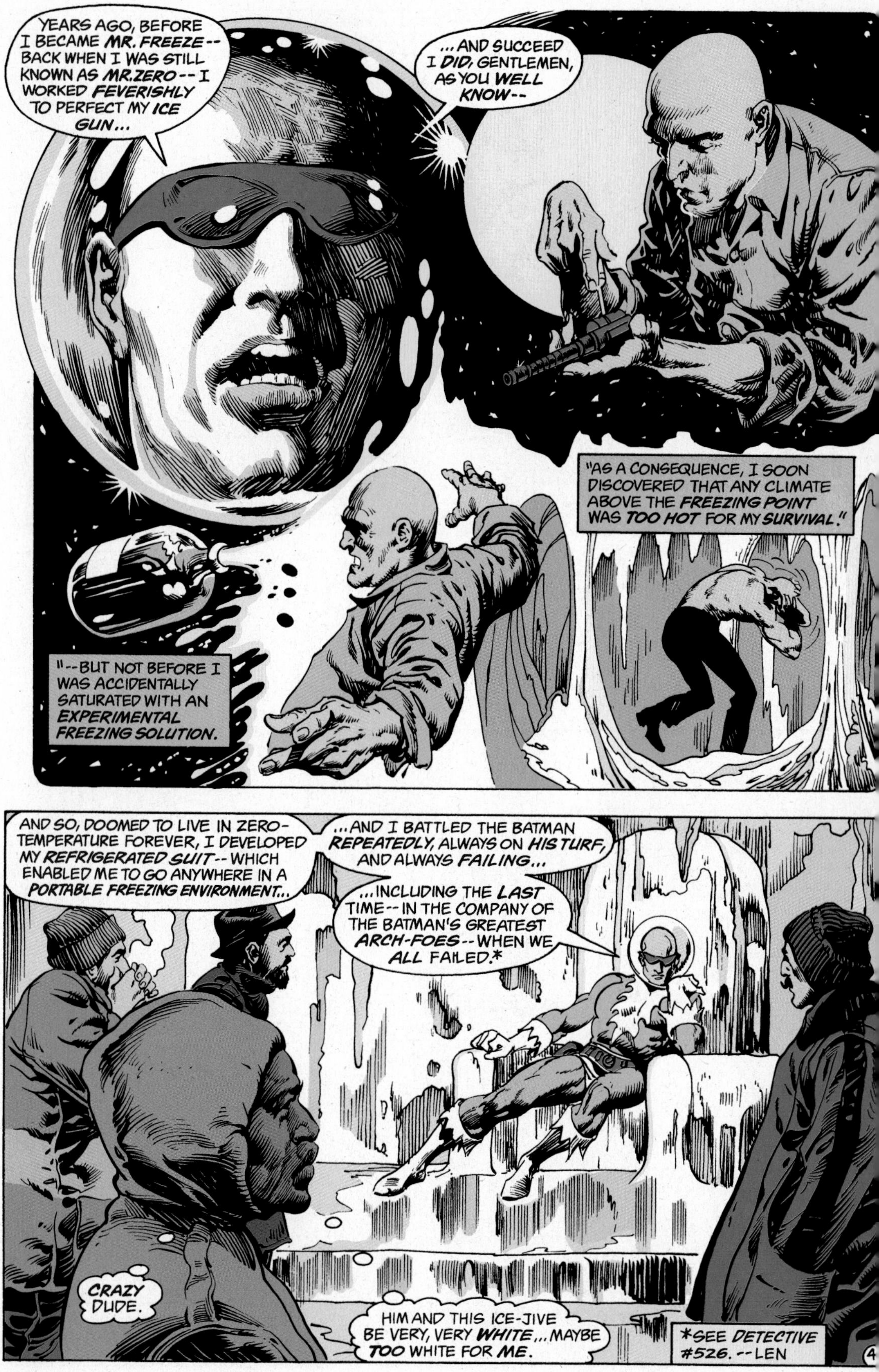
YEARS AGO, BEFORE I BECAME MR. FREEZE-- BACK WHEN I WAS STILL KNOWN AS MR.ZERO-- I WORKED FEVERISHLY TO PERFECT MY ICE GUN...
...AND SUCCEED I DID, GENTLEMEN, AS YOU WELL KNOW--
"--BUT NOT BEFORE I WAS ACCIDENTALLY SATURATED WITH AN EXPERIMENTAL FREEZING SOLUTION.
"AS A CONSEQUENCE, I SOON DISCOVERED THAT ANY CLIMATE ABOVE THE FREEZING POINT WAS TOO HOT FOR MY SURVIVAL."
AND SO, DOOMED TO LIVE IN ZERO-TEMPERATURE FOREVER, I DEVELOPED MY REFRIGERATED SUIT-- WHICH ENABLED ME TO GO ANYWHERE IN A PORTABLE FREEZING ENVIRONMENT...
...AND I BATTLED THE BATMAN REPEATEDLY, ALWAYS ON HIS TURF, AND ALWAYS FAILING...
...INCLUDING THE LAST TIME-- IN THE COMPANY OF THE BATMAN'S GREATEST ARCH-FOES-- WHEN WE ALL FAILED.*
CRAZY DUDE.
HIM AND THIS ICE-JIVE BE VERY, VERY WHITE... MAYBE TOO WHITE FOR ME.
*SEE DETECTIVE #526. --LEN
4

TOO MANY *CHIEFS* AND *NO BRAVES* --AND THAT'S WHY I'VE GATHERED *YOU* TOGETHER, TO FORM MY *GANG*.

YEAH--AND AS LONG AS THERE'S *MONEY* IN IT FOR ALL OF US, WE'RE WILLING TO *FOLLOW* YOU...

BUT *THIS* WILD SCHEME--! IT'S *TOO BIG* TO--

MY VISION -- AND SAMMY'S *DRAWINGS* --ARE EXAGGERATED, YES... BUT I *CAN* MAKE GOTHAM COLD ENOUGH TO *CRIPPLE* IT!

HOW--?!

LIKE *THIS*, LOU!

OKAY--YOUR ICE GUN IS *DYNAMITE!*

NO ONE'S ARGUING *THAT*-- IT CAN FREEZE A WHOLE POND WITH *ONE SHOT*-- BUT HOW'RE YOU GOING TO PLUNGE A *WHOLE CITY* INTO A NEW *ICE AGE?*

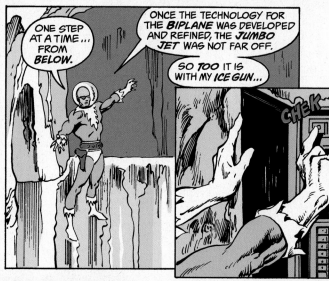

ONE STEP AT A TIME... FROM *BELOW*.

ONCE THE TECHNOLOGY FOR THE *BIPLANE* WAS DEVELOPED AND REFINED, THE *JUMBO JET* WAS NOT FAR OFF.

SO *TOO* IT IS WITH MY *ICE GUN*...

CHEK

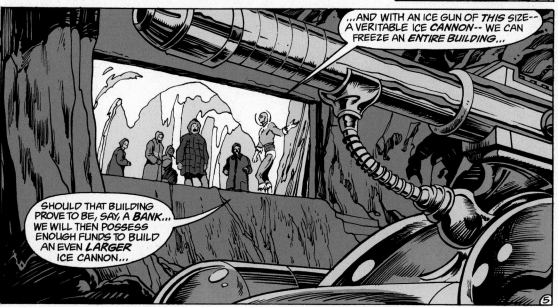

...AND WITH AN ICE GUN OF *THIS* SIZE-- A VERITABLE ICE *CANNON*-- WE CAN FREEZE AN *ENTIRE BUILDING*...

SHOULD THAT BUILDING PROVE TO BE, SAY, A *BANK*... WE WILL THEN POSSESS ENOUGH FUNDS TO BUILD AN EVEN *LARGER* ICE CANNON...

5

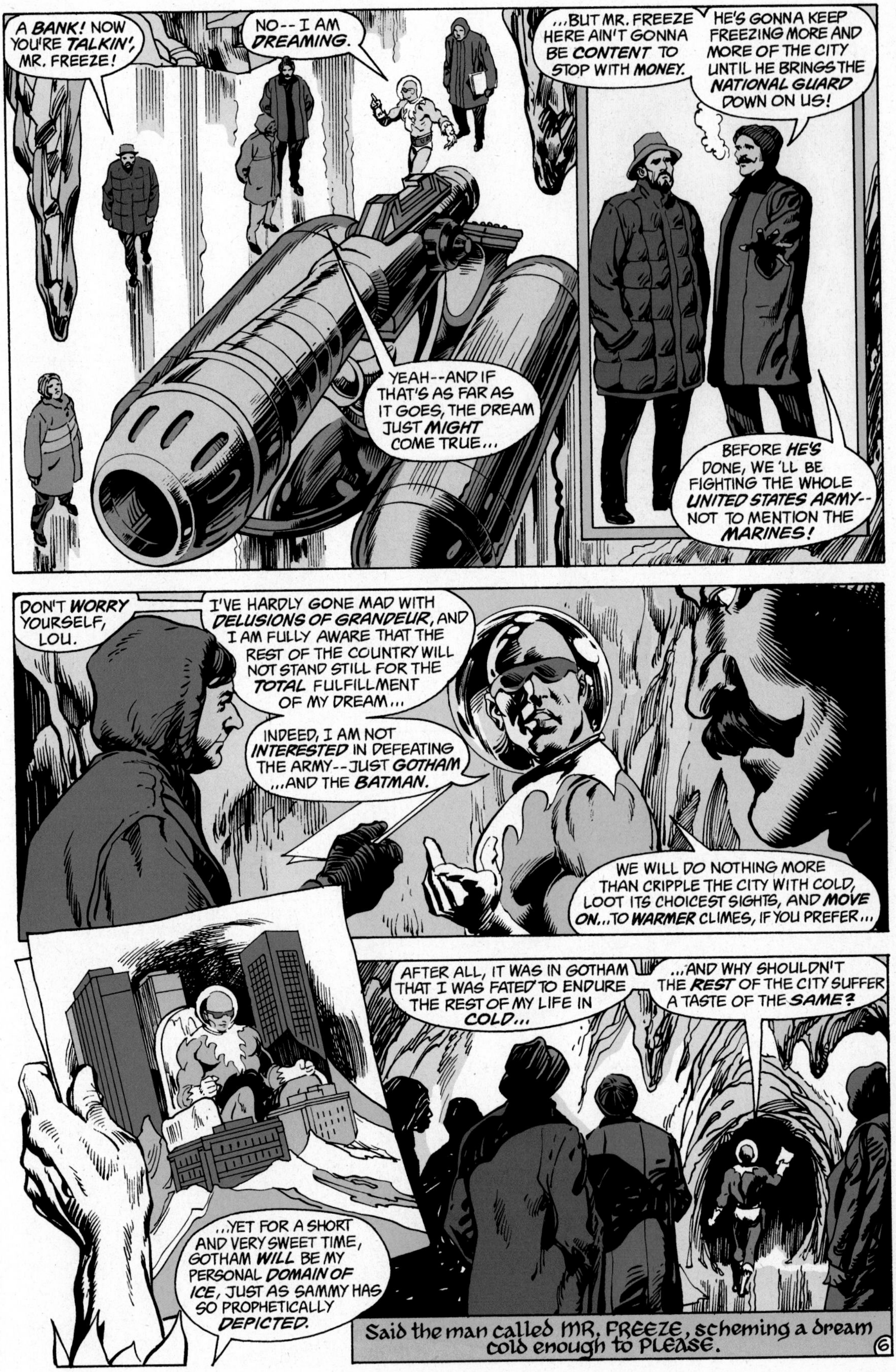
A BANK! NOW YOU'RE TALKIN', MR. FREEZE!
NO-- I AM DREAMING.
...BUT MR. FREEZE HERE AIN'T GONNA BE CONTENT TO STOP WITH MONEY.
HE'S GONNA KEEP FREEZING MORE AND MORE OF THE CITY UNTIL HE BRINGS THE NATIONAL GUARD DOWN ON US!
YEAH--AND IF THAT'S AS FAR AS IT GOES, THE DREAM JUST MIGHT COME TRUE...
BEFORE HE'S DONE, WE'LL BE FIGHTING THE WHOLE UNITED STATES ARMY-- NOT TO MENTION THE MARINES!
DON'T WORRY YOURSELF, LOU.
I'VE HARDLY GONE MAD WITH DELUSIONS OF GRANDEUR, AND I AM FULLY AWARE THAT THE REST OF THE COUNTRY WILL NOT STAND STILL FOR THE TOTAL FULFILLMENT OF MY DREAM...
INDEED, I AM NOT INTERESTED IN DEFEATING THE ARMY--JUST GOTHAM ...AND THE BATMAN.
WE WILL DO NOTHING MORE THAN CRIPPLE THE CITY WITH COLD, LOOT ITS CHOICEST SIGHTS, AND MOVE ON...TO WARMER CLIMES, IF YOU PREFER...
AFTER ALL, IT WAS IN GOTHAM THAT I WAS FATED TO ENDURE THE REST OF MY LIFE IN COLD...
...AND WHY SHOULDN'T THE REST OF THE CITY SUFFER A TASTE OF THE SAME?
...YET FOR A SHORT AND VERY SWEET TIME, GOTHAM WILL BE MY PERSONAL DOMAIN OF ICE, JUST AS SAMMY HAS SO PROPHETICALLY DEPICTED.
Said the man called MR. FREEZE, scheming a dream cold enough to PLEASE.
6

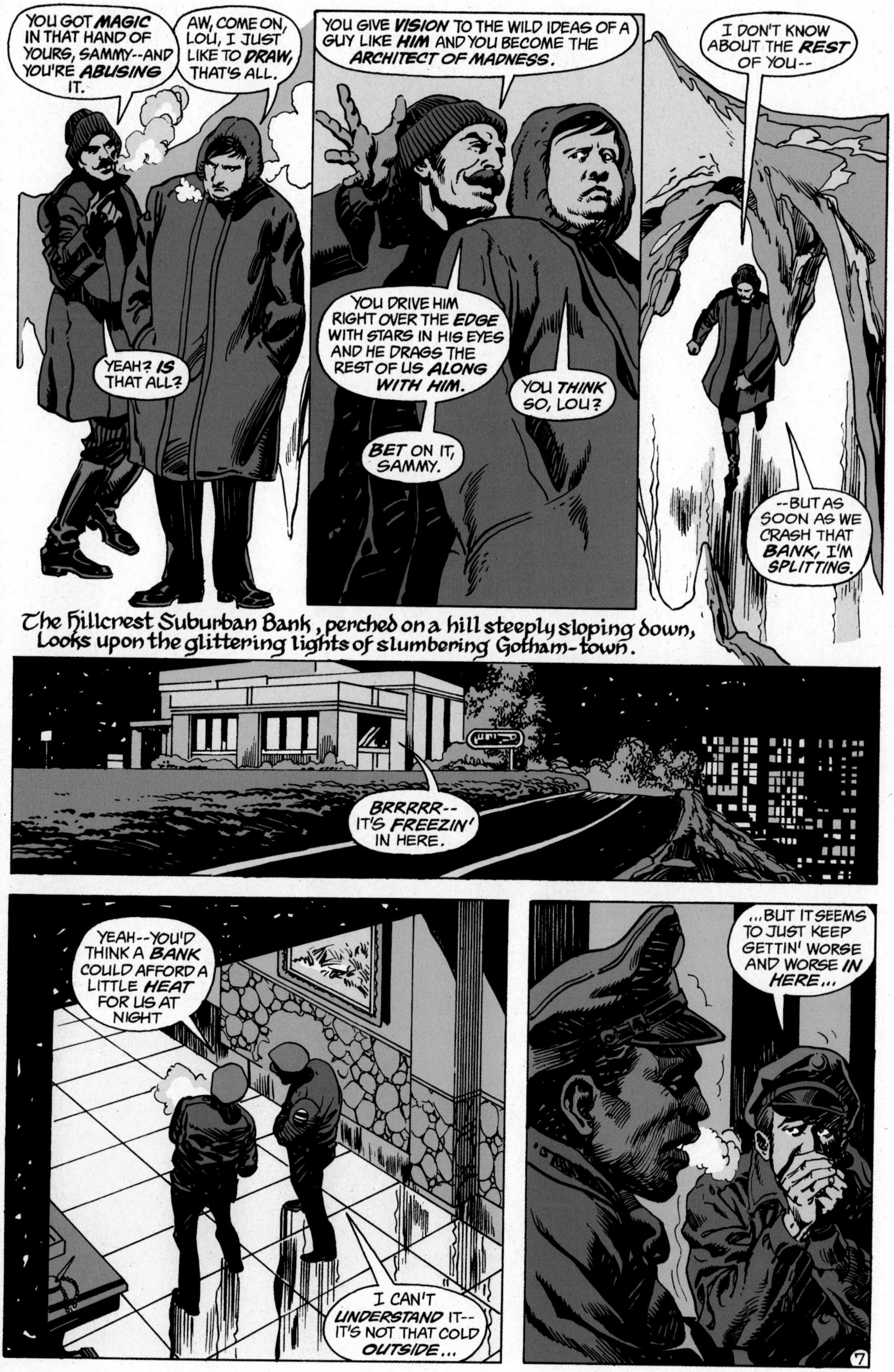
YOU GOT MAGIC IN THAT HAND OF YOURS, SAMMY--AND YOU'RE ABUSING IT.
AW, COME ON, LOU, I JUST LIKE TO DRAW, THAT'S ALL.
YEAH? IS THAT ALL?
YOU GIVE VISION TO THE WILD IDEAS OF A GUY LIKE HIM AND YOU BECOME THE ARCHITECT OF MADNESS.
YOU DRIVE HIM RIGHT OVER THE EDGE WITH STARS IN HIS EYES AND HE DRAGS THE REST OF US ALONG WITH HIM.
YOU THINK SO, LOU?
BET ON IT, SAMMY.
I DON'T KNOW ABOUT THE REST OF YOU--
--BUT AS SOON AS WE CRASH THAT BANK, I'M SPLITTING.
The Hillcrest Suburban Bank, perched on a hill steeply sloping down,
Looks upon the glittering lights of slumbering Gotham-town.
BRRRRR-- IT'S FREEZIN' IN HERE.
YEAH--YOU'D THINK A BANK COULD AFFORD A LITTLE HEAT FOR US AT NIGHT
I CAN'T UNDERSTAND IT-- IT'S NOT THAT COLD OUTSIDE...
...BUT IT SEEMS TO JUST KEEP GETTIN' WORSE AND WORSE IN HERE...
7

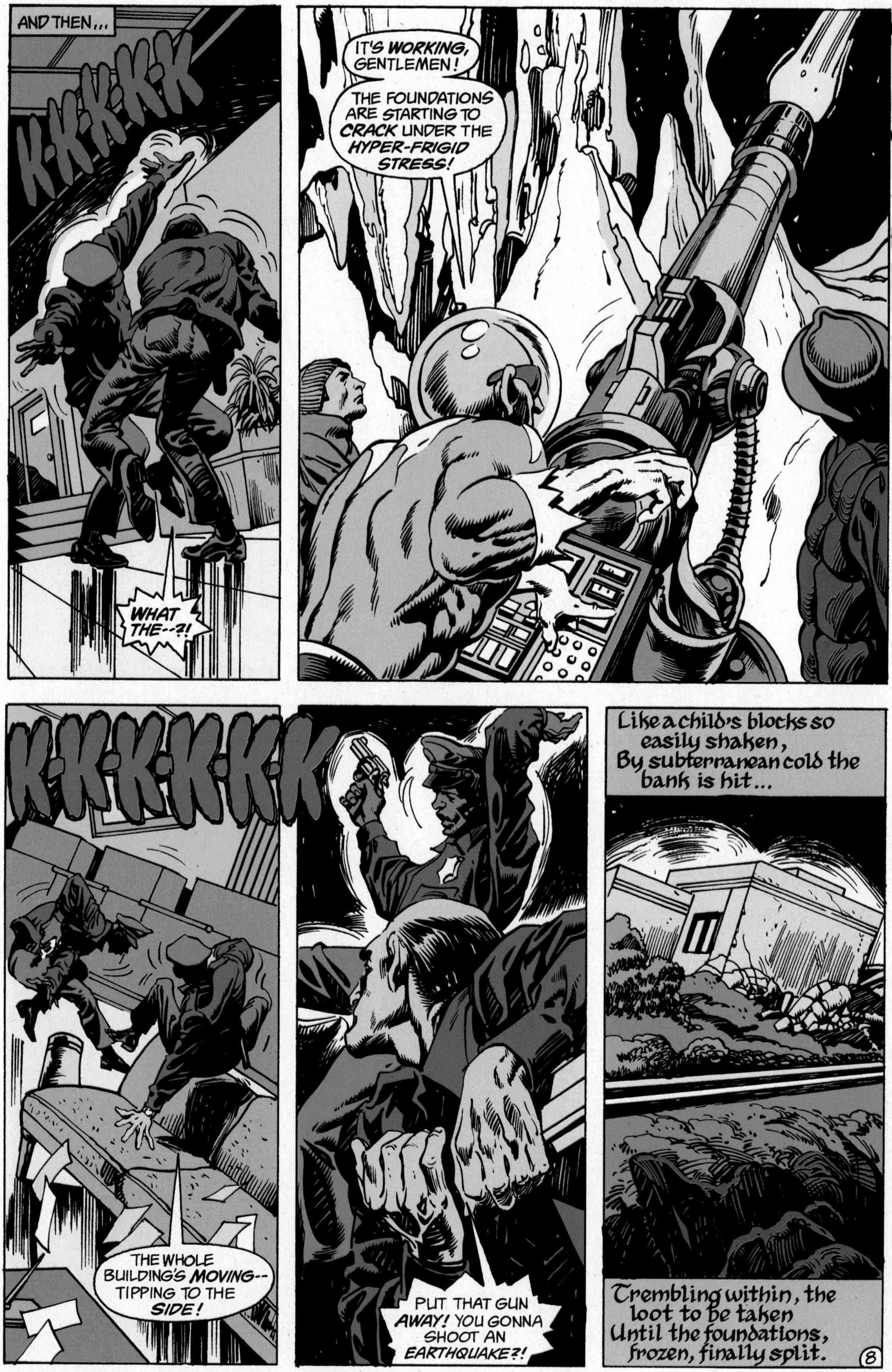
AND THEN...
K-K-K-K-K-K
WHAT THE--?!
IT'S WORKING, GENTLEMEN!
THE FOUNDATIONS ARE STARTING TO CRACK UNDER THE HYPER-FRIGID STRESS!
K-K-K-K-K-K-K
THE WHOLE BUILDING'S MOVING-- TIPPING TO THE SIDE!
PUT THAT GUN AWAY! YOU GONNA SHOOT AN EARTHQUAKE?!
Like a child's blocks so easily shaken,
By subterranean cold the bank is hit...
Trembling within, the loot to be taken
Until the foundations, frozen, finally split.
8

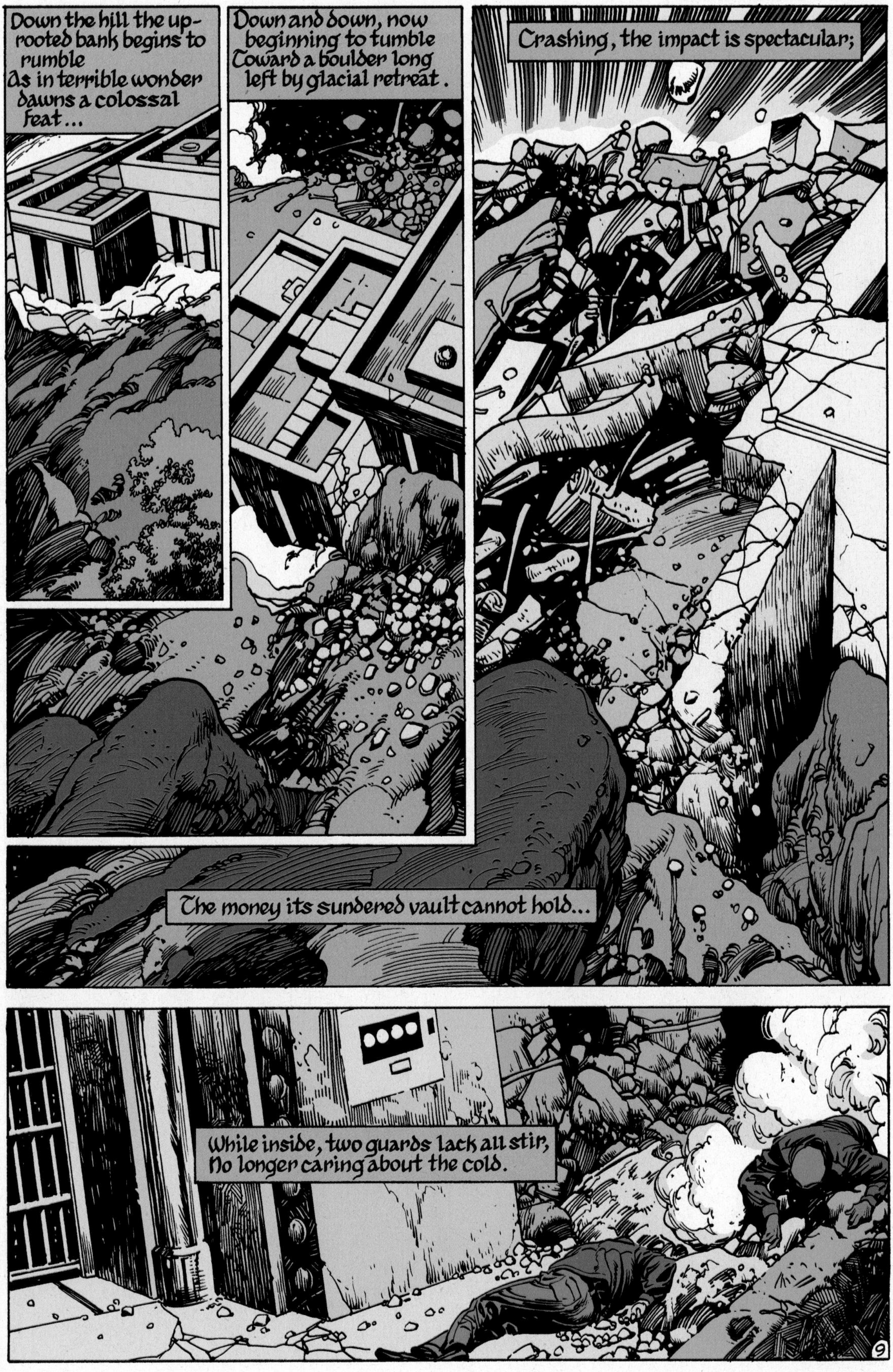
Down the hill the uprooted bank begins to rumble
As in terrible wonder dawns a colossal feat...
Down and down, now beginning to tumble
Toward a boulder long left by glacial retreat.
Crashing, the impact is spectacular;
The money its sundered vault cannot hold...
While inside, two guards lack all stir,
No longer caring about the cold.
9

From the hole where bank once stood
They rise like a frigid gust...

HURRY UP!

WE'RE *COMIN'*, BOSS--BUT THIS ICE IS *SLIPPERY*.

Then down the hill descend four hoods,

THERE'S THE *VAULT*.

Soon to leave this bank that went bust.

AND IT'LL BE A COLD DAY IN HELL BEFORE THEY FIGURE OUT *THIS* ONE, GENTLEMEN.

WAYNE MANOR:

AFTER MY PENGUIN CAPER IN *ANTARCTICA*, I JUST CAN'T SEEM TO GET *WARM* AGAIN.

AND HERE I WAS JUST ABOUT TO SUGGEST SOME NICE COLD *LEMONADE*...

...BUT IT LOOKS LIKE THINGS JUST *HEATED UP*, BRUCE --AND A LOT HOTTER THAN THIS *BORING* GAME.

THAT'S THE SMALLER, *MOBILE* BAT-SIGNAL, JASON --COMING FROM THE HILLS TO THE *WEST*.

WELL, IF YOU'RE READY TO PLAY *BATMAN*, I'M GAME FOR--

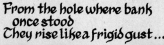

10

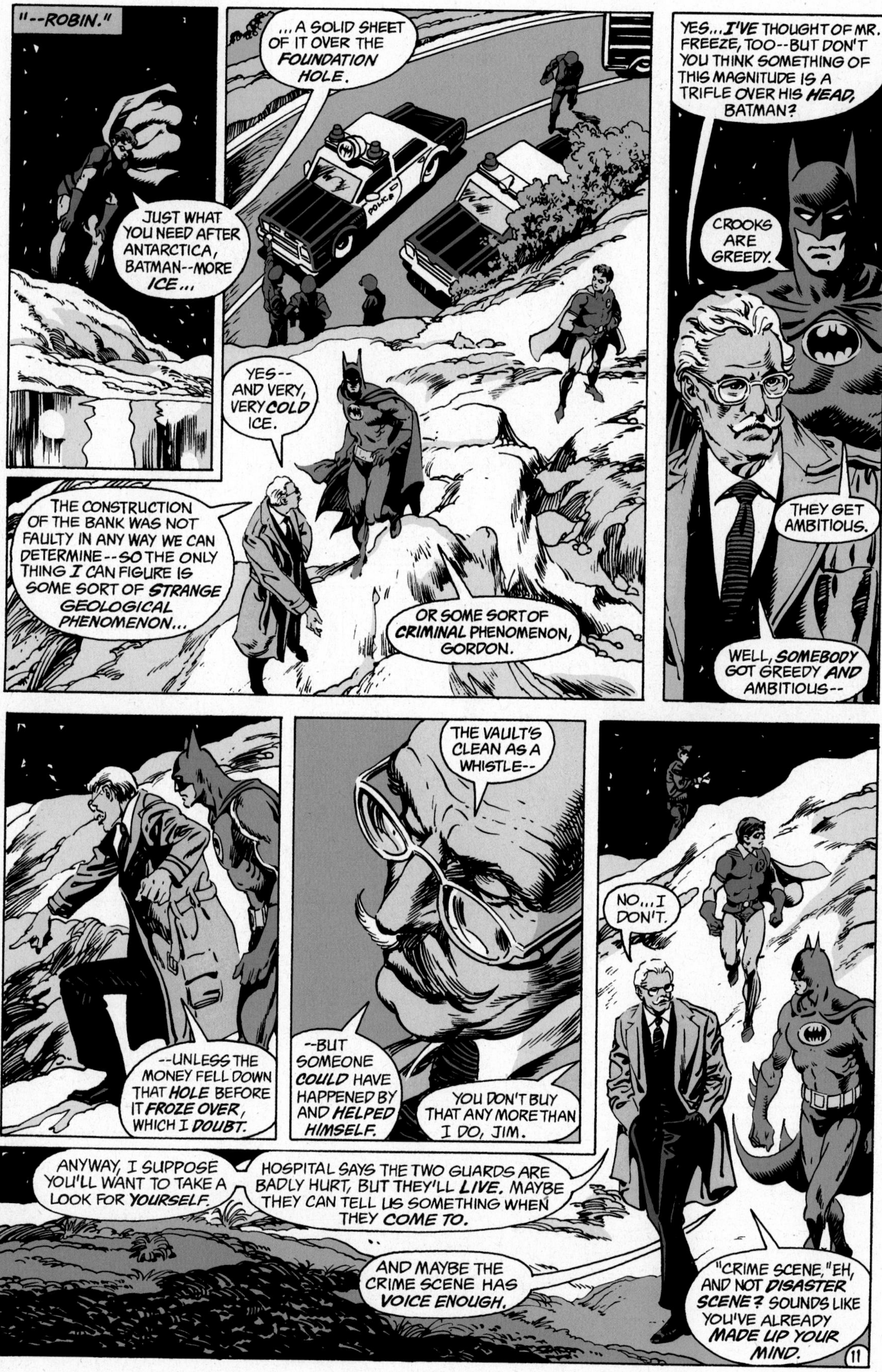
"--ROBIN."
JUST WHAT YOU NEED AFTER ANTARCTICA, BATMAN--MORE ICE...
...A SOLID SHEET OF IT OVER THE FOUNDATION HOLE.
YES--AND VERY, VERY COLD ICE.
THE CONSTRUCTION OF THE BANK WAS NOT FAULTY IN ANY WAY WE CAN DETERMINE--SO THE ONLY THING I CAN FIGURE IS SOME SORT OF STRANGE GEOLOGICAL PHENOMENON...
OR SOME SORT OF CRIMINAL PHENOMENON, GORDON.
YES...I'VE THOUGHT OF MR. FREEZE, TOO--BUT DON'T YOU THINK SOMETHING OF THIS MAGNITUDE IS A TRIFLE OVER HIS HEAD, BATMAN?
CROOKS ARE GREEDY.
THEY GET AMBITIOUS.
WELL, SOMEBODY GOT GREEDY AND AMBITIOUS--
--UNLESS THE MONEY FELL DOWN THAT HOLE BEFORE IT FROZE OVER, WHICH I DOUBT.
THE VAULT'S CLEAN AS A WHISTLE--
--BUT SOMEONE COULD HAVE HAPPENED BY AND HELPED HIMSELF.
YOU DON'T BUY THAT ANY MORE THAN I DO, JIM.
NO...I DON'T.
ANYWAY, I SUPPOSE YOU'LL WANT TO TAKE A LOOK FOR YOURSELF.
HOSPITAL SAYS THE TWO GUARDS ARE BADLY HURT, BUT THEY'LL LIVE. MAYBE THEY CAN TELL US SOMETHING WHEN THEY COME TO.
AND MAYBE THE CRIME SCENE HAS VOICE ENOUGH.
"CRIME SCENE," EH, AND NOT DISASTER SCENE? SOUNDS LIKE YOU'VE ALREADY MADE UP YOUR MIND.
11

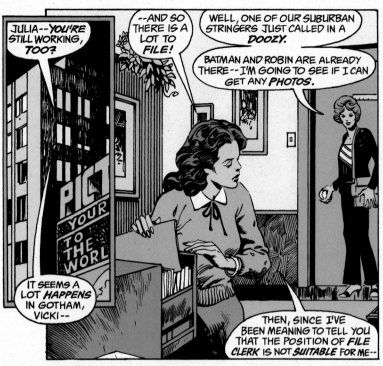

JULIA--YOU'RE STILL WORKING, TOO?

--AND SO THERE IS A LOT TO FILE!

WELL, ONE OF OUR SUBURBAN STRINGERS JUST CALLED IN A DOOZY. BATMAN AND ROBIN ARE ALREADY THERE-- I'M GOING TO SEE IF I CAN GET ANY PHOTOS.

IT SEEMS A LOT HAPPENS IN GOTHAM, VICKI--

THEN, SINCE I'VE BEEN MEANING TO TELL YOU THAT THE POSITION OF FILE CLERK IS NOT SUITABLE FOR ME--

--I SHALL COME ALONG AND DO SO.

OH?

MY FATHER AND MOTHER WERE PEOPLE OF ACTION-- AND THEY PUT IT IN MY BLOOD.

I THOUGHT YOUR FATHER WAS ALFRED-- BRUCE WAYNE'S BUTLER.

HE IS.

I WAS SPEAKING OF MY ADOPTIVE FATHER, THE RESISTANCE FIGHTER JACQUES REMARQUE-- ALTHOUGH ALFRED PENNYWORTH WAS ALSO A WAR HERO.

AND NOW YOU CRAVE THE ACTION OF A REPORTER'S LIFE?

WELL, COMING ALONG WILL AT LEAST KEEP YOU IN MY SIGHT-- AND AWAY FROM BRUCE WAYNE.

I'VE TOLD YOU, VICKI-- I HAVE NO ROMANTIC INTEREST IN MR. WAYNE.

HE'S TOO ARROGANT FOR MY TASTES--AND BESIDES, I PREFER A LESS IDLE MAN...

LIKE WHOM, FOR EXAMPLE?

OH...LIKE THE BATMAN, FOR EXAMPLE.

GOOD LUCK--YOU COULD SOONER SNARE A SHADOW.

AH, BUT BOLD MOVES ARE MY SPECIALTY.

⑫

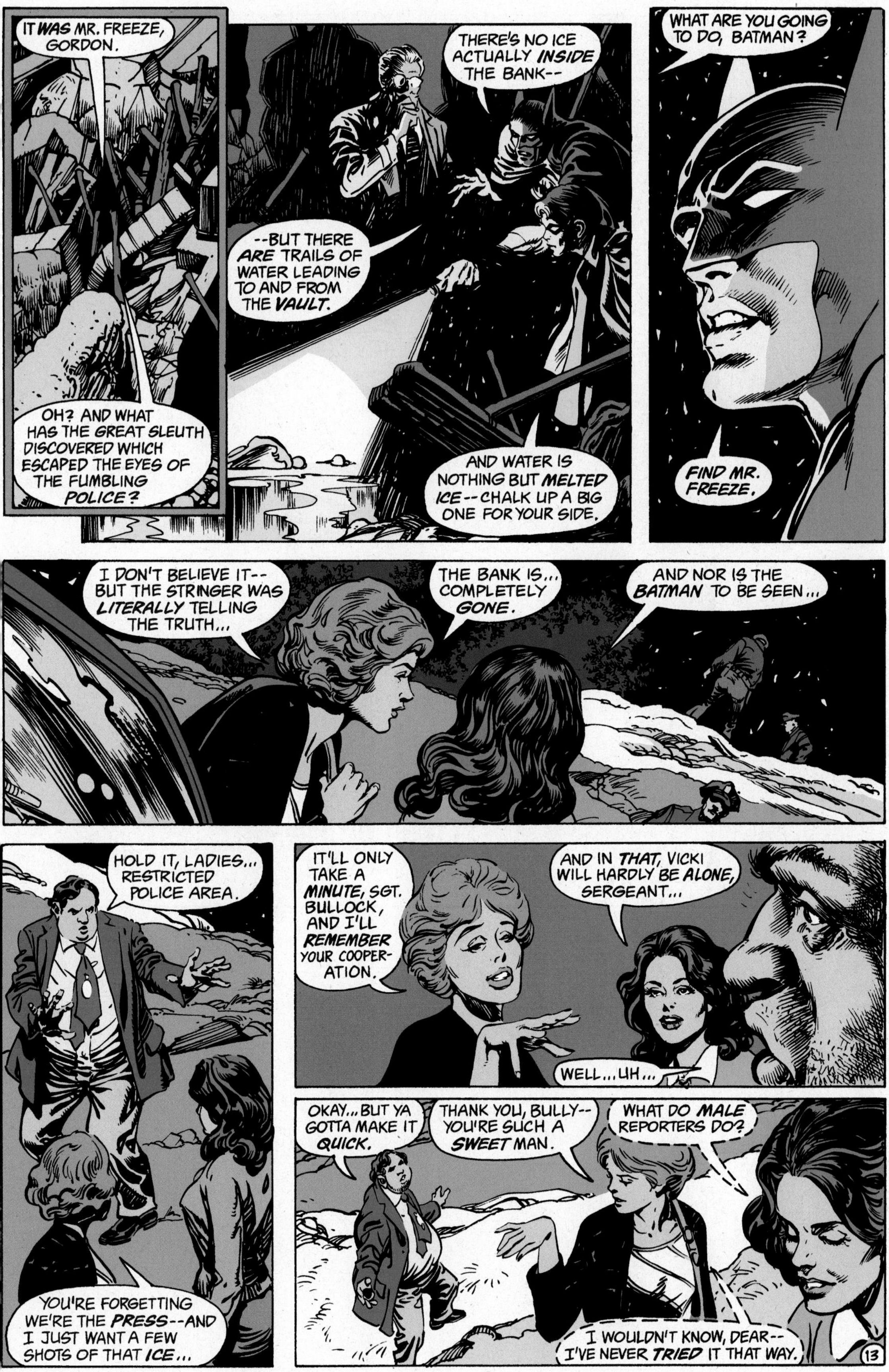
IT WAS MR. FREEZE, GORDON.
OH? AND WHAT HAS THE GREAT SLEUTH DISCOVERED WHICH ESCAPED THE EYES OF THE FUMBLING POLICE?
THERE'S NO ICE ACTUALLY INSIDE THE BANK--
--BUT THERE ARE TRAILS OF WATER LEADING TO AND FROM THE VAULT.
AND WATER IS NOTHING BUT MELTED ICE--CHALK UP A BIG ONE FOR YOUR SIDE.
WHAT ARE YOU GOING TO DO, BATMAN?
FIND MR. FREEZE.
I DON'T BELIEVE IT--BUT THE STRINGER WAS LITERALLY TELLING THE TRUTH...
THE BANK IS... COMPLETELY GONE.
AND NOR IS THE BATMAN TO BE SEEN...
HOLD IT, LADIES... RESTRICTED POLICE AREA.
YOU'RE FORGETTING WE'RE THE PRESS--AND I JUST WANT A FEW SHOTS OF THAT ICE...
IT'LL ONLY TAKE A MINUTE, SGT. BULLOCK, AND I'LL REMEMBER YOUR COOPERATION.
AND IN THAT, VICKI WILL HARDLY BE ALONE, SERGEANT...
WELL...UH...
OKAY... BUT YA GOTTA MAKE IT QUICK.
THANK YOU, BULLY--YOU'RE SUCH A SWEET MAN.
WHAT DO MALE REPORTERS DO?
I WOULDN'T KNOW, DEAR--I'VE NEVER TRIED IT THAT WAY.
13

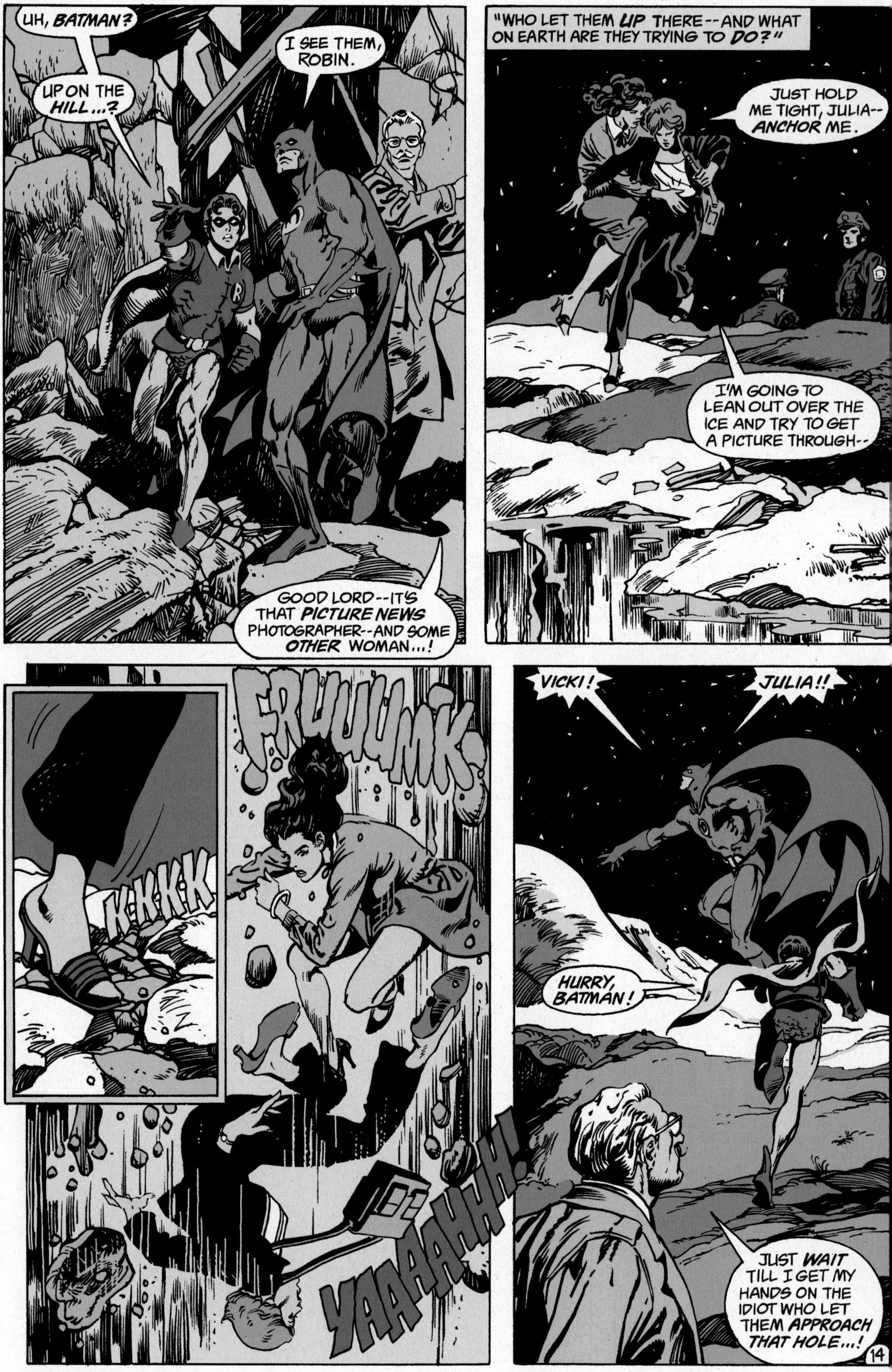
UH, BATMAN?
UP ON THE HILL...?
I SEE THEM, ROBIN.
GOOD LORD--IT'S THAT PICTURE NEWS PHOTOGRAPHER--AND SOME OTHER WOMAN...!
"WHO LET THEM UP THERE--AND WHAT ON EARTH ARE THEY TRYING TO DO?"
JUST HOLD ME TIGHT, JULIA--ANCHOR ME.
I'M GOING TO LEAN OUT OVER THE ICE AND TRY TO GET A PICTURE THROUGH--
KKKK
FRUUUMK
YAAAAHHH!
VICKI!
JULIA!!
HURRY, BATMAN!
JUST WAIT TILL I GET MY HANDS ON THE IDIOT WHO LET THEM APPROACH THAT HOLE...!
14

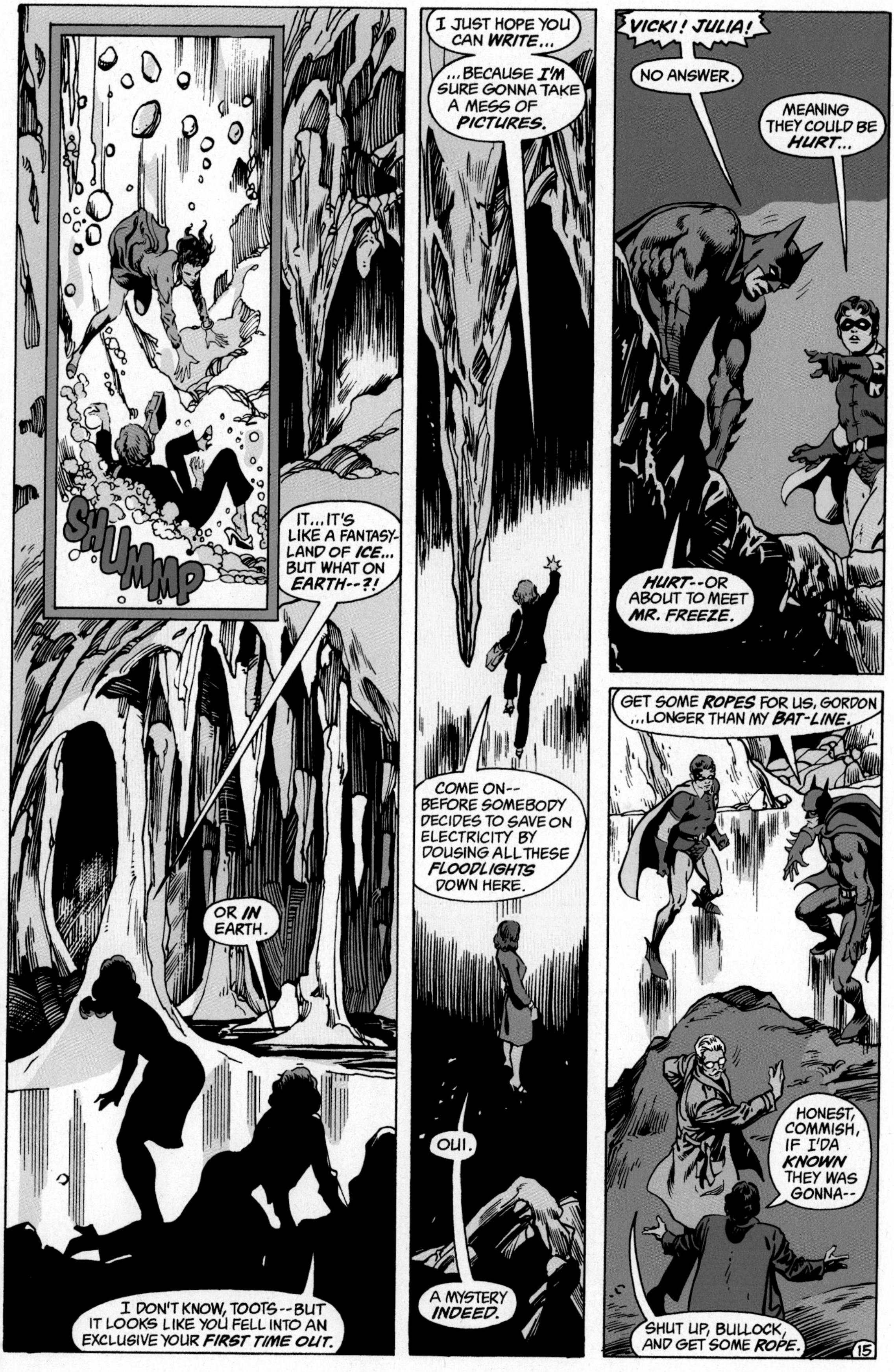
SHUMMP
IT...IT'S LIKE A FANTASY-LAND OF ICE... BUT WHAT ON EARTH--?!
OR IN EARTH.
I DON'T KNOW, TOOTS--BUT IT LOOKS LIKE YOU FELL INTO AN EXCLUSIVE YOUR FIRST TIME OUT.
I JUST HOPE YOU CAN WRITE...
...BECAUSE I'M SURE GONNA TAKE A MESS OF PICTURES.
COME ON--BEFORE SOMEBODY DECIDES TO SAVE ON ELECTRICITY BY DOUSING ALL THESE FLOODLIGHTS DOWN HERE.
OUI.
A MYSTERY INDEED.
VICKI! JULIA!
NO ANSWER.
MEANING THEY COULD BE HURT...
HURT--OR ABOUT TO MEET MR. FREEZE.
GET SOME ROPES FOR US, GORDON ...LONGER THAN MY BAT-LINE.
HONEST, COMMISH, IF I'DA KNOWN THEY WAS GONNA--
SHUT UP, BULLOCK, AND GET SOME ROPE.
15

WAYNE MANOR:

BING BONG

NOW, WHO COULD *THAT* BE AT THIS *LATE HOUR?*

YES? MAY I--

MY NAME IS *AMANDA GROSCZ*-- AND I'M FROM THE *GOTHAM CHILD WELFARE BUREAU.*

I'VE COME TO CHECK ON THE CHILD *JASON TODD* RESIDING HERE.

AH....AT *THIS* TIME OF THE--

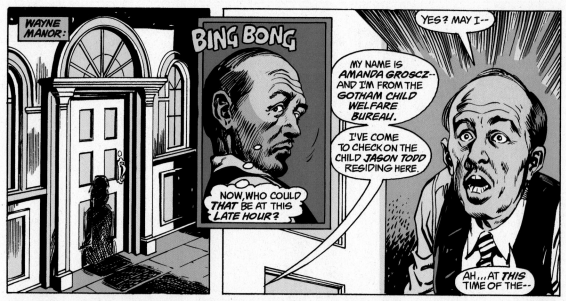

PRECISELY THE TIME A CHILD NEEDS TO BE *SECURE*-- AND SINCE I'M INVESTIGATING HIS *WELFARE,* A *PERFECT* TIME FOR ME TO *SEE* HIM.

HE...AH... *JASON* HAS GONE TO *BED*--HE'S *ASLEEP.*

WONDERFUL--THEN I'LL JUST *PEEK* IN ON HIS *ACCOMMODATIONS.*

AND MAY I REMIND YOU THAT I AM *AUTHORIZED BY THE CITY,* AND *MANDATED WITH THIS RIGHT,* MR. PENNYWORTH? NOW, WHERE IS THE CHILD'S *ROOM?*

I...I'M AFRAID JASON IS *OUT*...WITH *MASTER WAYNE* AT THE MOMENT...

YOU MEAN HE'S *NOT HERE?* DO YOU REALIZE IT IS GOING ON *ELEVEN P.M.?*

OF *COURSE* YOU DO--YOU JUST *COMPLAINED* OF THE *DREADFULLY LATE HOUR* YOURSELF.

VERY WELL, MR. PENNYWORTH, I THINK I'VE *LEARNED* EVERY- THING *WORTH* LEARNING.

BEYOND THE FACT THAT YOU *LIED* TO ME--AND BEYOND THE FACT THAT JASON TODD RESIDES HERE WITHOUT BENEFIT OF *LEGAL ADOPTION PAPERS*--THIS WILL LOOK *BAD* IN MY *REPORT.*

YES, INDEED-- *VERY BAD.*

16

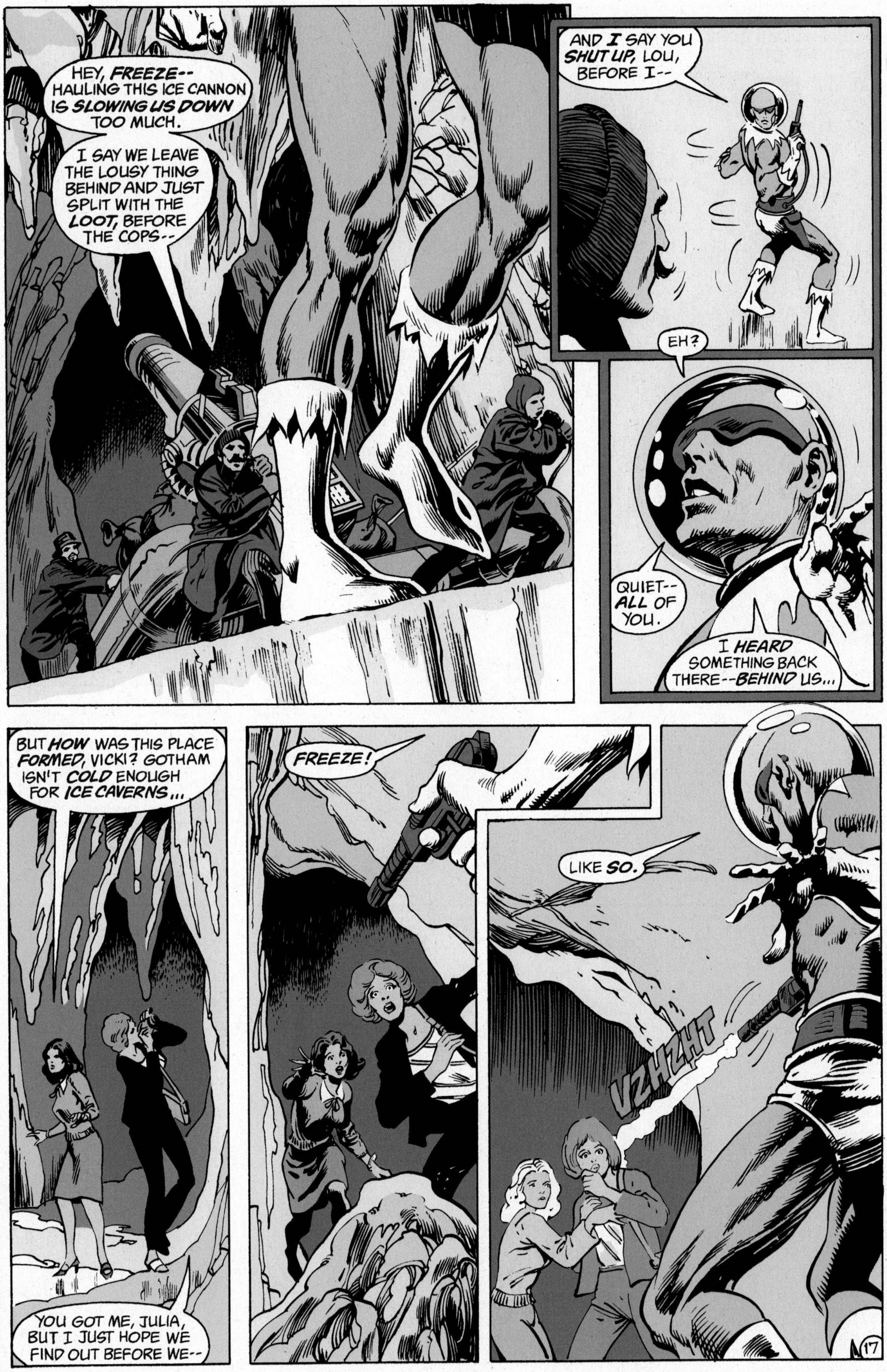
HEY, FREEZE-- HAULING THIS ICE CANNON IS SLOWING US DOWN TOO MUCH.
I SAY WE LEAVE THE LOUSY THING BEHIND AND JUST SPLIT WITH THE LOOT, BEFORE THE COPS--
AND I SAY YOU SHUT UP, LOU, BEFORE I--
EH?
QUIET-- ALL OF YOU.
I HEARD SOMETHING BACK THERE--BEHIND US...
BUT HOW WAS THIS PLACE FORMED, VICKI? GOTHAM ISN'T COLD ENOUGH FOR ICE CAVERNS...
YOU GOT ME, JULIA, BUT I JUST HOPE WE FIND OUT BEFORE WE--
FREEZE!
LIKE SO.
VZHZHT
17

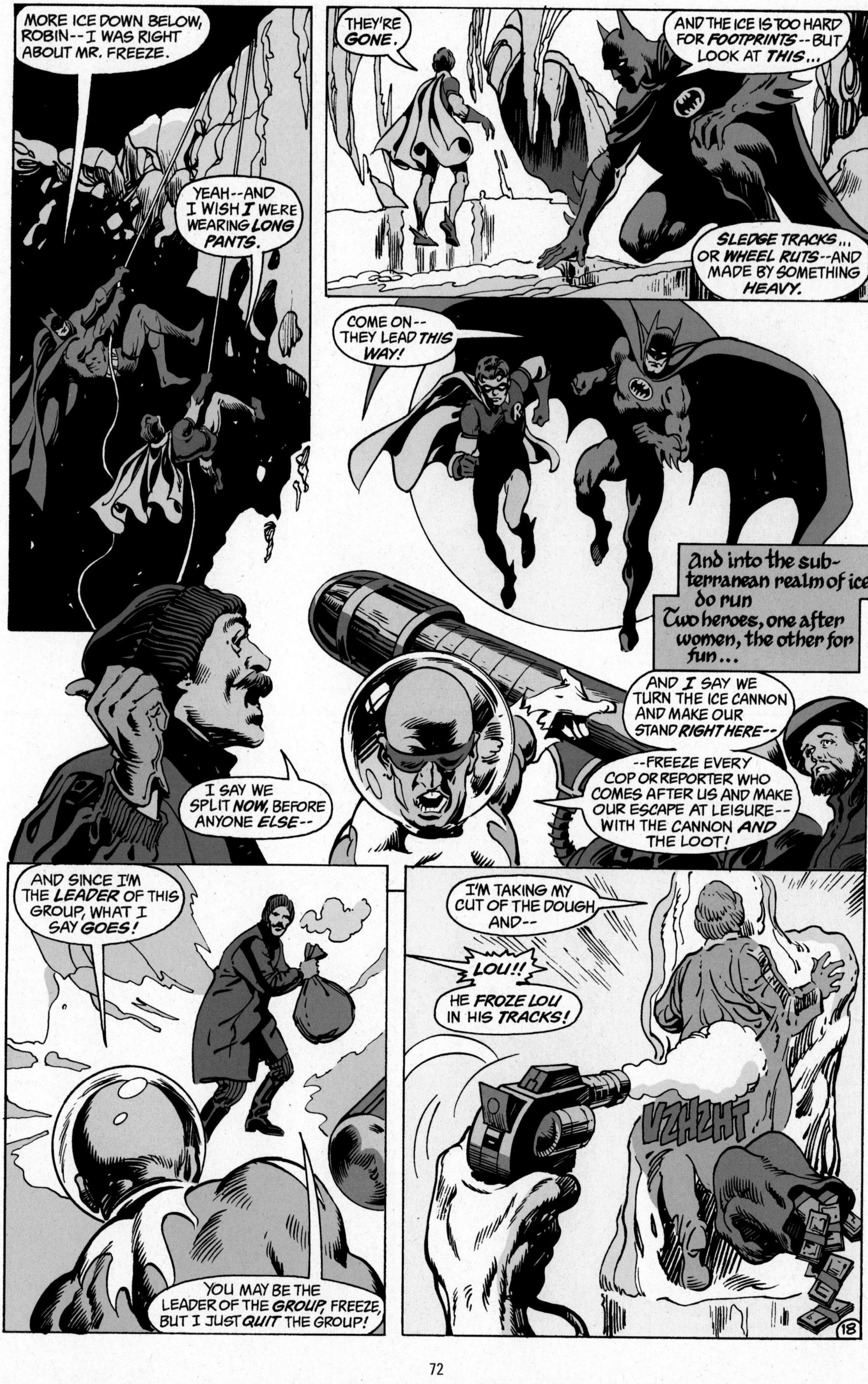
MORE ICE DOWN BELOW, ROBIN--I WAS RIGHT ABOUT MR. FREEZE.
YEAH--AND I WISH I WERE WEARING LONG PANTS.
THEY'RE GONE.
AND THE ICE IS TOO HARD FOR FOOTPRINTS--BUT LOOK AT THIS...
SLEDGE TRACKS... OR WHEEL RUTS--AND MADE BY SOMETHING HEAVY.
COME ON-- THEY LEAD THIS WAY!
And into the subterranean realm of ice do run Two heroes, one after women, the other for fun...
AND I SAY WE TURN THE ICE CANNON AND MAKE OUR STAND RIGHT HERE--
--FREEZE EVERY COP OR REPORTER WHO COMES AFTER US AND MAKE OUR ESCAPE AT LEISURE--WITH THE CANNON AND THE LOOT!
I SAY WE SPLIT NOW, BEFORE ANYONE ELSE--
AND SINCE I'M THE LEADER OF THIS GROUP, WHAT I SAY GOES!
YOU MAY BE THE LEADER OF THE GROUP, FREEZE, BUT I JUST QUIT THE GROUP!
I'M TAKING MY CUT OF THE DOUGH AND--
LOU!!
HE FROZE LOU IN HIS TRACKS!
VZHZHT
18

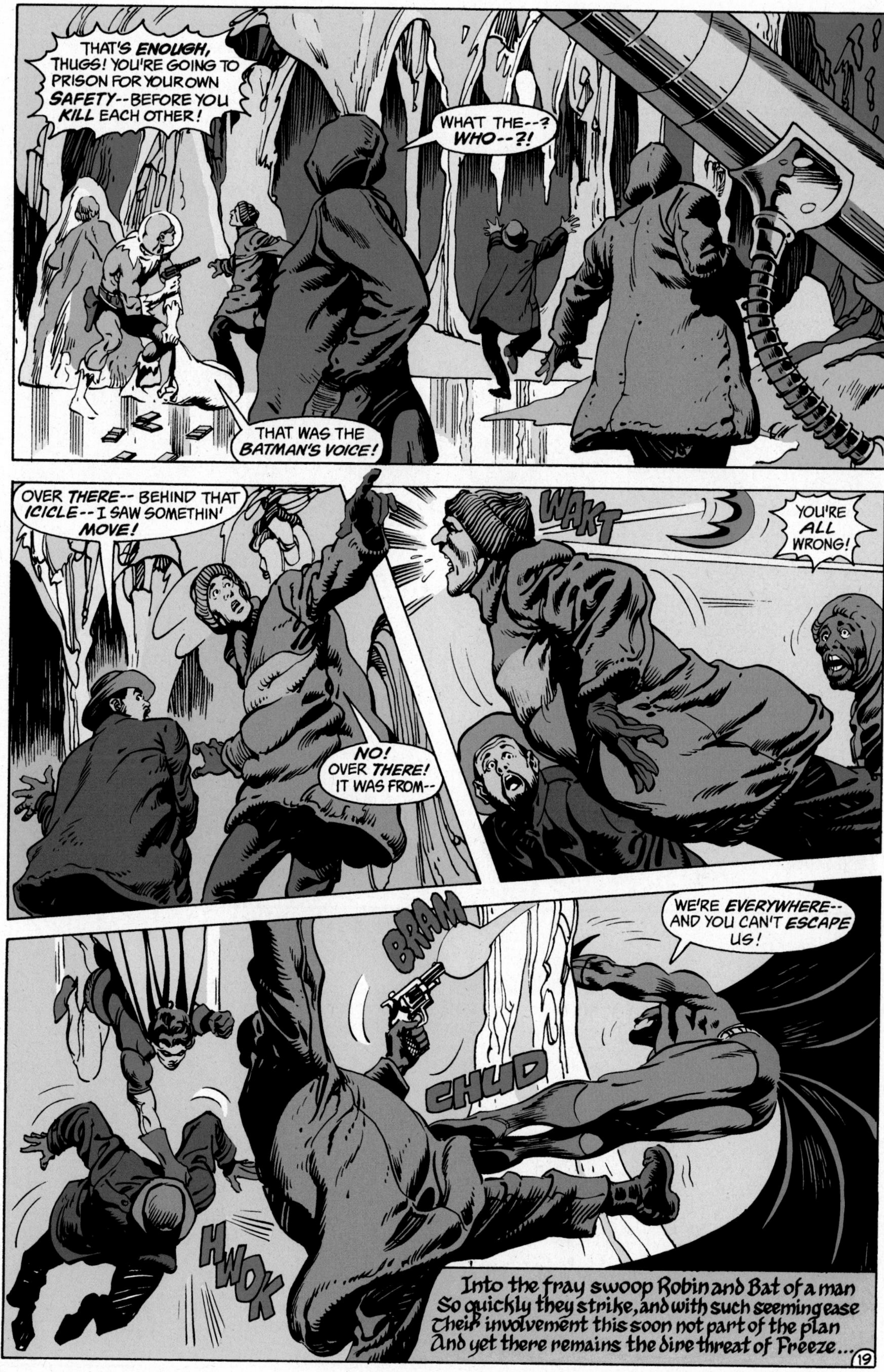
THAT'S ENOUGH, THUGS! YOU'RE GOING TO PRISON FOR YOUR OWN SAFETY--BEFORE YOU KILL EACH OTHER!
WHAT THE--? WHO--?!
THAT WAS THE BATMAN'S VOICE!
OVER THERE-- BEHIND THAT ICICLE--I SAW SOMETHIN' MOVE!
NO! OVER THERE! IT WAS FROM--
WAKT
YOU'RE ALL WRONG!
BRAM
WE'RE EVERYWHERE-- AND YOU CAN'T ESCAPE US!
CHUD
HWOK
Into the fray swoop Robin and Bat of a man
So quickly they strike, and with such seeming ease
Their involvement this soon not part of the plan
And yet there remains the dire threat of Freeze...
19

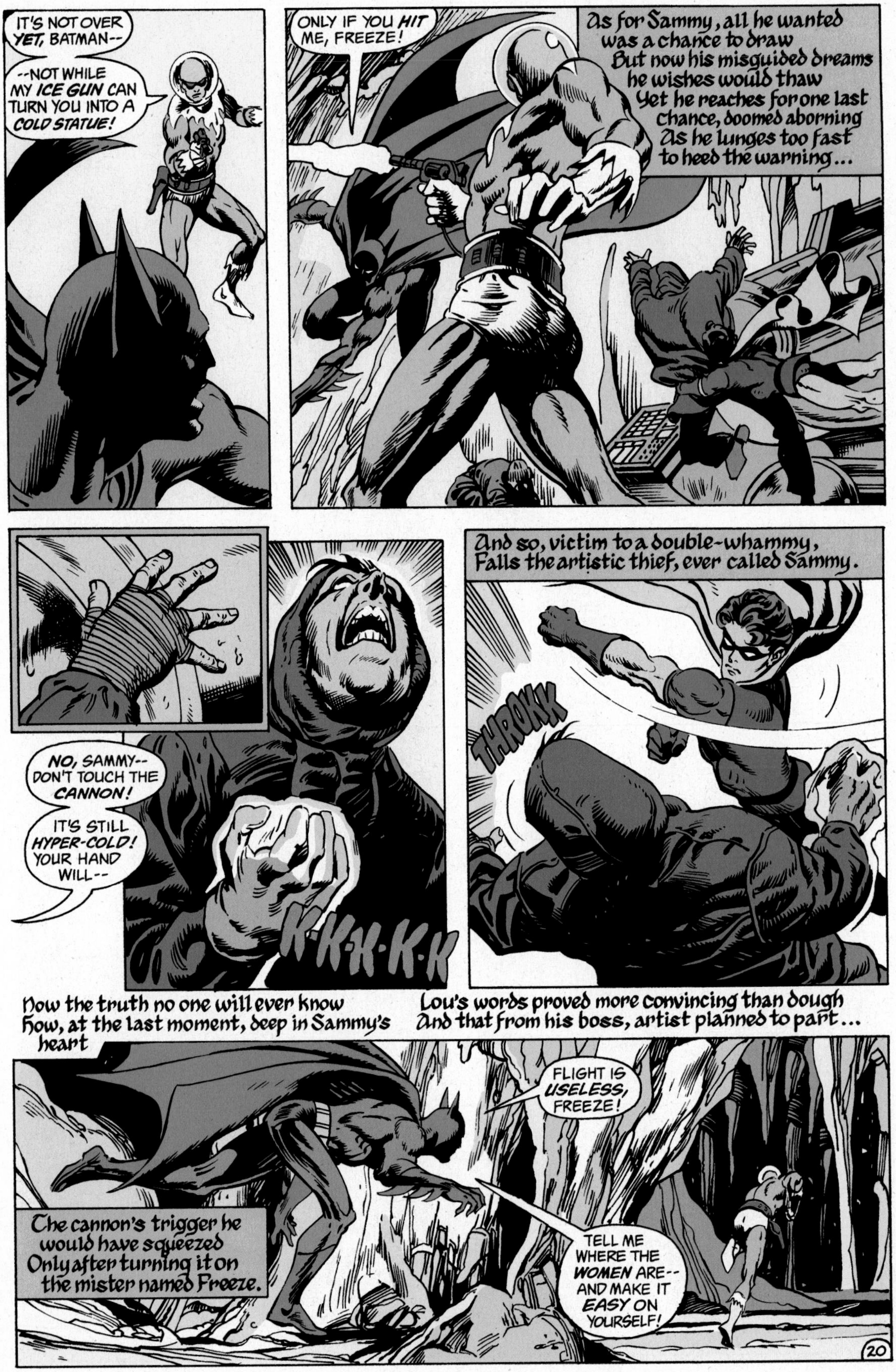
IT'S NOT OVER YET, BATMAN--
--NOT WHILE MY ICE GUN CAN TURN YOU INTO A COLD STATUE!
ONLY IF YOU HIT ME, FREEZE!
As for Sammy, all he wanted was a chance to draw But now his misguided dreams he wishes would thaw Yet he reaches for one last chance, doomed aborning As he lunges too fast to heed the warning...
NO, SAMMY-- DON'T TOUCH THE CANNON!
IT'S STILL HYPER-COLD! YOUR HAND WILL--
K-K-K-K-K
And so, victim to a double-whammy, Falls the artistic thief, ever called Sammy.
THROKK
Now the truth no one will ever know How, at the last moment, deep in Sammy's heart
Lou's words proved more convincing than dough And that from his boss, artist planned to part...
FLIGHT IS USELESS, FREEZE!
The cannon's trigger he would have squeezed Only after turning it on the mister named Freeze.
TELL ME WHERE THE WOMEN ARE-- AND MAKE IT EASY ON YOURSELF!
20

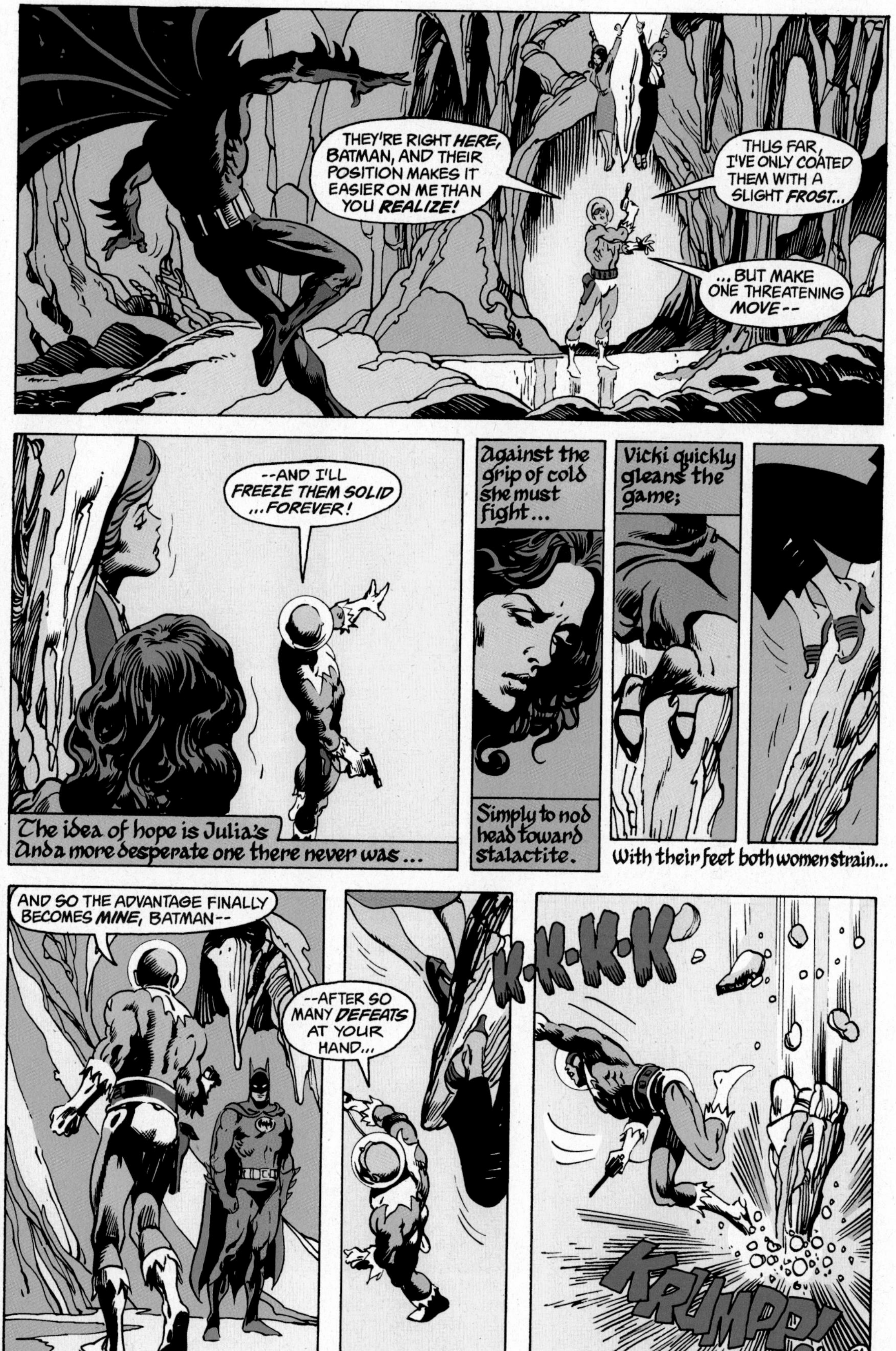
THEY'RE RIGHT HERE, BATMAN, AND THEIR POSITION MAKES IT EASIER ON ME THAN YOU REALIZE!
THUS FAR, I'VE ONLY COATED THEM WITH A SLIGHT FROST...
...BUT MAKE ONE THREATENING MOVE--
--AND I'LL FREEZE THEM SOLID ...FOREVER!
The idea of hope is Julia's
And a more desperate one there never was...
Against the grip of cold she must fight...
Simply to nod head toward stalactite.
Vicki quickly gleans the game;
With their feet both women strain...
AND SO THE ADVANTAGE FINALLY BECOMES MINE, BATMAN--
--AFTER SO MANY DEFEATS AT YOUR HAND...
K-K-K-K-K
KRUMPP!
21

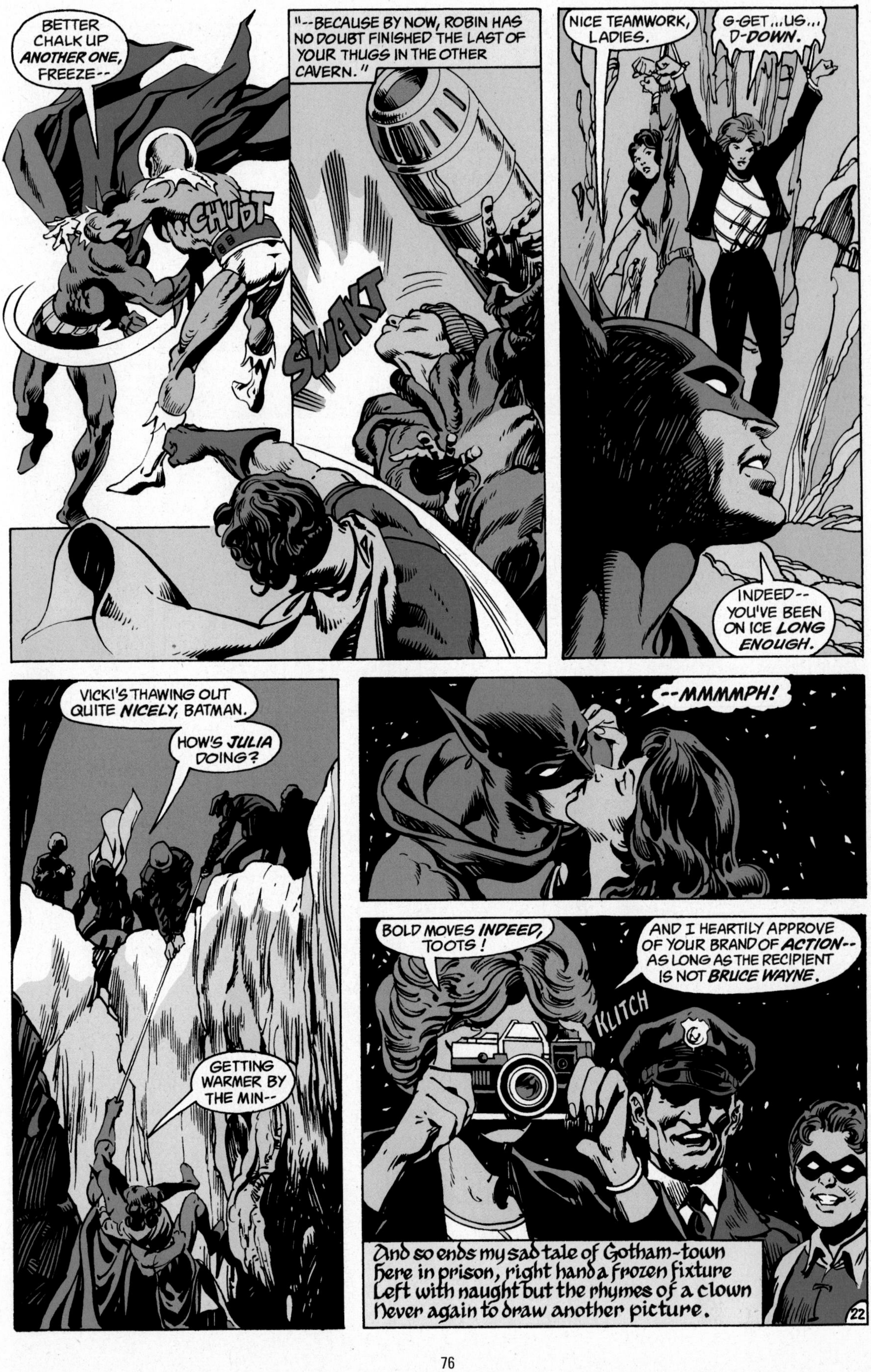
BETTER CHALK UP ANOTHER ONE, FREEZE--
CHUDT
"--BECAUSE BY NOW, ROBIN HAS NO DOUBT FINISHED THE LAST OF YOUR THUGS IN THE OTHER CAVERN."
SWAKT
NICE TEAMWORK, LADIES.
G-GET...US... D-DOWN.
INDEED-- YOU'VE BEEN ON ICE LONG ENOUGH.
VICKI'S THAWING OUT QUITE NICELY, BATMAN.
HOW'S JULIA DOING?
GETTING WARMER BY THE MIN--
--MMMMPH!
BOLD MOVES INDEED, TOOTS!
AND I HEARTILY APPROVE OF YOUR BRAND OF ACTION-- AS LONG AS THE RECIPIENT IS NOT BRUCE WAYNE.
KLITCH
And so ends my sad tale of Gotham-town
Here in prison, right hand a frozen fixture
Left with naught but the rhymes of a clown
Never again to draw another picture.
22

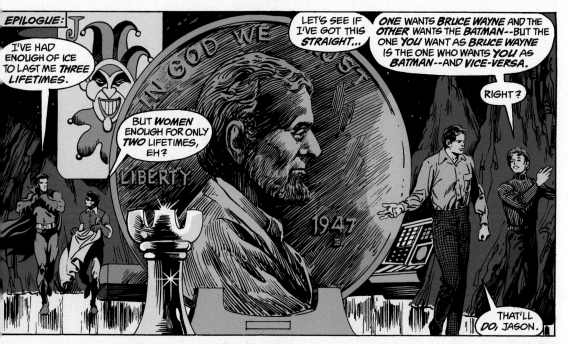

EPILOGUE:

I'VE HAD ENOUGH OF ICE TO LAST ME *THREE* LIFETIMES.

BUT *WOMEN* ENOUGH FOR ONLY *TWO* LIFETIMES, EH?

LET'S SEE IF I'VE GOT THIS *STRAIGHT*...

ONE WANTS *BRUCE WAYNE* AND THE *OTHER* WANTS THE *BATMAN*--BUT THE ONE *YOU* WANT AS *BRUCE WAYNE* IS THE ONE WHO WANTS *YOU* AS *BATMAN*--AND *VICE-VERSA*.

RIGHT?

THAT'LL *DO*, JASON.

OKAY--BUT IS IT JUST MY *IMAGINATION*... OR IS THE BATCAVE *CHILLIER* THAN *USUAL?*

IT HARDLY MATTERS, SINCE IMAGINATION IS MORE POWERFUL THAN REALITY, AND *MINE* IS SHIVERING JUST AS HARD AS *YOURS.*

HAVE TO DO SOMETHING ABOUT INCREASING THE *HEAT* DOWN HERE.

THANK GOD YOU'RE B-*BACK*, SIRS!

I...I DID MY B-*BEST*...TO *COVER* FOR YOU... B-BUT I'M AFRAID IT JUST WASN'T *ENOUGH!*

HUH? ARE *YOU* COLD *TOO*, ALFRED? WHAT ARE YOU *TALKING* ABOUT?

THEY'LL BE C-*COMING*...TO T-*TAKE*...MASTER JASON...*AWAY.*

IN THE NEXT *DETECTIVE* (ON SALE IN TWO WEEKS): *LOSING JASON* -- AND A BRAND-NEW VILLAIN IN THE NEXT *BATMAN: NIGHTSHADE!*

23

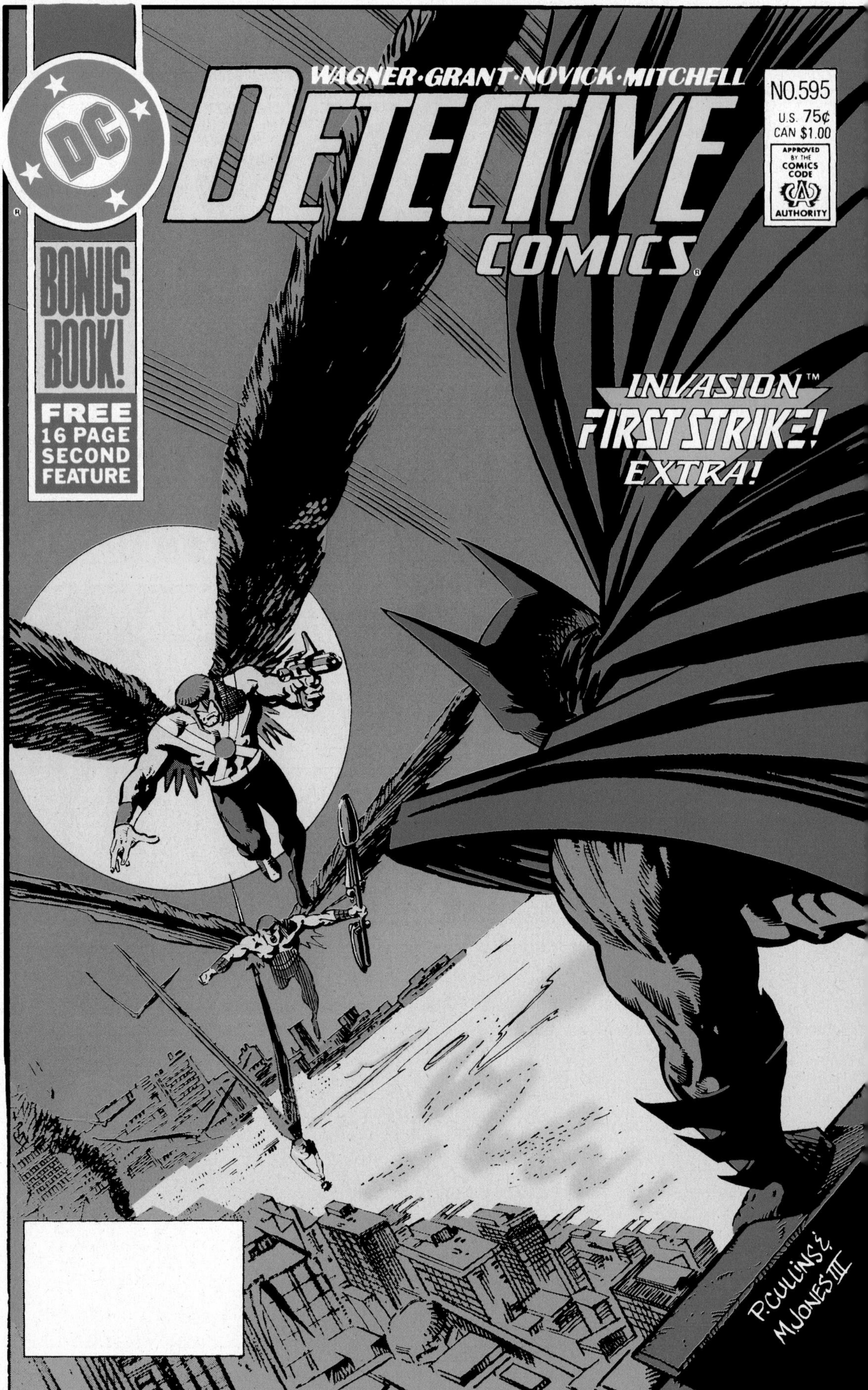
WAGNER·GRANT·NOVICK·MITCHELL
DETECTIVE COMICS
NO.595
U.S. 75¢
CAN $1.00
APPROVED BY THE COMICS CODE AUTHORITY
DC
BONUS BOOK!
FREE 16 PAGE SECOND FEATURE
INVASION™
FIRST STRIKE!
EXTRA!
P. CULLINS &
M. JONES III

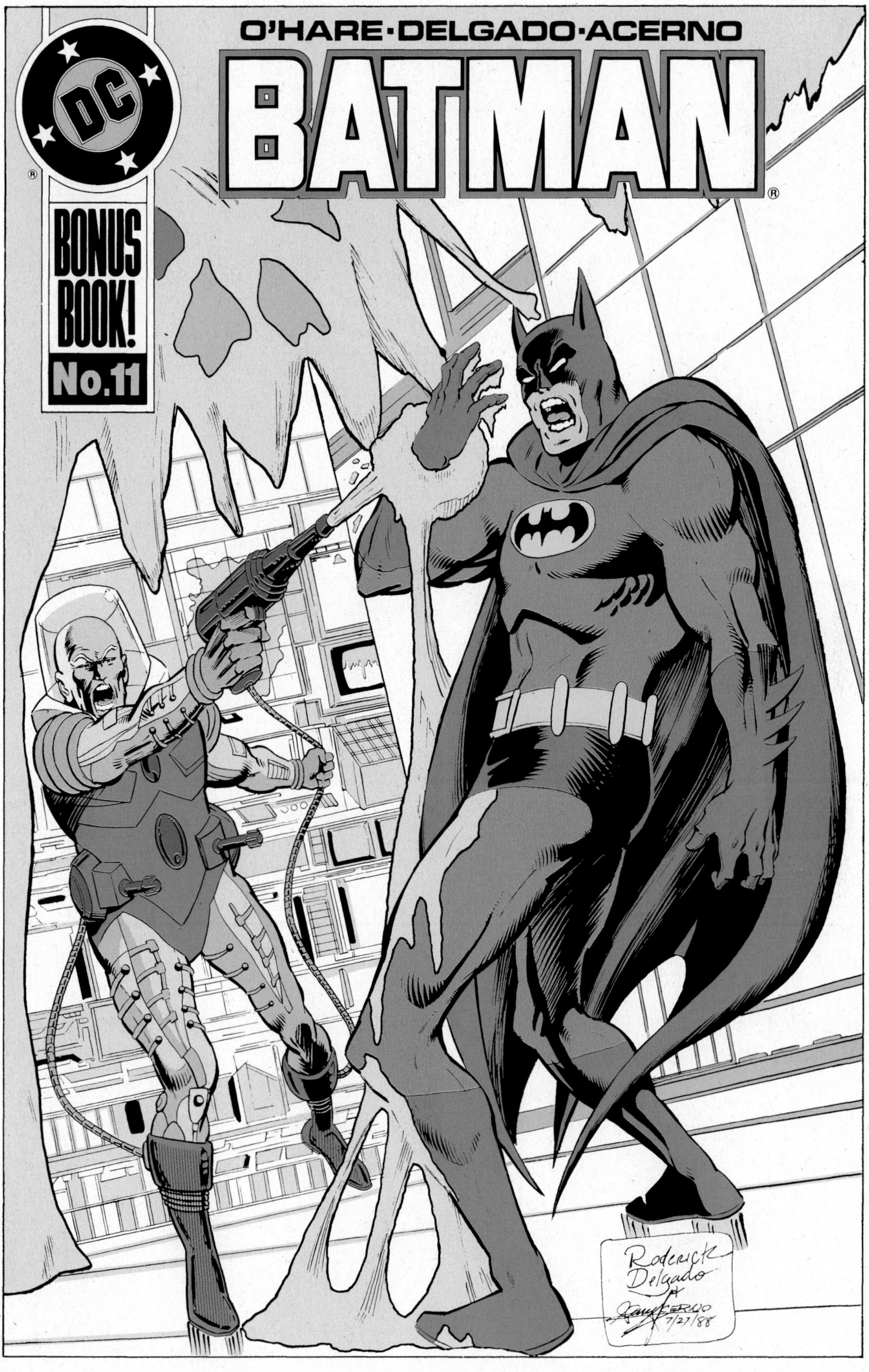
O'HARE·DELGADO·ACERNO
BATMAN
DC
BONUS BOOK!
No.11
Roderick Delgado

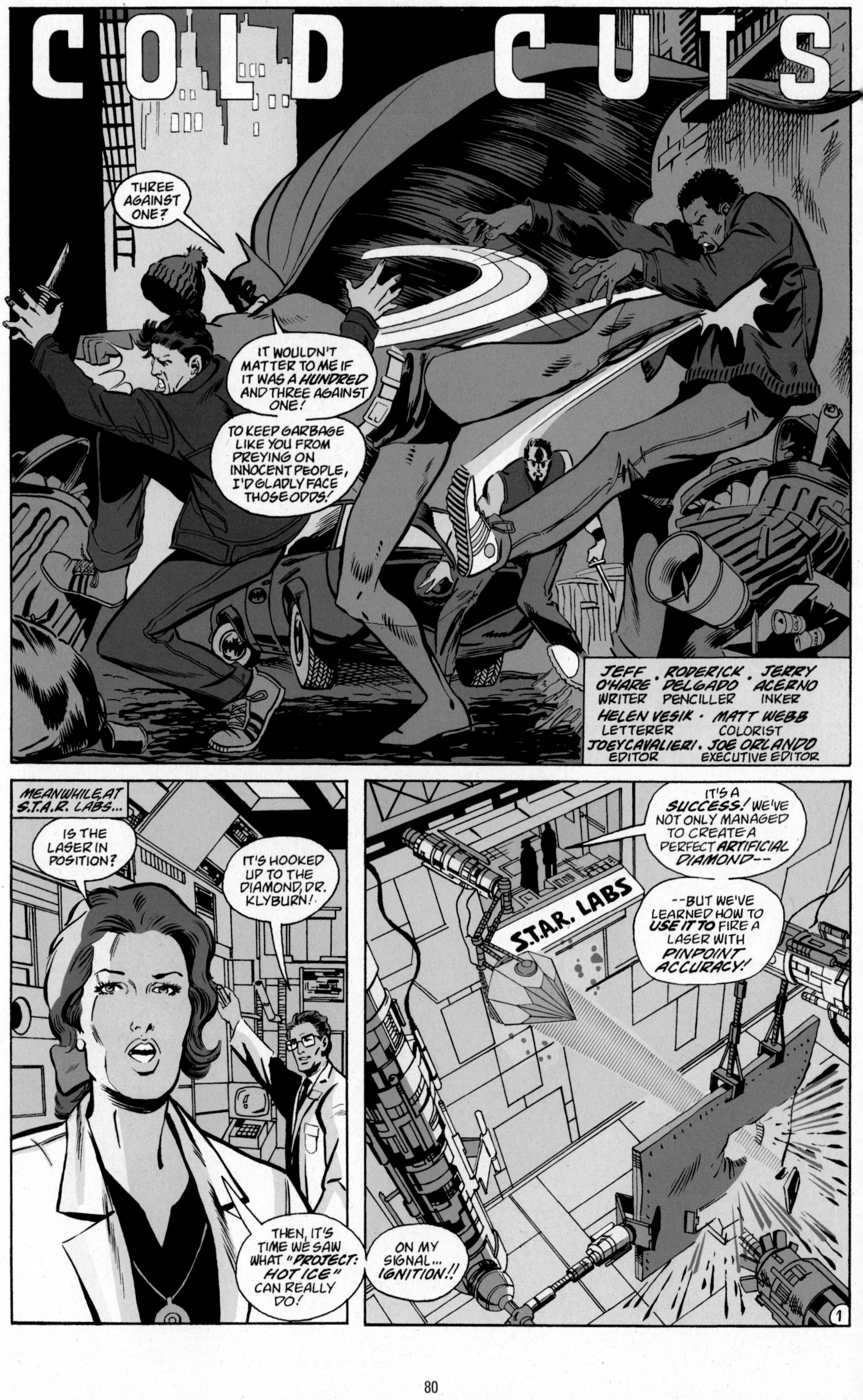
COLD CUTS
THREE AGAINST ONE?
IT WOULDN'T MATTER TO ME IF IT WAS A HUNDRED AND THREE AGAINST ONE!
TO KEEP GARBAGE LIKE YOU FROM PREYING ON INNOCENT PEOPLE, I'D GLADLY FACE THOSE ODDS!
JEFF O'HARE WRITER · RODERICK DELGADO PENCILLER · JERRY ACERNO INKER
HELEN VESIK LETTERER · MATT WEBB COLORIST
JOEY CAVALIERI EDITOR · JOE ORLANDO EXECUTIVE EDITOR
MEANWHILE, AT S.T.A.R. LABS...
IS THE LASER IN POSITION?
IT'S HOOKED UP TO THE DIAMOND, DR. KLYBURN!
THEN, IT'S TIME WE SAW WHAT "PROJECT: HOT ICE" CAN REALLY DO!
S.T.A.R. LABS
IT'S A SUCCESS! WE'VE NOT ONLY MANAGED TO CREATE A PERFECT ARTIFICIAL DIAMOND--
--BUT WE'VE LEARNED HOW TO USE IT TO FIRE A LASER WITH PINPOINT ACCURACY!
ON MY SIGNAL... IGNITION!!
1

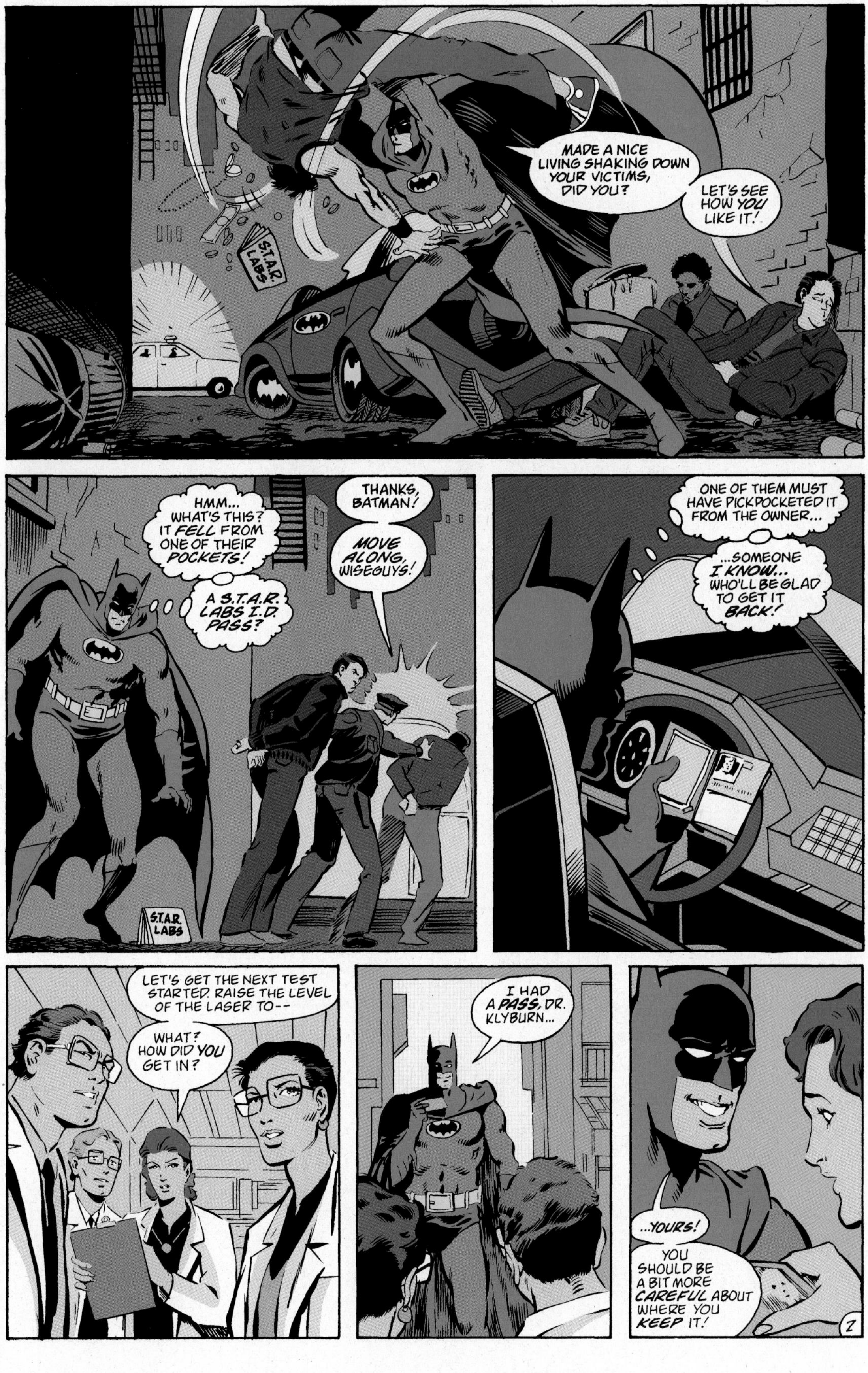

MADE A NICE LIVING SHAKING DOWN YOUR VICTIMS, DID YOU?
LET'S SEE HOW YOU LIKE IT!
S.T.A.R. LABS
HMM... WHAT'S THIS? IT FELL FROM ONE OF THEIR POCKETS!
A S.T.A.R. LABS I.D. PASS?
THANKS, BATMAN!
MOVE ALONG, WISEGUYS!
S.T.A.R. LABS
ONE OF THEM MUST HAVE PICKPOCKETED IT FROM THE OWNER...
...SOMEONE I KNOW... WHO'LL BE GLAD TO GET IT BACK!
LET'S GET THE NEXT TEST STARTED. RAISE THE LEVEL OF THE LASER TO--
WHAT? HOW DID YOU GET IN?
I HAD A PASS, DR. KLYBURN...
...YOURS!
YOU SHOULD BE A BIT MORE CAREFUL ABOUT WHERE YOU KEEP IT!
2

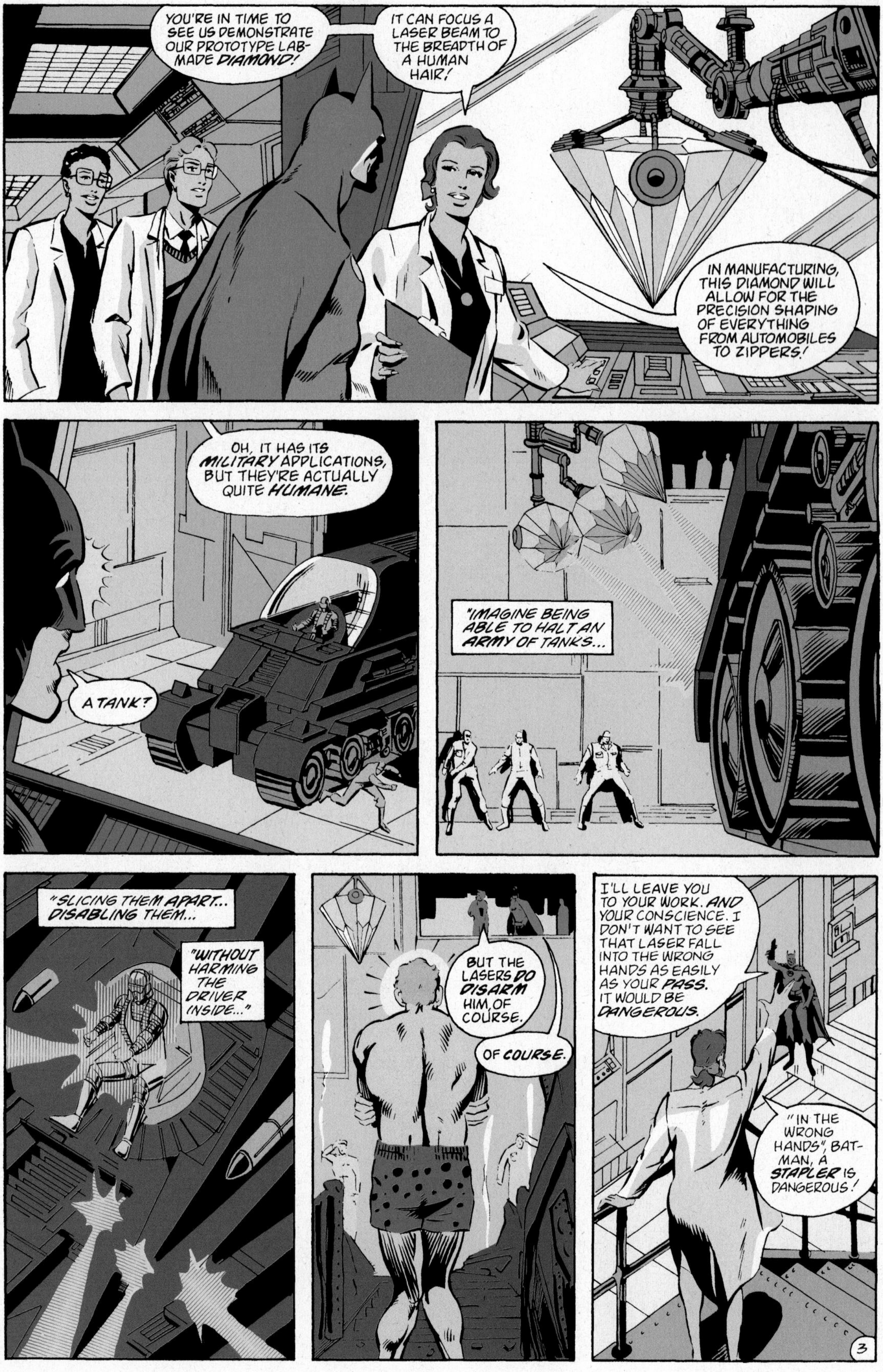
YOU'RE IN TIME TO SEE US DEMONSTRATE OUR PROTOTYPE LAB-MADE DIAMOND!
IT CAN FOCUS A LASER BEAM TO THE BREADTH OF A HUMAN HAIR!
IN MANUFACTURING, THIS DIAMOND WILL ALLOW FOR THE PRECISION SHAPING OF EVERYTHING FROM AUTOMOBILES TO ZIPPERS!
OH, IT HAS ITS MILITARY APPLICATIONS, BUT THEY'RE ACTUALLY QUITE HUMANE.
A TANK?
"IMAGINE BEING ABLE TO HALT AN ARMY OF TANKS...
"SLICING THEM APART... DISABLING THEM...
"WITHOUT HARMING THE DRIVER INSIDE..."
BUT THE LASERS DO DISARM HIM, OF COURSE.
OF COURSE.
I'LL LEAVE YOU TO YOUR WORK. AND YOUR CONSCIENCE. I DON'T WANT TO SEE THAT LASER FALL INTO THE WRONG HANDS AS EASILY AS YOUR PASS. IT WOULD BE DANGEROUS.
"IN THE WRONG HANDS", BAT-MAN, A STAPLER IS DANGEROUS!
3

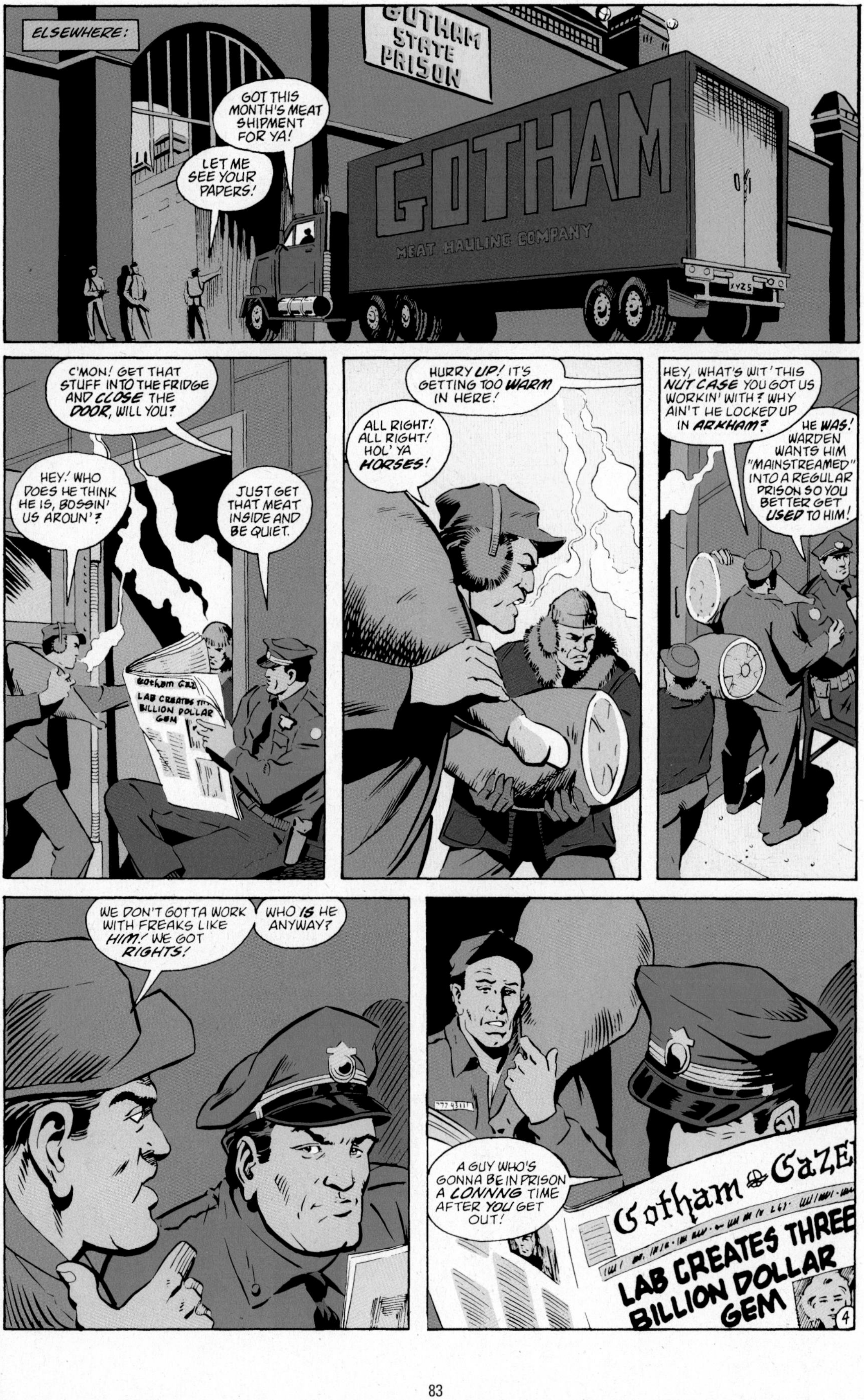
ELSEWHERE:
GOTHAM STATE PRISON
GOTHAM
MEAT HAULING COMPANY
GOT THIS MONTH'S MEAT SHIPMENT FOR YA!
LET ME SEE YOUR PAPERS!
C'MON! GET THAT STUFF INTO THE FRIDGE AND CLOSE THE DOOR, WILL YOU?
HEY! WHO DOES HE THINK HE IS, BOSSIN' US AROUN'?
JUST GET THAT MEAT INSIDE AND BE QUIET.
Gotham Gaz
LAB CREATES TH BILLION DOLLAR GEM
HURRY UP! IT'S GETTING TOO WARM IN HERE!
ALL RIGHT! ALL RIGHT! HOL' YA HORSES!
HEY, WHAT'S WIT' THIS NUT CASE YOU GOT US WORKIN' WITH? WHY AIN'T HE LOCKED UP IN ARKHAM?
HE WAS! WARDEN WANTS HIM "MAINSTREAMED" INTO A REGULAR PRISON SO YOU BETTER GET USED TO HIM!
WE DON'T GOTTA WORK WITH FREAKS LIKE HIM! WE GOT RIGHTS!
WHO IS HE ANYWAY?
A GUY WHO'S GONNA BE IN PRISON A LONNNG TIME AFTER YOU GET OUT!
Gotham Gaze
LAB CREATES THREE BILLION DOLLAR GEM
4

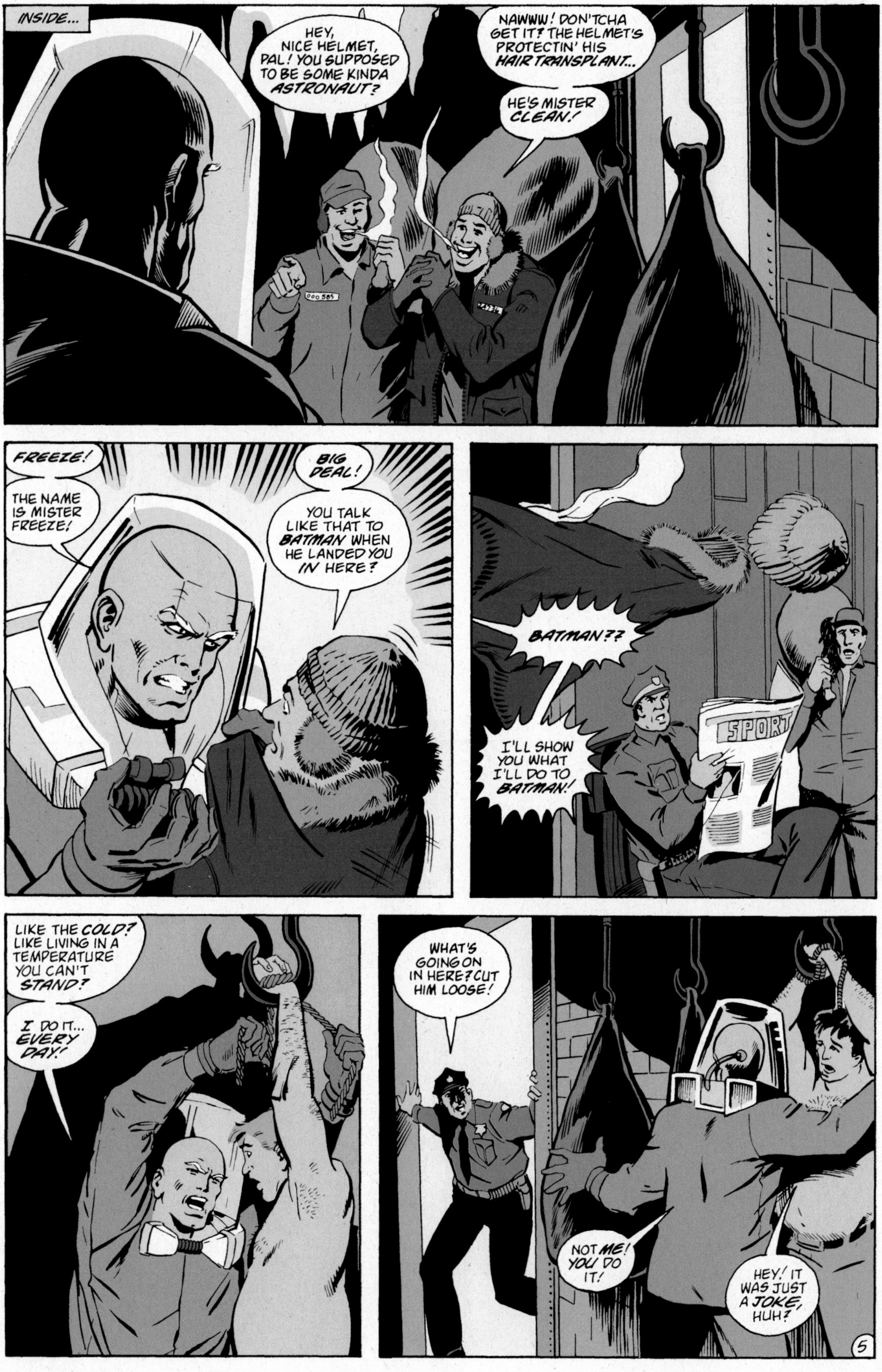
INSIDE...
HEY, NICE HELMET, PAL! YOU SUPPOSED TO BE SOME KINDA ASTRONAUT?
NAWWW! DON'TCHA GET IT? THE HELMET'S PROTECTIN' HIS HAIR TRANSPLANT...
HE'S MISTER CLEAN!
FREEZE!
THE NAME IS MISTER FREEZE!
BIG DEAL!
YOU TALK LIKE THAT TO BATMAN WHEN HE LANDED YOU IN HERE?
BATMAN??
I'LL SHOW YOU WHAT I'LL DO TO BATMAN!
SPORT
LIKE THE COLD? LIKE LIVING IN A TEMPERATURE YOU CAN'T STAND?
I DO IT... EVERY DAY!
WHAT'S GOING ON IN HERE? CUT HIM LOOSE!
NOT ME! YOU DO IT!
HEY! IT WAS JUST A JOKE, HUH?
5

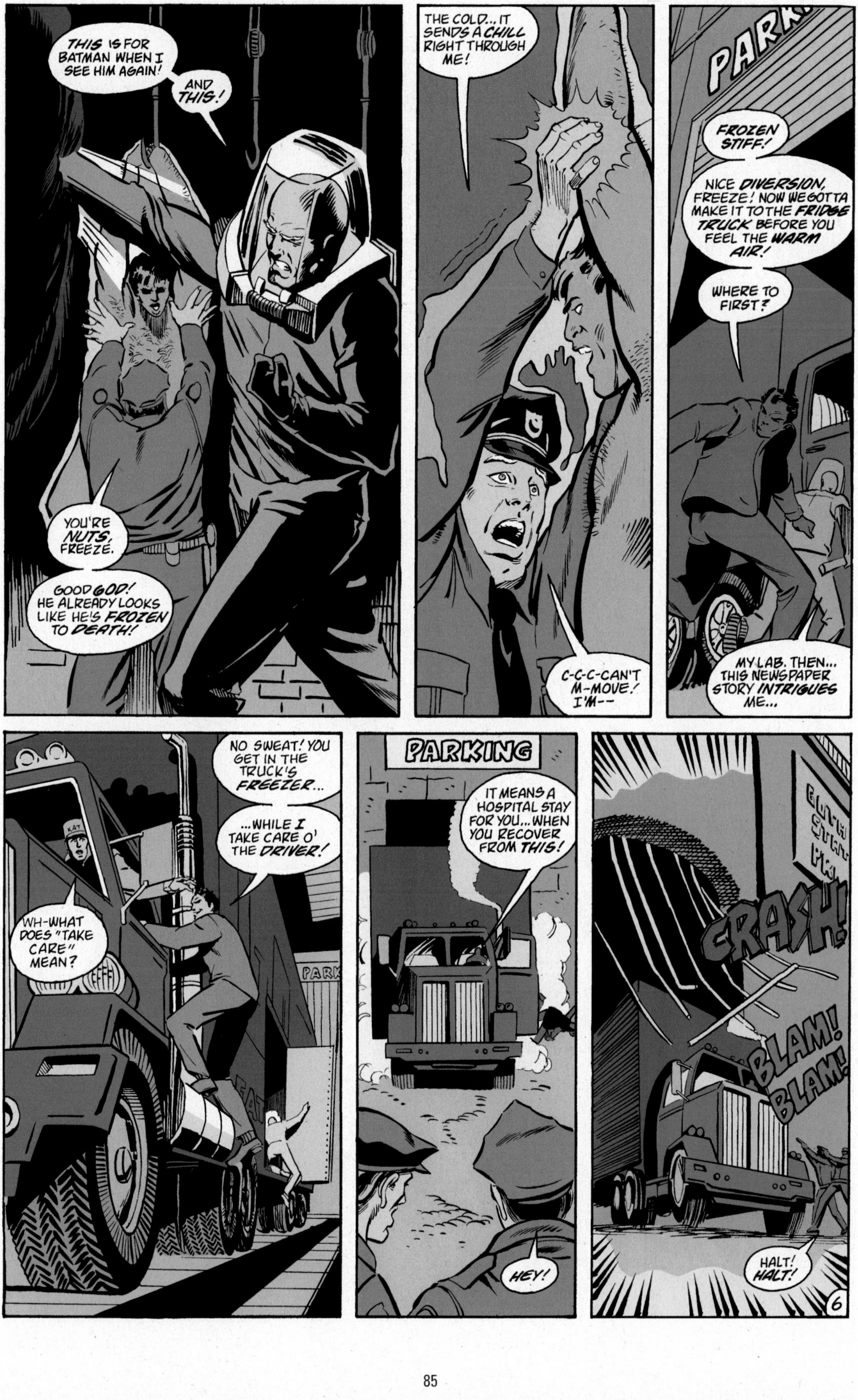
THIS IS FOR BATMAN WHEN I SEE HIM AGAIN!
AND THIS!
YOU'RE NUTS, FREEZE.
GOOD GOD! HE ALREADY LOOKS LIKE HE'S FROZEN TO DEATH!
THE COLD... IT SENDS A CHILL RIGHT THROUGH ME!
C-C-C-CAN'T M-MOVE! I'M--
PARK
FROZEN STIFF!
NICE DIVERSION, FREEZE! NOW WE GOTTA MAKE IT TO THE FRIDGE TRUCK BEFORE YOU FEEL THE WARM AIR!
WHERE TO FIRST?
MY LAB. THEN... THIS NEWSPAPER STORY INTRIGUES ME...
NO SWEAT! YOU GET IN THE TRUCK'S FREEZER...
...WHILE I TAKE CARE O' THE DRIVER!
WH-WHAT DOES "TAKE CARE" MEAN?
PARKING
IT MEANS A HOSPITAL STAY FOR YOU... WHEN YOU RECOVER FROM THIS!
HEY!
CRASH!
BLAM! BLAM!
HALT! HALT!
6

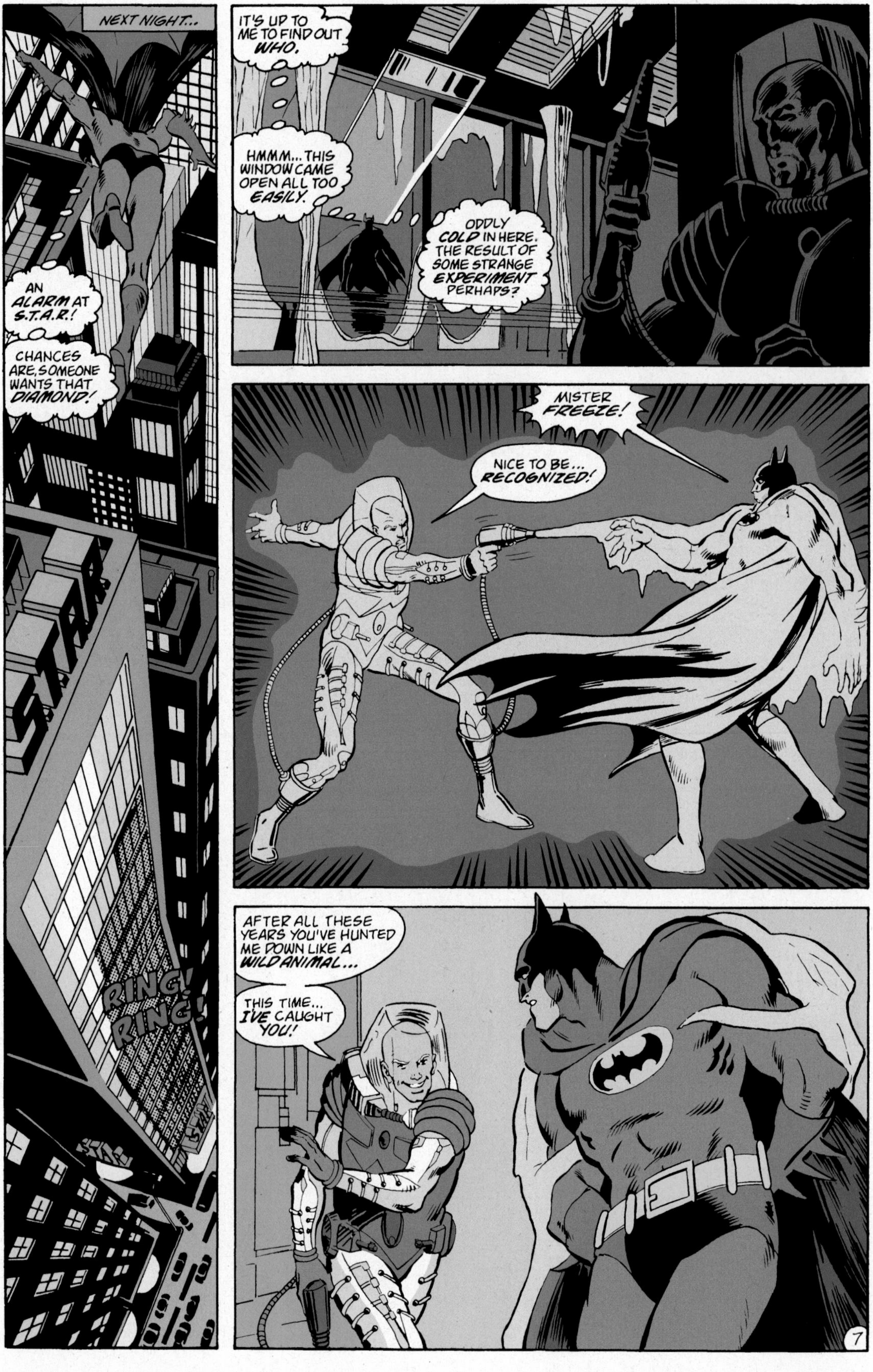
NEXT NIGHT...
AN ALARM AT S.T.A.R.!
CHANCES ARE, SOMEONE WANTS THAT DIAMOND!
RING! RING!
STAR
IT'S UP TO ME TO FIND OUT WHO.
HMMM... THIS WINDOW CAME OPEN ALL TOO EASILY.
ODDLY COLD IN HERE. THE RESULT OF SOME STRANGE EXPERIMENT PERHAPS?
MISTER FREEZE!
NICE TO BE... RECOGNIZED!
AFTER ALL THESE YEARS YOU'VE HUNTED ME DOWN LIKE A WILD ANIMAL...
THIS TIME... I'VE CAUGHT YOU!
7

THE ENTIRE *FLOOR* OF THIS *BUILDING* IS *ICED* *SHUT!* NO ONE CAN GET *IN...* AND *YOU* WON'T GET *OUT!*

THIS IS ALL FOR *YOUR* BENEFIT, BAT MAN! *YOU* WILL SUFFER... AS *I* HAVE SUFFERED!

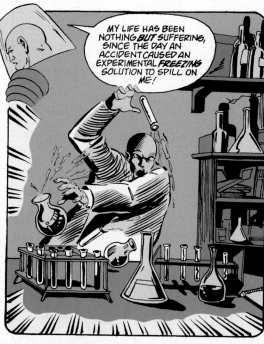

MY LIFE HAS BEEN NOTHING *BUT* SUFFERING, SINCE THE DAY AN ACCIDENT CAUSED AN EXPERIMENTAL *FREEZING* SOLUTION TO SPILL ON ME!

IMMEDIATELY, I COULD NO LONGER STAND NORMAL TEMPERATURES! I COULD SURVIVE ONLY IN A SUB-ZERO ENVIRONMENT!

I LIVED IN *VIRTUAL* ISOLATION EVER SINCE--

--SEPARATED FROM A WORLD THAT CAN'T *HELP* ME AND DOESN'T *CARE.*

YOU SPENT A LOT OF TIME MAKING SURE I REMAINED BEHIND *BARS,* BATMAN...

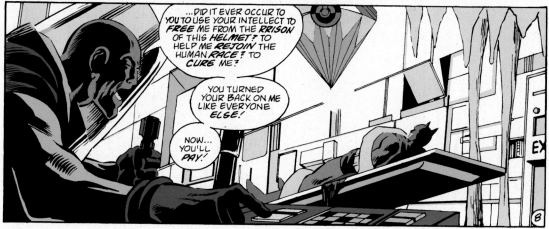

...DID IT EVER OCCUR TO YOU TO USE YOUR INTELLECT TO *FREE* ME FROM THE *PRISON* OF THIS *HELMET?* TO HELP ME *REJOIN* THE HUMAN *RACE?* TO *CURE* ME?

YOU TURNED YOUR BACK ON ME LIKE EVERYONE *ELSE!*

NOW... YOU'LL *PAY!*

8

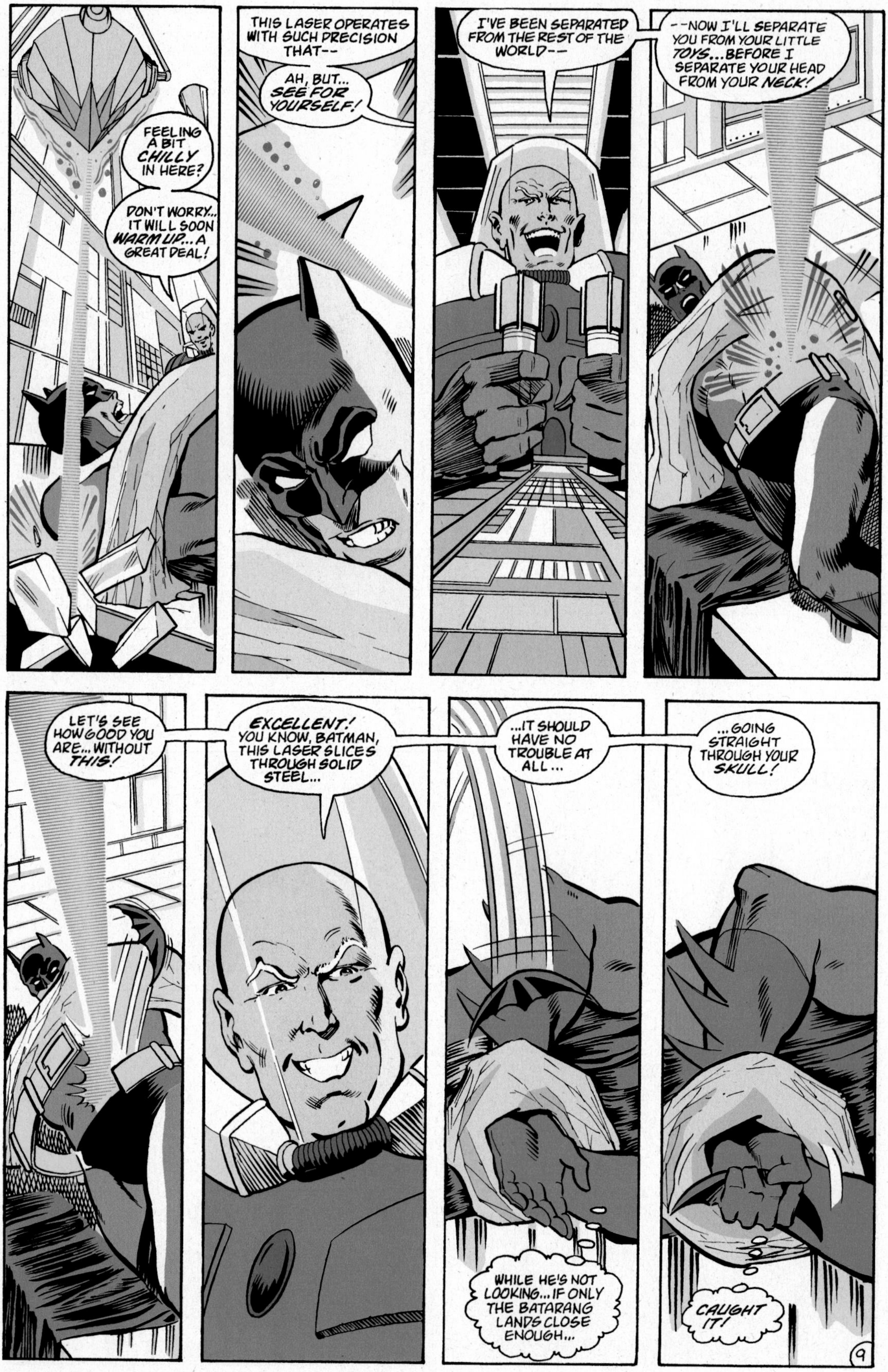

FEELING A BIT CHILLY IN HERE?
DON'T WORRY... IT WILL SOON WARM UP... A GREAT DEAL!
THIS LASER OPERATES WITH SUCH PRECISION THAT--
AH, BUT... SEE FOR YOURSELF!
I'VE BEEN SEPARATED FROM THE REST OF THE WORLD--
--NOW I'LL SEPARATE YOU FROM YOUR LITTLE TOYS... BEFORE I SEPARATE YOUR HEAD FROM YOUR NECK!
LET'S SEE HOW GOOD YOU ARE... WITHOUT THIS!
EXCELLENT! YOU KNOW, BATMAN, THIS LASER SLICES THROUGH SOLID STEEL...
...IT SHOULD HAVE NO TROUBLE AT ALL...
...GOING STRAIGHT THROUGH YOUR SKULL!
WHILE HE'S NOT LOOKING... IF ONLY THE BATARANG LANDS CLOSE ENOUGH...
CAUGHT IT!
9

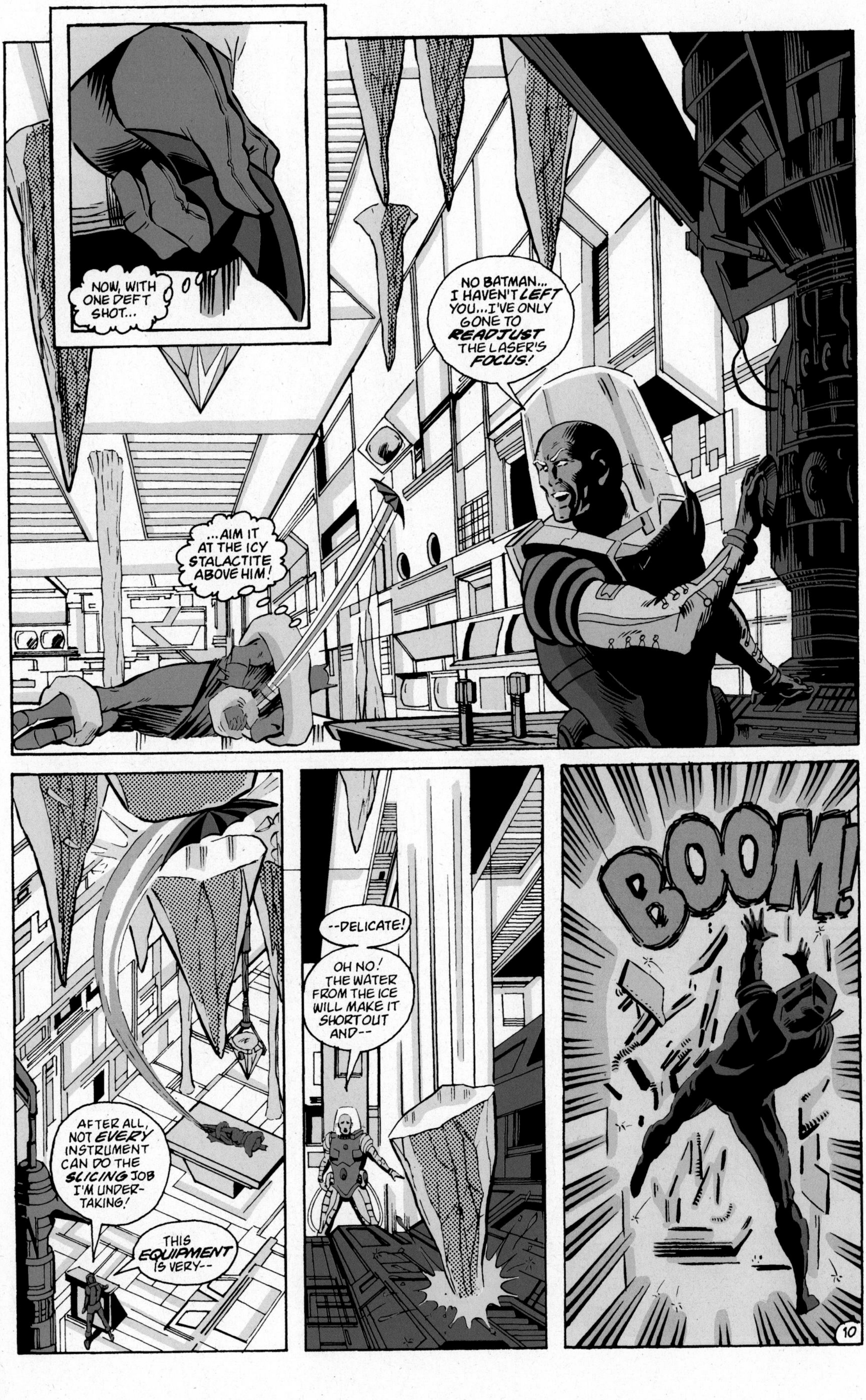
NOW, WITH ONE DEFT SHOT...
NO BATMAN... I HAVEN'T LEFT YOU...I'VE ONLY GONE TO READJUST THE LASER'S FOCUS!
...AIM IT AT THE ICY STALACTITE ABOVE HIM!
AFTER ALL, NOT EVERY INSTRUMENT CAN DO THE SLICING JOB I'M UNDER-TAKING!
THIS EQUIPMENT IS VERY--
--DELICATE!
OH NO! THE WATER FROM THE ICE WILL MAKE IT SHORT OUT AND--
BOOM!
10

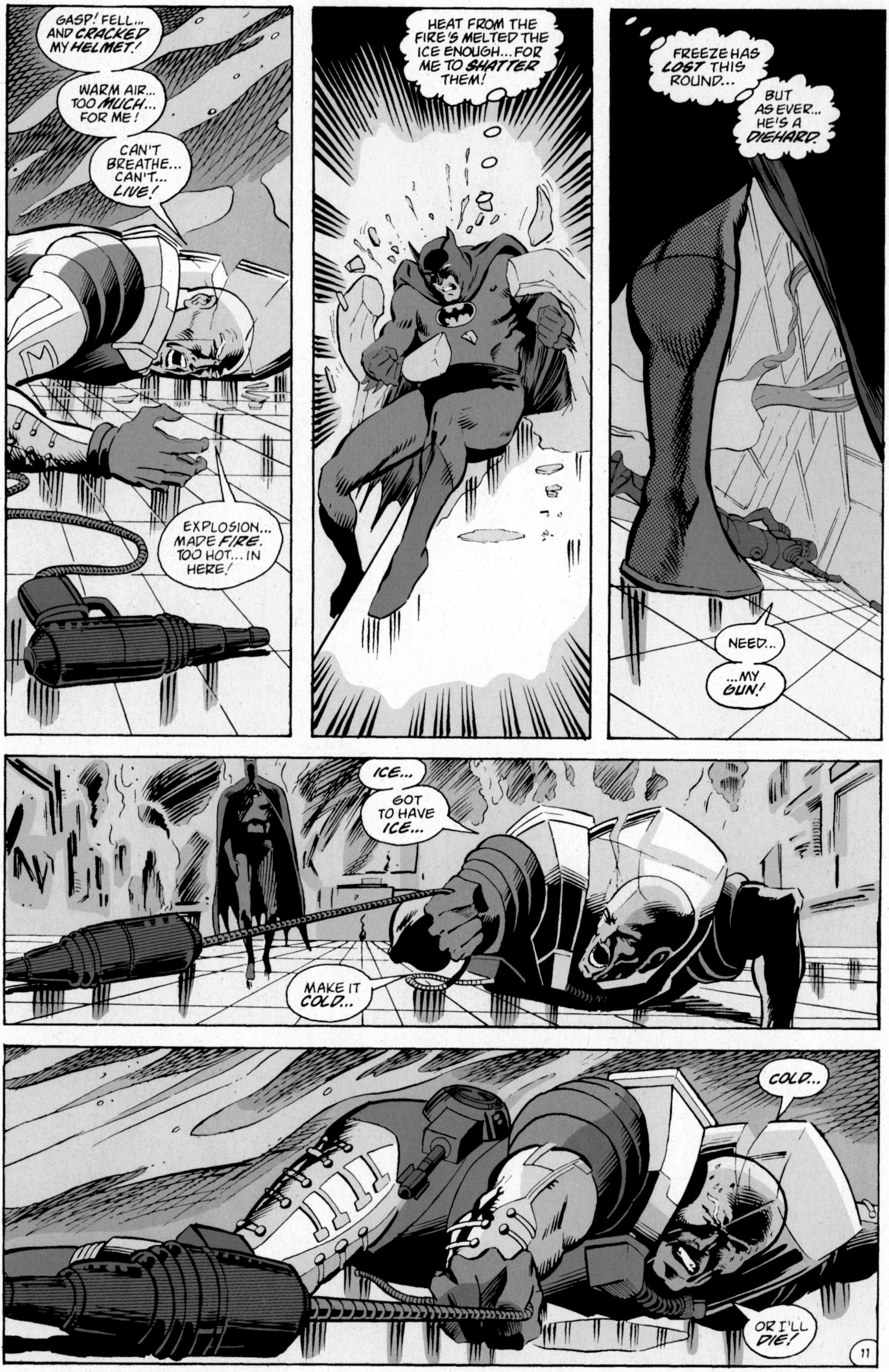
GASP! FELL... AND CRACKED MY HELMET!
WARM AIR... TOO MUCH... FOR ME!
CAN'T BREATHE... CAN'T... LIVE!
EXPLOSION... MADE FIRE. TOO HOT... IN HERE!
HEAT FROM THE FIRE'S MELTED THE ICE ENOUGH... FOR ME TO SHATTER THEM!
FREEZE HAS LOST THIS ROUND...
BUT AS EVER... HE'S A DIEHARD.
NEED...
...MY GUN!
ICE...
GOT TO HAVE ICE...
MAKE IT COLD...
COLD...
OR I'LL DIE!
11

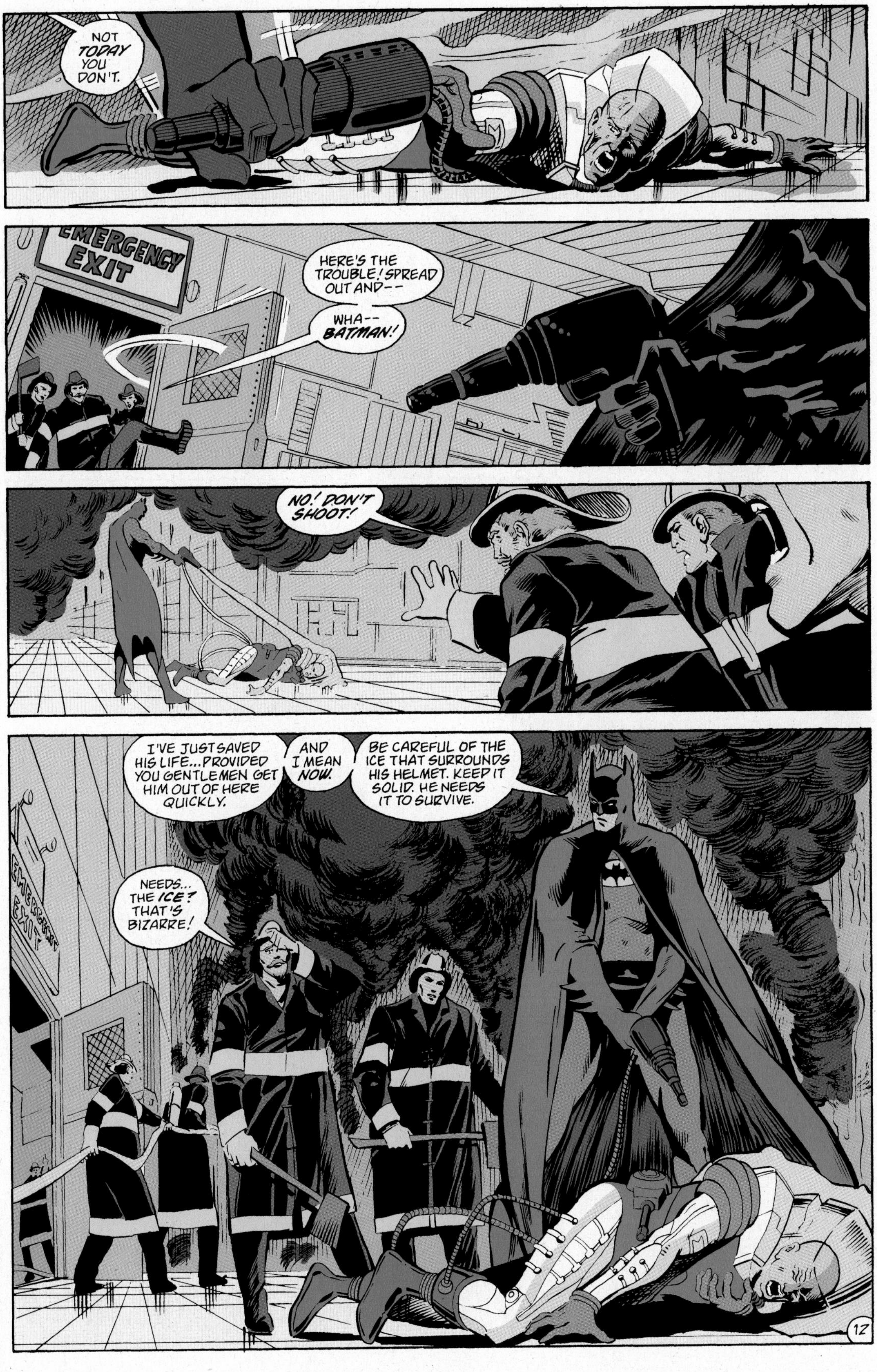
NOT TODAY YOU DON'T.
HERE'S THE TROUBLE! SPREAD OUT AND--
WHA-- BATMAN!
EMERGENCY EXIT
NO! DON'T SHOOT!
I'VE JUST SAVED HIS LIFE...PROVIDED YOU GENTLEMEN GET HIM OUT OF HERE QUICKLY.
AND I MEAN NOW.
BE CAREFUL OF THE ICE THAT SURROUNDS HIS HELMET. KEEP IT SOLID. HE NEEDS IT TO SURVIVE.
NEEDS... THE ICE? THAT'S BIZARRE!
EMERGENCY EXIT
12

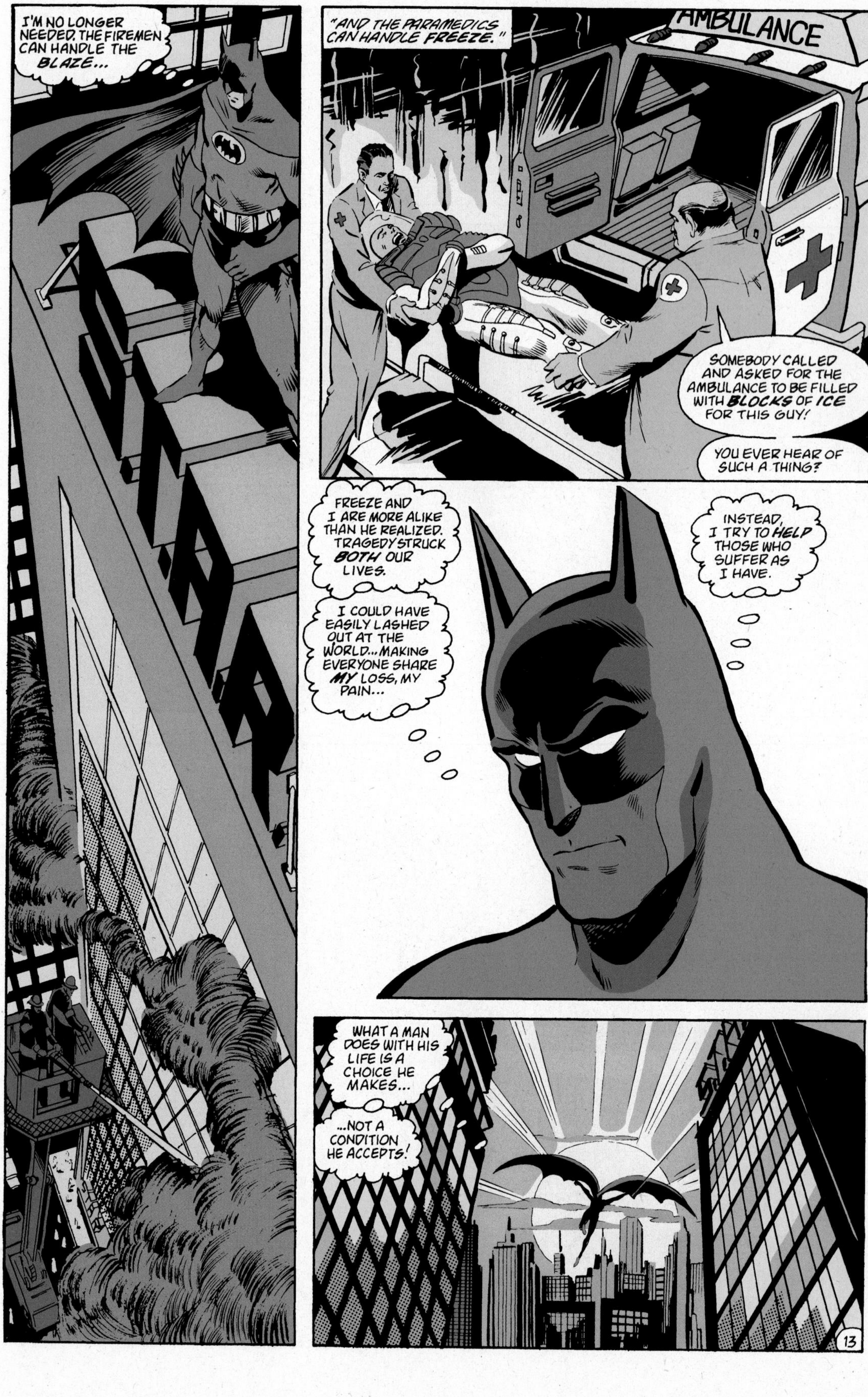
I'M NO LONGER NEEDED. THE FIREMEN CAN HANDLE THE BLAZE...
"AND THE PARAMEDICS CAN HANDLE FREEZE."
AMBULANCE
SOMEBODY CALLED AND ASKED FOR THE AMBULANCE TO BE FILLED WITH BLOCKS OF ICE FOR THIS GUY!
YOU EVER HEAR OF SUCH A THING?
FREEZE AND I ARE MORE ALIKE THAN HE REALIZED. TRAGEDY STRUCK BOTH OUR LIVES.
I COULD HAVE EASILY LASHED OUT AT THE WORLD... MAKING EVERYONE SHARE MY LOSS, MY PAIN...
INSTEAD, I TRY TO HELP THOSE WHO SUFFER AS I HAVE.
WHAT A MAN DOES WITH HIS LIFE IS A CHOICE HE MAKES...
...NOT A CONDITION HE ACCEPTS!
13

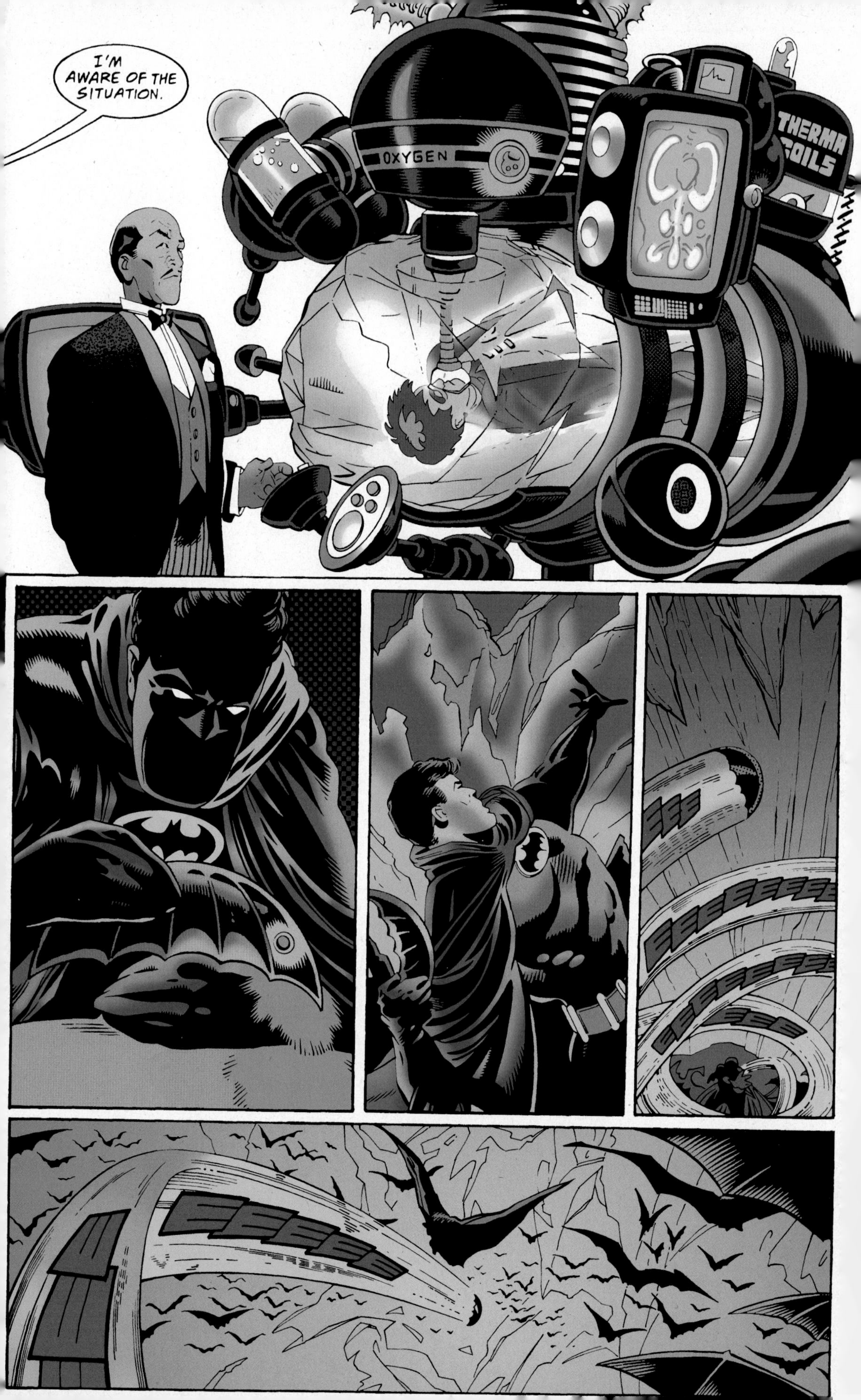
I'M AWARE OF THE SITUATION.
OXYGEN
THERMA COILS

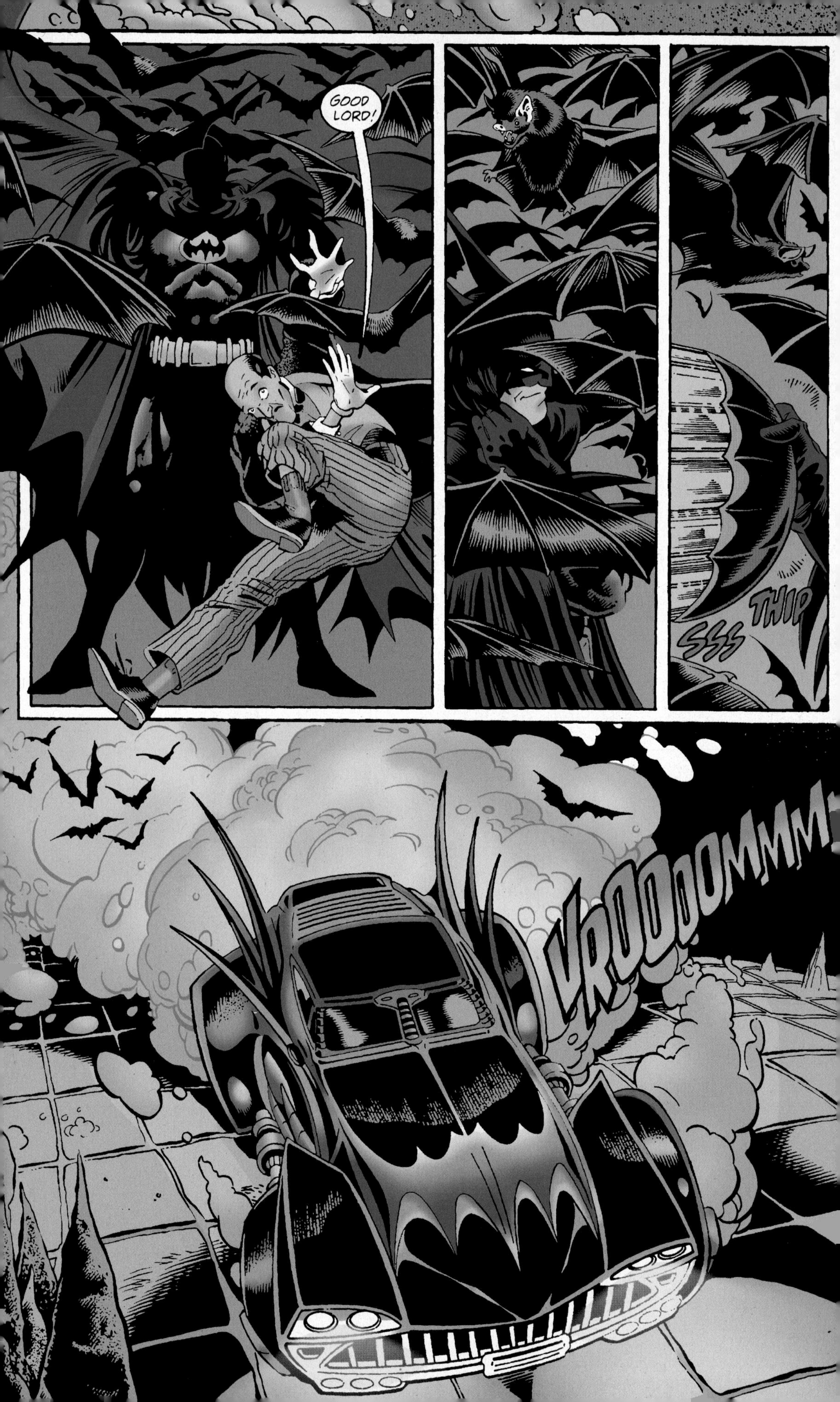
GOOD LORD!
SSS THIP
VROOOOOMMM

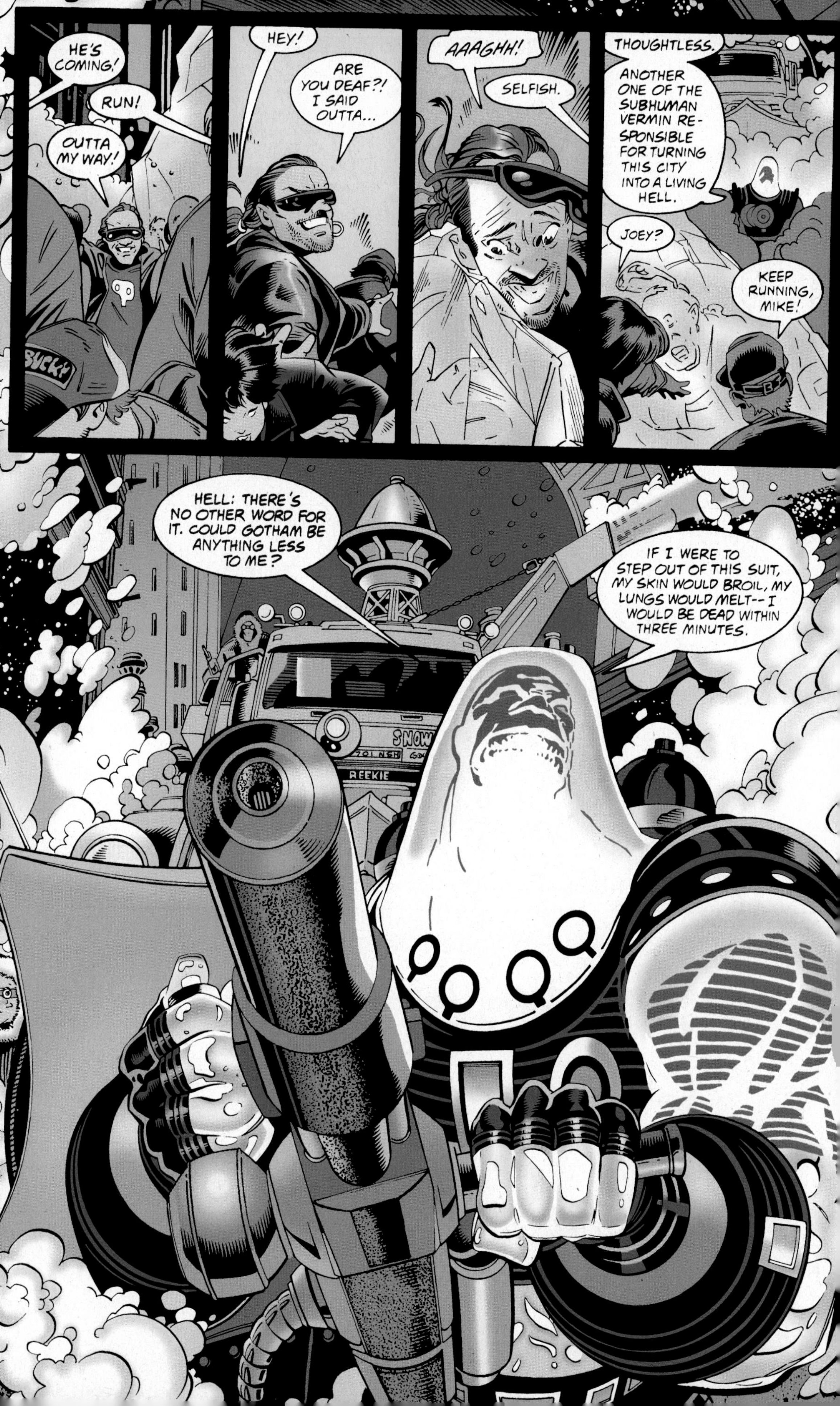
HE'S COMING!
RUN!
OUTTA MY WAY!
HEY!
ARE YOU DEAF?! I SAID OUTTA...
AAAGHH!
SELFISH.
THOUGHTLESS.
ANOTHER ONE OF THE SUBHUMAN VERMIN RESPONSIBLE FOR TURNING THIS CITY INTO A LIVING HELL.
JOEY?
KEEP RUNNING, MIKE!
HELL: THERE'S NO OTHER WORD FOR IT. COULD GOTHAM BE ANYTHING LESS TO ME?
IF I WERE TO STEP OUT OF THIS SUIT, MY SKIN WOULD BROIL, MY LUNGS WOULD MELT-- I WOULD BE DEAD WITHIN THREE MINUTES.
SNOW
REEKIE

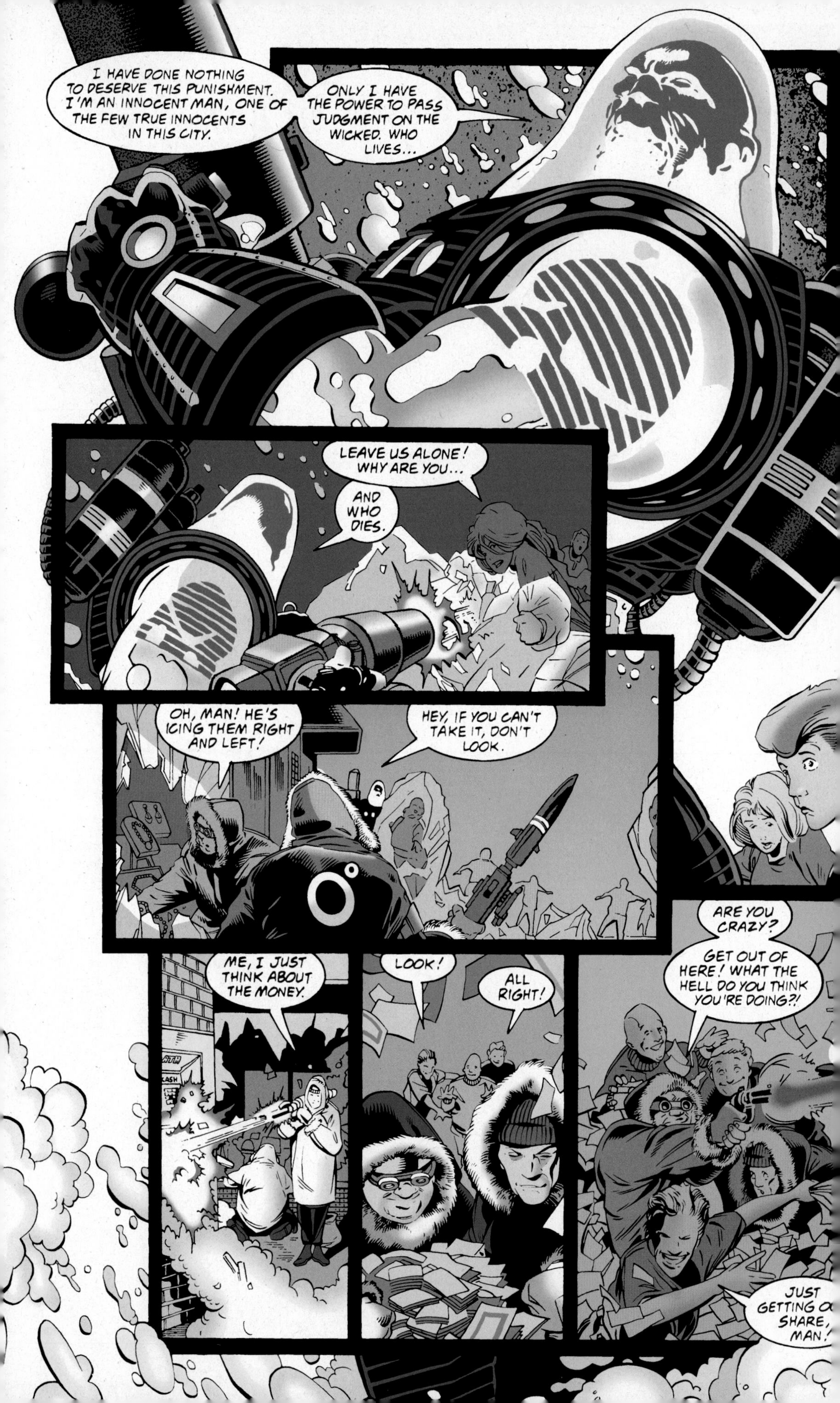
I HAVE DONE NOTHING TO DESERVE THIS PUNISHMENT. I'M AN INNOCENT MAN, ONE OF THE FEW TRUE INNOCENTS IN THIS CITY.
ONLY I HAVE THE POWER TO PASS JUDGMENT ON THE WICKED. WHO LIVES...
LEAVE US ALONE! WHY ARE YOU...
AND WHO DIES.
OH, MAN! HE'S ICING THEM RIGHT AND LEFT!
HEY, IF YOU CAN'T TAKE IT, DON'T LOOK.
ME, I JUST THINK ABOUT THE MONEY.
ATM
CASH
LOOK!
ALL RIGHT!
ARE YOU CRAZY?
GET OUT OF HERE! WHAT THE HELL DO YOU THINK YOU'RE DOING?!
JUST GETTING O SHARE, MAN!

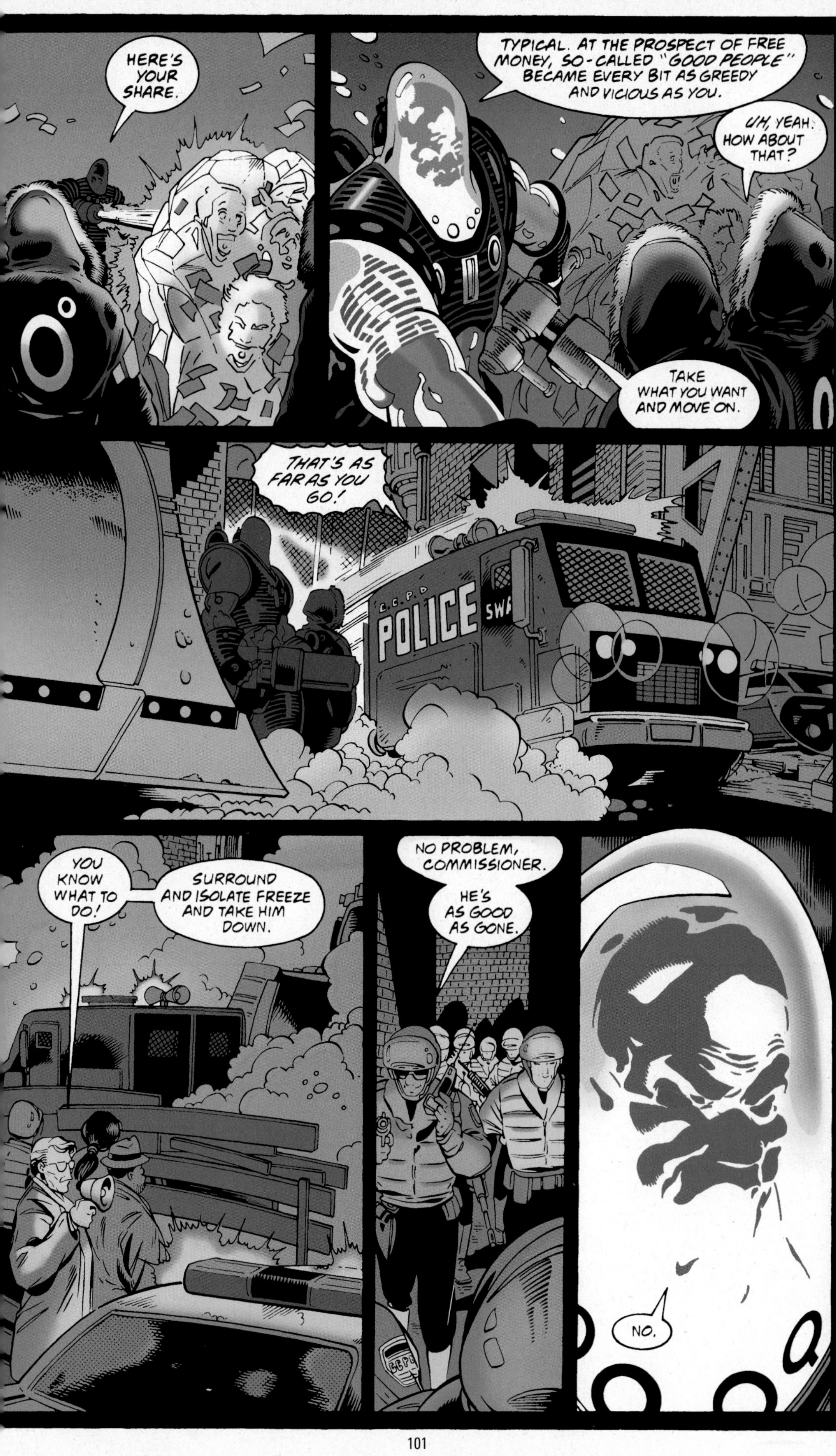
HERE'S YOUR SHARE.
TYPICAL. AT THE PROSPECT OF FREE MONEY, SO-CALLED "GOOD PEOPLE" BECAME EVERY BIT AS GREEDY AND VICIOUS AS YOU.
UH, YEAH. HOW ABOUT THAT?
TAKE WHAT YOU WANT AND MOVE ON.
THAT'S AS FAR AS YOU GO!
POLICE
YOU KNOW WHAT TO DO!
SURROUND AND ISOLATE FREEZE AND TAKE HIM DOWN.
NO PROBLEM, COMMISSIONER.
HE'S AS GOOD AS GONE.
NO.

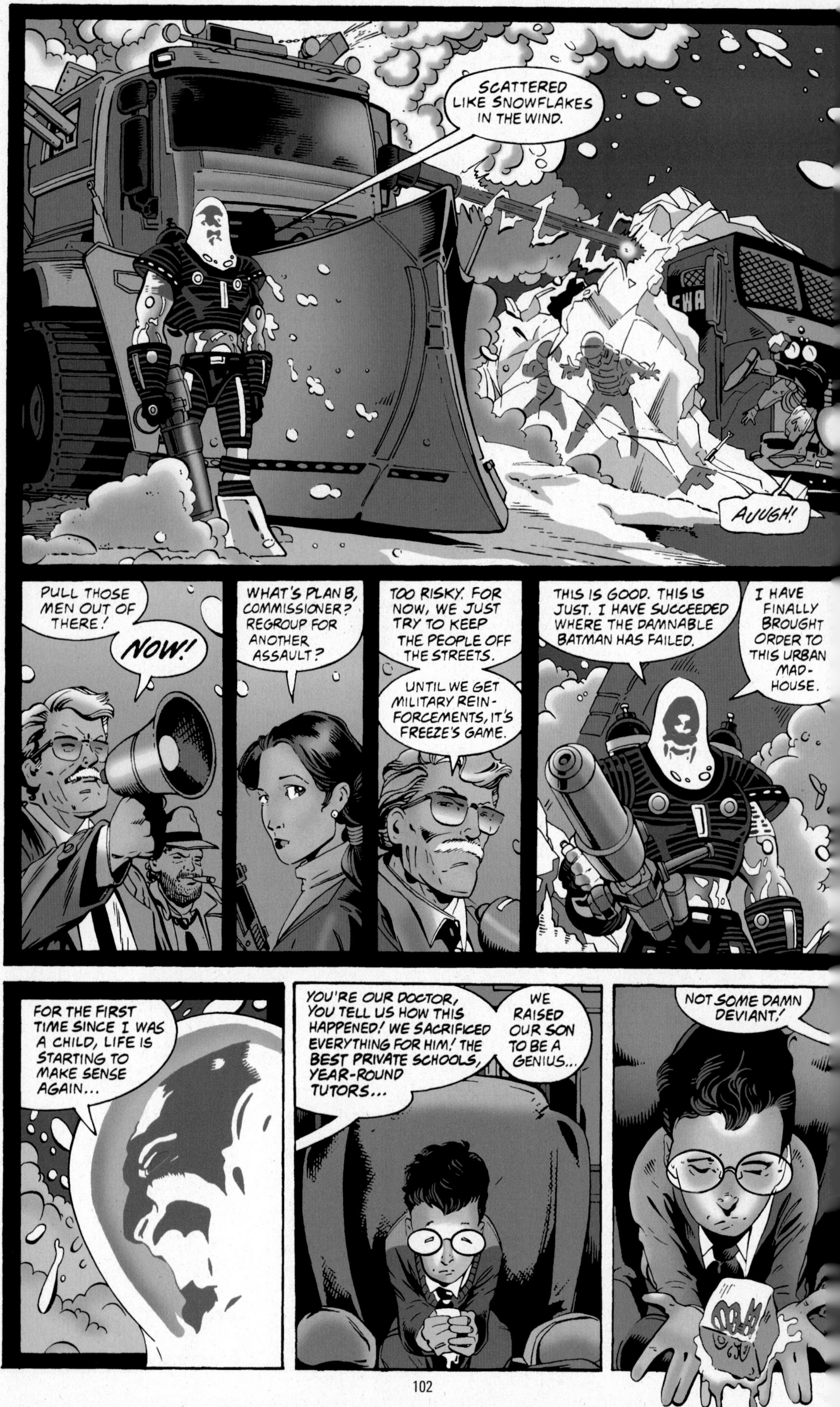

SCATTERED LIKE SNOWFLAKES IN THE WIND.
AUUGH!
PULL THOSE MEN OUT OF THERE!
NOW!
WHAT'S PLAN B, COMMISSIONER? REGROUP FOR ANOTHER ASSAULT?
TOO RISKY. FOR NOW, WE JUST TRY TO KEEP THE PEOPLE OFF THE STREETS.
UNTIL WE GET MILITARY REIN-FORCEMENTS, IT'S FREEZE'S GAME.
THIS IS GOOD. THIS IS JUST. I HAVE SUCCEEDED WHERE THE DAMNABLE BATMAN HAS FAILED.
I HAVE FINALLY BROUGHT ORDER TO THIS URBAN MAD-HOUSE.
FOR THE FIRST TIME SINCE I WAS A CHILD, LIFE IS STARTING TO MAKE SENSE AGAIN...
YOU'RE OUR DOCTOR, YOU TELL US HOW THIS HAPPENED! WE SACRIFICED EVERYTHING FOR HIM! THE BEST PRIVATE SCHOOLS, YEAR-ROUND TUTORS...
WE RAISED OUR SON TO BE A GENIUS...
NOT SOME DAMN DEVIANT!

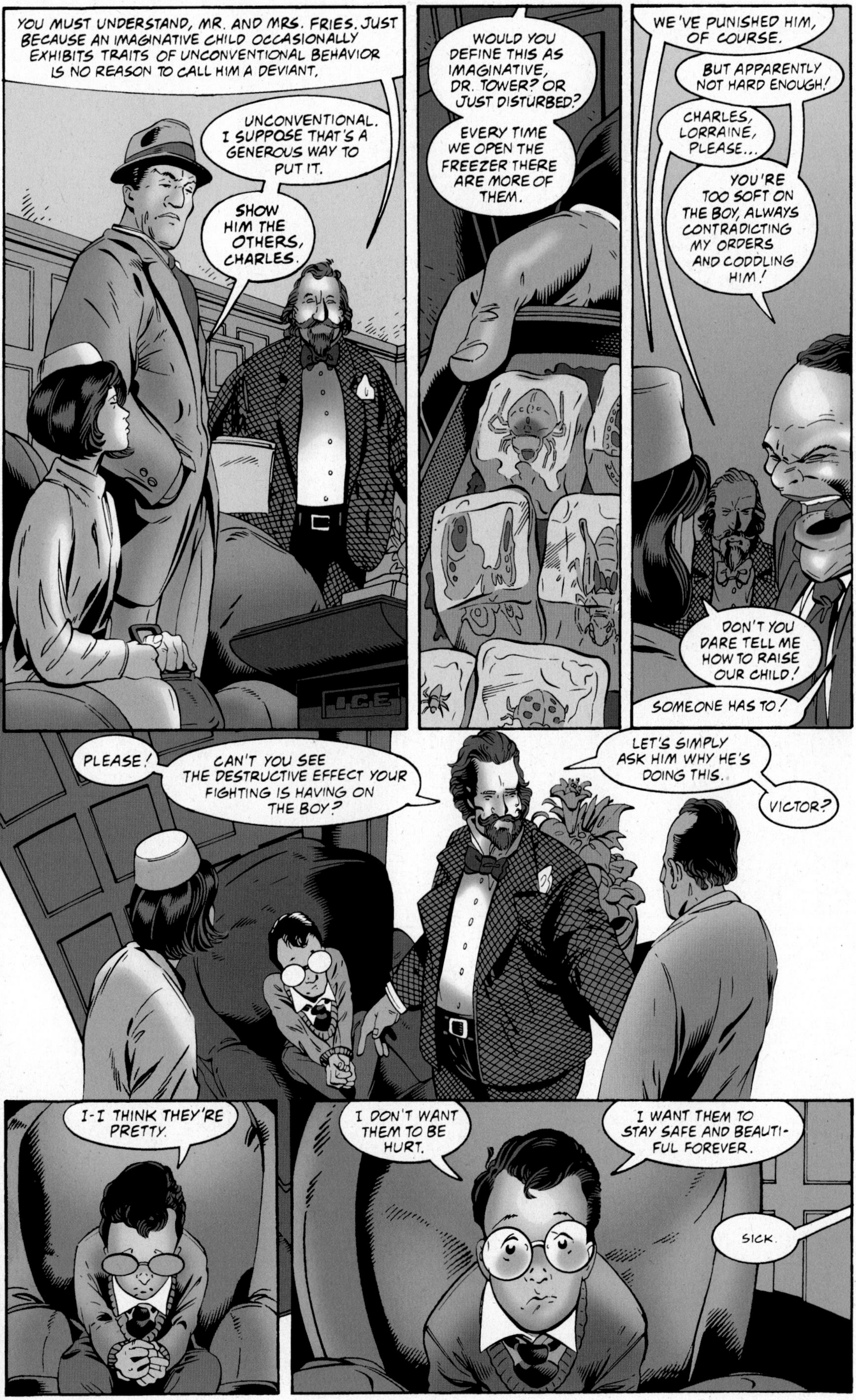
YOU MUST UNDERSTAND, MR. AND MRS. FRIES. JUST BECAUSE AN IMAGINATIVE CHILD OCCASIONALLY EXHIBITS TRAITS OF UNCONVENTIONAL BEHAVIOR IS NO REASON TO CALL HIM A DEVIANT.
UNCONVENTIONAL. I SUPPOSE THAT'S A GENEROUS WAY TO PUT IT.
SHOW HIM THE OTHERS, CHARLES.
WOULD YOU DEFINE THIS AS IMAGINATIVE, DR. TOWER? OR JUST DISTURBED?
EVERY TIME WE OPEN THE FREEZER THERE ARE MORE OF THEM.
I.C.E.
WE'VE PUNISHED HIM, OF COURSE.
BUT APPARENTLY NOT HARD ENOUGH!
CHARLES, LORRAINE, PLEASE...
YOU'RE TOO SOFT ON THE BOY, ALWAYS CONTRADICTING MY ORDERS AND CODDLING HIM!
DON'T YOU DARE TELL ME HOW TO RAISE OUR CHILD!
SOMEONE HAS TO!
PLEASE!
CAN'T YOU SEE THE DESTRUCTIVE EFFECT YOUR FIGHTING IS HAVING ON THE BOY?
LET'S SIMPLY ASK HIM WHY HE'S DOING THIS.
VICTOR?
I-I THINK THEY'RE PRETTY.
I DON'T WANT THEM TO BE HURT.
I WANT THEM TO STAY SAFE AND BEAUTIFUL FOREVER.
SICK.

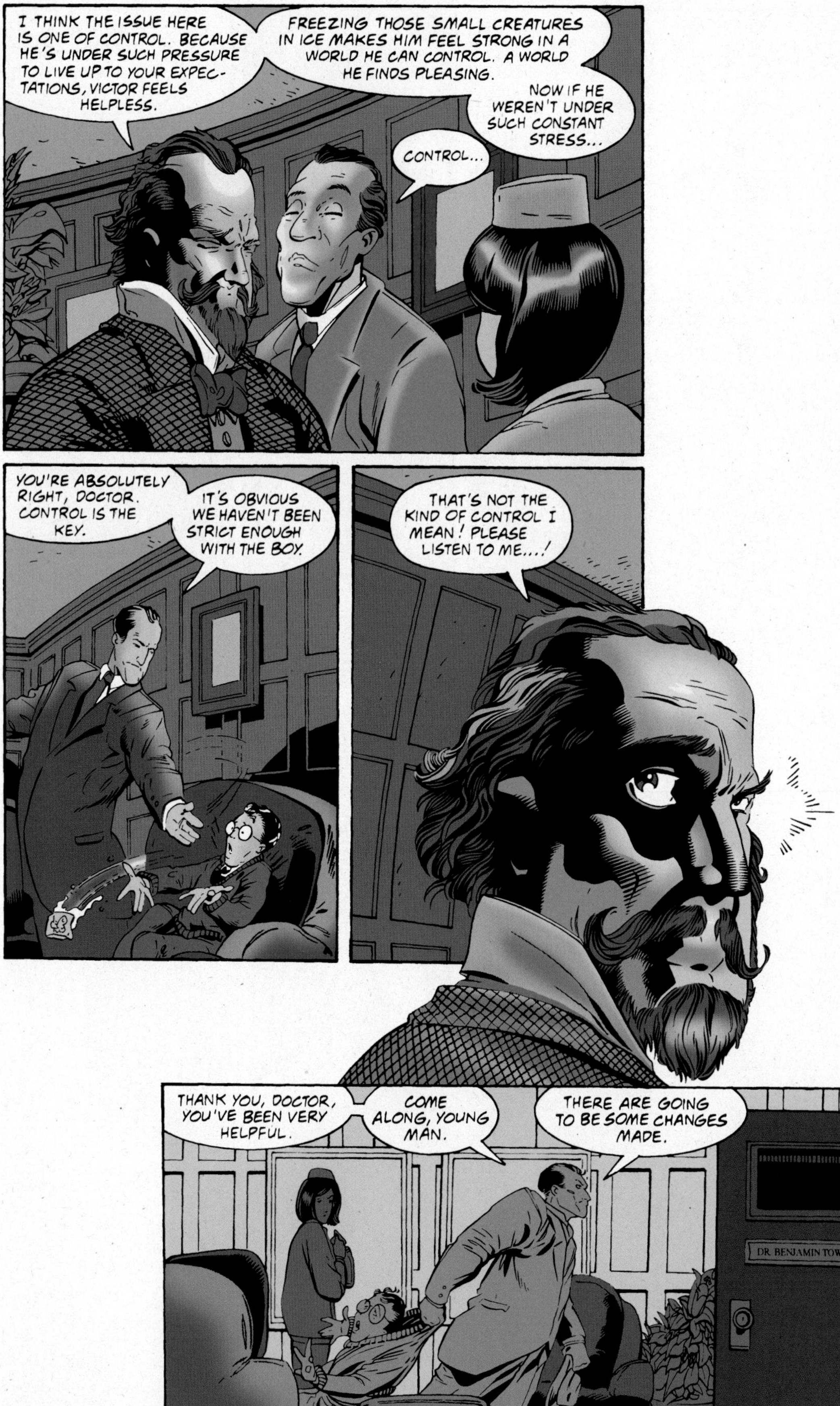
I THINK THE ISSUE HERE IS ONE OF CONTROL. BECAUSE HE'S UNDER SUCH PRESSURE TO LIVE UP TO YOUR EXPECTATIONS, VICTOR FEELS HELPLESS.
FREEZING THOSE SMALL CREATURES IN ICE MAKES HIM FEEL STRONG IN A WORLD HE CAN CONTROL. A WORLD HE FINDS PLEASING.
NOW IF HE WEREN'T UNDER SUCH CONSTANT STRESS...
CONTROL...
YOU'RE ABSOLUTELY RIGHT, DOCTOR. CONTROL IS THE KEY.
IT'S OBVIOUS WE HAVEN'T BEEN STRICT ENOUGH WITH THE BOY.
THAT'S NOT THE KIND OF CONTROL I MEAN! PLEASE LISTEN TO ME....!
THANK YOU, DOCTOR, YOU'VE BEEN VERY HELPFUL.
COME ALONG, YOUNG MAN.
THERE ARE GOING TO BE SOME CHANGES MADE.
DR. BENJAMIN TOWER

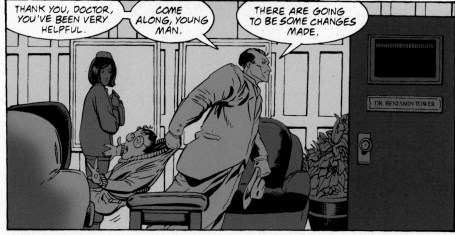

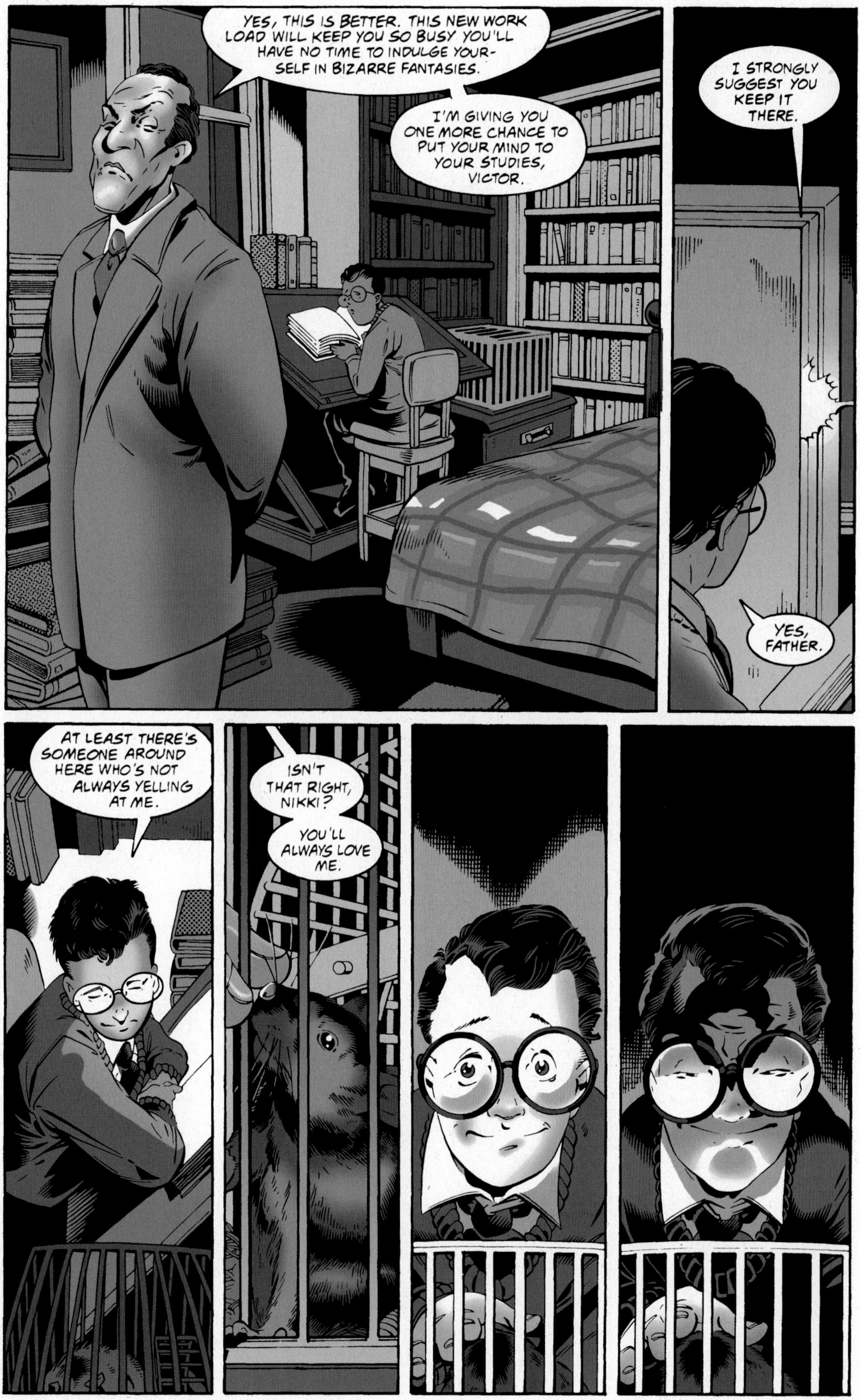
YES, THIS IS BETTER. THIS NEW WORK LOAD WILL KEEP YOU SO BUSY YOU'LL HAVE NO TIME TO INDULGE YOURSELF IN BIZARRE FANTASIES.
I'M GIVING YOU ONE MORE CHANCE TO PUT YOUR MIND TO YOUR STUDIES, VICTOR.
I STRONGLY SUGGEST YOU KEEP IT THERE.
YES, FATHER.
AT LEAST THERE'S SOMEONE AROUND HERE WHO'S NOT ALWAYS YELLING AT ME.
ISN'T THAT RIGHT, NIKKI?
YOU'LL ALWAYS LOVE ME.

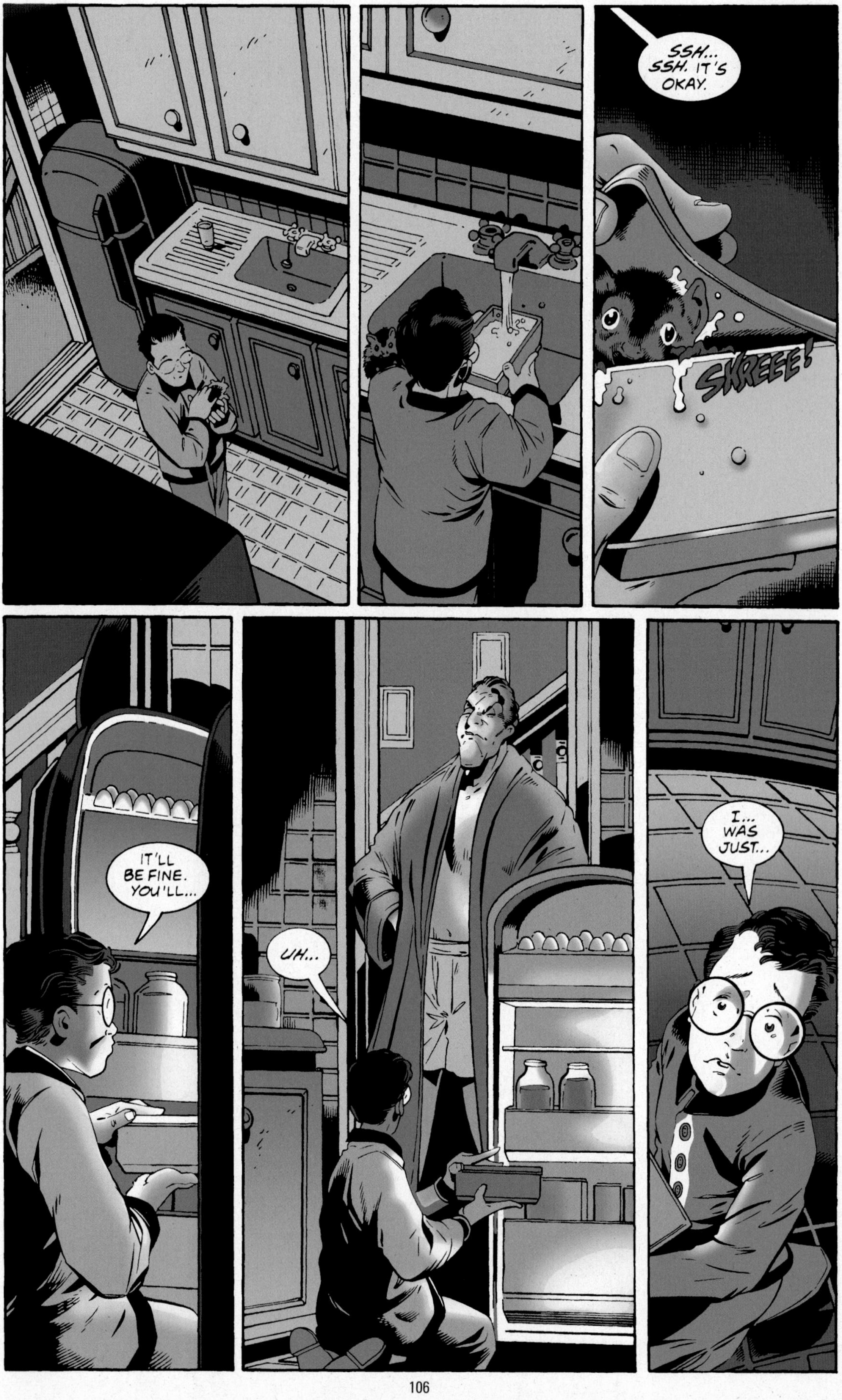
SSH... SSH. IT'S OKAY.
SKREEEE!
IT'LL BE FINE. YOU'LL...
UH...
I... WAS JUST...

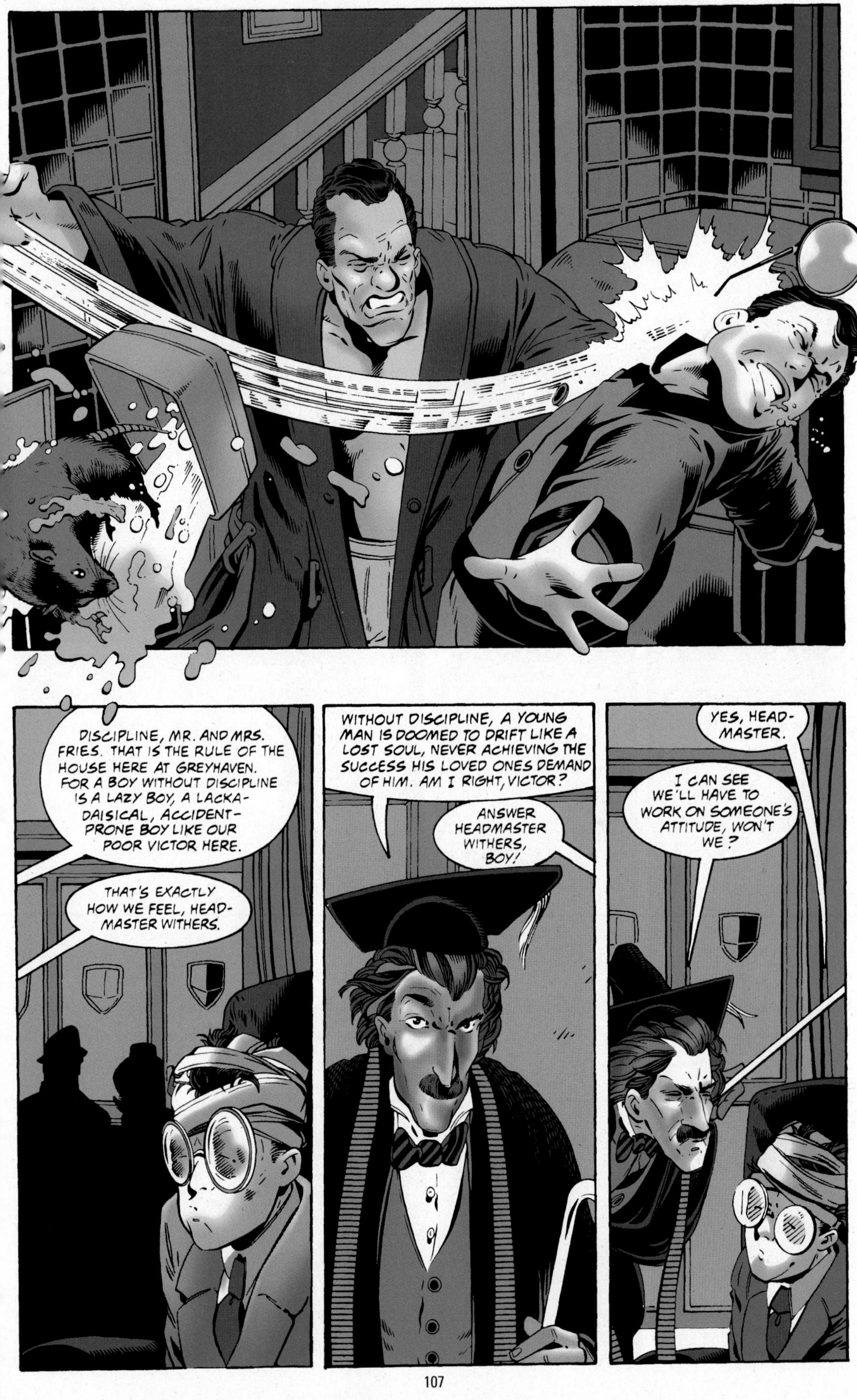
DISCIPLINE, MR. AND MRS. FRIES. THAT IS THE RULE OF THE HOUSE HERE AT GREYHAVEN. FOR A BOY WITHOUT DISCIPLINE IS A LAZY BOY, A LACKA-DAISICAL, ACCIDENT-PRONE BOY LIKE OUR POOR VICTOR HERE.
THAT'S EXACTLY HOW WE FEEL, HEAD-MASTER WITHERS.
WITHOUT DISCIPLINE, A YOUNG MAN IS DOOMED TO DRIFT LIKE A LOST SOUL, NEVER ACHIEVING THE SUCCESS HIS LOVED ONES DEMAND OF HIM. AM I RIGHT, VICTOR?
ANSWER HEADMASTER WITHERS, BOY!
YES, HEAD-MASTER.
I CAN SEE WE'LL HAVE TO WORK ON SOMEONE'S ATTITUDE, WON'T WE?

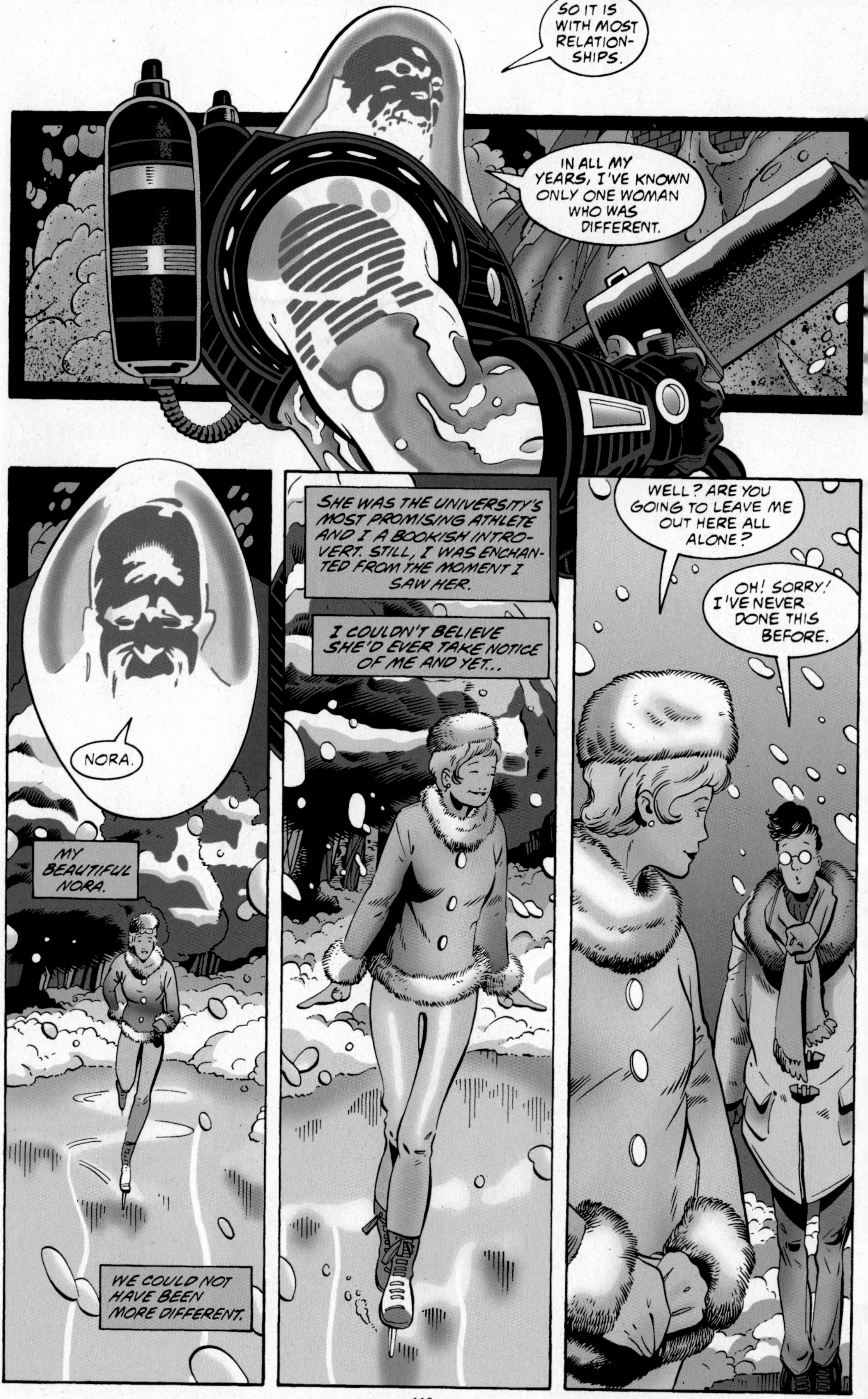

SO IT IS WITH MOST RELATION-SHIPS.
IN ALL MY YEARS, I'VE KNOWN ONLY ONE WOMAN WHO WAS DIFFERENT.
NORA.
MY BEAUTIFUL NORA.
WE COULD NOT HAVE BEEN MORE DIFFERENT.
SHE WAS THE UNIVERSITY'S MOST PROMISING ATHLETE AND I A BOOKISH INTRO-VERT. STILL, I WAS ENCHAN-TED FROM THE MOMENT I SAW HER.
I COULDN'T BELIEVE SHE'D EVER TAKE NOTICE OF ME AND YET...
WELL? ARE YOU GOING TO LEAVE ME OUT HERE ALL ALONE?
OH! SORRY! I'VE NEVER DONE THIS BEFORE.

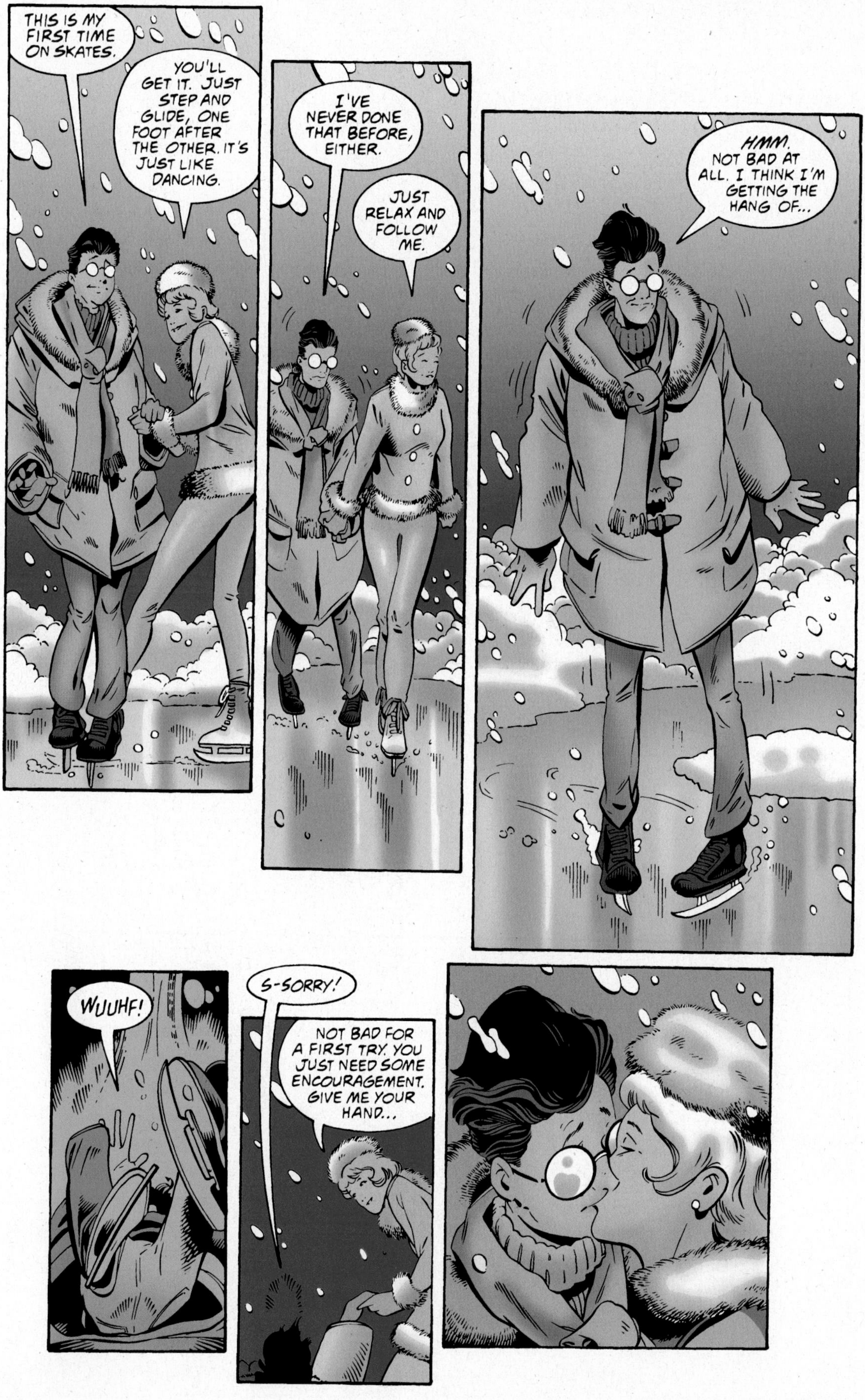
THIS IS MY FIRST TIME ON SKATES.
YOU'LL GET IT. JUST STEP AND GLIDE, ONE FOOT AFTER THE OTHER. IT'S JUST LIKE DANCING.
I'VE NEVER DONE THAT BEFORE, EITHER.
JUST RELAX AND FOLLOW ME.
HMM. NOT BAD AT ALL. I THINK I'M GETTING THE HANG OF...
WUUHF!
S-SORRY!
NOT BAD FOR A FIRST TRY. YOU JUST NEED SOME ENCOURAGEMENT. GIVE ME YOUR HAND...

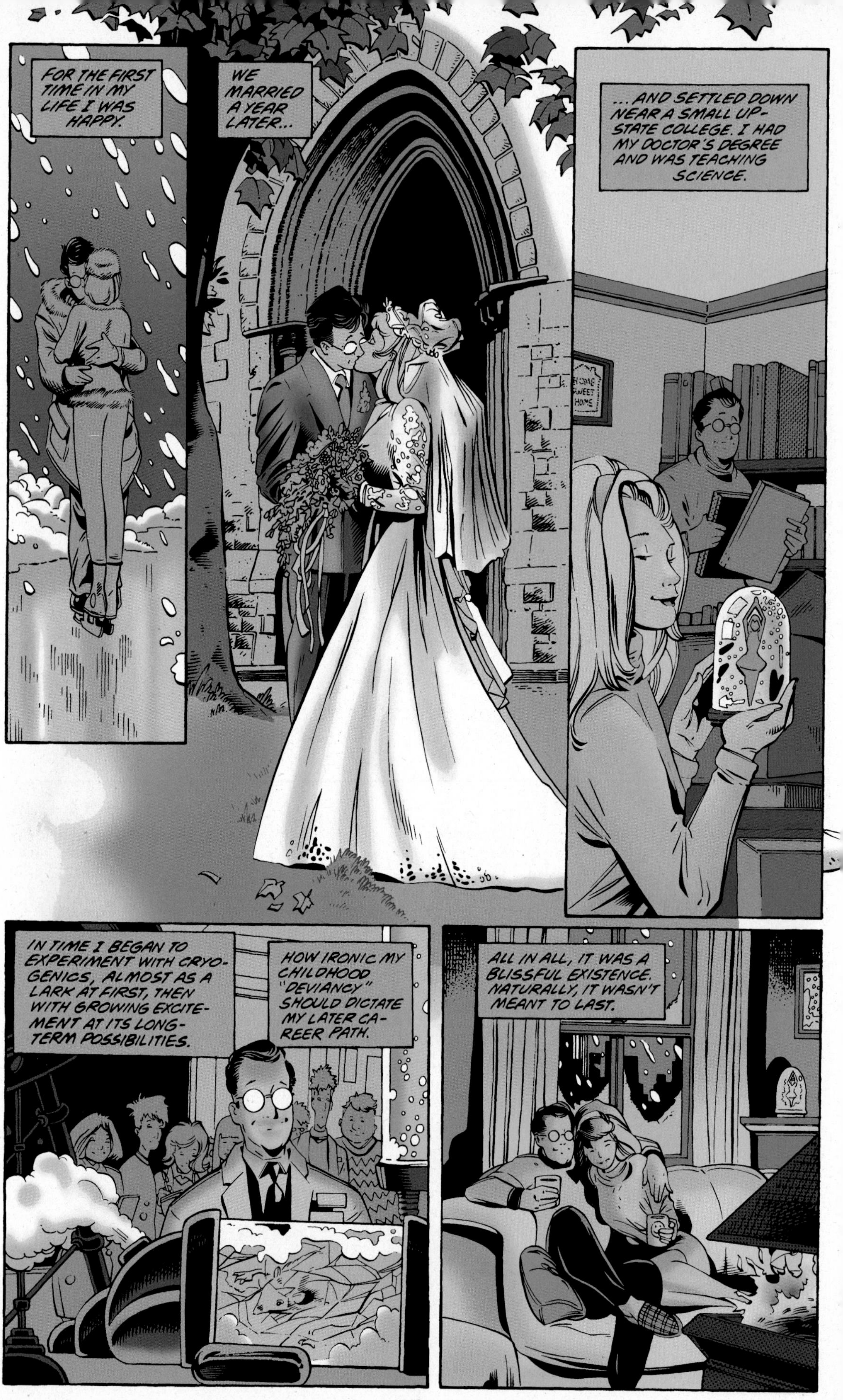
FOR THE FIRST TIME IN MY LIFE I WAS HAPPY.
WE MARRIED A YEAR LATER...
...AND SETTLED DOWN NEAR A SMALL UP-STATE COLLEGE. I HAD MY DOCTOR'S DEGREE AND WAS TEACHING SCIENCE.
IN TIME I BEGAN TO EXPERIMENT WITH CRYO-GENICS, ALMOST AS A LARK AT FIRST, THEN WITH GROWING EXCITE-MENT AT ITS LONG-TERM POSSIBILITIES.
HOW IRONIC MY CHILDHOOD "DEVIANCY" SHOULD DICTATE MY LATER CA-REER PATH.
ALL IN ALL, IT WAS A BLISSFUL EXISTENCE. NATURALLY, IT WASN'T MEANT TO LAST.

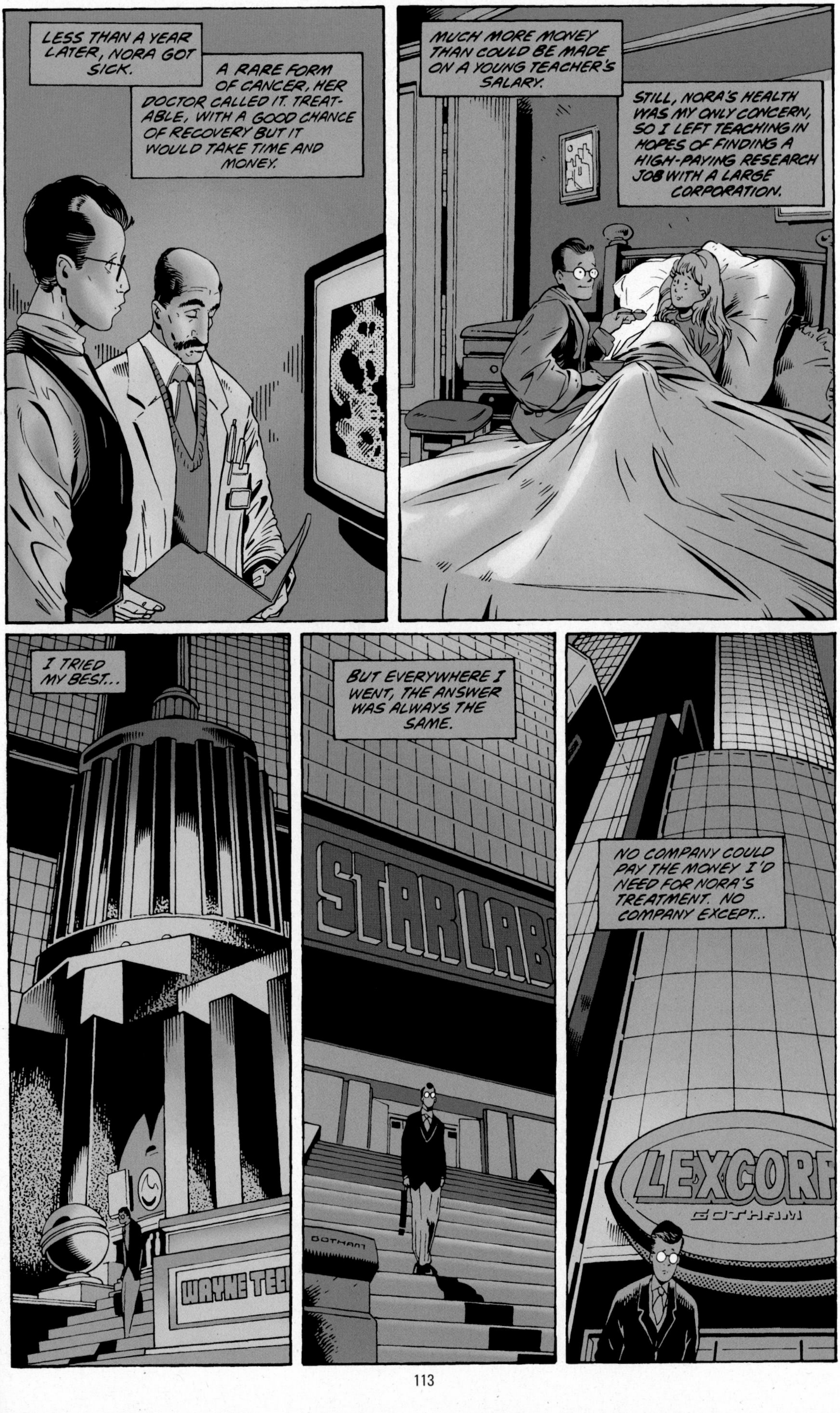
LESS THAN A YEAR LATER, NORA GOT SICK.
A RARE FORM OF CANCER, HER DOCTOR CALLED IT. TREAT-ABLE, WITH A GOOD CHANCE OF RECOVERY BUT IT WOULD TAKE TIME AND MONEY.
MUCH MORE MONEY THAN COULD BE MADE ON A YOUNG TEACHER'S SALARY.
STILL, NORA'S HEALTH WAS MY ONLY CONCERN, SO I LEFT TEACHING IN HOPES OF FINDING A HIGH-PAYING RESEARCH JOB WITH A LARGE CORPORATION.
I TRIED MY BEST...
WAYNE TEC
BUT EVERYWHERE I WENT, THE ANSWER WAS ALWAYS THE SAME.
STARLAB
GOTHAM
NO COMPANY COULD PAY THE MONEY I'D NEED FOR NORA'S TREATMENT. NO COMPANY EXCEPT...
LEXCORP
GOTHAM

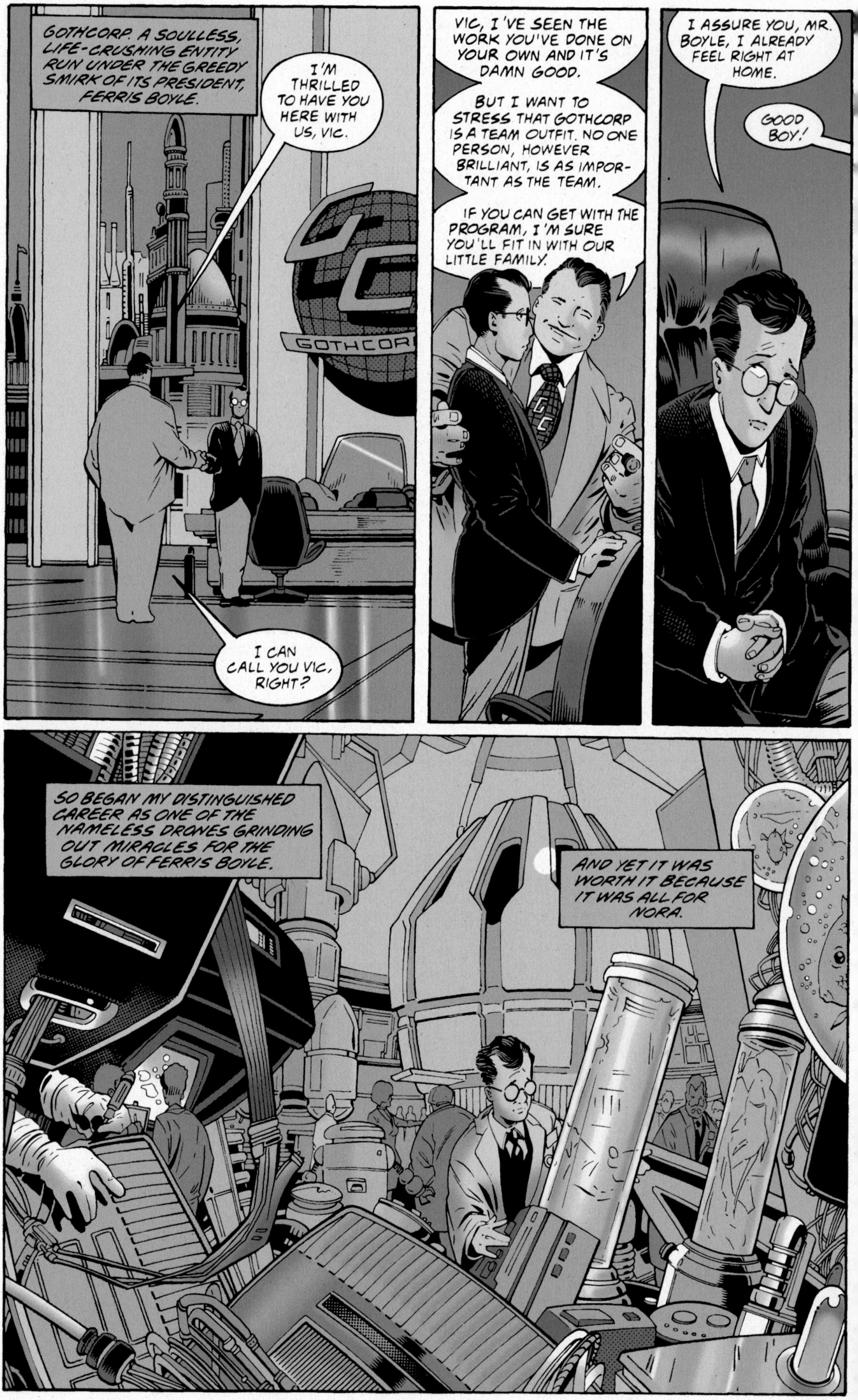
GOTHCORP. A SOULLESS, LIFE-CRUSHING ENTITY RUN UNDER THE GREEDY SMIRK OF ITS PRESIDENT, FERRIS BOYLE.
I'M THRILLED TO HAVE YOU HERE WITH US, VIC.
GOTHCORP
I CAN CALL YOU VIC, RIGHT?
VIC, I'VE SEEN THE WORK YOU'VE DONE ON YOUR OWN AND IT'S DAMN GOOD.
BUT I WANT TO STRESS THAT GOTHCORP IS A TEAM OUTFIT. NO ONE PERSON, HOWEVER BRILLIANT, IS AS IMPORTANT AS THE TEAM.
IF YOU CAN GET WITH THE PROGRAM, I'M SURE YOU'LL FIT IN WITH OUR LITTLE FAMILY.
I ASSURE YOU, MR. BOYLE, I ALREADY FEEL RIGHT AT HOME.
GOOD BOY!
SO BEGAN MY DISTINGUISHED CAREER AS ONE OF THE NAMELESS DRONES GRINDING OUT MIRACLES FOR THE GLORY OF FERRIS BOYLE.
AND YET IT WAS WORTH IT BECAUSE IT WAS ALL FOR NORA.

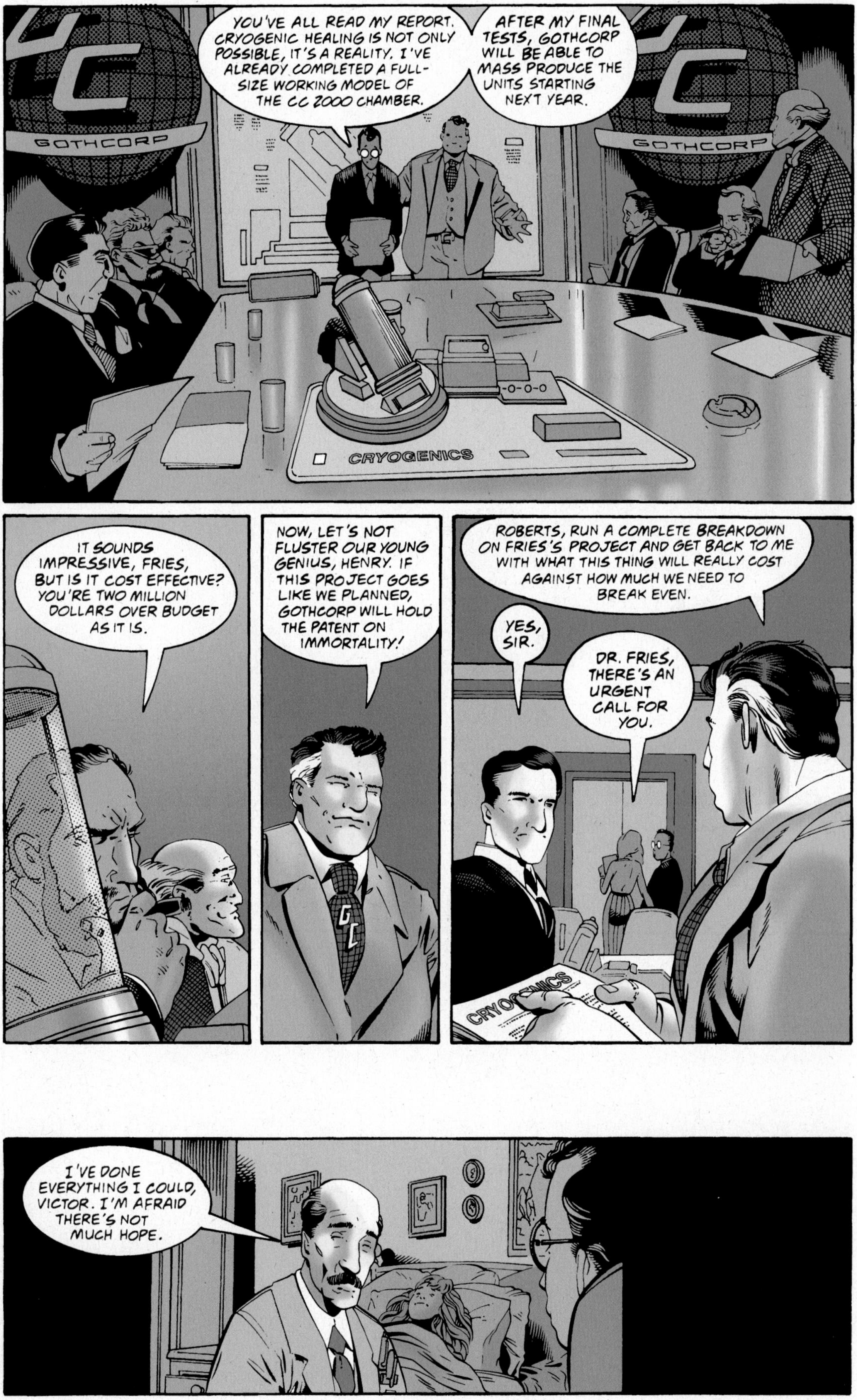
YOU'VE ALL READ MY REPORT. CRYOGENIC HEALING IS NOT ONLY POSSIBLE, IT'S A REALITY. I'VE ALREADY COMPLETED A FULL-SIZE WORKING MODEL OF THE CC 2000 CHAMBER.
AFTER MY FINAL TESTS, GOTHCORP WILL BE ABLE TO MASS PRODUCE THE UNITS STARTING NEXT YEAR.
GOTHCORP
GOTHCORP
CRYOGENICS
IT SOUNDS IMPRESSIVE, FRIES, BUT IS IT COST EFFECTIVE? YOU'RE TWO MILLION DOLLARS OVER BUDGET AS IT IS.
NOW, LET'S NOT FLUSTER OUR YOUNG GENIUS, HENRY. IF THIS PROJECT GOES LIKE WE PLANNED, GOTHCORP WILL HOLD THE PATENT ON IMMORTALITY!
ROBERTS, RUN A COMPLETE BREAKDOWN ON FRIES'S PROJECT AND GET BACK TO ME WITH WHAT THIS THING WILL REALLY COST AGAINST HOW MUCH WE NEED TO BREAK EVEN.
YES, SIR.
DR. FRIES, THERE'S AN URGENT CALL FOR YOU.
CRYOGENICS
I'VE DONE EVERYTHING I COULD, VICTOR. I'M AFRAID THERE'S NOT MUCH HOPE.

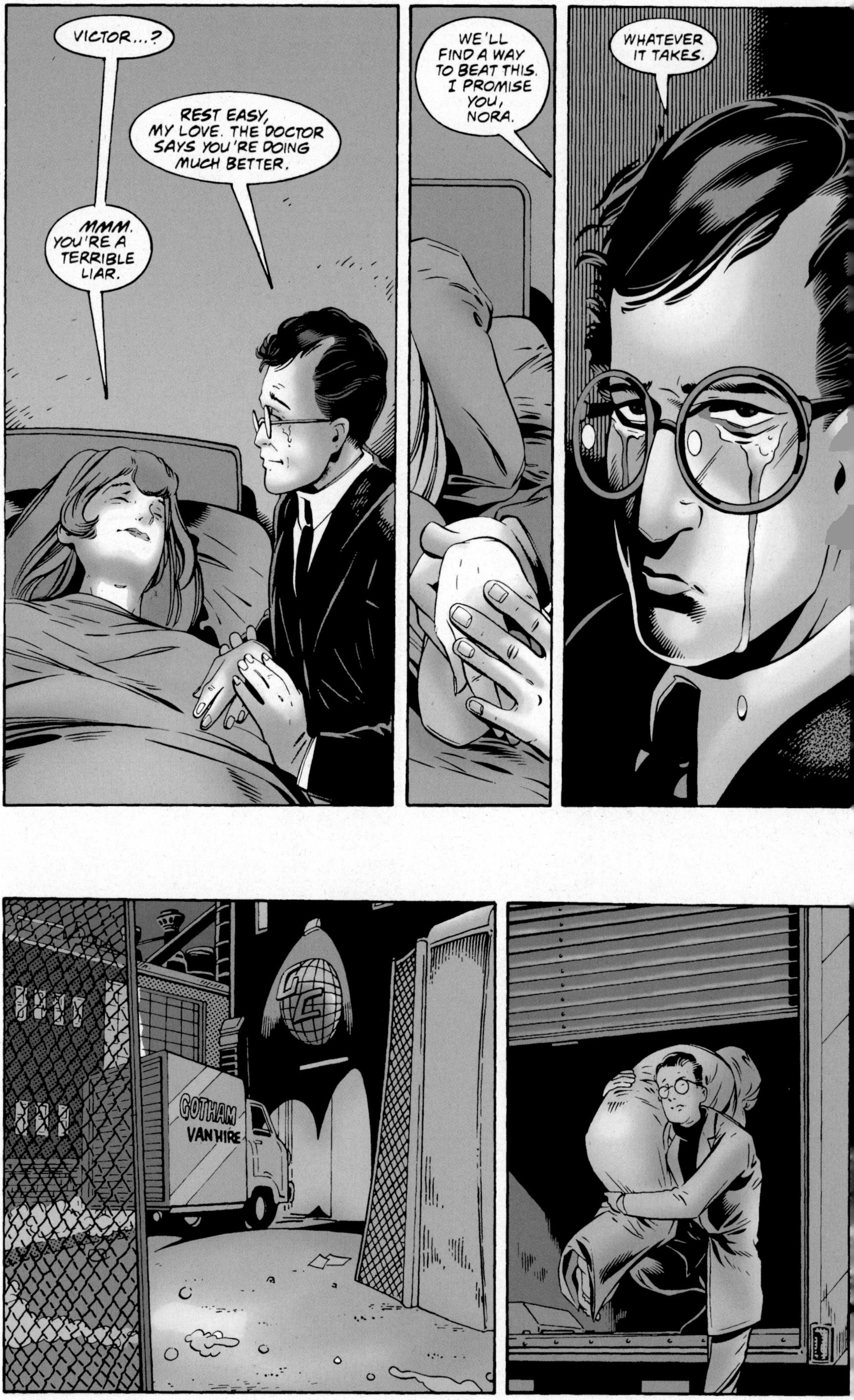
VICTOR...?
REST EASY, MY LOVE. THE DOCTOR SAYS YOU'RE DOING MUCH BETTER.
MMM. YOU'RE A TERRIBLE LIAR.
WE'LL FIND A WAY TO BEAT THIS. I PROMISE YOU, NORA.
WHATEVER IT TAKES.
GOTHAM
VANHIRE

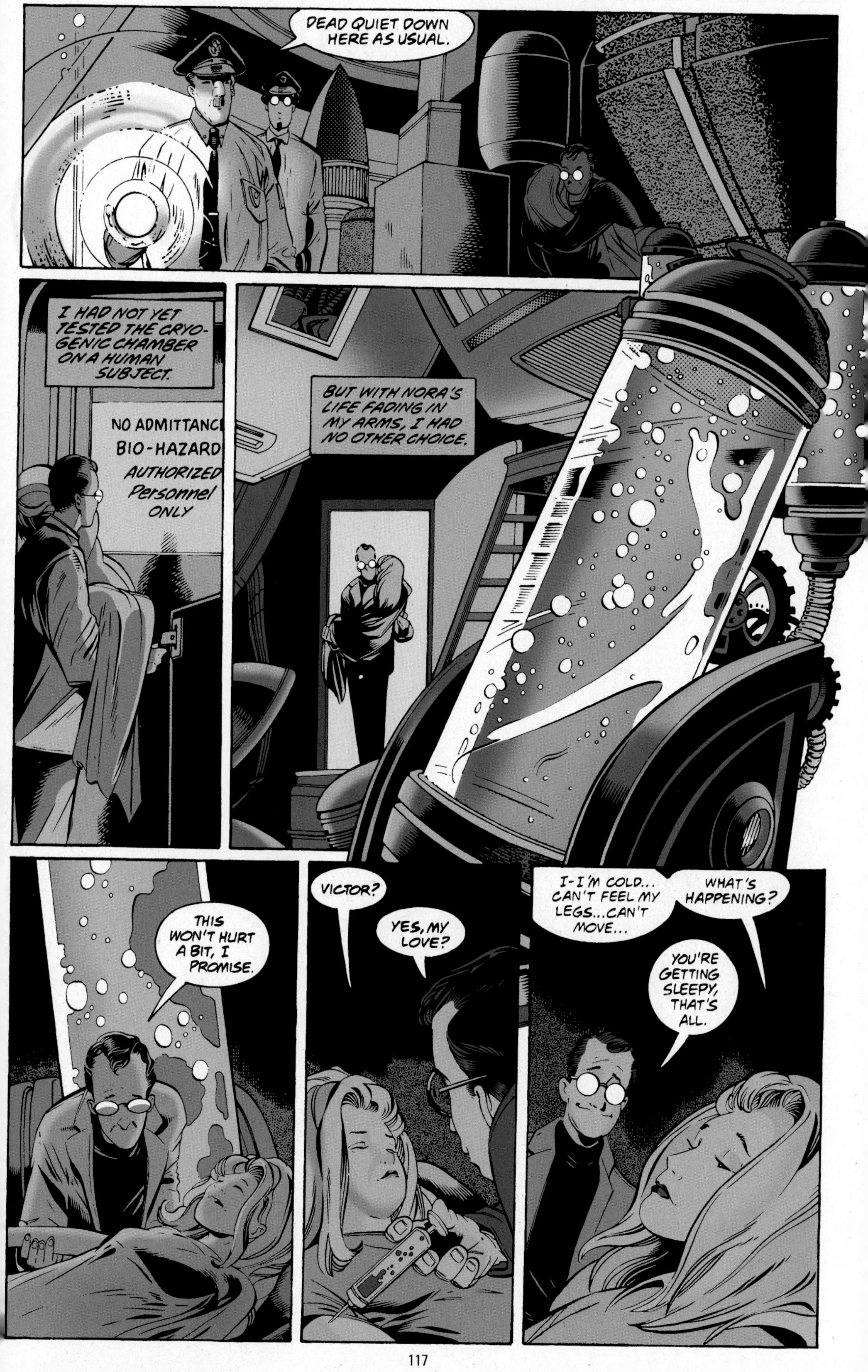
DEAD QUIET DOWN HERE AS USUAL.
I HAD NOT YET TESTED THE CRYOGENIC CHAMBER ON A HUMAN SUBJECT.
NO ADMITTANCE
BIO-HAZARD
AUTHORIZED Personnel ONLY
BUT WITH NORA'S LIFE FADING IN MY ARMS, I HAD NO OTHER CHOICE.
THIS WON'T HURT A BIT, I PROMISE.
VICTOR?
YES, MY LOVE?
I-I'M COLD... CAN'T FEEL MY LEGS...CAN'T MOVE...
WHAT'S HAPPENING?
YOU'RE GETTING SLEEPY, THAT'S ALL.

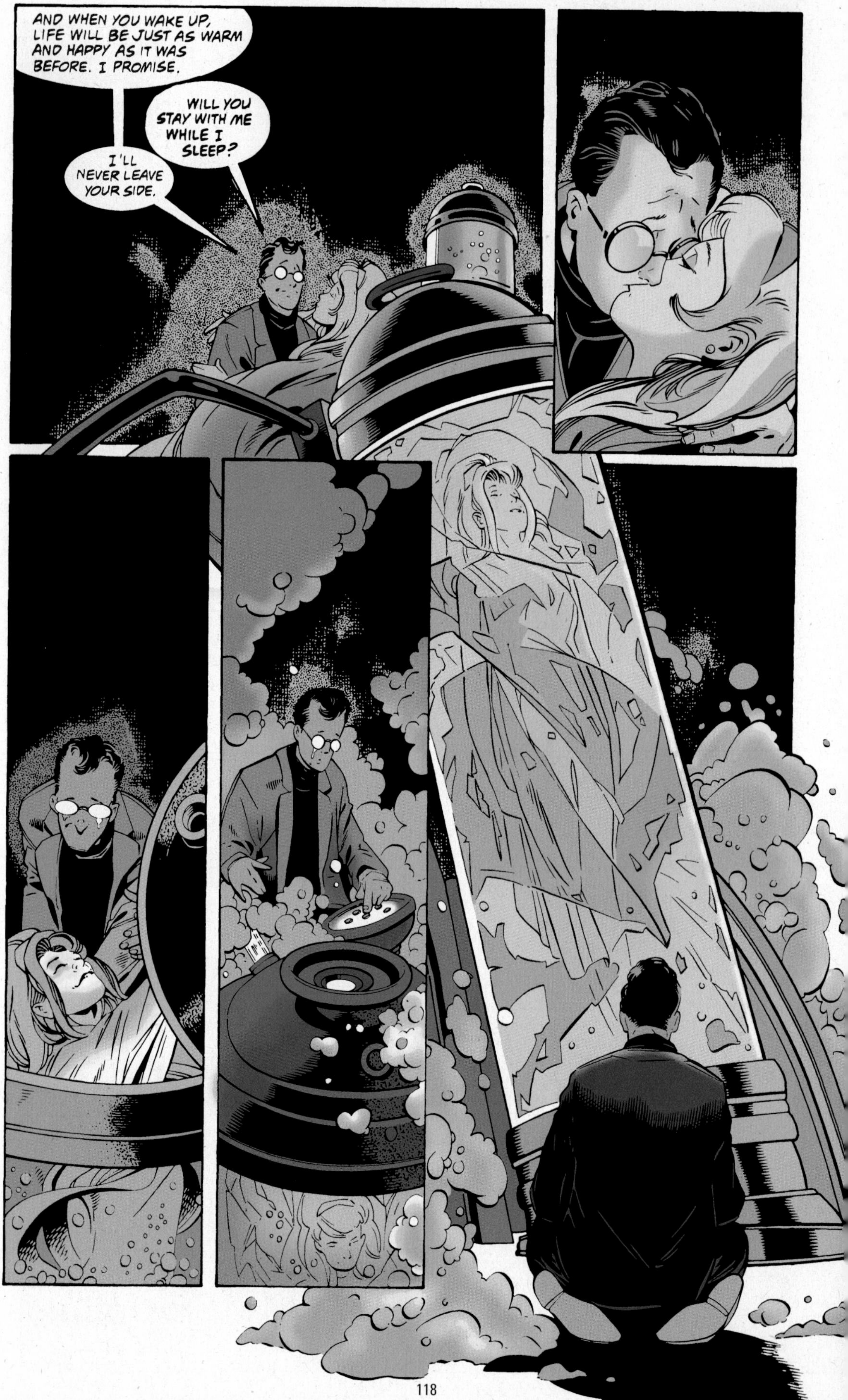
AND WHEN YOU WAKE UP, LIFE WILL BE JUST AS WARM AND HAPPY AS IT WAS BEFORE. I PROMISE.
WILL YOU STAY WITH ME WHILE I SLEEP?
I'LL NEVER LEAVE YOUR SIDE.

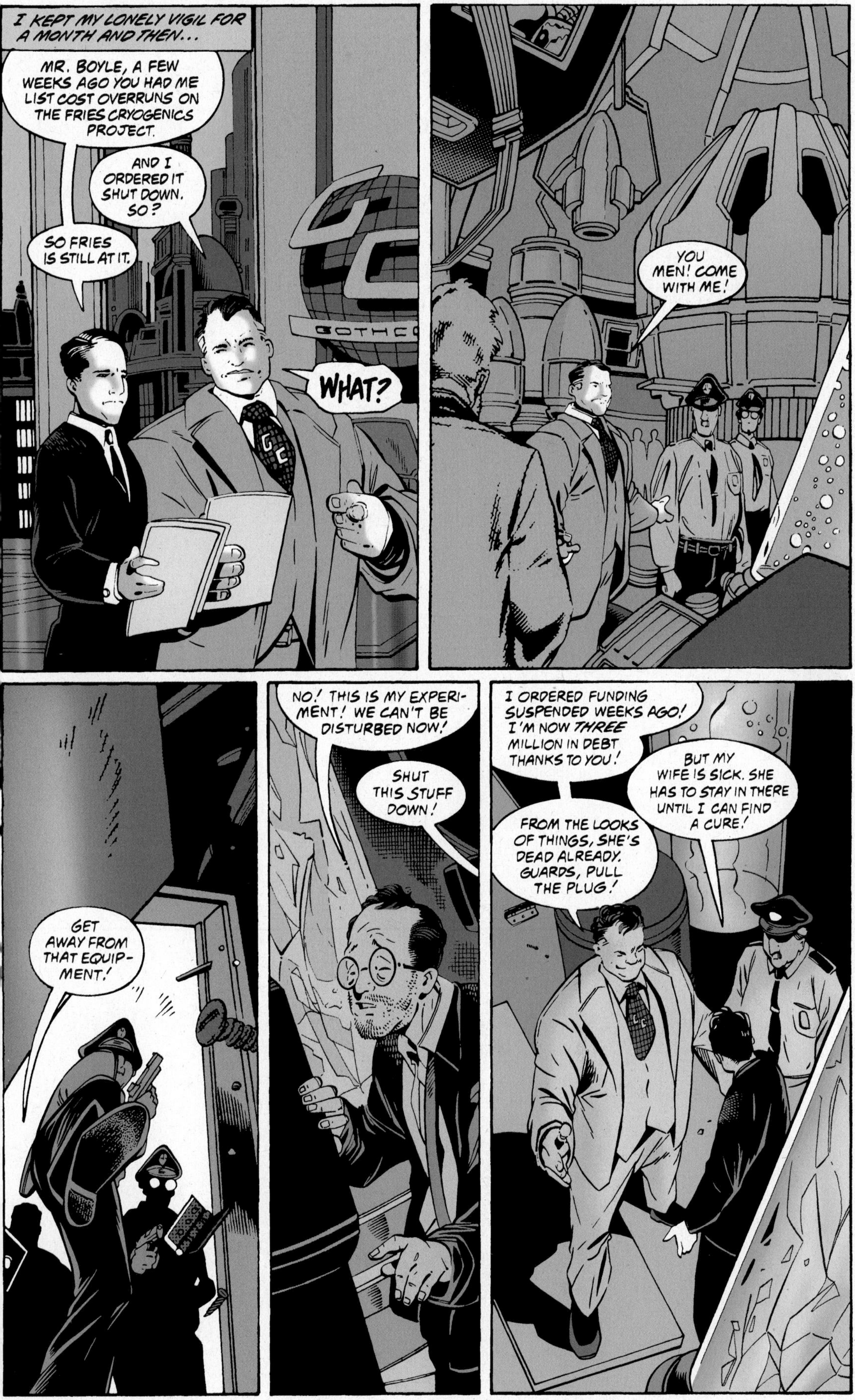
I KEPT MY LONELY VIGIL FOR A MONTH AND THEN...
MR. BOYLE, A FEW WEEKS AGO YOU HAD ME LIST COST OVERRUNS ON THE FRIES CRYOGENICS PROJECT.
AND I ORDERED IT SHUT DOWN. SO?
SO FRIES IS STILL AT IT.
WHAT?
GOTHCO
YOU MEN! COME WITH ME!
NO! THIS IS MY EXPERIMENT! WE CAN'T BE DISTURBED NOW!
SHUT THIS STUFF DOWN!
GET AWAY FROM THAT EQUIPMENT!
I ORDERED FUNDING SUSPENDED WEEKS AGO! I'M NOW THREE MILLION IN DEBT, THANKS TO YOU!
BUT MY WIFE IS SICK. SHE HAS TO STAY IN THERE UNTIL I CAN FIND A CURE!
FROM THE LOOKS OF THINGS, SHE'S DEAD ALREADY. GUARDS, PULL THE PLUG!

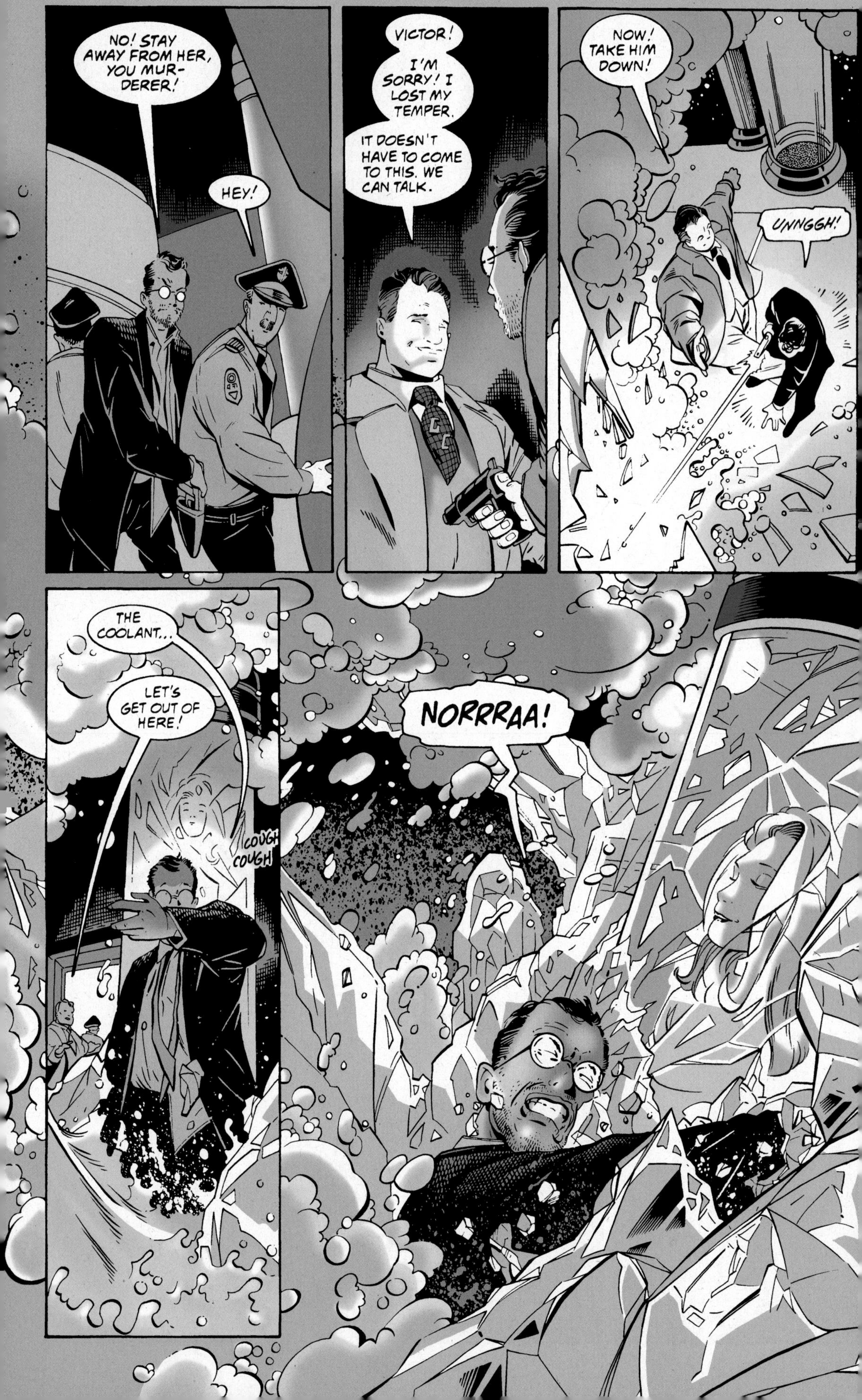
NO! STAY AWAY FROM HER, YOU MUR-DERER!
HEY!
VICTOR!
I'M SORRY! I LOST MY TEMPER.
IT DOESN'T HAVE TO COME TO THIS. WE CAN TALK.
NOW! TAKE HIM DOWN!
UNNGGH!
THE COOLANT...
LET'S GET OUT OF HERE!
COUGH COUGH
NORRRAA!

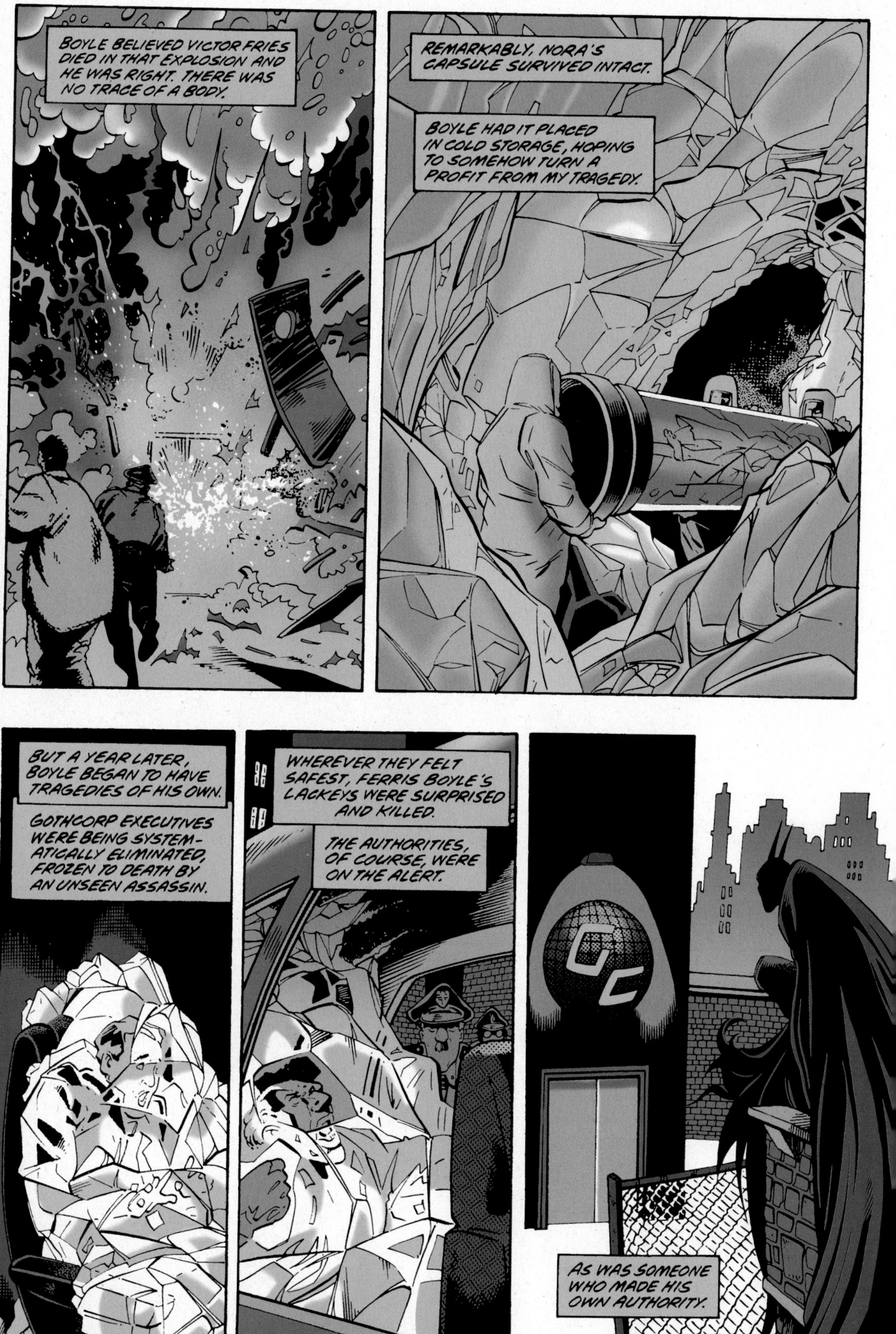
BOYLE BELIEVED VICTOR FRIES DIED IN THAT EXPLOSION AND HE WAS RIGHT. THERE WAS NO TRACE OF A BODY.
REMARKABLY, NORA'S CAPSULE SURVIVED INTACT.
BOYLE HAD IT PLACED IN COLD STORAGE, HOPING TO SOMEHOW TURN A PROFIT FROM MY TRAGEDY.
BUT A YEAR LATER, BOYLE BEGAN TO HAVE TRAGEDIES OF HIS OWN.
GOTHCORP EXECUTIVES WERE BEING SYSTEM-ATICALLY ELIMINATED, FROZEN TO DEATH BY AN UNSEEN ASSASSIN.
WHEREVER THEY FELT SAFEST, FERRIS BOYLE'S LACKEYS WERE SURPRISED AND KILLED.
THE AUTHORITIES, OF COURSE, WERE ON THE ALERT.
AS WAS SOMEONE WHO MADE HIS OWN AUTHORITY.

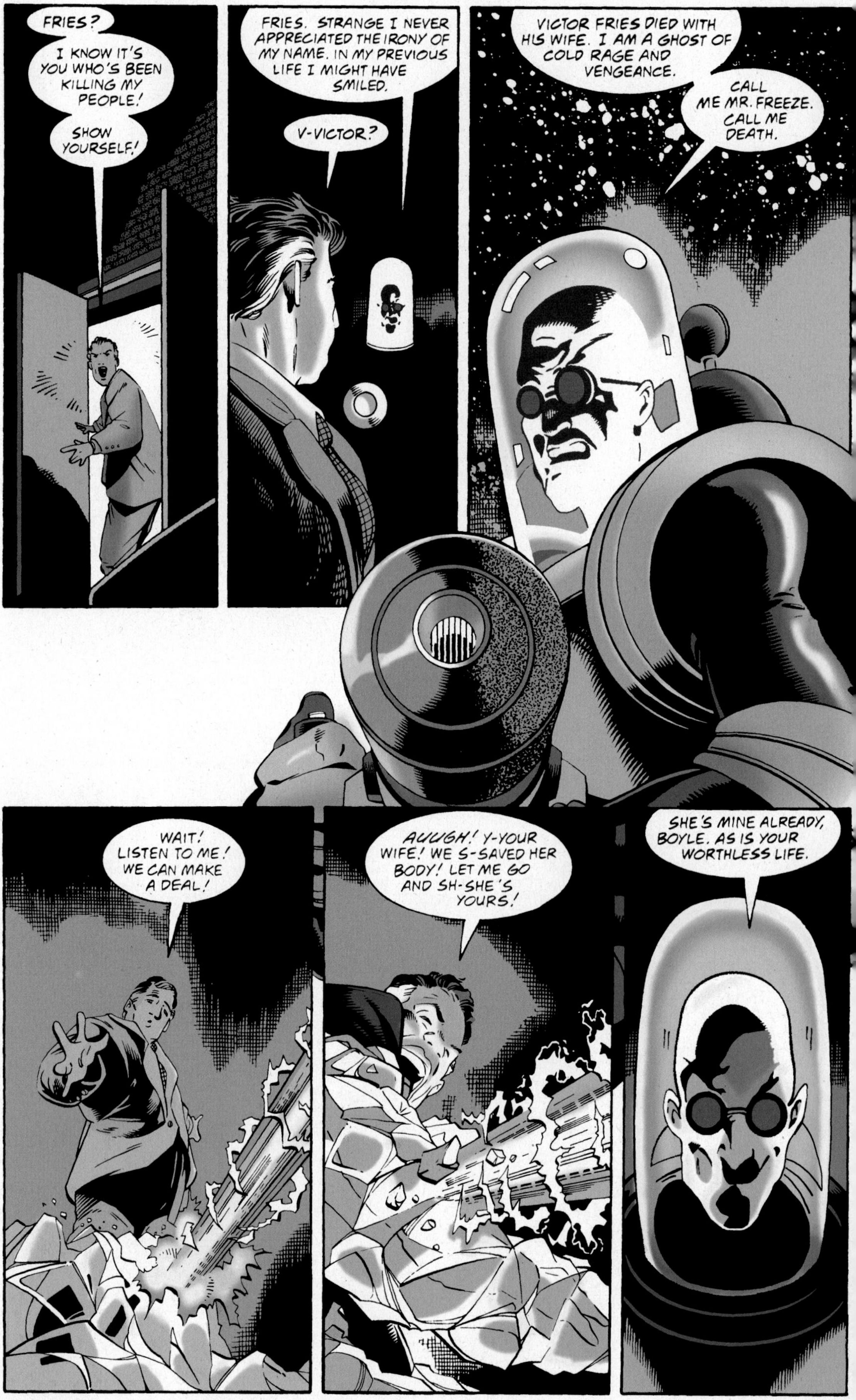
FRIES?
I KNOW IT'S YOU WHO'S BEEN KILLING MY PEOPLE!
SHOW YOURSELF!
FRIES. STRANGE I NEVER APPRECIATED THE IRONY OF MY NAME. IN MY PREVIOUS LIFE I MIGHT HAVE SMILED.
V-VICTOR?
VICTOR FRIES DIED WITH HIS WIFE. I AM A GHOST OF COLD RAGE AND VENGEANCE.
CALL ME MR. FREEZE. CALL ME DEATH.
WAIT! LISTEN TO ME! WE CAN MAKE A DEAL!
AUUGH! Y-YOUR WIFE! WE S-SAVED HER BODY! LET ME GO AND SH-SHE'S YOURS!
SHE'S MINE ALREADY, BOYLE. AS IS YOUR WORTHLESS LIFE.

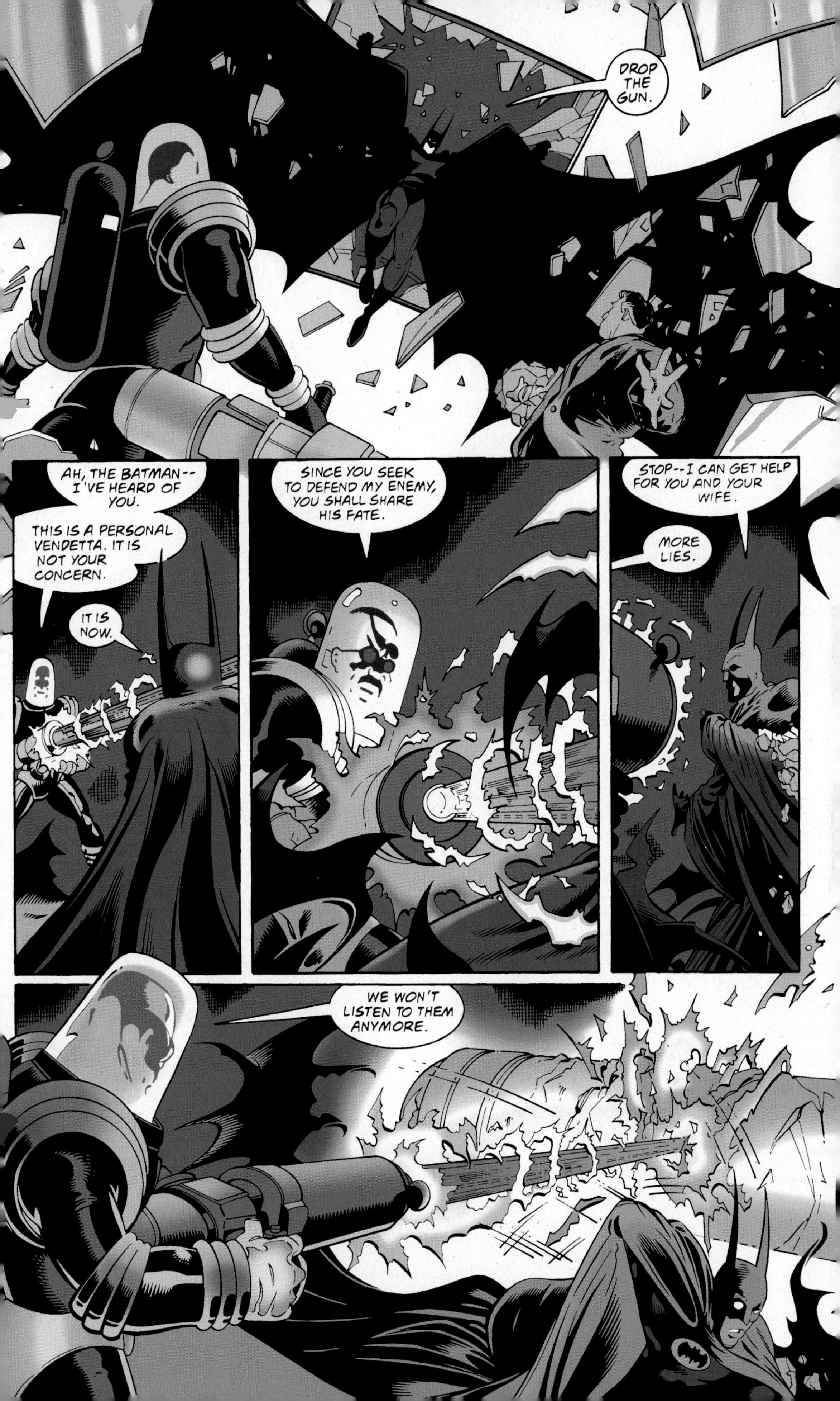
DROP THE GUN.
AH, THE BATMAN-- I'VE HEARD OF YOU.
THIS IS A PERSONAL VENDETTA. IT IS NOT YOUR CONCERN.
IT IS NOW.
SINCE YOU SEEK TO DEFEND MY ENEMY, YOU SHALL SHARE HIS FATE.
STOP--I CAN GET HELP FOR YOU AND YOUR WIFE.
MORE LIES.
WE WON'T LISTEN TO THEM ANYMORE.

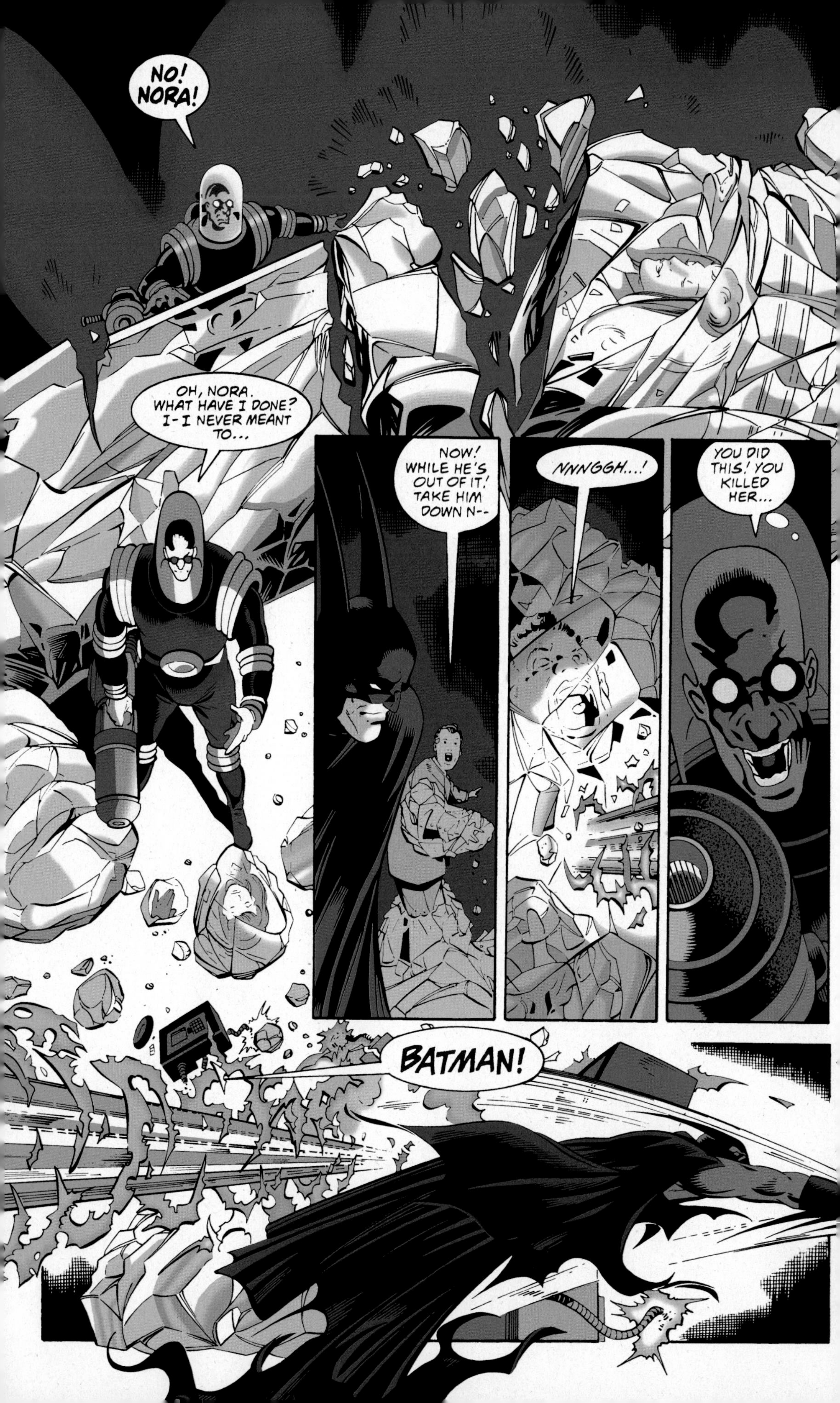
NO! NORA!
OH, NORA. WHAT HAVE I DONE? I-- I NEVER MEANT TO...
NOW! WHILE HE'S OUT OF IT! TAKE HIM DOWN N--
NNNGGH...!
YOU DID THIS! YOU KILLED HER...
BATMAN!

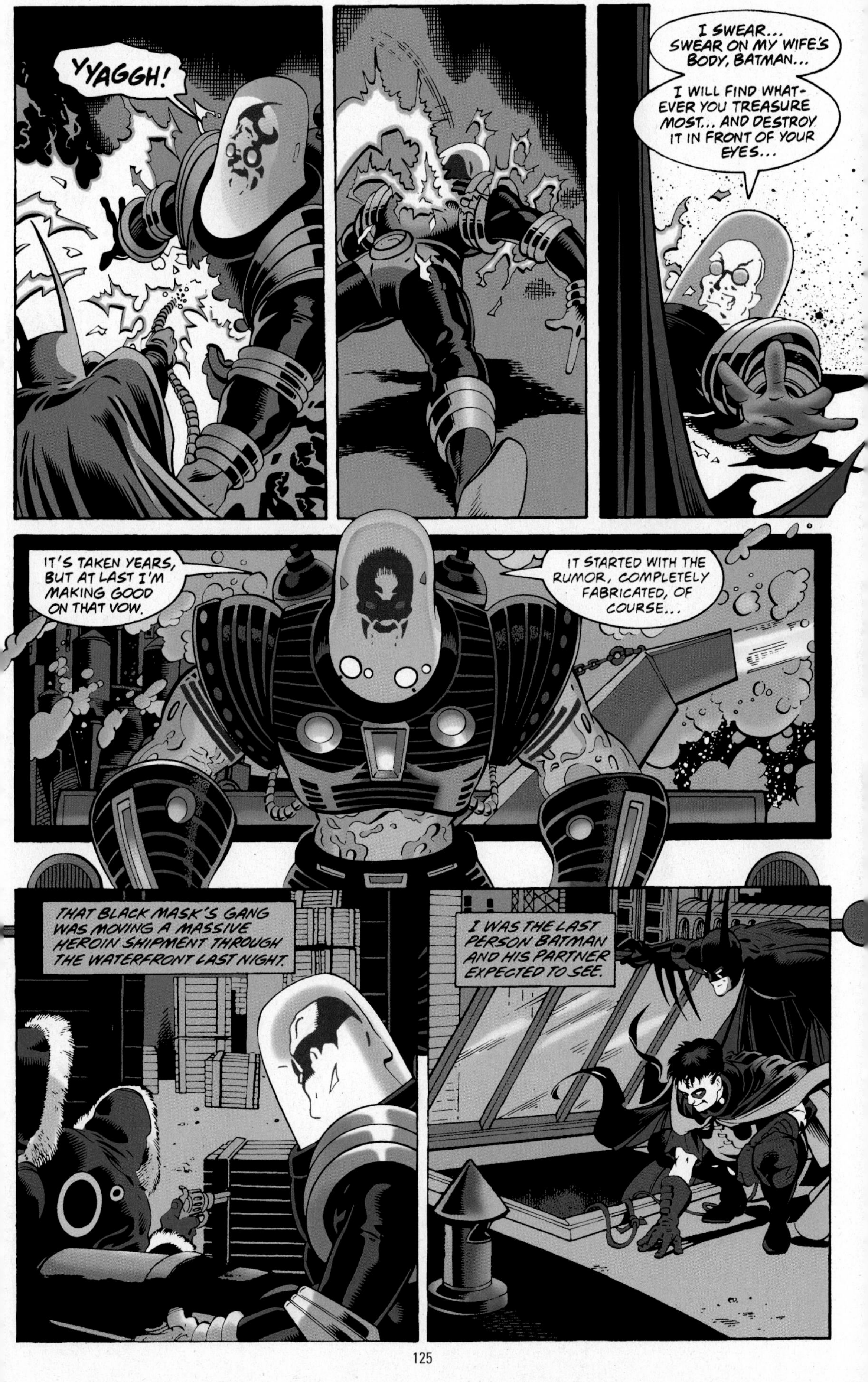
YYAGGH!
I SWEAR... SWEAR ON MY WIFE'S BODY, BATMAN...
I WILL FIND WHAT-EVER YOU TREASURE MOST... AND DESTROY IT IN FRONT OF YOUR EYES...
IT'S TAKEN YEARS, BUT AT LAST I'M MAKING GOOD ON THAT VOW.
IT STARTED WITH THE RUMOR, COMPLETELY FABRICATED, OF COURSE...
THAT BLACK MASK'S GANG WAS MOVING A MASSIVE HEROIN SHIPMENT THROUGH THE WATERFRONT LAST NIGHT.
I WAS THE LAST PERSON BATMAN AND HIS PARTNER EXPECTED TO SEE.

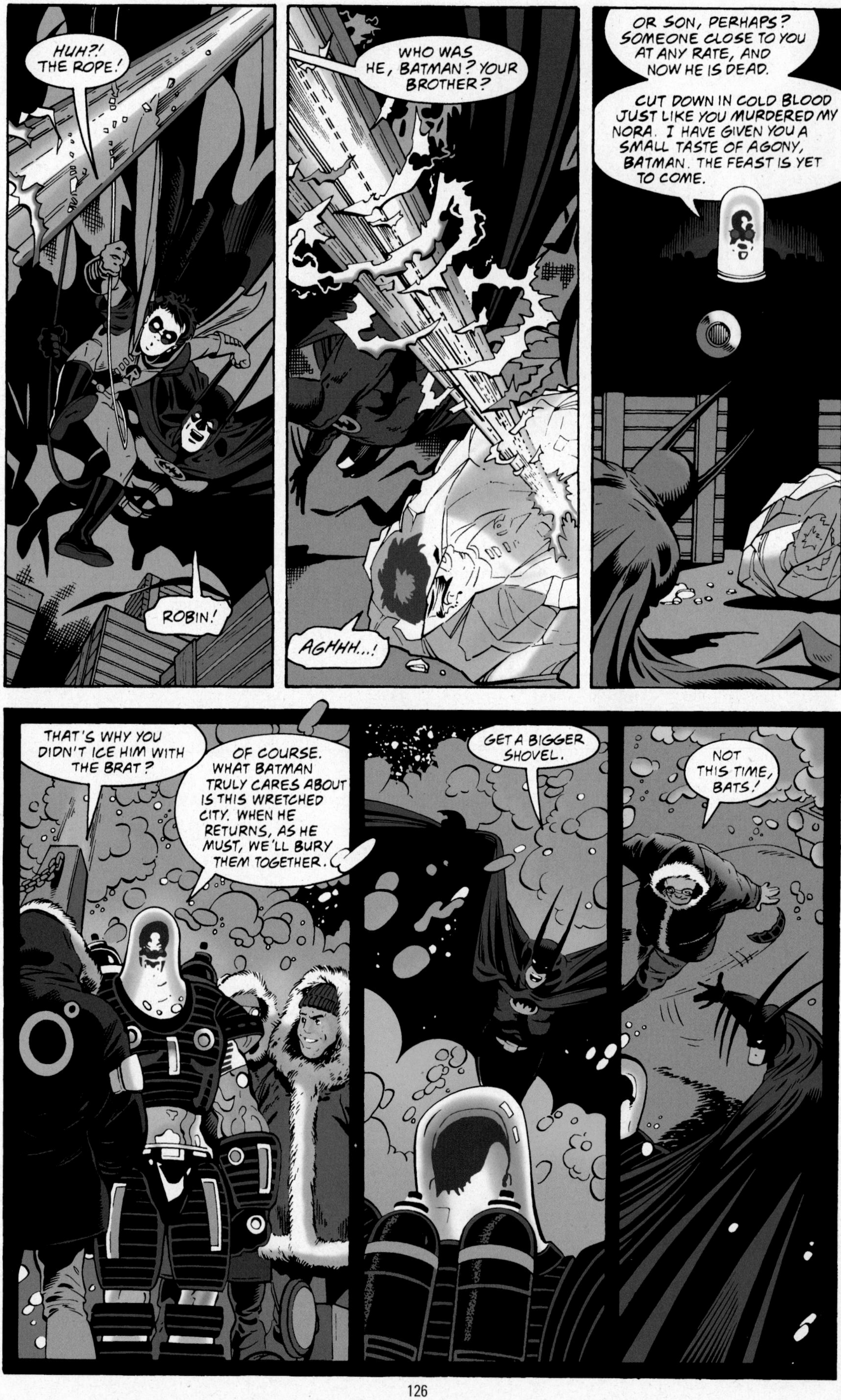
HUH?! THE ROPE!
ROBIN!
WHO WAS HE, BATMAN? YOUR BROTHER?
AGHHH...!
OR SON, PERHAPS? SOMEONE CLOSE TO YOU AT ANY RATE, AND NOW HE IS DEAD.
CUT DOWN IN COLD BLOOD JUST LIKE YOU MURDERED MY NORA. I HAVE GIVEN YOU A SMALL TASTE OF AGONY, BATMAN. THE FEAST IS YET TO COME.
THAT'S WHY YOU DIDN'T ICE HIM WITH THE BRAT?
OF COURSE. WHAT BATMAN TRULY CARES ABOUT IS THIS WRETCHED CITY. WHEN HE RETURNS, AS HE MUST, WE'LL BURY THEM TOGETHER.
GET A BIGGER SHOVEL.
NOT THIS TIME, BATS!

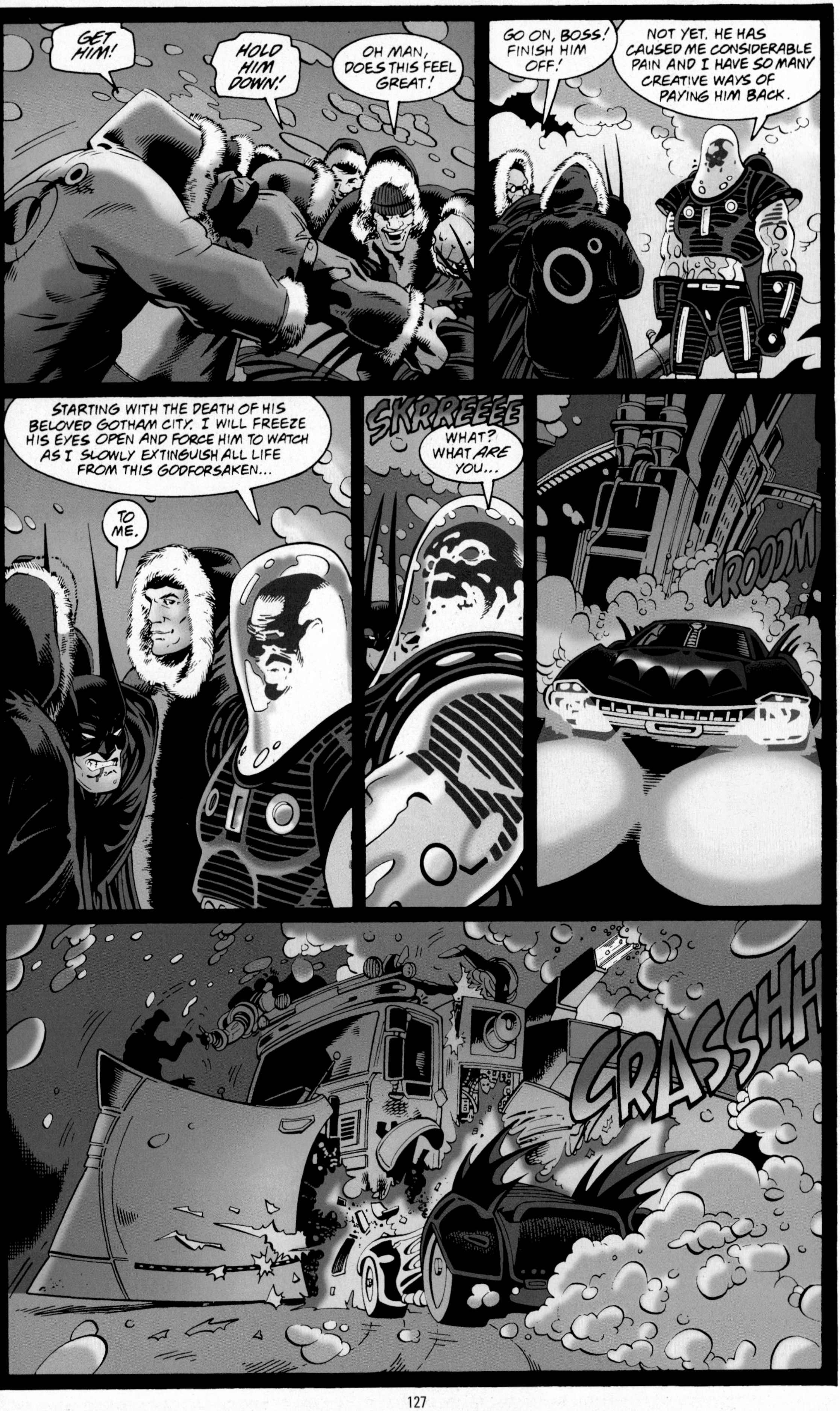
GET HIM!
HOLD HIM DOWN!
OH MAN, DOES THIS FEEL GREAT!
GO ON, BOSS! FINISH HIM OFF!
NOT YET. HE HAS CAUSED ME CONSIDERABLE PAIN AND I HAVE SO MANY CREATIVE WAYS OF PAYING HIM BACK.
STARTING WITH THE DEATH OF HIS BELOVED GOTHAM CITY. I WILL FREEZE HIS EYES OPEN AND FORCE HIM TO WATCH AS I SLOWLY EXTINGUISH ALL LIFE FROM THIS GODFORSAKEN...
TO ME.
SKRREEEE
WHAT? WHAT ARE YOU...
VROOOM
CRASSHH

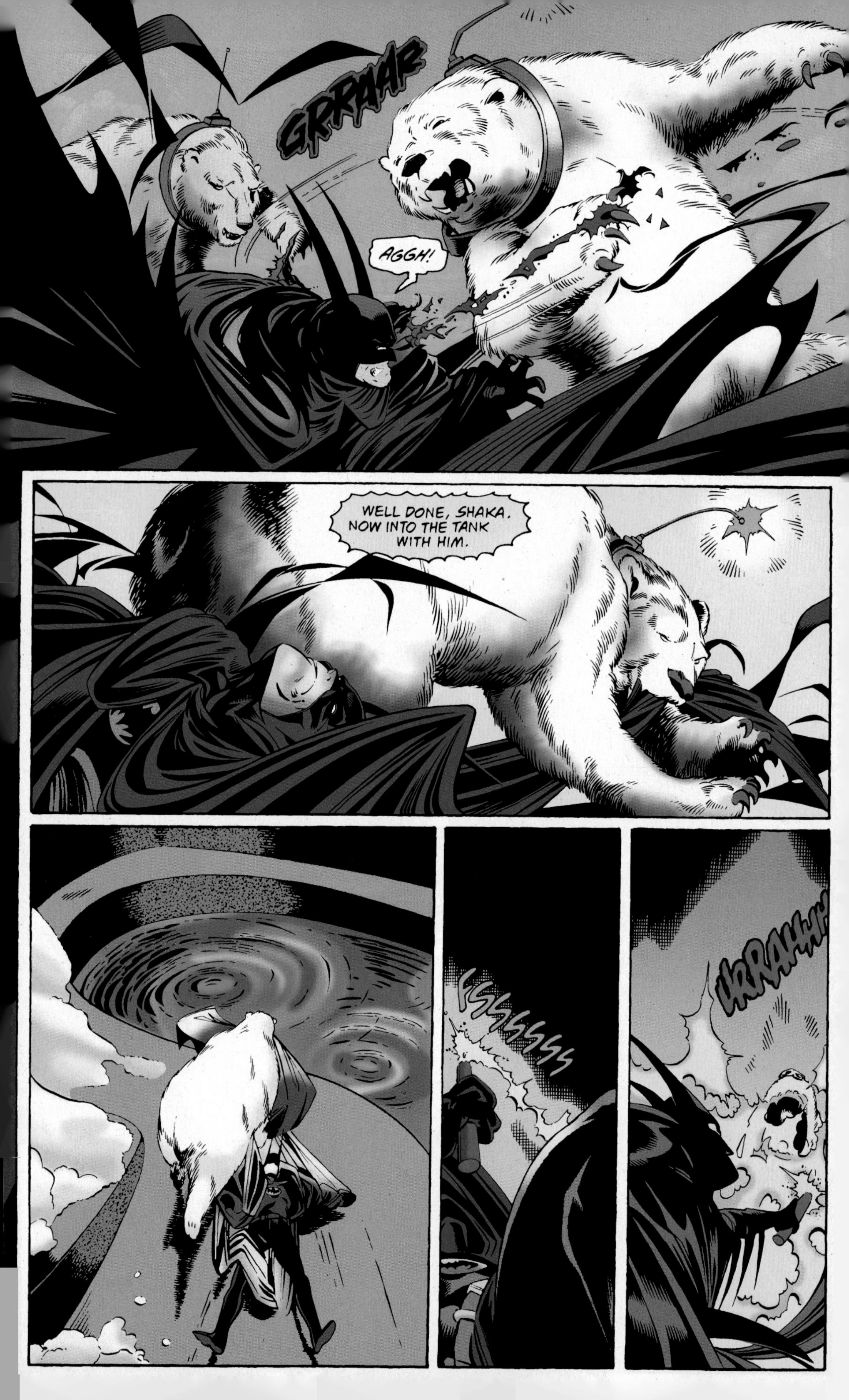
GRRAAR
AGGH!
WELL DONE, SHAKA. NOW INTO THE TANK WITH HIM.
FSSSSSSS

NO!

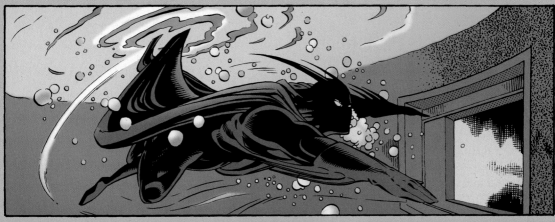

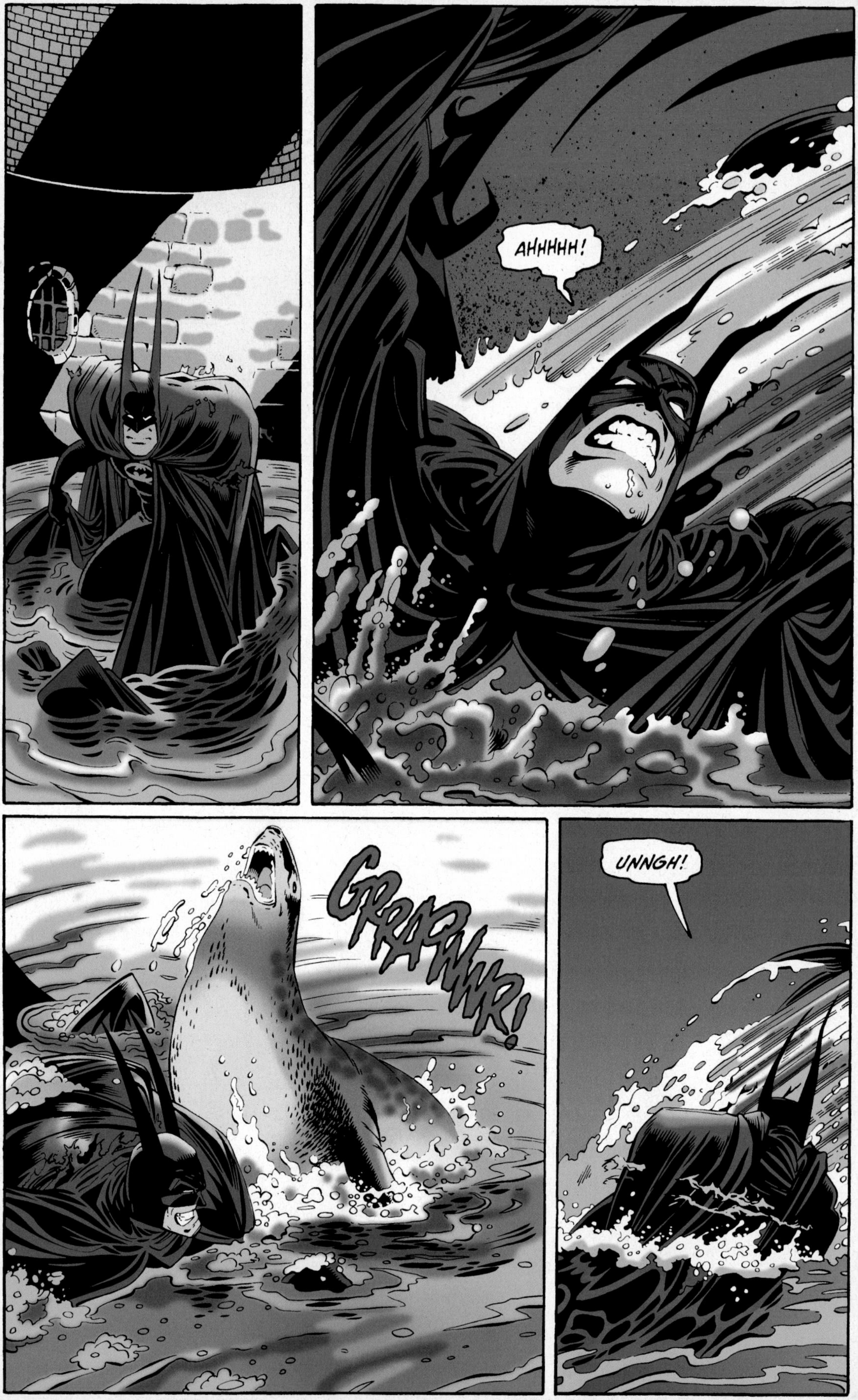
AHHHHH!
GRRAAWWR!
UNNGH!

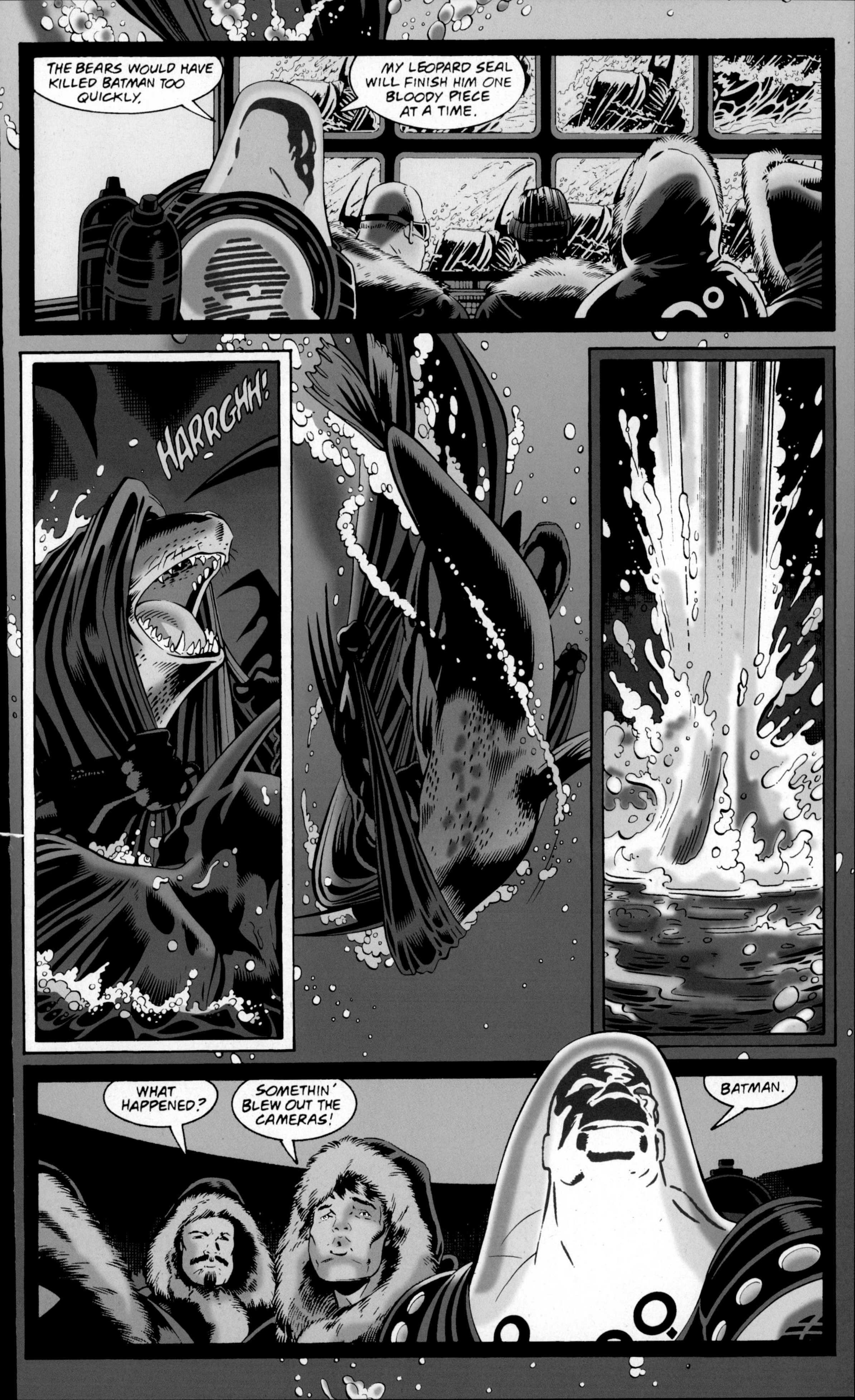
THE BEARS WOULD HAVE KILLED BATMAN TOO QUICKLY.
MY LEOPARD SEAL WILL FINISH HIM ONE BLOODY PIECE AT A TIME.
HARRGHH!
WHAT HAPPENED?
SOMETHIN' BLEW OUT THE CAMERAS!
BATMAN.

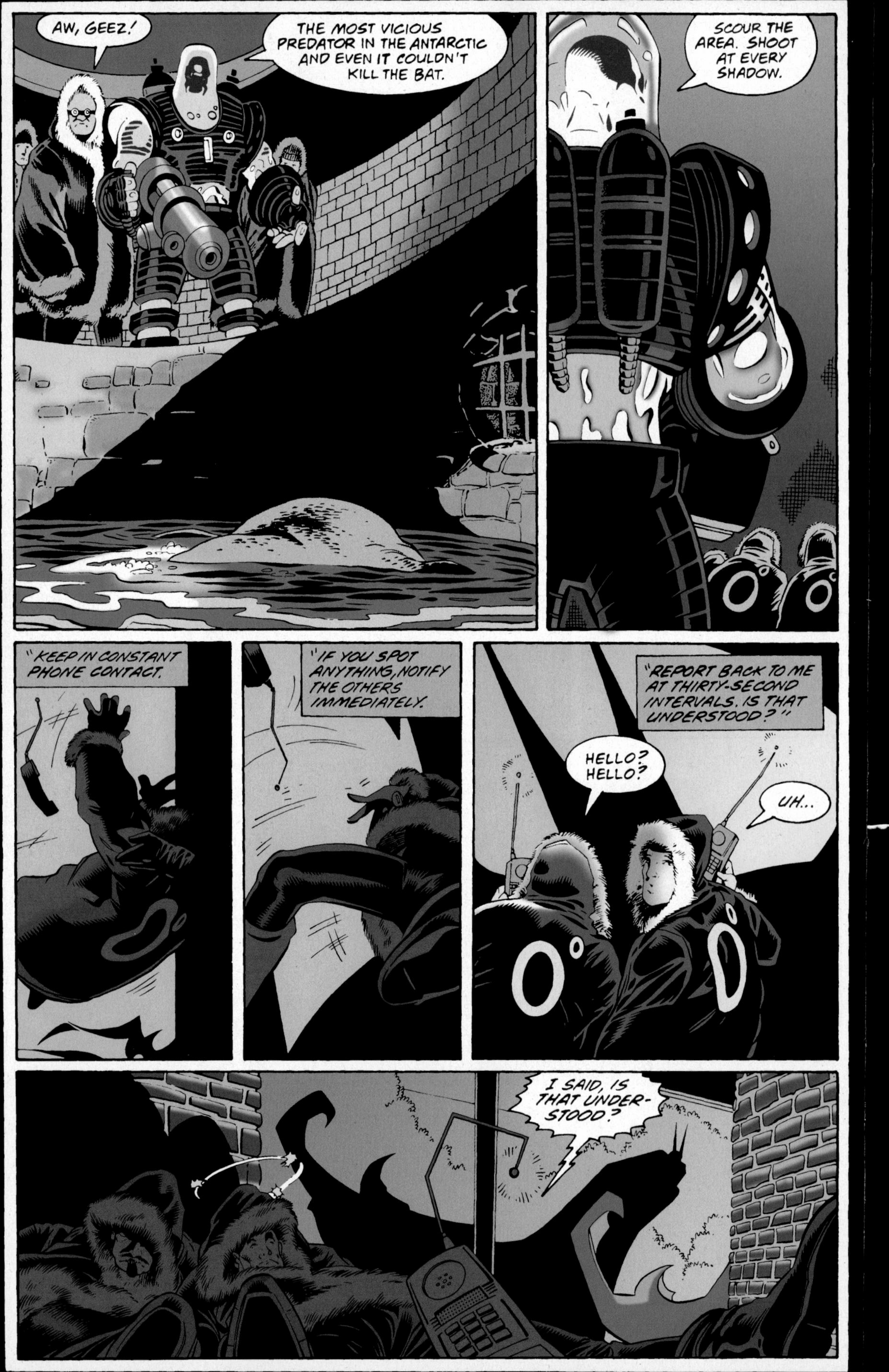
AW, GEEZ!
THE MOST VICIOUS PREDATOR IN THE ANTARCTIC AND EVEN IT COULDN'T KILL THE BAT.
SCOUR THE AREA. SHOOT AT EVERY SHADOW.
"KEEP IN CONSTANT PHONE CONTACT.
"IF YOU SPOT ANYTHING, NOTIFY THE OTHERS IMMEDIATELY.
"REPORT BACK TO ME AT THIRTY-SECOND INTERVALS. IS THAT UNDERSTOOD?"
HELLO? HELLO?
UH...
I SAID, IS THAT UNDER-STOOD?

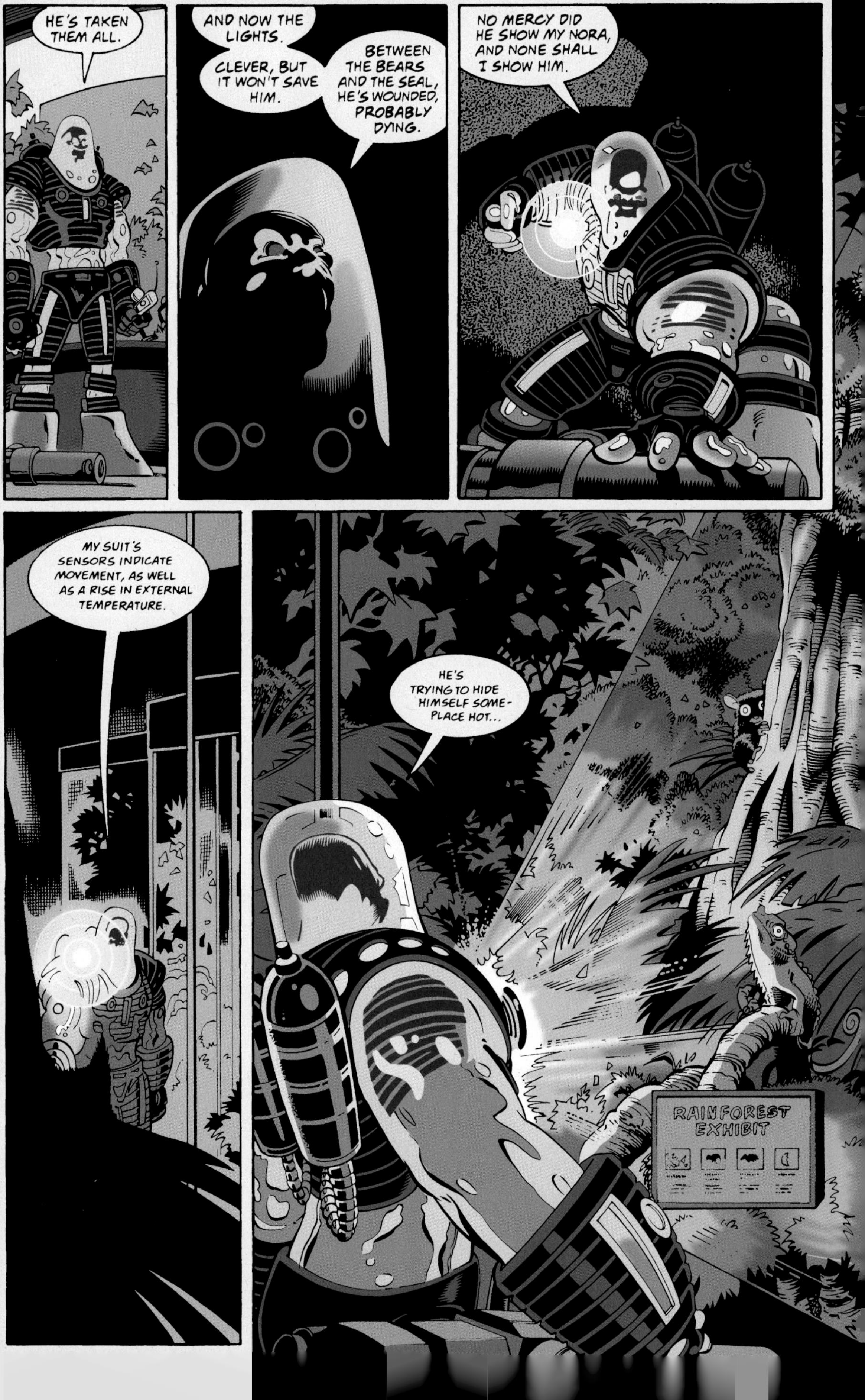
HE'S TAKEN THEM ALL.
AND NOW THE LIGHTS.
CLEVER, BUT IT WON'T SAVE HIM.
BETWEEN THE BEARS AND THE SEAL, HE'S WOUNDED, PROBABLY DYING.
NO MERCY DID HE SHOW MY NORA, AND NONE SHALL I SHOW HIM.
MY SUIT'S SENSORS INDICATE MOVEMENT, AS WELL AS A RISE IN EXTERNAL TEMPERATURE.
HE'S TRYING TO HIDE HIMSELF SOME-PLACE HOT...
RAINFOREST EXHIBIT

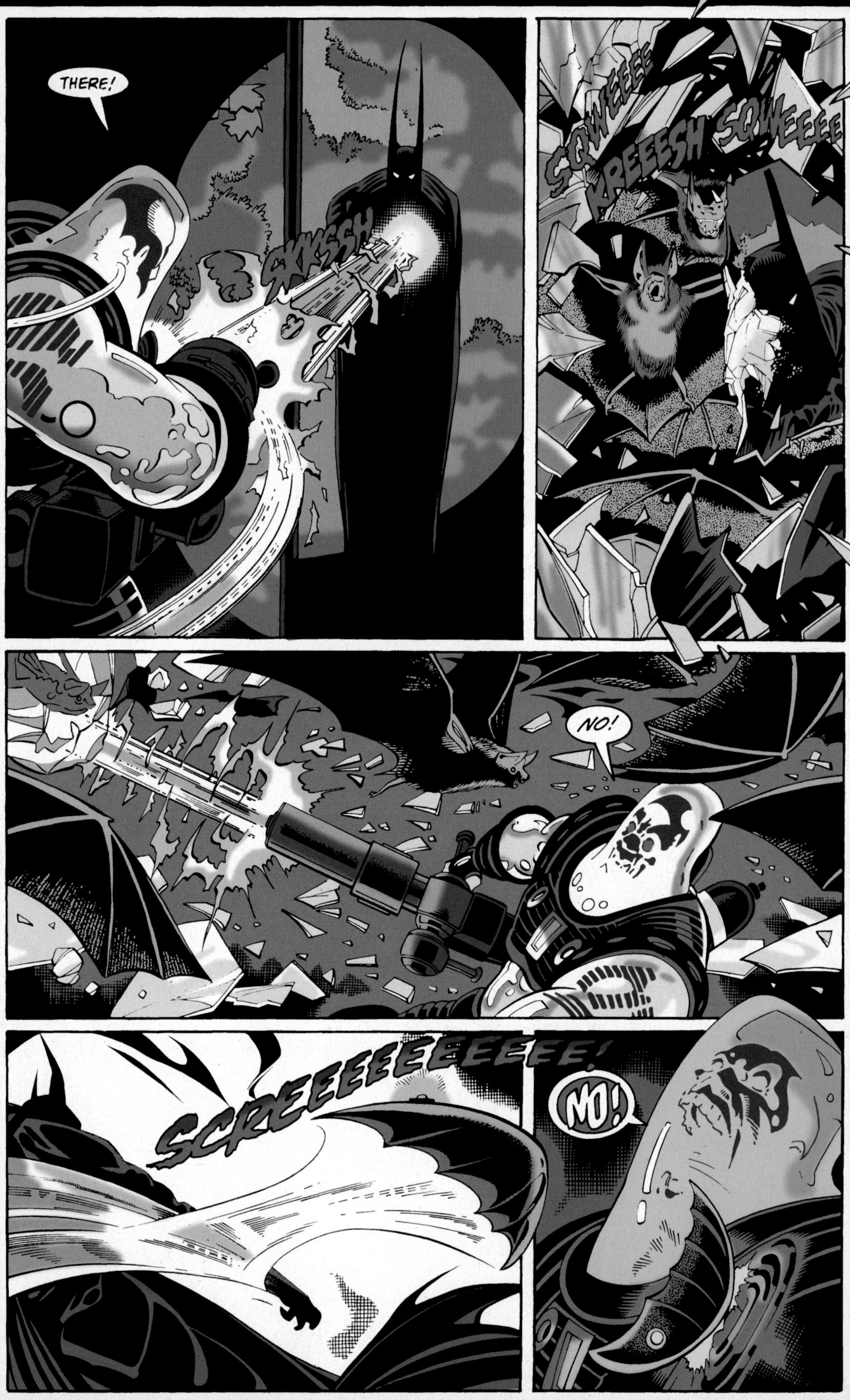
THERE!
SKHSSH
SQWEEEE
KREEESH
SQWEEEE
NO!
SCREEEEEEEEEEEE!
NO!

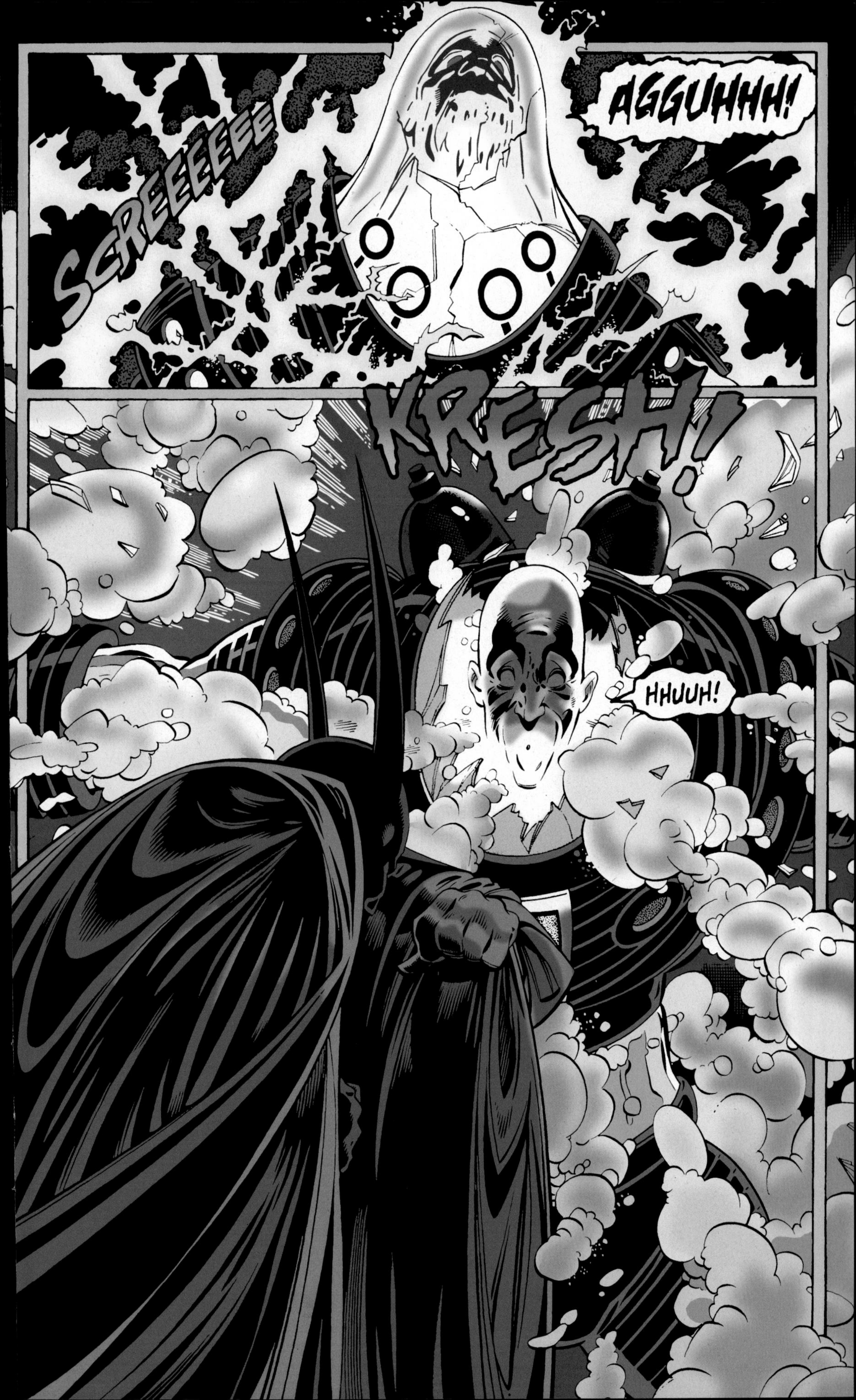
SCREEEEEEE
AGGUHHH!
KRESH!
HHUUH!

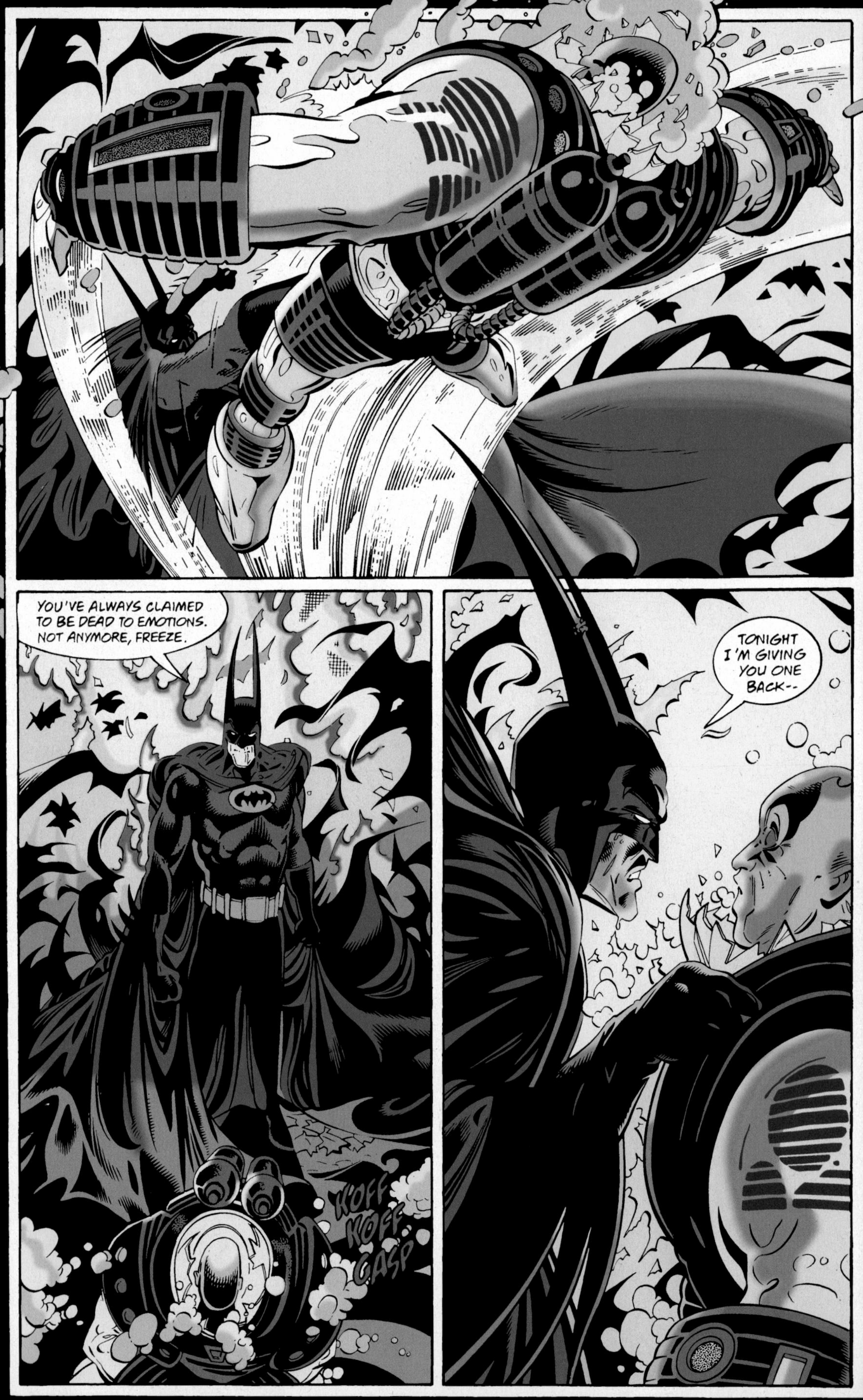
YOU'VE ALWAYS CLAIMED TO BE DEAD TO EMOTIONS. NOT ANYMORE, FREEZE.
KOFF KOFF GASP
TONIGHT I'M GIVING YOU ONE BACK--

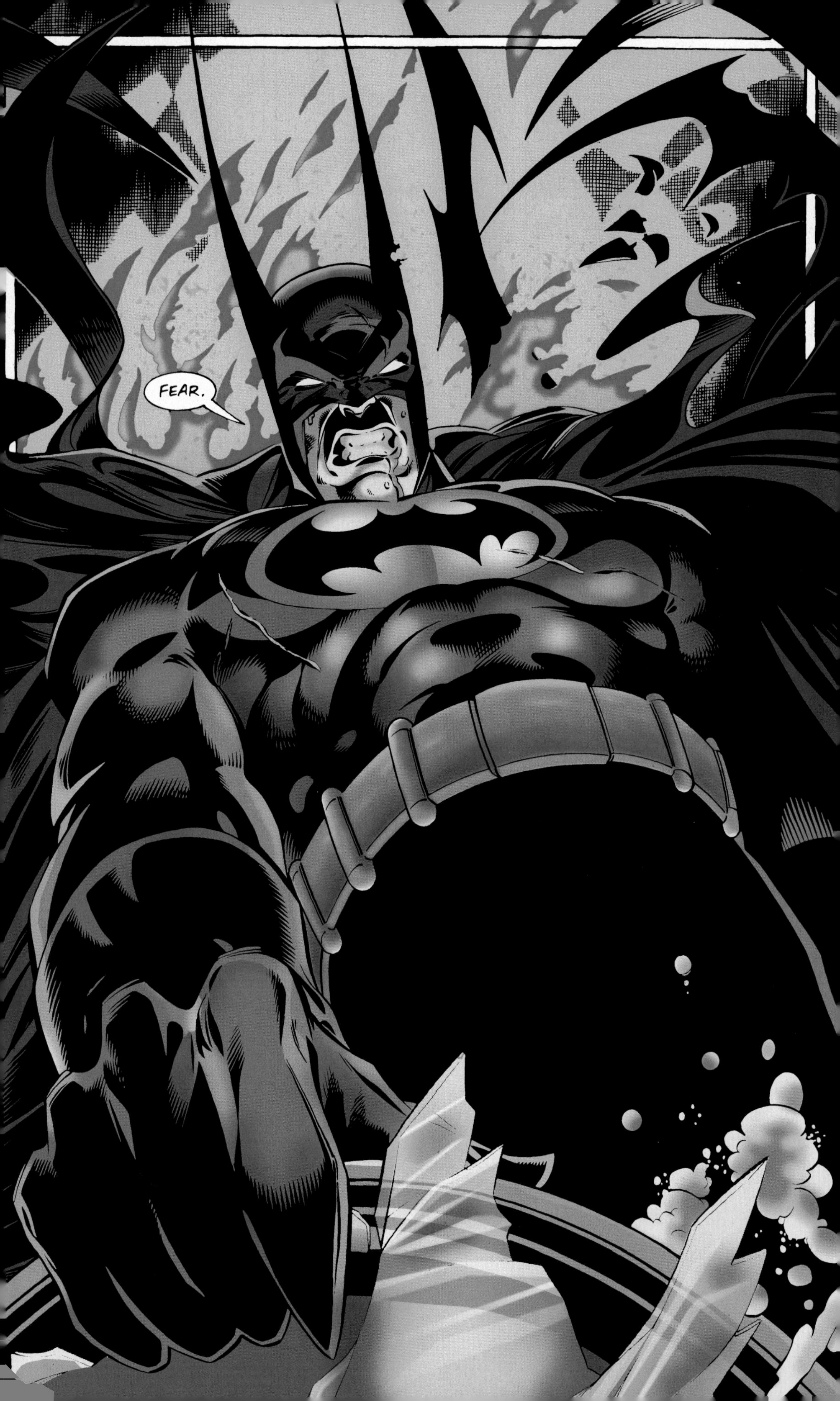
FEAR.

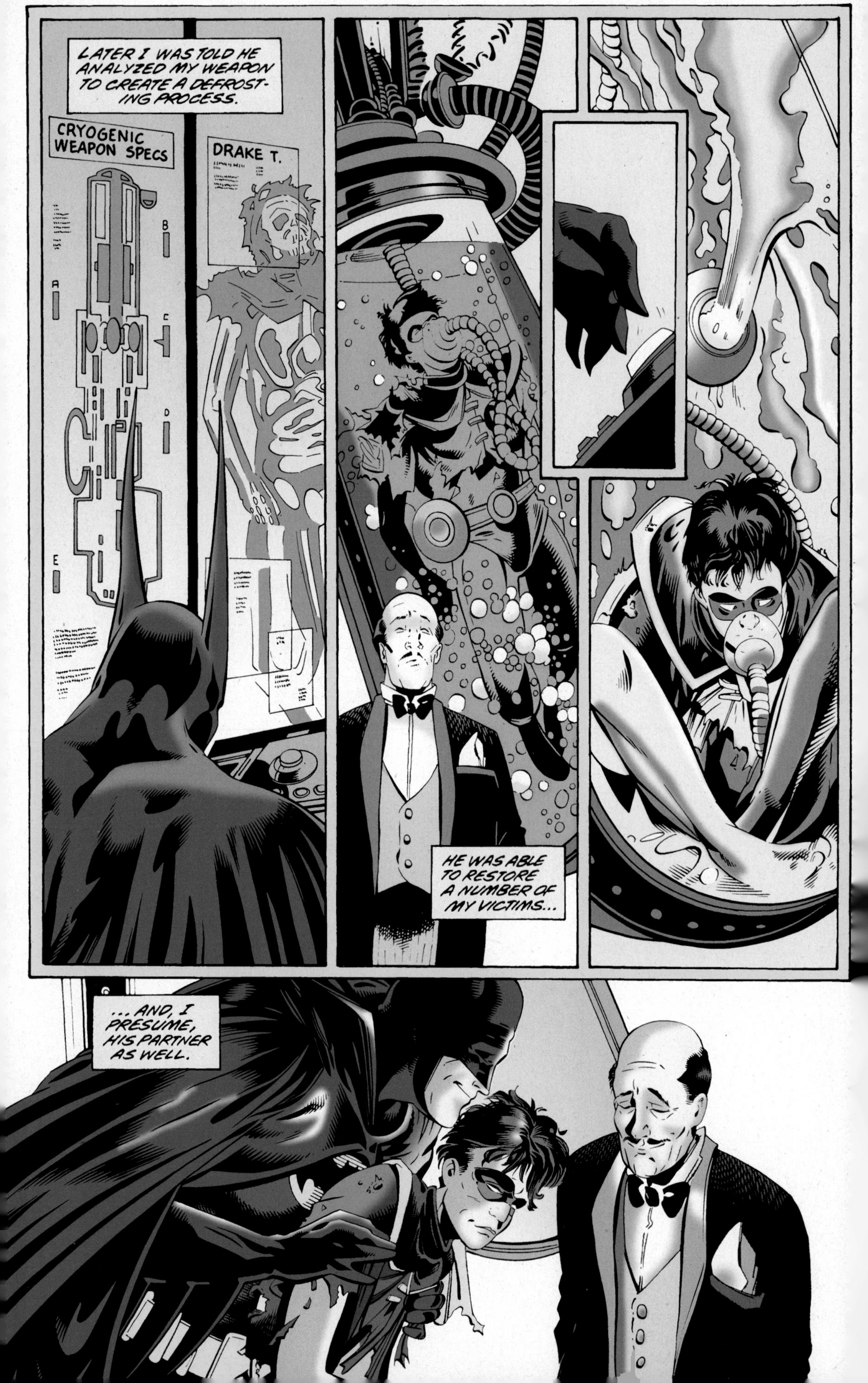
LATER I WAS TOLD HE ANALYZED MY WEAPON TO CREATE A DEFROSTING PROCESS.
CRYOGENIC WEAPON SPECS
DRAKE T.
HE WAS ABLE TO RESTORE A NUMBER OF MY VICTIMS...
...AND, I PRESUME, HIS PARTNER AS WELL.

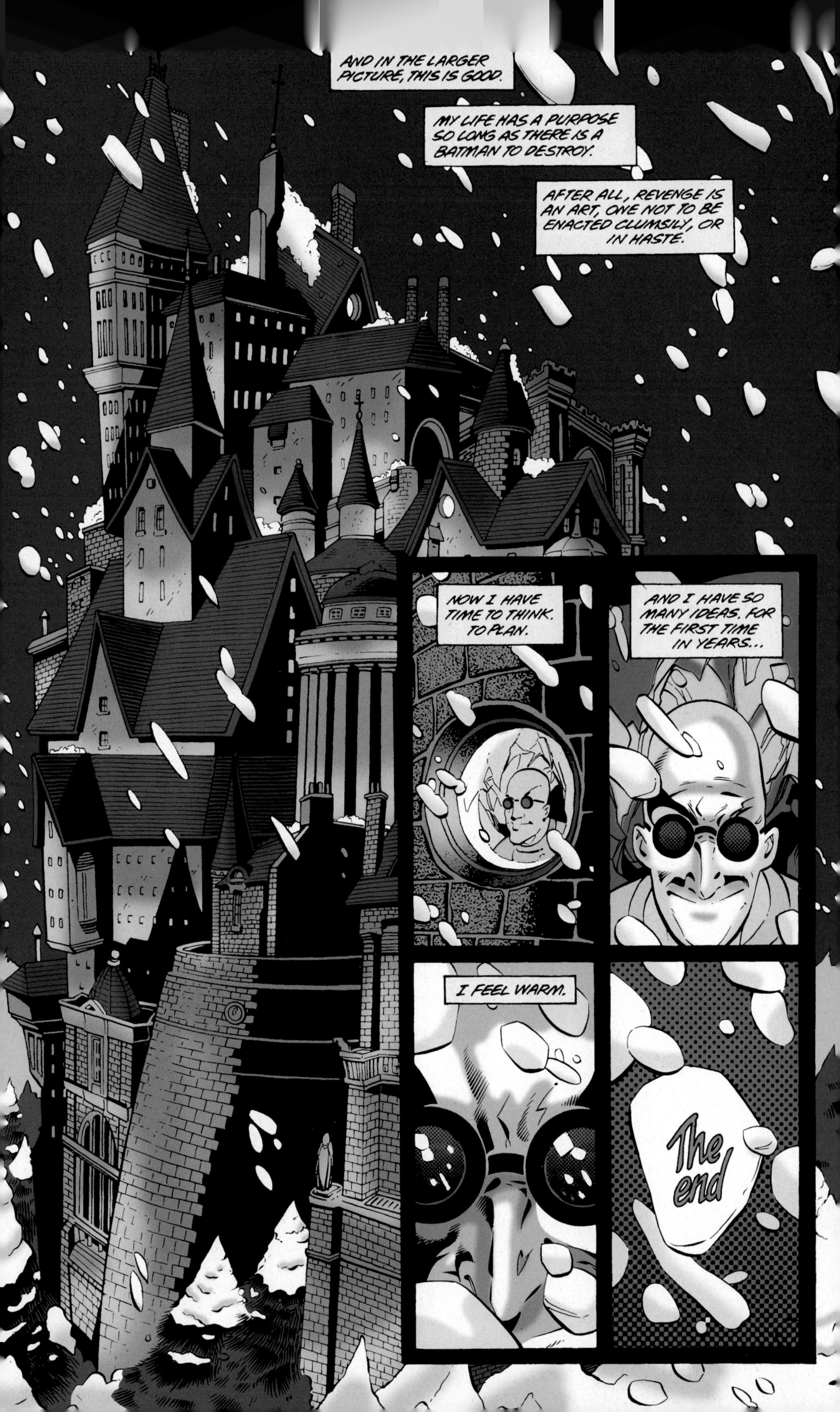
AND IN THE LARGER PICTURE, THIS IS GOOD.
MY LIFE HAS A PURPOSE SO LONG AS THERE IS A BATMAN TO DESTROY.
AFTER ALL, REVENGE IS AN ART, ONE NOT TO BE ENACTED CLUMSILY, OR IN HASTE.
NOW I HAVE TIME TO THINK. TO PLAN.
AND I HAVE SO MANY IDEAS. FOR THE FIRST TIME IN YEARS...
I FEEL WARM.
The end

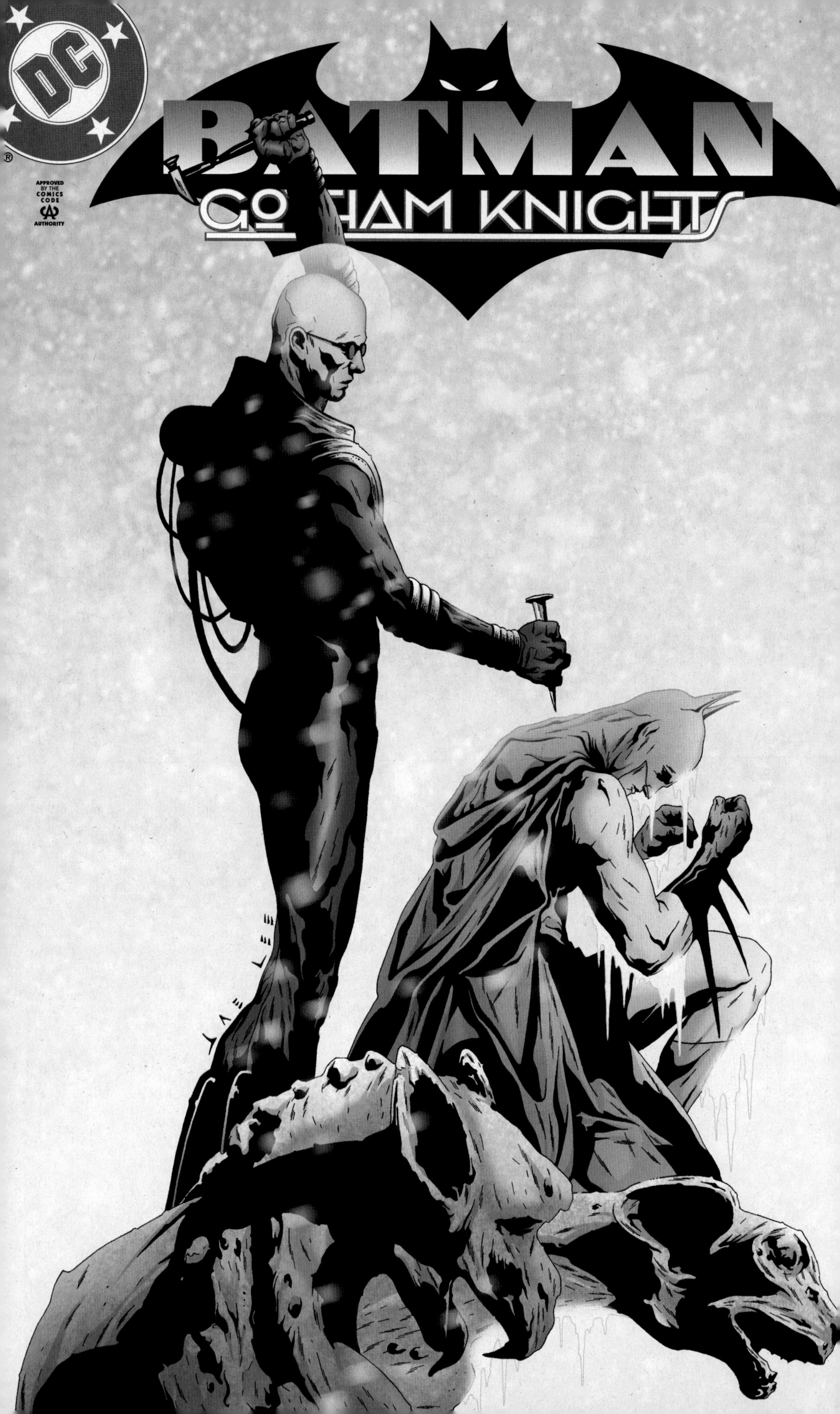
DC
BATMAN
GOTHAM KNIGHTS
APPROVED BY THE COMICS CODE AUTHORITY

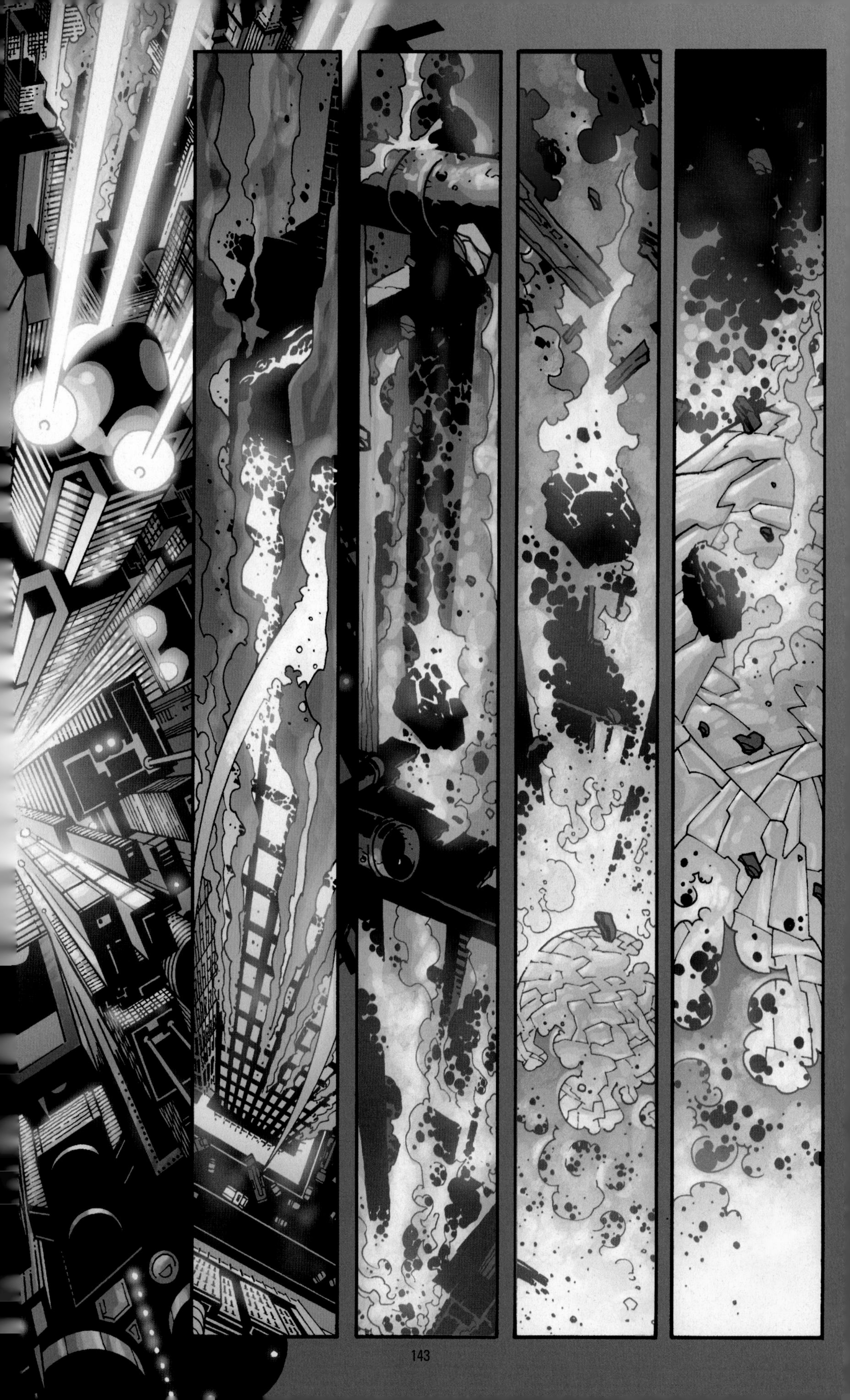

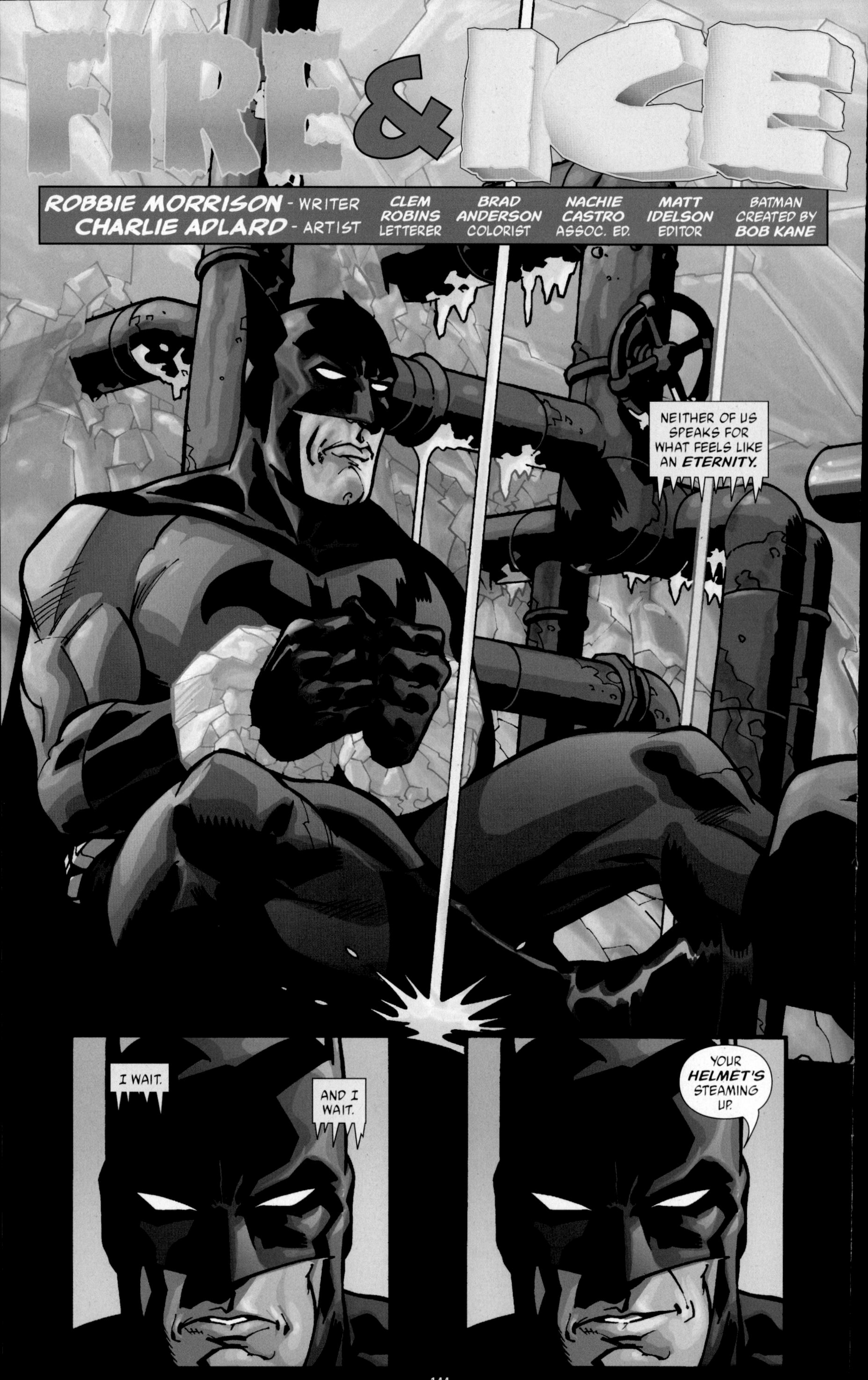
FIRE & ICE
ROBBIE MORRISON - WRITER
CHARLIE ADLARD - ARTIST
CLEM ROBINS LETTERER
BRAD ANDERSON COLORIST
NACHIE CASTRO ASSOC. ED.
MATT IDELSON EDITOR
BATMAN CREATED BY BOB KANE
NEITHER OF US SPEAKS FOR WHAT FEELS LIKE AN ETERNITY.
I WAIT.
AND I WAIT.
YOUR HELMET'S STEAMING UP.

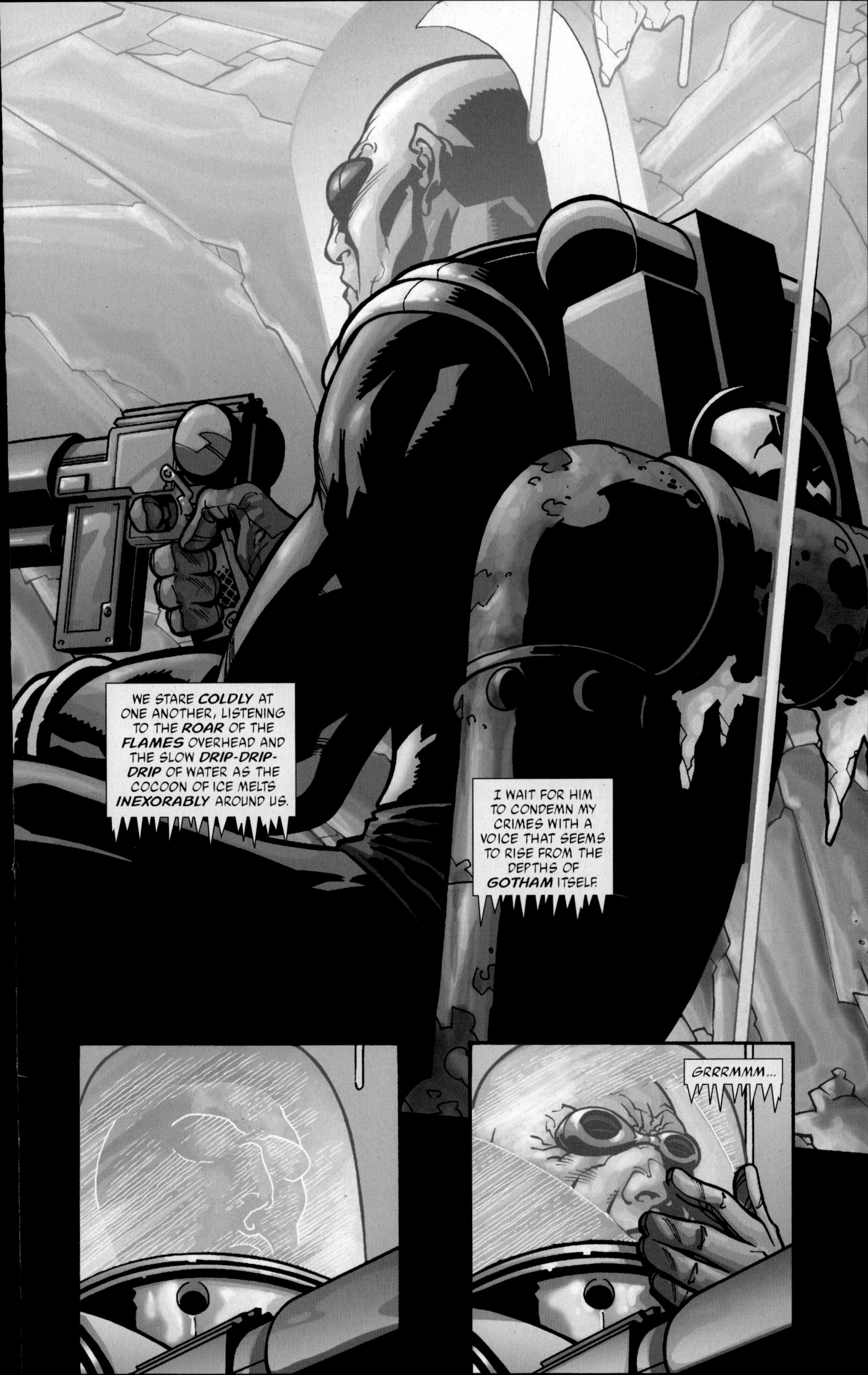
WE STARE COLDLY AT ONE ANOTHER, LISTENING TO THE ROAR OF THE FLAMES OVERHEAD AND THE SLOW DRIP-DRIP-DRIP OF WATER AS THE COCOON OF ICE MELTS INEXORABLY AROUND US.
I WAIT FOR HIM TO CONDEMN MY CRIMES WITH A VOICE THAT SEEMS TO RISE FROM THE DEPTHS OF GOTHAM ITSELF.
GRRRMMM...

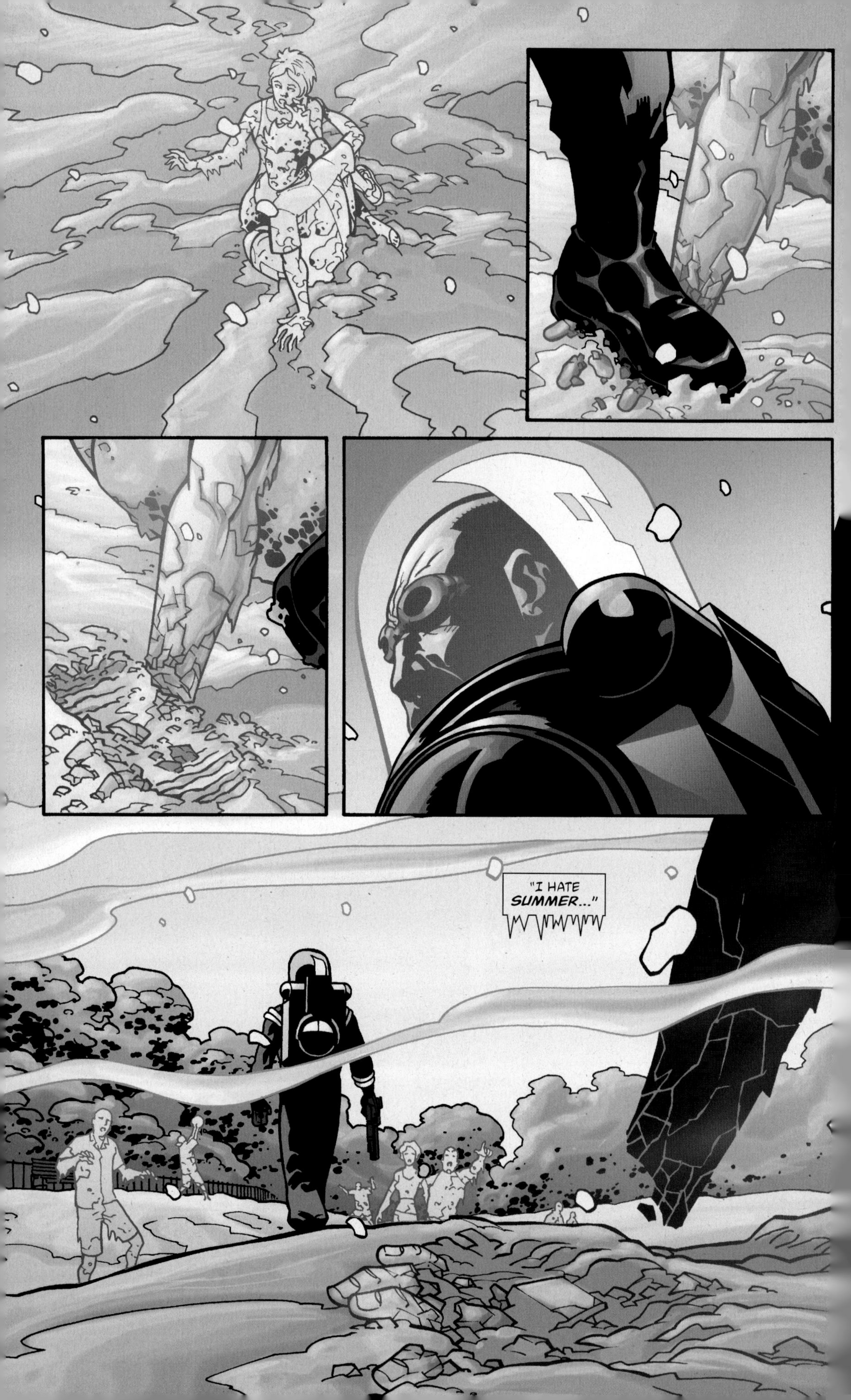
"I HATE
SUMMER..."

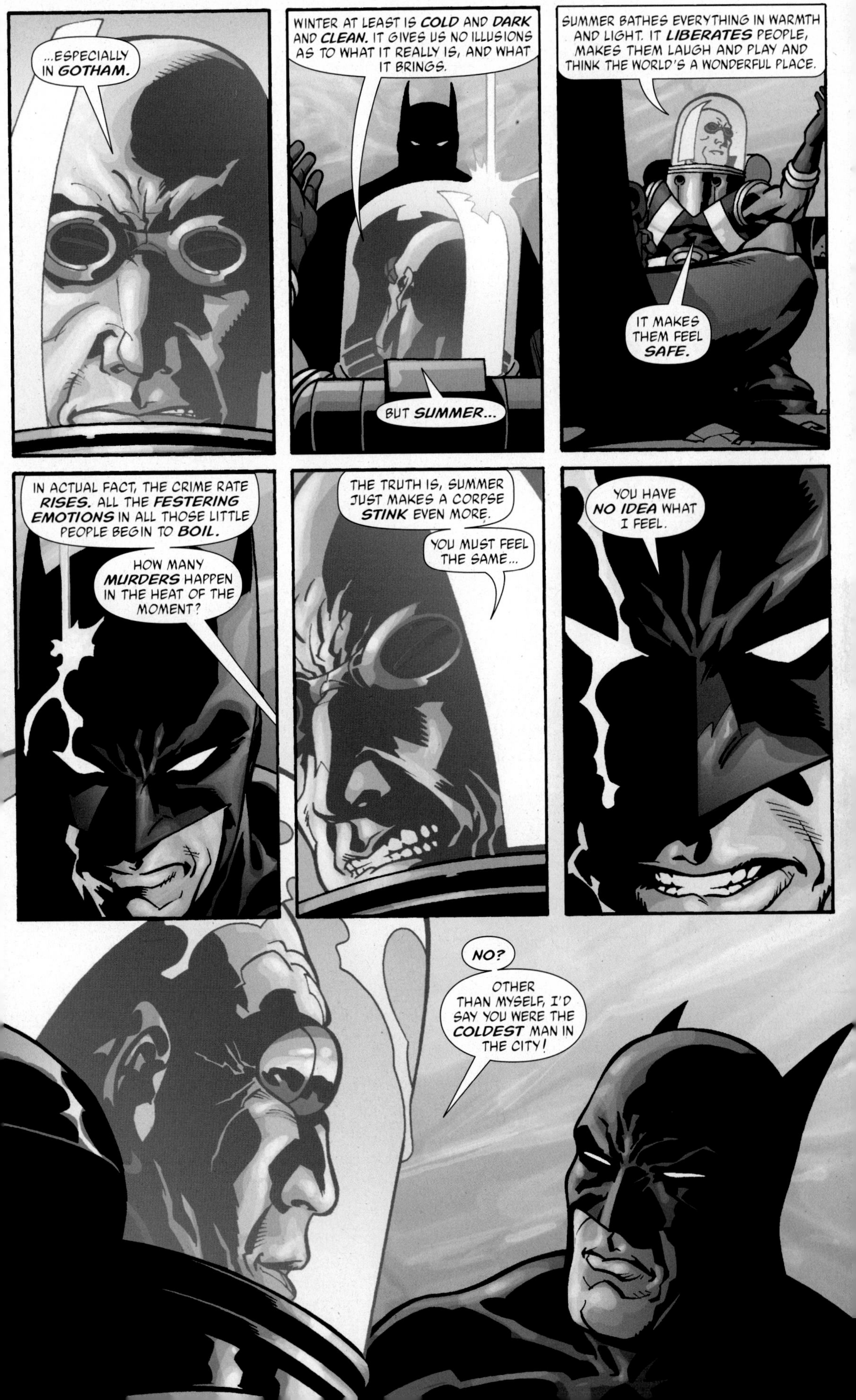
...ESPECIALLY IN GOTHAM.
WINTER AT LEAST IS COLD AND DARK AND CLEAN. IT GIVES US NO ILLUSIONS AS TO WHAT IT REALLY IS, AND WHAT IT BRINGS.
BUT SUMMER...
SUMMER BATHES EVERYTHING IN WARMTH AND LIGHT. IT LIBERATES PEOPLE, MAKES THEM LAUGH AND PLAY AND THINK THE WORLD'S A WONDERFUL PLACE.
IT MAKES THEM FEEL SAFE.
IN ACTUAL FACT, THE CRIME RATE RISES. ALL THE FESTERING EMOTIONS IN ALL THOSE LITTLE PEOPLE BEGIN TO BOIL.
HOW MANY MURDERS HAPPEN IN THE HEAT OF THE MOMENT?
THE TRUTH IS, SUMMER JUST MAKES A CORPSE STINK EVEN MORE.
YOU MUST FEEL THE SAME...
YOU HAVE NO IDEA WHAT I FEEL.
NO?
OTHER THAN MYSELF, I'D SAY YOU WERE THE COLDEST MAN IN THE CITY!

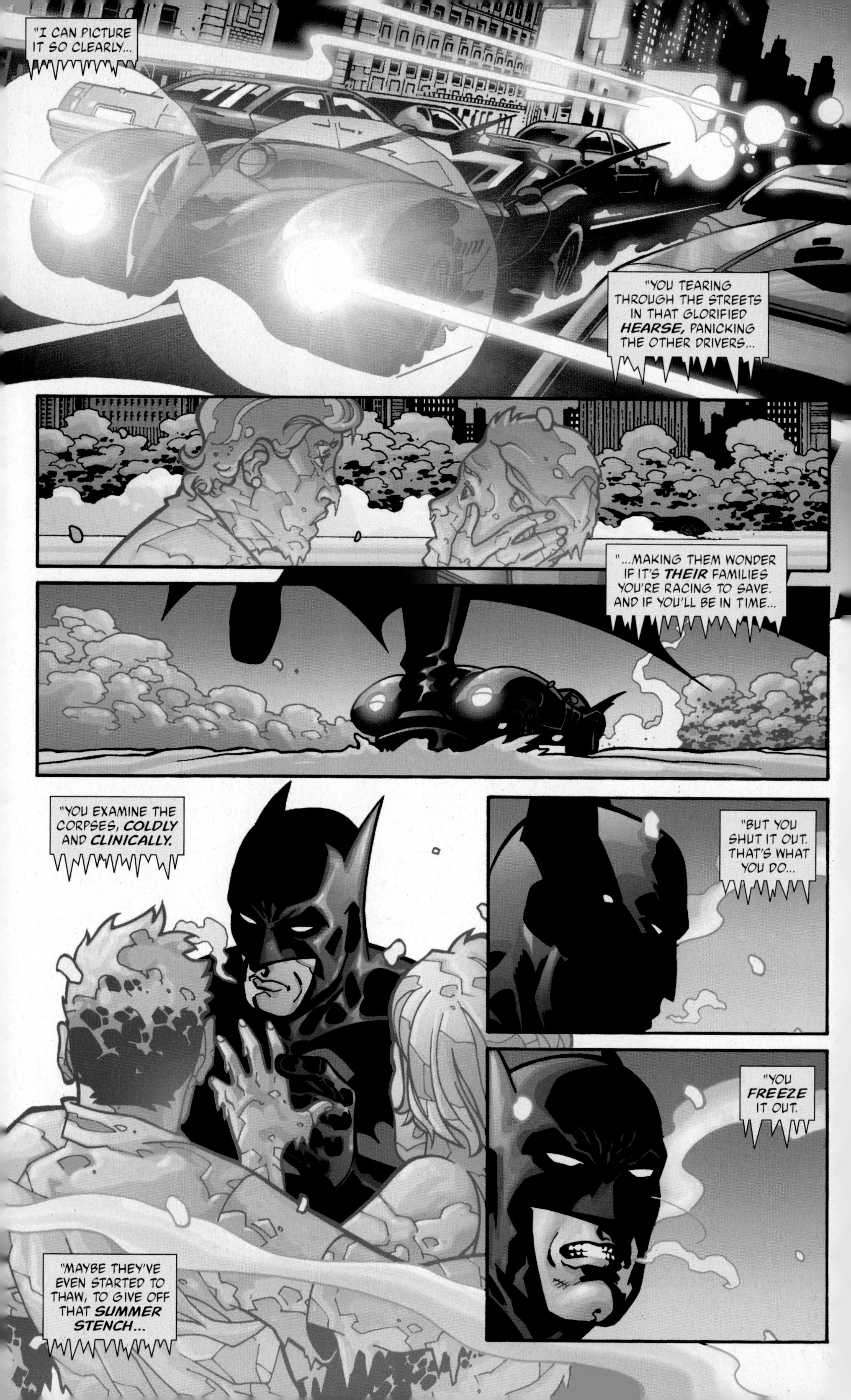
"I CAN PICTURE IT SO CLEARLY...
"YOU TEARING THROUGH THE STREETS IN THAT GLORIFIED HEARSE, PANICKING THE OTHER DRIVERS...
"...MAKING THEM WONDER IF IT'S THEIR FAMILIES YOU'RE RACING TO SAVE. AND IF YOU'LL BE IN TIME...
"YOU EXAMINE THE CORPSES, COLDLY AND CLINICALLY.
"MAYBE THEY'VE EVEN STARTED TO THAW, TO GIVE OFF THAT SUMMER STENCH...
"BUT YOU SHUT IT OUT. THAT'S WHAT YOU DO...
"YOU FREEZE IT OUT.

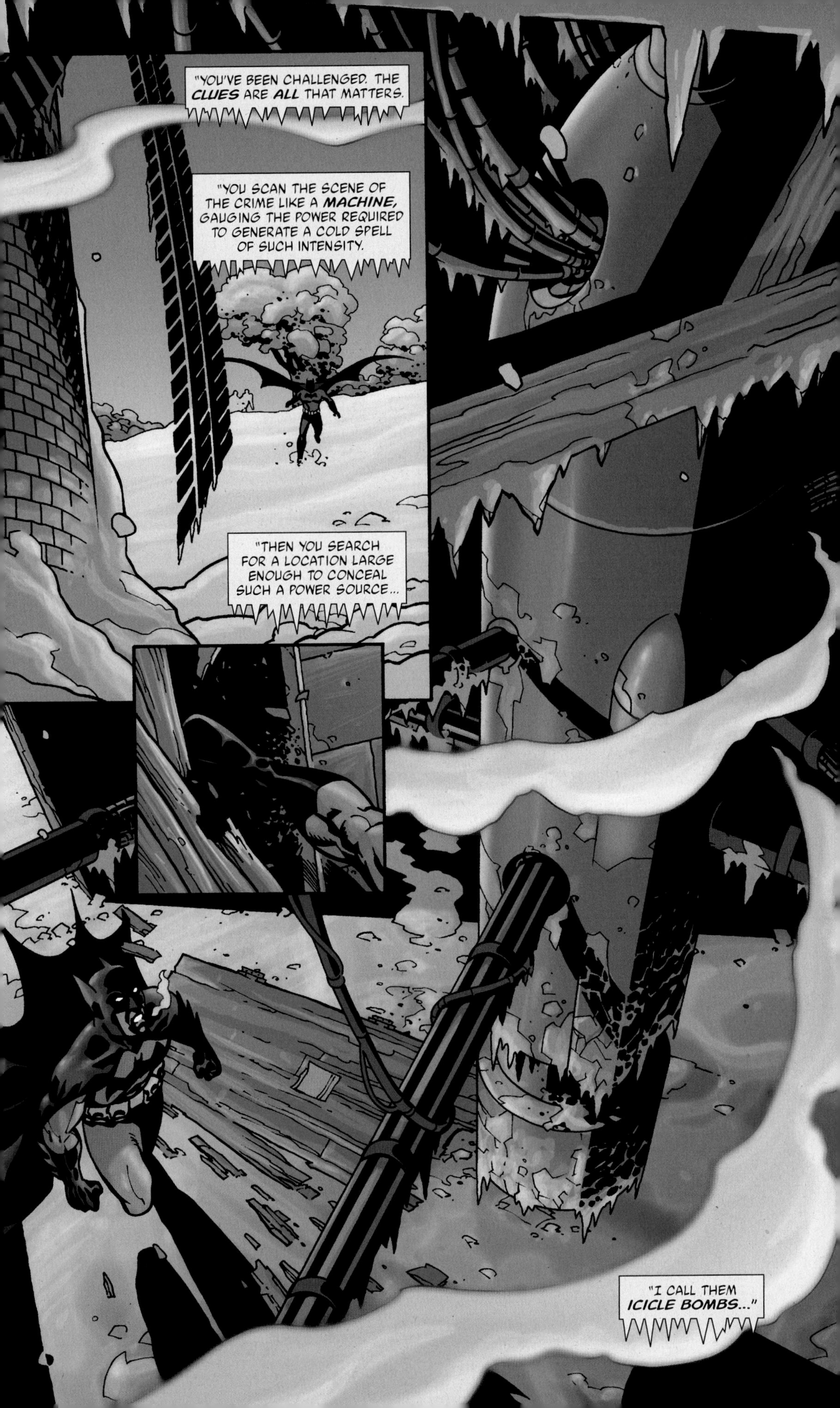
"YOU'VE BEEN CHALLENGED. THE **CLUES** ARE **ALL** THAT MATTERS.
"YOU SCAN THE SCENE OF THE CRIME LIKE A **MACHINE,** GAUGING THE POWER REQUIRED TO GENERATE A COLD SPELL OF SUCH INTENSITY.
"THEN YOU SEARCH FOR A LOCATION LARGE ENOUGH TO CONCEAL SUCH A POWER SOURCE...
"I CALL THEM **ICICLE BOMBS...**"

...THOUGH THAT MIGHT NOT IMPRESS A MAN WHO DRIVES A *BATMOBILE!*

WHEN DID YOU REALIZE IT WAS ME?

SUBTLETY ISN'T EXACTLY YOUR STRONG POINT, VICTOR.

STOP CALLING ME THAT.

IT'S JUST YOUR NAME, *VICTOR.*

NOT ANYMORE.

DON'T *PATRONIZE* ME, DETECTIVE. *YOU'RE* HARDLY QUALIFIED TO COMMENT ON SUCH MATTERS.

WHAT SORT OF *IDENTITY CRISIS* IS PLAYING OUT UNDER THAT MASK, I WONDER?

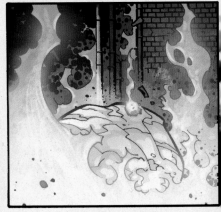

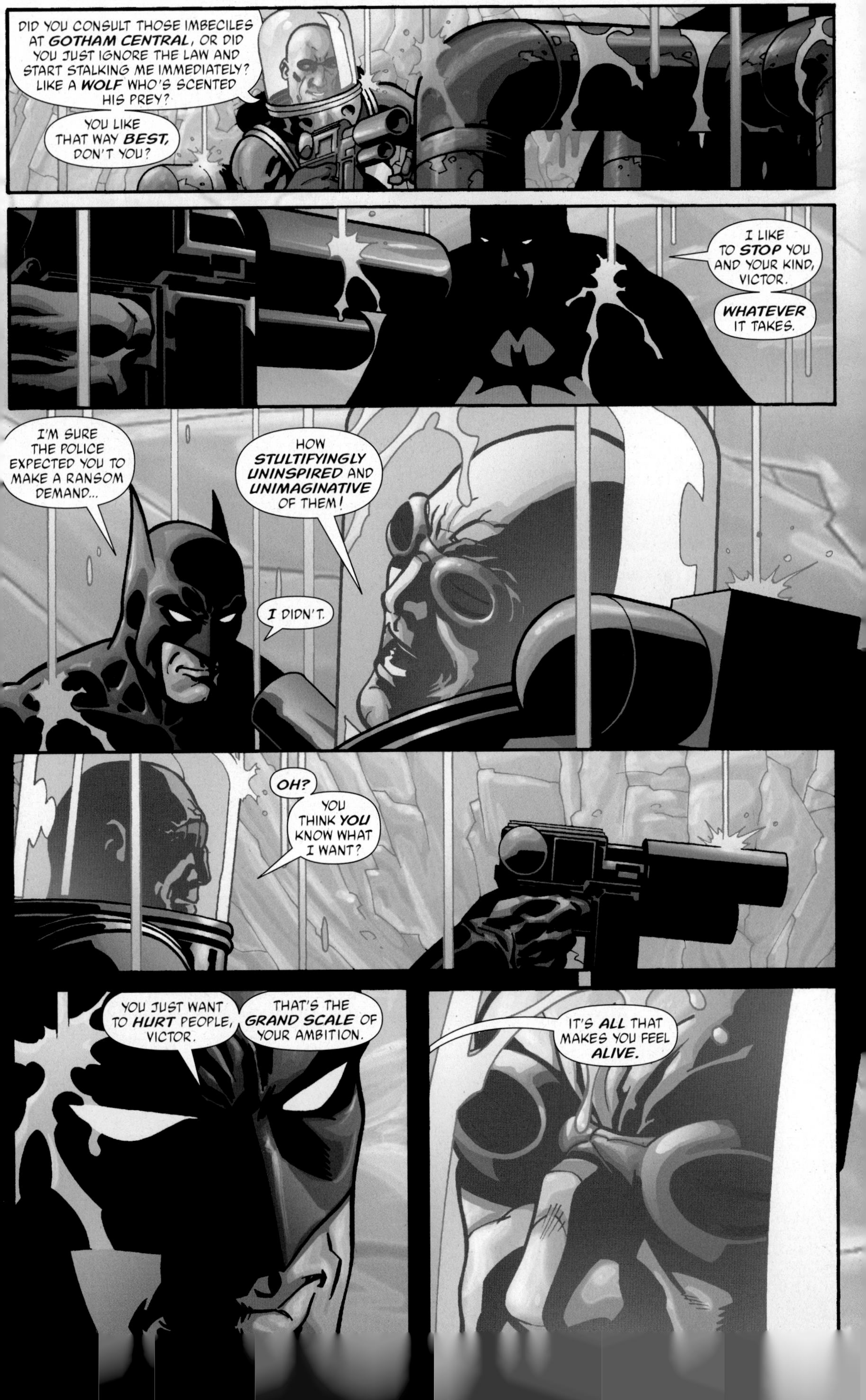
DID YOU CONSULT THOSE IMBECILES AT GOTHAM CENTRAL, OR DID YOU JUST IGNORE THE LAW AND START STALKING ME IMMEDIATELY? LIKE A WOLF WHO'S SCENTED HIS PREY?
YOU LIKE THAT WAY BEST, DON'T YOU?
I LIKE TO STOP YOU AND YOUR KIND, VICTOR.
WHATEVER IT TAKES.
I'M SURE THE POLICE EXPECTED YOU TO MAKE A RANSOM DEMAND...
HOW STULTIFYINGLY UNINSPIRED AND UNIMAGINATIVE OF THEM!
I DIDN'T.
OH?
YOU THINK YOU KNOW WHAT I WANT?
YOU JUST WANT TO HURT PEOPLE, VICTOR.
THAT'S THE GRAND SCALE OF YOUR AMBITION.
IT'S ALL THAT MAKES YOU FEEL ALIVE.

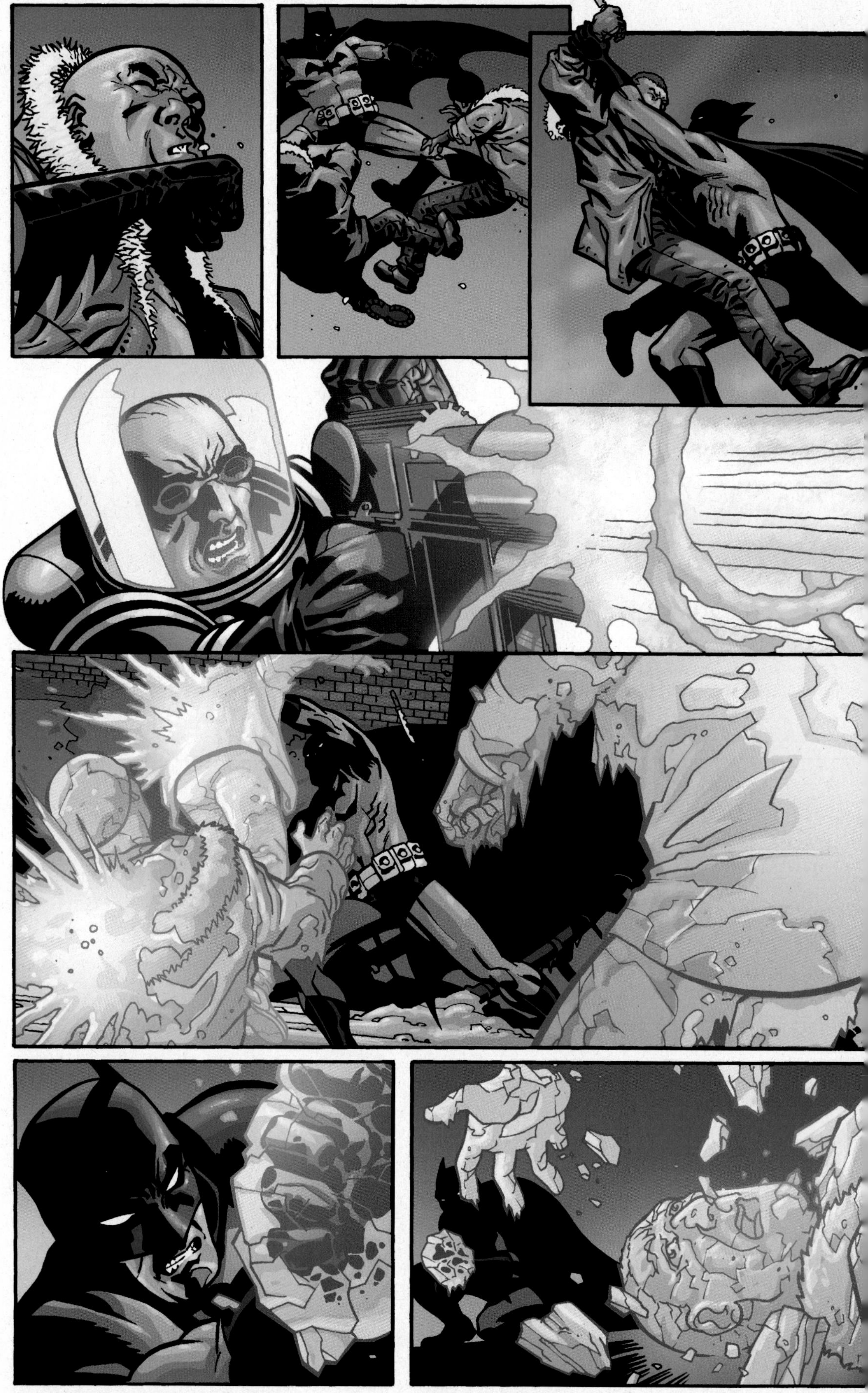

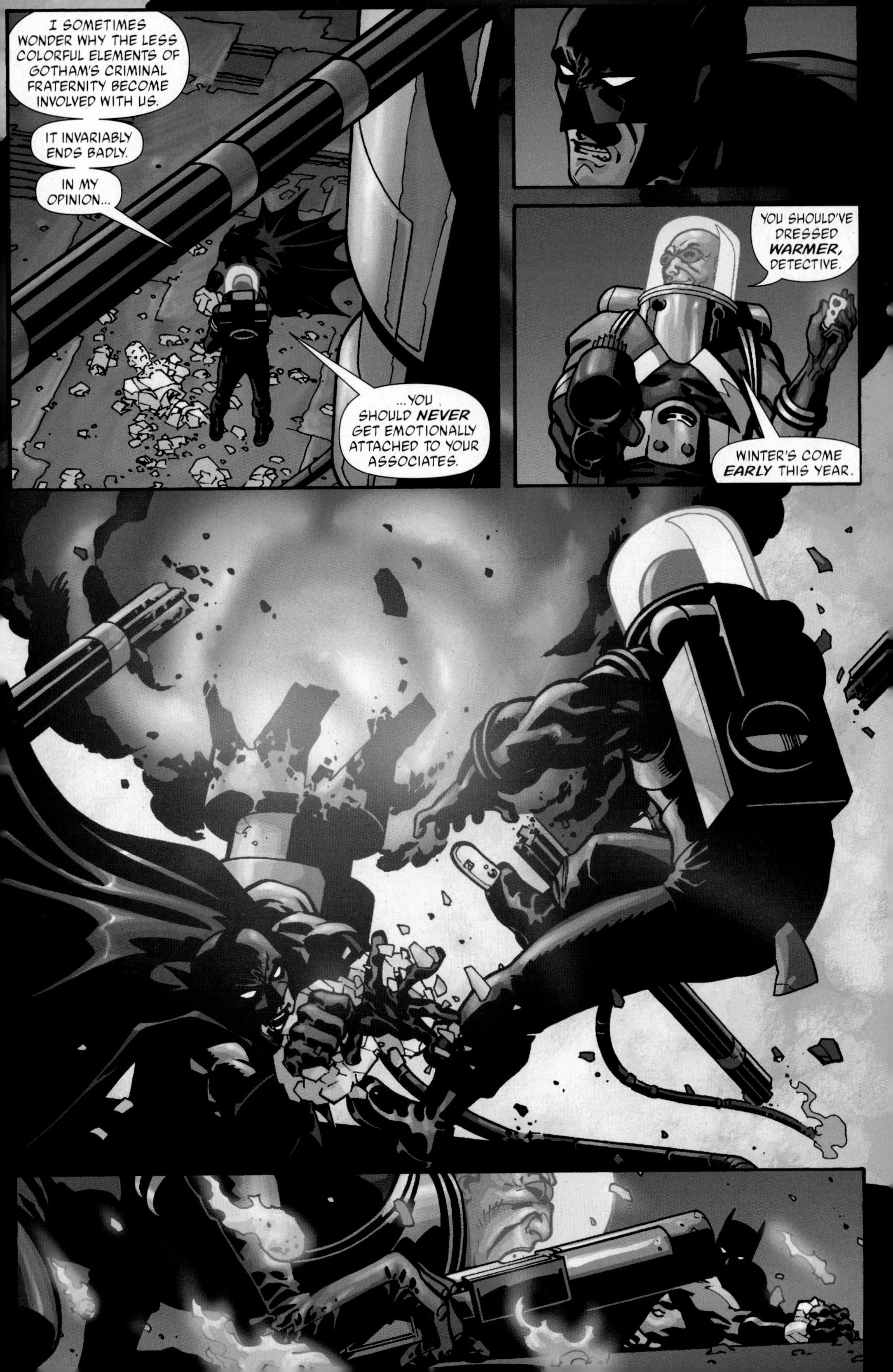
I SOMETIMES WONDER WHY THE LESS COLORFUL ELEMENTS OF GOTHAM'S CRIMINAL FRATERNITY BECOME INVOLVED WITH US.
IT INVARIABLY ENDS BADLY.
IN MY OPINION...
...YOU SHOULD NEVER GET EMOTIONALLY ATTACHED TO YOUR ASSOCIATES.
YOU SHOULD'VE DRESSED WARMER, DETECTIVE.
WINTER'S COME EARLY THIS YEAR.

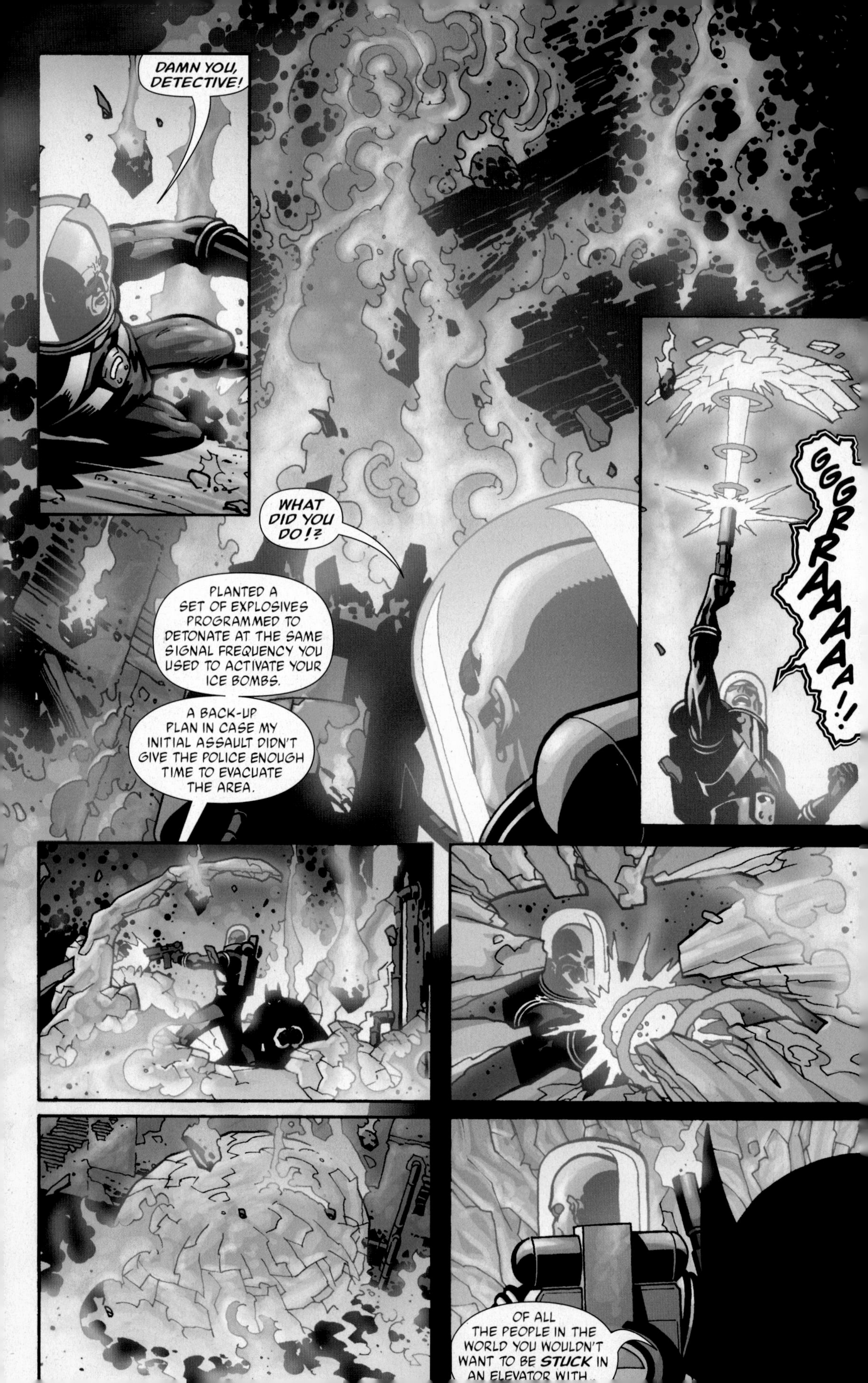
DAMN YOU, DETECTIVE!
WHAT DID YOU DO!?
PLANTED A SET OF EXPLOSIVES PROGRAMMED TO DETONATE AT THE SAME SIGNAL FREQUENCY YOU USED TO ACTIVATE YOUR ICE BOMBS.
A BACK-UP PLAN IN CASE MY INITIAL ASSAULT DIDN'T GIVE THE POLICE ENOUGH TIME TO EVACUATE THE AREA.
GGGRRAAAAA!!
OF ALL THE PEOPLE IN THE WORLD YOU WOULDN'T WANT TO BE STUCK IN AN ELEVATOR WITH...

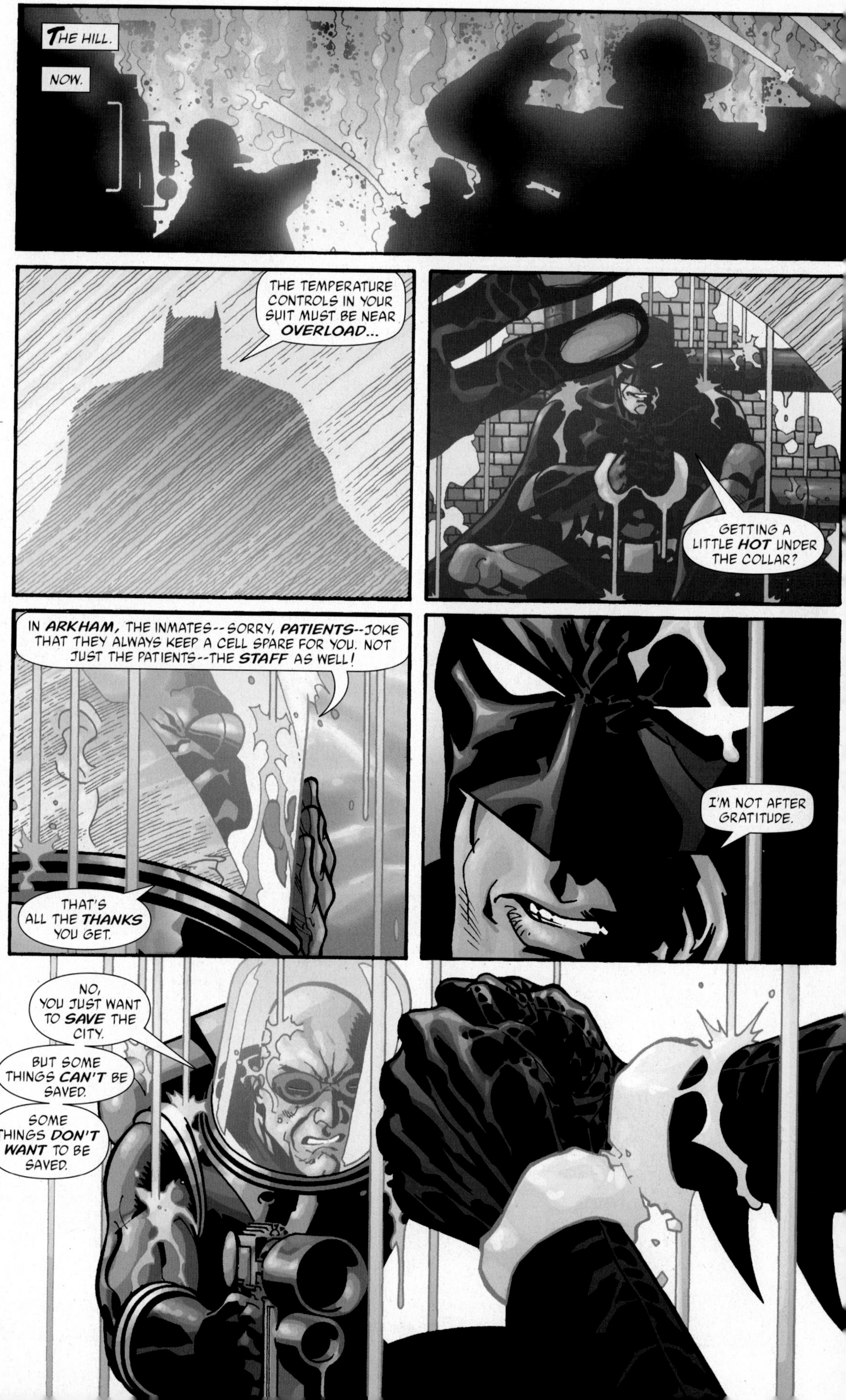
THE HILL.
NOW.
THE TEMPERATURE CONTROLS IN YOUR SUIT MUST BE NEAR OVERLOAD...
GETTING A LITTLE HOT UNDER THE COLLAR?
IN ARKHAM, THE INMATES--SORRY, PATIENTS--JOKE THAT THEY ALWAYS KEEP A CELL SPARE FOR YOU. NOT JUST THE PATIENTS--THE STAFF AS WELL!
THAT'S ALL THE THANKS YOU GET.
I'M NOT AFTER GRATITUDE.
NO, YOU JUST WANT TO SAVE THE CITY.
BUT SOME THINGS CAN'T BE SAVED.
SOME THINGS DON'T WANT TO BE SAVED.

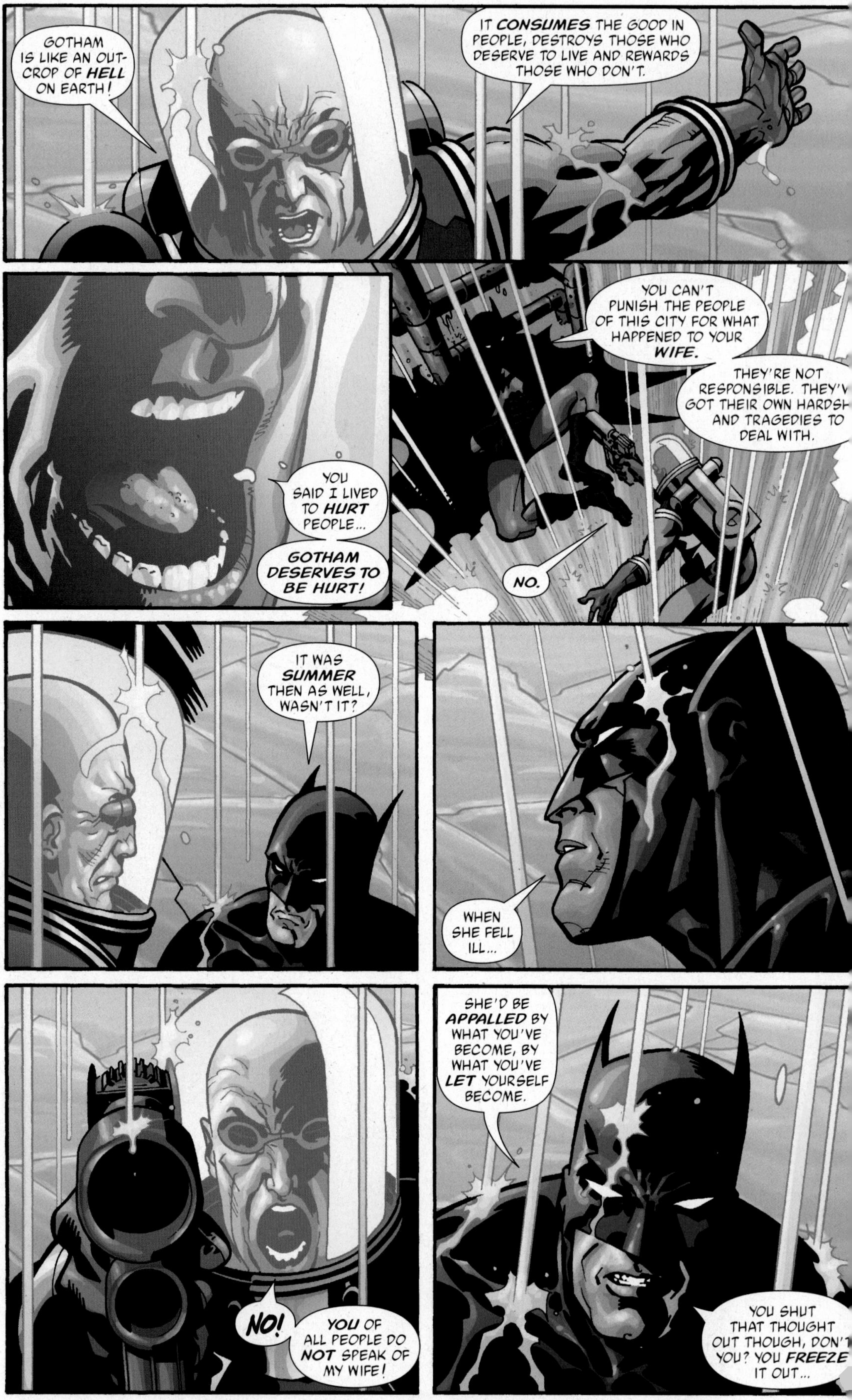
GOTHAM IS LIKE AN OUT-CROP OF HELL ON EARTH!
IT CONSUMES THE GOOD IN PEOPLE, DESTROYS THOSE WHO DESERVE TO LIVE AND REWARDS THOSE WHO DON'T.
YOU SAID I LIVED TO HURT PEOPLE...
GOTHAM DESERVES TO BE HURT!
YOU CAN'T PUNISH THE PEOPLE OF THIS CITY FOR WHAT HAPPENED TO YOUR WIFE.
THEY'RE NOT RESPONSIBLE. THEY'V GOT THEIR OWN HARDSH AND TRAGEDIES TO DEAL WITH.
NO.
IT WAS SUMMER THEN AS WELL, WASN'T IT?
WHEN SHE FELL ILL...
NO!
YOU OF ALL PEOPLE DO NOT SPEAK OF MY WIFE!
SHE'D BE APPALLED BY WHAT YOU'VE BECOME, BY WHAT YOU'VE LET YOURSELF BECOME.
YOU SHUT THAT THOUGHT OUT THOUGH, DON'T YOU? YOU FREEZE IT OUT...

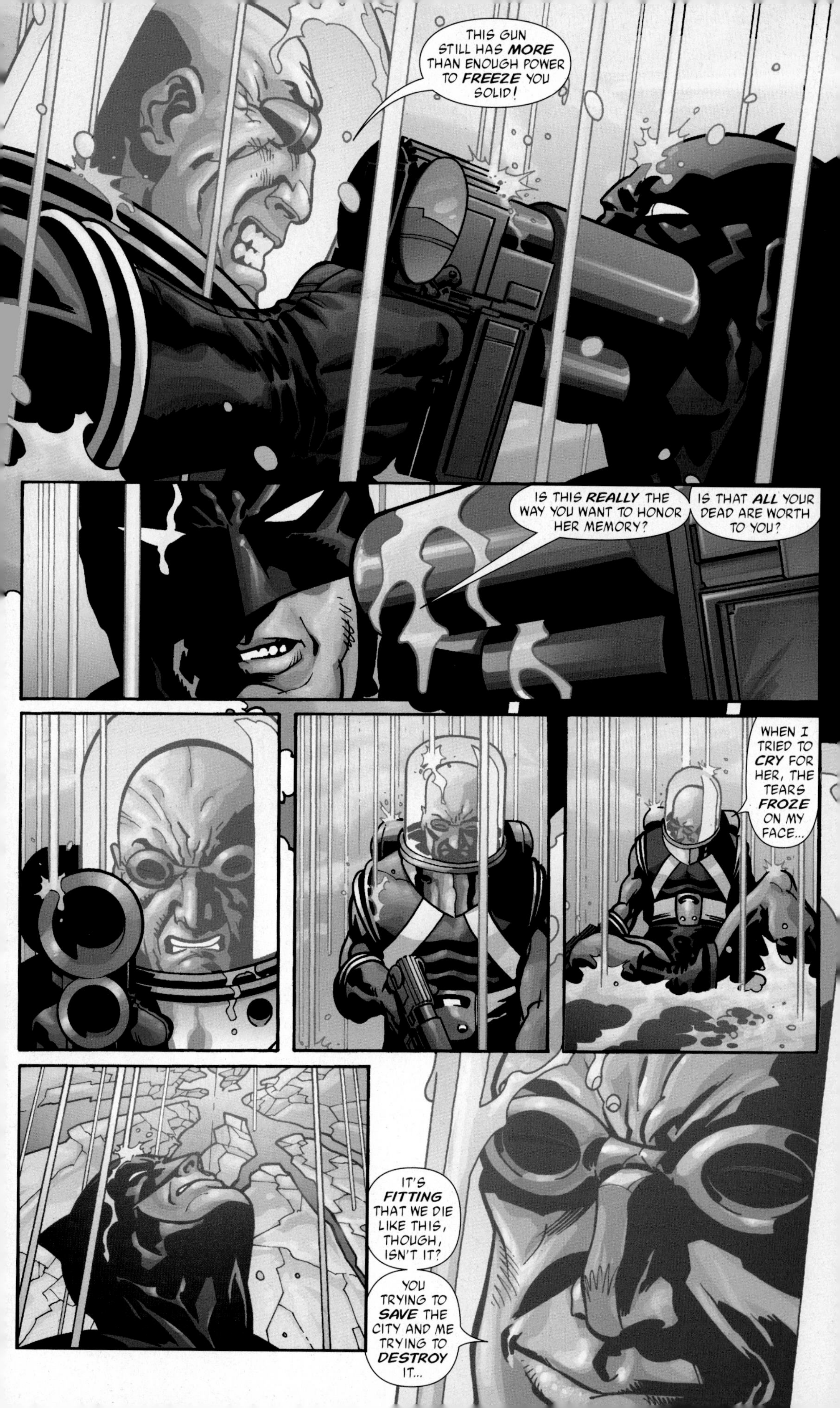
THIS GUN STILL HAS MORE THAN ENOUGH POWER TO FREEZE YOU SOLID!
IS THIS REALLY THE WAY YOU WANT TO HONOR HER MEMORY?
IS THAT ALL YOUR DEAD ARE WORTH TO YOU?
WHEN I TRIED TO CRY FOR HER, THE TEARS FROZE ON MY FACE...
IT'S FITTING THAT WE DIE LIKE THIS, THOUGH, ISN'T IT?
YOU TRYING TO SAVE THE CITY AND ME TRYING TO DESTROY IT...

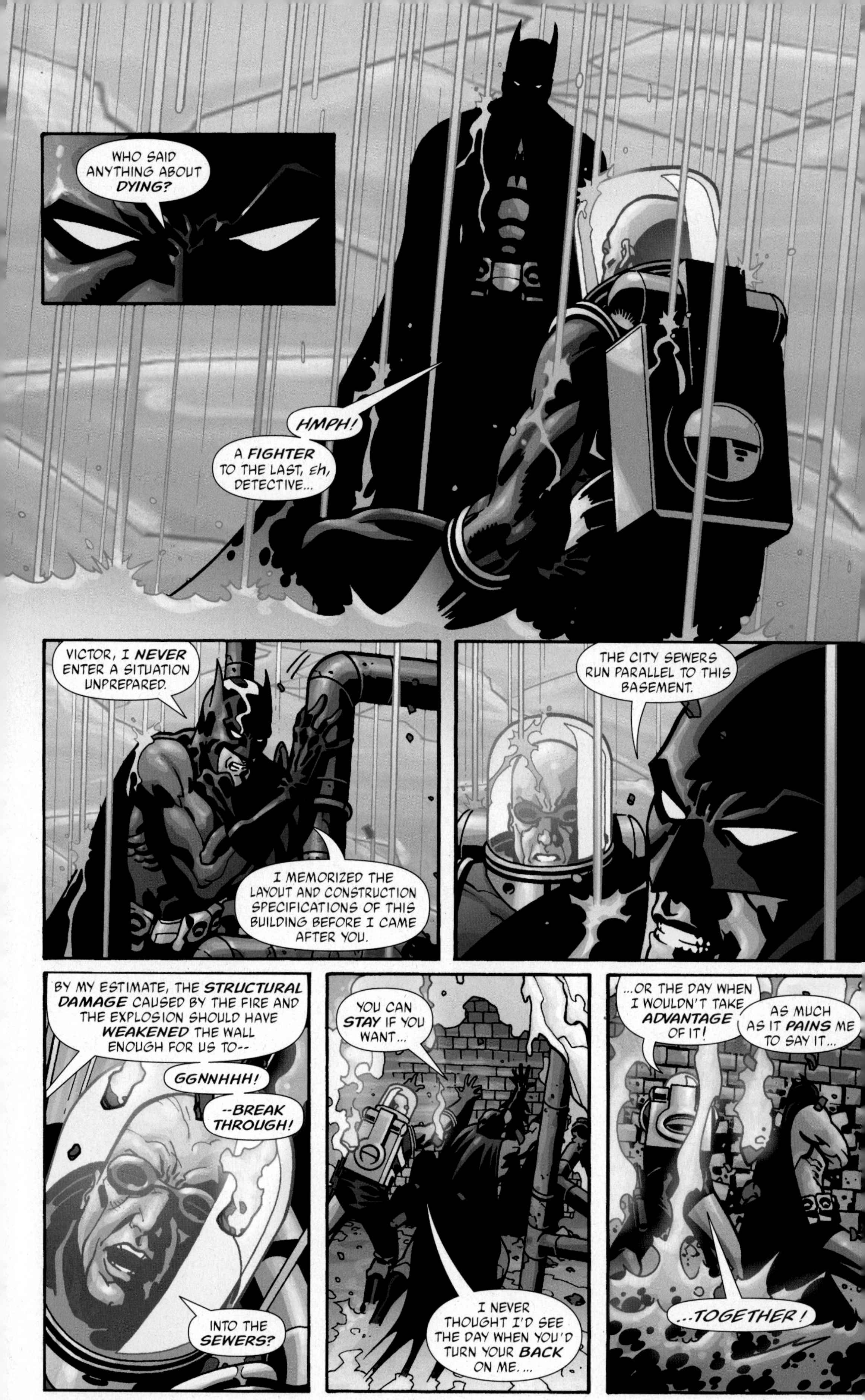

WHO SAID ANYTHING ABOUT DYING?
HMPH!
A FIGHTER TO THE LAST, EH, DETECTIVE...
VICTOR, I NEVER ENTER A SITUATION UNPREPARED.
I MEMORIZED THE LAYOUT AND CONSTRUCTION SPECIFICATIONS OF THIS BUILDING BEFORE I CAME AFTER YOU.
THE CITY SEWERS RUN PARALLEL TO THIS BASEMENT.
BY MY ESTIMATE, THE STRUCTURAL DAMAGE CAUSED BY THE FIRE AND THE EXPLOSION SHOULD HAVE WEAKENED THE WALL ENOUGH FOR US TO--
GGNNHHH!
--BREAK THROUGH!
INTO THE SEWERS?
YOU CAN STAY IF YOU WANT...
I NEVER THOUGHT I'D SEE THE DAY WHEN YOU'D TURN YOUR BACK ON ME....
...OR THE DAY WHEN I WOULDN'T TAKE ADVANTAGE OF IT!
AS MUCH AS IT PAINS ME TO SAY IT...
...TOGETHER!

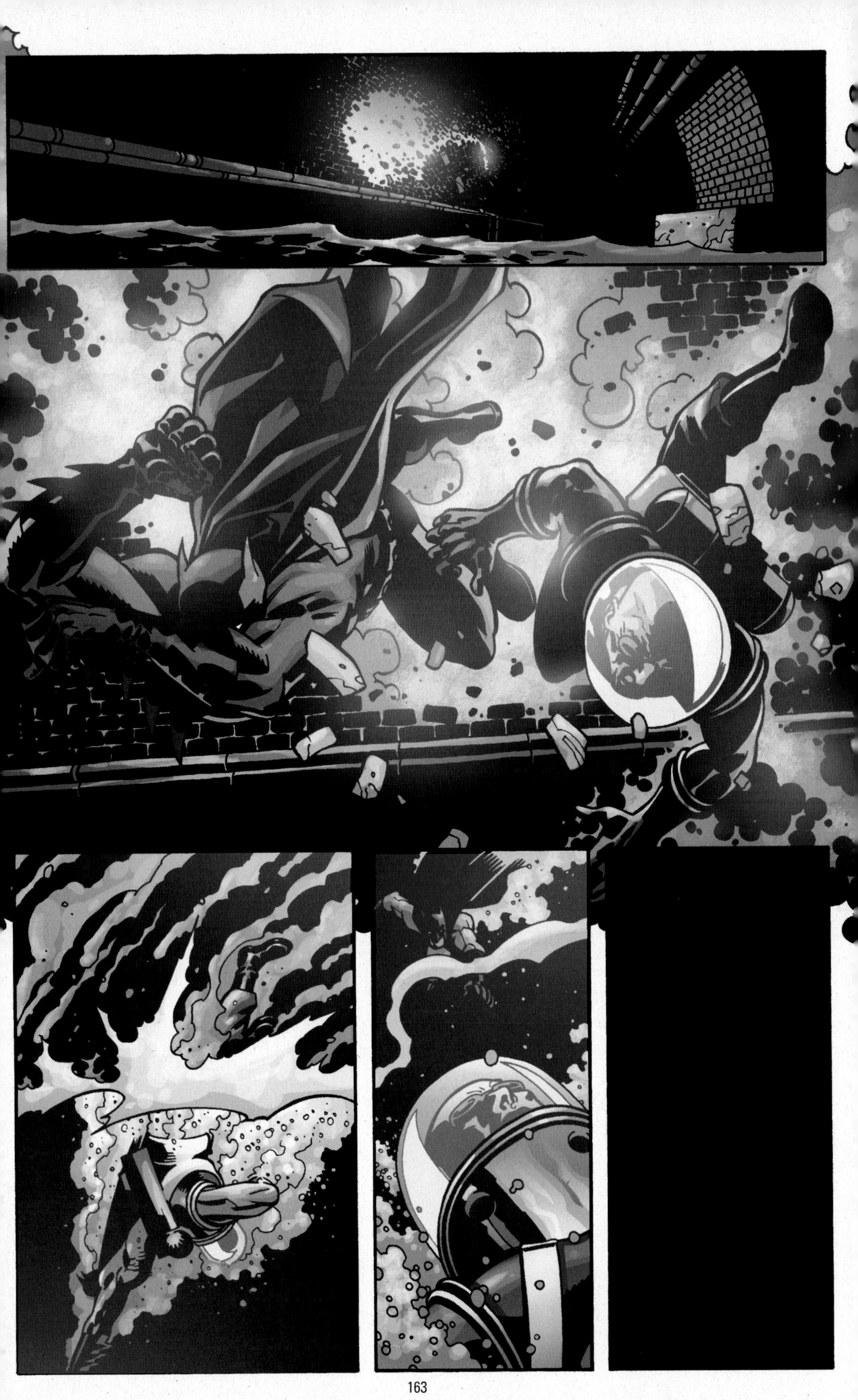

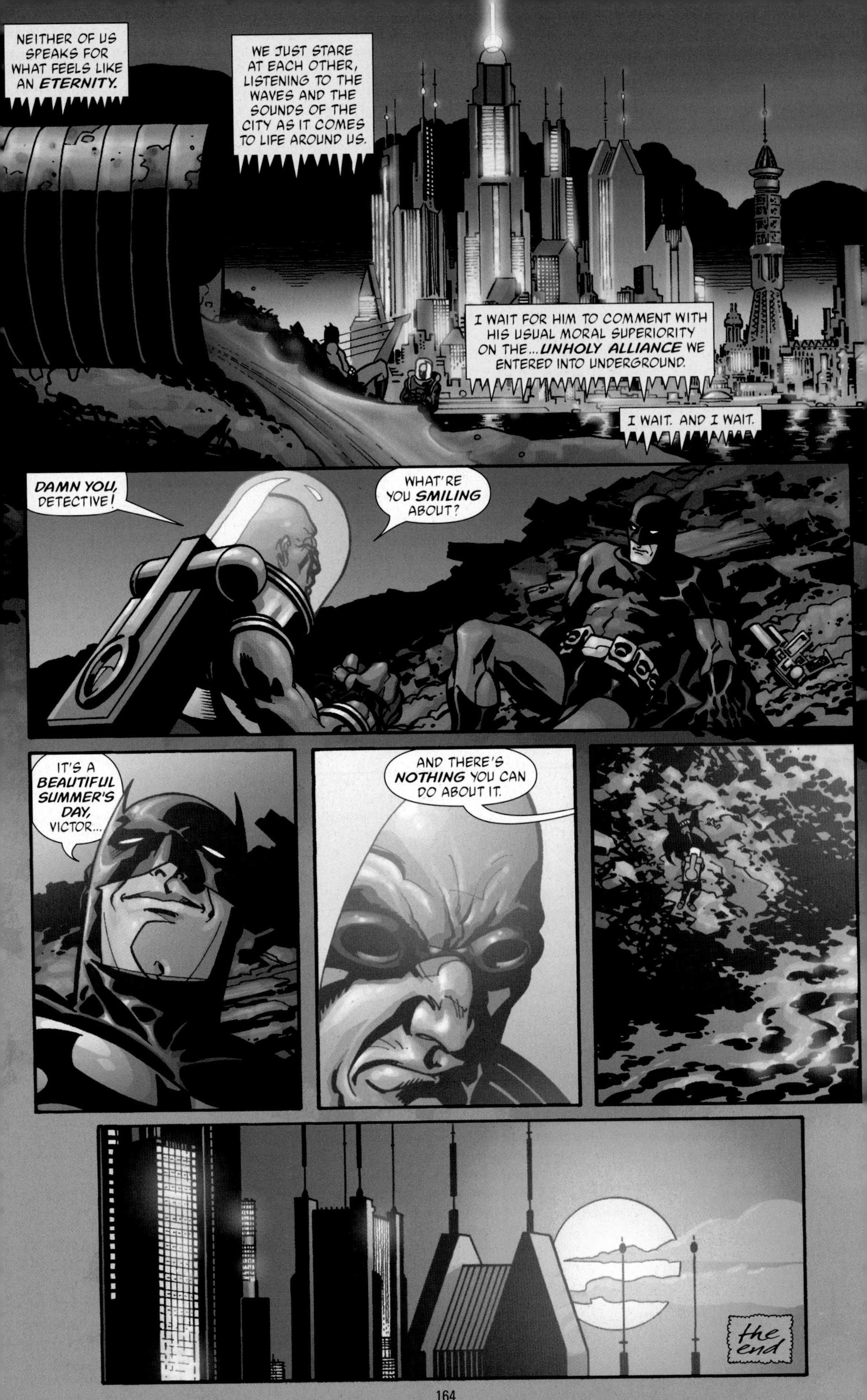
NEITHER OF US SPEAKS FOR WHAT FEELS LIKE AN ETERNITY.
WE JUST STARE AT EACH OTHER, LISTENING TO THE WAVES AND THE SOUNDS OF THE CITY AS IT COMES TO LIFE AROUND US.
I WAIT FOR HIM TO COMMENT WITH HIS USUAL MORAL SUPERIORITY ON THE... UNHOLY ALLIANCE WE ENTERED INTO UNDERGROUND.
I WAIT. AND I WAIT.
DAMN YOU, DETECTIVE!
WHAT'RE YOU SMILING ABOUT?
IT'S A BEAUTIFUL SUMMER'S DAY, VICTOR...
AND THERE'S NOTHING YOU CAN DO ABOUT IT.
the end

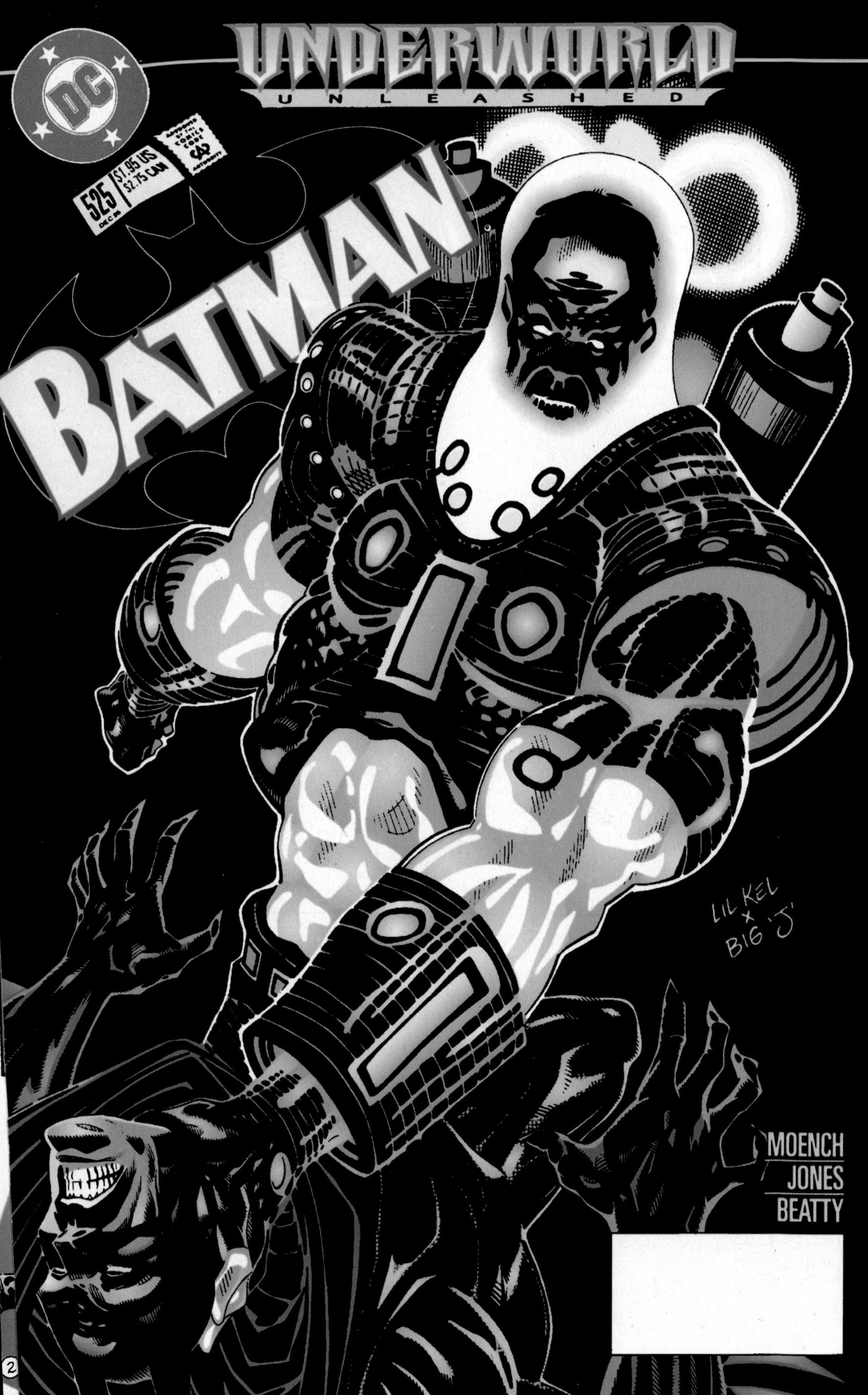
UNDERWORLD
UNLEASHED
525
$1.95 US
$2.75 CAN
BATMAN
LIL KEL
x
BIG 'J'
MOENCH
JONES
BEATTY

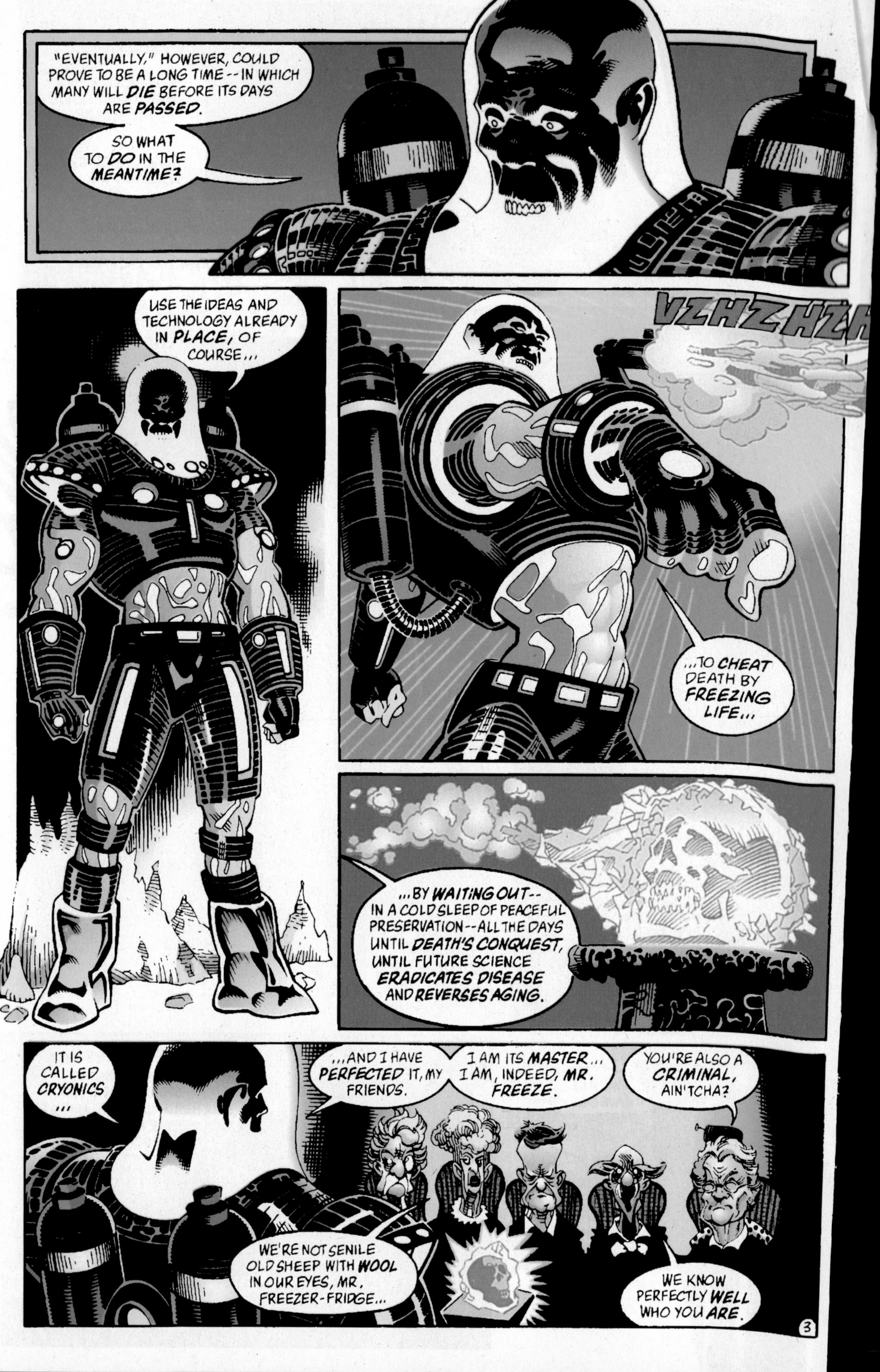

"EVENTUALLY," HOWEVER, COULD PROVE TO BE A LONG TIME--IN WHICH MANY WILL DIE BEFORE ITS DAYS ARE PASSED.
SO WHAT TO DO IN THE MEANTIME?
USE THE IDEAS AND TECHNOLOGY ALREADY IN PLACE, OF COURSE...
VZHZHZH
...TO CHEAT DEATH BY FREEZING LIFE...
...BY WAITING OUT-- IN A COLD SLEEP OF PEACEFUL PRESERVATION--ALL THE DAYS UNTIL DEATH'S CONQUEST, UNTIL FUTURE SCIENCE ERADICATES DISEASE AND REVERSES AGING.
IT IS CALLED CRYONICS ...
...AND I HAVE PERFECTED IT, MY FRIENDS.
I AM ITS MASTER... I AM, INDEED, MR. FREEZE.
YOU'RE ALSO A CRIMINAL, AIN'TCHA?
WE'RE NOT SENILE OLD SHEEP WITH WOOL IN OUR EYES, MR. FREEZER-FRIDGE...
WE KNOW PERFECTLY WELL WHO YOU ARE.
3

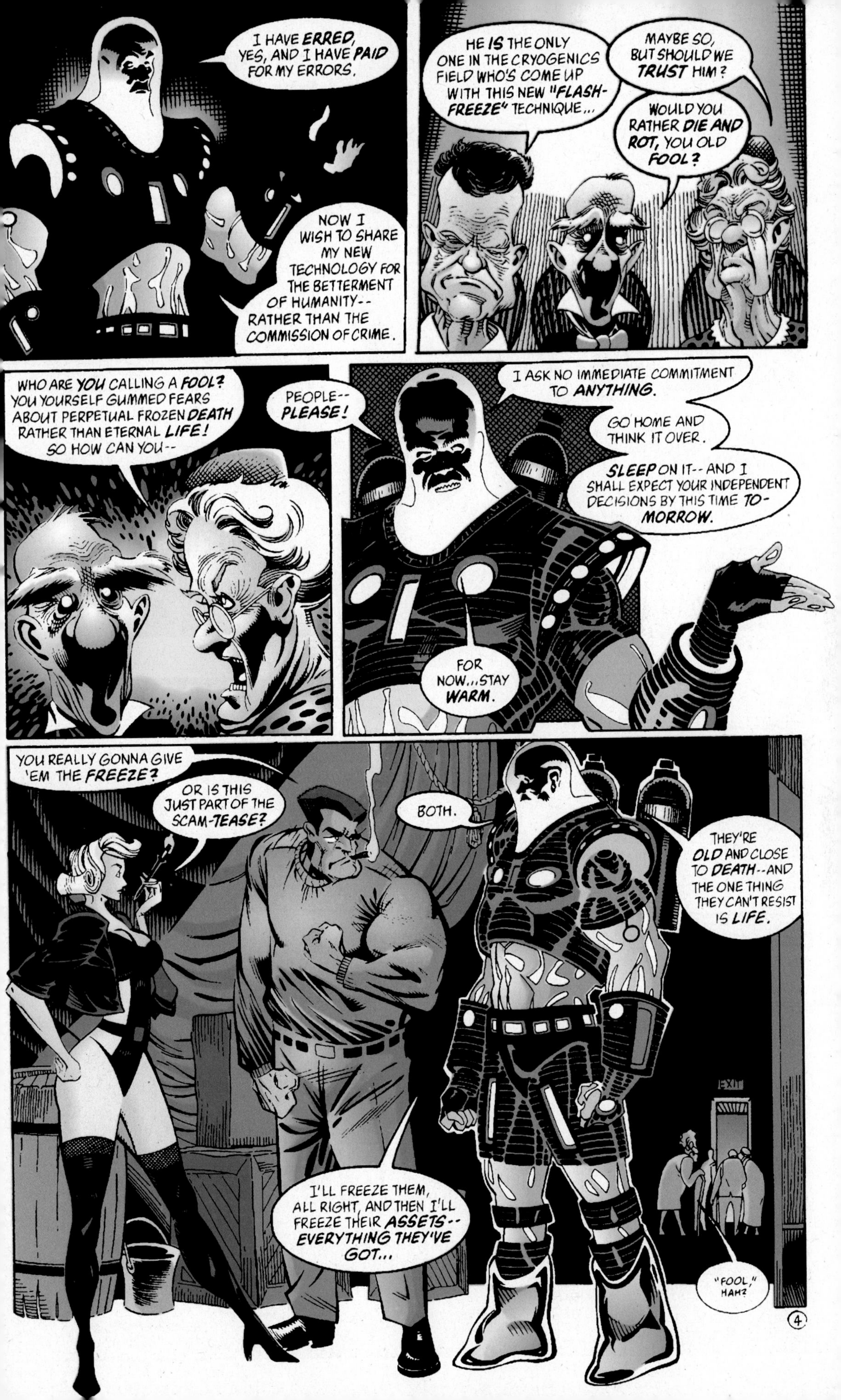
I HAVE ERRED, YES, AND I HAVE PAID FOR MY ERRORS.
NOW I WISH TO SHARE MY NEW TECHNOLOGY FOR THE BETTERMENT OF HUMANITY-- RATHER THAN THE COMMISSION OF CRIME.
HE IS THE ONLY ONE IN THE CRYOGENICS FIELD WHO'S COME UP WITH THIS NEW "FLASH-FREEZE" TECHNIQUE...
MAYBE SO, BUT SHOULD WE TRUST HIM?
WOULD YOU RATHER DIE AND ROT, YOU OLD FOOL?
WHO ARE YOU CALLING A FOOL? YOU YOURSELF GUMMED FEARS ABOUT PERPETUAL FROZEN DEATH RATHER THAN ETERNAL LIFE! SO HOW CAN YOU--
PEOPLE-- PLEASE!
I ASK NO IMMEDIATE COMMITMENT TO ANYTHING.
GO HOME AND THINK IT OVER.
SLEEP ON IT-- AND I SHALL EXPECT YOUR INDEPENDENT DECISIONS BY THIS TIME TO-MORROW.
FOR NOW... STAY WARM.
YOU REALLY GONNA GIVE 'EM THE FREEZE?
OR IS THIS JUST PART OF THE SCAM-TEASE?
BOTH.
THEY'RE OLD AND CLOSE TO DEATH--AND THE ONE THING THEY CAN'T RESIST IS LIFE.
I'LL FREEZE THEM, ALL RIGHT, AND THEN I'LL FREEZE THEIR ASSETS-- EVERYTHING THEY'VE GOT...
EXIT
"FOOL," HAH?

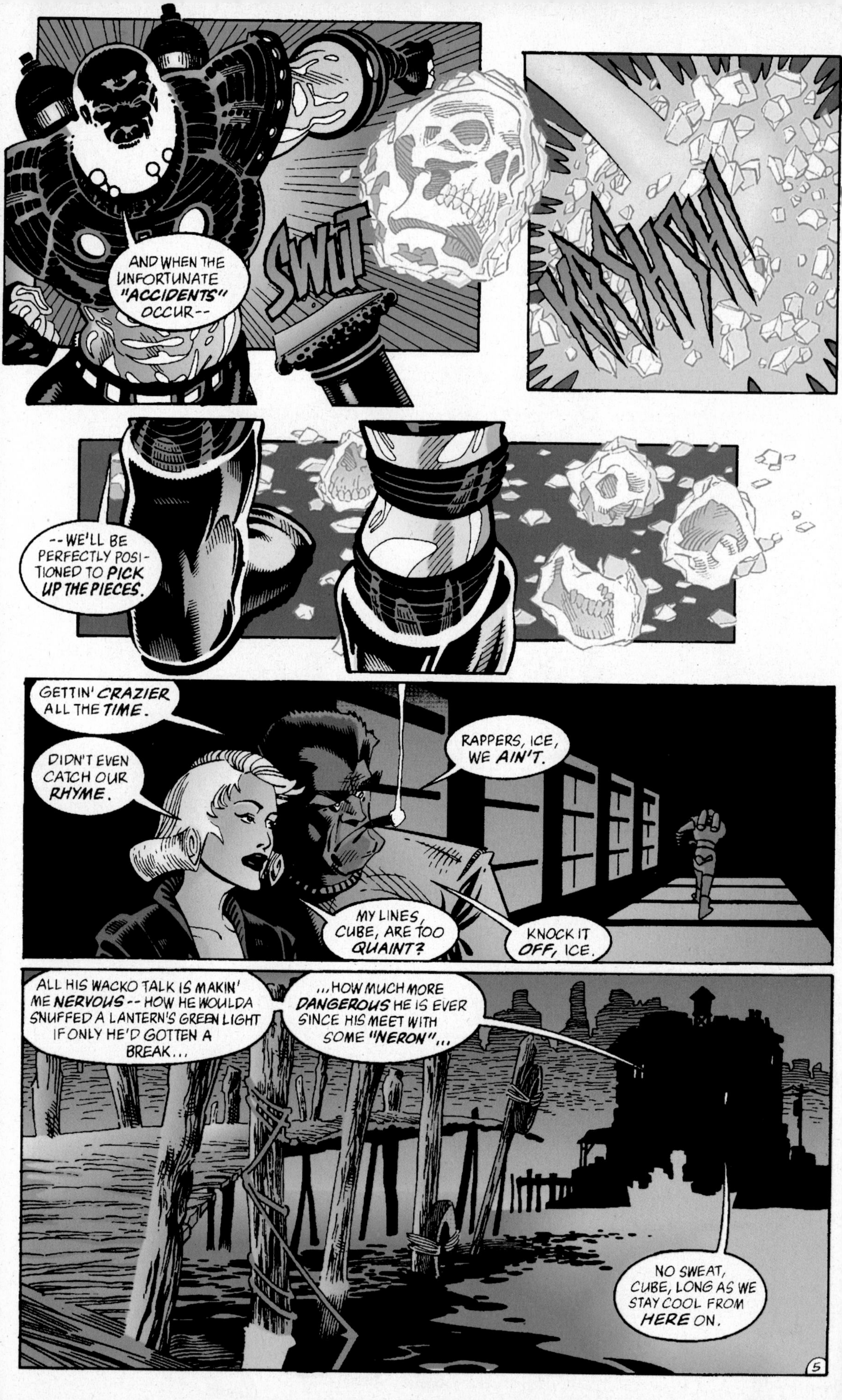
AND WHEN THE UNFORTUNATE "ACCIDENTS" OCCUR--
SWUT
--WE'LL BE PERFECTLY POSITIONED TO PICK UP THE PIECES.
GETTIN' CRAZIER ALL THE TIME.
DIDN'T EVEN CATCH OUR RHYME.
RAPPERS, ICE, WE AIN'T.
MY LINES, CUBE, ARE TOO QUAINT?
KNOCK IT OFF, ICE.
ALL HIS WACKO TALK IS MAKIN' ME NERVOUS -- HOW HE WOULDA SNUFFED A LANTERN'S GREEN LIGHT IF ONLY HE'D GOTTEN A BREAK...
...HOW MUCH MORE DANGEROUS HE IS EVER SINCE HIS MEET WITH SOME "NERON"...
NO SWEAT, CUBE, LONG AS WE STAY COOL FROM HERE ON.

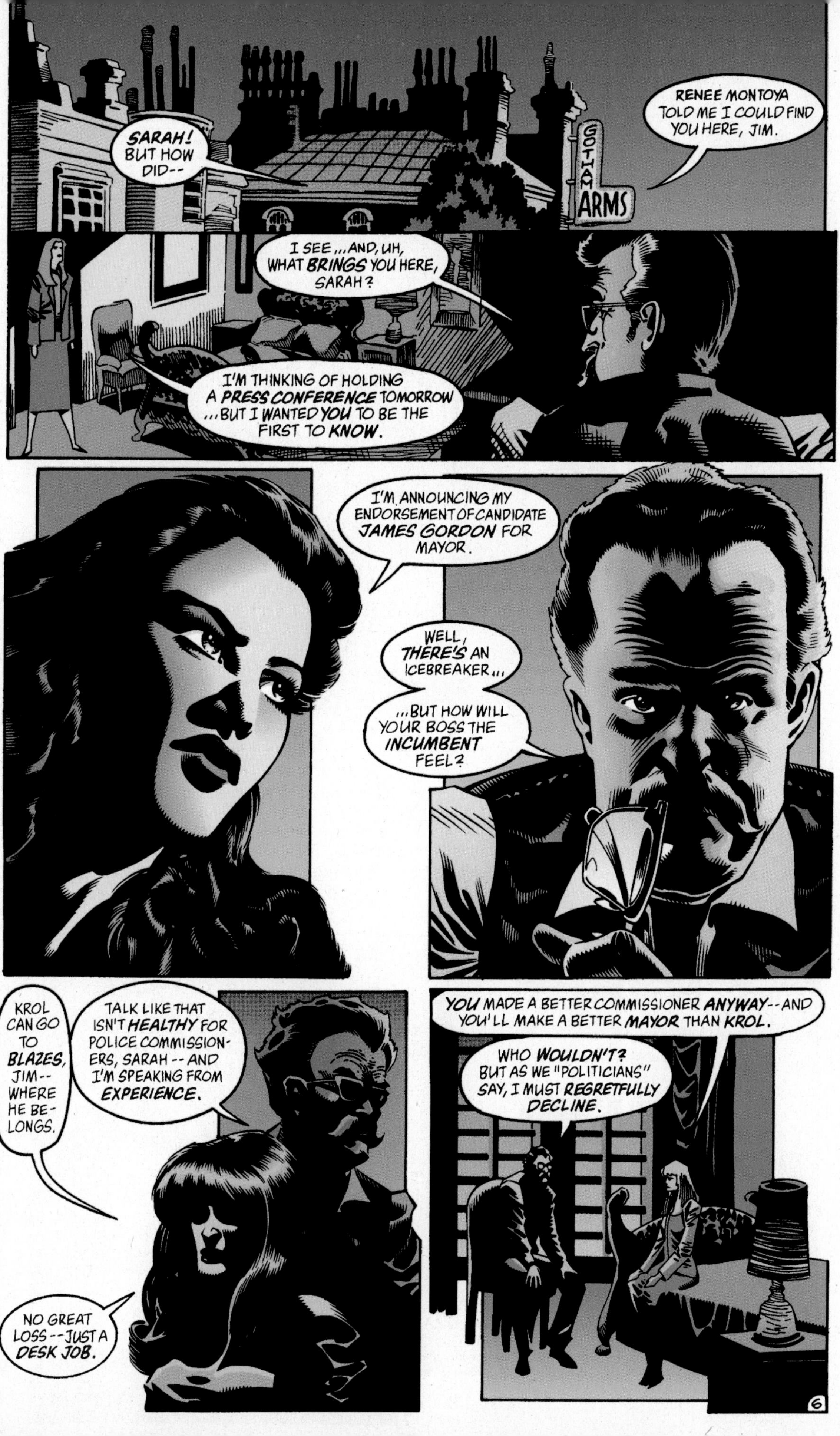
SARAH! BUT HOW DID--
RENEE MONTOYA TOLD ME I COULD FIND YOU HERE, JIM.
GOTHAM ARMS
I SEE ... AND, UH, WHAT BRINGS YOU HERE, SARAH?
I'M THINKING OF HOLDING A PRESS CONFERENCE TOMORROW ... BUT I WANTED YOU TO BE THE FIRST TO KNOW.
I'M ANNOUNCING MY ENDORSEMENT OF CANDIDATE JAMES GORDON FOR MAYOR.
WELL, THERE'S AN ICEBREAKER...
...BUT HOW WILL YOUR BOSS THE INCUMBENT FEEL?
KROL CAN GO TO BLAZES, JIM-- WHERE HE BELONGS.
TALK LIKE THAT ISN'T HEALTHY FOR POLICE COMMISSIONERS, SARAH -- AND I'M SPEAKING FROM EXPERIENCE.
NO GREAT LOSS -- JUST A DESK JOB.
YOU MADE A BETTER COMMISSIONER ANYWAY -- AND YOU'LL MAKE A BETTER MAYOR THAN KROL.
WHO WOULDN'T? BUT AS WE "POLITICIANS" SAY, I MUST REGRETFULLY DECLINE.
6

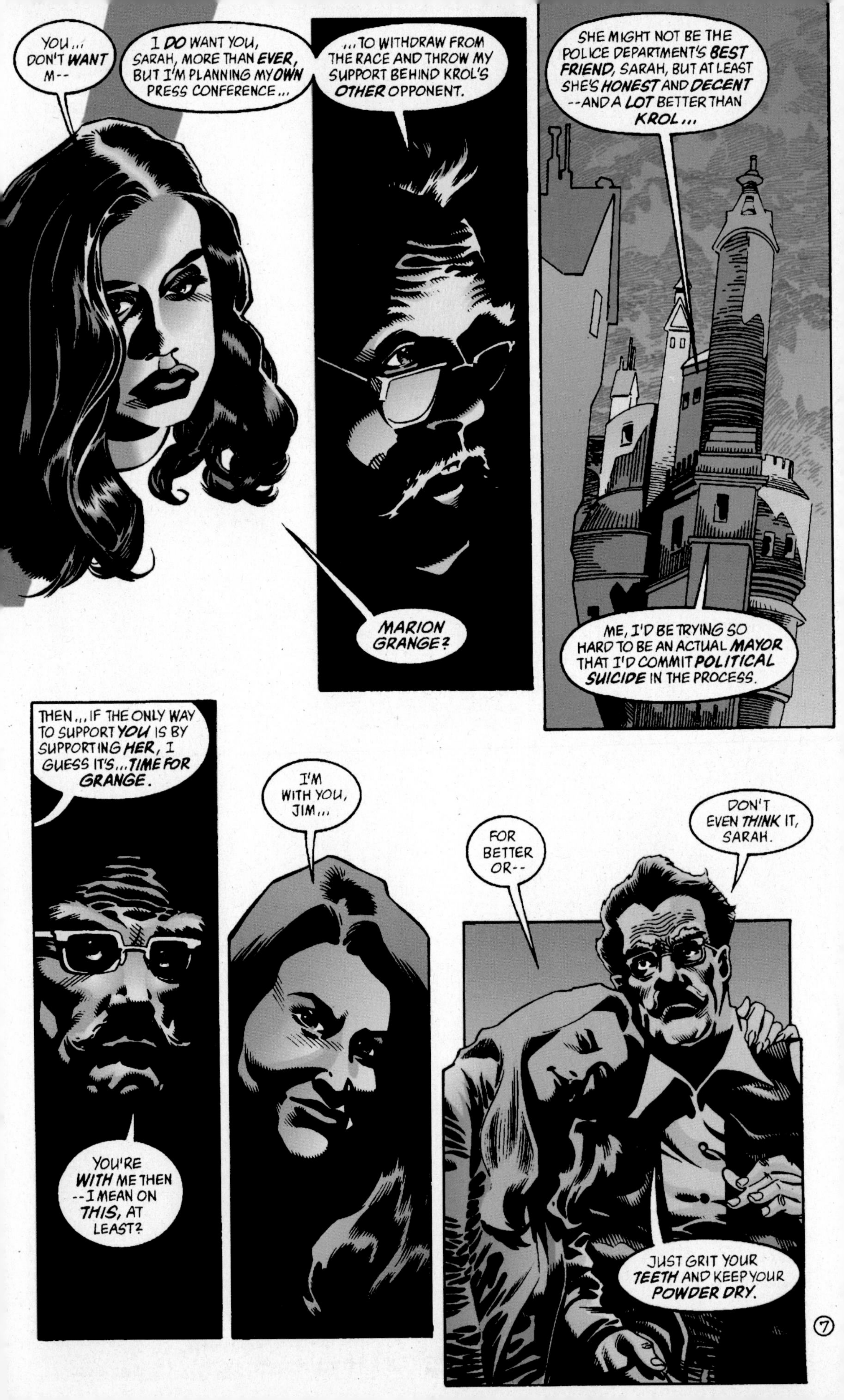
YOU... DON'T WANT M--
I DO WANT YOU, SARAH, MORE THAN EVER, BUT I'M PLANNING MY OWN PRESS CONFERENCE...
...TO WITHDRAW FROM THE RACE AND THROW MY SUPPORT BEHIND KROL'S OTHER OPPONENT.
MARION GRANGE?
SHE MIGHT NOT BE THE POLICE DEPARTMENT'S BEST FRIEND, SARAH, BUT AT LEAST SHE'S HONEST AND DECENT --AND A LOT BETTER THAN KROL...
ME, I'D BE TRYING SO HARD TO BE AN ACTUAL MAYOR THAT I'D COMMIT POLITICAL SUICIDE IN THE PROCESS.
THEN... IF THE ONLY WAY TO SUPPORT YOU IS BY SUPPORTING HER, I GUESS IT'S... TIME FOR GRANGE.
YOU'RE WITH ME THEN --I MEAN ON THIS, AT LEAST?
I'M WITH YOU, JIM...
FOR BETTER OR--
DON'T EVEN THINK IT, SARAH.
JUST GRIT YOUR TEETH AND KEEP YOUR POWDER DRY.

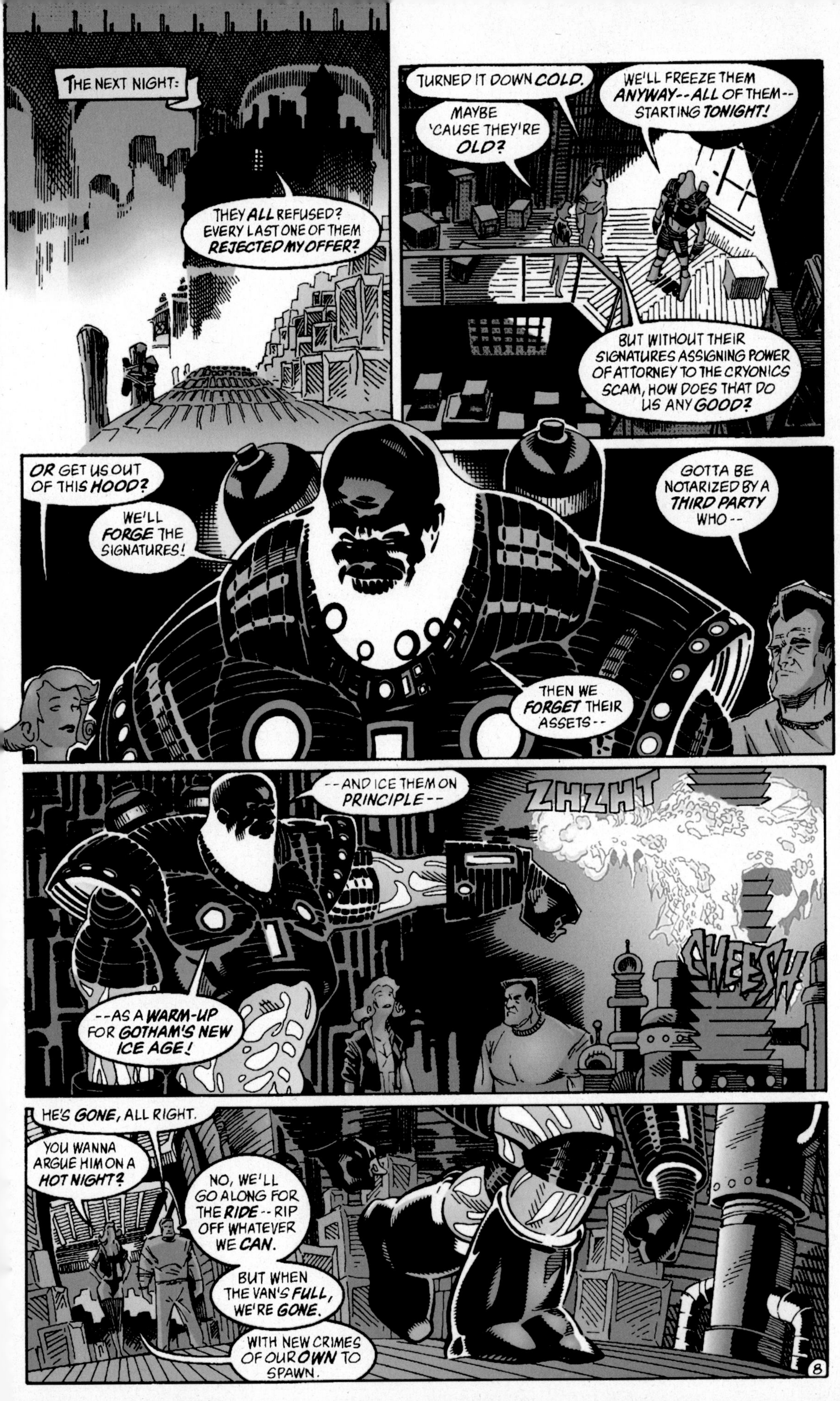
THE NEXT NIGHT:
THEY ALL REFUSED? EVERY LAST ONE OF THEM REJECTED MY OFFER?
TURNED IT DOWN COLD.
MAYBE 'CAUSE THEY'RE OLD?
WE'LL FREEZE THEM ANYWAY--ALL OF THEM--STARTING TONIGHT!
BUT WITHOUT THEIR SIGNATURES ASSIGNING POWER OF ATTORNEY TO THE CRYONICS SCAM, HOW DOES THAT DO US ANY GOOD?
OR GET US OUT OF THIS HOOD?
WE'LL FORGE THE SIGNATURES!
GOTTA BE NOTARIZED BY A THIRD PARTY WHO--
THEN WE FORGET THEIR ASSETS--
--AND ICE THEM ON PRINCIPLE--
ZHZHT
CHEESH
--AS A WARM-UP FOR GOTHAM'S NEW ICE AGE!
HE'S GONE, ALL RIGHT.
YOU WANNA ARGUE HIM ON A HOT NIGHT?
NO, WE'LL GO ALONG FOR THE RIDE--RIP OFF WHATEVER WE CAN.
BUT WHEN THE VAN'S FULL, WE'RE GONE.
WITH NEW CRIMES OF OUR OWN TO SPAWN.
8

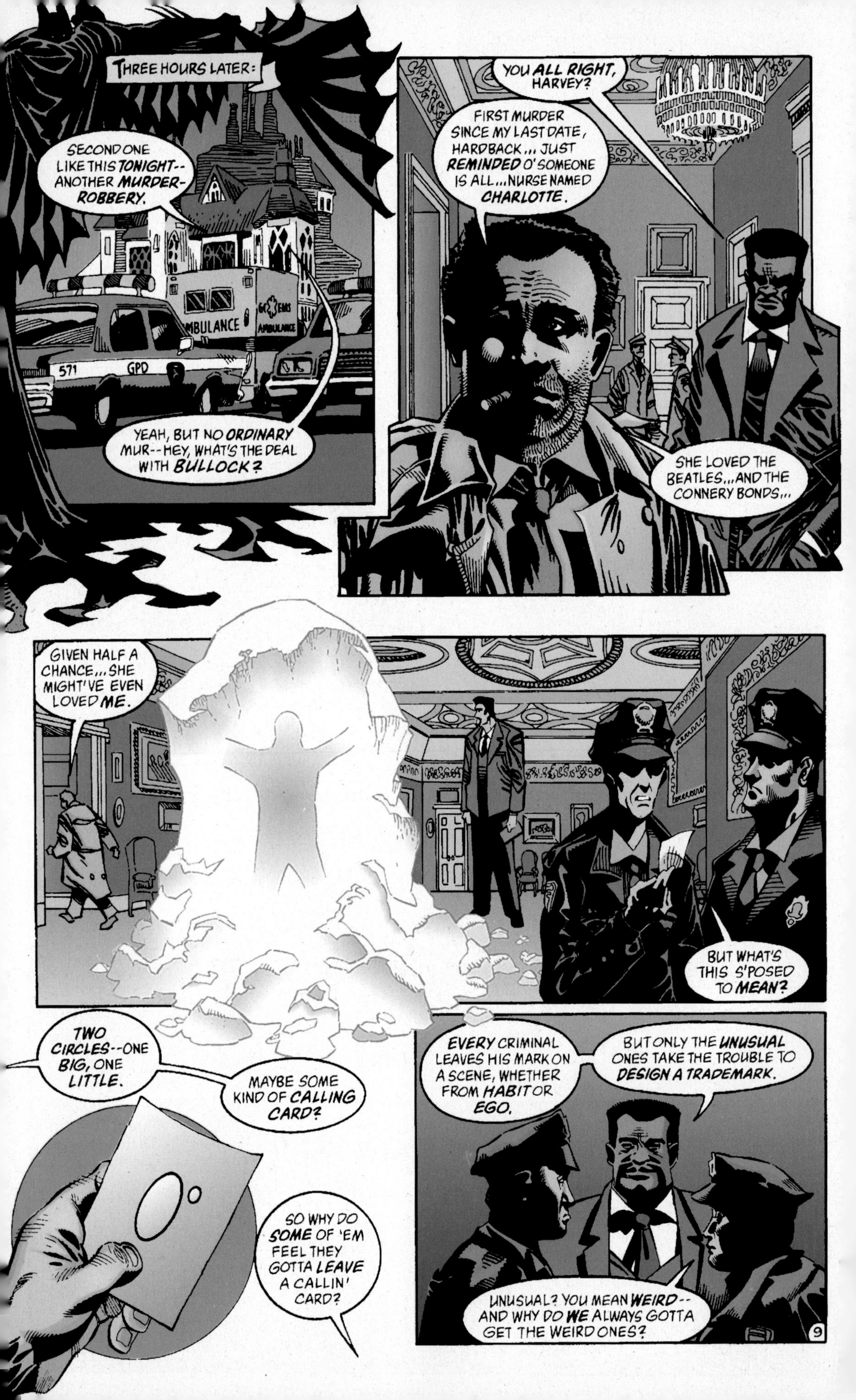
THREE HOURS LATER:
SECOND ONE LIKE THIS TONIGHT-- ANOTHER MURDER-ROBBERY.
YEAH, BUT NO ORDINARY MUR--HEY, WHAT'S THE DEAL WITH BULLOCK?
571 GPD
AMBULANCE
YOU ALL RIGHT, HARVEY?
FIRST MURDER SINCE MY LAST DATE, HARDBACK... JUST REMINDED O' SOMEONE IS ALL... NURSE NAMED CHARLOTTE.
SHE LOVED THE BEATLES... AND THE CONNERY BONDS...
GIVEN HALF A CHANCE... SHE MIGHT'VE EVEN LOVED ME.
BUT WHAT'S THIS S'POSED TO MEAN?
TWO CIRCLES--ONE BIG, ONE LITTLE.
MAYBE SOME KIND OF CALLING CARD?
SO WHY DO SOME OF 'EM FEEL THEY GOTTA LEAVE A CALLIN' CARD?
EVERY CRIMINAL LEAVES HIS MARK ON A SCENE, WHETHER FROM HABIT OR EGO.
BUT ONLY THE UNUSUAL ONES TAKE THE TROUBLE TO DESIGN A TRADEMARK.
UNUSUAL? YOU MEAN WEIRD-- AND WHY DO WE ALWAYS GOTTA GET THE WEIRD ONES?

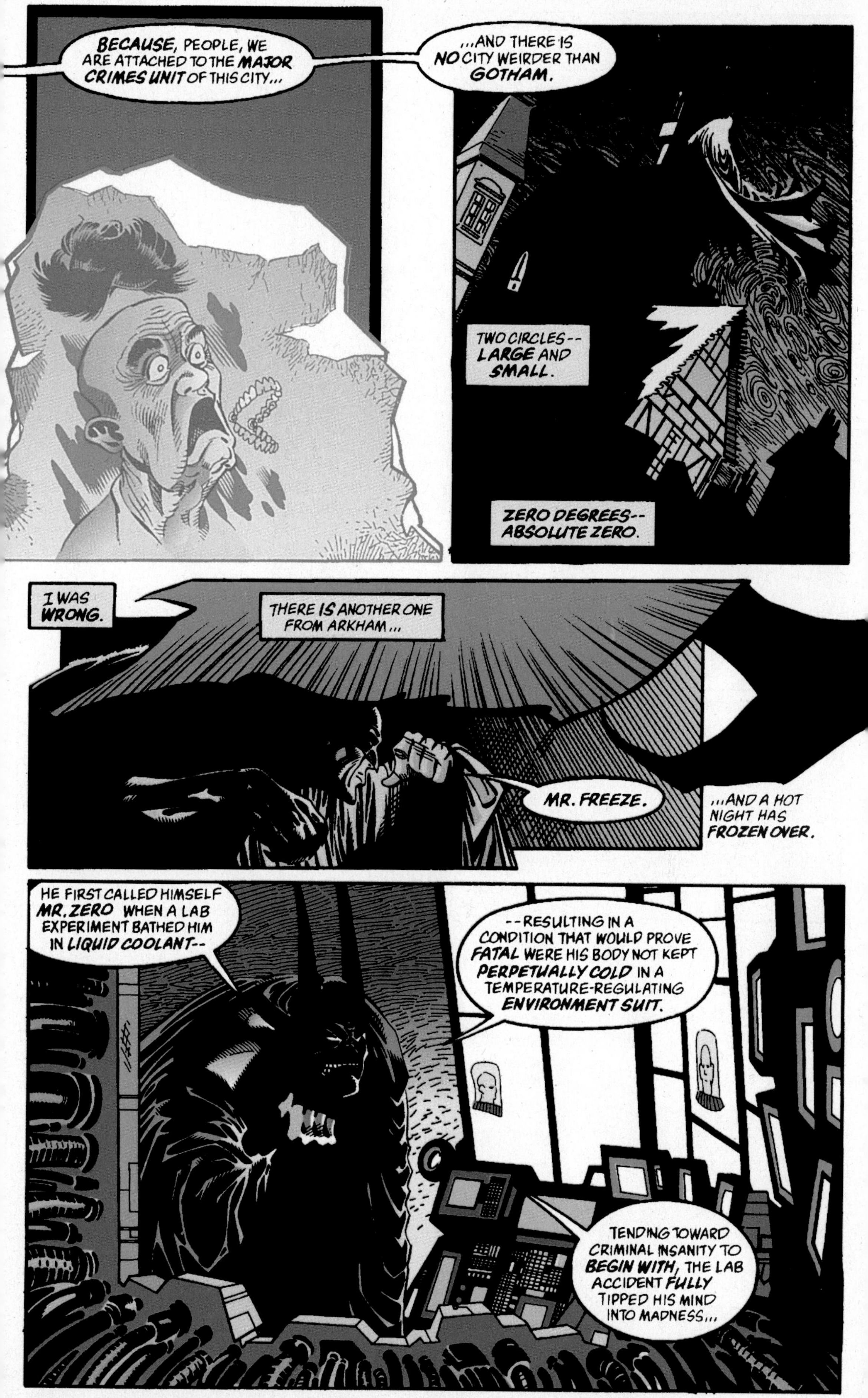
BECAUSE, PEOPLE, WE ARE ATTACHED TO THE MAJOR CRIMES UNIT OF THIS CITY...
...AND THERE IS NO CITY WEIRDER THAN GOTHAM.
TWO CIRCLES-- LARGE AND SMALL.
ZERO DEGREES-- ABSOLUTE ZERO.
I WAS WRONG.
THERE IS ANOTHER ONE FROM ARKHAM...
MR. FREEZE.
...AND A HOT NIGHT HAS FROZEN OVER.
HE FIRST CALLED HIMSELF MR. ZERO WHEN A LAB EXPERIMENT BATHED HIM IN LIQUID COOLANT--
--RESULTING IN A CONDITION THAT WOULD PROVE FATAL WERE HIS BODY NOT KEPT PERPETUALLY COLD IN A TEMPERATURE-REGULATING ENVIRONMENT SUIT.
TENDING TOWARD CRIMINAL INSANITY TO BEGIN WITH, THE LAB ACCIDENT FULLY TIPPED HIS MIND INTO MADNESS...

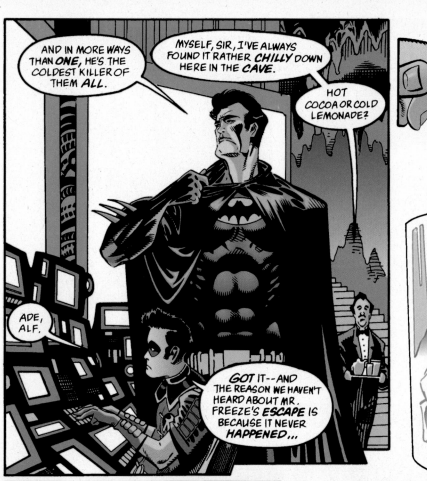

AND IN MORE WAYS THAN *ONE*, HE'S THE *COLDEST* KILLER OF THEM *ALL*.

MYSELF, SIR, I'VE ALWAYS FOUND IT RATHER *CHILLY* DOWN HERE IN THE *CAVE*.

HOT COCOA OR COLD LEMONADE?

HE WAS *RELEASED* FOLLOWING A "*POSITIVE PSY-CHOLOGICAL REVIEW.*"

ADE, ALF.

GOT IT--AND THE REASON WE HAVEN'T HEARD ABOUT MR. *FREEZE'S* *ESCAPE* IS BECAUSE IT NEVER *HAPPENED*...

MUST'VE BEEN ONE *COOL CUSTOMER* DURING HIS EVALUATION TO FOOL--

NO *QUIPS*, ROBIN--WE DON'T HAVE THE TIME TO *WASTE*.

HIGH VAULTED "CEILINGS," SO TO SPEAK...

PERPETUALLY *DRAFTY*...

INVADE THE *POLICE COMPUTER LOG*--NOW.

OKAY, OKAY, TAKE IT *EASY*.

IT *ISN'T EASY*, ROBIN, AND IT ISN'T *FUN*.

IT'S *LIFE AND DEATH*.

ALL *RIGHT*.

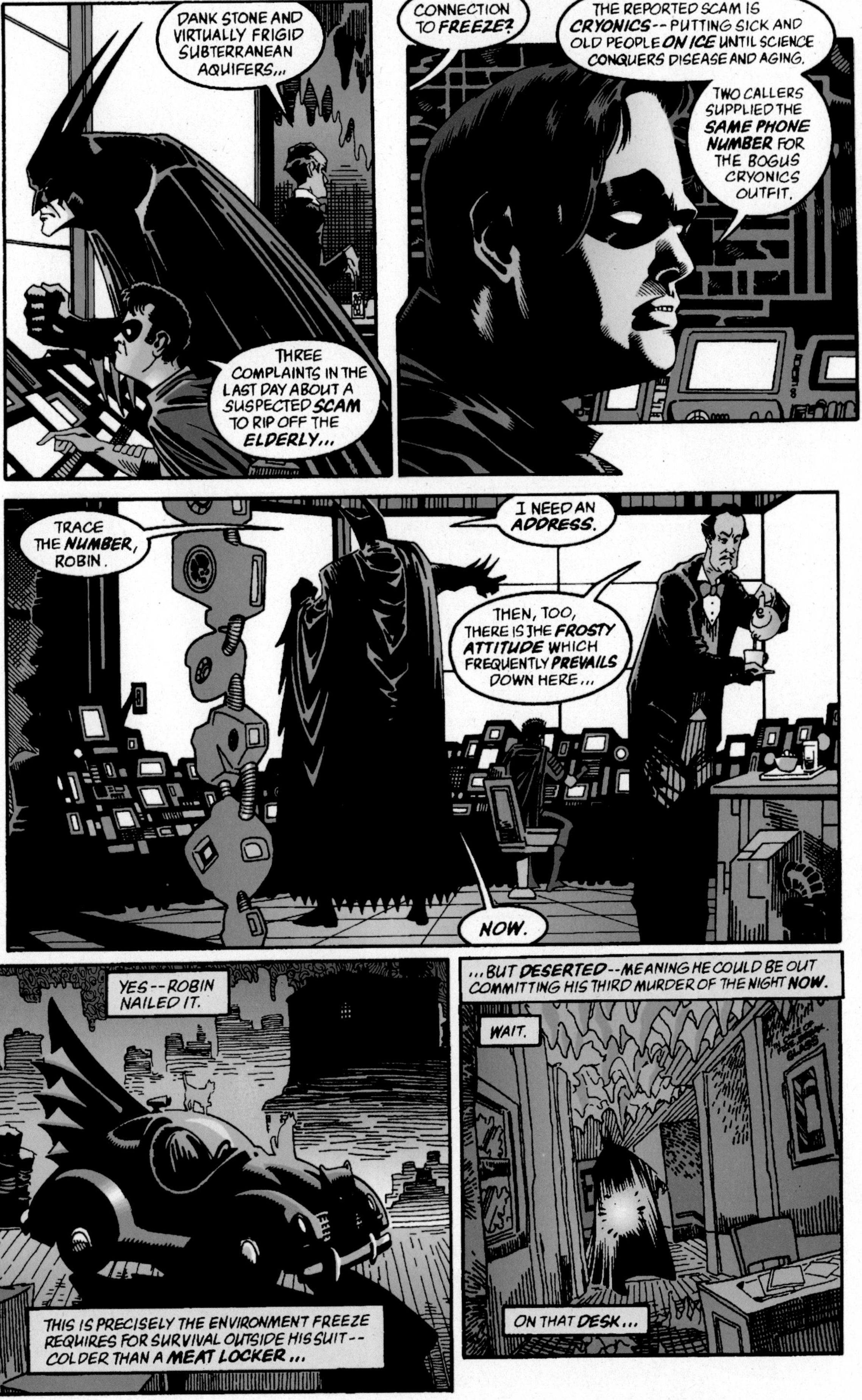

DANK STONE AND VIRTUALLY FRIGID SUBTERRANEAN AQUIFERS...
THREE COMPLAINTS IN THE LAST DAY ABOUT A SUSPECTED SCAM TO RIP OFF THE ELDERLY...
CONNECTION TO FREEZE?
THE REPORTED SCAM IS CRYONICS--PUTTING SICK AND OLD PEOPLE ON ICE UNTIL SCIENCE CONQUERS DISEASE AND AGING.
TWO CALLERS SUPPLIED THE SAME PHONE NUMBER FOR THE BOGUS CRYONICS OUTFIT.
TRACE THE NUMBER, ROBIN.
I NEED AN ADDRESS.
THEN, TOO, THERE IS THE FROSTY ATTITUDE WHICH FREQUENTLY PREVAILS DOWN HERE...
NOW.
YES--ROBIN NAILED IT.
THIS IS PRECISELY THE ENVIRONMENT FREEZE REQUIRES FOR SURVIVAL OUTSIDE HIS SUIT--COLDER THAN A MEAT LOCKER...
...BUT DESERTED--MEANING HE COULD BE OUT COMMITTING HIS THIRD MURDER OF THE NIGHT NOW.
WAIT.
ON THAT DESK...

A LIST--

And the world shall end in ice.

~~Comstock~~
~~Jaynes~~
Vandemeer
Kaminski
Sperling

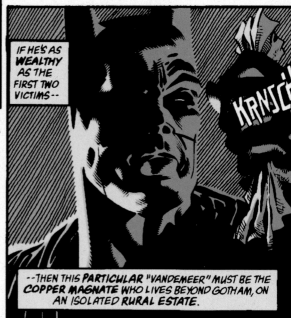

IF HE'S AS WEALTHY AS THE FIRST TWO VICTIMS--

KRNSCH

--AND THE FIRST TWO NAMES, CROSSED OFF, MATCH THE **MURDER VICTIMS**-- PUTTING THE **THIRD** NAME IN OBVIOUS **JEOPARDY**.

--THEN THIS PARTICULAR "VANDEMEER" MUST BE THE **COPPER MAGNATE** WHO LIVES BEYOND GOTHAM, ON AN ISOLATED RURAL ESTATE.

--UNDER THE CRUSHING WEIGHT OF A **PERSONAL GLACIER!**

AND UNLESS I **OUTRACE** THE **FLOW OF ICE,** ANOTHER LONG LIFE COULD SOON END--

RANSOME! THERE'S A **DRAFT** IN HERE!

HAVE YOU LEFT A BLOODY **WINDOW** OPEN AGAIN?

RANSOME--?!

VRAOWW

COMING, MR. VANDEMEER!

BUT I DON'T BELIEVE ANY OF THE WINDOWS ARE--

STU

⌐UHN--!⌐

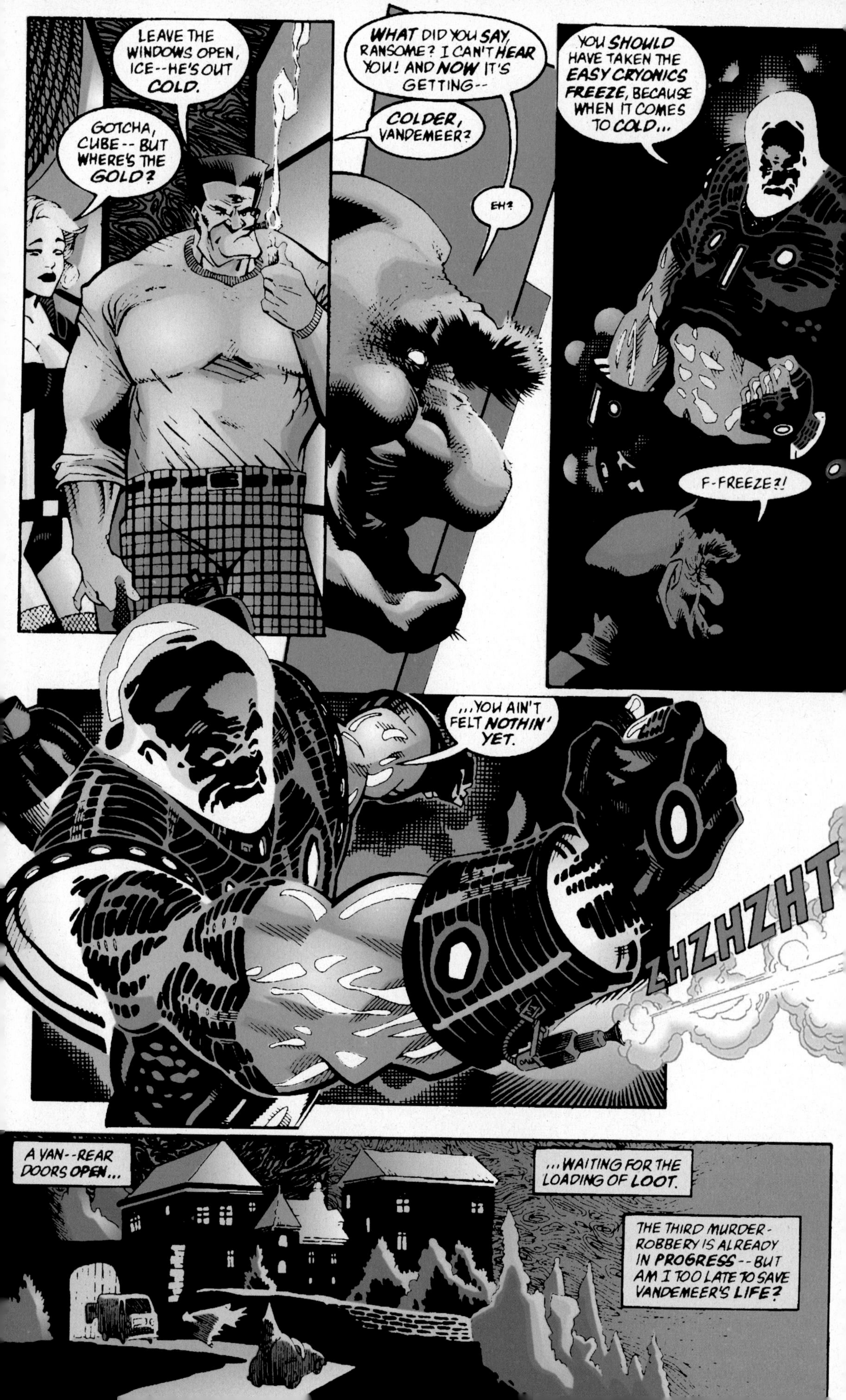
LEAVE THE WINDOWS OPEN, ICE--HE'S OUT COLD.
GOTCHA, CUBE--BUT WHERE'S THE GOLD?
WHAT DID YOU SAY, RANSOME? I CAN'T HEAR YOU! AND NOW IT'S GETTING--
COLDER, VANDEMEER?
EH?
YOU SHOULD HAVE TAKEN THE EASY CRYONICS FREEZE, BECAUSE WHEN IT COMES TO COLD...
F-FREEZE?!
...YOU AIN'T FELT NOTHIN' YET.
ZHZHZHT
A VAN--REAR DOORS OPEN...
...WAITING FOR THE LOADING OF LOOT.
THE THIRD MURDER-ROBBERY IS ALREADY IN PROGRESS--BUT AM I TOO LATE TO SAVE VANDEMEER'S LIFE?

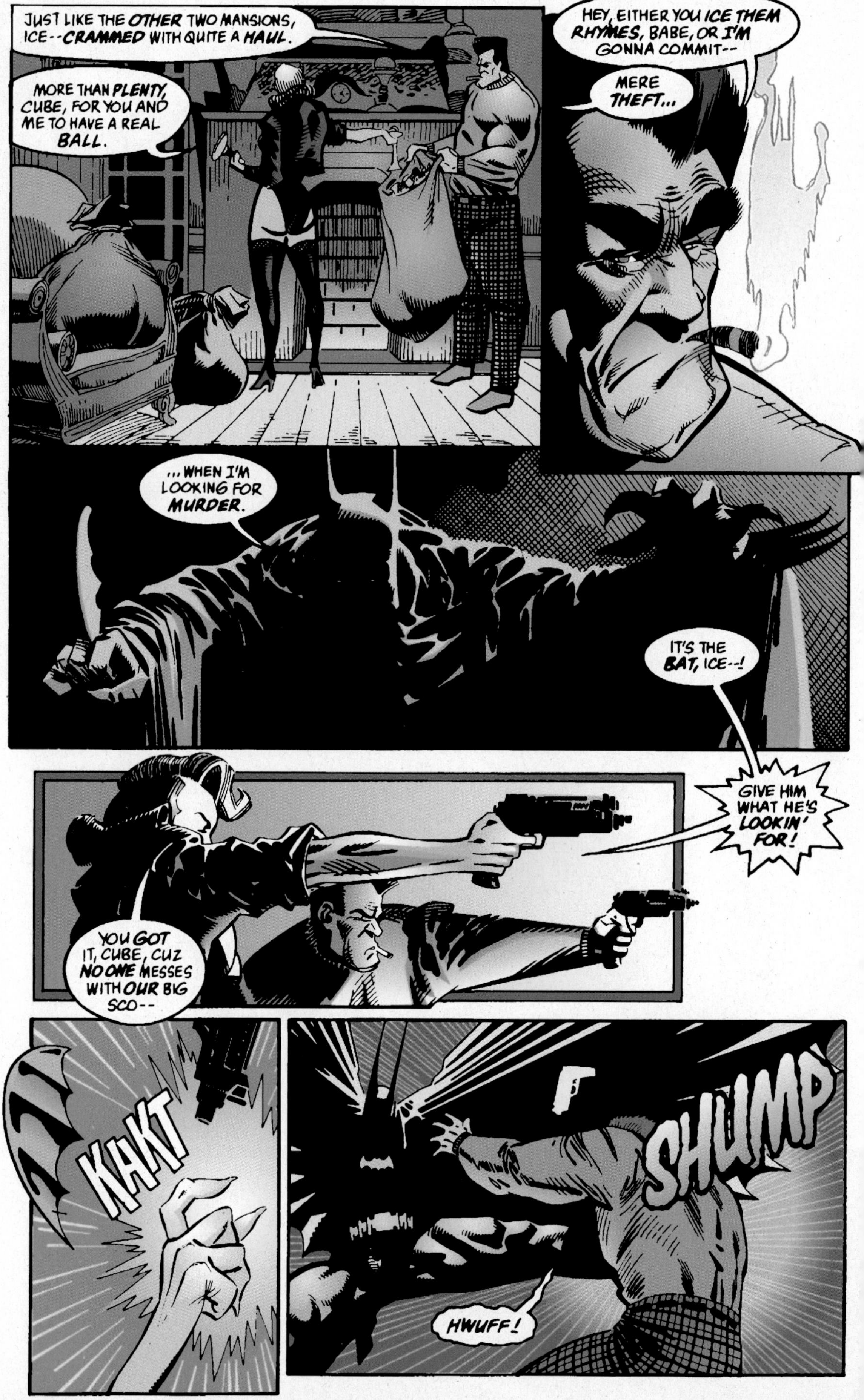

JUST LIKE THE OTHER TWO MANSIONS, ICE--CRAMMED WITH QUITE A HAUL.
MORE THAN PLENTY, CUBE, FOR YOU AND ME TO HAVE A REAL BALL.
HEY, EITHER YOU ICE THEM RHYMES, BABE, OR I'M GONNA COMMIT--
MERE THEFT...
...WHEN I'M LOOKING FOR MURDER.
IT'S THE BAT, ICE--!
GIVE HIM WHAT HE'S LOOKIN' FOR!
YOU GOT IT, CUBE, CUZ NO ONE MESSES WITH OUR BIG SCO--
KAKT
SHUMP
HWUFF!

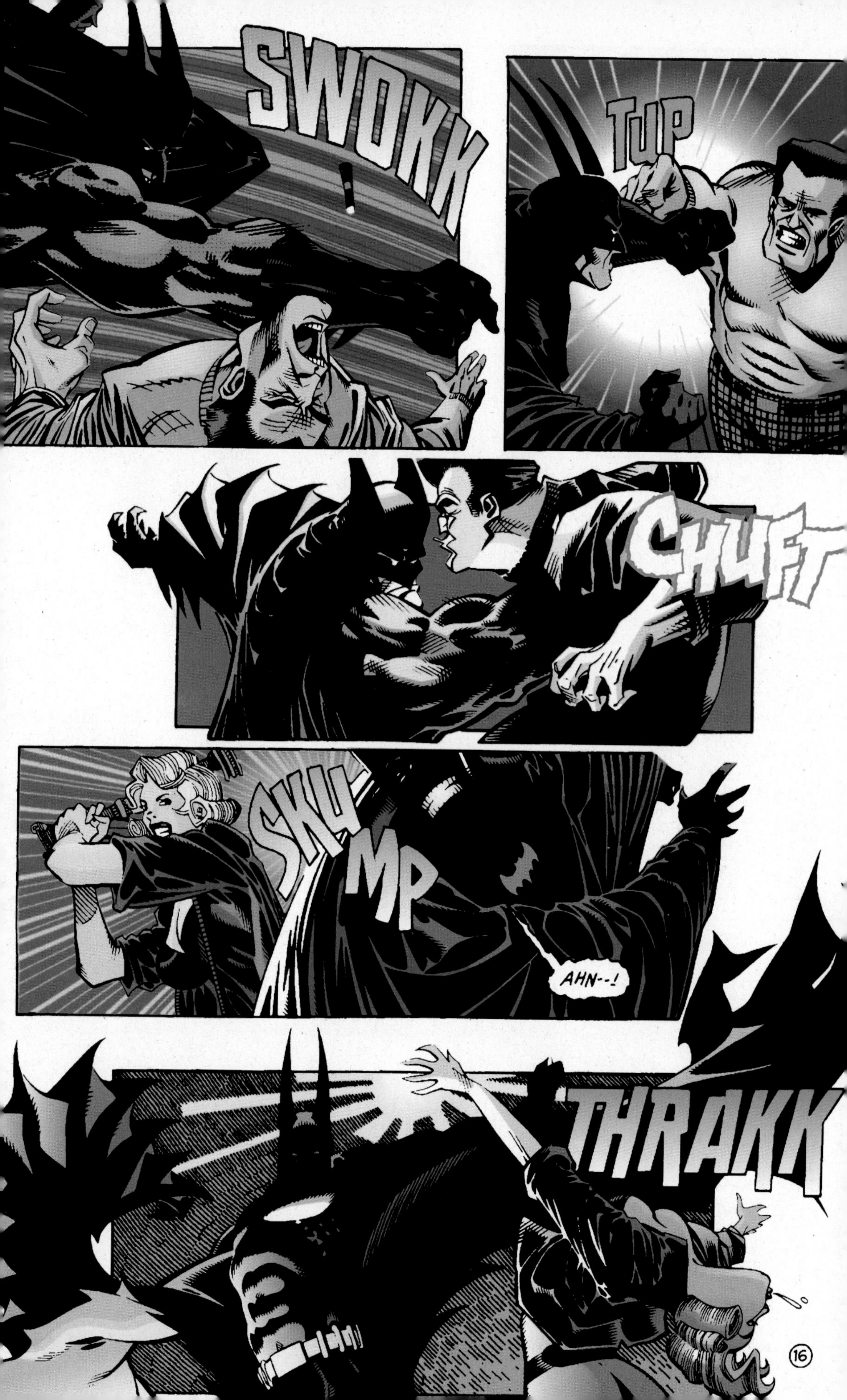
SWOKK
TUP
CHUFT
SKUMP
AHN--!
THRAKK

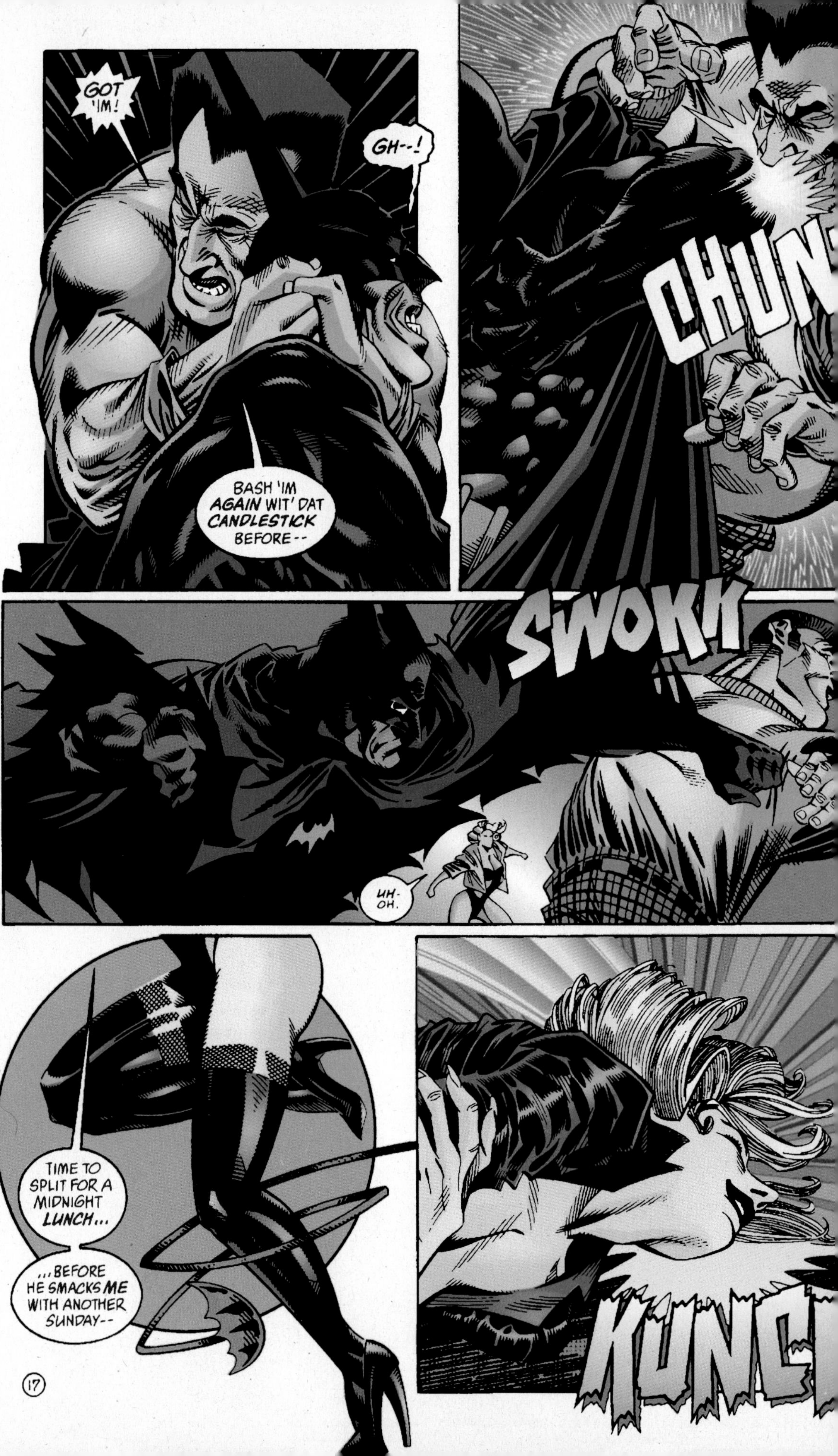

GOT 'IM!
GH--!
BASH 'IM AGAIN WIT' DAT CANDLESTICK BEFORE--
SWOKK
UH-OH.
TIME TO SPLIT FOR A MIDNIGHT LUNCH...
...BEFORE HE SMACKS ME WITH ANOTHER SUNDAY--

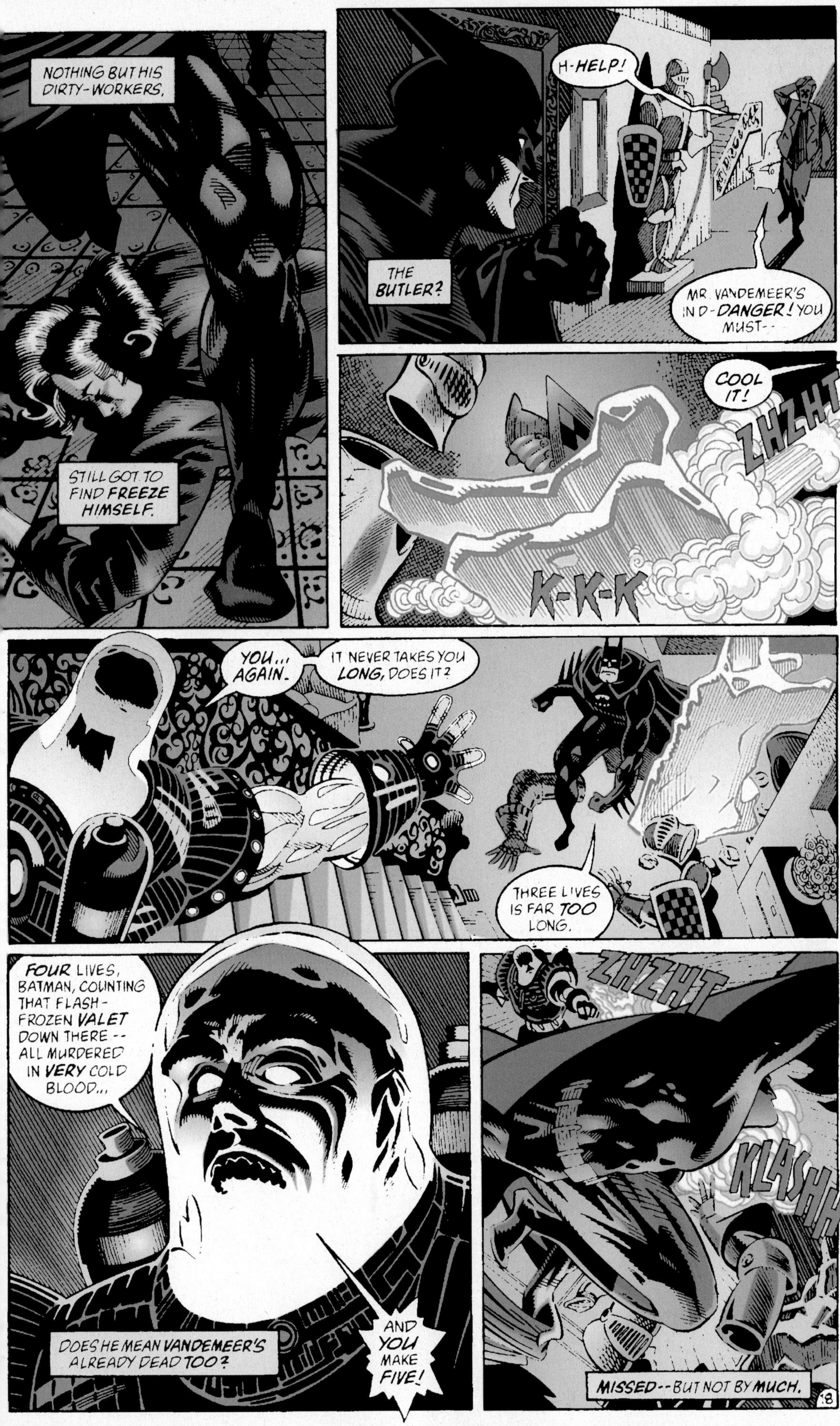
NOTHING BUT HIS DIRTY-WORKERS.
STILL GOT TO FIND FREEZE HIMSELF.
H-HELP!
THE BUTLER?
MR. VANDEMEER'S IN D-DANGER! YOU MUST--
COOL IT!
ZHZHT
K-K-K
YOU... AGAIN.
IT NEVER TAKES YOU LONG, DOES IT?
THREE LIVES IS FAR TOO LONG.
FOUR LIVES, BATMAN, COUNTING THAT FLASH-FROZEN VALET DOWN THERE -- ALL MURDERED IN VERY COLD BLOOD...
DOES HE MEAN VANDEMEER'S ALREADY DEAD TOO?
AND YOU MAKE FIVE!
ZHZHT
KLASHH
MISSED--BUT NOT BY MUCH.

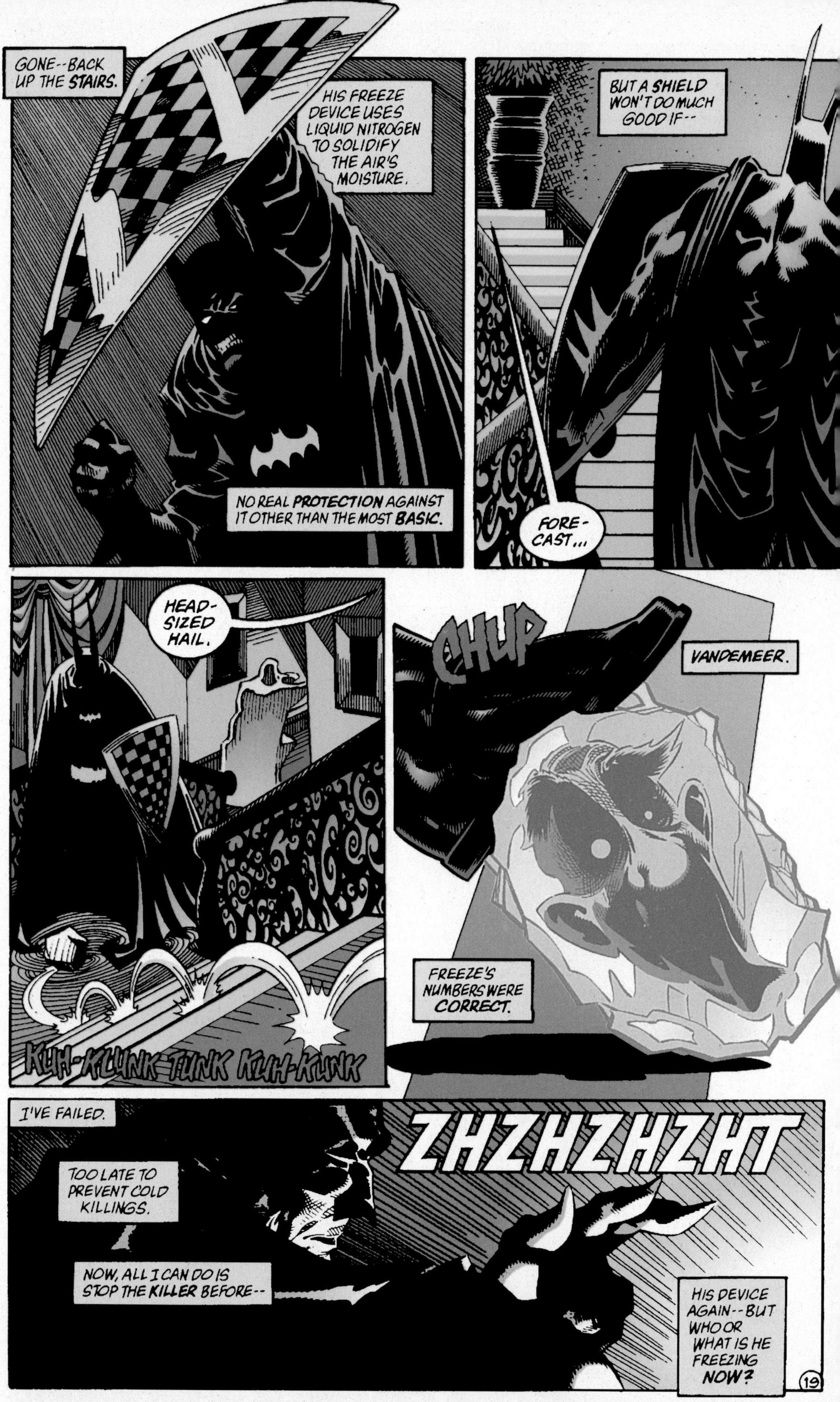

GONE--BACK UP THE STAIRS.
HIS FREEZE DEVICE USES LIQUID NITROGEN TO SOLIDIFY THE AIR'S MOISTURE.
NO REAL PROTECTION AGAINST IT OTHER THAN THE MOST BASIC.
BUT A SHIELD WON'T DO MUCH GOOD IF--
FORE-CAST...
HEAD-SIZED HAIL.
KUH-KLUNK TUNK KUH-KUNK
CHUP
VANDEMEER.
FREEZE'S NUMBERS WERE CORRECT.
I'VE FAILED.
ZHZHZHZHZHT
TOO LATE TO PREVENT COLD KILLINGS.
NOW, ALL I CAN DO IS STOP THE KILLER BEFORE--
HIS DEVICE AGAIN--BUT WHO OR WHAT IS HE FREEZING NOW?

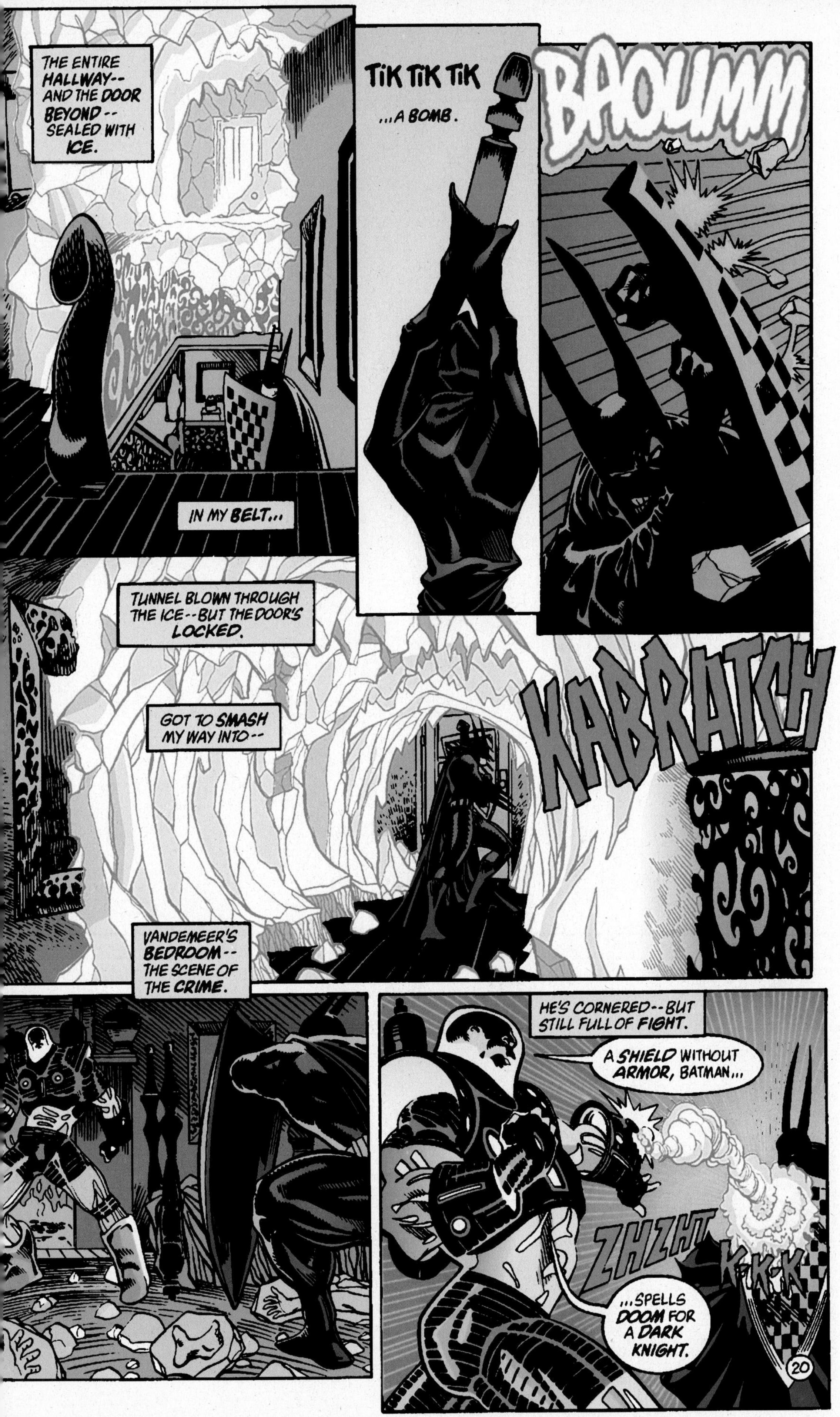
THE ENTIRE HALLWAY-- AND THE DOOR BEYOND-- SEALED WITH ICE.
IN MY BELT...
TIK TIK TIK
...A BOMB.
BAOUMM
TUNNEL BLOWN THROUGH THE ICE--BUT THE DOOR'S LOCKED.
GOT TO SMASH MY WAY INTO--
KABRATCH
VANDEMEER'S BEDROOM-- THE SCENE OF THE CRIME.
HE'S CORNERED--BUT STILL FULL OF FIGHT.
A SHIELD WITHOUT ARMOR, BATMAN...
ZHZHT
KKK
...SPELLS DOOM FOR A DARK KNIGHT.
20

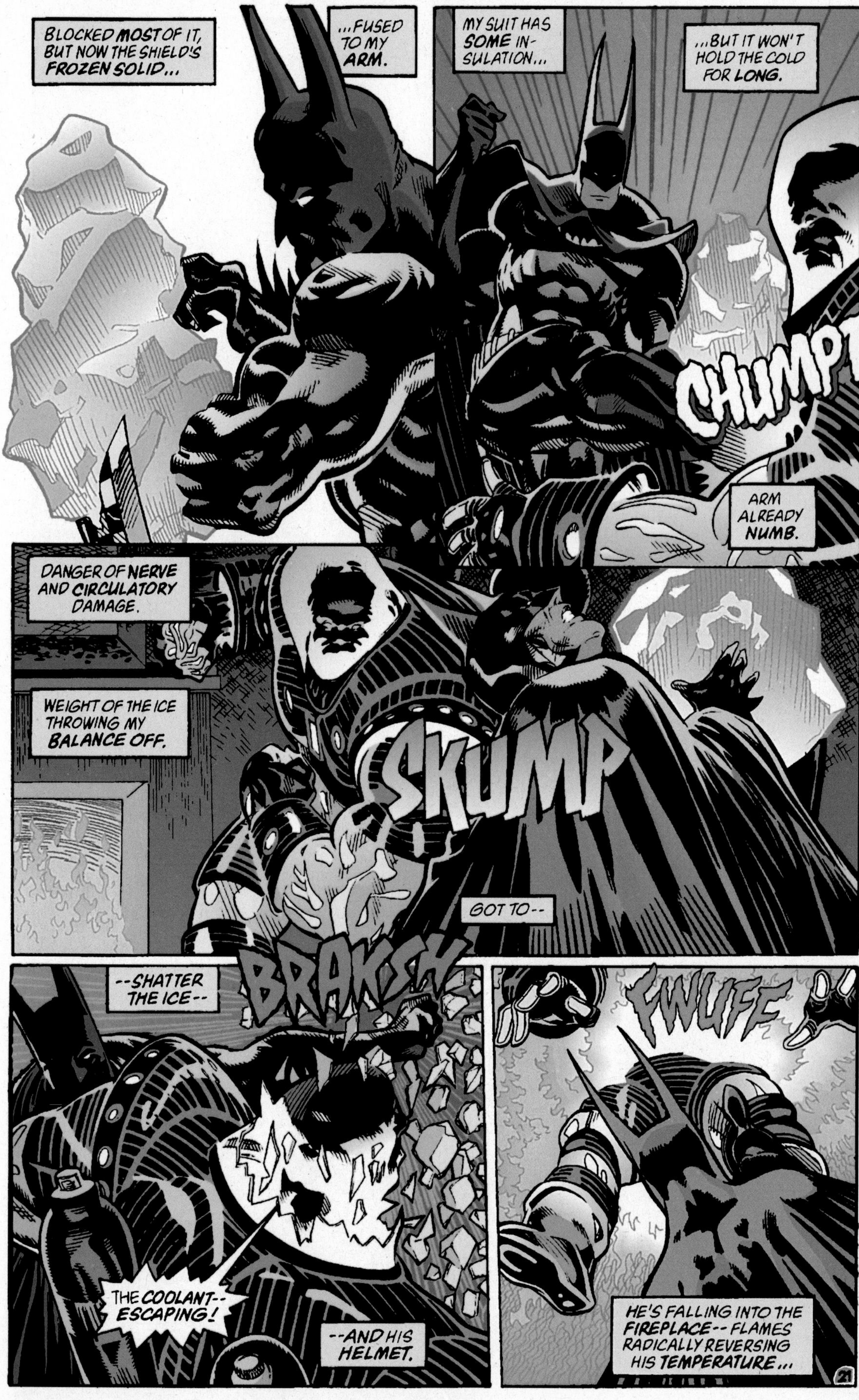
BLOCKED MOST OF IT, BUT NOW THE SHIELD'S FROZEN SOLID...
...FUSED TO MY ARM.
MY SUIT HAS SOME IN-SULATION...
...BUT IT WON'T HOLD THE COLD FOR LONG.
CHUMP
ARM ALREADY NUMB.
DANGER OF NERVE AND CIRCULATORY DAMAGE.
WEIGHT OF THE ICE THROWING MY BALANCE OFF.
SKUMP
GOT TO--
BRAKSH
--SHATTER THE ICE--
THE COOLANT--ESCAPING!
--AND HIS HELMET.
FWUFF
HE'S FALLING INTO THE FIREPLACE--FLAMES RADICALLY REVERSING HIS TEMPERATURE...
21

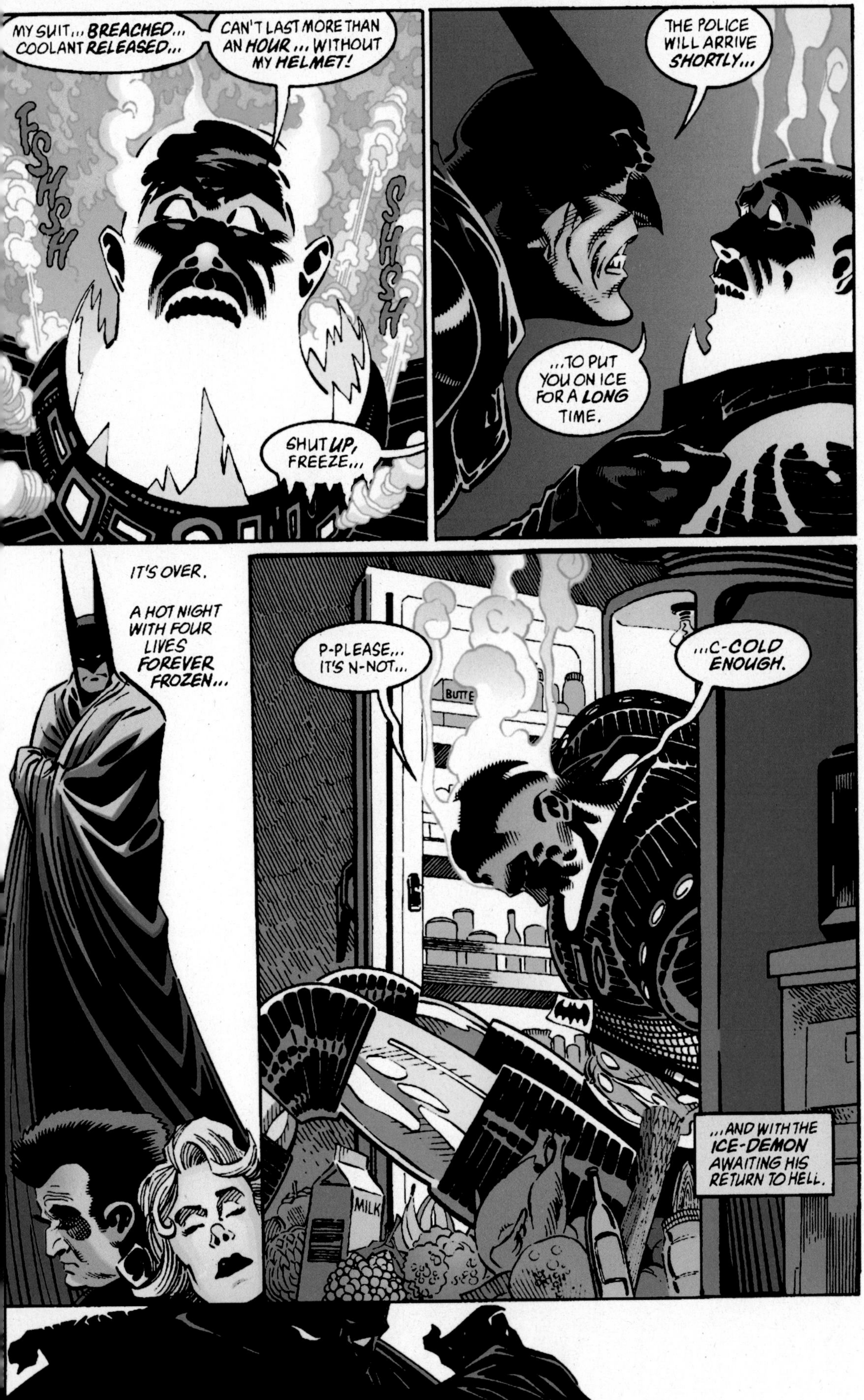
MY SUIT... BREACHED... COOLANT RELEASED...
CAN'T LAST MORE THAN AN HOUR... WITHOUT MY HELMET!
FSHSH
SHSH
SHUT UP, FREEZE...
THE POLICE WILL ARRIVE SHORTLY...
...TO PUT YOU ON ICE FOR A LONG TIME.
IT'S OVER.
A HOT NIGHT WITH FOUR LIVES FOREVER FROZEN...
P-PLEASE... IT'S N-NOT...
...C-COLD ENOUGH.
BUTTE
MILK
...AND WITH THE ICE-DEMON AWAITING HIS RETURN TO HELL.

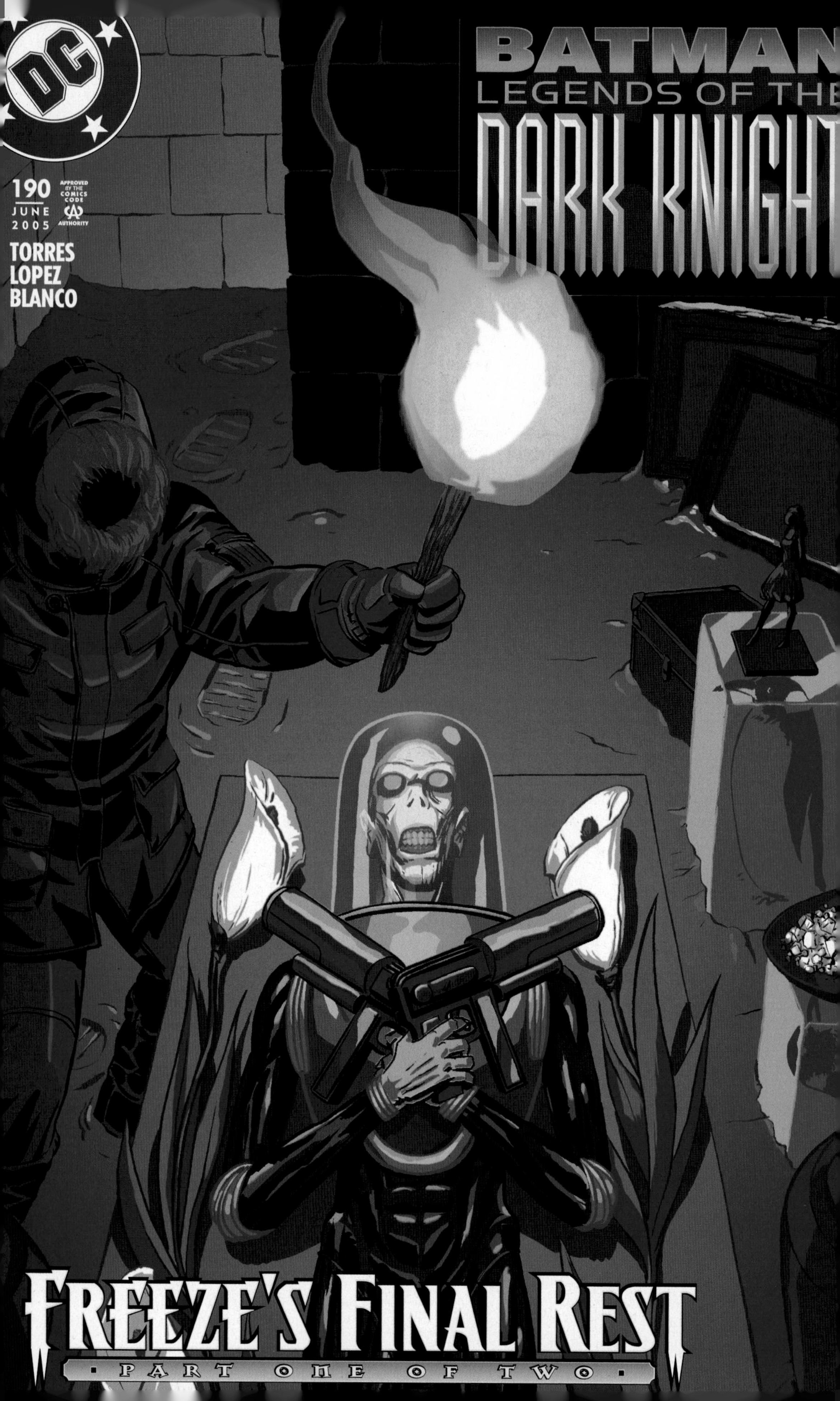

DC
BATMAN
LEGENDS OF THE
DARK KNIGHT
190
JUNE
2005
APPROVED BY THE COMICS CODE AUTHORITY
TORRES
LOPEZ
BLANCO
FREEZE'S FINAL REST
PART ONE OF TWO

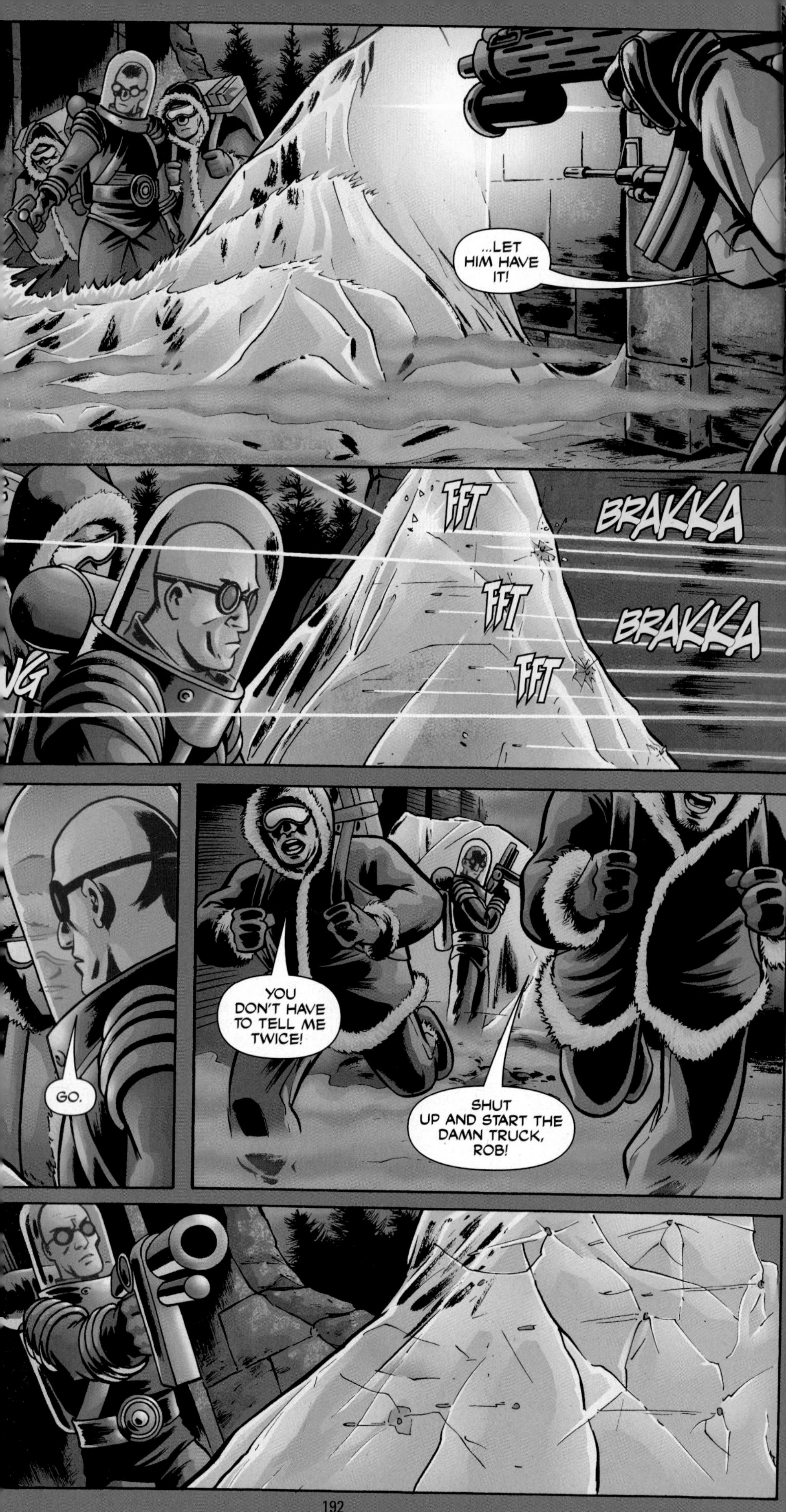
...LET HIM HAVE IT!
FFT
BRAKKA
FFT
BRAKKA
FFT
GO.
YOU DON'T HAVE TO TELL ME TWICE!
SHUT UP AND START THE DAMN TRUCK, ROB!

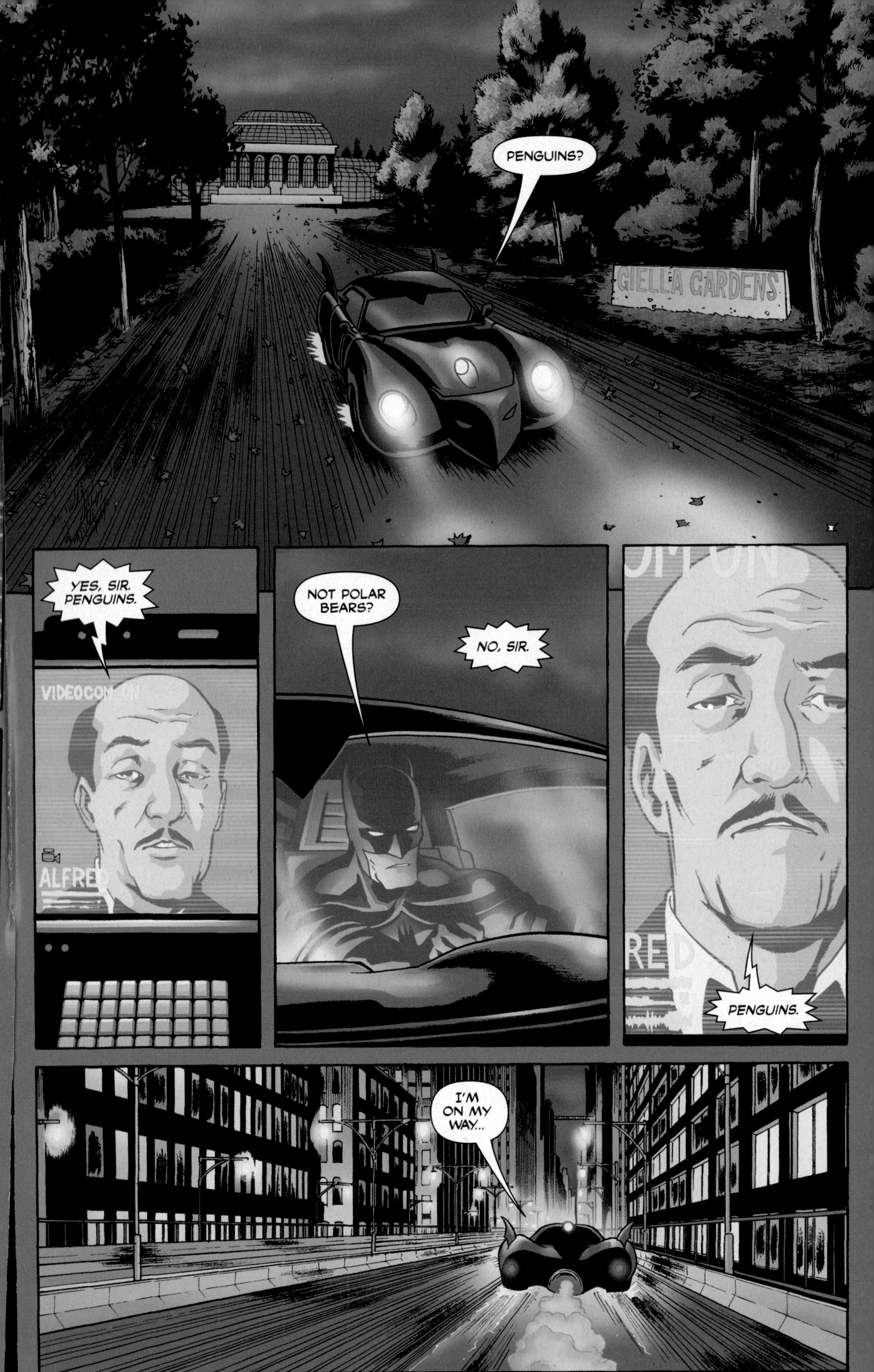
PENGUINS?
GIELLA GARDENS
YES, SIR. PENGUINS.
VIDEOCOM ON
ALFRED
NOT POLAR BEARS?
NO, SIR.
PENGUINS.
I'M ON MY WAY...

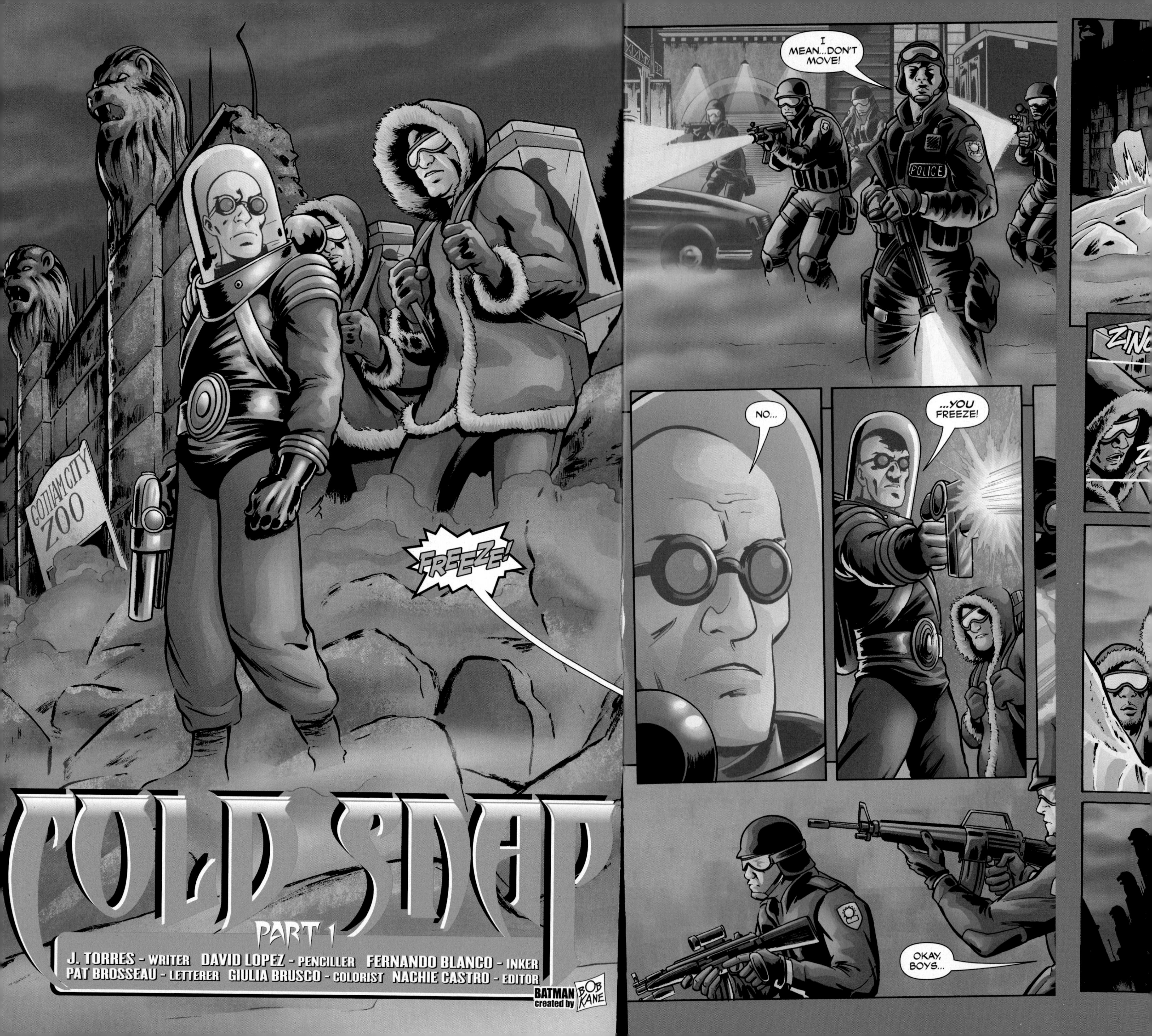
GOTHAM CITY ZOO
FREEZE!
COLD SNAP
PART 1
J. TORRES - WRITER DAVID LOPEZ - PENCILLER FERNANDO BLANCO - INKER
PAT BROSSEAU - LETTERER GIULIA BRUSCO - COLORIST NACHIE CASTRO - EDITOR
BATMAN created by BOB KANE
I MEAN...DON'T MOVE!
POLICE
NO...
...YOU FREEZE!
OKAY, BOYS...

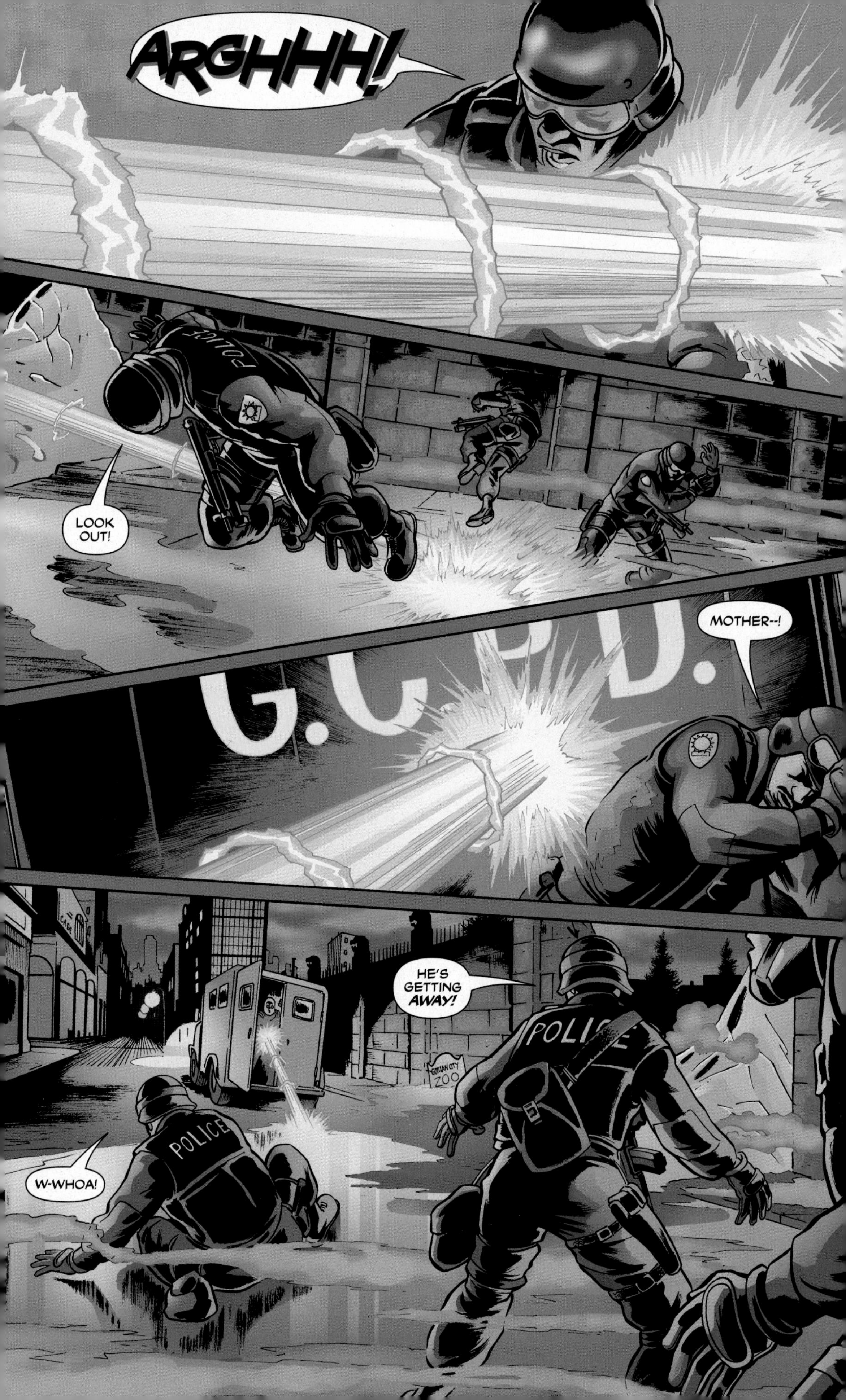
ARGHHH!
LOOK OUT!
MOTHER--!
G.C.P.D.
HE'S GETTING AWAY!
GOTHAM CITY ZOO
POLICE
W-WHOA!

"FREEZE LET THEM OFF EASY.

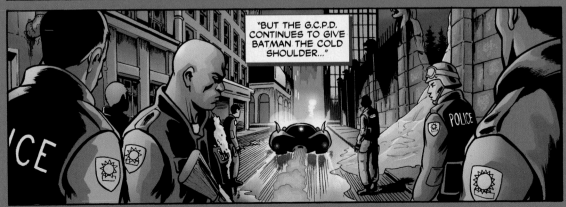

"BUT THE G.C.P.D. CONTINUES TO GIVE BATMAN THE COLD SHOULDER..."

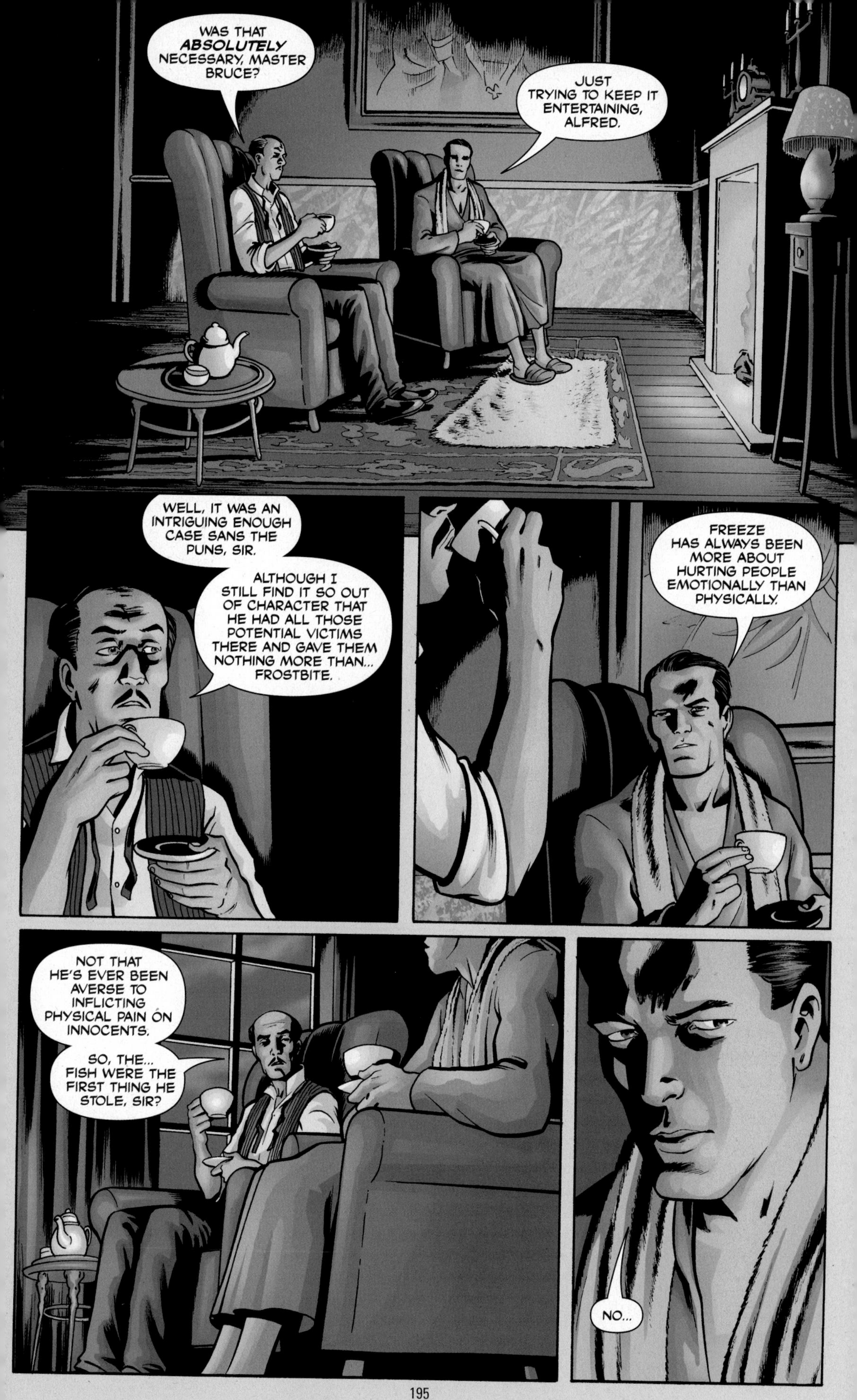
WAS THAT *ABSOLUTELY* NECESSARY, MASTER BRUCE?
JUST TRYING TO KEEP IT ENTERTAINING, ALFRED.
WELL, IT WAS AN INTRIGUING ENOUGH CASE SANS THE PUNS, SIR.
ALTHOUGH I STILL FIND IT SO OUT OF CHARACTER THAT HE HAD ALL THOSE POTENTIAL VICTIMS THERE AND GAVE THEM NOTHING MORE THAN... FROSTBITE.
FREEZE HAS ALWAYS BEEN MORE ABOUT HURTING PEOPLE EMOTIONALLY THAN PHYSICALLY.
NOT THAT HE'S EVER BEEN AVERSE TO INFLICTING PHYSICAL PAIN ON INNOCENTS.
SO, THE... FISH WERE THE FIRST THING HE STOLE, SIR?
NO...

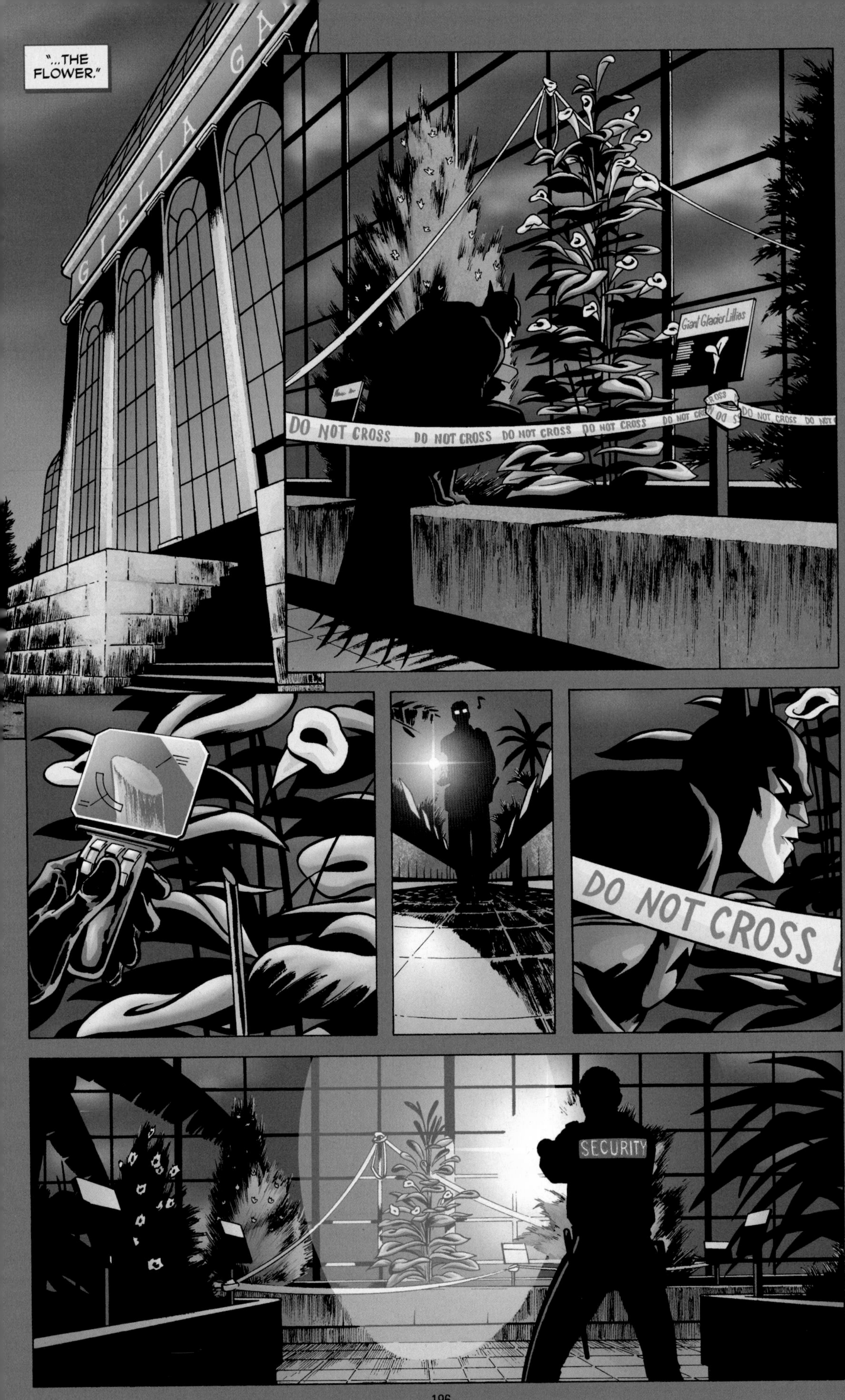

"...THE FLOWER."
GIELLA GA
Giant Glacier Lillies
DO NOT CROSS
DO NOT CROSS
SECURITY

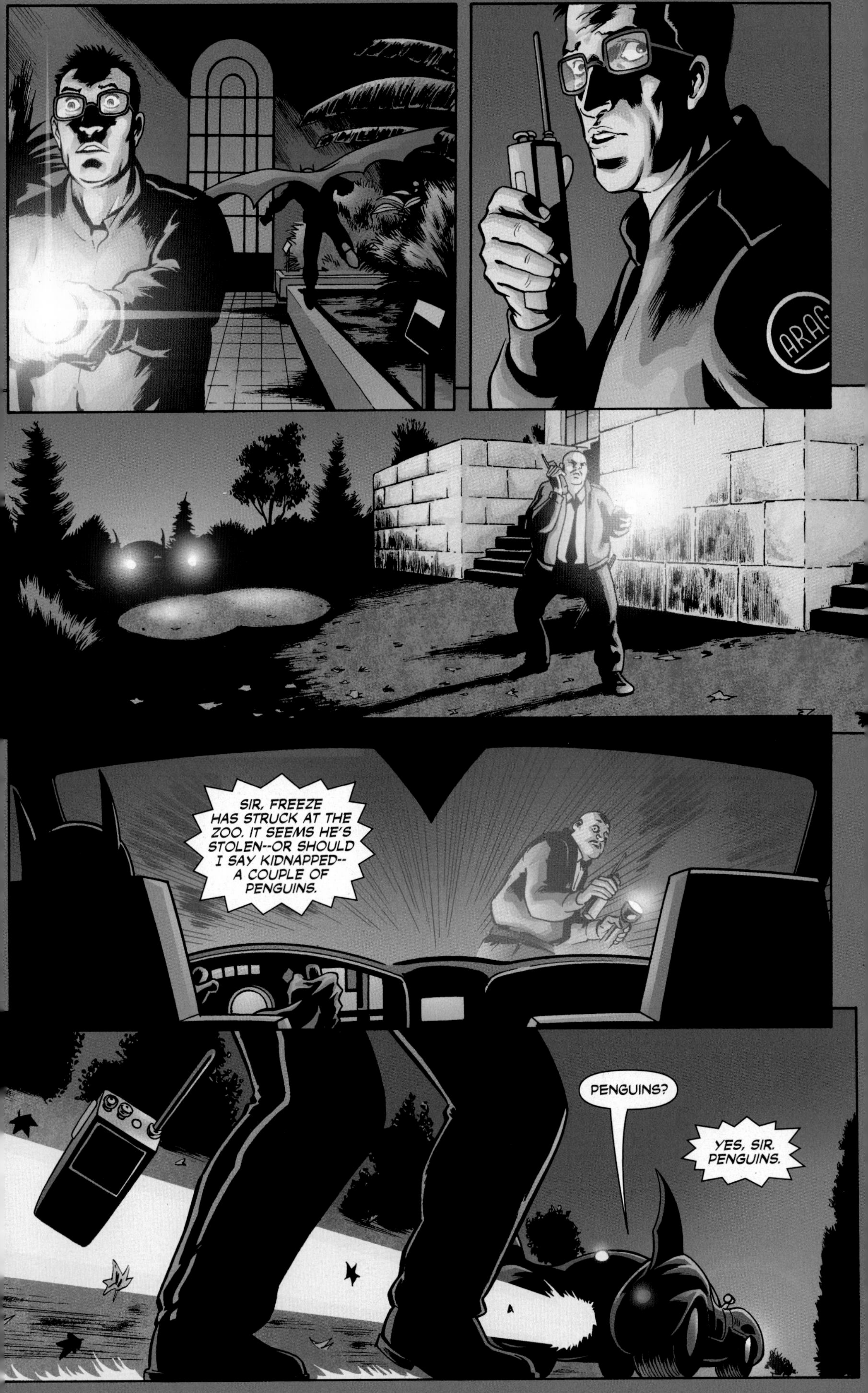
SIR, FREEZE HAS STRUCK AT THE ZOO. IT SEEMS HE'S STOLEN--OR SHOULD I SAY KIDNAPPED--A COUPLE OF PENGUINS.
PENGUINS?
YES, SIR. PENGUINS.

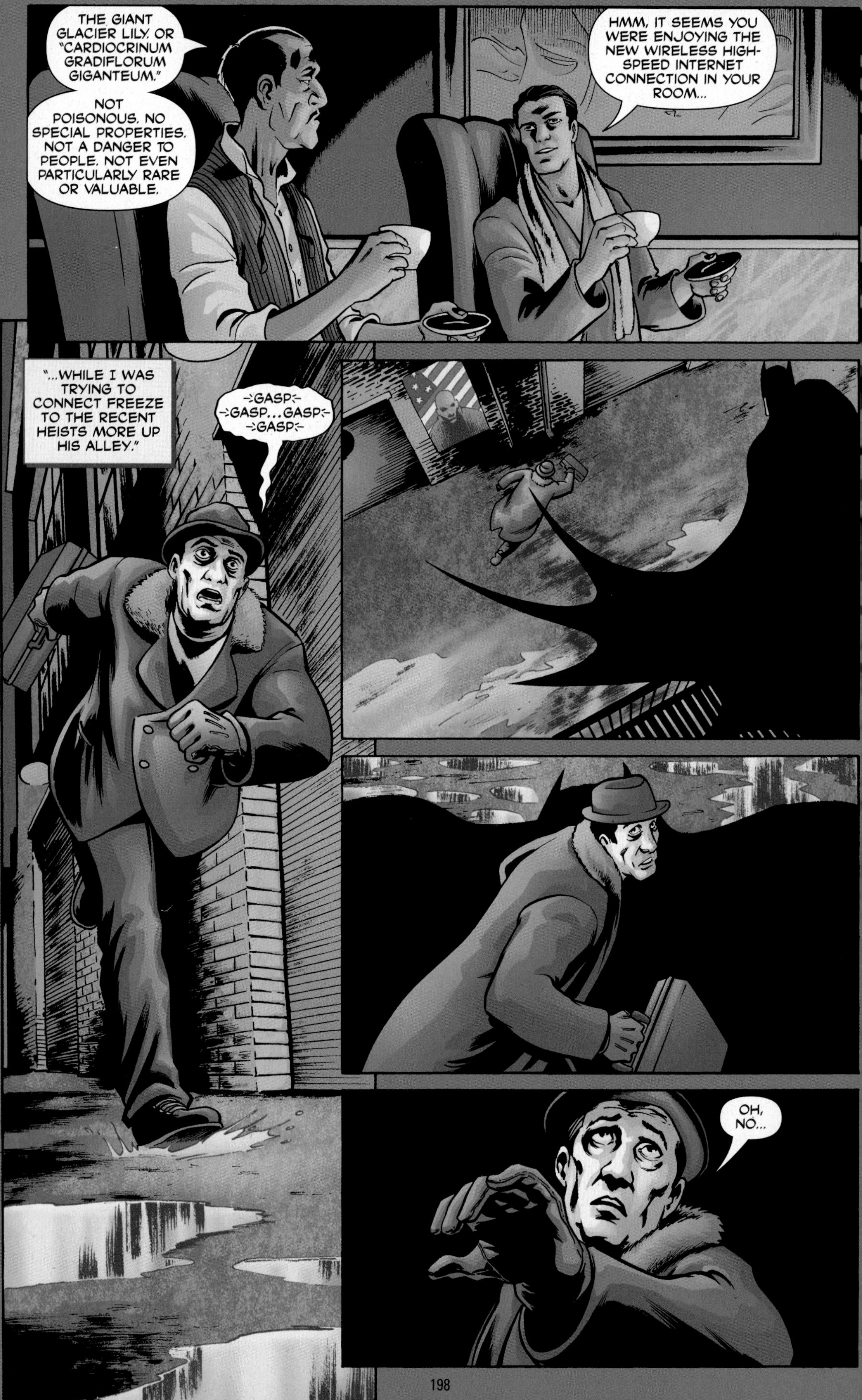
THE GIANT GLACIER LILY, OR "CARDIOCRINUM GRADIFLORUM GIGANTEUM."
NOT POISONOUS. NO SPECIAL PROPERTIES. NOT A DANGER TO PEOPLE. NOT EVEN PARTICULARLY RARE OR VALUABLE.
HMM, IT SEEMS YOU WERE ENJOYING THE NEW WIRELESS HIGH-SPEED INTERNET CONNECTION IN YOUR ROOM...
"...WHILE I WAS TRYING TO CONNECT FREEZE TO THE RECENT HEISTS MORE UP HIS ALLEY."
GASP GASP...GASP GASP
OH, NO...

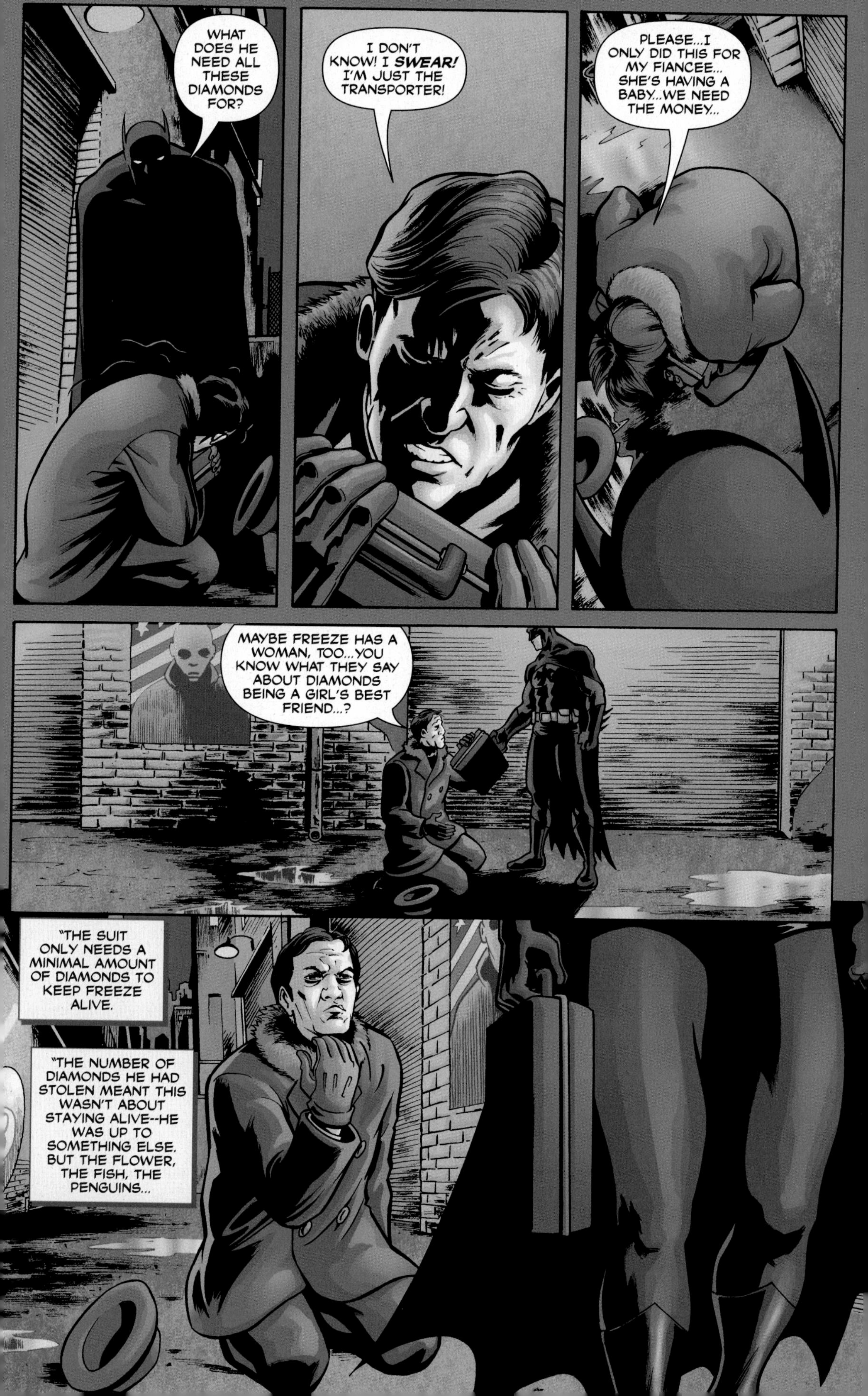
WHAT DOES HE NEED ALL THESE DIAMONDS FOR?
I DON'T KNOW! I SWEAR! I'M JUST THE TRANSPORTER!
PLEASE...I ONLY DID THIS FOR MY FIANCEE... SHE'S HAVING A BABY...WE NEED THE MONEY...
MAYBE FREEZE HAS A WOMAN, TOO...YOU KNOW WHAT THEY SAY ABOUT DIAMONDS BEING A GIRL'S BEST FRIEND...?
"THE SUIT ONLY NEEDS A MINIMAL AMOUNT OF DIAMONDS TO KEEP FREEZE ALIVE.
"THE NUMBER OF DIAMONDS HE HAD STOLEN MEANT THIS WASN'T ABOUT STAYING ALIVE--HE WAS UP TO SOMETHING ELSE. BUT THE FLOWER, THE FISH, THE PENGUINS...

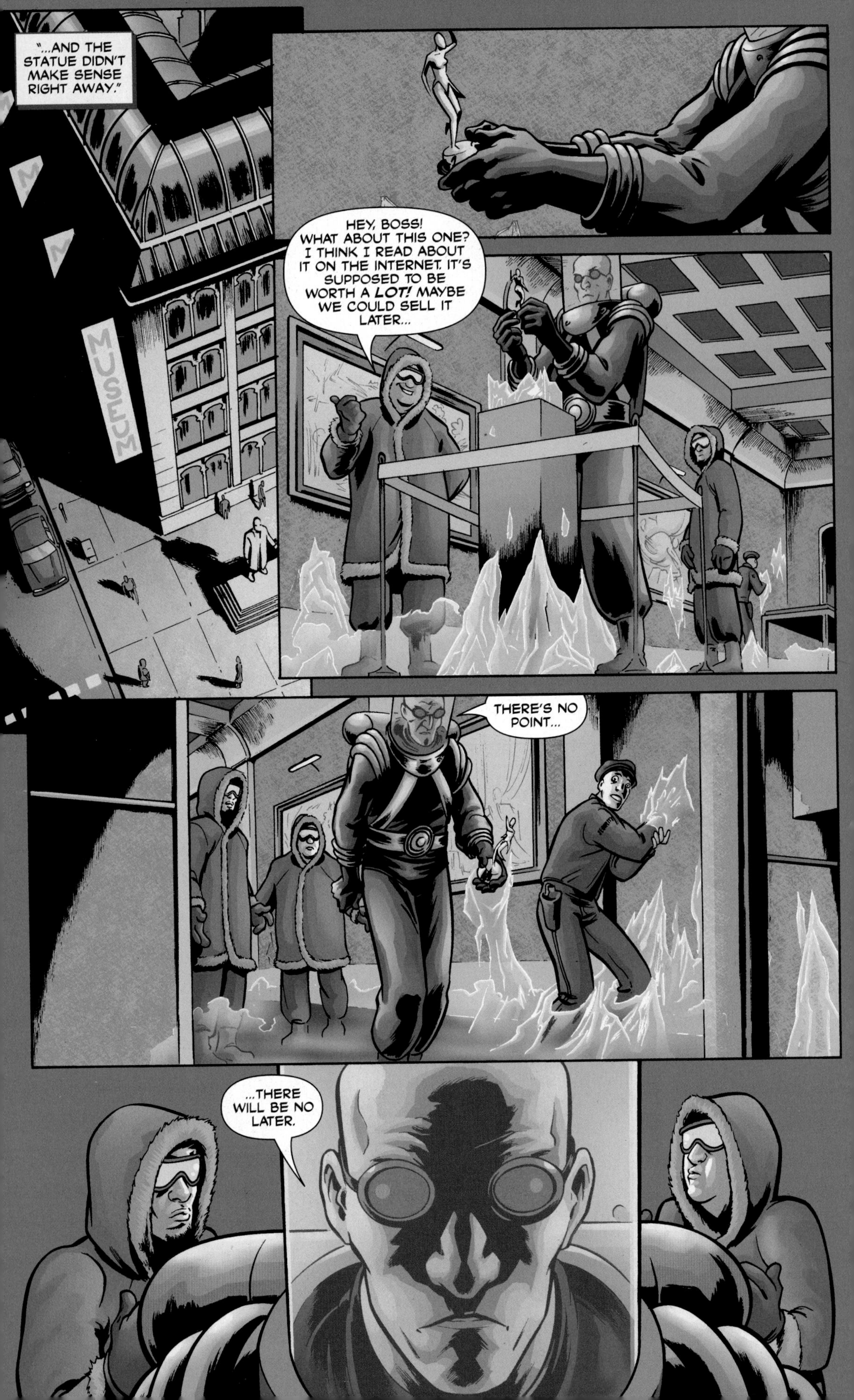
"...AND THE STATUE DIDN'T MAKE SENSE RIGHT AWAY."
MUSEUM
HEY, BOSS! WHAT ABOUT THIS ONE? I THINK I READ ABOUT IT ON THE INTERNET. IT'S SUPPOSED TO BE WORTH A *LOT!* MAYBE WE COULD SELL IT LATER...
THERE'S NO POINT...
...THERE WILL BE NO LATER.

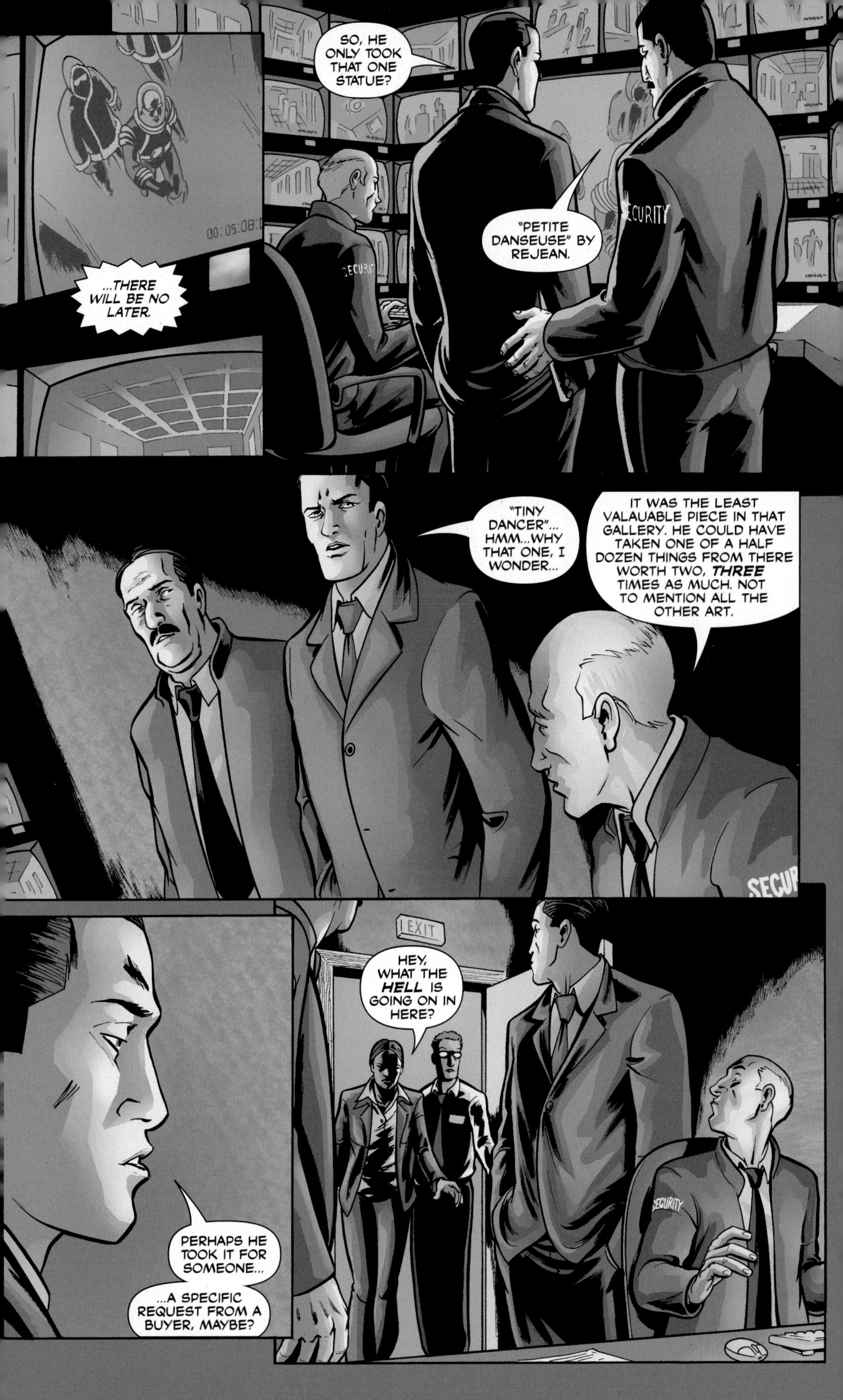
...THERE WILL BE NO LATER.
00:05:08:
SO, HE ONLY TOOK THAT ONE STATUE?
"PETITE DANSEUSE" BY REJEAN.
SECURITY
"TINY DANCER"... HMM...WHY THAT ONE, I WONDER...
IT WAS THE LEAST VALAUABLE PIECE IN THAT GALLERY. HE COULD HAVE TAKEN ONE OF A HALF DOZEN THINGS FROM THERE WORTH TWO, THREE TIMES AS MUCH. NOT TO MENTION ALL THE OTHER ART.
PERHAPS HE TOOK IT FOR SOMEONE...
...A SPECIFIC REQUEST FROM A BUYER, MAYBE?
EXIT
HEY, WHAT THE HELL IS GOING ON IN HERE?
SECURITY

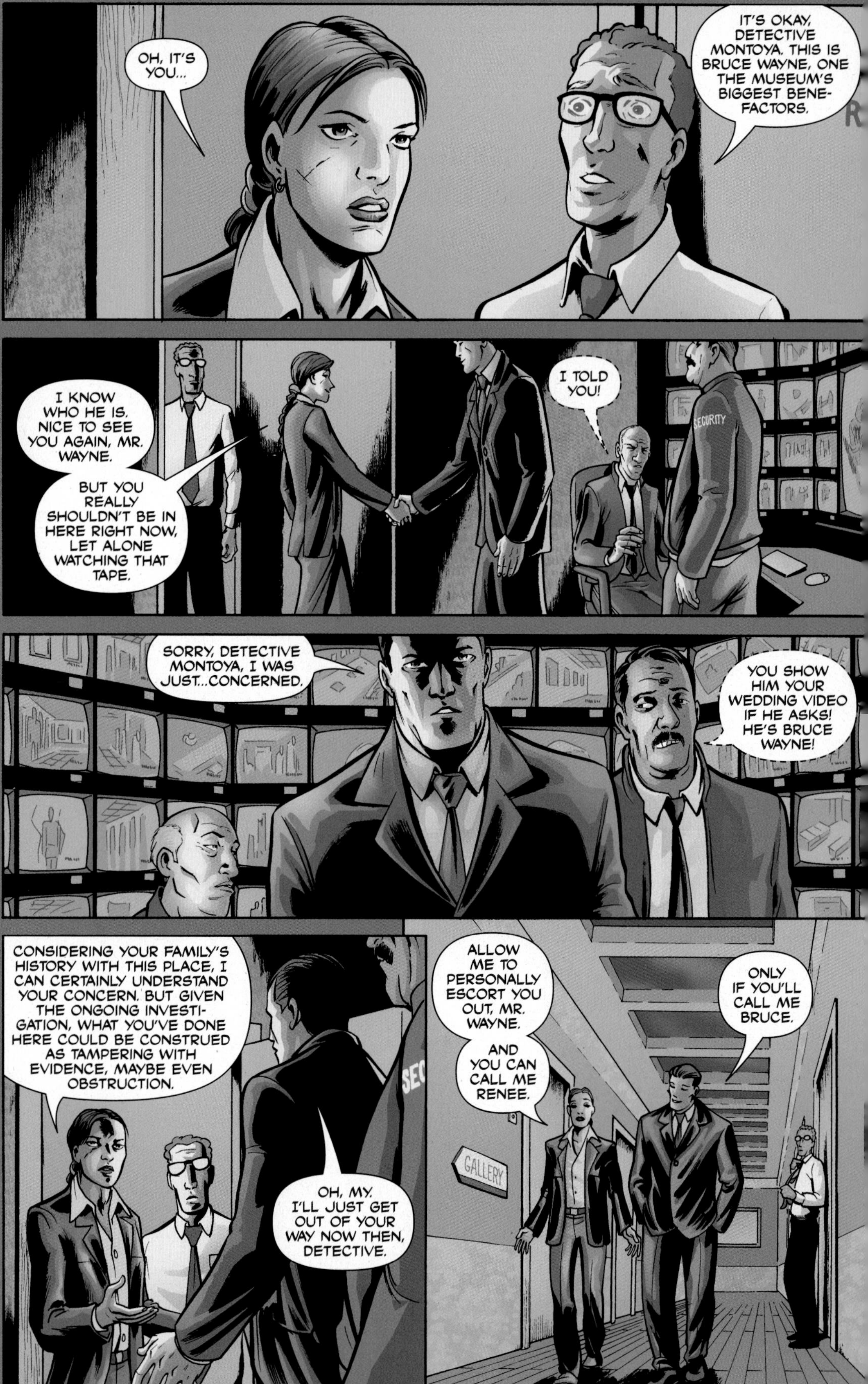

OH, IT'S YOU...
IT'S OKAY, DETECTIVE MONTOYA. THIS IS BRUCE WAYNE, ONE THE MUSEUM'S BIGGEST BENE-FACTORS.
I KNOW WHO HE IS. NICE TO SEE YOU AGAIN, MR. WAYNE.
BUT YOU REALLY SHOULDN'T BE IN HERE RIGHT NOW, LET ALONE WATCHING THAT TAPE.
I TOLD YOU!
SECURITY
SORRY, DETECTIVE MONTOYA, I WAS JUST...CONCERNED.
YOU SHOW HIM YOUR WEDDING VIDEO IF HE ASKS! HE'S BRUCE WAYNE!
CONSIDERING YOUR FAMILY'S HISTORY WITH THIS PLACE, I CAN CERTAINLY UNDERSTAND YOUR CONCERN. BUT GIVEN THE ONGOING INVESTI-GATION, WHAT YOU'VE DONE HERE COULD BE CONSTRUED AS TAMPERING WITH EVIDENCE, MAYBE EVEN OBSTRUCTION.
OH, MY. I'LL JUST GET OUT OF YOUR WAY NOW THEN, DETECTIVE.
ALLOW ME TO PERSONALLY ESCORT YOU OUT, MR. WAYNE.
AND YOU CAN CALL ME RENEE.
GALLERY
ONLY IF YOU'LL CALL ME BRUCE.

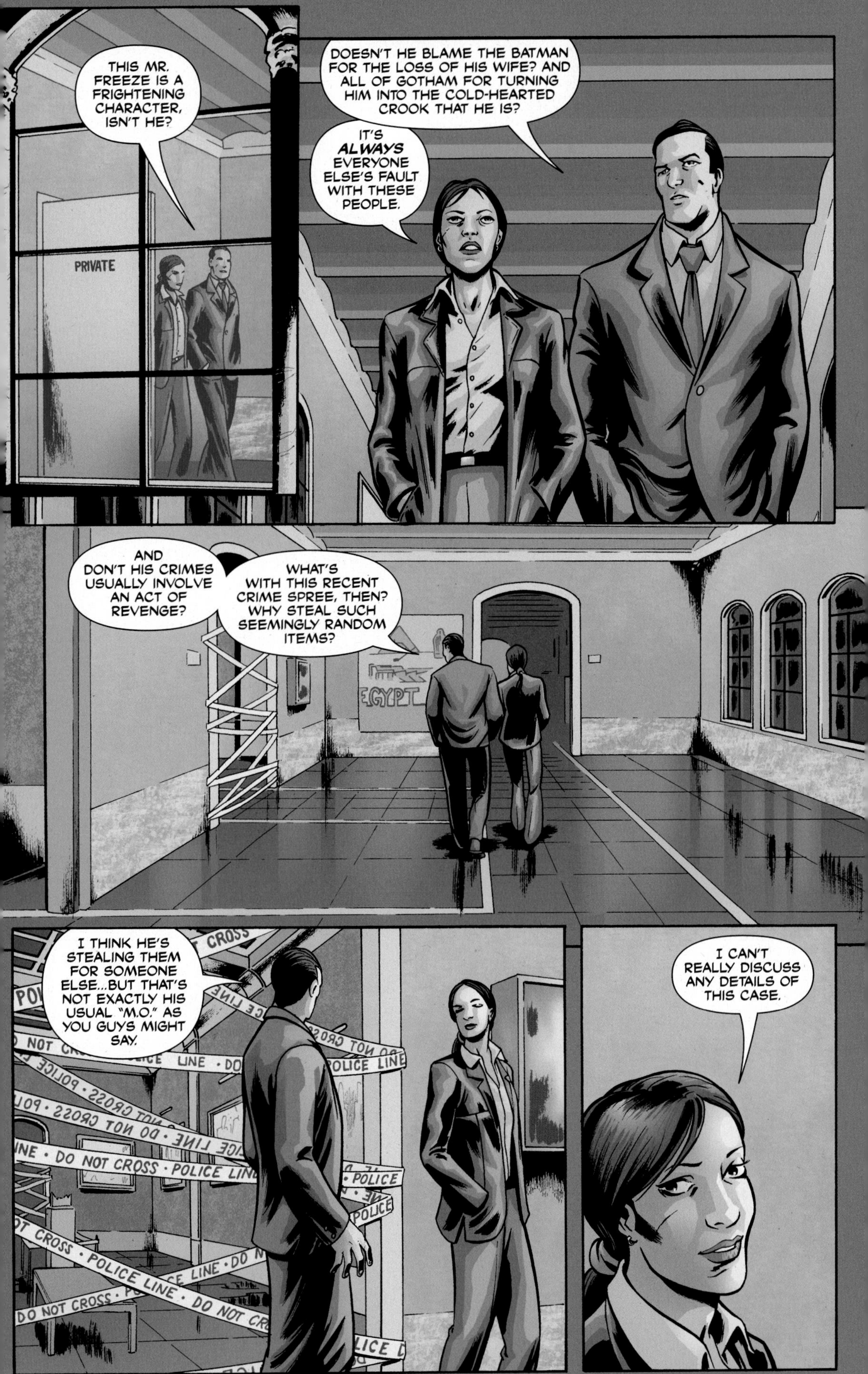
THIS MR. FREEZE IS A FRIGHTENING CHARACTER, ISN'T HE?
PRIVATE
DOESN'T HE BLAME THE BATMAN FOR THE LOSS OF HIS WIFE? AND ALL OF GOTHAM FOR TURNING HIM INTO THE COLD-HEARTED CROOK THAT HE IS?
IT'S **ALWAYS** EVERYONE ELSE'S FAULT WITH THESE PEOPLE.
AND DON'T HIS CRIMES USUALLY INVOLVE AN ACT OF REVENGE?
WHAT'S WITH THIS RECENT CRIME SPREE, THEN? WHY STEAL SUCH SEEMINGLY RANDOM ITEMS?
EGYPT
I THINK HE'S STEALING THEM FOR SOMEONE ELSE...BUT THAT'S NOT EXACTLY HIS USUAL "M.O." AS YOU GUYS MIGHT SAY.
POLICE LINE · DO NOT CROSS
I CAN'T REALLY DISCUSS ANY DETAILS OF THIS CASE.

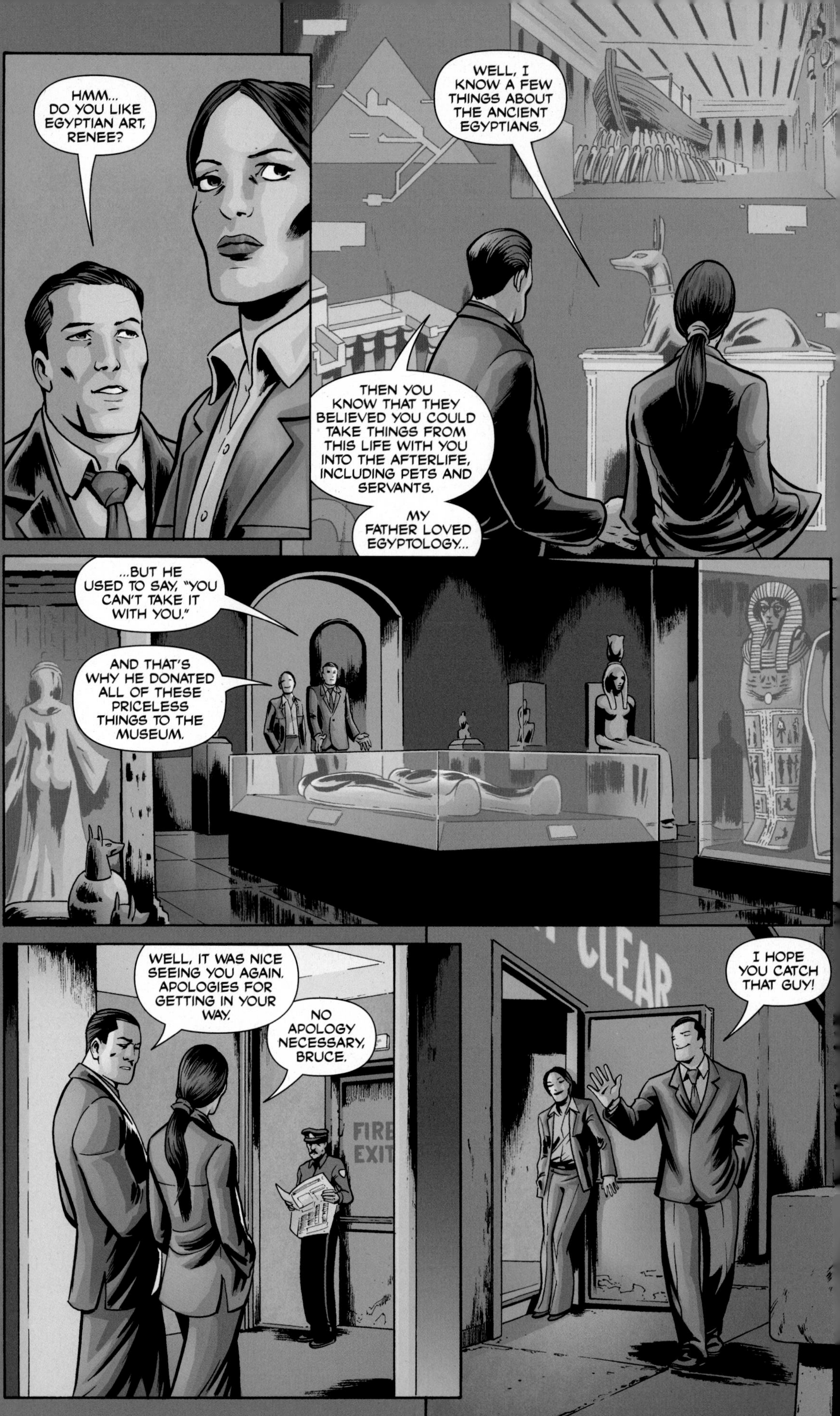
HMM... DO YOU LIKE EGYPTIAN ART, RENEE?
WELL, I KNOW A FEW THINGS ABOUT THE ANCIENT EGYPTIANS.
THEN YOU KNOW THAT THEY BELIEVED YOU COULD TAKE THINGS FROM THIS LIFE WITH YOU INTO THE AFTERLIFE, INCLUDING PETS AND SERVANTS.
MY FATHER LOVED EGYPTOLOGY...
...BUT HE USED TO SAY, "YOU CAN'T TAKE IT WITH YOU."
AND THAT'S WHY HE DONATED ALL OF THESE PRICELESS THINGS TO THE MUSEUM.
WELL, IT WAS NICE SEEING YOU AGAIN. APOLOGIES FOR GETTING IN YOUR WAY.
NO APOLOGY NECESSARY, BRUCE.
FIRE EXIT
CLEAR
I HOPE YOU CATCH THAT GUY!

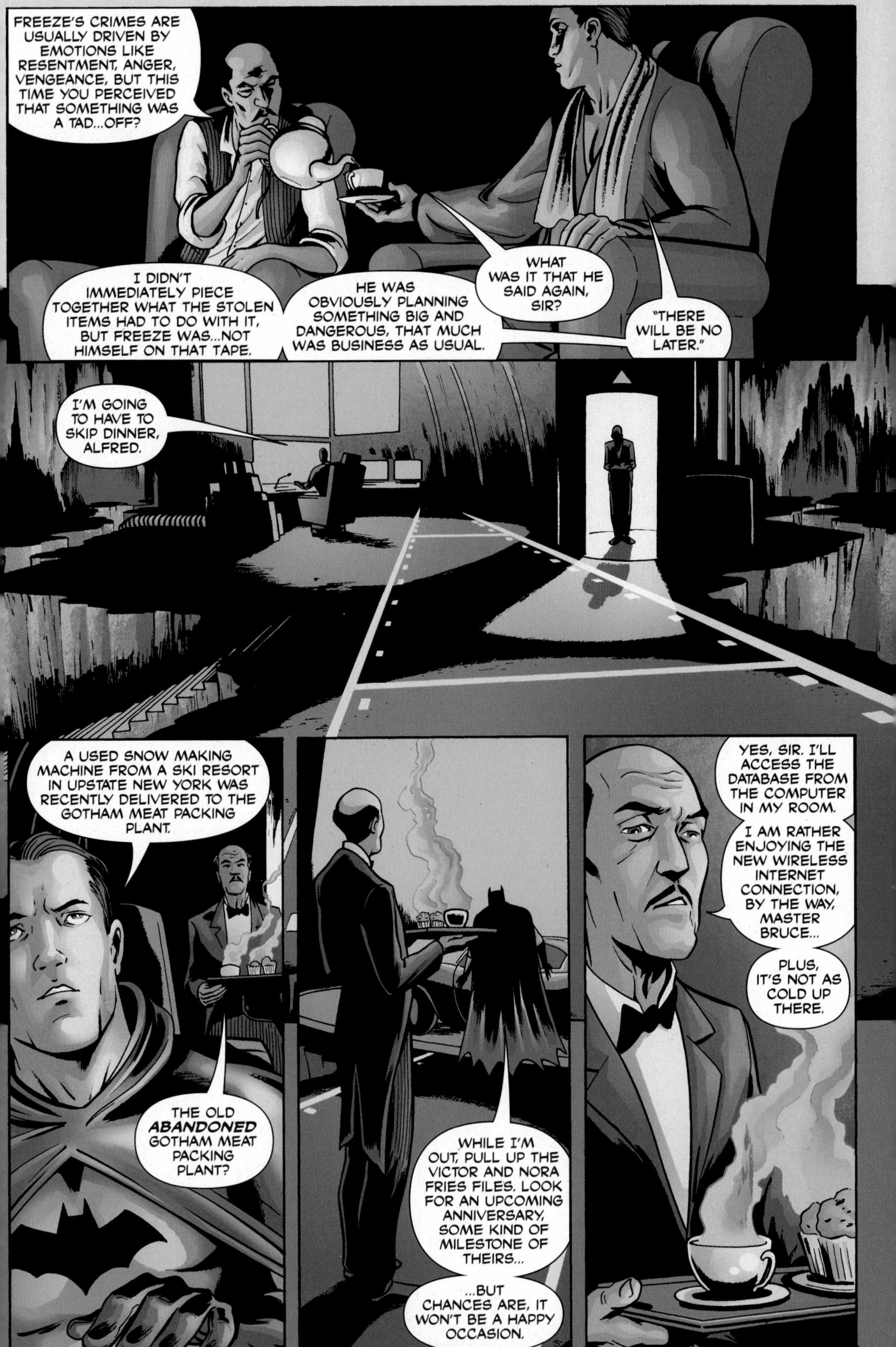
FREEZE'S CRIMES ARE USUALLY DRIVEN BY EMOTIONS LIKE RESENTMENT, ANGER, VENGEANCE, BUT THIS TIME YOU PERCEIVED THAT SOMETHING WAS A TAD...OFF?
I DIDN'T IMMEDIATELY PIECE TOGETHER WHAT THE STOLEN ITEMS HAD TO DO WITH IT, BUT FREEZE WAS...NOT HIMSELF ON THAT TAPE.
HE WAS OBVIOUSLY PLANNING SOMETHING BIG AND DANGEROUS, THAT MUCH WAS BUSINESS AS USUAL.
WHAT WAS IT THAT HE SAID AGAIN, SIR?
"THERE WILL BE NO LATER."
I'M GOING TO HAVE TO SKIP DINNER, ALFRED.
A USED SNOW MAKING MACHINE FROM A SKI RESORT IN UPSTATE NEW YORK WAS RECENTLY DELIVERED TO THE GOTHAM MEAT PACKING PLANT.
THE OLD *ABANDONED* GOTHAM MEAT PACKING PLANT?
WHILE I'M OUT, PULL UP THE VICTOR AND NORA FRIES FILES. LOOK FOR AN UPCOMING ANNIVERSARY, SOME KIND OF MILESTONE OF THEIRS...
...BUT CHANCES ARE, IT WON'T BE A HAPPY OCCASION.
YES, SIR. I'LL ACCESS THE DATABASE FROM THE COMPUTER IN MY ROOM.
I AM RATHER ENJOYING THE NEW WIRELESS INTERNET CONNECTION, BY THE WAY, MASTER BRUCE...
PLUS, IT'S NOT AS COLD UP THERE.

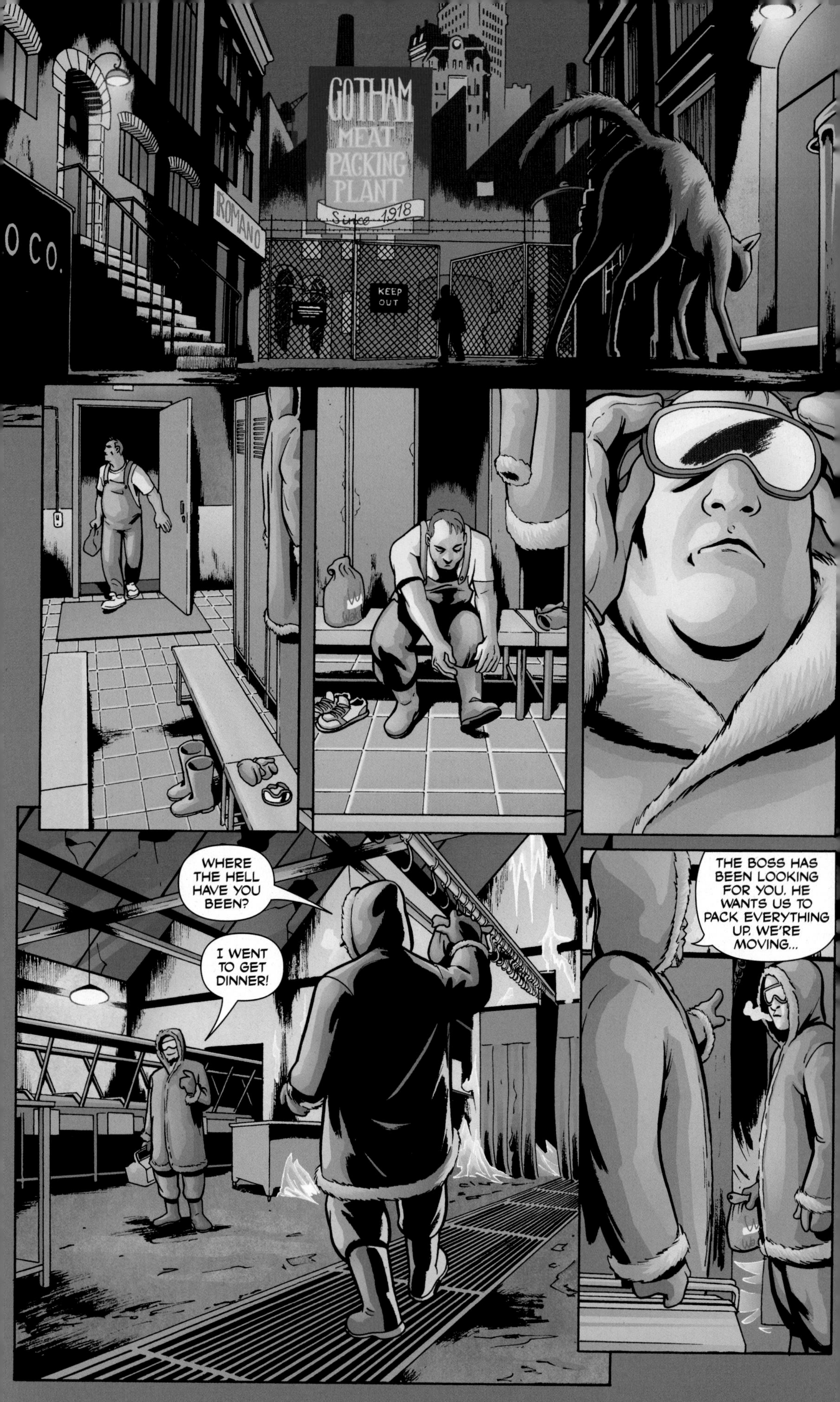

GOTHAM MEAT PACKING PLANT
Since 1918
ROMANO
O CO.
KEEP OUT
WHERE THE HELL HAVE YOU BEEN?
I WENT TO GET DINNER!
THE BOSS HAS BEEN LOOKING FOR YOU. HE WANTS US TO PACK EVERYTHING UP. WE'RE MOVING...

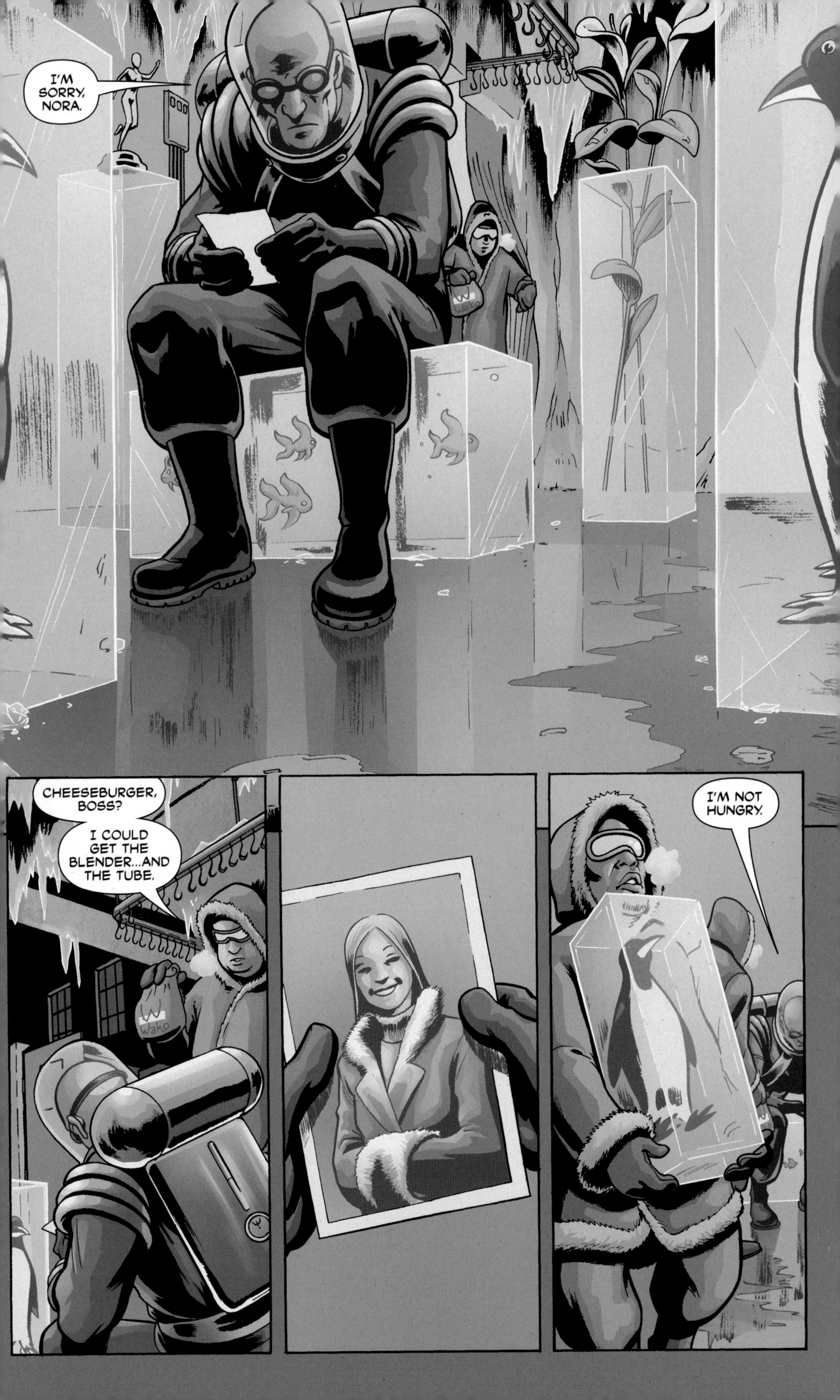
I'M SORRY, NORA.
CHEESEBURGER, BOSS?
I COULD GET THE BLENDER...AND THE TUBE.
I'M NOT HUNGRY.

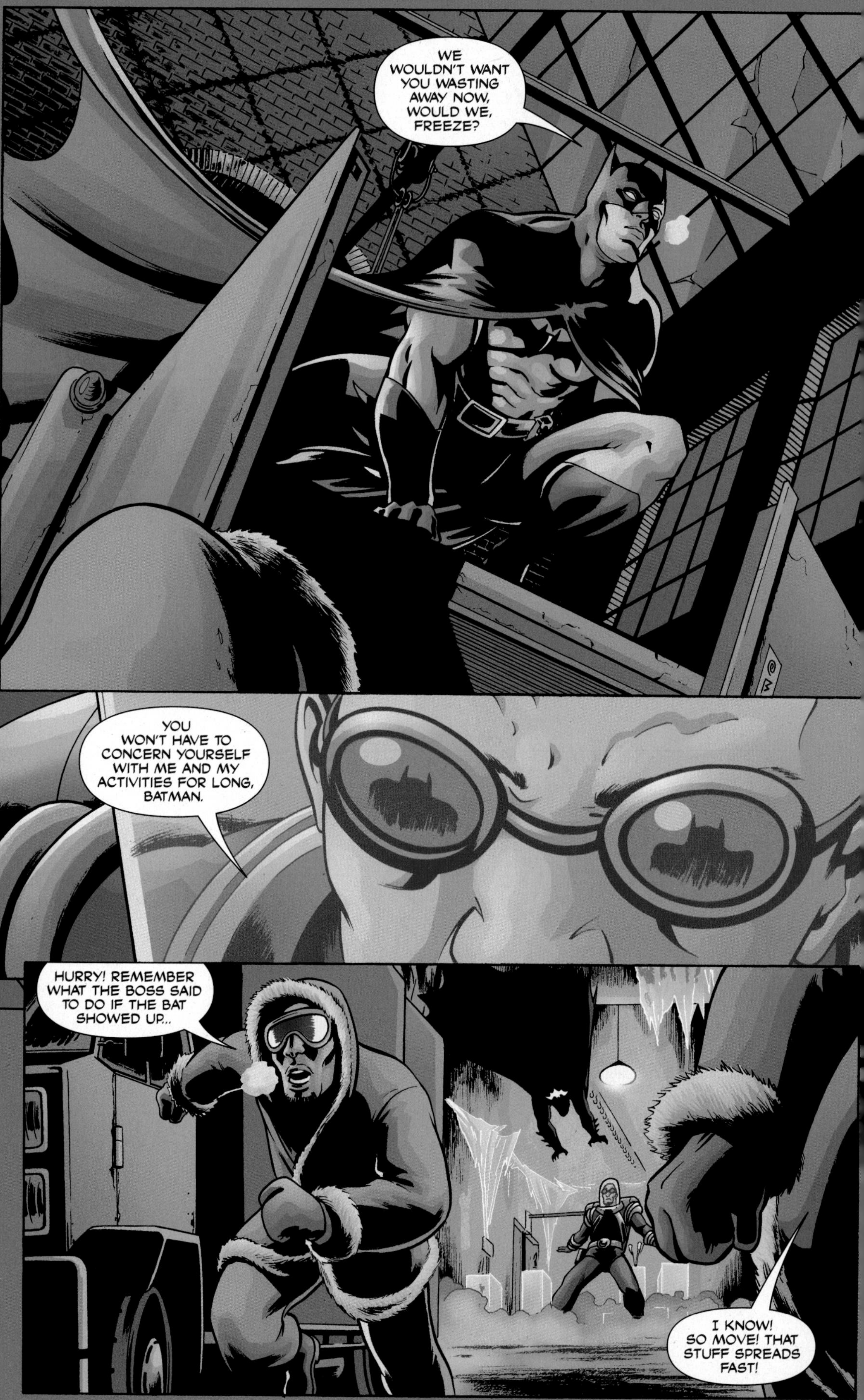

WE WOULDN'T WANT YOU WASTING AWAY NOW, WOULD WE, FREEZE?
YOU WON'T HAVE TO CONCERN YOURSELF WITH ME AND MY ACTIVITIES FOR LONG, BATMAN.
HURRY! REMEMBER WHAT THE BOSS SAID TO DO IF THE BAT SHOWED UP...
I KNOW! SO MOVE! THAT STUFF SPREADS FAST!

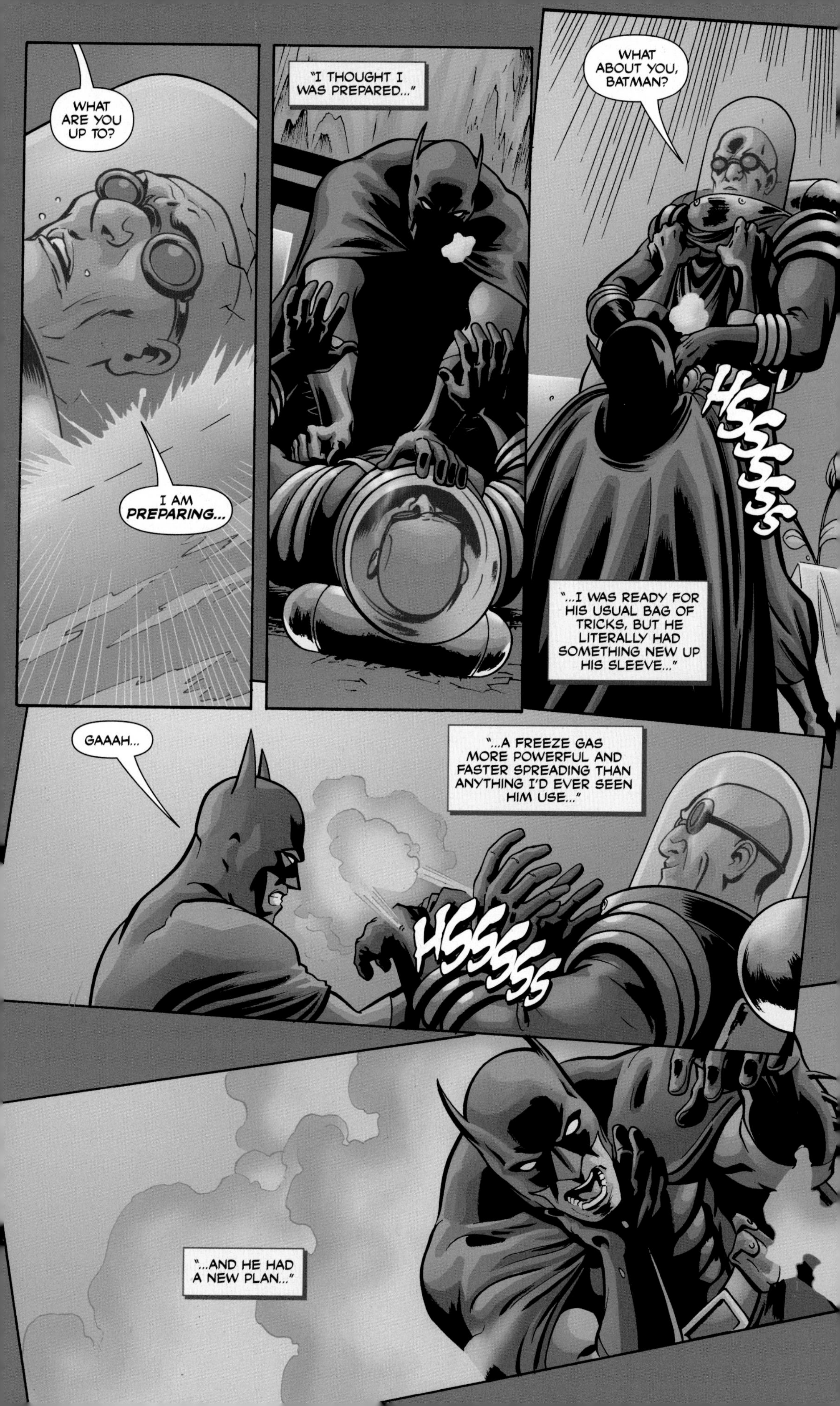
WHAT ARE YOU UP TO?
I AM *PREPARING*...
"I THOUGHT I WAS PREPARED..."
WHAT ABOUT YOU, BATMAN?
HSSSSSS
"...I WAS READY FOR HIS USUAL BAG OF TRICKS, BUT HE LITERALLY HAD SOMETHING NEW UP HIS SLEEVE..."
GAAAH...
"...A FREEZE GAS MORE POWERFUL AND FASTER SPREADING THAN ANYTHING I'D EVER SEEN HIM USE..."
HSSSSSS
"...AND HE HAD A NEW PLAN..."

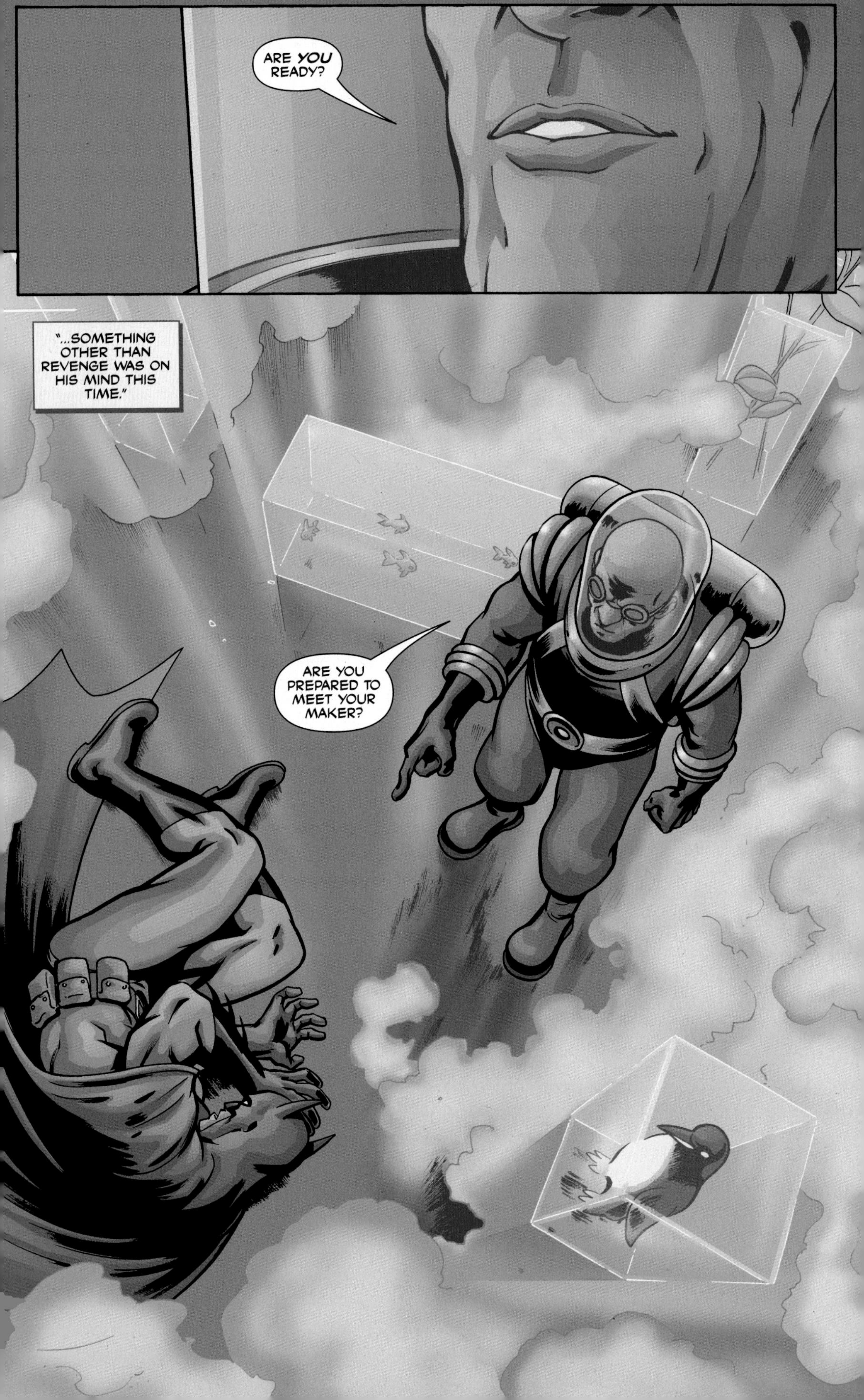
ARE YOU READY?
"...SOMETHING OTHER THAN REVENGE WAS ON HIS MIND THIS TIME."
ARE YOU PREPARED TO MEET YOUR MAKER?

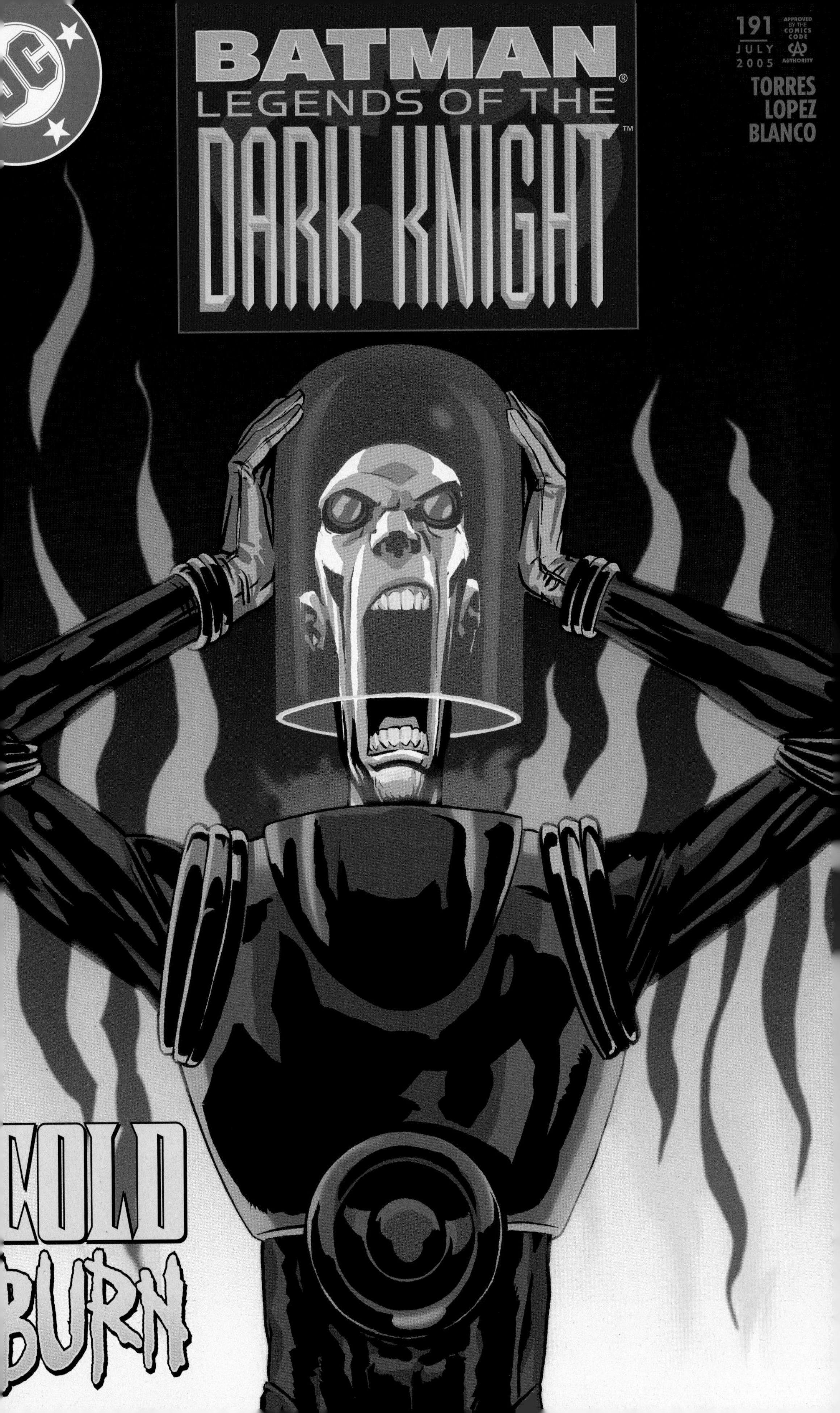

191
JULY
2005
APPROVED BY THE COMICS CODE AUTHORITY
BATMAN
LEGENDS OF THE
DARK KNIGHT
TORRES
LOPEZ
BLANCO
COLD
BURN

DID HE ACTUALLY SAY, "ARE YOU PREPARED TO MEET YOUR MAKER"?

I'M AFRAID SO, ALFRED.

"THEN HE SAYS..."

I GROW WEARY OF ALL THIS, AS I'M SURE YOU HAVE...

"...SO WHY DON'T WE GIVE IT A REST."

HOW EVER DO YOU SORT OUT THE *CAMP* FROM THE CRIES FOR *HELP*, MASTER BRUCE?

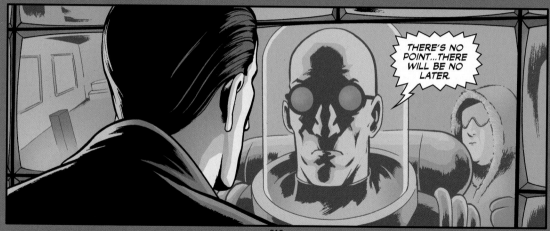

THERE'S NO POINT...THERE WILL BE NO LATER.

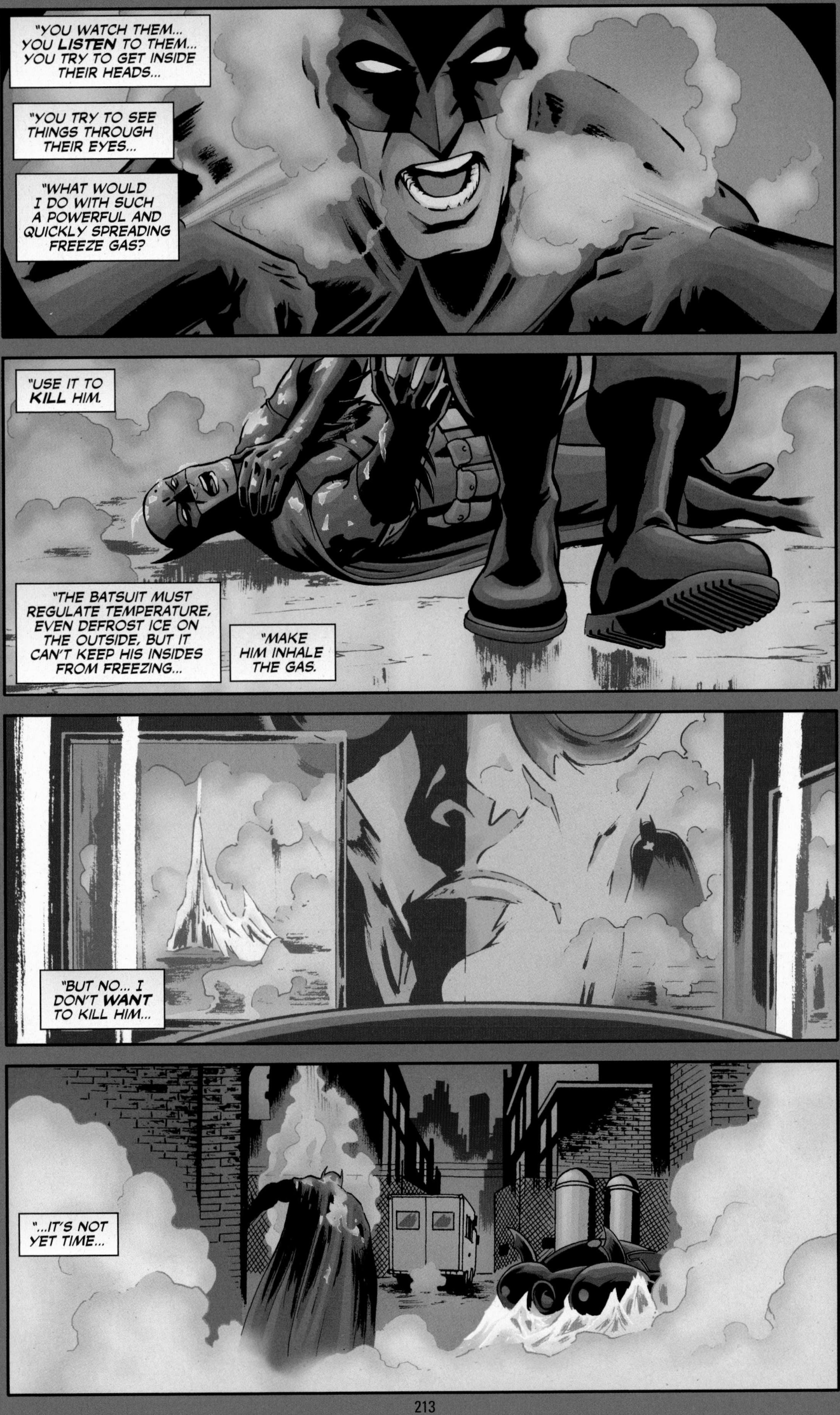
"YOU WATCH THEM... YOU LISTEN TO THEM... YOU TRY TO GET INSIDE THEIR HEADS...
"YOU TRY TO SEE THINGS THROUGH THEIR EYES...
"WHAT WOULD I DO WITH SUCH A POWERFUL AND QUICKLY SPREADING FREEZE GAS?
"USE IT TO KILL HIM.
"THE BATSUIT MUST REGULATE TEMPERATURE, EVEN DEFROST ICE ON THE OUTSIDE, BUT IT CAN'T KEEP HIS INSIDES FROM FREEZING...
"MAKE HIM INHALE THE GAS.
"BUT NO... I DON'T WANT TO KILL HIM...
"...IT'S NOT YET TIME...

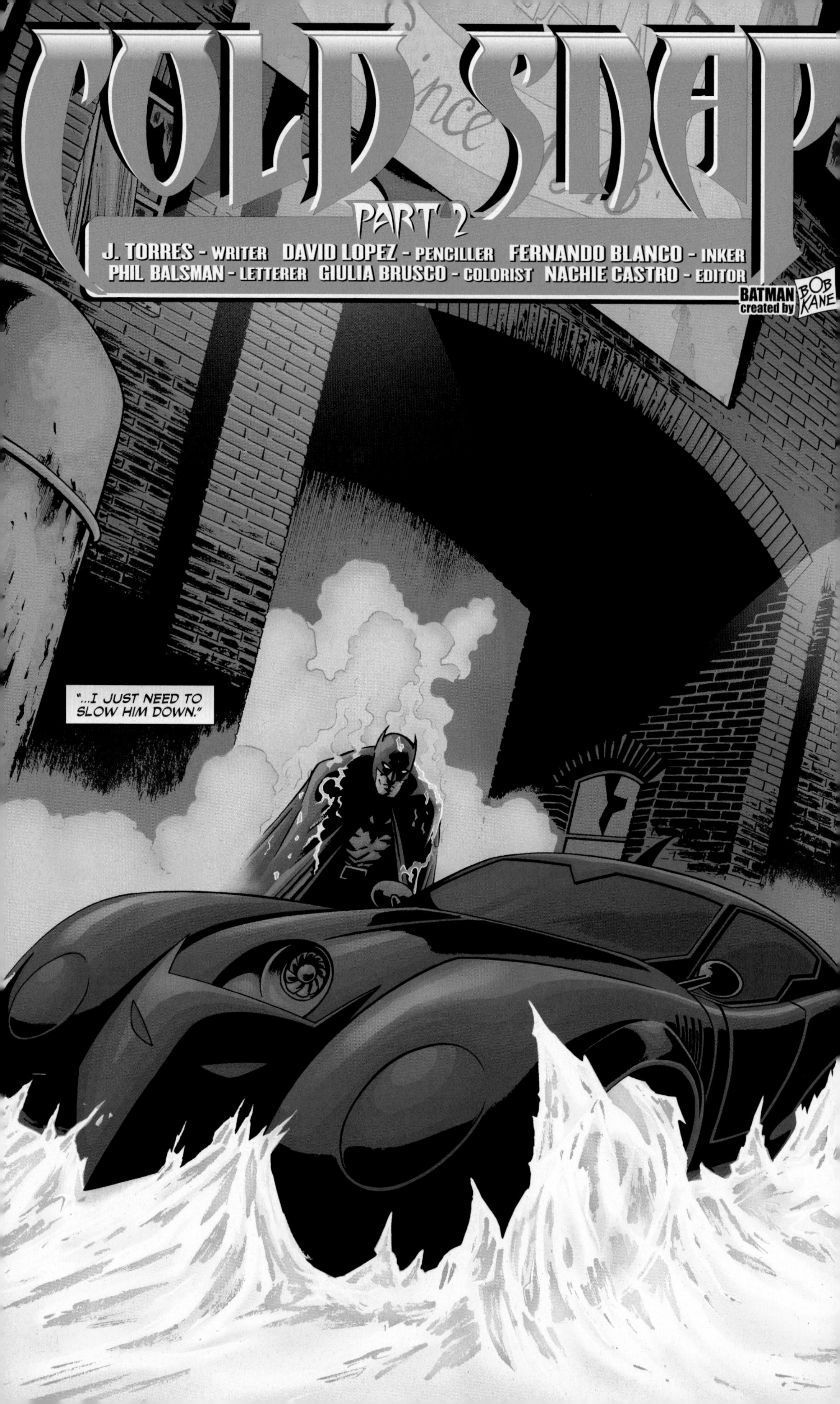
COLD SNAP
PART 2
J. TORRES - WRITER DAVID LOPEZ - PENCILLER FERNANDO BLANCO - INKER
PHIL BALSMAN - LETTERER GIULIA BRUSCO - COLORIST NACHIE CASTRO - EDITOR
BATMAN created by BOB KANE
"...I JUST NEED TO SLOW HIM DOWN."

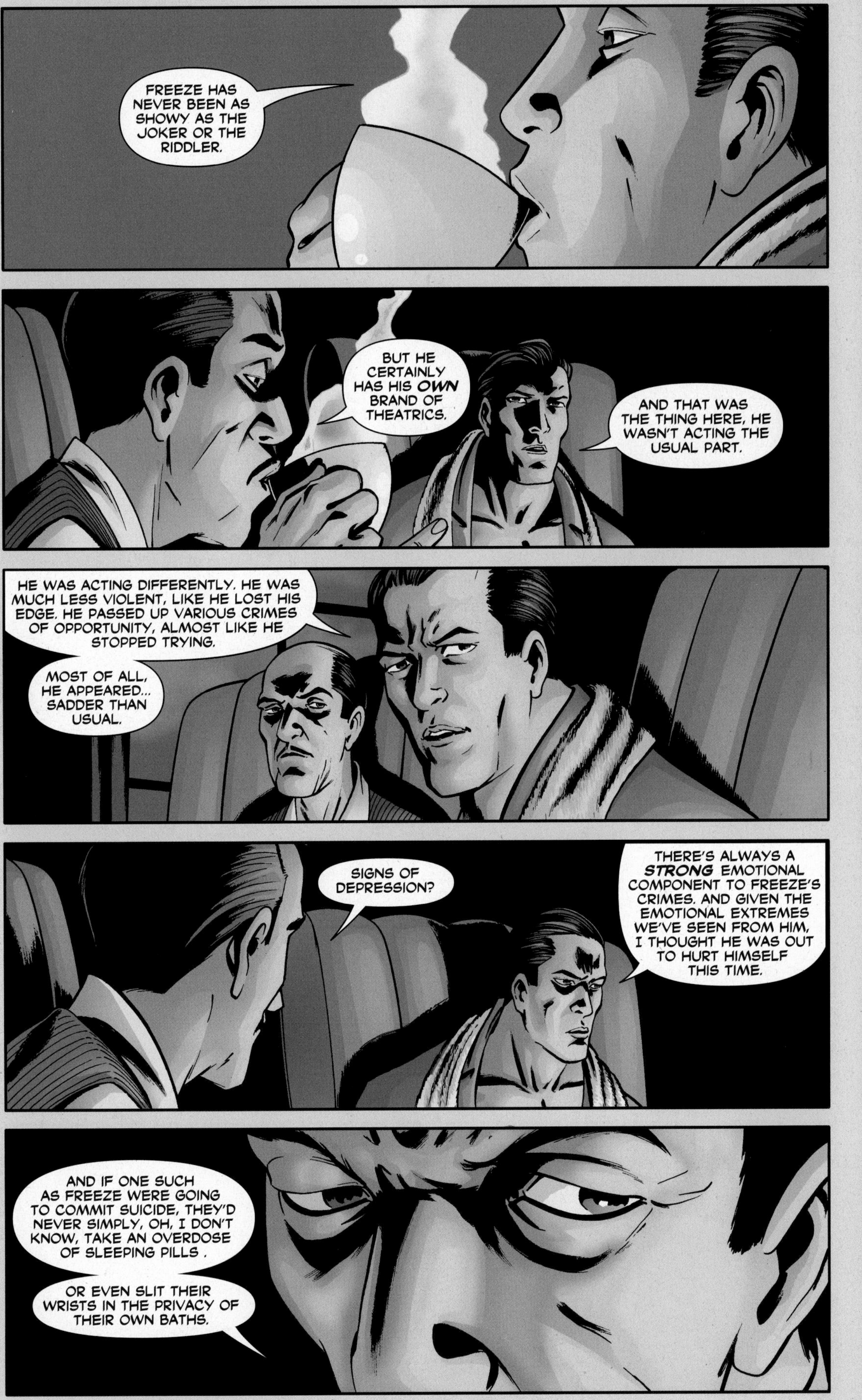
FREEZE HAS NEVER BEEN AS SHOWY AS THE JOKER OR THE RIDDLER.
BUT HE CERTAINLY HAS HIS OWN BRAND OF THEATRICS.
AND THAT WAS THE THING HERE, HE WASN'T ACTING THE USUAL PART.
HE WAS ACTING DIFFERENTLY. HE WAS MUCH LESS VIOLENT, LIKE HE LOST HIS EDGE. HE PASSED UP VARIOUS CRIMES OF OPPORTUNITY, ALMOST LIKE HE STOPPED TRYING.
MOST OF ALL, HE APPEARED... SADDER THAN USUAL.
SIGNS OF DEPRESSION?
THERE'S ALWAYS A STRONG EMOTIONAL COMPONENT TO FREEZE'S CRIMES. AND GIVEN THE EMOTIONAL EXTREMES WE'VE SEEN FROM HIM, I THOUGHT HE WAS OUT TO HURT HIMSELF THIS TIME.
AND IF ONE SUCH AS FREEZE WERE GOING TO COMMIT SUICIDE, THEY'D NEVER SIMPLY, OH, I DON'T KNOW, TAKE AN OVERDOSE OF SLEEPING PILLS .
OR EVEN SLIT THEIR WRISTS IN THE PRIVACY OF THEIR OWN BATHS.

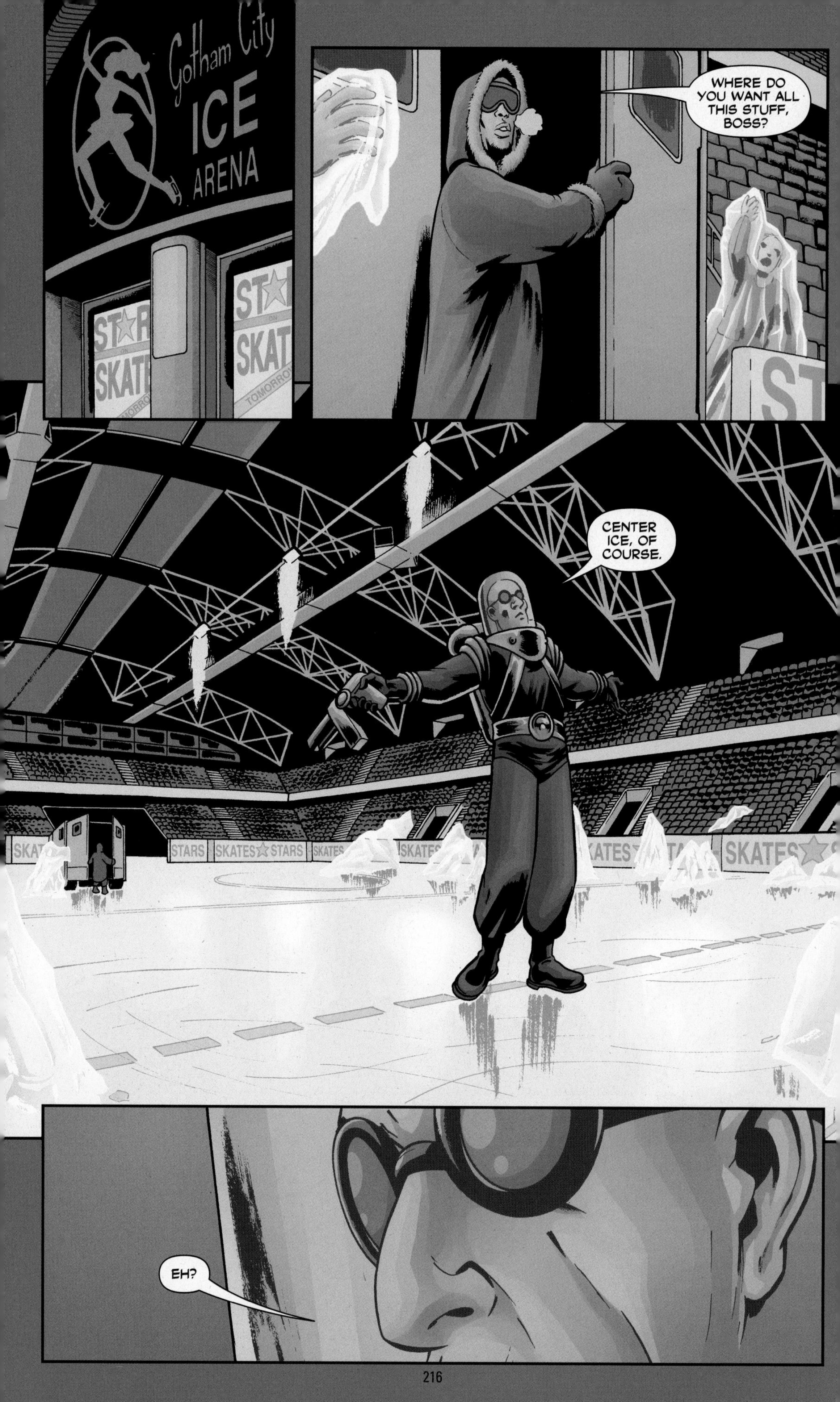
Gotham City ICE ARENA
STARS ON SKATES
TOMORROW
WHERE DO YOU WANT ALL THIS STUFF, BOSS?
CENTER ICE, OF COURSE.
STARS SKATES STARS SKATES
EH?

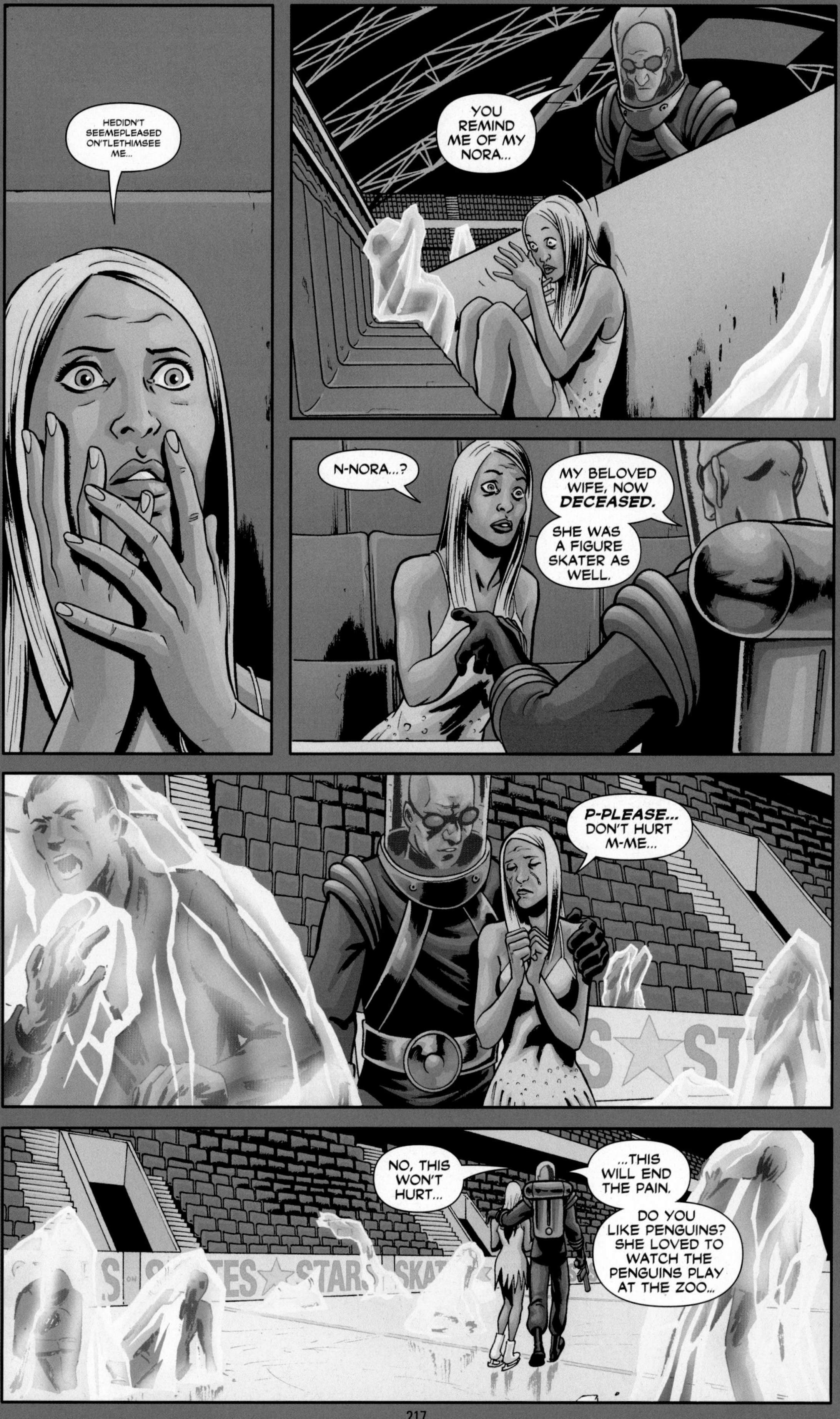

HEDIDN'T SEEMEPLEASED ON'TLETHIMSEE ME...
YOU REMIND ME OF MY NORA...
N-NORA...?
MY BELOVED WIFE, NOW *DECEASED.*
SHE WAS A FIGURE SKATER AS WELL.
P-PLEASE... DON'T HURT M-ME...
NO, THIS WON'T HURT...
...THIS WILL END THE PAIN.
DO YOU LIKE PENGUINS? SHE LOVED TO WATCH THE PENGUINS PLAY AT THE ZOO...

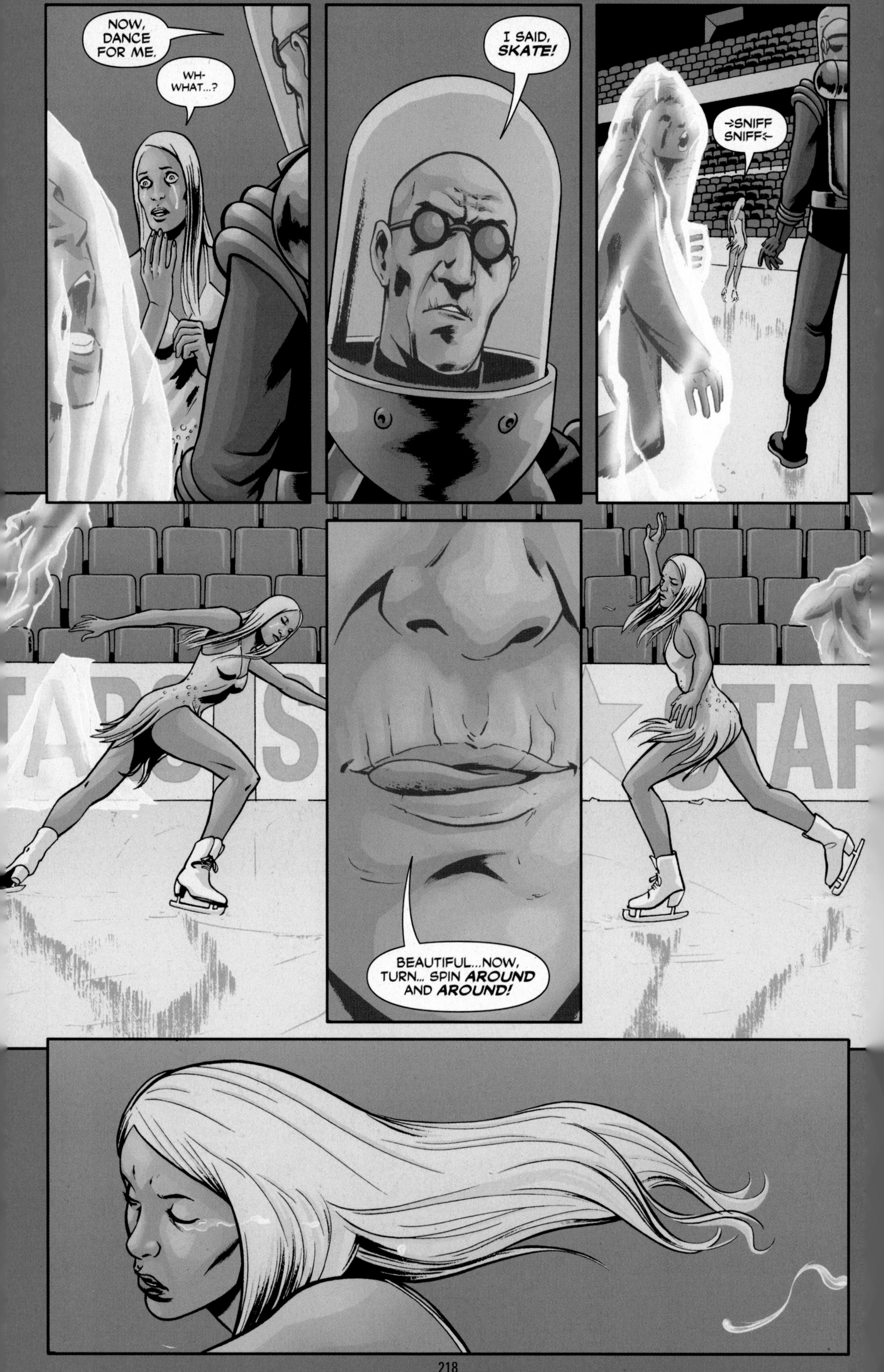

NOW, DANCE FOR ME.
WH- WHAT...?
I SAID, SKATE!
SNIFF SNIFF
BEAUTIFUL...NOW, TURN... SPIN AROUND AND AROUND!

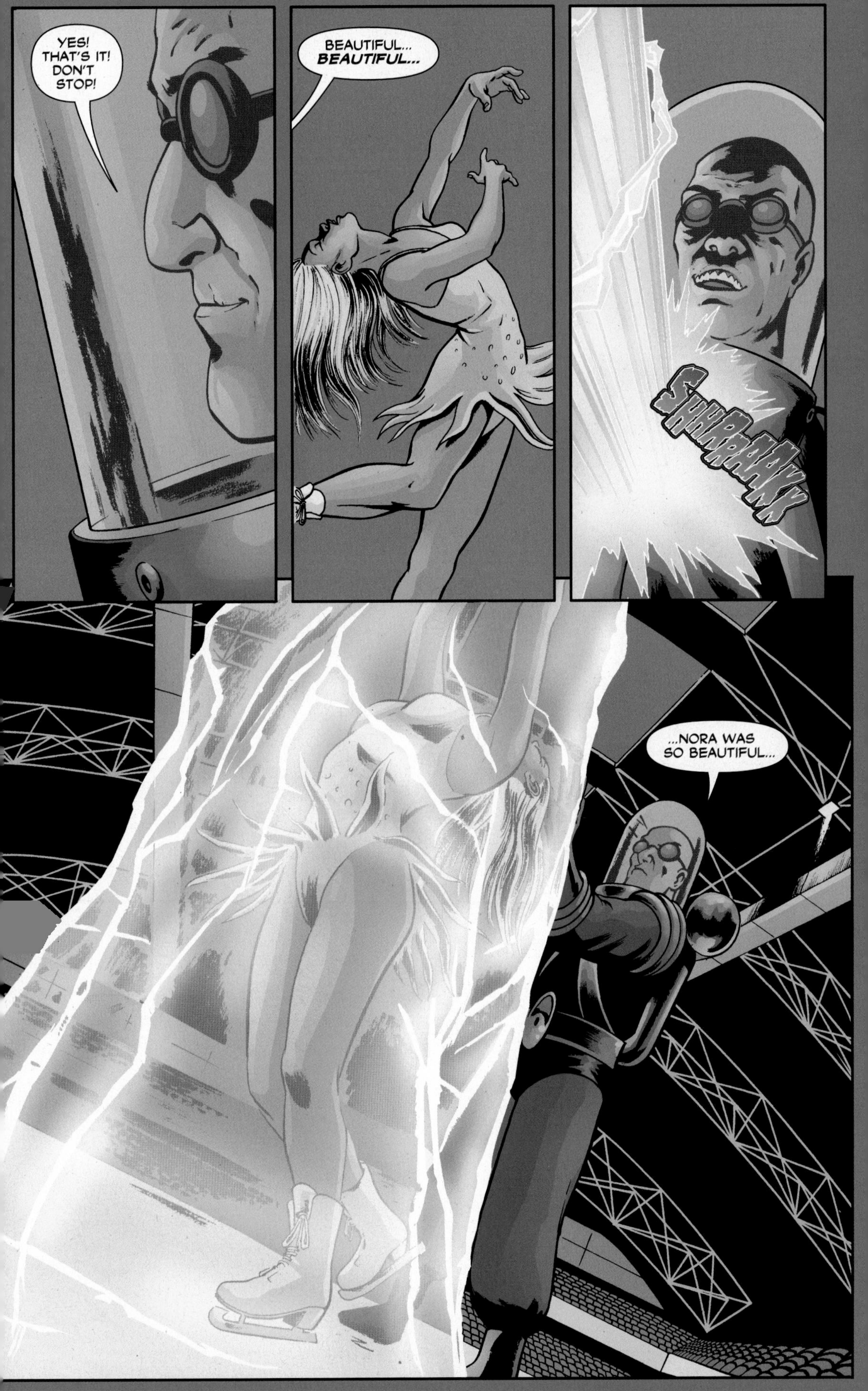
YES! THAT'S IT! DON'T STOP!
BEAUTIFUL... BEAUTIFUL...
SHHRAAKK
...NORA WAS SO BEAUTIFUL...

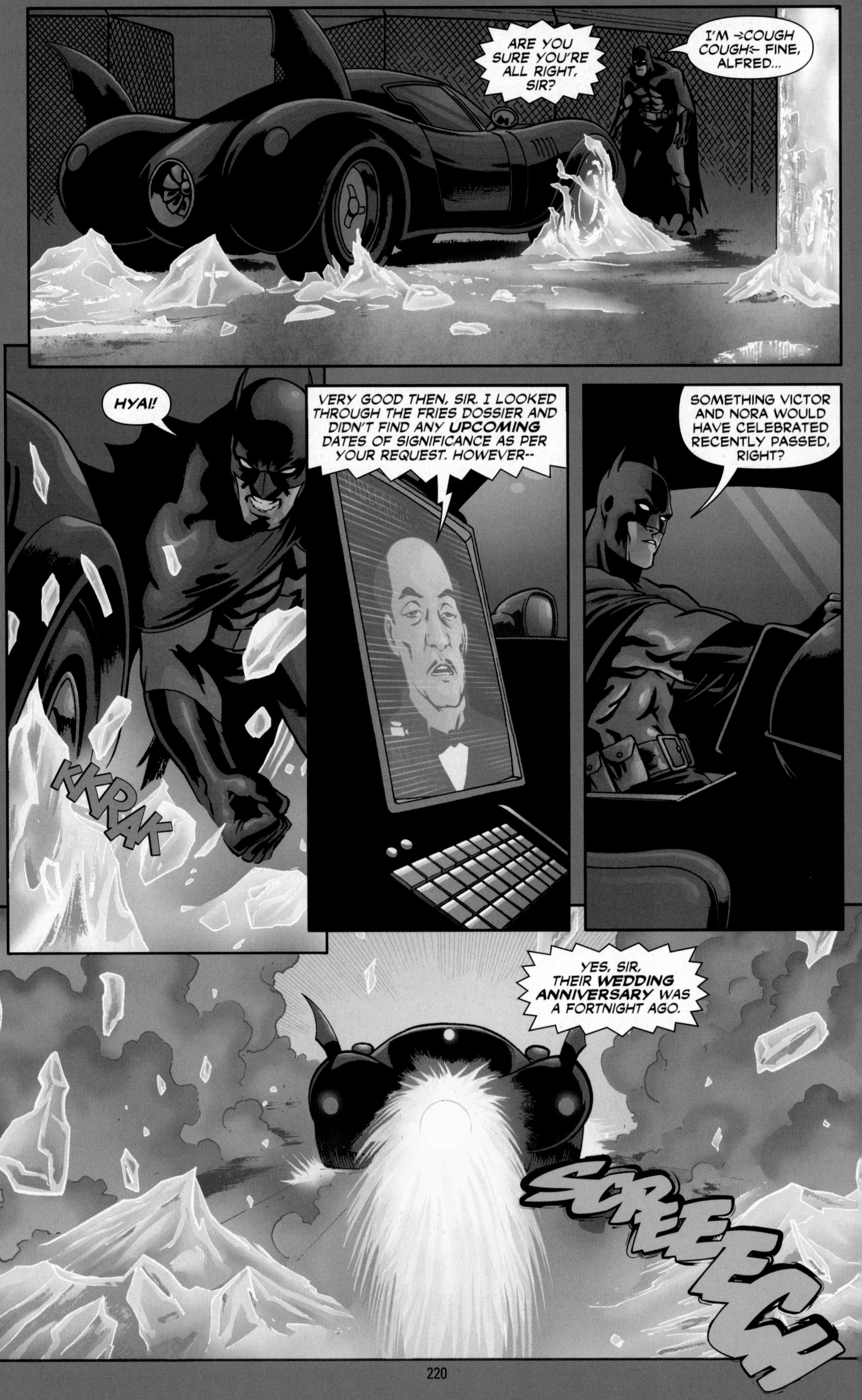

ARE YOU SURE YOU'RE ALL RIGHT, SIR?
I'M →COUGH COUGH← FINE, ALFRED...
HYAI!
KKRAK
VERY GOOD THEN, SIR. I LOOKED THROUGH THE FRIES DOSSIER AND DIDN'T FIND ANY **UPCOMING** DATES OF SIGNIFICANCE AS PER YOUR REQUEST. HOWEVER--
SOMETHING VICTOR AND NORA WOULD HAVE CELEBRATED RECENTLY PASSED, RIGHT?
YES, SIR, THEIR **WEDDING ANNIVERSARY** WAS A FORTNIGHT AGO.
SCREEEECH

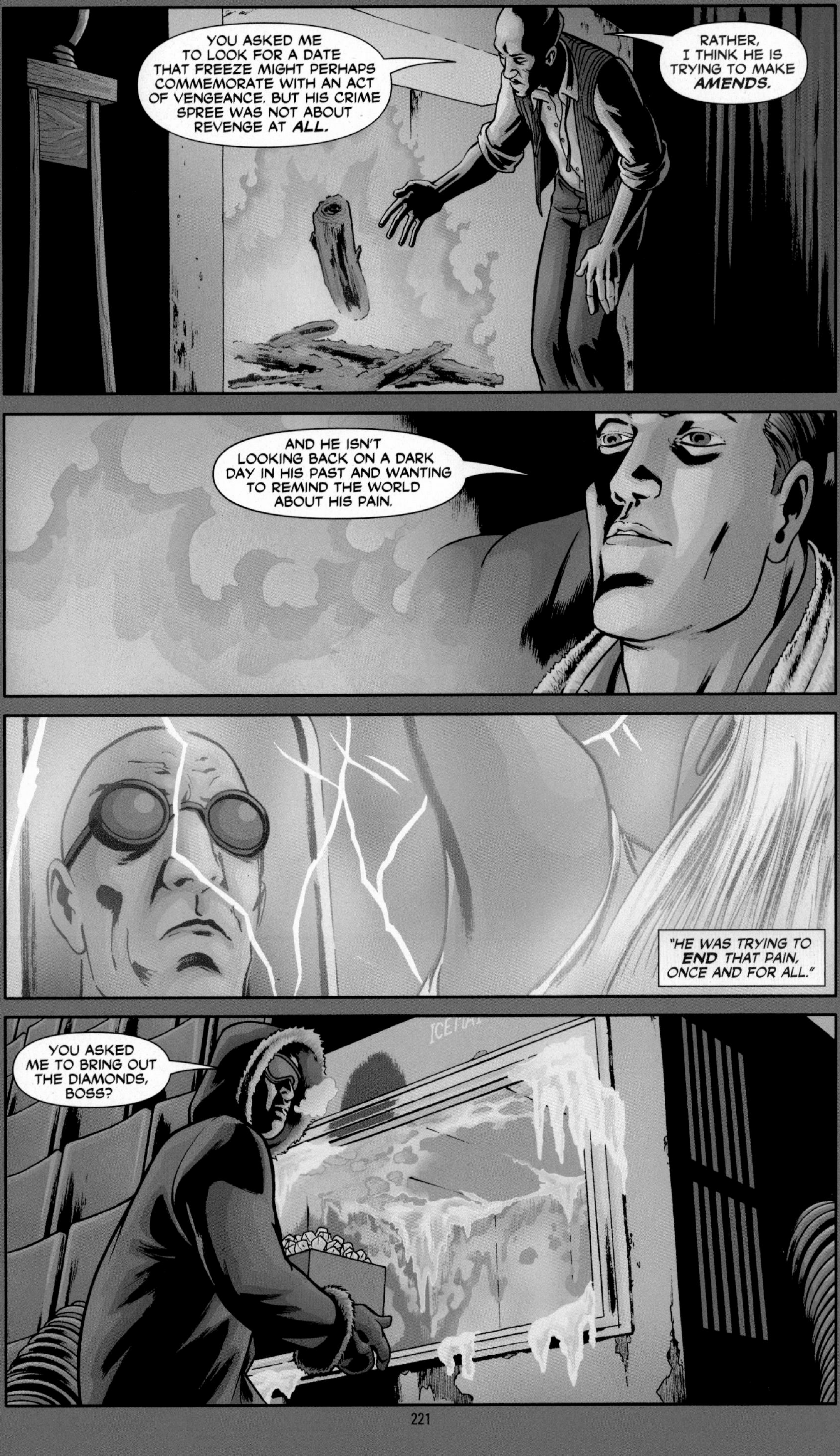
YOU ASKED ME TO LOOK FOR A DATE THAT FREEZE MIGHT PERHAPS COMMEMORATE WITH AN ACT OF VENGEANCE. BUT HIS CRIME SPREE WAS NOT ABOUT REVENGE AT ***ALL.***
RATHER, I THINK HE IS TRYING TO MAKE ***AMENDS.***
AND HE ISN'T LOOKING BACK ON A DARK DAY IN HIS PAST AND WANTING TO REMIND THE WORLD ABOUT HIS PAIN.
"HE WAS TRYING TO ***END*** THAT PAIN, ONCE AND FOR ALL."
YOU ASKED ME TO BRING OUT THE DIAMONDS, BOSS?

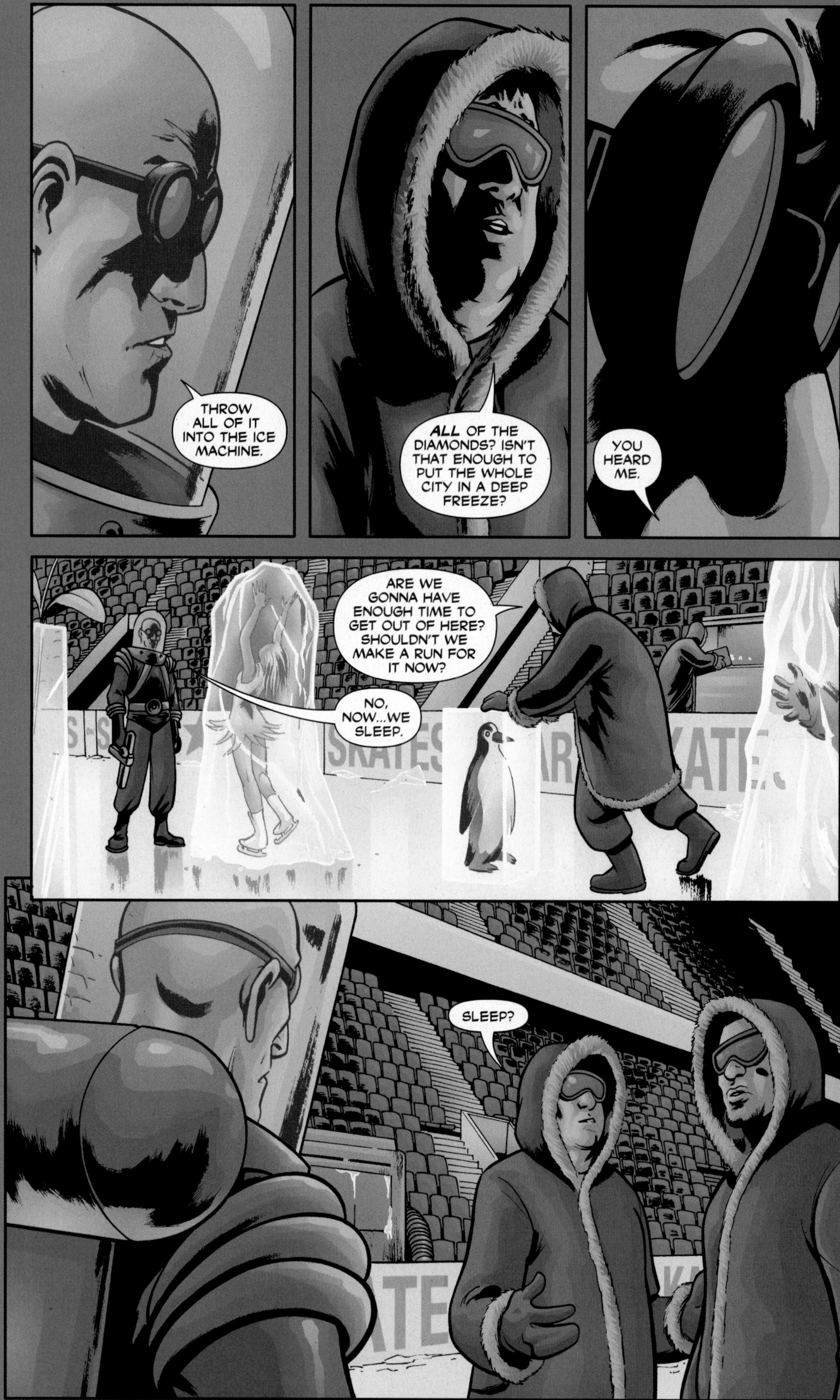
THROW ALL OF IT INTO THE ICE MACHINE.
ALL OF THE DIAMONDS? ISN'T THAT ENOUGH TO PUT THE WHOLE CITY IN A DEEP FREEZE?
YOU HEARD ME.
ARE WE GONNA HAVE ENOUGH TIME TO GET OUT OF HERE? SHOULDN'T WE MAKE A RUN FOR IT NOW?
NO, NOW...WE SLEEP.
SKATES
SLEEP?

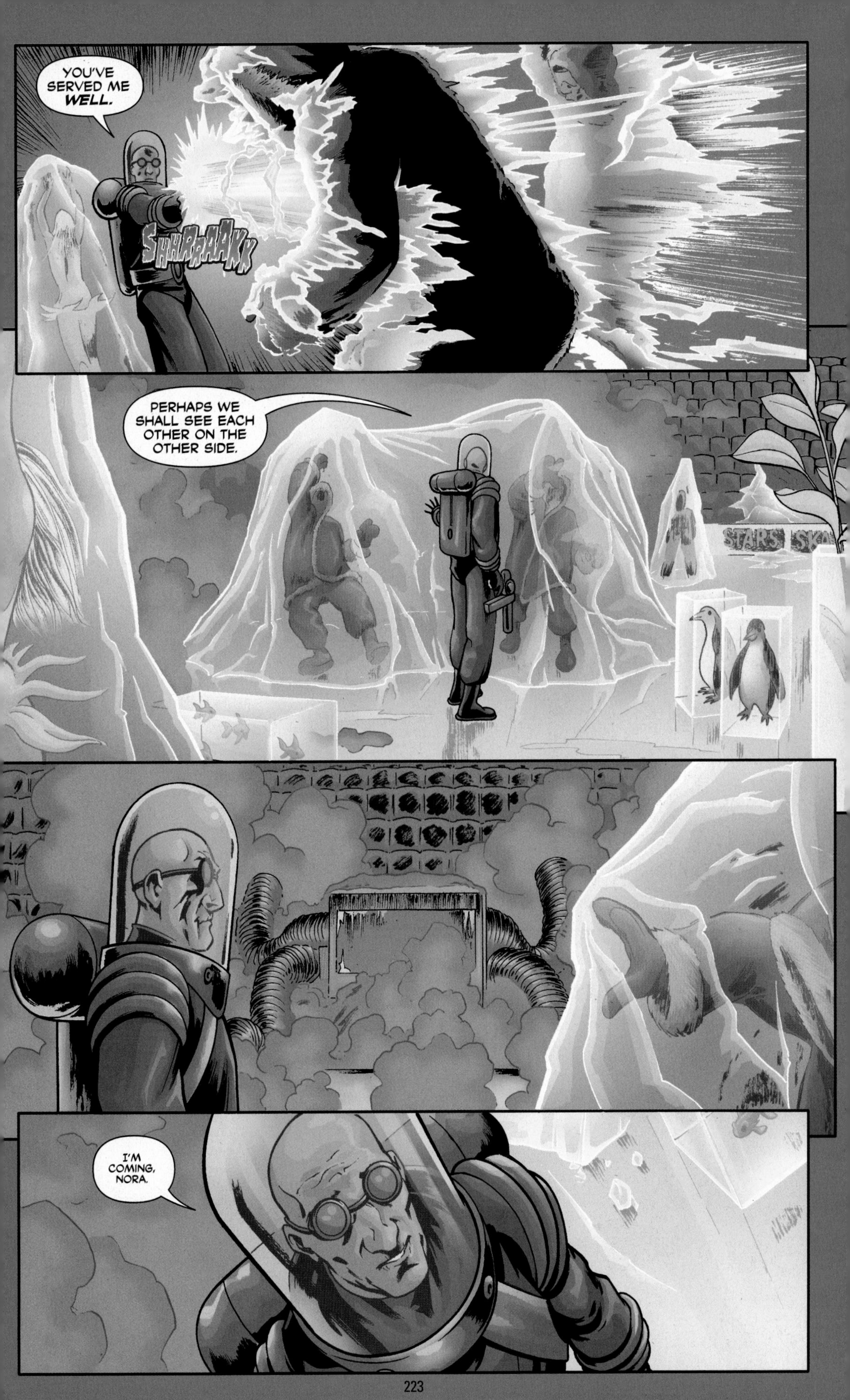
YOU'VE SERVED ME WELL.
SHHRRAAKK
PERHAPS WE SHALL SEE EACH OTHER ON THE OTHER SIDE.
STARS
I'M COMING, NORA.

"SOME SAY THE WORLD WILL END IN FIRE, SOME SAY IN ICE..."

"FROM WHAT I'VE TASTED OF DESIRE, I HOLD WITH THOSE WHO FAVOR FIRE."

"BUT IF IT HAD TO PERISH TWICE, I THINK I KNOW ENOUGH OF HATE TO KNOW THAT FOR DESTRUCTION ICE IS ALSO GREAT..."

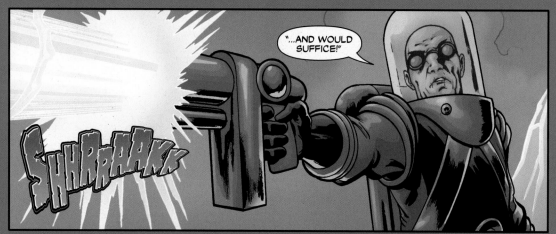

"...AND WOULD SUFFICE!"

SHHRRAAKK

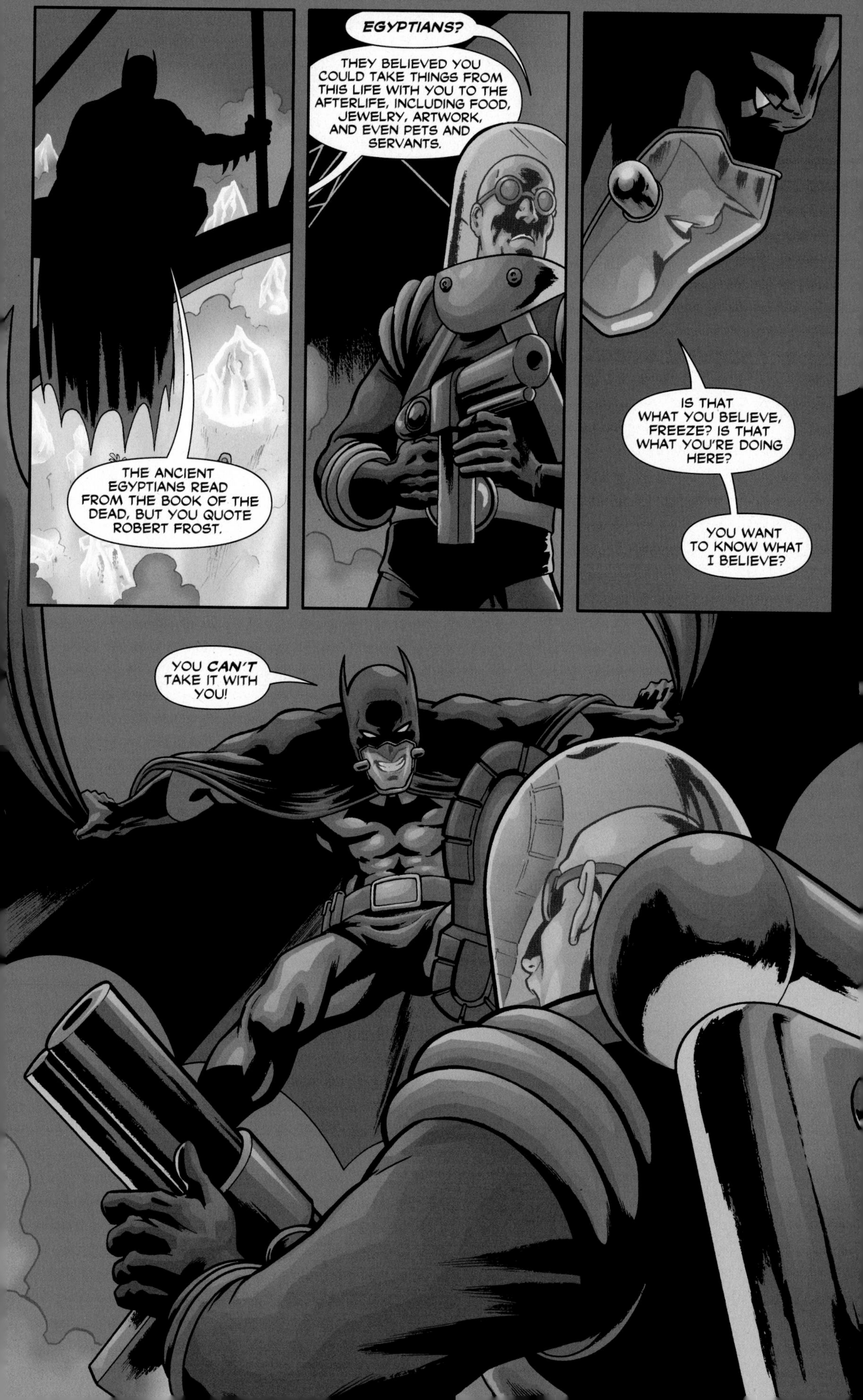

THE ANCIENT EGYPTIANS READ FROM THE BOOK OF THE DEAD, BUT YOU QUOTE ROBERT FROST.
EGYPTIANS?
THEY BELIEVED YOU COULD TAKE THINGS FROM THIS LIFE WITH YOU TO THE AFTERLIFE, INCLUDING FOOD, JEWELRY, ARTWORK, AND EVEN PETS AND SERVANTS.
IS THAT WHAT YOU BELIEVE, FREEZE? IS THAT WHAT YOU'RE DOING HERE?
YOU WANT TO KNOW WHAT I BELIEVE?
YOU *CAN'T* TAKE IT WITH YOU!

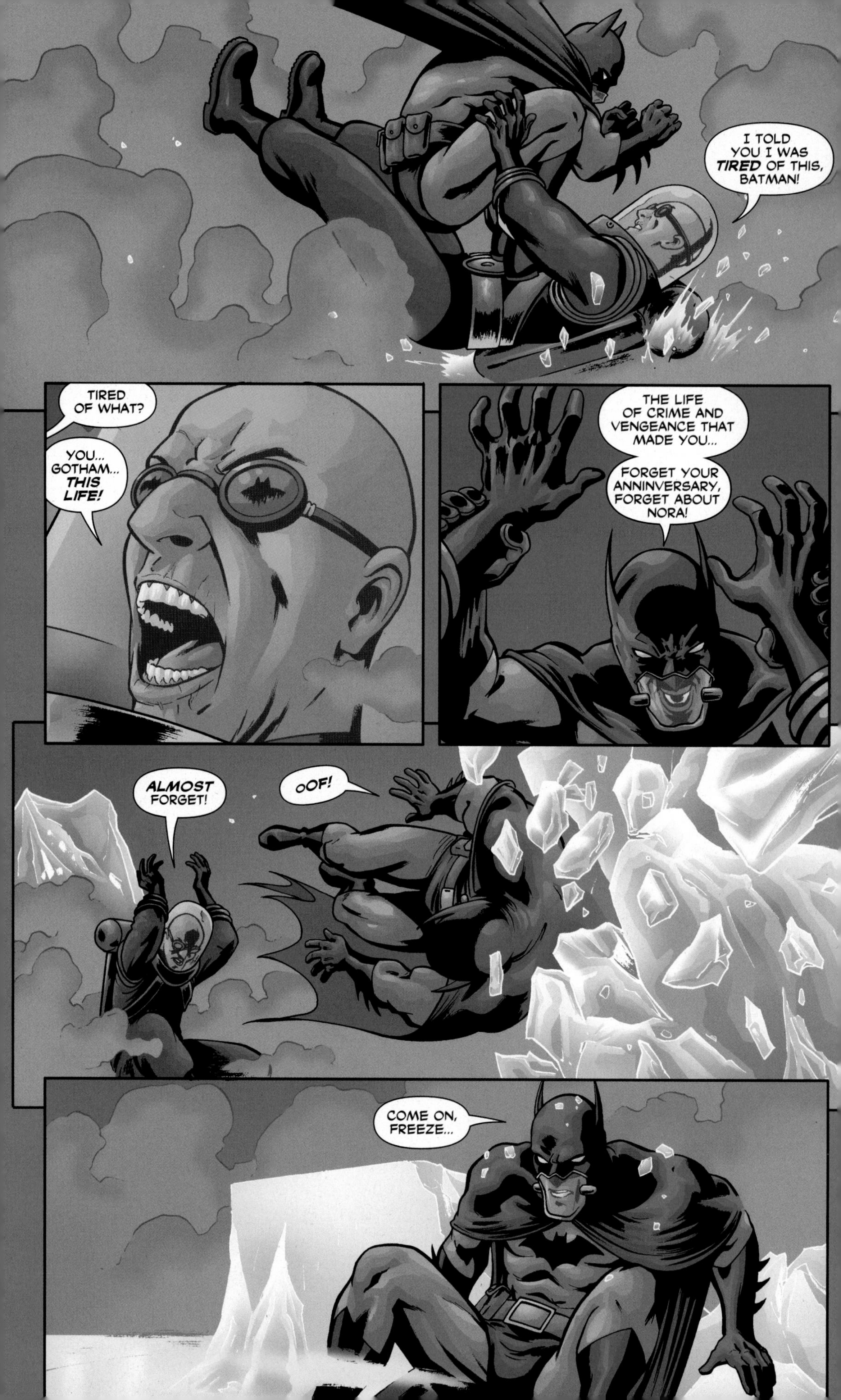
I TOLD YOU I WAS TIRED OF THIS, BATMAN!
TIRED OF WHAT?
YOU... GOTHAM... THIS LIFE!
THE LIFE OF CRIME AND VENGEANCE THAT MADE YOU...
FORGET YOUR ANNINVERSARY, FORGET ABOUT NORA!
ALMOST FORGET!
OOF!
COME ON, FREEZE...

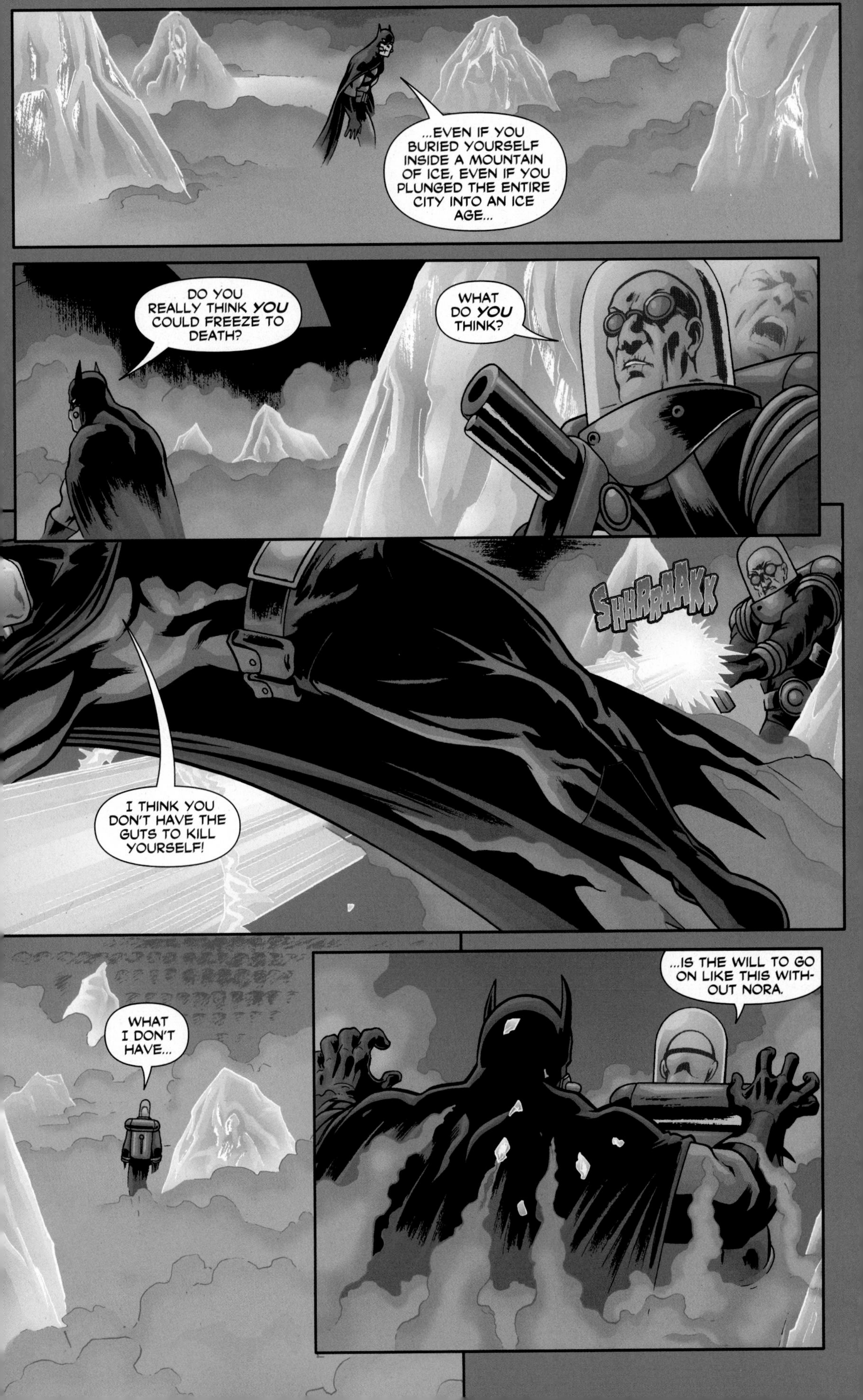
...EVEN IF YOU BURIED YOURSELF INSIDE A MOUNTAIN OF ICE, EVEN IF YOU PLUNGED THE ENTIRE CITY INTO AN ICE AGE...
DO YOU REALLY THINK YOU COULD FREEZE TO DEATH?
WHAT DO YOU THINK?
SHHRRAAKK
I THINK YOU DON'T HAVE THE GUTS TO KILL YOURSELF!
WHAT I DON'T HAVE...
...IS THE WILL TO GO ON LIKE THIS WITH-OUT NORA.

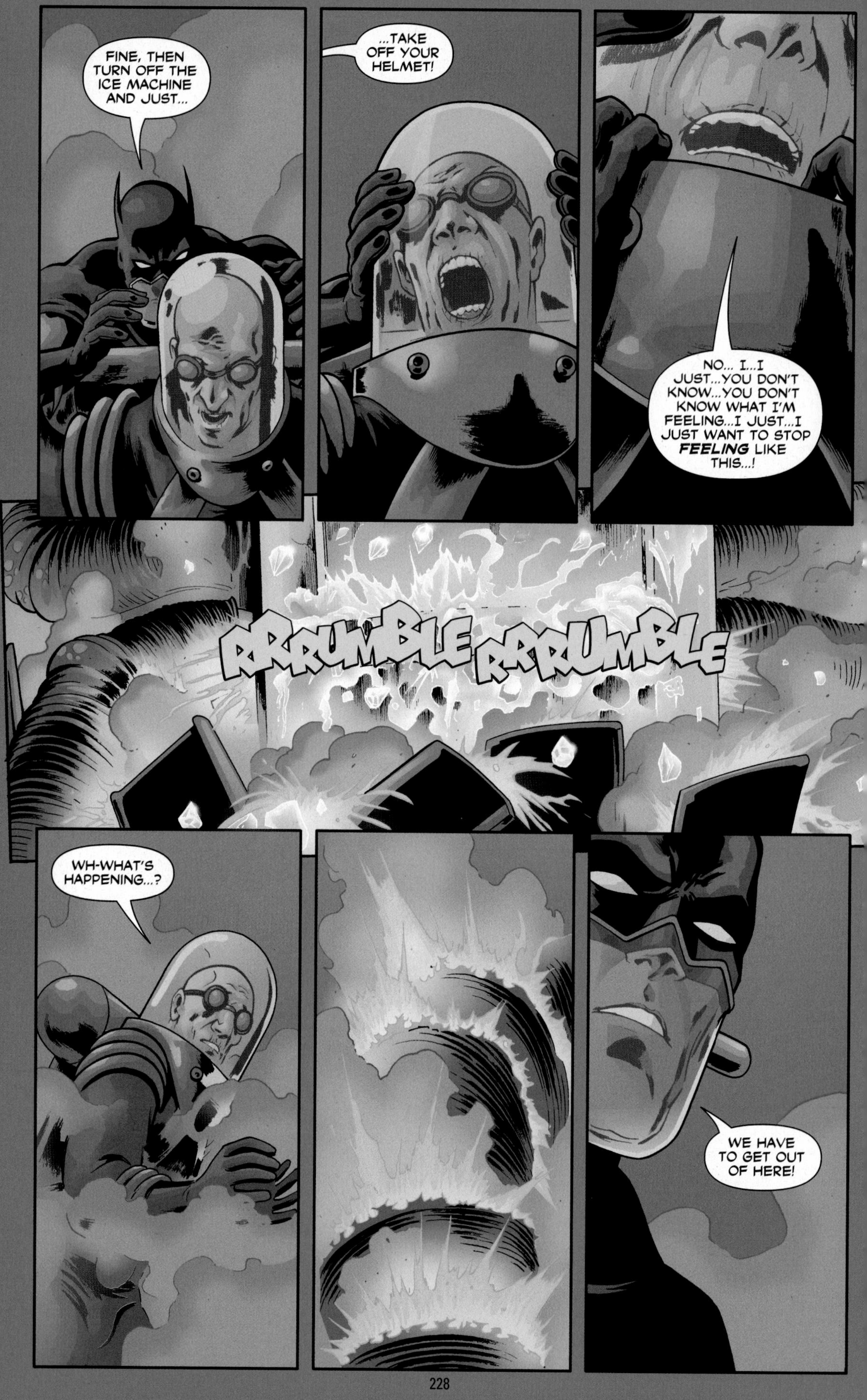
FINE, THEN TURN OFF THE ICE MACHINE AND JUST...
...TAKE OFF YOUR HELMET!
NO... I...I JUST...YOU DON'T KNOW...YOU DON'T KNOW WHAT I'M FEELING...I JUST...I JUST WANT TO STOP FEELING LIKE THIS...!
RRRUMBLE RRRUMBLE
WH-WHAT'S HAPPENING...?
WE HAVE TO GET OUT OF HERE!

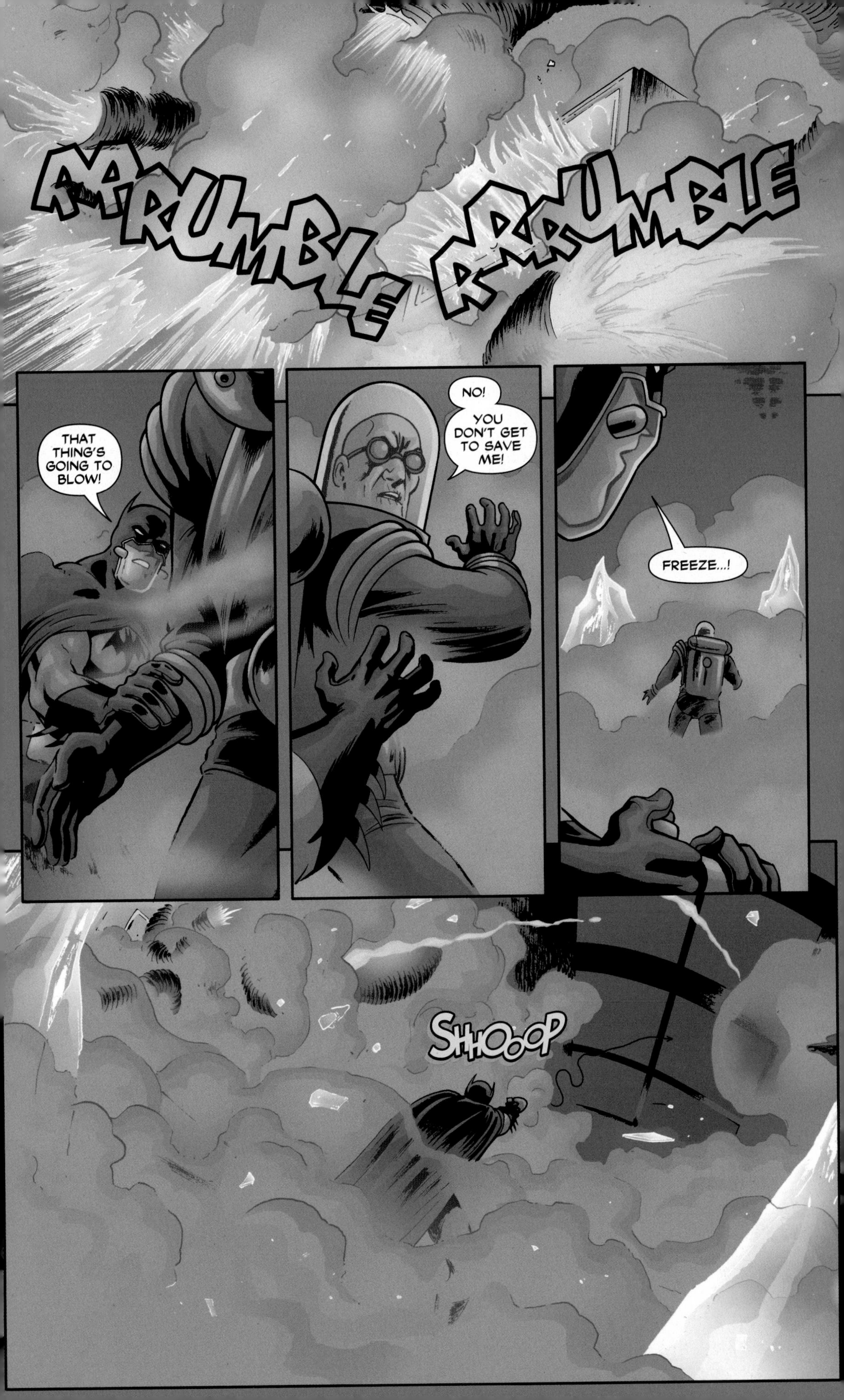

RRRUMBLE RRRUMBLE
THAT THING'S GOING TO BLOW!
NO!
YOU DON'T GET TO SAVE ME!
FREEZE...!
SHHOOOP

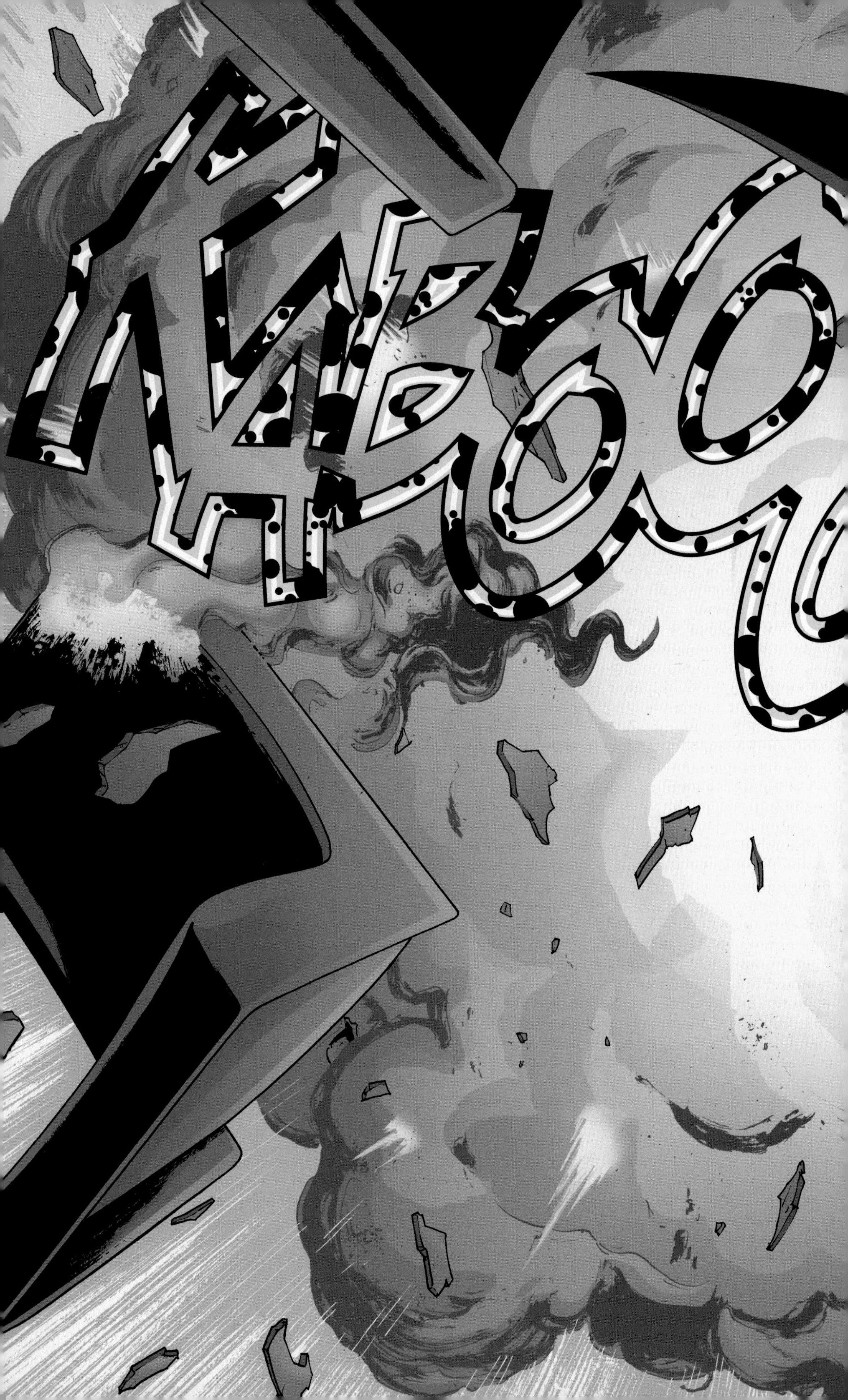

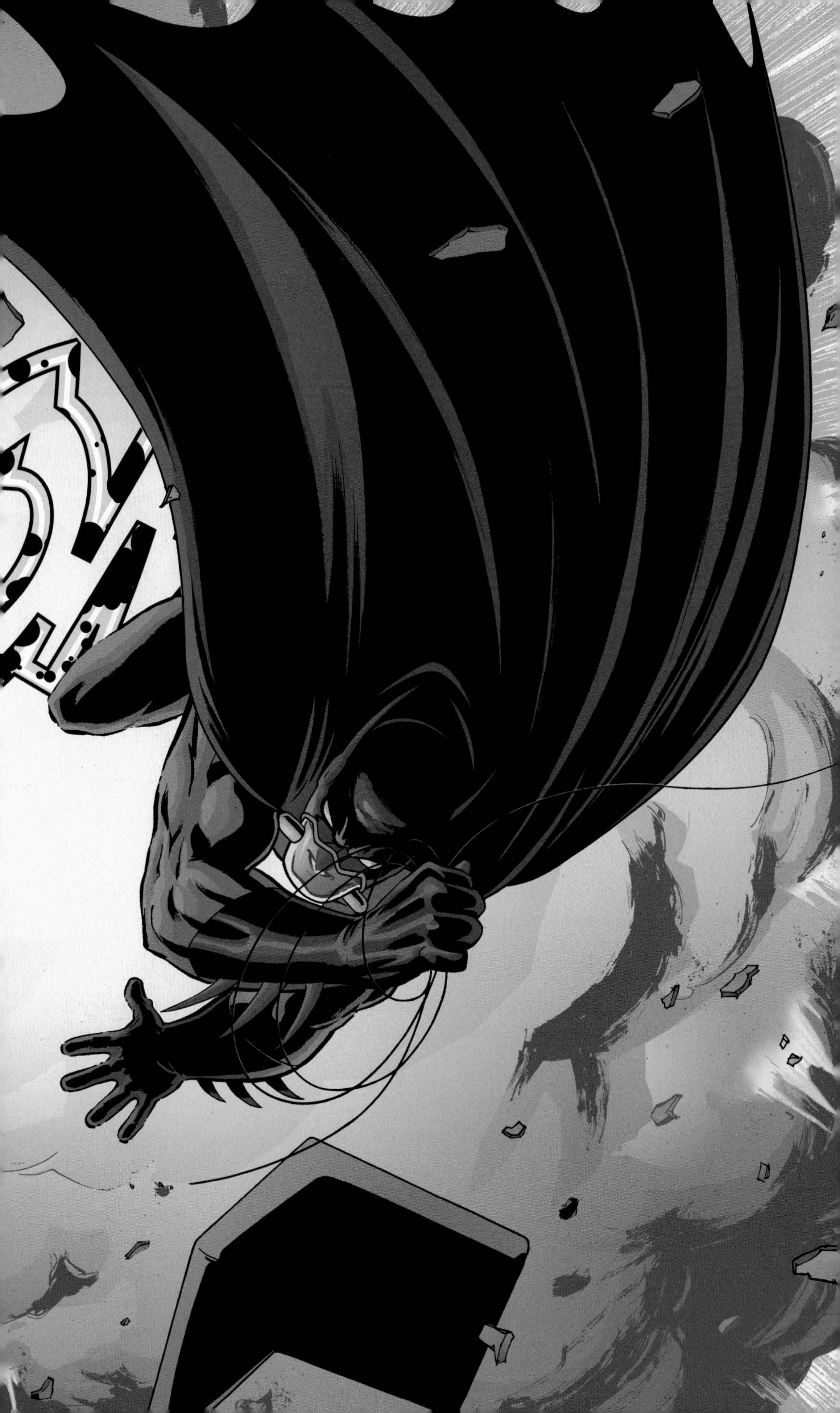

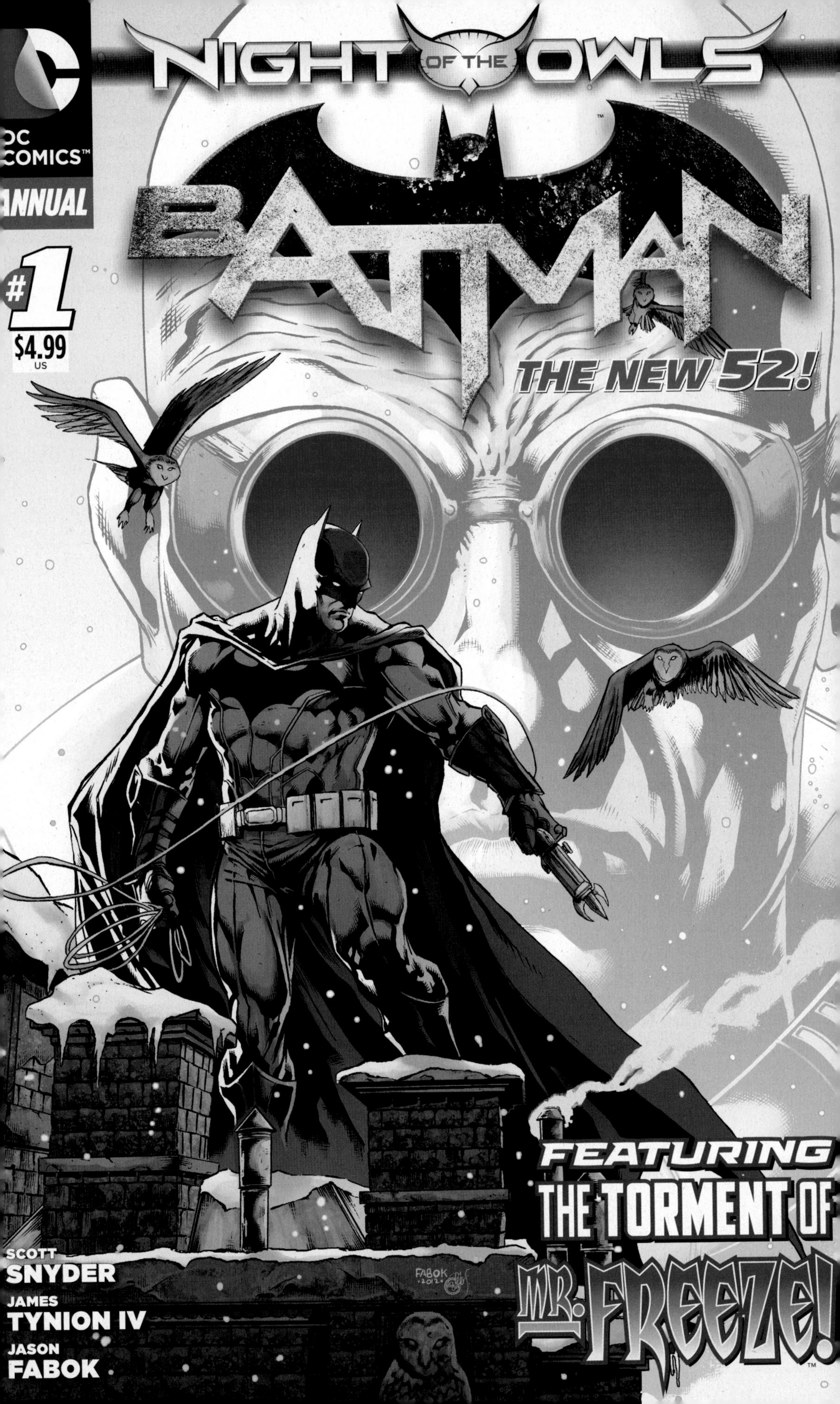

NIGHT OF THE OWLS
DC COMICS™
ANNUAL
BATMAN
#1
$4.99 US
THE NEW 52!
FEATURING
THE TORMENT OF
MR. FREEZE!
SCOTT SNYDER
JAMES TYNION IV
JASON FABOK
FABOK 2012

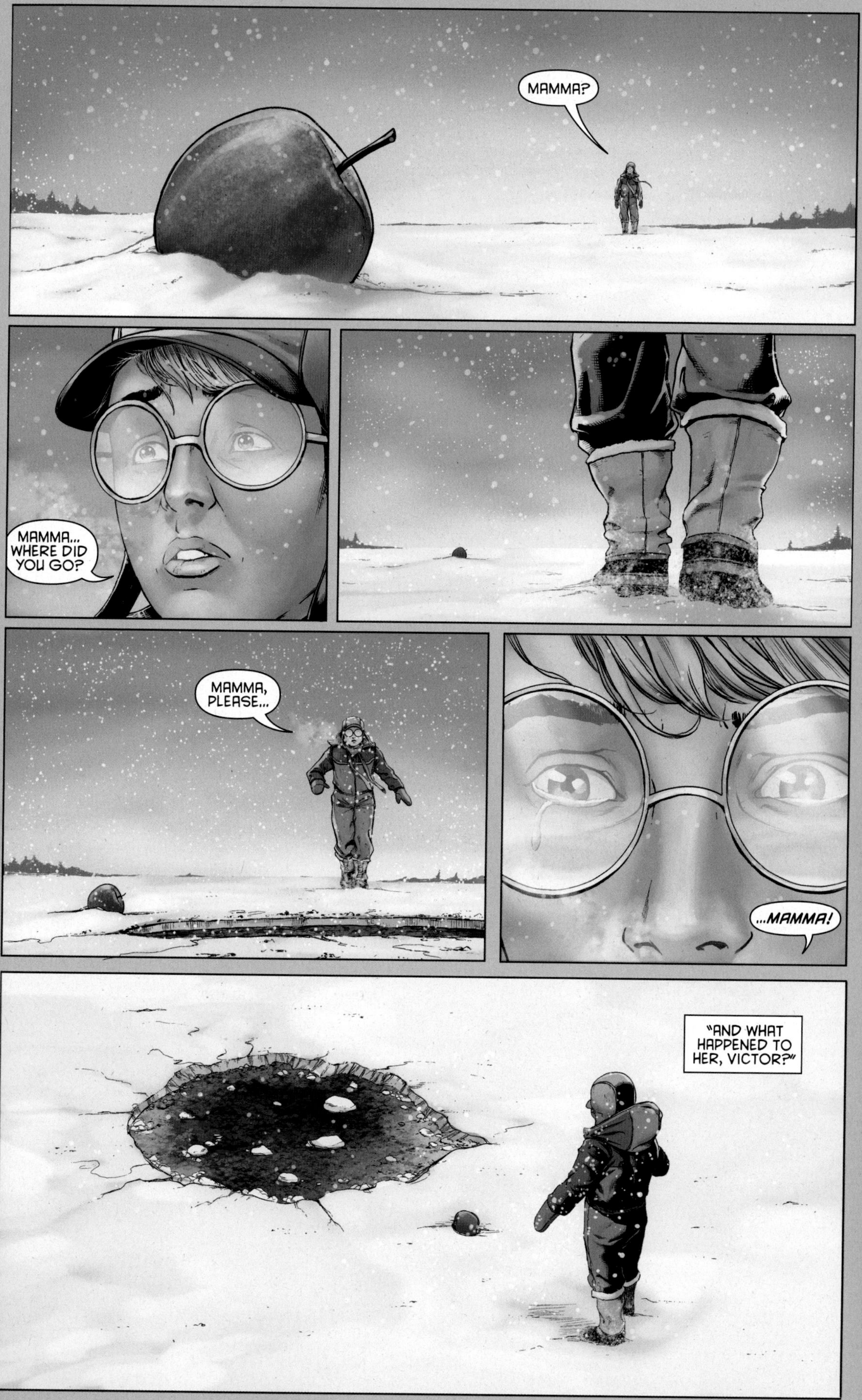
MAMMA?
MAMMA... WHERE DID YOU GO?
MAMMA, PLEASE...
...MAMMA!
"AND WHAT HAPPENED TO HER, VICTOR?"

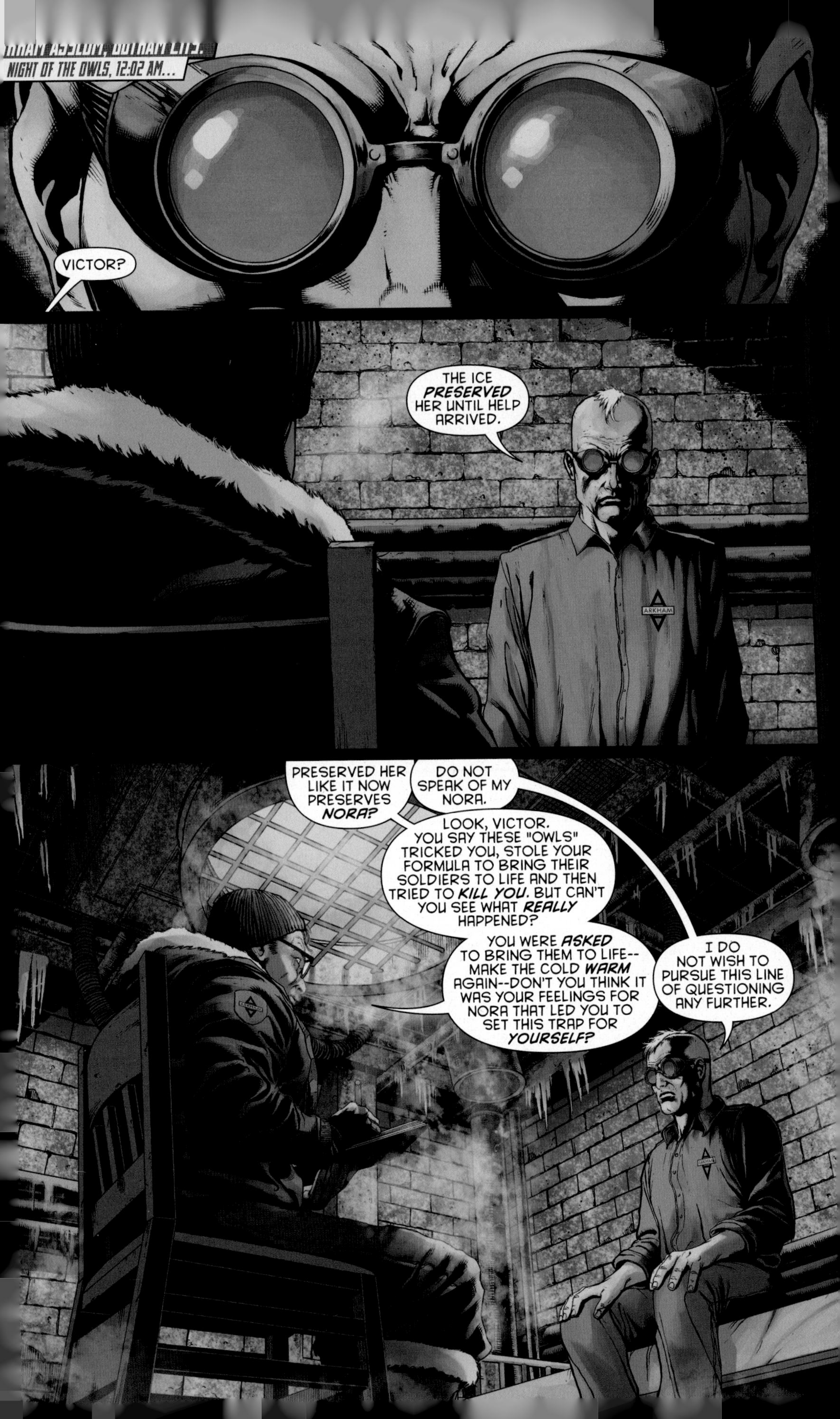

NIGHT OF THE OWLS, 12:02 AM...
VICTOR?
THE ICE *PRESERVED* HER UNTIL HELP ARRIVED.
PRESERVED HER LIKE IT NOW PRESERVES *NORA?*
DO NOT SPEAK OF MY NORA.
LOOK, VICTOR. YOU SAY THESE "OWLS" TRICKED YOU, STOLE YOUR FORMULA TO BRING THEIR SOLDIERS TO LIFE AND THEN TRIED TO *KILL YOU*. BUT CAN'T YOU SEE WHAT *REALLY* HAPPENED?
YOU WERE *ASKED* TO BRING THEM TO LIFE-- MAKE THE COLD *WARM* AGAIN--DON'T YOU THINK IT WAS YOUR FEELINGS FOR NORA THAT LED YOU TO SET THIS TRAP FOR *YOURSELF?*
I DO NOT WISH TO PURSUE THIS LINE OF QUESTIONING ANY FURTHER.
ARKHAM

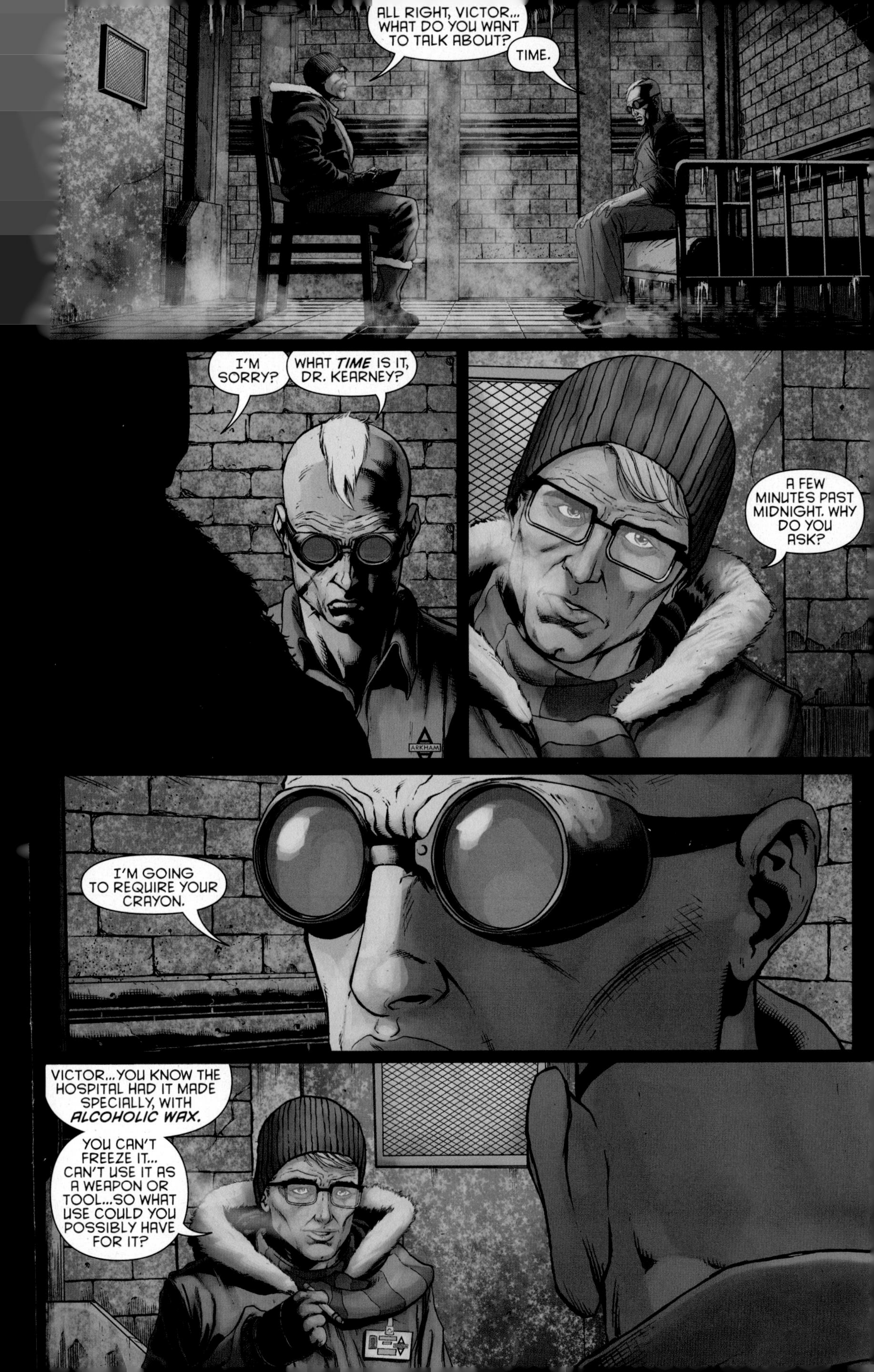

ALL RIGHT, VICTOR... WHAT DO YOU WANT TO TALK ABOUT?
TIME.
I'M SORRY?
WHAT *TIME* IS IT, DR. KEARNEY?
A FEW MINUTES PAST MIDNIGHT. WHY DO YOU ASK?
I'M GOING TO REQUIRE YOUR CRAYON.
VICTOR...YOU KNOW THE HOSPITAL HAD IT MADE SPECIALLY, WITH ***ALCOHOLIC WAX.***
YOU CAN'T FREEZE IT... CAN'T USE IT AS A WEAPON OR TOOL...SO WHAT USE COULD YOU POSSIBLY HAVE FOR IT?

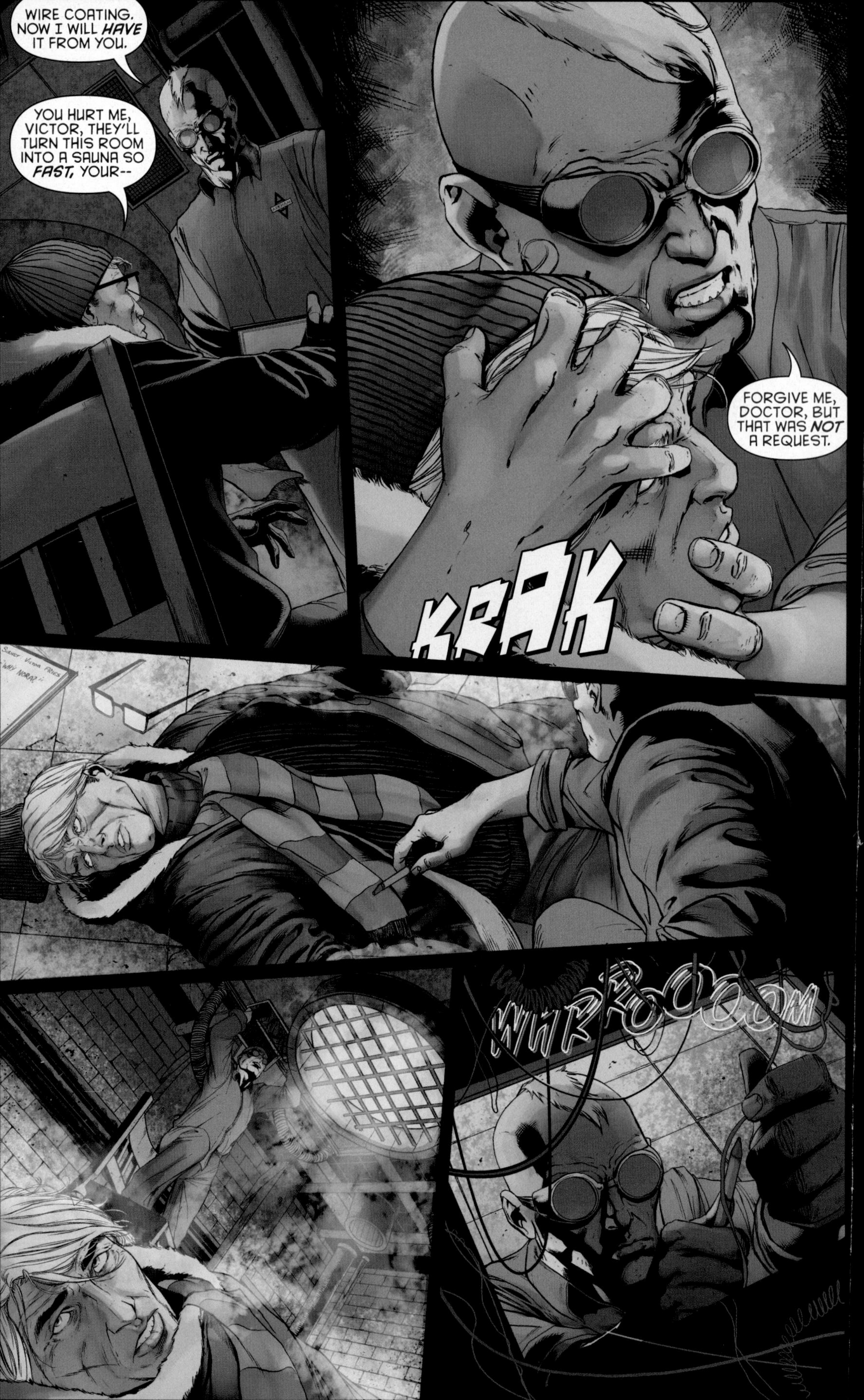
WIRE COATING. NOW I WILL *HAVE* IT FROM YOU.
YOU HURT ME, VICTOR, THEY'LL TURN THIS ROOM INTO A SAUNA SO *FAST,* YOUR--
FORGIVE ME, DOCTOR, BUT THAT WAS *NOT* A REQUEST.
KRAK
WHRROOOOM

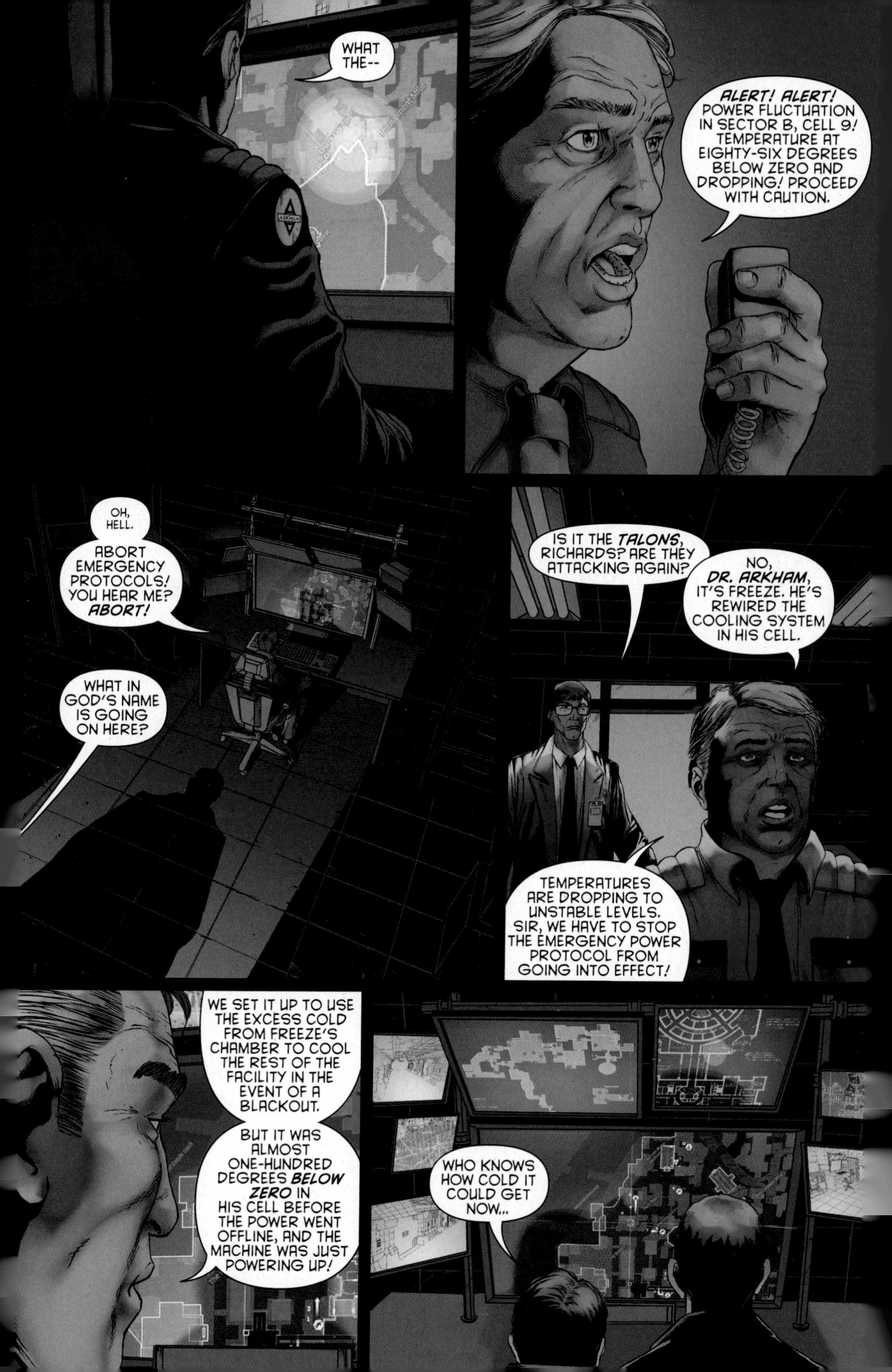
WHAT THE--
ALERT! ALERT! POWER FLUCTUATION IN SECTOR B, CELL 9! TEMPERATURE AT EIGHTY-SIX DEGREES BELOW ZERO AND DROPPING! PROCEED WITH CAUTION.
OH, HELL.
ABORT EMERGENCY PROTOCOLS! YOU HEAR ME? ABORT!
WHAT IN GOD'S NAME IS GOING ON HERE?
IS IT THE TALONS, RICHARDS? ARE THEY ATTACKING AGAIN?
NO, DR. ARKHAM, IT'S FREEZE. HE'S REWIRED THE COOLING SYSTEM IN HIS CELL.
TEMPERATURES ARE DROPPING TO UNSTABLE LEVELS. SIR, WE HAVE TO STOP THE EMERGENCY POWER PROTOCOL FROM GOING INTO EFFECT!
WE SET IT UP TO USE THE EXCESS COLD FROM FREEZE'S CHAMBER TO COOL THE REST OF THE FACILITY IN THE EVENT OF A BLACKOUT.
BUT IT WAS ALMOST ONE-HUNDRED DEGREES BELOW ZERO IN HIS CELL BEFORE THE POWER WENT OFFLINE, AND THE MACHINE WAS JUST POWERING UP!
WHO KNOWS HOW COLD IT COULD GET NOW...

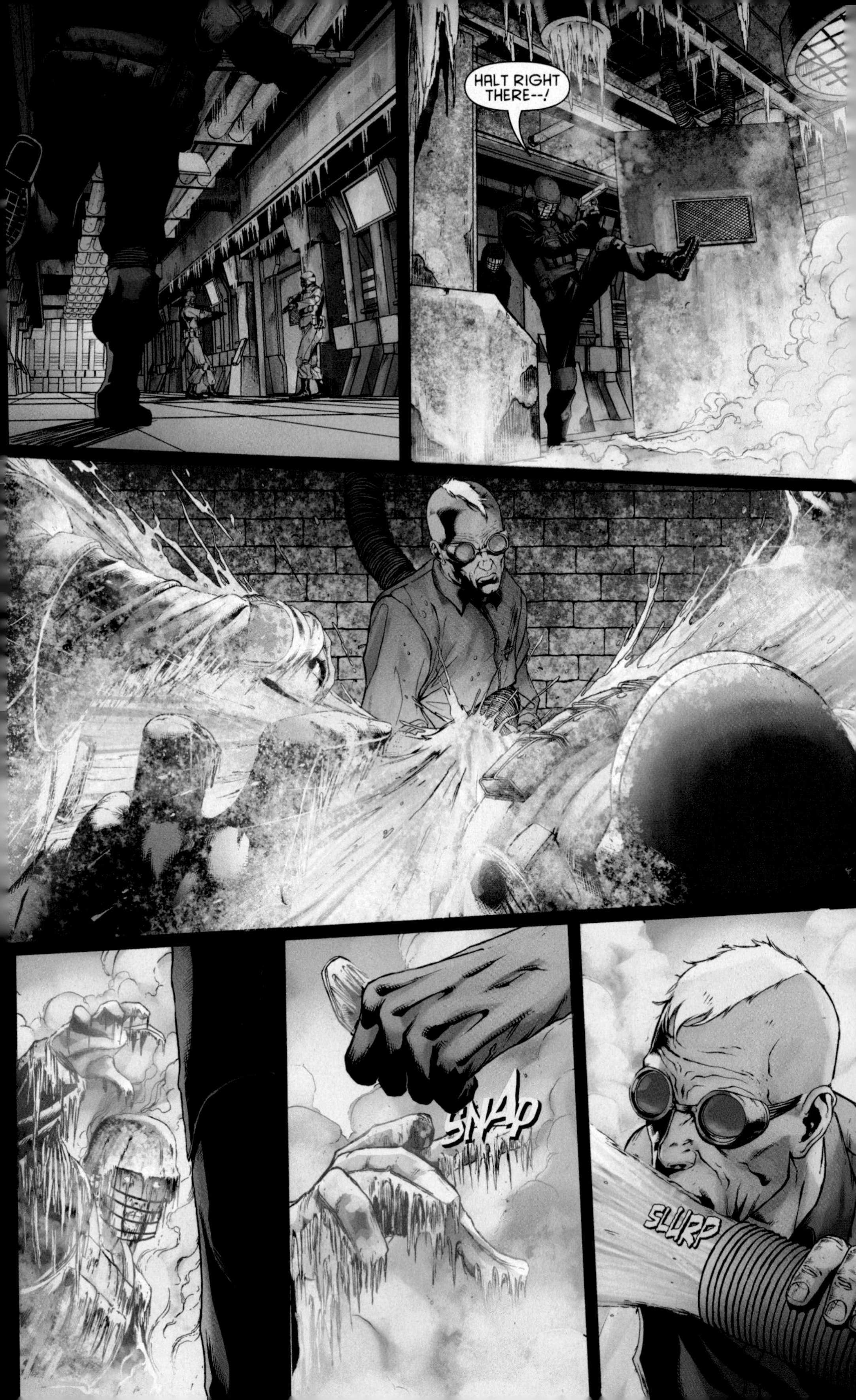
HALT RIGHT THERE--!
SNAP
SLURP

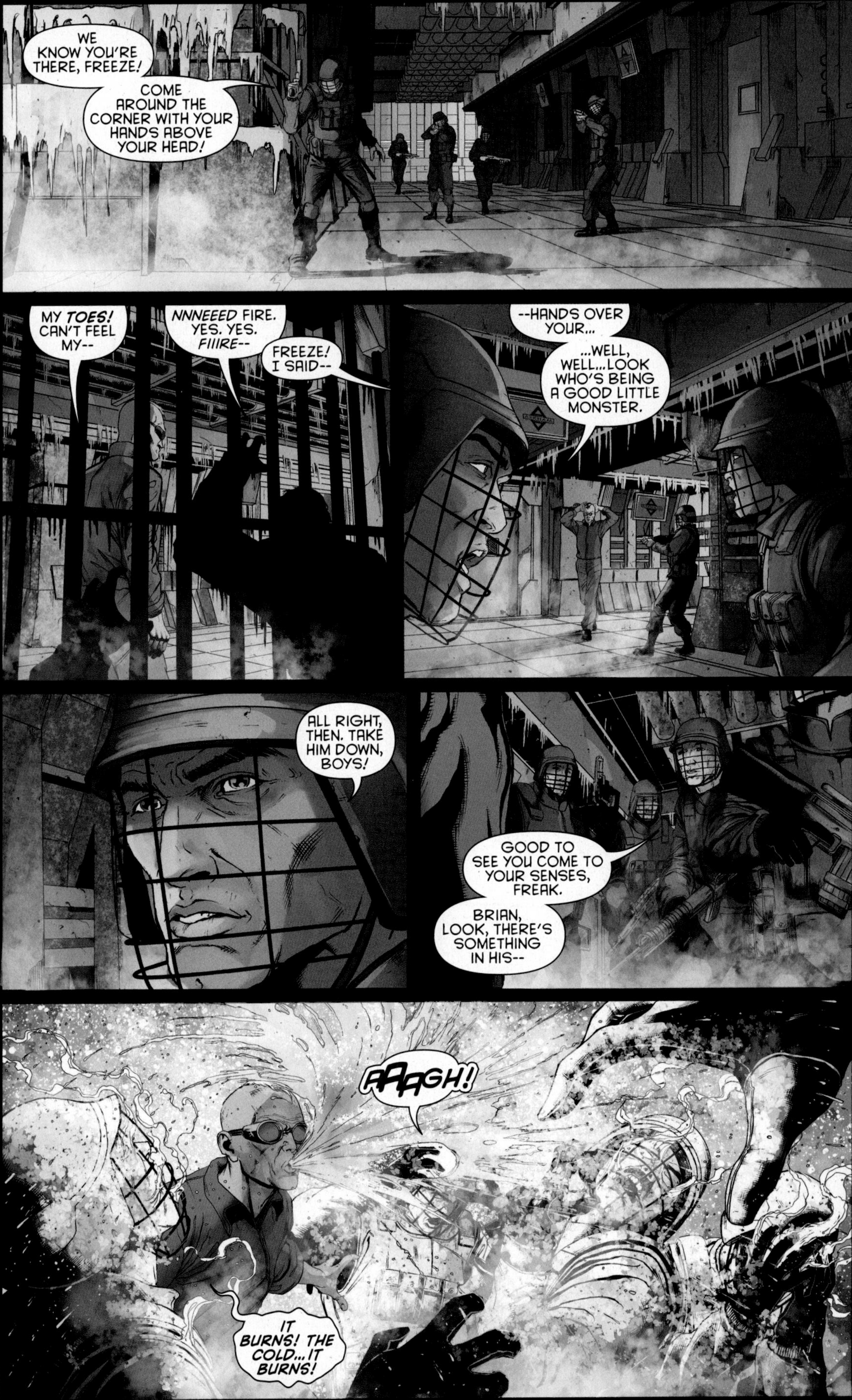
WE KNOW YOU'RE THERE, FREEZE!
COME AROUND THE CORNER WITH YOUR HANDS ABOVE YOUR HEAD!
MY *TOES!* CAN'T FEEL MY--
NNNEEED FIRE. YES. YES. *FIIIRE*--
FREEZE! I SAID--
--HANDS OVER YOUR...
...WELL, WELL...LOOK WHO'S BEING A GOOD LITTLE MONSTER.
ALL RIGHT, THEN. TAKE HIM DOWN, BOYS!
GOOD TO SEE YOU COME TO YOUR SENSES, FREAK.
BRIAN, LOOK, THERE'S SOMETHING IN HIS--
AAAGH!
IT BURNS! THE COLD...IT BURNS!

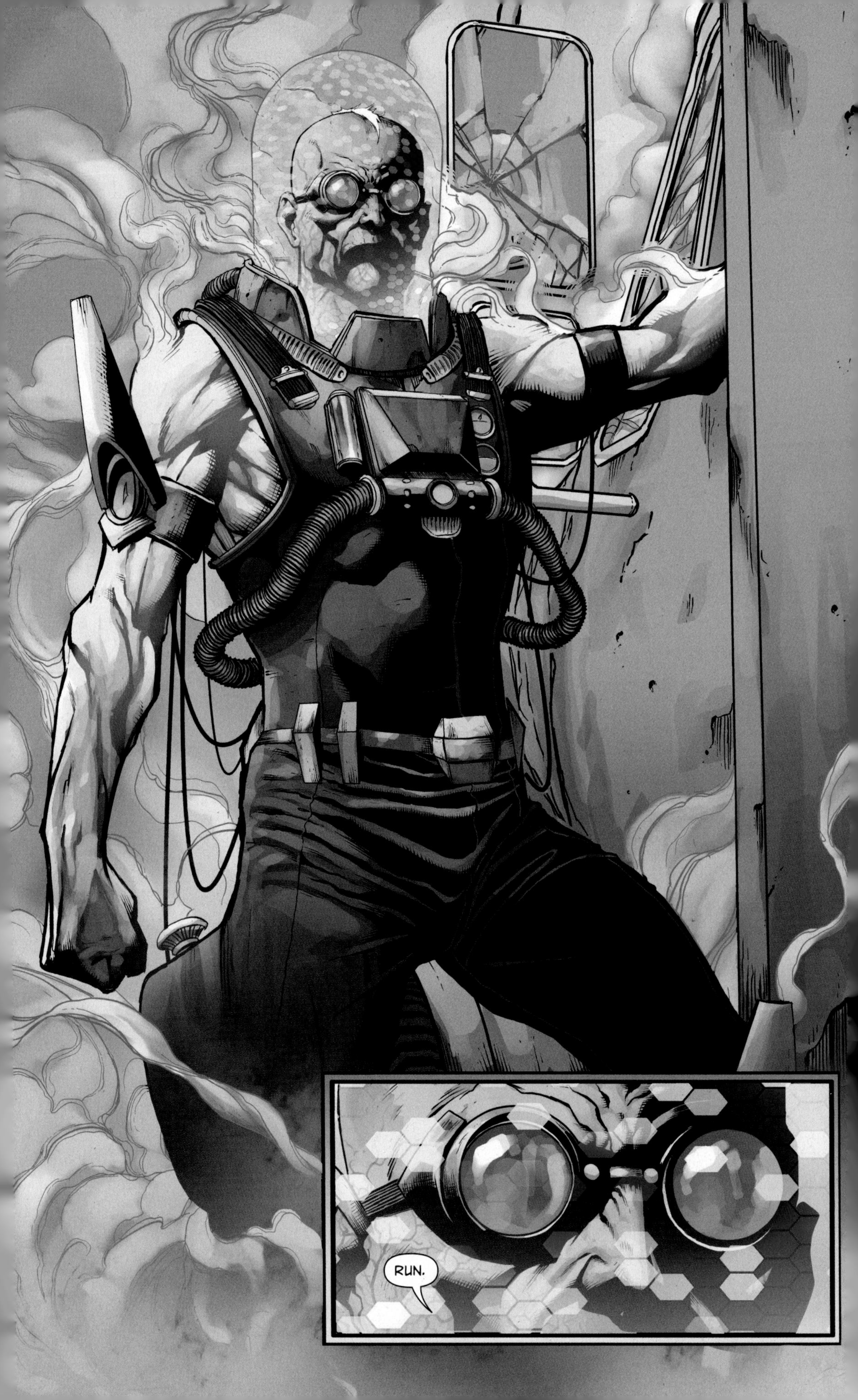
RUN.

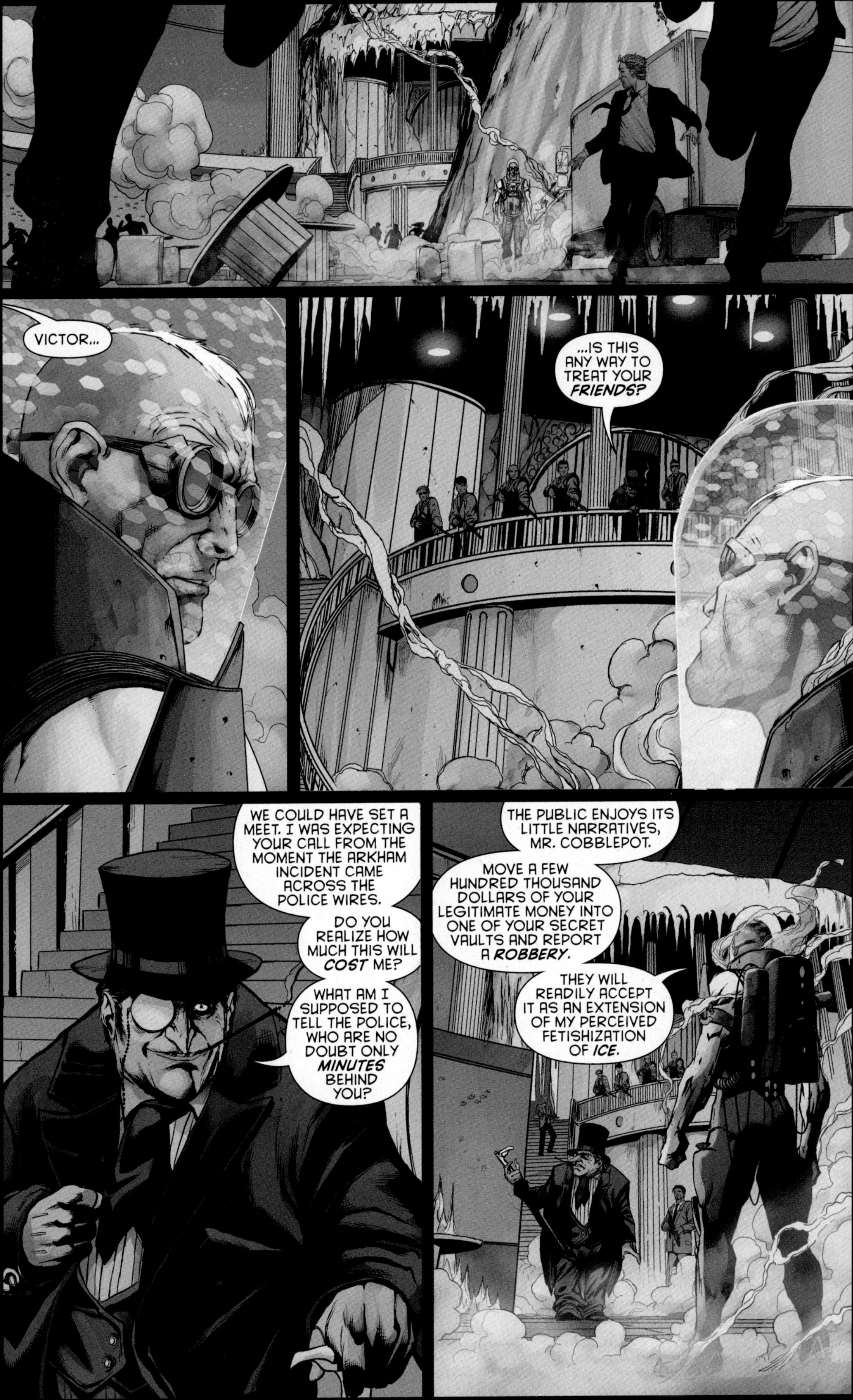
VICTOR...
...IS THIS ANY WAY TO TREAT YOUR FRIENDS?
WE COULD HAVE SET A MEET. I WAS EXPECTING YOUR CALL FROM THE MOMENT THE ARKHAM INCIDENT CAME ACROSS THE POLICE WIRES.
DO YOU REALIZE HOW MUCH THIS WILL COST ME?
WHAT AM I SUPPOSED TO TELL THE POLICE, WHO ARE NO DOUBT ONLY MINUTES BEHIND YOU?
THE PUBLIC ENJOYS ITS LITTLE NARRATIVES, MR. COBBLEPOT.
MOVE A FEW HUNDRED THOUSAND DOLLARS OF YOUR LEGITIMATE MONEY INTO ONE OF YOUR SECRET VAULTS AND REPORT A ROBBERY.
THEY WILL READILY ACCEPT IT AS AN EXTENSION OF MY PERCEIVED FETISHIZATION OF ICE.

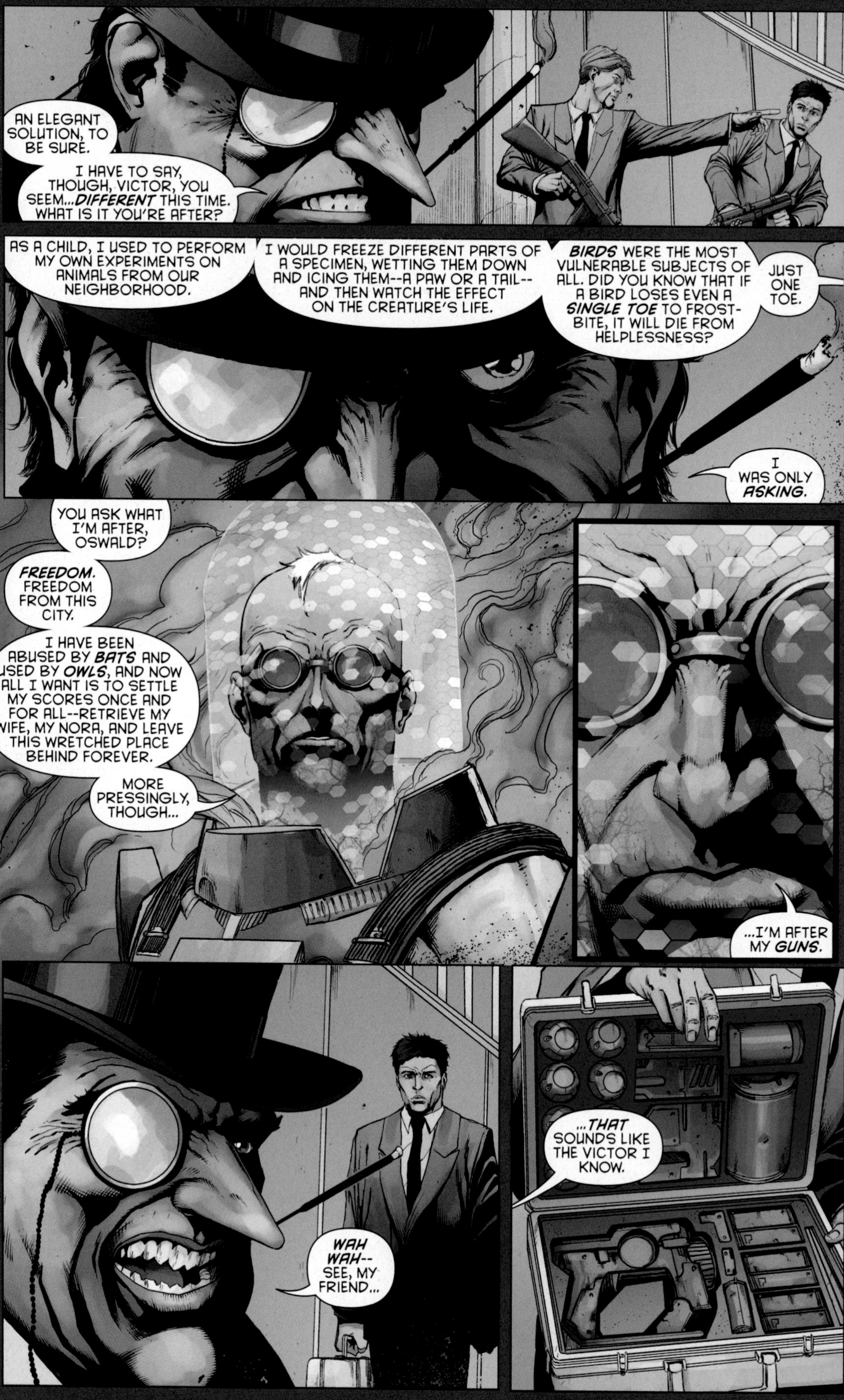
AN ELEGANT SOLUTION, TO BE SURE.
I HAVE TO SAY, THOUGH, VICTOR, YOU SEEM...*DIFFERENT* THIS TIME. WHAT IS IT YOU'RE AFTER?
AS A CHILD, I USED TO PERFORM MY OWN EXPERIMENTS ON ANIMALS FROM OUR NEIGHBORHOOD.
I WOULD FREEZE DIFFERENT PARTS OF A SPECIMEN, WETTING THEM DOWN AND ICING THEM--A PAW OR A TAIL--AND THEN WATCH THE EFFECT ON THE CREATURE'S LIFE.
BIRDS WERE THE MOST VULNERABLE SUBJECTS OF ALL. DID YOU KNOW THAT IF A BIRD LOSES EVEN A *SINGLE TOE* TO FROST-BITE, IT WILL DIE FROM HELPLESSNESS?
JUST ONE TOE.
I WAS ONLY *ASKING*.
YOU ASK WHAT I'M AFTER, OSWALD?
FREEDOM. FREEDOM FROM THIS CITY.
I HAVE BEEN ABUSED BY *BATS* AND USED BY *OWLS*, AND NOW ALL I WANT IS TO SETTLE MY SCORES ONCE AND FOR ALL--RETRIEVE MY WIFE, MY NORA, AND LEAVE THIS WRETCHED PLACE BEHIND FOREVER.
MORE PRESSINGLY, THOUGH...
...I'M AFTER MY *GUNS*.
WAH WAH--SEE, MY FRIEND...
...*THAT* SOUNDS LIKE THE VICTOR I KNOW.

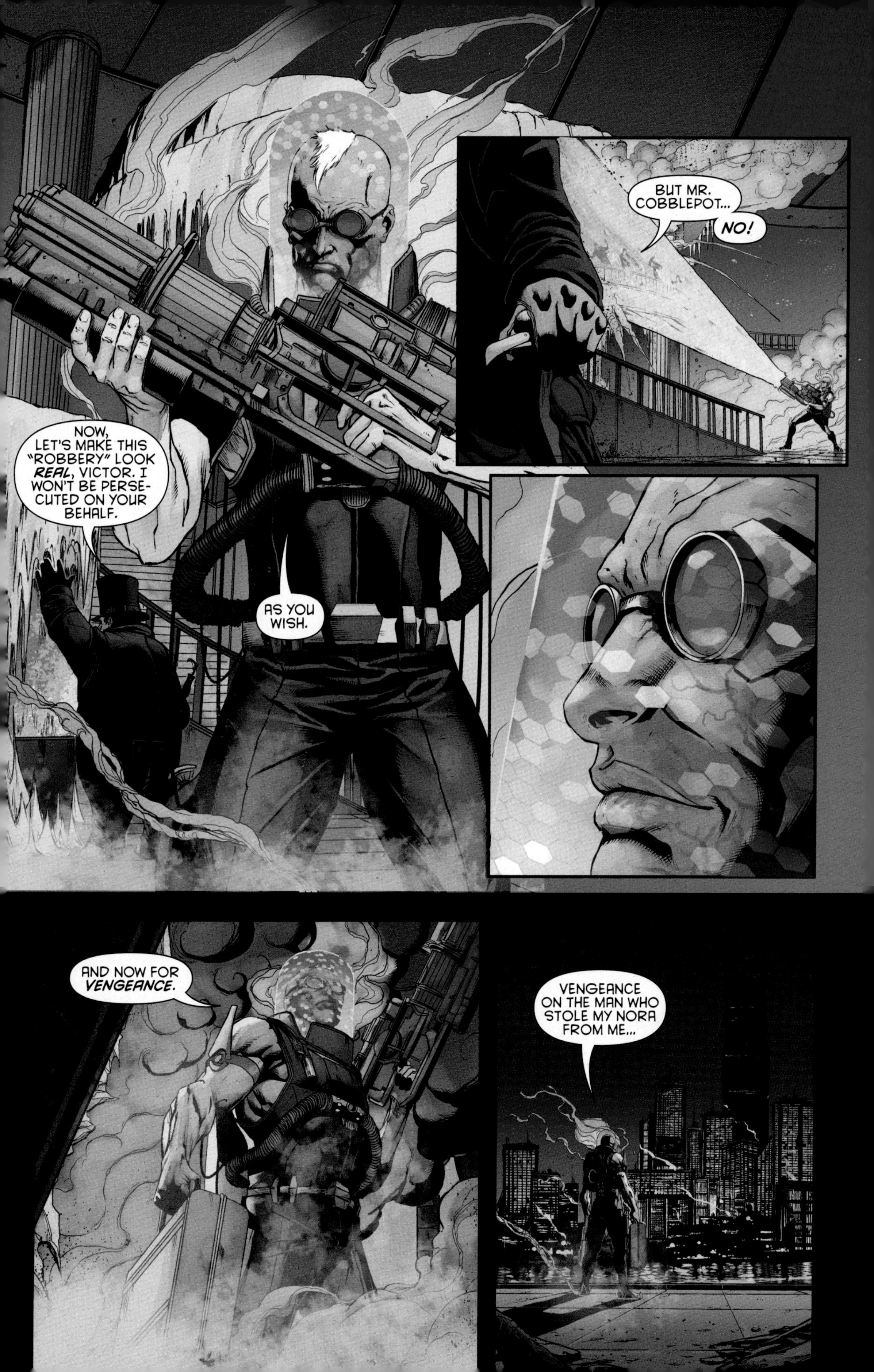
NOW, LET'S MAKE THIS "ROBBERY" LOOK *REAL*, VICTOR. I WON'T BE PERSECUTED ON YOUR BEHALF.
AS YOU WISH.
BUT MR. COBBLEPOT...
NO!
AND NOW FOR *VENGEANCE*.
VENGEANCE ON THE MAN WHO STOLE MY NORA FROM ME...

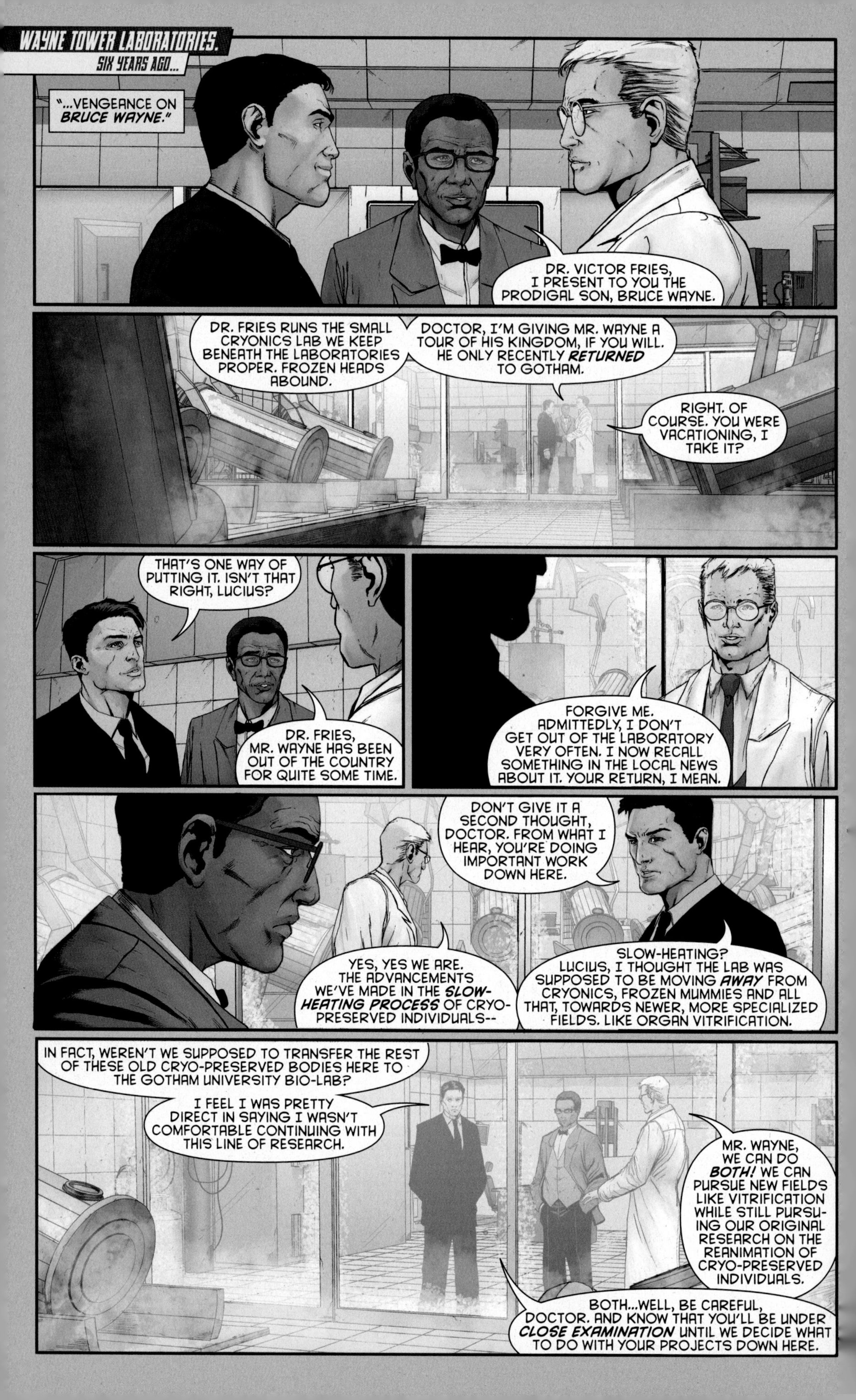
WAYNE TOWER LABORATORIES.
SIX YEARS AGO...
"...VENGEANCE ON BRUCE WAYNE."
DR. VICTOR FRIES, I PRESENT TO YOU THE PRODIGAL SON, BRUCE WAYNE.
DR. FRIES RUNS THE SMALL CRYONICS LAB WE KEEP BENEATH THE LABORATORIES PROPER. FROZEN HEADS ABOUND.
DOCTOR, I'M GIVING MR. WAYNE A TOUR OF HIS KINGDOM, IF YOU WILL. HE ONLY RECENTLY RETURNED TO GOTHAM.
RIGHT. OF COURSE. YOU WERE VACATIONING, I TAKE IT?
THAT'S ONE WAY OF PUTTING IT. ISN'T THAT RIGHT, LUCIUS?
DR. FRIES, MR. WAYNE HAS BEEN OUT OF THE COUNTRY FOR QUITE SOME TIME.
FORGIVE ME. ADMITTEDLY, I DON'T GET OUT OF THE LABORATORY VERY OFTEN. I NOW RECALL SOMETHING IN THE LOCAL NEWS ABOUT IT. YOUR RETURN, I MEAN.
DON'T GIVE IT A SECOND THOUGHT, DOCTOR. FROM WHAT I HEAR, YOU'RE DOING IMPORTANT WORK DOWN HERE.
YES, YES WE ARE. THE ADVANCEMENTS WE'VE MADE IN THE SLOW-HEATING PROCESS OF CRYO-PRESERVED INDIVIDUALS--
SLOW-HEATING? LUCIUS, I THOUGHT THE LAB WAS SUPPOSED TO BE MOVING AWAY FROM CRYONICS, FROZEN MUMMIES AND ALL THAT, TOWARDS NEWER, MORE SPECIALIZED FIELDS. LIKE ORGAN VITRIFICATION.
IN FACT, WEREN'T WE SUPPOSED TO TRANSFER THE REST OF THESE OLD CRYO-PRESERVED BODIES HERE TO THE GOTHAM UNIVERSITY BIO-LAB?
I FEEL I WAS PRETTY DIRECT IN SAYING I WASN'T COMFORTABLE CONTINUING WITH THIS LINE OF RESEARCH.
MR. WAYNE, WE CAN DO BOTH! WE CAN PURSUE NEW FIELDS LIKE VITRIFICATION WHILE STILL PURSUING OUR ORIGINAL RESEARCH ON THE REANIMATION OF CRYO-PRESERVED INDIVIDUALS.
BOTH...WELL, BE CAREFUL, DOCTOR. AND KNOW THAT YOU'LL BE UNDER CLOSE EXAMINATION UNTIL WE DECIDE WHAT TO DO WITH YOUR PROJECTS DOWN HERE.

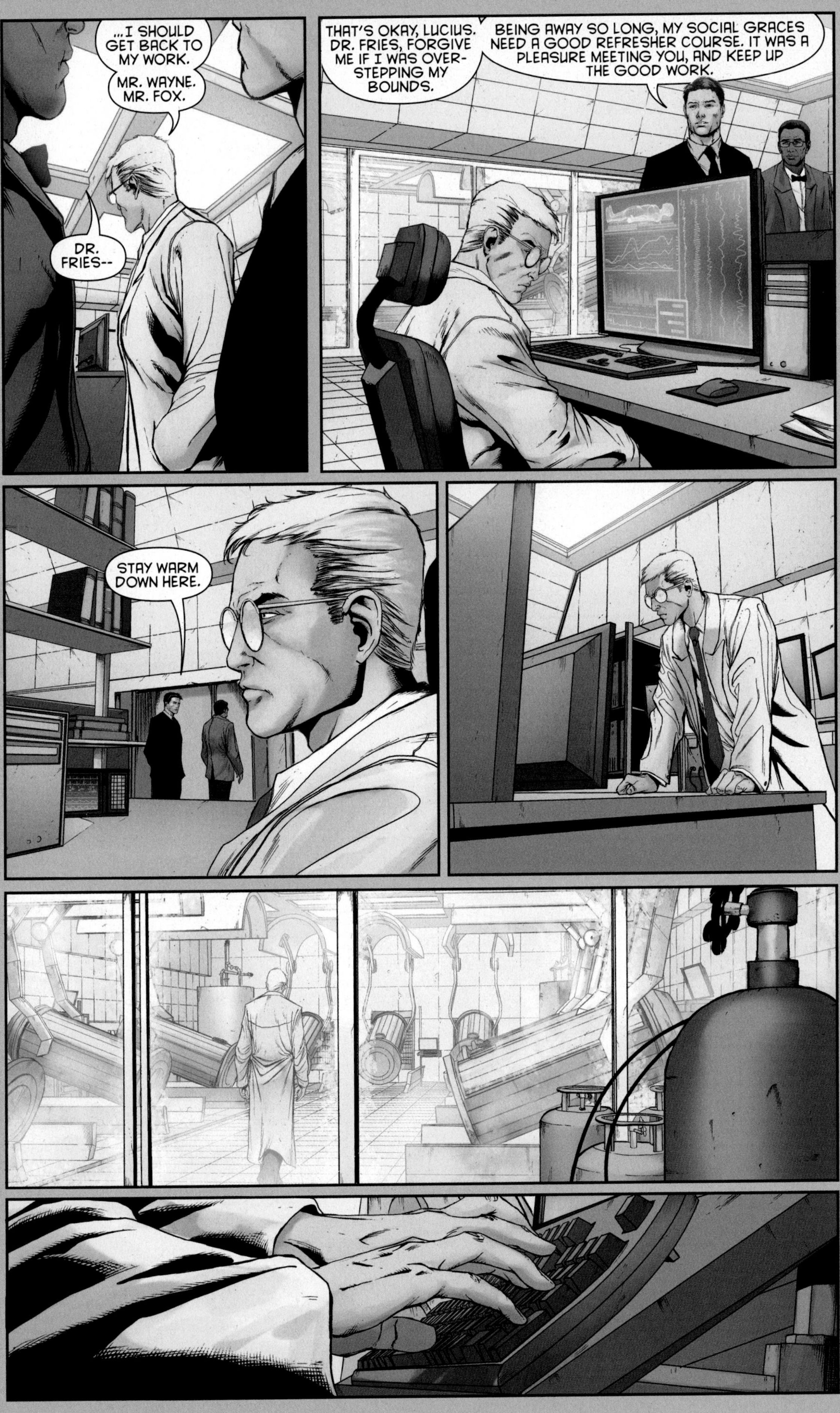
...I SHOULD GET BACK TO MY WORK.
MR. WAYNE. MR. FOX.
DR. FRIES--
THAT'S OKAY, LUCIUS. DR. FRIES, FORGIVE ME IF I WAS OVER-STEPPING MY BOUNDS.
BEING AWAY SO LONG, MY SOCIAL GRACES NEED A GOOD REFRESHER COURSE. IT WAS A PLEASURE MEETING YOU, AND KEEP UP THE GOOD WORK.
STAY WARM DOWN HERE.

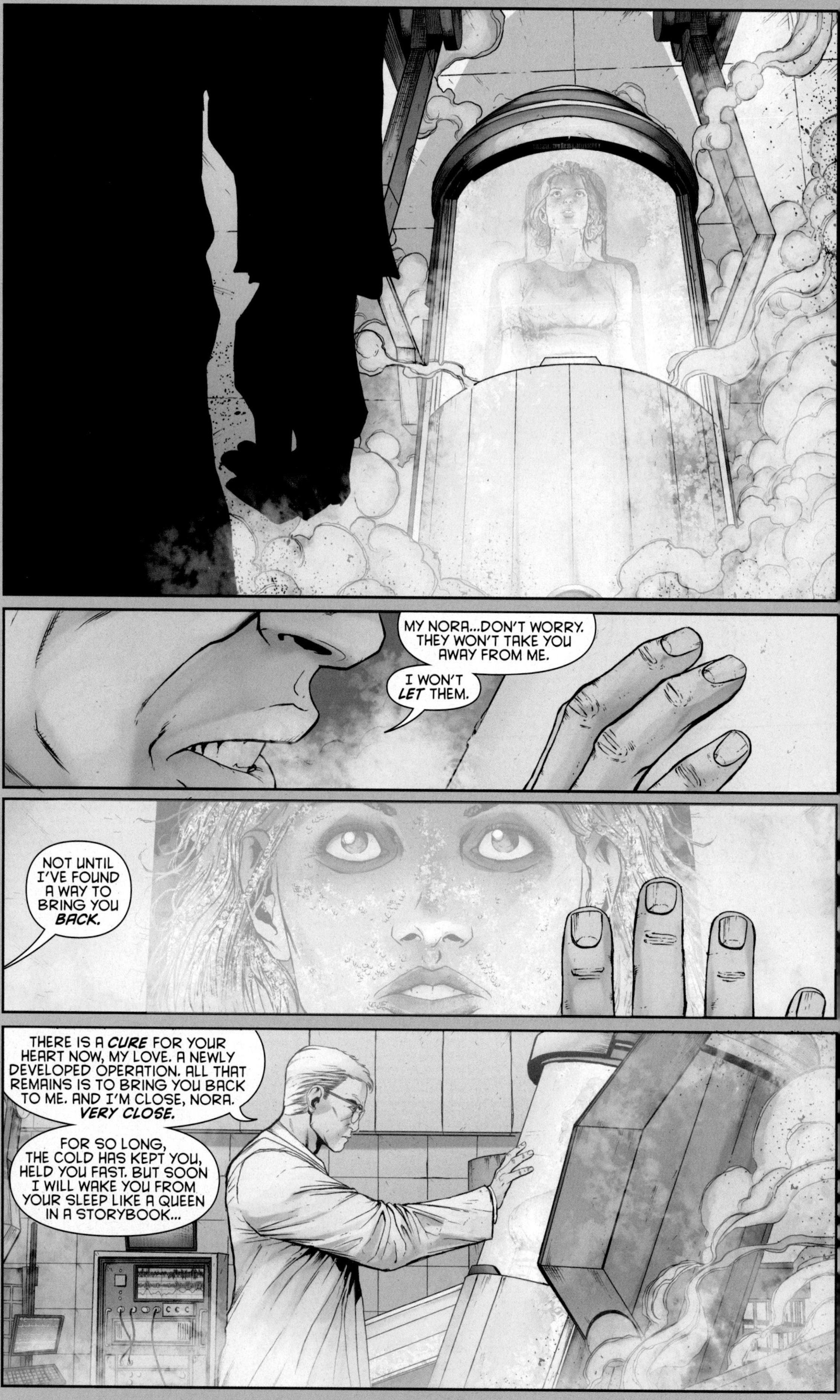
MY NORA...DON'T WORRY. THEY WON'T TAKE YOU AWAY FROM ME.
I WON'T *LET* THEM.
NOT UNTIL I'VE FOUND A WAY TO BRING YOU *BACK.*
THERE IS A *CURE* FOR YOUR HEART NOW, MY LOVE. A NEWLY DEVELOPED OPERATION. ALL THAT REMAINS IS TO BRING YOU BACK TO ME. AND I'M CLOSE, NORA. *VERY CLOSE.*
FOR SO LONG, THE COLD HAS KEPT YOU, HELD YOU FAST. BUT SOON I WILL WAKE YOU FROM YOUR SLEEP LIKE A QUEEN IN A STORYBOOK...

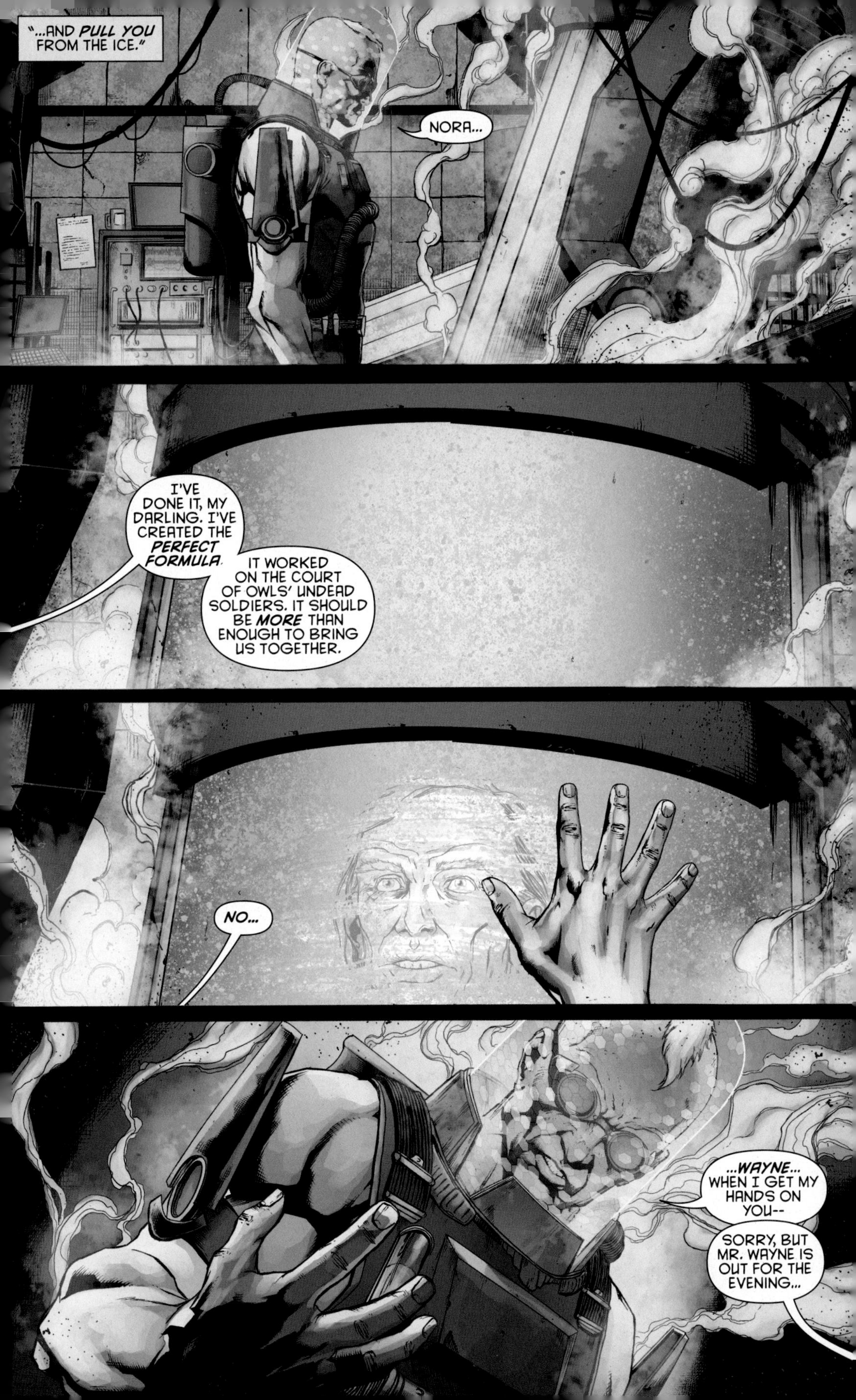
"...AND PULL YOU FROM THE ICE."
NORA...
I'VE DONE IT, MY DARLING. I'VE CREATED THE PERFECT FORMULA.
IT WORKED ON THE COURT OF OWLS' UNDEAD SOLDIERS. IT SHOULD BE MORE THAN ENOUGH TO BRING US TOGETHER.
NO...
...WAYNE... WHEN I GET MY HANDS ON YOU--
SORRY, BUT MR. WAYNE IS OUT FOR THE EVENING...

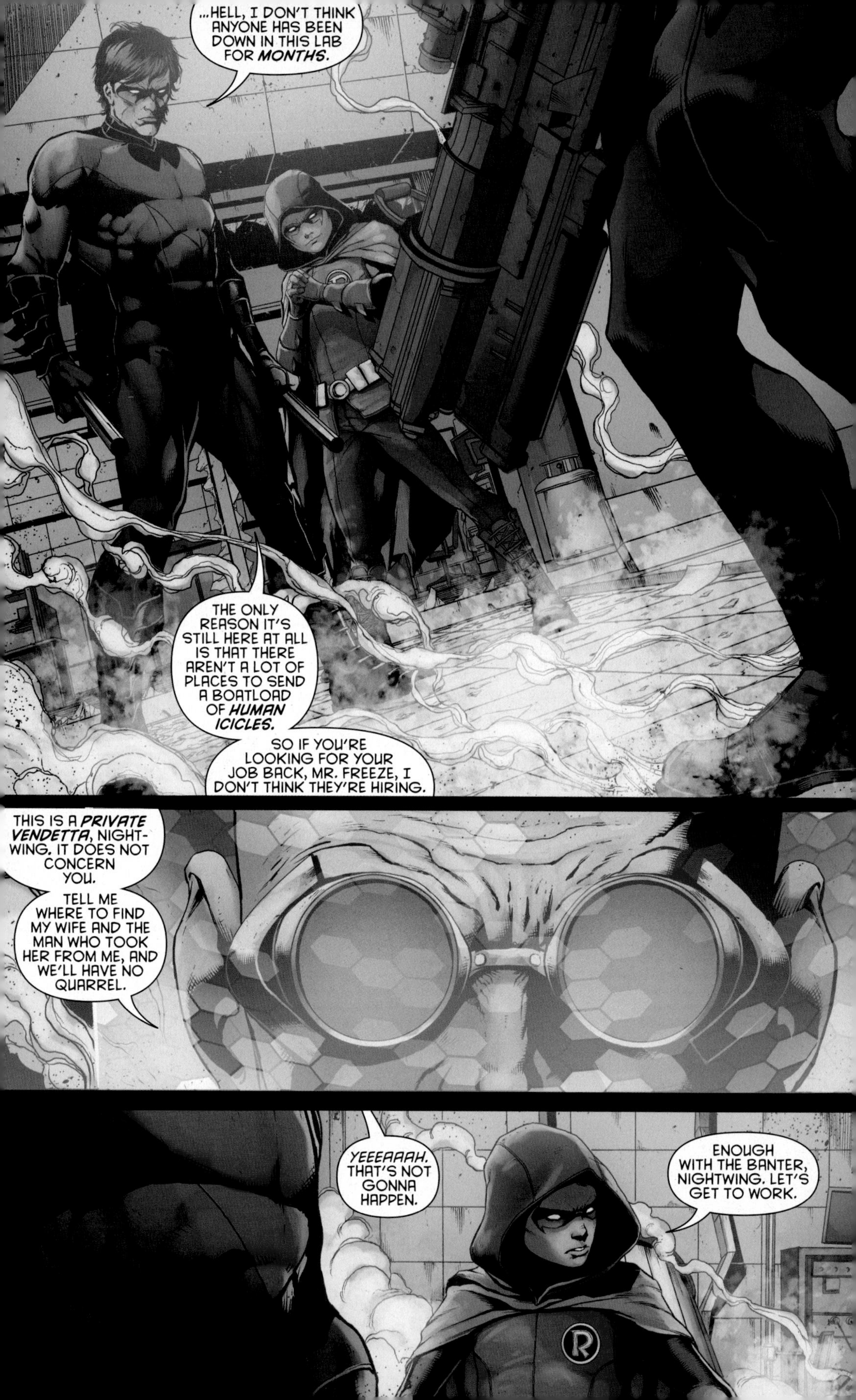
...HELL, I DON'T THINK ANYONE HAS BEEN DOWN IN THIS LAB FOR *MONTHS*.
THE ONLY REASON IT'S STILL HERE AT ALL IS THAT THERE AREN'T A LOT OF PLACES TO SEND A BOATLOAD OF *HUMAN ICICLES*.
SO IF YOU'RE LOOKING FOR YOUR JOB BACK, MR. FREEZE, I DON'T THINK THEY'RE HIRING.
THIS IS A *PRIVATE VENDETTA*, NIGHT-WING. IT DOES NOT CONCERN YOU.
TELL ME WHERE TO FIND MY WIFE AND THE MAN WHO TOOK HER FROM ME, AND WE'LL HAVE NO QUARREL.
YEEEAAAH. THAT'S NOT GONNA HAPPEN.
ENOUGH WITH THE BANTER, NIGHTWING. LET'S GET TO WORK.

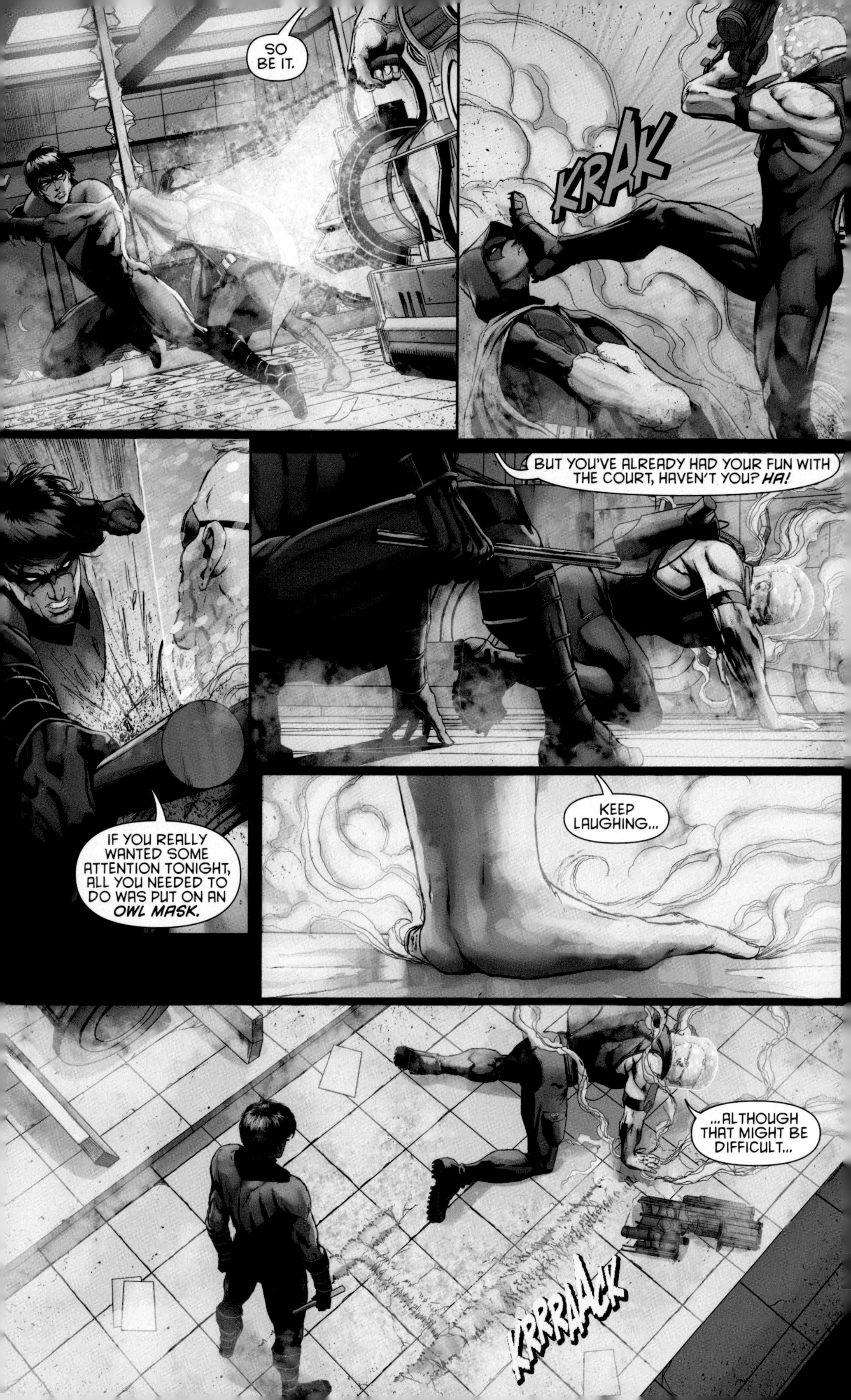
SO BE IT.
KRAK
BUT YOU'VE ALREADY HAD YOUR FUN WITH THE COURT, HAVEN'T YOU? HA!
IF YOU REALLY WANTED SOME ATTENTION TONIGHT, ALL YOU NEEDED TO DO WAS PUT ON AN OWL MASK.
KEEP LAUGHING...
...ALTHOUGH THAT MIGHT BE DIFFICULT...
KRRRAACK

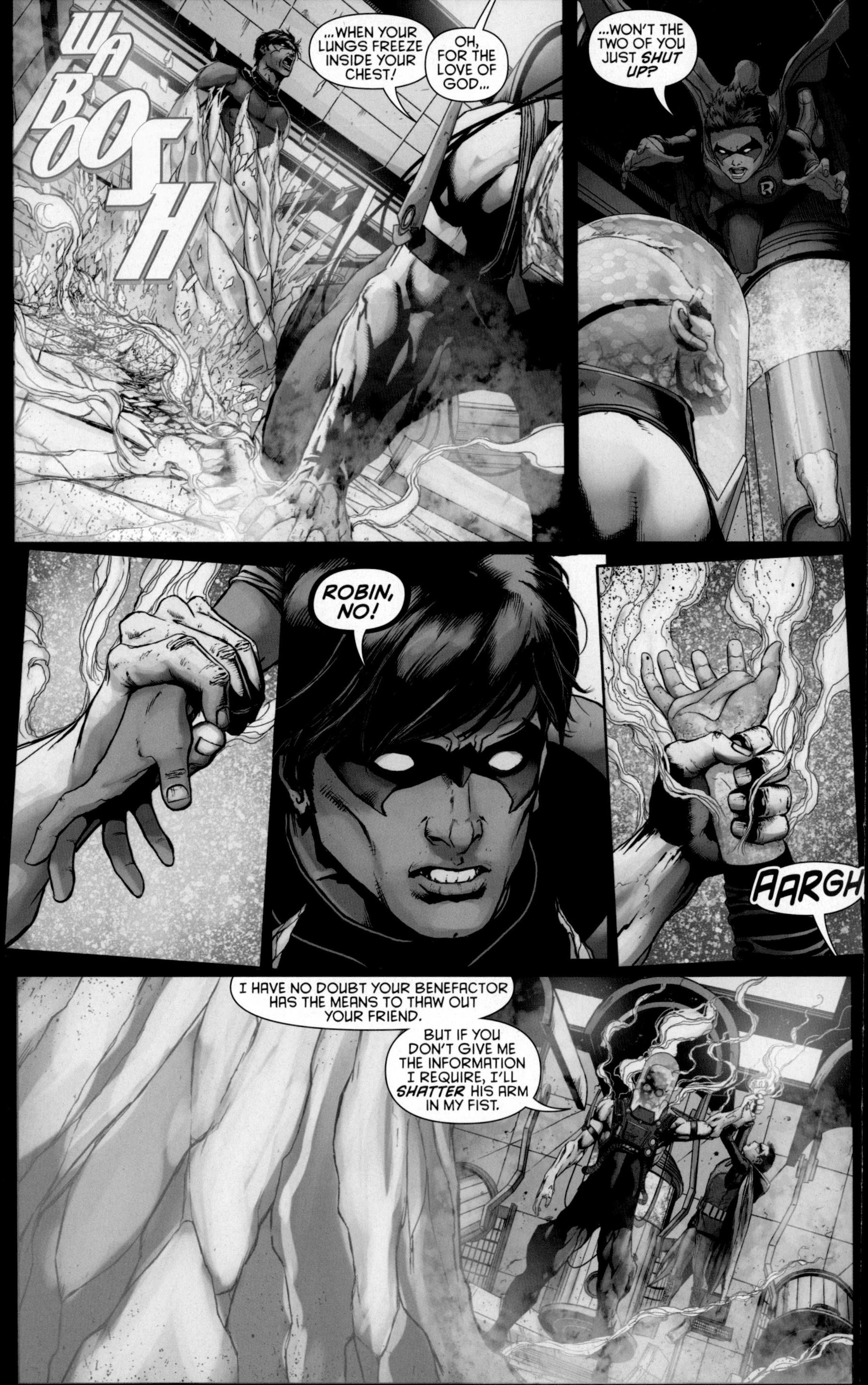
WA BOOSH
...WHEN YOUR LUNGS FREEZE INSIDE YOUR CHEST!
OH, FOR THE LOVE OF GOD...
...WON'T THE TWO OF YOU JUST SHUT UP?
ROBIN, NO!
AARGH
I HAVE NO DOUBT YOUR BENEFACTOR HAS THE MEANS TO THAW OUT YOUR FRIEND.
BUT IF YOU DON'T GIVE ME THE INFORMATION I REQUIRE, I'LL SHATTER HIS ARM IN MY FIST.

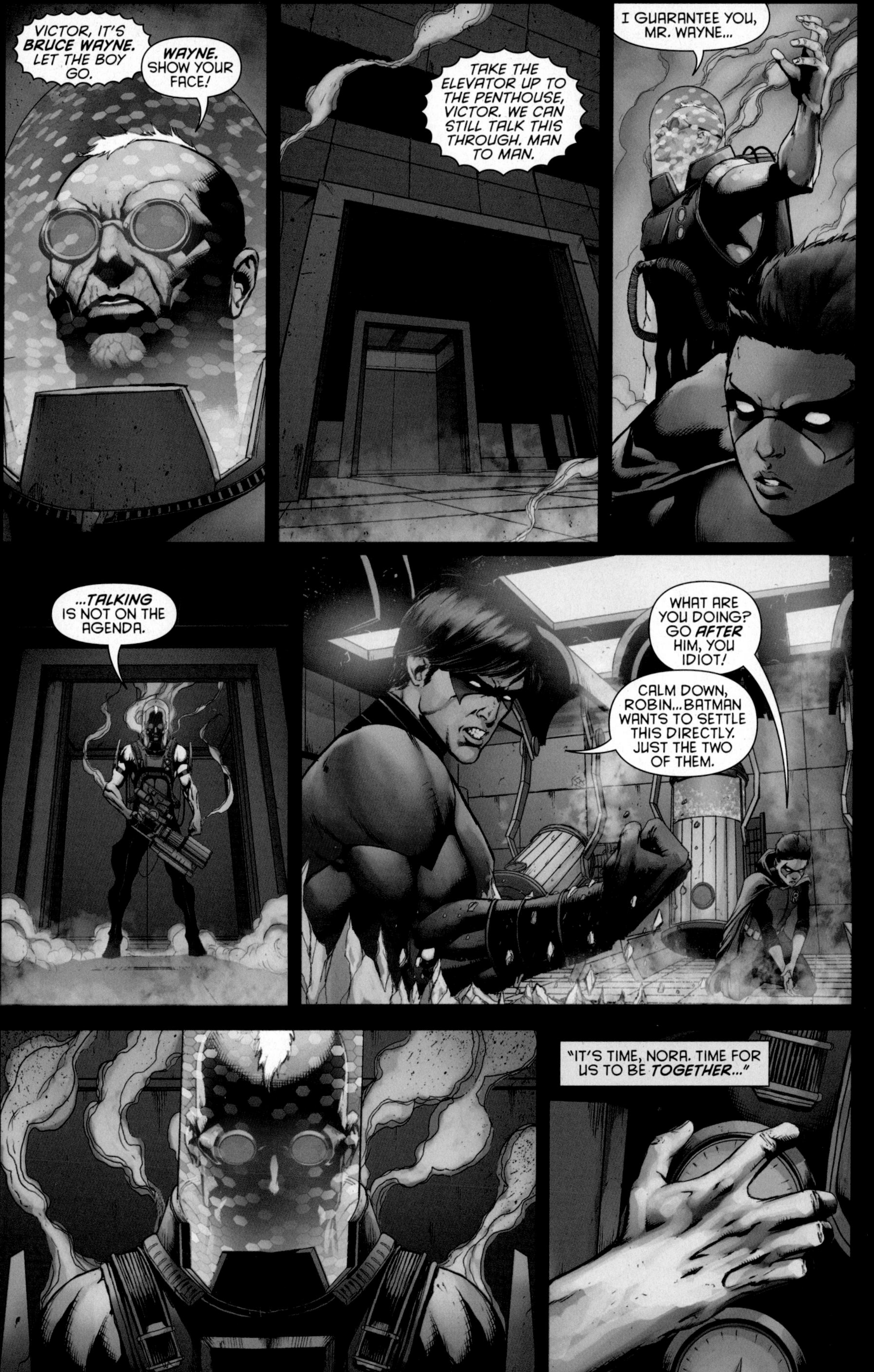
VICTOR, IT'S **BRUCE WAYNE.** LET THE BOY GO.
WAYNE. SHOW YOUR FACE!
TAKE THE ELEVATOR UP TO THE PENTHOUSE, VICTOR. WE CAN STILL TALK THIS THROUGH. MAN TO MAN.
I GUARANTEE YOU, MR. WAYNE...
...**TALKING** IS NOT ON THE AGENDA.
WHAT ARE YOU DOING? GO **AFTER** HIM, YOU IDIOT!
CALM DOWN, ROBIN...BATMAN WANTS TO SETTLE THIS DIRECTLY. JUST THE TWO OF THEM.
"IT'S TIME, NORA. TIME FOR US TO BE **TOGETHER**..."

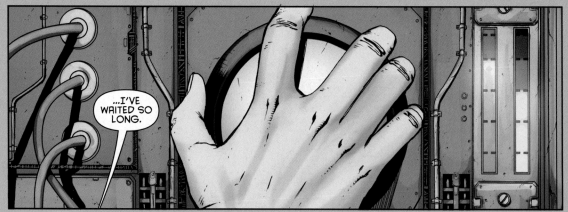

...I'VE WAITED SO LONG.

BUT THIS--THIS *NEW COMPOUND* IS EVERYTHING WE'VE BEEN WAITING FOR, MY LOVE.

AND IT WILL WORK. I *WILL* BRING YOU BACK.

NO, VICTOR...

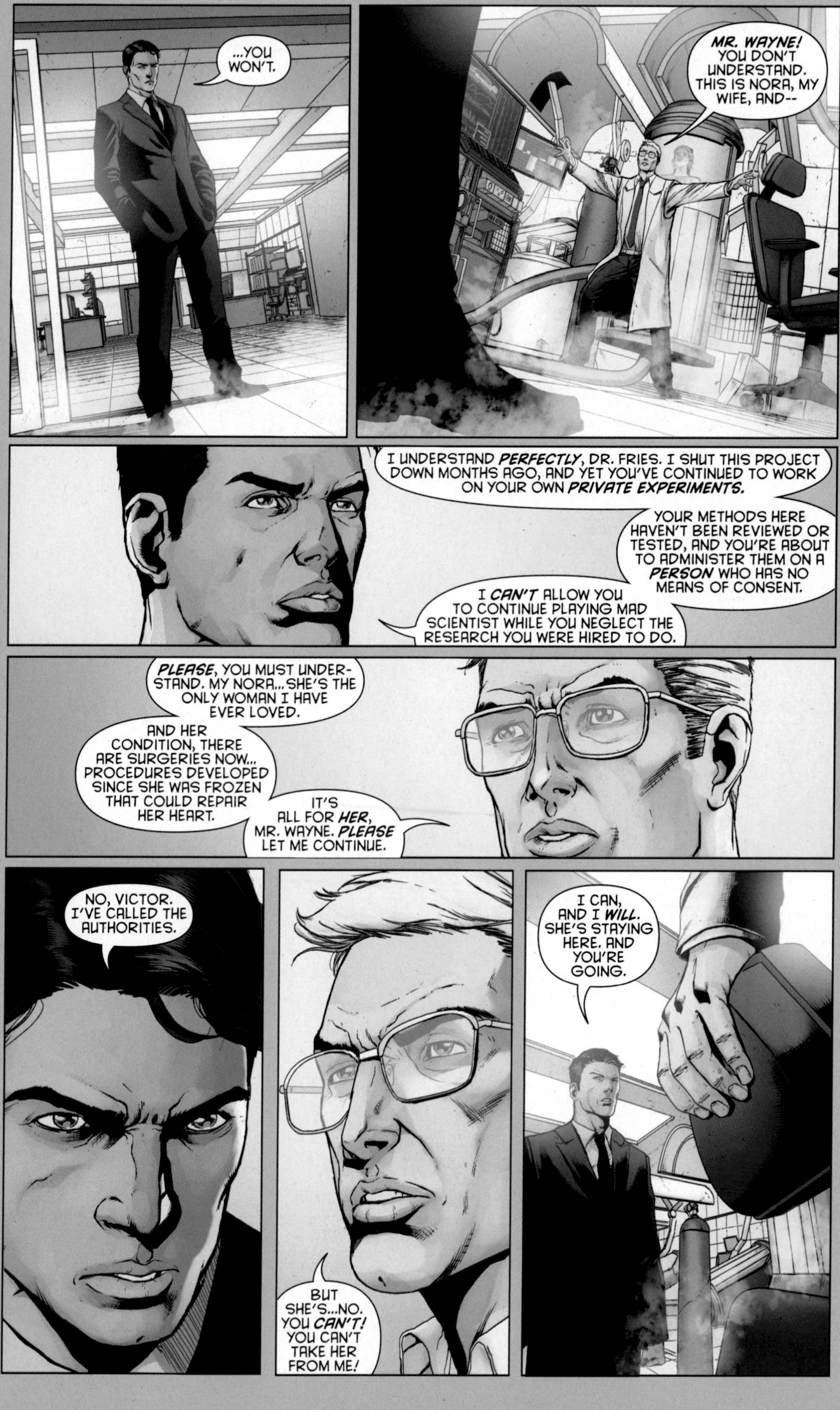
...YOU WON'T.
MR. WAYNE! YOU DON'T UNDERSTAND. THIS IS NORA, MY WIFE, AND--
I UNDERSTAND PERFECTLY, DR. FRIES. I SHUT THIS PROJECT DOWN MONTHS AGO, AND YET YOU'VE CONTINUED TO WORK ON YOUR OWN PRIVATE EXPERIMENTS.
YOUR METHODS HERE HAVEN'T BEEN REVIEWED OR TESTED, AND YOU'RE ABOUT TO ADMINISTER THEM ON A PERSON WHO HAS NO MEANS OF CONSENT.
I CAN'T ALLOW YOU TO CONTINUE PLAYING MAD SCIENTIST WHILE YOU NEGLECT THE RESEARCH YOU WERE HIRED TO DO.
PLEASE, YOU MUST UNDERSTAND. MY NORA... SHE'S THE ONLY WOMAN I HAVE EVER LOVED.
AND HER CONDITION, THERE ARE SURGERIES NOW... PROCEDURES DEVELOPED SINCE SHE WAS FROZEN THAT COULD REPAIR HER HEART.
IT'S ALL FOR HER, MR. WAYNE. PLEASE LET ME CONTINUE.
NO, VICTOR. I'VE CALLED THE AUTHORITIES.
BUT SHE'S...NO. YOU CAN'T! YOU CAN'T TAKE HER FROM ME!
I CAN, AND I WILL. SHE'S STAYING HERE. AND YOU'RE GOING.

NO!

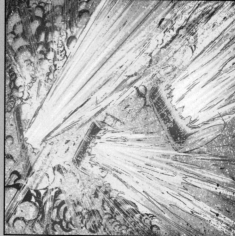

VICTOR, GET OUT OF THE WAY!

AAAHHH!

NOOO.... RRRAA. NORA...

"THIS IS *INCREDIBLE*, I'VE NEVER SEEN ANYTHING LIKE IT."

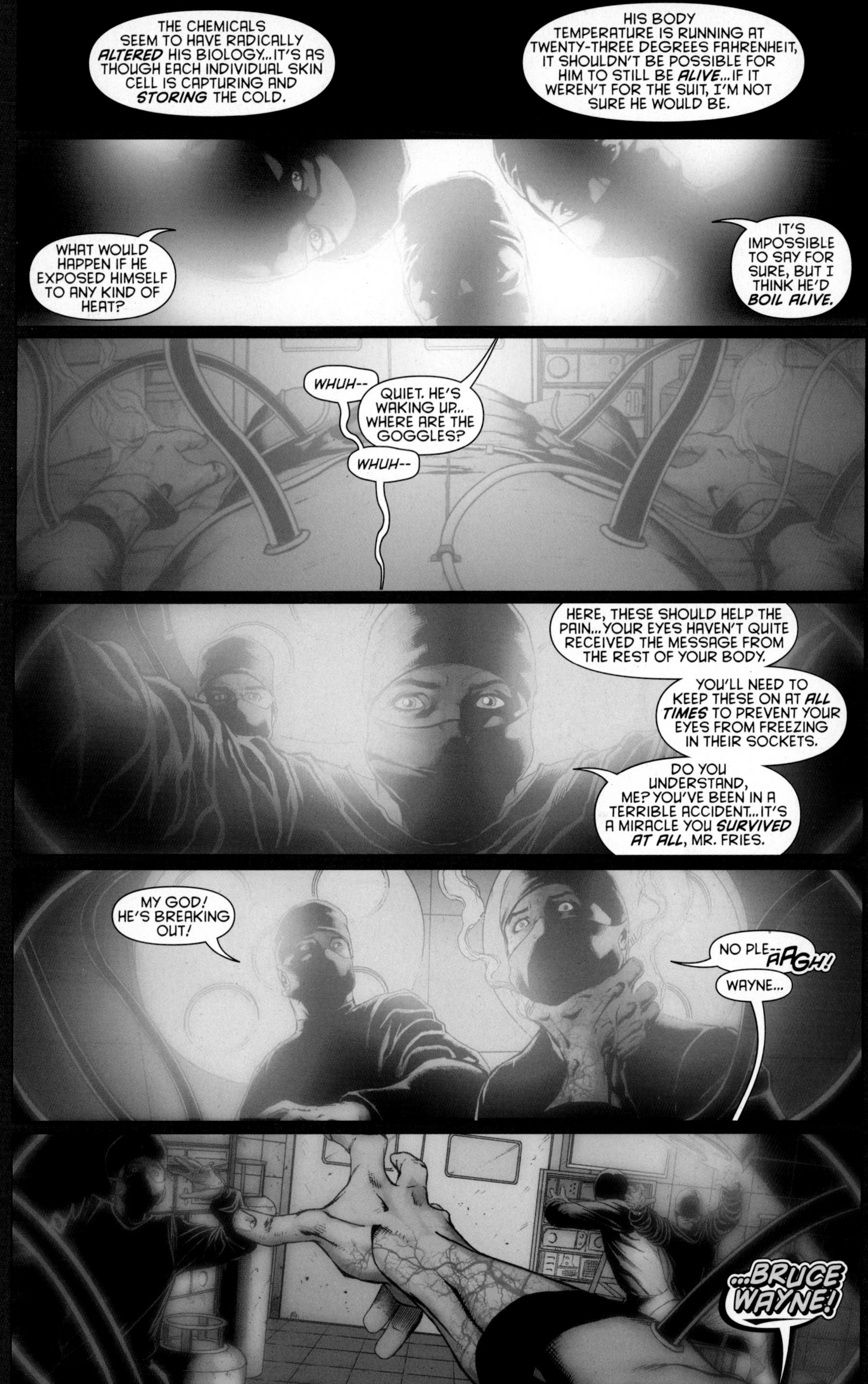
THE CHEMICALS SEEM TO HAVE RADICALLY ALTERED HIS BIOLOGY... IT'S AS THOUGH EACH INDIVIDUAL SKIN CELL IS CAPTURING AND STORING THE COLD.
HIS BODY TEMPERATURE IS RUNNING AT TWENTY-THREE DEGREES FAHRENHEIT, IT SHOULDN'T BE POSSIBLE FOR HIM TO STILL BE ALIVE... IF IT WEREN'T FOR THE SUIT, I'M NOT SURE HE WOULD BE.
WHAT WOULD HAPPEN IF HE EXPOSED HIMSELF TO ANY KIND OF HEAT?
IT'S IMPOSSIBLE TO SAY FOR SURE, BUT I THINK HE'D BOIL ALIVE.
WHUH--
QUIET. HE'S WAKING UP... WHERE ARE THE GOGGLES?
WHUH--
HERE, THESE SHOULD HELP THE PAIN... YOUR EYES HAVEN'T QUITE RECEIVED THE MESSAGE FROM THE REST OF YOUR BODY.
YOU'LL NEED TO KEEP THESE ON AT ALL TIMES TO PREVENT YOUR EYES FROM FREEZING IN THEIR SOCKETS.
DO YOU UNDERSTAND, ME? YOU'VE BEEN IN A TERRIBLE ACCIDENT... IT'S A MIRACLE YOU SURVIVED AT ALL, MR. FRIES.
MY GOD! HE'S BREAKING OUT!
NO PLE--AAGH!
WAYNE...
...BRUCE WAYNE!

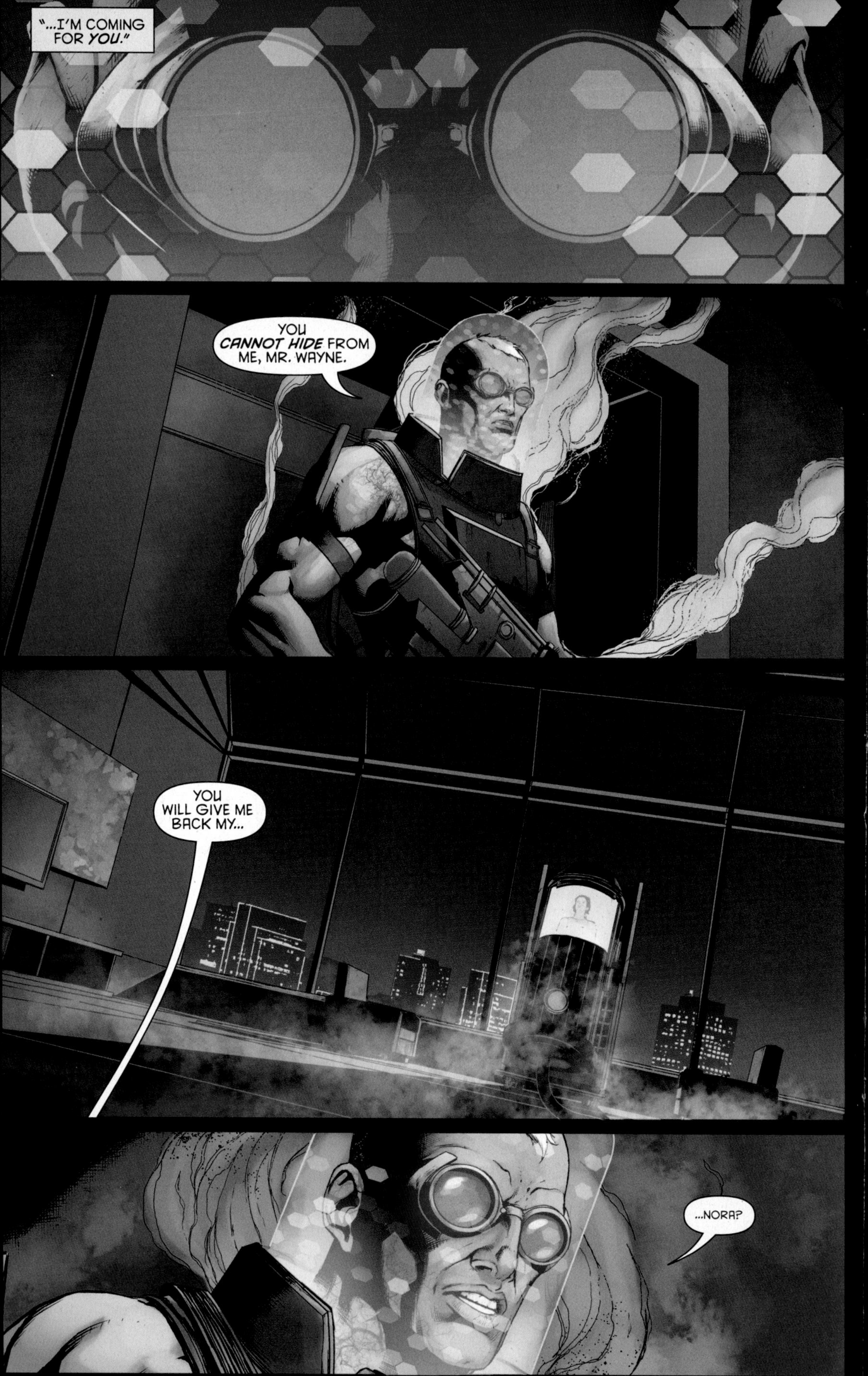
"...I'M COMING FOR *YOU*."
YOU *CANNOT HIDE* FROM ME, MR. WAYNE.
YOU WILL GIVE ME BACK MY...
...NORA?

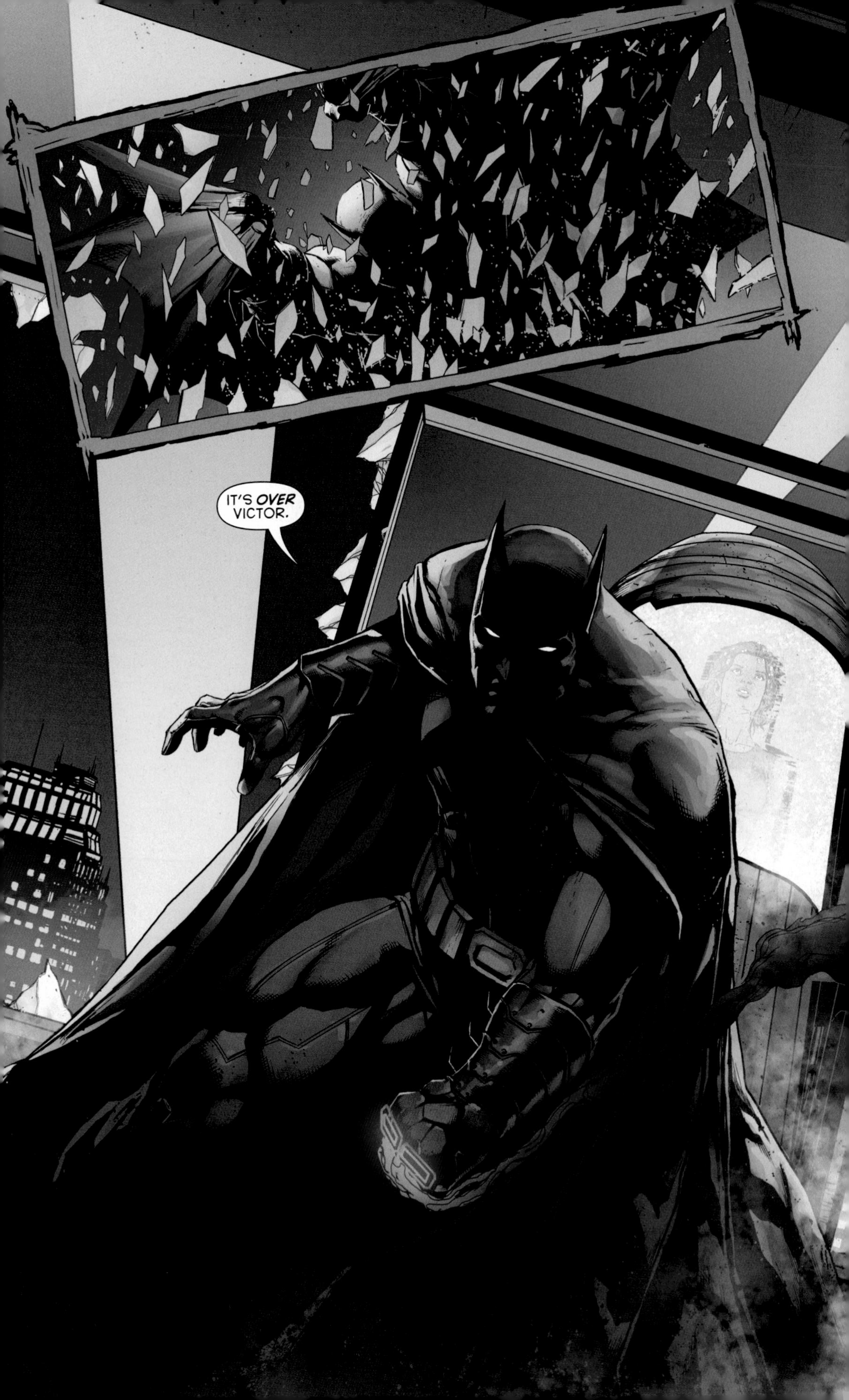
IT'S OVER VICTOR.

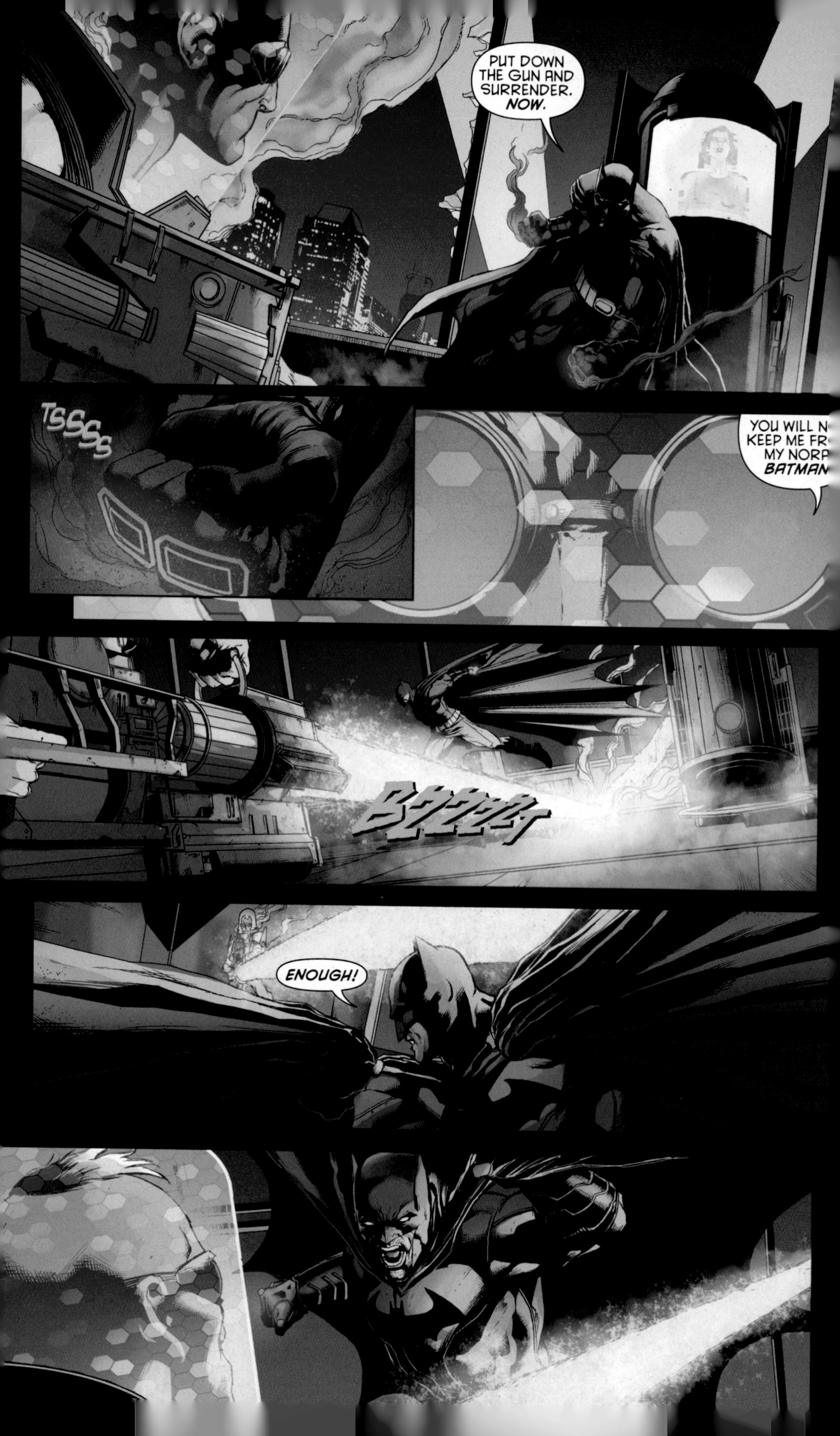
PUT DOWN THE GUN AND SURRENDER. NOW.
TSSSS
YOU WILL N
KEEP ME FR
MY NORA
BATMAN
ENOUGH!

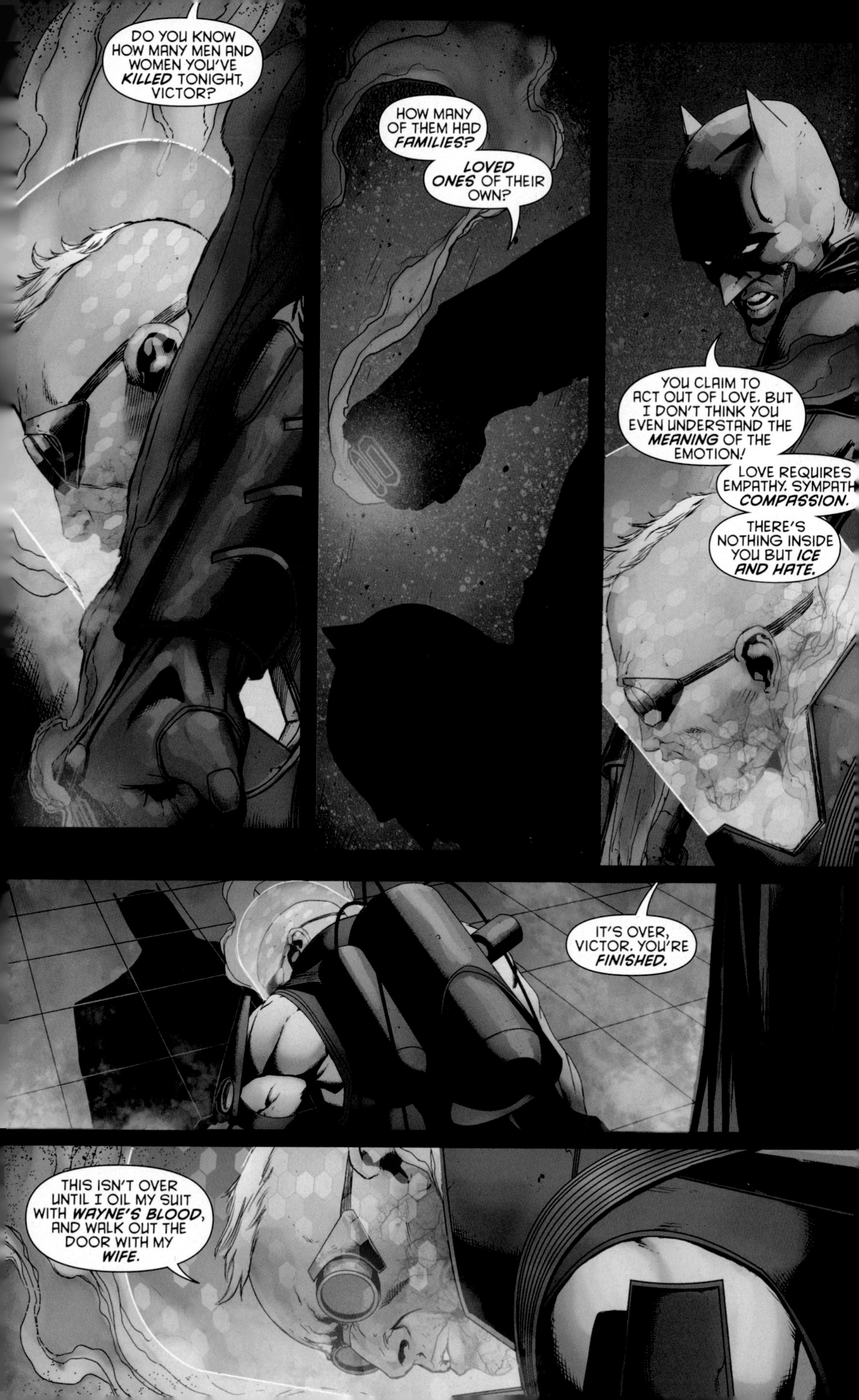
DO YOU KNOW HOW MANY MEN AND WOMEN YOU'VE *KILLED* TONIGHT, VICTOR?
HOW MANY OF THEM HAD *FAMILIES?*
LOVED ONES OF THEIR OWN?
YOU CLAIM TO ACT OUT OF LOVE. BUT I DON'T THINK YOU EVEN UNDERSTAND THE *MEANING* OF THE EMOTION!
LOVE REQUIRES EMPATHY. SYMPATH *COMPASSION.*
THERE'S NOTHING INSIDE YOU BUT *ICE AND HATE.*
IT'S OVER, VICTOR. YOU'RE *FINISHED.*
THIS ISN'T OVER UNTIL I OIL MY SUIT WITH *WAYNE'S BLOOD*, AND WALK OUT THE DOOR WITH MY *WIFE.*

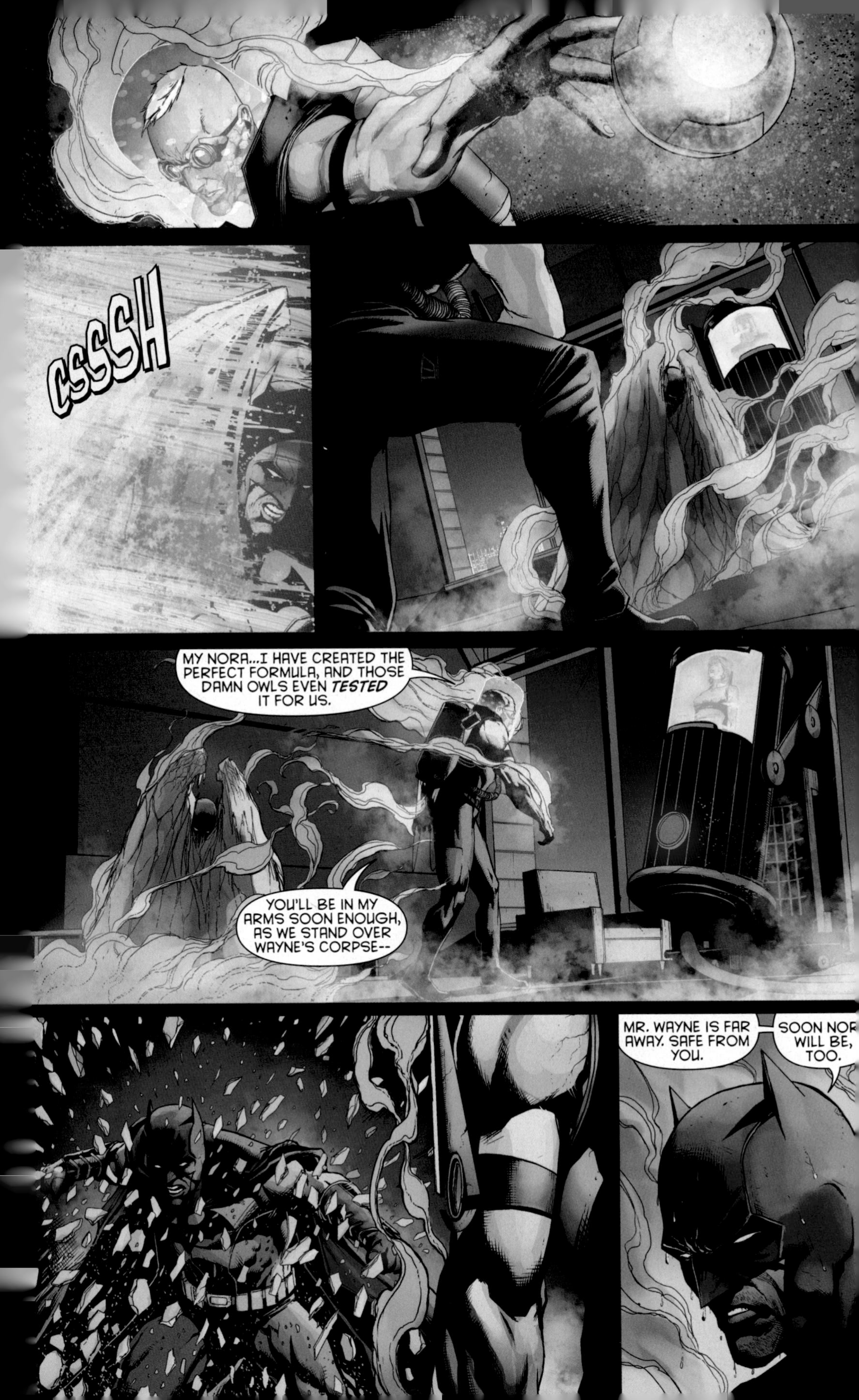
CSSSH
MY NORA...I HAVE CREATED THE PERFECT FORMULA, AND THOSE DAMN OWLS EVEN TESTED IT FOR US.
YOU'LL BE IN MY ARMS SOON ENOUGH, AS WE STAND OVER WAYNE'S CORPSE--
MR. WAYNE IS FAR AWAY. SAFE FROM YOU.
WILL BE, TOO.

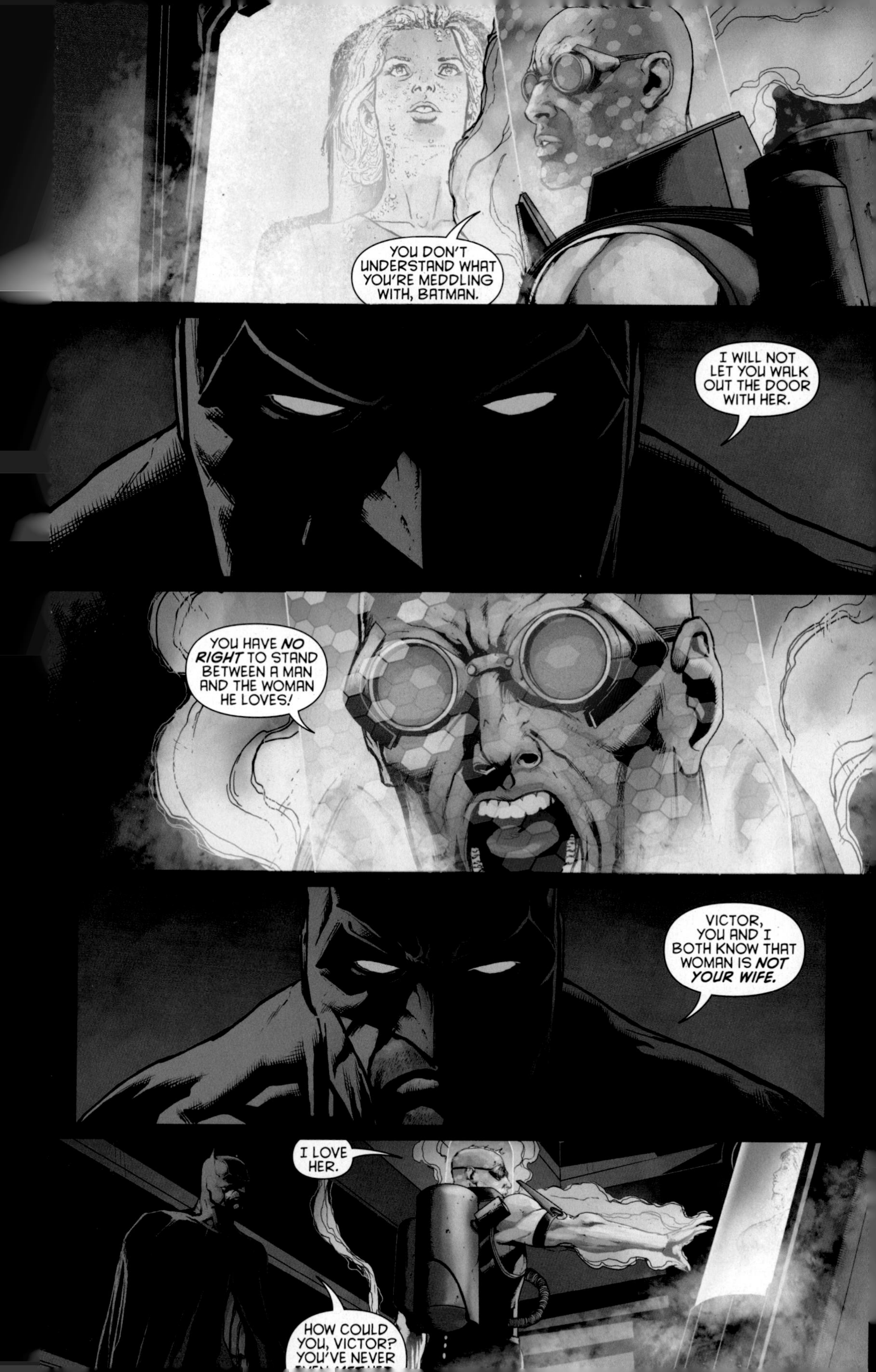
YOU DON'T UNDERSTAND WHAT YOU'RE MEDDLING WITH, BATMAN.
I WILL NOT LET YOU WALK OUT THE DOOR WITH HER.
YOU HAVE **NO RIGHT** TO STAND BETWEEN A MAN AND THE WOMAN HE LOVES!
VICTOR, YOU AND I BOTH KNOW THAT WOMAN IS **NOT YOUR WIFE.**
I LOVE HER.
HOW COULD YOU, VICTOR? YOU'VE NEVER

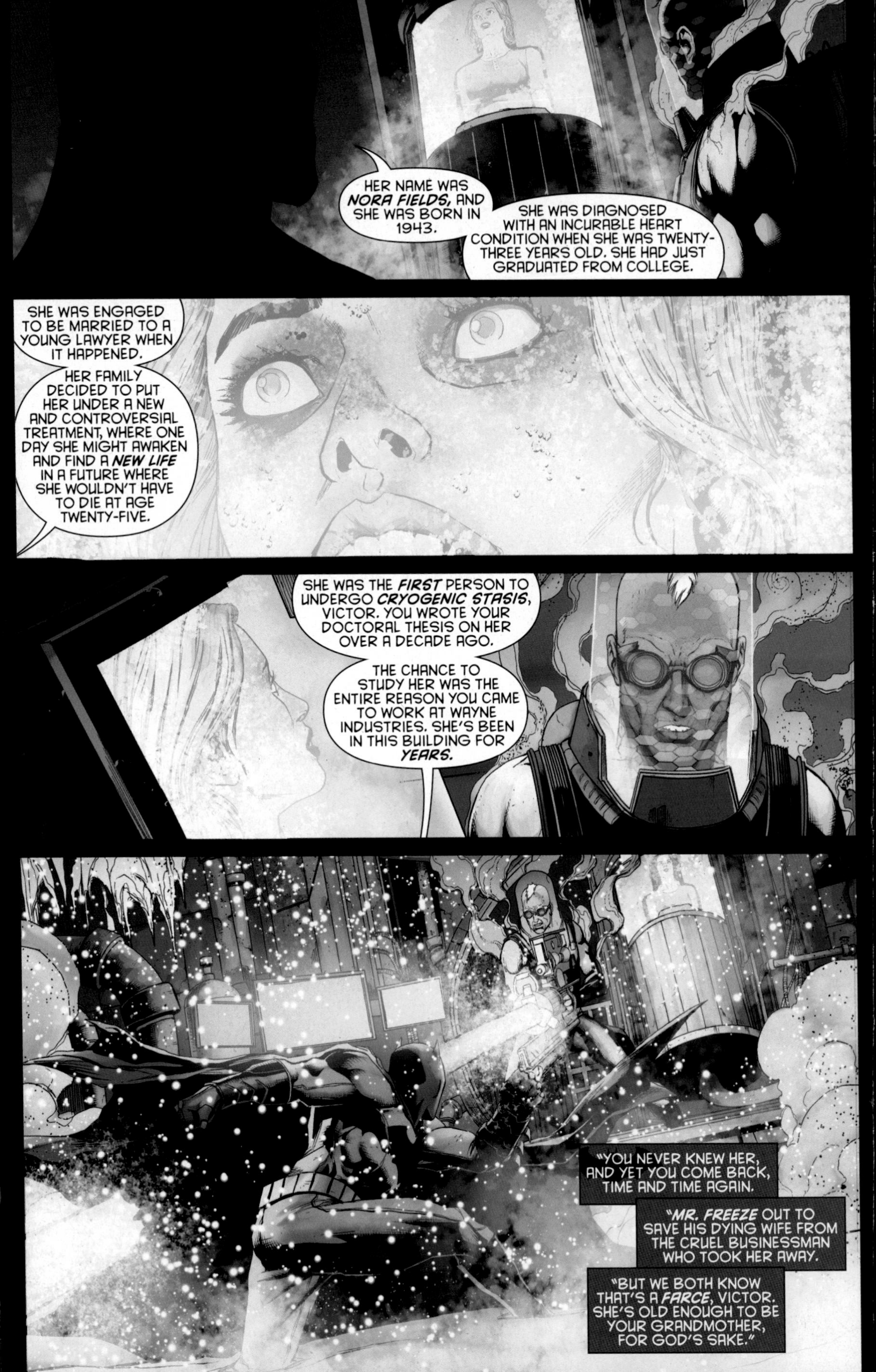
HER NAME WAS NORA FIELDS, AND SHE WAS BORN IN 1943.
SHE WAS DIAGNOSED WITH AN INCURABLE HEART CONDITION WHEN SHE WAS TWENTY-THREE YEARS OLD. SHE HAD JUST GRADUATED FROM COLLEGE.
SHE WAS ENGAGED TO BE MARRIED TO A YOUNG LAWYER WHEN IT HAPPENED.
HER FAMILY DECIDED TO PUT HER UNDER A NEW AND CONTROVERSIAL TREATMENT, WHERE ONE DAY SHE MIGHT AWAKEN AND FIND A NEW LIFE IN A FUTURE WHERE SHE WOULDN'T HAVE TO DIE AT AGE TWENTY-FIVE.
SHE WAS THE FIRST PERSON TO UNDERGO CRYOGENIC STASIS, VICTOR. YOU WROTE YOUR DOCTORAL THESIS ON HER OVER A DECADE AGO.
THE CHANCE TO STUDY HER WAS THE ENTIRE REASON YOU CAME TO WORK AT WAYNE INDUSTRIES. SHE'S BEEN IN THIS BUILDING FOR YEARS.
"YOU NEVER KNEW HER, AND YET YOU COME BACK, TIME AND TIME AGAIN.
"MR. FREEZE OUT TO SAVE HIS DYING WIFE FROM THE CRUEL BUSINESSMAN WHO TOOK HER AWAY.
"BUT WE BOTH KNOW THAT'S A FARCE, VICTOR. SHE'S OLD ENOUGH TO BE YOUR GRANDMOTHER, FOR GOD'S SAKE."

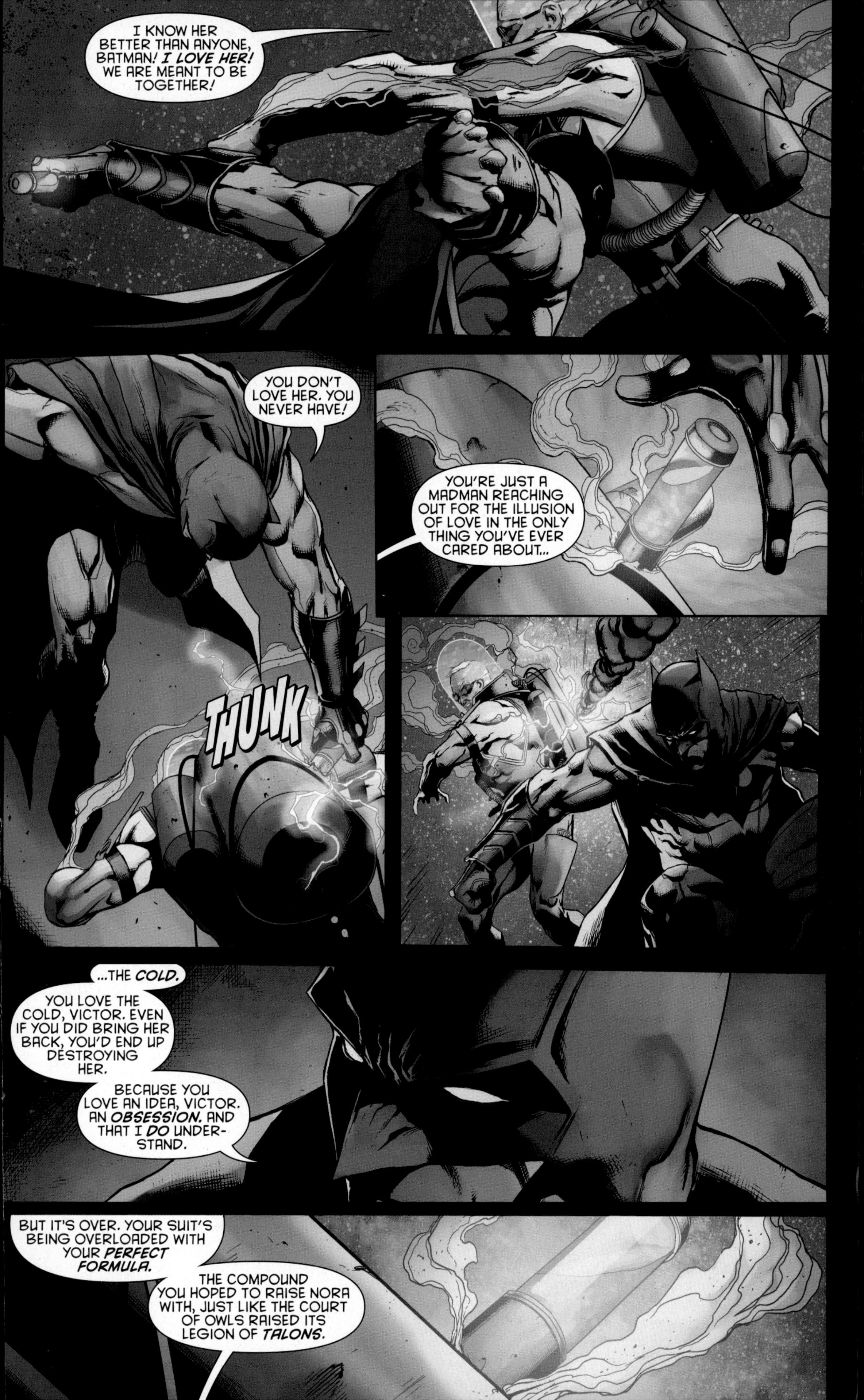
I KNOW HER BETTER THAN ANYONE, BATMAN! *I LOVE HER!* WE ARE MEANT TO BE TOGETHER!
YOU DON'T LOVE HER. YOU NEVER HAVE!
YOU'RE JUST A MADMAN REACHING OUT FOR THE ILLUSION OF LOVE IN THE ONLY THING YOU'VE EVER CARED ABOUT...
THUNK
...THE *COLD.*
YOU LOVE THE COLD, VICTOR. EVEN IF YOU DID BRING HER BACK, YOU'D END UP DESTROYING HER.
BECAUSE YOU LOVE AN IDEA, VICTOR. AN *OBSESSION.* AND THAT I *DO* UNDER-STAND.
BUT IT'S OVER. YOUR SUIT'S BEING OVERLOADED WITH YOUR *PERFECT FORMULA.*
THE COMPOUND YOU HOPED TO RAISE NORA WITH, JUST LIKE THE COURT OF OWLS RAISED ITS LEGION OF *TALONS.*

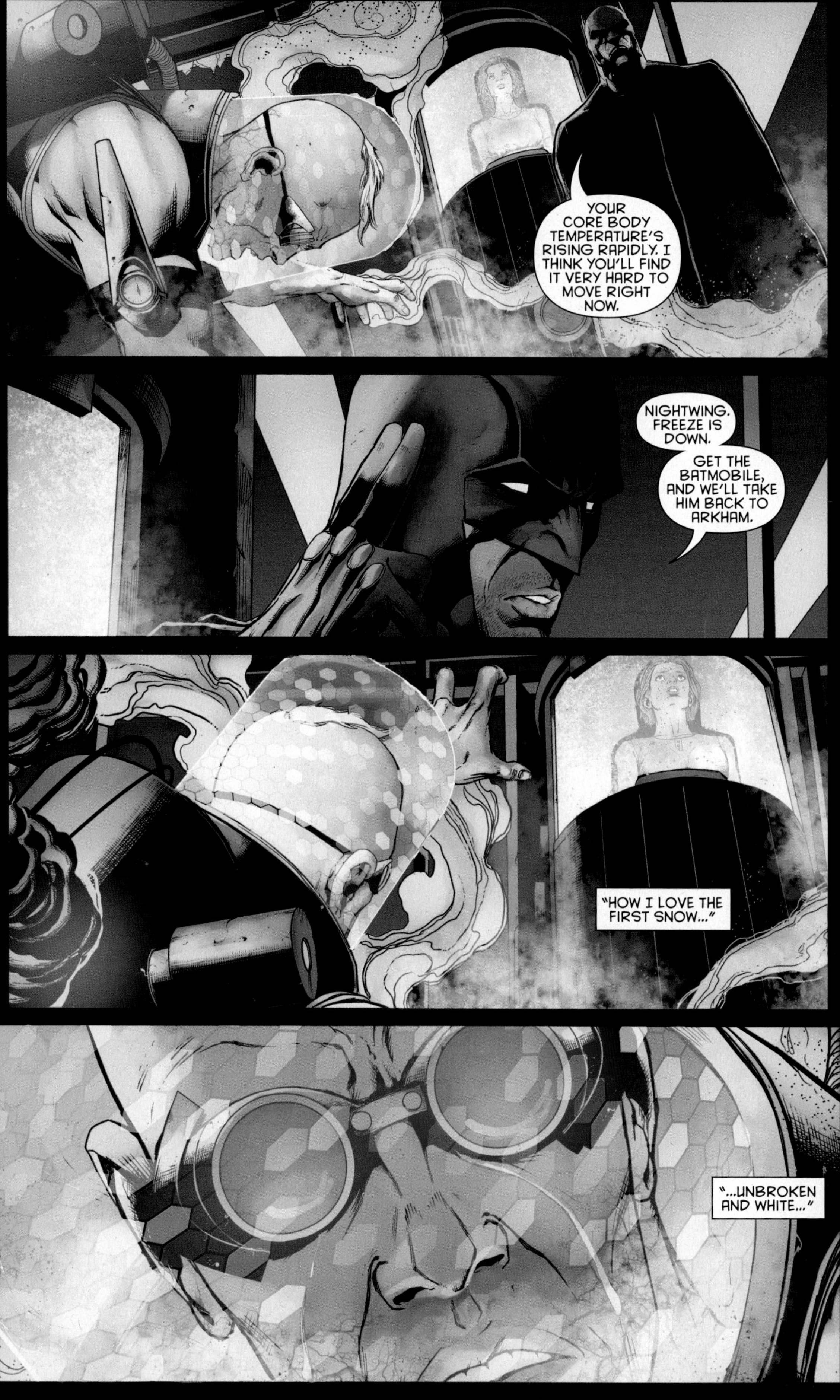
YOUR CORE BODY TEMPERATURE'S RISING RAPIDLY. I THINK YOU'LL FIND IT VERY HARD TO MOVE RIGHT NOW.
NIGHTWING. FREEZE IS DOWN.
GET THE BATMOBILE, AND WE'LL TAKE HIM BACK TO ARKHAM.
"HOW I LOVE THE FIRST SNOW..."
"...UNBROKEN AND WHITE..."

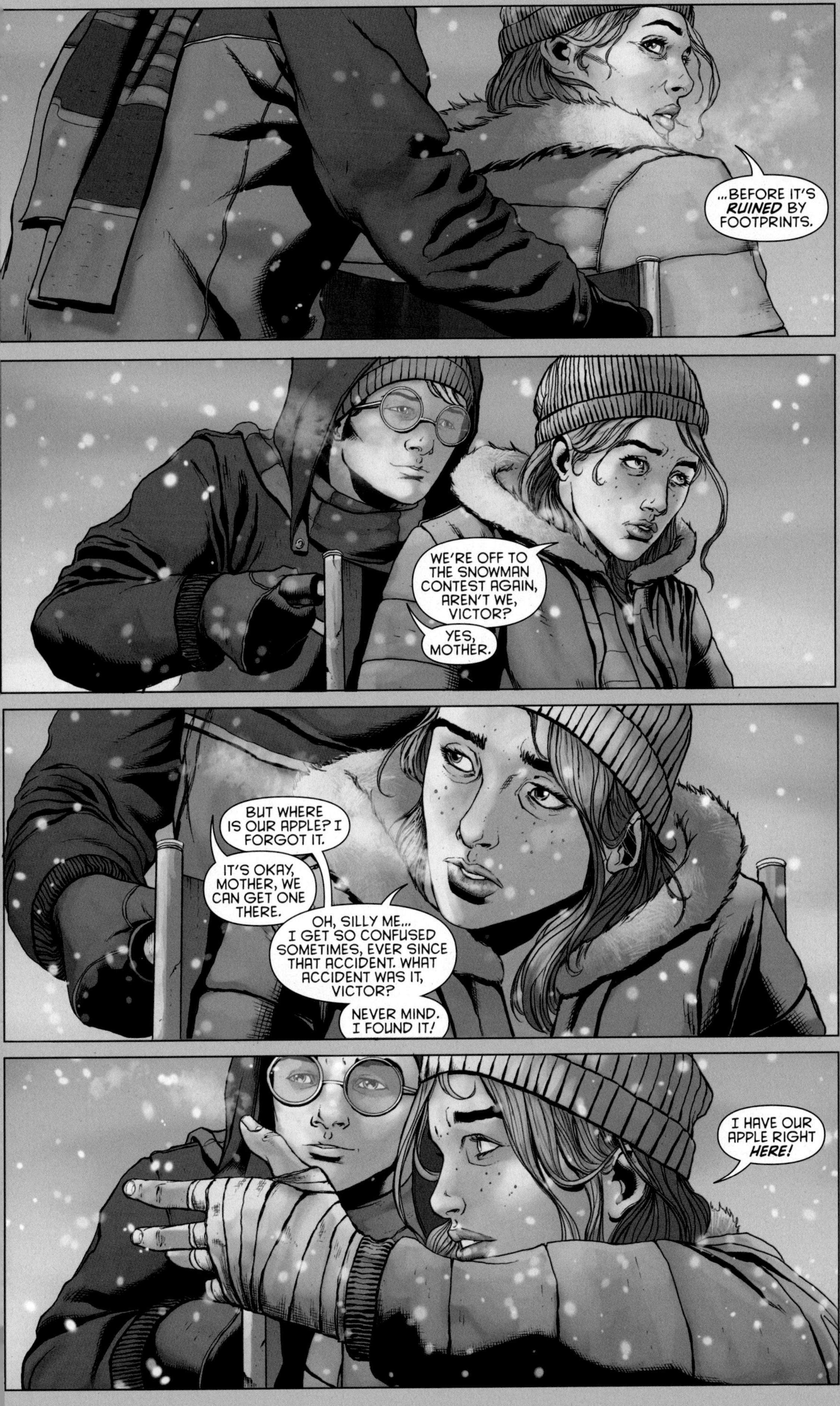
...BEFORE IT'S *RUINED* BY FOOTPRINTS.
WE'RE OFF TO THE SNOWMAN CONTEST AGAIN, AREN'T WE, VICTOR?
YES, MOTHER.
BUT WHERE IS OUR APPLE? I FORGOT IT.
IT'S OKAY, MOTHER, WE CAN GET ONE THERE.
OH, SILLY ME... I GET SO CONFUSED SOMETIMES, EVER SINCE THAT ACCIDENT. WHAT ACCIDENT WAS IT, VICTOR?
NEVER MIND. I FOUND IT!
I HAVE OUR APPLE RIGHT *HERE!*

I ALREADY *CARVED* IT, TOO! YOU SEE, VICTOR?

I SEE, MOTHER.

NOW REST.

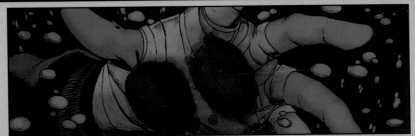

THE END